MINUTES

OF THE

Tenth Biennial Convention

OF

The United Lutheran Church in America

Columbus, Ohio
October 14-21, 1936

THE UNITED LUTHERAN PUBLICATION HOUSE
PHILADELPHIA, PA.

THE UNITED LUTHERAN CHURCH IN AMERICA

CALENDAR, 1936-1938

OFFICERS

President—Rev. F. H. Knubel, D.D., LL.D., S.T.D.
39 East 35th Street, New York, N. Y.

Secretary—Rev. W. H. Greever, D.D., LL.D.
39 East 35th Street, New York, N. Y.

Treasurer—E. Clarence Miller, LL.D.
1508 Walnut Street, Philadelphia, Pa.

EXECUTIVE BOARD

Term Expires 1940

Rev. E. B. Burgess, D.D., LL.D., 39 East 35th St., New York, N. Y.
Rev. H. W. A. Hanson, D.D., LL.D., Gettysburg, Pa.
Rev. E. P. Pfatteicher, Ph.D., D.D., LL.D., 1228 Spruce St.,
Philadelphia, Pa.
Carl M. Distler, Esq., 401 American Bldg., Baltimore, Md.
Robbin B. Wolf, LL.D., 711 Plaza Bldg., Pittsburgh, Pa.
Hon. John L. Zimmerman, LL.D., Springfield, Ohio.

Term Expires 1938

Rev. A. E. Bell, D.D., 2263 Maplewood Ave., Toledo, Ohio.
Rev. Jacob L. Morgan, D.D., 319 W. Horah St., Salisbury, N. C.
Rev. Rees Edgar Tulloss, Ph.D., D.D., 1617 Woodedge Ave.,
Springfield, Ohio
Mr. J. K. Jensen, Janesville, Wis.
James C. Kinard, LL.D., Newberry College, Newberry, S. C.
Hon. Claude T. Reno, 719 Hamilton St., Allentown, Pa.

Members Ex-Officio

Rev. F. H. Knubel, President
Rev. W. H. Greever, Secretary
Mr. E. Clarence Miller, Treasurer

Place of next Convention—Baltimore, Md.

Minutes of the Tenth Biennial Convention of The United Lutheran Church in America

THE SERVICE—INTRODUCTORY

FIRST LUTHERAN CHURCH
Columbus, Ohio
Wednesday, October 14, 1936, 7.30 P. M.

Preparatory to the opening of the Tenth Biennial Convention of The United Lutheran Church in America, delegates from the Constituent Synods, a large number of visitors and many members of the churches of the convention city, assembled to participate in The Service, at the First Lutheran Church, Columbus, Ohio, on Wednesday evening, October 14, 1936, at seven-thirty o'clock. The Secretary conducted The Service, including the Order for Public Confession and the Administration of the Sacrament of the Lord's Supper. The Reverends J. J. Raun, President of the California Synod; C. A. Linn, President of the Georgia-Alabama Synod; H. E. Turney, President of the Indiana Synod; and Thomas Hartig, President of the Manitoba Synod, assisted in the Administration of the Sacrament.

The text of the Sermon, which was preached by the President, was taken from the fifty-first Psalm, using the words of the Offertory; the theme, "Changed Lives."

FIRST SESSION

DESHLER-WALLICK HOTEL
Columbus, Ohio
Thursday, October 15, 1936, 8.45 A. M.

Matins were conducted by the Rev. W. L. Stough.

The President called the Convention to order, and, after the use of the Order for the Opening of Synods, declared the Tenth Biennial Convention of The United Lutheran Church in America open for business.

By general consent the report of the completed roll of delegates was deferred.

The roll, as established at noon, Friday, October 16, follows:

ROLL OF DELEGATES BY SYNODS

1. Ministerium of Pennsylvania
Organized August 15, 1748

Clerical

Ernst P. Pfatteicher, Ph.D., D.D., LL.D.
Charles M. Jacobs, D.D., LL.D., L.H.D.
H. Offermann, D.D.
John A. W. Haas, D.D., LL.D.
Paul J. Hoh, S.T.M.
Conrad Wilker, D.D.
Fred J. Fiedler
William L. Stough, D.D.
Corson C. Snyder, S.T.M.
Allen L. Benner, D.D.
Gustav H. Bechtold, D.D.
William M. Weaver, S.T.D.
Aden B. MacIntosh, D.D.
George Gebert, D.D.
Luther D. Reed, D.D.
Ernst F. Bachmann, D.D.
Ira F. Frankenfield
Harvey S. Kidd
John C. Mattes, D.D.
John H. Waidelich, D.D.
Fr. Flothmeier
Rufus E. Kern
Earl S. Erb
Paul P. Huyett
Frank M. Urich, D.D.
Harry P. Miller
Paul C. Weber
Geo. Smith Kressley, Litt.D.
Leo F. Duerr
James F. Lambert, D.D.
Frank Croman
William F. Herrmann
Ernest A. Weber
Gomer C. Rees, D.D.
Elmer R. Deibert
G. Elson Ruff
J. Howard Worth, D.D.
Karl S. Henry
Nathan B. Yerger

Lay

James F. Henninger
E. Clarence Miller, LL.D.
Otto W. Osterlund, P.D., P.H.M.
J. Myron Shimer
H. Torrey Walker
William H. Hager
Peter P. Hagan
Earle W. Bader
Ralph H. Schatz
J. Milton Deck
John Greiner, Jr.
William M. Mearig
Harry Hodges
Dr. C. C. Billig
Dr. J. A. Trexler
Matthias L. March
Grant Hultberg, D. C. L.
Clyde E. Gerberich
Robert D. Raeder
Maurice D. Walborn
Hans Boesch
Grant Warner
Ross M. Vickers
L. G. Heilman
Gus A. Schilbe
D. M. Reitz
Frank Davidheiser
John Stiles
George A. Eichler
Albert Broadmeyer (a)
Herman C. Kersteen
Fred Angerhofer
Henry S. Jacobs
Adam G. Hausmann
Albert T. McCabe
C. F. Haussmann
LeRoi E. Snyder
Dr. Otto J. Specker
Henry Heuer

2. United Synod of New York

*October 23, 1786

Clerical

Ellis B. Burgess, D.D., LL.D.
Paul C. White, Ph. D.
Frederick Noeldeke
Edward L. Keller, Ph. D.
Henry B. Dickert
E. H. von Hahmann, Ph.D., D.D.
Harold S. Miller
William O. Bruckner
F. Arnold Bavendam
Henry C. Freimuth
Frederick R. Knubel
Frederick H. Knubel, D.D., LL.D.,
    S.T.D.
Chalmers E. Frontz, D.D.
Theodore O. Posselt, D.D.
H. T. Weiskotten, Ph.D.
Paul Andrew Kirsch
Samuel Trexler, D.D.
Chrisenberry A. Ritchie
George C. Ackerly
Oscar V. Werner
David G. Jaxheimer
Oscar Krauch
Robert E. Schlotter
John Dimpfl
Behrend Mehrtens
Wilmer M. Zuehlke
Henry J. Pflum, Jr., D.D.
Arthur H. Schmoyer
Herbert A. Bosch
Andrew L. Dillenbeck, D.D.
John H. Dudde
Frederick E. Reissig
Norman D. Goehring (a)
A. Steimle, D.D.
C. K. Fegley
Theodore J. T. Erdmann
F. C. Ellerman

Lay

Fred H. Schlobohm
Henry Walter
Fred W. Gravenhorst (a)
S. Frederick Telleen
Frederick Henrich
William H. Stackel
Charles G. Schamu
Ross E. Smith
Henry Beisler
Heiby W. Ungerer
William Eck
Frank S. Houck
Philip H. Ketterer
Oscar Andersen
Howard L. Logan
Charles F. Obenhack
I. Searles Runyon
John C. Schaeffer
Walter W. Weller (a)
H. M. Greenwald
L. A. Wilke
Frederick W. Stechmann
Paul G. Wehle
F. J. Scheuerman
Hon. M. Neumann
Charles L. Kenyon
Frank G. Hergert
John Holzkamp
Emil Vogel
Joseph M. Lotsch
Charles Licht
Martin C. Schwaner
Herman Merkle
Fred Hussey
H. L. Stiles (a)
Harry T. Applen (a)
H. Grant Van Hoesen (a)

* Date of organization of the Ministerium of New York and Adjacent States and Countries, which on June 5, 1929, merged with the Evangelical Lutheran Synod of New York (organized 1830, see Minutes U. L. C. A., 1926, p. 8) and the Evangelical Lutheran Synod of New York and New England (organized in 1902), to form The United Lutheran Synod of New York.

3. United Synod of North Carolina
May 2, 1803

Clerical	Lay
Jacob L. Morgan, D.D.	Charles S. Heilig
B. E. Petrea	B. Capps
P. E. Monroe, D.D.	M. L. Rhodes
M. L. Stirewalt, D.D.	C. W. Isenhour
J. A. Yount	Paul B. Beatty
V. C. Ridenhour, D.D.	C. E. Gwin
J. D. Mauney	Prof. G. F. McAllister, Ped.D.
V. R. Cromer	L. G. Bolick
W. G. Cobb	Prof. K. B. Patterson

* Date of organization of the Evangelical Lutheran Synod and Ministerium of North Carolina, which on March 2, 1921, with the Evangelical Lutheran Tennessee Synod (organized July 17, 1820) merged into the United Evangelical Lutheran Synod of North Carolina under an amended charter of the former of the two synods which merged.

4. Maryland Synod
Organized October 11, 1820

Clerical	Lay
J. W. Ott, D.D.	Virgil W. Doub
A. J. Traver, D.D.	E. W. Herrmann
A. R. Wentz, Ph.D., D.D.	Thomas P. Hickman
Henry Einspruch	Ira Hoover
J. Frank Fife	Austin W. Howard
O. F. Blackwelder, D.D.	Frederick W. Kakel
L. Ralph Tabor	M. P. Moller, Jr.
J. E. Harms, D.D.	L. Russell Alden
William A. Wade, D.D.	George R. Sauble
John L. Deaton, D.D.	Austin M. Cooper

5. Synod of South Carolina
Organized January 14, 1824

Clerical	Lay
Thos. F. Suber	Jas. C. Kinard, LL.D.
P. D. Brown, D.D.	J. D. W. Zerbst
W. H. Greever, D.D., LL.D.	R. C. Counts
C. A. Freed, D.D.	B. B. Hare
W. C. Davis, D.D.	R. Torrence
Karl W. Kinard	E. H. Schirmer

6. Synod of West Pennsylvania
Organized September 5, 1825

Clerical	Lay
S. L. Hench	Alvin R. Nissly
George E. Sheffer	S. M. Goodyear
W. W. Barkley	W. K. S. Hershey
William C. Day	Dr. George A. Meyers
Ralph R. Gresh	W. E. Tilberg
E. S. Falkenstein	John B. Baumgardner
Harvey Bickel	Charles C. Culp
Clarence A. Neal	William H. Menges
G. E. Miller	George W. Hafer
Dwight F. Putman	Franklin Menges

7. Synod of Virginia
*August 10, 1829

Clerical	Lay
J. J. Scherer, Jr., D.D.	W. T. Stauffer
R. Homer Anderson, D.D.	R. E. Mapes
A. M. Huffman	H. C. Ahalt
Chas. J. Smith, D.D., LL.D.	Hon. J. L. Almond, Jr.
Hugh J. Rhyne	C. S. Kerlin
Charles M. Teufel, D.D.	W. F. Coyner, Jr.
A. W. Ballentine	C. M. Speese
J. L. Sieber, D.D.	J. H. Rexrode

* Date of organization of the Evangelical Lutheran Synod and Ministerium of Virginia, which, on March 17, 1922, with the Evangelical Lutheran Synod and Ministerium of Southwestern Virginia (composed of the former Evangelical Lutheran Synod and Ministerium of Southwestern Virginia, organized September 20, 1842, and the Evangelical Lutheran Holston Synod, organized September 29, 1860), merged into the Lutheran Synod of Virginia.

8. Synod of Ohio
*November 7, 1836

Clerical	Lay
Joseph Sittler, D.D.	Albert Baker
Franklin Clark Fry	Dorner L. Keyser
Grover E. Swoyer, D.D.	Erle C. Greiner
Arthur H. Smith, D.D.	John L. Zimmerman, Sr., LL.D.
Lewis P. Speaker, D.D.	C. G. Shatzer, Sc.D.
Joseph W. Frease	I. F. Mellinger
Simon A. Metzger	A. D. Rowlands
Ralph W. Loew	Philip Wolfe
H. C. Ter Vehn	Elmer Tracht
C. L. Warstler	B. T. Steiner
G. A. Royer	A. E. Albright
E. C. Herman, D.D.	George F. Schweikert
E. C. Xander, D.D.	George Rinkliff
C. W. Cassel, S.T.M.	Leonard Shipman (a)
E. E. Snyder, D.D.	Virgil E. Zigler, M.D.
George W. Miley, D.D.	Edward Rinderknecht
Paul R. Clouser	C. A. Krout
J. A. Miller	E. J. Young
Howard E. Dunmire	Miles S. Kuhns

* Date of organization of East Ohio Synod which, on November 3, 1920, with the Synod of Miami (organized October 16, 1844), Wittenberg Synod (organized June 8, 1847) and the District Synod of Ohio (organized August 26, 1857) merged into the Synod of Ohio of The United Lutheran Church in America.

9. East Pennsylvania Synod
Organized May 2, 1842

Clerical	Lay
E. Martin Grove, D.D.	E. G. Hoover
Chester S. Simonton, D.D.	William H. Emhardt
Stanley Billheimer, D.D.	John George Kurzenknabe
J. Harold Mumper, S.T.M.	David P. Deatrick, D.D.S.
Harry F. Baughman, D.D.	O. Roy Frankenfield
George A. Greiss, D.D.	Harold U. Landis
T. Benton Peery, S.T.D.	A. H. Durboraw
S. Winfield Herman, D.D.	C. H. Boyer
Charles L. Mogel, S.T.M.	E. S. Gerberich
Lewis C. Manges, D.D.	R. A. Hartman
Robert L. Lang	Harry A. Fritsch
E. Allan Chamberlin	B. B. Slifer
H. S. Rhoads	Ivan J. Snyder
Guy E. McCarney	J. E. Miller

10. Alleghany Synod
Organized September 9, 1842

Clerical	Lay
Paul L. Foulk	William Gleichert
L. W. Gross	S. Z. Miller
Clarence H. Hershey	V. D. Mulhollen
Howard K. Hilner	L. C. Smith
G. I. Melhorn	J. B. Sorrick
E. M. Morgan, D.D.	M. N. Staily
V. D. Naugle	C. C. Fleck

11. Pittsburgh Synod
Organized January 15, 1845

Clerical	Lay
H. H. Bagger, D.D.	C. C. Goodman
E. H. Daugherty	Jesse E. Martsolf
Earl S. Rudisill, Ph.D., D.D.	O. F. H. Bert, Sc.D.
J. F. Bermon	Robt. J. Lehmann
H. O. F. Simoleit	D. R. Fisher
Theo. Buch, D.D.	H. G. Gebert
Elmer F. Rice, D.D.	J. W. Gilchrist
Chas. W. White, D.D.	James Gregg
C. E. Krumbholz, D.D.	C. W. Herman Hess
G. Arthur Fry, D.D.	J. L. Lang
A. W. Steinfurth, D.D.	J. A. A. Geidel
Geo. N. Lauffer, D.D.	Harry B. Snyder
Jacob O. Kroen	George B. Forsythe
Geo. J. Muller	John J. Gluntz
Wm. A. Logan, D.D.	Raymond Goehring
Geo. L. Ulrich	Wm. Leubin
Frank P. Fisher	A. A. Culler
Wm. A. Zundel	W. J. Weishaar
Samuel Boerstler	J. S. Gilhousen
John J. Myers, D.D.	E. A. Emrick
Frank C. Snyder	Carl A. Braun

12. Indiana Synod
October 28, 1848

Clerical	Lay
H. E. Turney, D.D.	George A. Fisher, Sc.D.
R. H. Benting, D.D.	Henry J. Herbst
G. C. Goering	John F. Holaday
A. H. Keck, D.D.	C. B. Huntington
C. Franklin Koch	Otto K. Jensen
P. H. Krauss, D.D.	J. P. Lantz
C. E. Gardner, D.D.	Edward T. Mallett

* Date of organization of the Olive Branch Synod, which, on June 24, 1920, with portions of the Chicago Synod (organized 1896), united to form the Indiana Synod of The United Lutheran Church in America.

13. Illinois Synod
September 8, 1851

Clerical	Lay
Roy G. Catlin, D.D.	Carl Schulz
C. A. Naumann	Wm. Sachse
J. Bannen Swope	Ralph C. Klamer
L. O. Cooperrider	Erwin H. List
Luther Hogshead, D.D.	Wm. A. Dennis
Fred A. Millhouse	R. C. Appleman
Ernest S. Ewald	A. W. Larson
Dwight P. Bair, D.D.	Walter J. Pfaff
W. L. Wilson	W. E. White
Alfred L. Grewe	Edward H. Essig
George Beiswanger, D.D.	J. S. Umberger

* Date of organization of the Northern Illinois Synod, which on June 10, 1920, with the Southern Illinois (organized 1856), the Central Illinois (organized 1862), and portions of the Chicago (organized 1896) Synods, formed the Illinois Synod of The United Lutheran Church in America.

14. Texas Synod
Organized November 10, 1851

Clerical	Lay
Paul Kuehner	Joseph Pannen
Fred W. Kern	Wm. Goebel

15. Susquehanna Synod
February 21, 1855

Clerical	Lay
I. S. Sassaman, D.D.	C. M. Hausknecht
H. Walter Webner	L. M. Hoffman, M.D. (a)
W. M. Allison	H. S. Stetler
C. H. Stein, D.D.	Lewis E. Cox
Joseph E. Law	C. R. Klepfer
Paul W. DeLauter	J. R. Miller
W. C. Hanning	Dr. A. Monroe Hall
M. Hadwin Fischer, Ph.D.	Hon. Charles Steele

* Date of organization of the Synod of Central Pennsylvania which, on September 5, 1923, with the Susquehanna Synod (organized November 5, 1867) merged under the name of the Susquehanna Synod of Central Pennsylvania of the Evangelical Lutheran Church. The newly organized synod held its first session May 22, 1924. The name was changed April 11, 1932, to The Susquehanna Synod of The United Lutheran Church in America.

16. Mississippi Synod
Organized July 25, 1855

Clerical	Lay
John W. Mangum	E. A. Dubard

17. Synod of Iowa
Organized September 3, 1855

Clerical	Lay
L. H. Lesher	J. L. Berger
J. H. Dawson, Ph.D.	Wm. E. Haydon
A. J. Beil	F. L. R. Hansen

18. Georgia-Alabama Synod
Organized July 20, 1860

Clerical	Lay
C. A. Linn, Ph.D.	W. B. Clarke
W. A. Reiser	W. B. Spann (a)

19. Synod of Canada
*July 21, 1861

Clerical	Lay
L. H. Kalbfleisch	Walter Vogt
A. J. Datars	L. Zimmerman (a)
O. Stockmann	A. Metzger
C. S. Roberts	A. L. Brown
J. Schmieder	P. L. Shantz
S. Cooper	John H. Ziegler

* Date of organization of the Evangelical Lutheran Synod of Canada with which, on June 12, 1925, the Synod of Central Canada (organized November 11, 1908) united.

20. Synod of Kansas
Organized November 5, 1868

Clerical	Lay
E. Victor Roland	John F. Reinhardt LL.D.
B. R. Lantz, D.D.	Ed. A. Goult
Andreas Bard, D.D.	L. T. Bang
Charles A. Puls	L. W. Bauerle

21. Synod of Nebraska
Organized September 1, 1871

Clerical	Lay
W. H. Saas	Wm. Rohlfing (a)
H. C. Cordts	S. J. Flora
A. H. Pinkall	E. G. Miller
H. Dowler	Otto Nelson
Wm. Ira Guss, D.D.	G. E. Hickman

22. Wartburg Synod
Organized 1875

Clerical	Lay
Wm. F. Buch, D.D.	Christ Hummel
E. H. Klotsche, Ph.D.	Aug. Rinne (a)
J. A. Goeken (a)	P. Steinbach (a)
R. B. Garten, D.D.	O. Meyer (a)
R. R. Belter	R. E. Lang (a)

23. German Synod of Nebraska
Organized July 24, 1890

Clerical	Lay
F. W. Nolte	Geo. Hilbers
G. F. R. Duhrkop	R. G. Jenny
M. Koolen, D.D.	Harlan Borin (a)
H. O. Rhode	Fred Reuter (a)
E. Walter, D.D.	Fred Laue (a)
A. B. J. Lentz	Wm. Klug (a)

24. Synod of California
Organized April 2, 1891

Clerical	Lay
James J. Raun, Ph.D.	F. C. Noel
H. A. Anspach	Robert R. Inslee
Daniel J. Snyder, D.D.	George F. Kohl
Clarence F. Crouser	Emil Sass

25. Rocky Mountain Synod
Organized May 6, 1891

Clerical	Lay
C. L. Ramme	P. E. Richardson
George P. Krebs	E. H. Rights

26. Synod of the Northwest
Organized September 23, 1891

Clerical	Lay
R. H. Gerberding, D.D.	C. E. Anderson
Paul E. Bishop	Frederick Bullwinkel
D. E. Bosserman	Chas. A. Gottschalk
A. A. Hahn	J. K. Jensen
Geo. C. Koehler, S.T.M.	J. W. Jouno
J. F. Marlatte	Fred C. Mueller
P. H. Roth, D.D.	Martin Veaux
P. W. Roth, D.D.	Dr. F. C. Christensen
A. A. Zinck, D.D.	George W. Ekstrand

27. Manitoba Synod
Organized July 16, 1897

Clerical	Lay
Thos. Hartig	
G. A. Heimann	

28. Pacific Synod
Organized September 26, 1901

Clerical	*Lay*
A. M. Knudsen	M. W. Days
T. A. Schoenberg	Carl B. Merz
A. K. Walborn	P. W. Klug

29. Nova Scotia Synod
Organized July 10, 1903

Clerical	*Lay*
E. V. Nonamaker	Wynn A. Crouse

30. Synod of West Virginia
Organized April 17, 1912

Clerical	*Lay*
C. A. Portz	E. F. Joachim
W. M. Erhard	B. H. Sincell (a)

31. Slovak Lutheran "Zion" Synod
Organized June 10, 1919

Clerical	*Lay*
Paul A. Putra	
J. Albert Billy	

32. Michigan Synod
*June 10, 1920

Clerical	*Lay*
Herbert E. Schildroth	Otto G. Schoenlein
H. C. Castor	George Keen
F. P. Madsen	C. G. Lembke

* Date on which churches of the Northern Indiana Synod and of the Chicago Synod organized to form the Michigan Synod of The United Lutheran Church in America.

33. Synod of Florida
Organized September 24, 1928

Clerical	*Lay*
G. F. Snyder, D.D.	C. R. Carman

34. Kentucky-Tennessee Synod
Organized June 6, 1934

Clerical	*Lay*
Irwin W. Gernert	Lawrence F. Speckman
Ivan Heft	Robert F. Fehr

(Associated Synods)
The Andhra Evangelical Lutheran Church

Clerical	*Lay*

The Evangelical Lutheran Church in Japan
Clerical

C. W. Hepner, D.D., Ph.D.
Kyoshi Watanabe

(a)—Absent.

On motion the reports, as printed in the Bulletin, were received. By common consent it was decided that reports shall not be adopted as a whole, action being taken only upon resolutions and recommendations.

On motion the order of business was adopted as follows:

PROGRAM OF THE CONVENTION

All meetings will be held in the convention hall at the hotel, excepting as indicated in this program.

The offerings at all evening services will be applied to the deficit in the treasury of the Board of Foreign Missions, excepting the offering at the evening service devoted to the Deaconess Cause, which offering shall be given to the Board of Deaconess Work.

WEDNESDAY, OCTOBER 14—Night, 7:30 o'clock.
At First Church, Main and Twenty-second Streets.
The Service. President's Sermon. Sacrament of the Altar.

THURSDAY, OCTOBER 15—Morning, 8:45 to 12 o'clock.
1. Devotions. (Matins will be used. The Committee on Devotions will appoint those who are to conduct all devotions.)
2. Formal opening of the Convention.
3. Organization of the Convention—Roll. Receipt of reports as printed in the Bulletin. Order of Business. Special items from report of the Executive Board: Registration of Delegates; Committee on Minutes; Amendment to Constitution; Restudy of Procedure with reference to Nominations and Elections, (a) and (b); Committee on Place of Next Convention. Appointment of special committees. General rules of procedure.
4. Approval of minutes of last convention.
5. Formal Reception of Officials of the Lutheran World Convention.
6. Reports of the President and of the Secretary.
7. Election of the President and of the Secretary.
8. Treasurer's Report, with audit.
9. Election of the Treasurer.
10. Report of the Executive Board.
    Actions at this and succeeding sessions to be taken on the following items from the report. Any delegate may call up for consideration or question other items, not included in the following. These are given in the order in which they are found in the report. Year 1938 for Board of American Missions; Better Adjustment of Work of Auxiliaries; Basis of Apportionment; Calendar of Special Days and Seasons;

Alleghany Synod; Merger of Inner Mission Board, Board of Deaconess Work, Committee on Evangelism, and Committee on Moral and Social Welfare; Transfer of Mountain Work to Board of American Missions; Amendment to ruling on Plan of Operation of the Board of American Missions; Changes in Rules of the Board of Ministerial Pensions and Relief; Devotional Literature; Rules and Regulations of the Commission on Investments; Budget; Uniform Rate of Annuities; Supplementary Support for Executive Board.

THURSDAY, OCTOBER 15—Afternoon, 2 to 5 o'clock.
1. Devotions.
2. Continuation of action on the Executive Board's report.
3. (At 4.30 o'clock)—Necrologist's Obituary Record. Memorial service, with special tribute to the former president of the Lutheran World Convention, the Rev. J. A. Morehead, by the Rev. C. J. Smith.

THURSDAY, OCTOBER 15—Night, 8 o'clock.
Mass Meeting. Addresses by Officers of the Lutheran World Convention.

FRIDAY, OCTOBER 16—Morning, 8:45 to 12 o'clock.
(Before the opening of the morning session the chairmen of synodical delegations must secure ballots in the voting room for those elections which are to be held this day at noon. Each chairman will distribute the ballots to his delegation.)
1. Devotions.
2. Reports of Nominating Committees as to members of the Executive Board, of the Commission of Adjudication, of the Committee on Church Papers, and of the Executive Committee of the Laymen's Movement.
3. Board of Foreign Missions.
4. ' Unfinished Business.
5. At 11:30—Special Devotional Period. Theme: "The Nations of the World." Leader: Rev. W. H. Traub. (The nations today need nothing so much as the prayers of the Christian Church.)
(Immediately after the close of the session the election will be held for membership on the Executive Board, the Commission of Adjudication, the Committee on Church Papers, and the Executive Committee of the Laymen's Movement. Polls close at 2 o'clock.)

FRIDAY, OCTOBER 16—Afternoon, 2 to 5 o'clock.
1. Devotions.
2. Minutes.

3. Representatives and General Resolutions. (As arranged by the Committee of Reference and Counsel for this place and for stated places on following days.)
4. Board of American Missions.
5. Committee on Evangelism.
6. Commission of Adjudication.
7. Commission on Investments. (This Commission will hold a special meeting immediately after adjournment this afternoon. Delegates are invited to present to the Commission's chairman in advance matters relating to the investments of our Boards for the Commission's consideration.)
8. Committee on Church Papers.
9. Unfinished Business.

FRIDAY, OCTOBER 16—Night, 8:30 o'clock.

Celebration of the Centennial Anniversary of the Protestant Diaconate. A Pageant presenting history, present work, and a glimpse of the future of the Deaconess. In Music Hall, Capital University.

SATURDAY, OCTOBER 17—Morning, 8:45 to 11:45 o'clock.

(Before the opening of the morning session the chairmen of delegations must secure ballots for today's elections.)
1. Devotions.
2. Report of Nominating Committee for today's elections.
3. Report of tellers upon Friday's elections.
4. Board of Education.
5. Parish and Church School Board.
6. Unfinished Business.
(Immediately after adjournment the election will be held for membership on all boards and elective committees not included in the Friday election.)

SATURDAY, OCTOBER 17—Afternoon and Evening.

Wittenberg College guest day. Automobile trip to Springfield. Football game, buffet supper, and student program. Also opportunity for those interested to visit Oesterlen Home.

SUNDAY, OCTOBER 18.

The Columbus Committee has arranged and will announce the preachers at all church services.
Evening—Courtesy Evening planned for the U. L. C. A. by Capital University. In Music Hall, Capital University.

MONDAY, OCTOBER 19—Morning, 8:45 to 12 o'clock.

1. Devotions.
2. Report of tellers upon Saturday's elections.
3. Board of Publication.
4. Inner Mission Board.
5. Board of Deaconess Work.
6. Unfinished Business.
7. At 11:30—Special devotional period. Theme: "The Pastors of the U. L. C. A." Leader: Rev. A. M. Knudsen. (More than 250 of them are at the convention. More than 2,500 others are not delegates. All of them need and desire the Church's constant prayers. They are the Shepherds.)

MONDAY, OCTOBER 19—Afternoon, 2 to 5 o'clock.

1. Devotions.
2. Minutes.
3. Representatives and General Resolutions.
4. Board of Ministerial Pensions and Relief.
5. Laymen's Movement.
6. Committee on Memorials from Constituent Synods.
7. Committee on Moral and Social Welfare.
8. Unfinished Business.

MONDAY, OCTOBER 19—Evening.

Banquet arranged by the Laymen's Movement. Full particulars will be announced.

TUESDAY, OCTOBER 20—Morning, 8:45 to 12 o'clock.

1. Devotions.
2. Committee on Lutheran Brotherhoods.
   Hearing of the representative of the Brotherhood.
3. Committee on Women's Work.
   Hearing of the representative of the Women's Missionary Society.
4. Committee on Associations of Young People.
   Hearing of the representative of the Luther League in America.
5. Committee on Women as Congregational Representatives.
6. Unfinished Business.

TUESDAY, OCTOBER 20—Afternoon, 2 to 5 o'clock.

1. Devotions.
2. Minutes.
3. Representatives and General Resolutions.

4. Commission on Relations to American Lutheran Church Bodies.
5. Commissioners to the National Lutheran Council.
6. Executive Committee of the Lutheran World Convention.
7. Committee on President's Report.
8. Unfinished Business.

WEDNESDAY, OCTOBER 21—Morning, 8:45 to 12 o'clock, and afternoon, 2 to 5 o'clock. (Portions of the program for this day may be advanced to Tuesday night, if the convention decides to hold a session that night.)

1. Devotions.
2. Minutes.
3. Recognition of the Centennial of the Ohio Synod—Address by the Rev. A. H. Smith.
4. Committee on Common Service Book.
5. Committee on Church Music.
6. Committee on Church Architecture.
7. Committee on Statistics and Church Year Book.
8. Committee on German Interests.
9. Committee on Publicity.
10. Committee on Conference with Y. M. C. A.
11. Committee on Church and State.
12. Committee on Transportation.
13. Archivist.
14. Lutheran Laymen's Radio Committee.
15. Committee on Army and Navy Work.
16. Report of Representative in Advisory Council of the American Bible Society.
17. Committee on Place of Next Convention.
18. Committee on Leave of Absence.
19. Lutheran Historical Society.
20. Lutheran Church Book and Literature Society.
21. Unfinished Business.
22. Printing of Minutes.
23. Final Minutes.
24. Formal Close of the Convention.

The special items from the report of the Executive Board, necessary to the organization of the Convention, were presented for consideration. (See pp. 56, 64, 86, 87.)

XIII, 1, (c), Registration of Delegates. Adopted.

The President announced his ruling in connection with this item, as presented to the Executive Board, and this ruling was accepted by the Convention.

XIII, 2, (a), Committee on Minutes. Adopted.

IV, A, 1, Amendment to the Constitution. The recommendation, to submit this Constitutional amendment to the Constituent Synods, was adopted unanimously.

II, 15, Restudy of Procedure with Reference to Nominations and Elections. (a) and (b) adopted.

XIII, 1, (g), Committee on Place of Next Convention. Adopted. The Rev. J. W. Ott, President of the Maryland Synod, was named convener.

There being no objection, the President ruled that Special Committees stand as appointed and announced.

SPECIAL COMMITTEES

COMMITTEE OF REFERENCE AND COUNSEL

This committee is appointed to consider all general resolutions before they are submitted to the Convention; to arrange with the president for the hearing of representatives sent to the Convention; generally to assist the president in the daily program.

Clergymen	Laymen
Frank M. Urich	John Greiner, Jr.
Chalmers E. Frontz	S. Frederick Telleen
O. F. Blackwelder	L. Russel Alden
Hugh J. Rhyne	Charles C. Culp
E. C. Xander	Erle C. Greiner
Stanley Billheimer	B. B. Slifer
A. W. Steinfurth	Erwin H. List
Alfred L. Grewe	Otto Nelson
H. C. Cordts	Fred C. Mueller
H. A. Anspach	Robert Fehr
P. H. Roth	A. A. Culler
S. Cooper	
A. L. Dillenbeck	

COMMITTEE ON PRESIDENT'S REPORT

Clergymen	Laymen
J. Schmieder	J. A. Trexler
Franklin Clark Fry	Frederick Henrich
G. H. Bechtold	I. Searles Runyon
Arthur H. Schmoyer	J. L. Almond, Jr.
Harry F. Baughman	A. E. Albright
V. D. Naugle	George Rinkliff
H. O. F. Simoleit	O. F. H. Bert
L. O. Cooperrider	George A. Fisher
H. Walter Webner	Robert R. Inslee
W. A. Reiser	Ralph H. Schatz
Andreas Bard	F. L. R. Hansen
John H. Dudde	Charles Steele
W. M. Erhard	

COMMITTEE ON LEAVE OF ABSENCE

Clergymen	Laymen
W. C. Davis	A. W. Howard
George Smith Kressley	J. D. W. Zerbst
William O. Bruckner	George W. Hafer
Henry Einspruch	Henry J. Herbst
W. W. Barkley	James Gregg
E. C. Herman	George B. Forsythe
Harold Mumper	L. G. Bolick
Paul L. Foulk	J. E. Miller
H. C. Castor	J. S. Umberger
H. O. Rhode	
W. L. Wilson	
A. K. Walborn	

COMMITTEE ON MEMORIALS FROM CONSTITUENT SYNODS

Clergymen	Laymen
P. W. Roth	James F. Henninger
H. T. Weiskotten	Heiby W. Ungerer
P. E. Monroe	M. P. Moller, Jr.
Ralph R. Gresh	A. H. Durboraw
George A. Greiss	Wm. Gleichert
Clarence H. Hershey	C. B. Huntington
C. F. Koch	Carl Schulz
A. J. Beil	L. T. Bang
C. S. Roberts	J. W. Jouno
R. B. Garten	George Keen
Paul E. Bishop	W. F. Coyner, Jr.
J. H. Dawson	K. B. Patterson
Behrend Mehrtens	
Oscar Krauch	

COMMITTEE TO NOMINATE EXECUTIVE COMMITTEE OF LAYMEN'S MOVEMENT

Clergymen	Laymen
J. Luther Sieber	E. A. Dubard
A. B. J. Lentz	Carl B. Merz
G. A. Heimann	Wynn A. Crouse

COMMITTEE TO NOMINATE MEMBERS OF EXECUTIVE BOARD, COMMISSION OF ADJUDICATION AND CHURCH PAPERS COMMITTEE

Clergymen	Laymen
Lewis C. Manges	Virgil W. Doub
Aden B. MacIntosh	W. T. Stauffer
V. C. Ridenhour	L. C. Smith
Grover E. Swoyer	William Sachse
George N. Lauffer	Wm. E. Haydon
W. C. Hanning	Walter Vogt
B. R. Lantz	E. F. Joachim
F. P. Madsen	Charles L. Kenyon
G. F. Snyder	

COMMITTEE TO NOMINATE MEMBERS OF ALL OTHER BOARDS

Clergymen	*Laymen*
A. J. Traver	J. Milton Deck
Harold S. Miller	M. L. Rhodes
Karl W. Kinard	George A. Meyers
E. S. Falkenstein	Philip Wolfe
R. H. Benting	William H. Emhardt
C. L. Ramme	C. C. Goodman
Paul A. Putra	W. B. Clarke
Ivan Heft	Emil Sass
Fred W. Kern	F. C. Christensen

COMMITTEE ON DEVOTIONAL SERVICES

Clergymen	*Laymen*
G. Arthur Fry	Frederick W. Stechmann
Fred J. Fiedler	W. K. S. Hershey
Harry P. Miller	H. C. Ahalt
Edward L. Keller	O. Roy Frankenfield
David G. Jaxheimer	Harry B. Snyder
J. A. Yount	Carl A. Braun
Charles M. Teufel	Fred Hussey
George W. Miley	Miles S. Kuhns
T. Benton Peery	E. H. Schirmer
G. I. Melhorn	
Luther Hogshead	
Dwight F. Putman	
John L. Deaton	
J. A. Miller	

COMMITTEE OF TELLERS No. 1

To conduct the election of the president and of the secretary, and also the Friday elections.

Laymen

C. G. Shatzer	S. Z. Miller
William M. Mearig	H. G. Gebert
C. W. Isenhour	Otto K. Jensen
Thomas P. Hickman	Ralph C. Klamer
B. B. Hare	C. M. Hausknecht
W. E. Tilberg	J. L. Berger
R. E. Mapes	Joseph Pannen
Harry A. Fritsch	

COMMITTEE OF TELLERS No. 2

To conduct the election of the treasurer and also the Saturday elections.

Laymen

P. E. Richardson	C. E. Anderson
A. Metzger	Otto G. Schoenlein
John F. Reinhardt	C. R. Carman
S. J. Flora	Lawrence F. Speckman
George Hilbers	Clyde E. Gerberich
George F. Kohl	Charles G. Schamu
E. A. Emrick	P. W. Klug

SPECIAL COMMITTEE ON MINUTES
Clergymen

Charles A. Puls
Paul C. White

William L. Stough
John J. Myers

The following rules of procedure were adopted:

(1) That any delegate may, from the floor, move a resolution which fits perfectly to any report coming before the Convention, but that resolutions of a general character must be handed to the Committee of Reference and Counsel, with whom the mover may confer;

(2) That in discussion the time of speakers be limited to five minutes; and

(3) That the privilege of the floor be granted to members of the Executive Board, to all members of the Commission of Adjudication, and to officers of other boards when their reports are before the Convention.

A printed copy of the Minutes of the Savannah Convention, 1934, certified by F. H. Knubel, as President, and W. H. Greever, as Secretary, under seal, was submitted and approved. The President thereupon declared that copy of the Minutes to be the official protocol of the proceedings of the Ninth Biennial Convention of The United Lutheran Church in America.

The Rev. Lewis P. Speaker was introduced, and, after extending cordial words of welcome to the Convention, in the name of the churches of The United Lutheran Church in America in Columbus, he presented a gavel, with historical connections, from one of the oldest settlements west of the Allegheny mountains, at Marietta, Ohio. The gavel was accepted by the President with proper comments.

As a special feature of the program, the distinguished visitors from Germany, representing the Lutheran World Convention, were introduced as follows: Bishop August Marahrens of Hanover, Bishop Hans Meiser of Bavaria, and Dr. Hanns Lilje of Berlin. The introduction was made by Prof. Abdel Ross Wentz of Gettysburg Seminary, who delivered a very happy address in the German language. Bishop Marahrens responded by presenting the greetings of the Lutheran World Convention, with special reference to the Scandinavian representatives who were unable to be present. Dr. Wentz afterwards gave the substance of his address in English, and the address of Bishop Marahrens was interpreted by Dr. Lilje.

The President presented his report as printed in the Bulletin and it was referred to the Committee on President's Report. (For Committee's report, and action thereon, see pp. 418, 420, 431.)

REPORT OF THE PRESIDENT

My report two years ago indicated that the period before 1934 was the most critical one in our history. The past biennium was not equally critical. Nevertheless, a religious review of the time since 1934, whether within the U. L. C. A. or within all Christian groups, reveals a continued restlessness and alarm along with cries for radical action. The dissatisfied call to leaders to "do something" still echoes strongly. The most pronounced expression of alarm relates to the dangers for the Church from atheistic communism. We are told for instance that "there are treacherous forces at work through the press, over the radio, in the forum and even back of the sacred pulpit, spreading propaganda to destroy that faith born with the smile of a Babe under the Star of Bethlehem. A revival of the gospel of the Son of God should be brought about to chase away the darkness caused by this shadow of the vulture wings of atheistic communism."

The dangers from this source are real, but they do not justify some present procedures, they do not call for hysterical action and high-pressure methods. In a period when bewildered excitement continues, the Church must manifest sturdy steadiness. For instance, Christians individually must realize that to be a Christian means to hold to a Savior Who holds us, to possess studied religious convictions instead of flippant, cant opinions, and to live by those convictions. The need of the present is furthermore that in all nations Christians unitedly insist that governments must not interfere with the proper and full freedom of the Church. The need is also that Protestant pastors everywhere recognize that today the Church is repenting of recent liberal follies and is restudying Reformation principles, that the redemptive emphasis in preaching carries God's supreme message and is the sure answer to atheism, and that sturdy holiness is a pastor's ordination pledge. These needs of the time provide the special reason why during this convention of the Church we shall twice turn aside from our business to pray, first for the troubled, bewildered nations of the world today and then for our thousands of pastors. It seems impossible to leave this portion of the report without saying that in a serious time like the present we Lutherans cannot permit ourselves to be drawn from the confessional, redemptive heart of the Gospel by any merely attractive and novel doctrinal and educational ideas and jargon. Sometimes our people, even occasionally some of our leaders, seem to be tempted by such bright lights.

The above is just a quick outline of present conditions in Christianity generally and therefore in every Church group. They cannot be further discussed in this report, because of a definite responsibility laid upon the president to deal with a specific measure. The nature of that responsibility will become manifest as we proceed to examine the particular conditions in the U. L. C. A. during the past two years. It must be remembered that the critical situation during the previous biennium led to the wholehearted adoption of a program of six propositions for improvement in our life and work. They were presented at the last convention. Much of our effort during the last two years has been guided by the desire to give effect to those propositions. We have aimed for instance to lay "stronger emphasis than ever upon the regular apportionment as the chief and constant source of the funds for the general work of the Church." That was one proposition. Another sought "a better adjustment in the methods used by synods in distributing the funds received from congregations." To this end the constituent synods have quite generally manifested a great willingness. A number of practical instances could be cited of steps taken by individual synods whereby the people and the synods and the U. L. C. A. are all considered fairly in the distribution of benevolent moneys. Still another of those six propositions asked that there be "a better adjustment of the work of the Women's Missionary Society to the work of the Church as a whole." This was enlarged so as to relate to all auxiliary organizations, and a special committee has worked upon suggestions which will come before this convention as a part of the Executive Board's report. They need no additional attention in this report.

The first proposition in that list of six called for "the development of a stronger spiritual life in the Church." This item has never been forgotten, and is naturally an abiding responsibility in every biennium. I am making no specific statements concerning it, partly because this report must center upon another of the propositions but also because the Church's spiritual life is practically the theme of the president's sermon to this convention.

I turn then to that other proposition approved two years ago. It occupies the remainder of this report. It demands "a stronger educational promotion throughout all parishes." A few years ago, when the editor of The Lutheran gathered opinions from several sources and summarized in a single article the main achievements of each of our biennial conventions, he concluded the article by saying "The United Lutheran Church does not hold the place in the affections and esteem of its membership to which its capacity to serve and the fidelity of its trustees entitle it. It might well be one distinctive objective of the eighth convention to consider how it may make every member of every congregation in our body U. L. C. A. conscious." That was an appeal for promotional activity by the Church. Every interested one among us has recognized frequently that most of those among us are not truly interested. Not long ago I was hearing again that fine Reformation cantata, "The City of God." I was stirred by that sad refrain of the prophet concerning God's people, "They have forgotten Thee." One's mind inevitably asks as to the extent to which that cry is true of our people today—their ignorance, their indifference, their unwillingness. Is it not equally true that the Church has neglected to remind, to inform, to arouse her people?

The appeal of *The Lutheran's* editor was not a new one. For at least the last fifteen years insistence has come from various sources that we plan a better promotional work. Had we the space an interesting story could be told of past efforts and their disheartening failure. The inclusion of that promotional proposition among the six offered to the last convention was therefore the cry of all our past neglect telling us that now, in these critical years, we must neglect no more. Savannah acted, by the appointment of a special committee of nine members. That committee became deeply conscious of the need—and also of the difficulties. The Executive Board is reporting to this convention the results of the nine men's deliberations. The responsibility for the preparation of promotional plans was placed upon the president, entirely contrary to his desire. This is the specific measure previously mentioned as being laid upon him. The task was assumed with a hearty will, the counsel of many was sought through conversations, correspondence, and conference, and the result is now submitted to this convention for action.

What is promotion? A definition, of a sort, may be gained by distinguishing promotion from publicity and from education. Such a definition will at least provide us with a working plan, setting limits to our purpose. Publicity is the advertising of the Church to those on the outside; promotion is the advertising of the Church to its own members. As regards education, promotion is the first step in an educational process. It aims primarily to arouse interest, although it also begets purpose and seeks to bring that purpose to action. When the interest has been aroused, the Church's educational agencies will proceed with the people. Promotion therefore is the Church's effort to arouse the active interest of her own people in her faith and her life and her work.

The next question is one of choice. Any wideawake Christian can quickly suggest a number of good, practical plans for promotion. Schemes for promotion are multitudinous today in all spheres of life. Wisdom demands therefore a careful survey of our whole situation, a canvass of all suggested methods, and the choice of just a few (the fewer the better) for earnest trial until experience shows the need of a change. My decision, reached as a consequence of such survey and canvass, was that we ought establish no new agency for this work. Several denominations have in the past established special promotional agencies and seem in each instance to have regretted that step. Our own tendency has been furthermore to reduce the number of our agencies, apparently with satisfactory results. Another decision reached was to examine the promotional operations now conducted by us, to select the best ones, and to intensify them. A study of the suggestions about to be made will reveal that they consist chiefly of an intensification of things we are now doing, or perhaps a new application of them. Three primary suggestions are submitted for approval. It is proposed that they be tried for a period of two years before a judgment is finally formed as to their wisdom and helpfulness.

The first of these is to be carried out by the Board of Publication. I believe that a great injustice is done to that Board in the ordinary thoughts of even our best informed members. How often men are heard to remark that the Board of Publication, as distinguished from other boards, is a business board. This implies that its responsibility is just the printing and sale of literature. As a result, we wrongly urge that Board to believe that it has no direct part in the Church's great task of proclaiming God's redemption. We remove all inspiring joy from its service. We tempt it to become a shrewd, worldly mechanism, to bring the spirit of the world into the Church. Our mistake is that we forget what "publication," "publish" means. Even the dictionary designates as a first definition, "to make public; to make known to people in general." A Board of Publication is then first of all an agency for publicity or for promotion. It is the chief agency for promotion possessed by the U. L. C. A. Indeed when the special committee of nine men were studying the plans for promotion, the president advocated that the *entire* responsibility for this work be assigned to that Board. He was overruled, but it is evident that whatever plans are adopted a large share of responsibility for promotion must be assumed by this, our chief promotional agency. It would seem indeed that those who framed our constitution must have possessed the promotional spirit and must have understood the true sphere of the Board of Publication, for when they described the Church's objects, they included this terse, pregnant item: "The preparation and publication of such literature as shall *promote* (note that word) the dissemination of knowledge as to the doctrines, practice, progress, and needs of the Lutheran Church."

One of the fine instruments of promotion put forth by the Board of Publication is the Church paper. My first proposition is that we merely intensify something we now use, that we intensify the spread of the Church paper. The main idea, for which approval is asked, is that *the Board of Publication be instructed to arrange so that three times a year, for two years, a special number of "The Lutheran" is sent to every family within the U. L. C. A.* Those who have a sense of promotional values will recognize quickly that this quiet, repeated visit of the whole Church in every home of the Church should have stirring effects. Such men will also appreciate that a satisfactory accomplishment of this idea requires

careful decision on many details. Many difficulties must also be overcome. No attempt can be made here to discuss the details and the difficulties. As in all other things, if there be first the good will to do that
which ought to be done a way will be found to do it.

A few points concerning the idea may nevertheless be mentioned. I
believe that these special numbers should be prepared by a special editor.
and that he should become the guide of all promotional activity carried
on by the Board of Publication. He would be under the directing supervision of the manager of the Board of Publication, and would be in touch
with the president of the Church as long as the latter continues to direct
the Church's whole promotional activity. This contact of the editor with
the president would furthermore provide the former with steady knowledge of all central developments in the Church's plans. The editor would
keep living contact also with executives of the Church's Boards, so that
their purposes may be clearly understood and faithfully portrayed. The
editor would read widely on modern developments in missions of all
types. Since he must write for people who do not know a Church paper,
his task would be a distinctly different one from that of the regular
editor of *The Lutheran.*

Will there not be a large item of cost to the Board of Publication for
these special numbers? The answer to this question may naturally be
that these special numbers will, if carefully prepared, bring back important
financial returns to the Publication House. The true answer to the objection of cost, if it be an objection, is however that the cost is small if
our people are won, if the United Lutheran Church gains a place in their
affections and esteem which it does not now possess.

The above, as the first of three suggestions, covers a promotional approach to our people entirely through our literature. Effective promotion
should however provide also for our personal approach. Indeed the
former will not have sufficient influence without the latter. In the past,
when the three bodies which formed the U. L. C. A. were comparatively
small organizations, representatives of the operating boards could visit
a great majority of the congregations. This was personal promotion of an
effective character. Frequent calls are heard for a renewal of this method.
One of our constituent synods has sent a memorial to this convention,
reciting the helpfulness of this method in arousing our people to a new
sense of loyalty and responsibility in the Church's vital fields of endeavor.
The synod asks this convention to direct the boards to make possible
the personal appearance of representatives in the congregations of the
U. L. C. A., bearing information and inspiration regarding the specific
and general work of the Church. That memorial represents no passing
whim of a few individuals. It is one more of the voices which will increase in number and force until the Church undertakes a worthy pro-

gram of promotion. The president in his long study of promotion investigated this very proposition thoroughly, namely, the possibility of complete plans for congregational visitation by representatives of boards. Figuring all the possibly available individuals from all boards for such visits and keeping them all at the task fifty-two weeks in the year, there could be only one visit to a congregation every three years—one visit in three years concerning the work of all the boards. That is not satisfactory promotion. The boards must continue congregational visitation to the best of their ability, but this method cannot be relied upon to meet our whole need.

Another idea is therefore offered, as a plan of personal promotion, to be carried out by the seven boards of the Church which receive about 95 cents out of every dollar of the apportionment. They are the Boards of Foreign Missions, American Missions, Education, Parish and Church School, Inner Mission, Deaconess Work, and Ministerial Pensions. Working always with these seven boards in securing the apportionment is also the Laymen's Movement. Let us not suppose that these agencies have been neglectful of the Church's promotional necessity. They have faithfully sent representatives annually to the meetings of all synods, but both the synods and the boards have quite unanimously agreed that something more effective is needed. The boards have all prepared promotional literature of various character, but have not found methods of distribution that are fully satisfactory to themselves. They have special days and seasons of the year assigned to them, but they believe that this opportunity should be opened more widely for their use. These Boards should be provided with better promotional opportunities.

The plan now proposed will be recognized to be, as was true with the Board of Publication, merely an intensification or new application of methods that have been used hitherto. It has been shown that the boards cannot reach all the congregations individually with a personal message. They can however reach personally representatives (including the pastors) of all the congregations if the representatives of say every twenty congregations will come together in a group. Those representatives can then carry a board's message and its literature to their own congregations. Themselves inspired by personal contact with the board's representatives at their group meeting they can personally inspire their congregations. To say the least this will be more effective than the board's long-distance touch with a congregation by means of cold print and postage stamps. Such meetings of groups of congregational representatives are even now a common and constant occurrence. Each synod for instance has its conferences and their meetings. The officials of all synods are eager that conference meetings become more powerful influences of a true character than they are at present. A number of synods furthermore, working under the inspiration of their presidents, now have group meetings of smaller size than the conferences. They are used for various important purposes. Several of the boards have secured the appointment of synodical and congregational committees for personal contacts. Still further, the executive secretary of the Layman's Movement has set up in a number of synods, under the guidance of their officers, special groups of volunteer congregational representatives. Additional opportunities present themselves, as for example synodical summer schools. In any event it is evident that with steady effort, with elastic arrangements to suit the special conditions in synods, through the guiding help of synodical officials, and by a fuller use of existing committees and conferences, the boards can personally reach each year representatives of all congregations, gathered in varying groups.

The idea is that each board shall personally present its cause to such groups in connection with its use of its special season. Each board will prepare its own literature as hitherto, but will intensify its whole promotional endeavor at its special season. A thoughtful individual will now realize that for the seven boards concerned, each with its own season, this would mean seven meetings annually of the groups of congregational representatives. That is indeed the ideal. An executive secretary of one board when learning of the plan pointed out that as an ideal it is unattainable, but he urged that we work in that direction. An examination of the special seasons reveals that a very easy and somewhat advantageous combination reduces the number of annual meetings needed to four. In some synods a beginning with one or two meetings must be made. Existing group meetings in each synod will be the point of departure for this work as we move toward the ideal.

The thoughtful man sees a second real difficulty. How can a single board provide personal representatives for its special season at several hundred group meetings (because we have four thousand congregations)? Here we discover one of the most beautiful features of the plan. That single board will indeed be in charge for its own special season, but it is to be assisted in its presentation by the forces of all the other boards. Will it not be beautiful in the eyes of the Church if the secretaries of all the boards are vigorously advocating foreign missions to groups of congregational representatives at the Epiphany season? Will it not be a rich experience to foreign missionaries on furlough if they advocate the claims of the deaconess service once a year? The representatives of an individual board in its special season will be the secretaries of all boards, missionaries of all kinds, members of all boards, synodical officials, and committees, and each synod's delegates to the last convention of the U. L. C. A. Thus a single board can be personally represented at several hundred group meetings. Hundreds of advocates will be serving that board at its special season.

A last difficulty from the thoughtful man. How shall all the arrangements for several hundred group meetings and for the assignment of a board's representatives to the groups be made? A committee should be constituted of the executive secretaries of the eight agencies with the president of the Church (as long as he continues active in the Church's promotional program). This committee will make the arrangements mentioned, it having been stated that each board itself prepares the plans and literature for its special season. The agent of the committee in arranging with synodical officers for the group meetings would be the secretary of the Laymen's Movement. This would be merely a continuation of work he has long done under the guidance of synodical officers.

The second idea is then that *the Boards of Foreign Missions, American Missions, Education, Parish and Church School, Inner Mission, Deaconess Work, and Ministerial Pensions and the Laymen's Movement be instructed to arrange for a promotional activity during their special seasons in general as explained in this report, and also to appoint their executive secretaries as members of a joint committee for the special purposes assigned to the committee in this report.*

A third promotional plan of strong influence is also suggested. It would be conducted by those agencies of the Church which are commonly known as auxiliaries. These societies of men and women and young people desire loyally to serve the Church. From its beginning the Luther League's motto has been "Of the Church, by the Church, for the Church." The Women's Missionary Society has manifested a readiness to assume even new responsibilities for the good of the Church's work. It undertook for instance during the past year a form of activity which it designates as "Missionary Advance," whereby the women are seeking to have their congregational societies become active in a most definite manner, so that the entire congregation develops interest in the whole work of the whole Church. The congregational society will not be working just to strengthen itself, but to strengthen the congregation as a whole. It will in this as in all things consult and co-operate with the pastor of the congregation. Some sentences from the society's constitution and other literature illuminate this entire purpose.

"Every member of the congregation interested in Missions."

"One of the leading objects of the Women's Missionary Society is to promote and stimulate the interest of the whole Church in the work of missions by disseminating information and promoting missionary education."

"Loyal support of the regular apportionment of the Church by every member of a congregational society shall be a recognized policy of the Society."

"A church-wide missionary society, comprising men, women and children, would be the ideal."

Manifestly this plan of the Women's Missionary Society contemplates a constant promotional activity carried on *by a group within the congregation,* and manifestly this group desires to become more positively than ever a leaven within the congregation, working in the interest of the Church as a whole. The activity is to be commended, and it is desirable that the Lutheran Brotherhood and the Luther League undertake also to emphasize even more positively than hitherto that their congregational units become actuated by a similar sense of responsibility for the congregations of which they are parts. These auxiliaries alone would furnish many supplementary representatives for the personal approaches planned by the boards as outlined above.

The third idea then is that *this Convention commends the loyalty of the Lutheran Brotherhood, the Women's Missionary Society, and the Luther League, and instructs them to further their present purposes whereby their congregational units will be vigorous promotional agents for the interest of the entire congregation in the whole work of the whole Church.*

The three primary suggestions made above were chosen after fullest consideration and conference, and they are believed to constitute something in the nature of a rounded and complete program. While each is independent they will be found in actual trial to complement and assist one another. In the course of discussions of the program it developed however that two supplements must be suggested.

The first of these relates to the annual meetings of synods. It was stated that both synods and boards are dissatisfied with all previous arrangements for the presentation of causes at the meetings of synods. This was emphasized at the recent conference of synodical presidents and also at the recent conference of board secretaries. The Executive Board of the Church has discussed the matter at the request of both conferences, and it may present a supplemental report to this convention relating to this topic. Whether or not the Executive Board submits such a report, the president would undertake to suggest a two-year trial of a plan whereby the Executive Board would, at the expense of its own treasury, arrange to send just one representative of the whole Church to each meeting of each constituent Synod. All of the operating boards would meanwhile cease to send representatives according to the plan hitherto provided for synodical meetings at the expense of those boards.

The second supplement relates to the pastors. Various officers with whom the president has conferred have emphasized strongly the undeniable fact that the most effective promotional work can be done in congregations by their own pastors. Any plan of promotion which is to be complete must make provision so that our pastors are instructed and inspired unto promotional activity. It has however been stated that the pastors themselves are asking for assistance to this end from the Church at large. One man consulted suggested that arrangements be made for an occasional letter from the president of the Church direct to all the pastors. He says that the biennial convention minutes form now the only instance of direct communication from the Church as a whole to the pastors. "It is the pastors' text-book, but it is not much studied by the rank and file. The pastors would be exceedingly glad to get such a circular letter from the president. There is a feeling (I do not know how general it is) that the pastors know little of what is being thought out centrally in the U. L. C. A.. If they knew more, they would be sure to take more interest in and give more support to what is being developed."

Another makes quite a different suggestion. He believes that the Executive Board should arrange to send an authoritative representative of the Church at regular intervals to all theological seminaries in order to instruct the coming pastors thoroughly concerning the purposes and work of the Church. In connection with this suggestion it is to be remembered that even now a number of our agencies ask for time from our seminaries in order to present their special interests to the students. Perhaps the seminaries would welcome the coming rather of a single individual with a "balanced meal" of the Church's provisions. It must also be remembered that even if the Church as a whole does not at present control the seminaries she is greatly concerned that the young men be well prepared to understand the definite activities carried on by the Church.

As a summary of this entire discussion of promotion the following recommendations for action are submitted to the Convention. Action is not asked upon any details in this report excepting as specified in these recommendations. (For action see pp. 418, 420, 431.)

1. The Board of Publication is instructed to arrange so that three times a year a special number of *The Lutheran* is sent to every family within the U. L. C. A. (Substitute adopted, see p. 420.)

2. The Boards of Foreign Missions, American Missions, Education, Parish and Church School, Inner Mission, Deaconess Work, and Ministerial Pensions, and the Laymen's Movement are instructed to arrange for a promotional activity, during their special seasons, in general (not in detail) as explained in this report, and also to appoint their executive secretaries as members of a joint committee for the special purposes assigned to the committee in this report.

3. This Convention commends the loyalty of the Lutheran Brotherhood, the Women's Missionary Society, and the Luther League, and instructs them to further their present purposes whereby their congregational units will be vigorous promotional agents for the interest of the entire congregation in the whole work of the whole Church.

4. The plans above outlined shall be tried faithfully for a period of two years, and are to be reconsidered two years hence. (Omitted by committee as unnecessary to the plan, see pp. 419, 431.)

5. During these two years the three groups of agencies mentioned in recommendations 1, 2, and 3 are instructed to carry out these plans in co-operation with the president of the Church. If agreement cannot be co-operatively reached in any important matter, the point of difference is to be decided by the Executive Board of the Church. (Amended by omission of "During these two years," see pp. 419, 431.)

6. The Executive Board is instructed to consider the feasibility and desirability of an arrangement whereby it will send (at the expense of its own treasury) to each meeting of each constituent synod an authoritative representative of the Church as a whole. If its decision is favorable, it is instructed to proceed. It is in that event also hereby authorized to declare as rescinded all previous actions of the Church concerning the presentation of causes at the meetings of constituent synods.

7. The Executive Board is instructed to consider the second supplementary item in this report (concerning pastors) and is authorized to act in accordance with its decisions and arrangements.

8. All constituent synods are asked to co-operate whole-heartedly in all efforts to make these plans effective, including the use of the delegates to this convention, since they hold office as delegates for the biennium.

If the Convention votes negatively upon recommendations 1 to 5 the following recommendation is offered:

In view of the demand throughout the Church for a thorough plan of promotional activity, the Board of Publication as one group, the Boards of Foreign Missions, American Missions, Education, Parish and Church School, Inner Mission, Deaconess Work, and Ministerial Pensions, and the Laymen's Movement as a second group, and the Lutheran Brotherhood, the Women's Missionary Society, and the Luther League as a third group, are instructed as three separate groups to enter at once upon a study of promotional activities which they can and will carry out for the Church as a whole, and to submit the results of their study for approval to the Executive Board of the Church not later than July 1, 1937. They shall then proceed farther as decided by the Executive Board in consultation with them.

———————

A few items of official action during the biennium must be included in this report, since they are not reported elsewhere.

Immediately after the last convention all special responsibilities from that convention were carried out. This included the official transmission to all other Lutheran bodies in this country of the declaration on Lutheran Church relationships adopted at Savannah. All commissions and committees were also appointed. The authorized Commission on Lutheran Church Relationships and the authorized Committee on Promotion were not named until after the minutes were printed and are therefore reported now. The appointment of the president as a member of both agencies was in accordance with the instructions of the convention.

Committee on Promotion: Rev. F. H. Knubel, Rev. W. H. Greever, Mr. E. Clarence Miller, Mr. Arthur P. Black, Mr. Harry L. Hess, Mr. Grant Hultberg, Rev. H. A. Bosch, Mr. H. E. Isenhour, and Rev. A. J. Traver.

Committee on Lutheran Church Relationships: Rev. F. H. Knubel, Rev. Henry H. Bagger, Rev. Charles M. Jacobs, Rev. John Frederick Krueger, Rev. H. Offermann, Mr. E. F. Eilert, Mr. J. K. Jensen, Mr. E. Clarence Miller, Mr. Edward Rinderknecht. Rev. Paul H. Krauss was later appointed to the vacancy caused by the death of Dr. Krueger.

Dr. Krueger's death also caused a vacancy in the Common Service Book Committee. Rev. E. H. Klotsche was appointed to fill that vacancy.

A few elections in 1934 required that the individuals concerned, because of our constitution's requirements, withdraw from certain agencies. Hon. Claude T. Reno and Prof. J. C. Kinard chose to accept membership on the Executive Board. Mr. Henry Beisler chose to accept membership on the Board of American Missions.

The following appointments of individuals were made as representatives to various meetings. Augustana Synod, 1936, Rev. Paul H. Roth. Installation of Dr. P. O. Bersell as president of the Augustana Synod, Rev. R. H. Gerberding. Suomi Synod, 1936, Rev. John F. Seibert. Icelandic Synod, 1935, Rev. Thos. Hartig; 1936, Rev. Edward T. Horn. American Federation of Lutheran Brotherhoods, Mr. Arthur P. Black. Finnish Apostolic Lutheran Church, 1936, Rev. E. A. Tappert.

The Secretary presented his report as printed in the Bulletin, and it was accepted.

REPORT OF THE SECRETARY

1. Regular Duties.

The current duties pertaining to conferences, correspondence, and official records have been performed during the biennium by conscientious application of time and judgment and by the fullest possible use of resources. Four items are submitted for information.

(a) *Memorials.* The following memorials have been received and, with such material as accompanies them for interpretation, have been placed in the hands of the Chairman of the Committee on Memorials, while mimeographed copies have been prepared for distribution to all delegates in the Convention:

(1)   From the Georgia-Alabama Synod pertaining to new work among the negroes of the South.

(2)   From the German Synod of Nebraska pertaining to (a) ministerial education, and, (b) the consolidation of church periodicals.

(3)   From the Iowa Synod referring to representatives of boards and institutions of the U. L. C. A. in possible work among congregations.

(4)   From the Synod of New York referring to (a) changes in the present pension system, and, (b) ministerial education.

(5)   From the Texas Synod referring to the adoption of "bishop" as the title for executive heads of the synods.

(b) *Directories.* Special effort has been made during this biennium to bring all directories of the Church into complete and accurate form, and to make them easily accessible for whatever use the Church may have for them. The amount of work involved in this effort cannot be realized without a day by day contact. It has included the frequent issue of a bulletin service giving up-to-date changes of addresses, notices of deaths, etc., to all of the Boards, Institutions and Officers of the Constituent Synods.

(c) *Comprehensive Index.* The compilation of a comprehensive index, covering all Minutes of the United Lutheran Church from the first convention and including the 1936 convention, has been undertaken, by authority from the Executive Board, and is well along in its preparation for publication. This will be an index to much collateral material as well as to all records of action.

(d) *Convention Bulletin.* Copy was prepared and arrangements were made for the publication of eight hundred copies of the Bulletin for this Convention, by instructions from the Executive Board.

Note: In the extension work of the office, particularly in the effort to perfect directories, there has been a fine co-operation on the part of Board and synodical officials which I wish to acknowledge with genuine appreciation. It is also right that great credit be given for the improvement in directories to the initiative, judgment and efficiency of Miss Mabel Groneberg, office secretary, to whom the actual work of the Comprehensive Index has been committed.

2. Special Assignments.

(a) *Statistics.* The statistics for the U. L. C. A. have been compiled for publication in the Church Year Book for 1936 and 1937, and for publication in the Minutes of this Convention. (See report of Statistical and Church Year Book Committee.)

(b) *Church Year Book.* The editorial work was done for the Church Year Book for 1936 for publication by the Board of Publication, and all material for the 1937 Year Book, except such as is furnished by this convention, is in the hands of the printer.

The space for the main editorial material for 1936 was used for a summary of the actions of the Savannah Convention, and that space will be used for a similar summary of actions of the Columbus Convention in the 1937 Year Book. As a special feature this should increase the circulation and use of the Year Book.

(c) *Publicity.* (See report of Publicity Committee.)

(d) *Transportation.* (See report of Committee on Transportation.)

(e) *Management of Lutheran Church House.* The Church House at 39 East 35th Street, New York, has had no change in occupancy during this biennium, being headquarters for the officers of the U. L. C. A., for the Board of American Missions, for the Inner Mission Board, for the United Lutheran Synod of New York, and for the National Lutheran Council. The property has been conditioned as occasion has arisen (see financial report to the Executive Board), the occupants have been given the benefit of three months' maintenance within the biennium, maintenance has been improved at lowered cost and $5,000.00 has been allocated to a depreciation fund. Our report as treasurer, as submitted by the auditor, is an item in the report of the Executive Board.

3. Miscellaneous.

I have performed delegated duties at twelve conventions of synods, in numerous special conferences, at one Conference of Synod Presidents, and with various committees, and have accepted invitations for addresses on special occasions, and for the preparation of articles for publication.

W. H. GREEVER.

The Convention proceeded to the election of a President, under the direction of Committee of Tellers No. 1.

The Treasurer presented his report, calling attention to its different divisions, and offering special explanations by way of information.

REPORT OF TREASURER OF THE UNITED LUTHERAN CHURCH IN AMERICA

EXECUTIVE BOARD OF THE UNITED LUTHERAN CHURCH IN AMERICA
STATEMENT OF RECEIPTS AND DISBURSEMENTS ON ACCOUNT OF APPORTIONMENT
For Year Ended June 30, 1935

Balance in Apportionment Fund—July 1, 1934.................................... $4,409.00

RECEIPTS

Ministerium of Pennsylvania...$163,933.14
United Synod of New York 85,125.00

North Carolina Synod	18,830.39
Maryland Synod	71,680.63
South Carolina Synod	15,950.00
West Pennsylvania Synod	71,825.00
Virginia Synod	12,136.32
Ohio Synod	69,109.87
East Pennsylvania Synod	64,886.00
Alleghany Synod	34,377.00
Pittsburgh Synod	68,442.70
Indiana Synod	17,724.40
Illinois Synod	31,000.30
Texas Synod	2,350.18
Susquehanna Synod	31,976.45
Mississippi Synod	351.18
Iowa Synod	6,950.00
Michigan Synod	6,406.21
Georgia-Alabama Synod	5,083.39
Canada Synod	4,545.74
Kansas Synod	8,823.24
Nebraska Synod	7,930.57
Wartburg Synod	2,800.00
German Synod of Nebraska	1,865.55
California Synod	5,525.65
Rocky Mountain Synod	2,532.66
Synod of the Northwest	30,134.43
Manitoba Synod	948.16
Pacific Synod	3,172.08
Nova Scotia Synod	760.07
West Virginia Synod	4,600.00
Slovak Zion Synod	99.83
Florida Synod	1,508.10
Kentucky-Tennessee Synod	6,714.54
Miscellaneous	476.28
Lutheran Publication House	40,000.00

Total Receipts for year ended June 30, 1935.............. 900,575.06

$904,984.06

DISBURSEMENTS

Board of American Missions	$342,980.00
Board of Foreign Missions	270,770.00
Inner Mission Board	15,344.00
Board of Ministerial Pensions and Relief	106,054.00
Board of Education	81,232.00
Board of Deaconess Work	18,050.00
Parish and Church School Boards	9,928.00
National Lutheran Council	10,380.00
National Lutheran Home for the Aged	1,485.00
Tabitha Home	2,708.00
Lowman Home	542.00
American Bible Society	2,257.00
General Fund—United Lutheran Church Treasury..	38,270.00

Total Disbursements for the year ended June 30,
1935 .... 900,000.00

Balance in Apportionment Fund June 30, 1935.............................. $4,984.06

DISTRIBUTION BY MONTHS

August	$70,000.00
September	50,000.00
October	60,000.00
November	60,000.00
December	90,000.00
January	209,055.00
February	79,640.00
March	49,775.00
April	39,820.00
May	69,685.00
June	122,025.00
Total	$900,000.00

STATEMENT OF RECEIPTS AND DISBURSEMENTS ON ACCOUNT OF SPECIALS
For Year Ended June 30, 1935
RECEIPTS

Ministerium of Pennsylvania	$13,194.16
United Synod of New York	7,520.89
North Carolina Synod	994.52
Maryland Synod	1,578.65
South Carolina Synod	539.30
West Pennsylvania Synod	9,626.18
Virginia Synod	1,609.55
Ohio Synod	5,700.94
East Pennsylvania Synod	9,935.00
Alleghany Synod	1,657.75
Pittsburgh Synod	6,778.71
Indiana Synod	78.39
Illinois Synod	2,215.78
Texas Synod	173.80
Susquehanna Synod	37.69
Mississippi Synod	18.43
Iowa Synod	255.53
Michigan Synod	160.83
Georgia-Alabama Synod	226.97
Canada Synod	962.92
Kansas Synod	194.70
Nebraska Synod	844.29
Wartburg Synod	515.59
German Synod of Nebraska	575.22
California Synod	583.12
Rocky Mountain Synod	170.40
Synod of the Northwest	3,124.88
Manitoba Synod	145.34
Pacific Synod	242.62
Nova Scotia Synod	73.62
West Virginia Synod	98.06
Slovak Zion Synod	141.44
Florida Synod	96.11
Kentucky-Tennessee Synod	507.17
Miscellaneous	183.80
Women's Missionary Society	245,812.12
Total	$316,574.47

SPECIAL SYNODICAL HOME MISSION SUPPORT

Receipts: Virginia Synod $2,037.96
        United Synod of New York 2,815.34

                                                                                    $4,853.30

Total Specials Received $321,427.77

STATEMENT OF RECEIPTS AND DISBURSEMENTS ON ACCOUNT OF SPECIALS
For Year Ended June 30, 1935
DISBURSEMENTS

Board of American Missions	$68,747.60
Board of Foreign Missions	221,668.88
Inner Mission Board	9,621.83
Board of Ministerial Pensions and Relief	11,072.57
Board of Education	2,285.09
Board of Deaconess Work	20.16
National Lutheran Council	1,556.08
Tabitha Home	140.73
American Bible Society	19.00
Grace College	387.93
Saskatoon College and Seminary	67.55
Philadelphia Theological Seminary	18.69
Midland College	33.00
Konnarock Training School	11.19
Iron Mountain Lutheran Boys' School	137.95
Pacific Theological Seminary	25.00
Nachusa Lutheran Orphanage	568.80
Lutheran Orient Mission	40.00
American Mission to Lepers	39.50
Bethesda Leper Home	25.00
Mulberry Lutheran Home	20.00
Good Shepherd Home	11.00
National Home Finding Society	6.00
Bible Institute Colportage	6.00
Women's Missionary Society	44.92

Total $316,574.47

SPECIAL SYNODICAL HOME MISSION SUPPORT
DISBURSEMENTS

Board of American Missions $4,853.30

Total Specials Disbursed $321,427.77

RECONCILIATION OF CASH
For Year Ended June 30, 1935

	General Fund United Lutheran Church Treasury	Apportion- ment Fund	Special Funds	Trust Funds	Totals
Balance— June 30, 1934	$20,454.27	$4,409.00	....	$3,283.39	$28,146.66
Receipts for Year	38,653.97	900,575.06	$321,427.77	1,194.12	1,261.850.92
	$59,108.24	$904,984.06	$321,427.77	$4,477.51	$1,289,997.58
Disbursed in Year	63,090.00	900,000.00	321,427.77	....	1,284,517.77
Balance June 30, 1935	$3,981.76*	$4,984.06	....	$4,477.51	$5,479.81

*Overdraft.

STATEMENT OF RECEIPTS AND DISBURSEMENTS ON ACCOUNT OF APPORTIONMENT
For Year Ended June 30, 1936

Balance in Apportionment Fund—July 1, 1935.............................. $4,984.06

RECEIPTS

Ministerium of Pennsylvania	$161,837.51
United Synod of New York	93,520.00
North Carolina Synod	18,050.06
Maryland Synod	69,867.79
South Carolina Synod	17,750.00
West Pennsylvania Synod	76,090.00
Virginia Synod	14,481.46
Ohio Synod	81,935.16
East Pennsylvania Synod	65,094.00
Alleghany Synod	37,006.00
Pittsburgh Synod	69,314.63
Indiana Synod	16,503.63
Illinois Synod	27,500.00
Texas Synod	2,483.29
Susquehanna Synod	34,533.00
Mississippi Synod	369.32
Iowa Synod	7,000.00
Michigan Synod	6,867.00
Georgia-Alabama Synod	5,373.97
Canada Synod	4,766.24
Kansas Synod	8,110.00
Nebraska Synod	7,296.43
Wartburg Synod	3,100.00
German Synod of Nebraska	2,054.46
California Synod	5,095.07

Rocky Mountain Synod	3,178.00
Synod of the Northwest	29,235.58
Manitoba Synod	864.00
Pacific Synod	3,352.16
Nova Scotia Synod	663.05
West Virginia Synod	4,350.00
Slovak Zion Synod	38.60
Florida Synod	1,515.96
Kentucky-Tennessee Synod	7,699.94
Miscellaneous	255.00
Lutheran Publication House	30,000.00

Total Receipts for year ended June 30, 1936 ....   917,151.31

$922,135.37

STATEMENT OF RECEIPTS AND DISBURSEMENTS ON ACCOUNT OF APPORTIONMENT

For Year Ended June 30, 1936

DISBURSEMENTS

Board of American Missions	$353,372.00
Board of Foreign Missions	276,500.00
Board of Inner Missions	15,669.00
Board of Ministerial Pensions and Relief	108,296.00
Board of Education	82,948.00
Board of Deaconess Work	18,431.00
Parish and Church School Board	10,141.00
National Lutheran Council	10,597.00
Tabitha Home	2,212.00
Lowman Home	444.00
American Bible Society	2,304.00
General Fund—United Lutheran Church Treasury	39,086.00

Total Disbursements for the year ended June 30, 1936 ....   920,000.00

Balance in Apportionment Fund June 30, 1936 .... $2,135.37

DISTRIBUTION BY MONTHS

August, 1935	$100,000.00
September, 1935	50,000.00
October, 1935	60,000.00
November, 1935	70,000.00
December, 1935	90,000.00
January, 1936	210,000.00
February, 1936	70,000.00
March, 1936	40,000.00
April, 1936	50,000.00
May, 1936	70,000.00
June, 1936	110,000.00

Total $920,000.00

STATEMENT OF RECEIPTS AND DISBURSEMENTS ON ACCOUNT OF SPECIALS
For Year Ended June 30, 1936
RECEIPTS

Ministerium of Pennsylvania	$10,006.56
United Synod of New York	8,119.05
North Carolina Synod	518.36
Maryland Synod	1,965.15
South Carolina Synod	1,133.75
West Pennsylvania Synod	8,418.41
Virginia Synod	1,491.69
Ohio Synod	4,797.64
East Pennsylvania Synod	8,359.00
Alleghany Synod	703.75
Pittsburgh Synod	6,828.26
Indiana Synod	486.84
Illinois Synod	2,447.37
Texas Synod	345.18
Susquehanna Synod	675.78
Mississippi Synod	13.43
Iowa Synod	374.73
Michigan Synod	137.76
Georgia-Alabama Synod	183.79
Canada Synod	911.11
Kansas Synod	142.24
Nebraska Synod	847.57
Wartburg Synod	688.18
German Synod of Nebraska	595.81
California Synod	158.40
Rocky Mountain Synod	270.04
Synod of the Northwest	4,872.53
Manitoba Synod	529.53
Pacific Synod	360.09
Slovak Zion Synod	143.10
Florida Synod	59.82
Kentucky-Tennessee Synod	421.96
Miscellaneous	1,686.25
Women's Missionary Society	264,104.19
Income on Trust Funds (Designated)	2,834.60
	$335,631.92

SPECIAL SYNODICAL HOME MISSION SUPPORT

Receipts: Virginia Synod	$3,857.02
United Synod of New York	7,351.54
	$11,208.56
Total Specials Received	$346,840.48

STATEMENT OF RECEIPTS AND DISBURSEMENTS ON ACCOUNT OF SPECIALS
For Year Ended June 30, 1936

DISBURSEMENTS

Board of American Missions	$79,906.83
Board of Foreign Missions	231,043.28
Inner Mission Board	7,209.16
Board of Ministerial Pensions and Relief	8,801.72
Board of Education	2,326.25
Board of Deaconess Work	14.73
National Lutheran Council	2,877.42
Tabitha Home	106.71
American Bible Soceity	12.29
Grace College	250.00
Carthage College	3.80
Midland College	34.18
Saskatoon College and Seminary	34.00
Pacific Theological Seminary	15.00
Philadelphia Theological Seminary	10.15
Iron Mountain Lutheran Boys' School	83.43
Nachusa Lutheran Orphanage	630.63
Lutheran Orphans' Home of the South	258.67
American Mission to Lepers	34.49
Bethesda Leper Colony	30.85
Women's Missionary Society	22.48
Lutheran Orient Mission	45.00
Lutheran Inner Mission Society	23.15
Flood Relief	600.00
Sundry Specials	83.15
	$334,457.37

SPECIAL SYNODICAL HOME MISSION SUPPORT

Disbursements:	
Board of American Missions	$10,913.59
Balance on hand June 30, 1936—Virginia Synod	294.97
Balance of Undistributed Specials at June 30, 1936	1,174.55
	$12,383.11
Total Specials Disbursed and Undistributed	$346,840.48

RECONCILIATION OF CASH
For Year Ended June 30, 1936

	General Fund United Lutheran Church Treasury	Apportion- ment Fund	Specials Fund	Trust Funds	Totals
Balance— June 30, 1936	$3,981.76*	$4,984.06	....	$4,477.51	$5,479.81

Receipts for year....	40,404.00	917,151.31	$346,840.48	17,005.47	1,321,401.26
	$36,422.24	$922,135.37	$346,840.48	$21,482.98	$1,326,881.07
Disbursed in year	34,557.89	920,000.00	345,370.96	13,962.88	1,313,891.73
Cash Balance— June 30, 1936	$1,864.35	$2,135.37	$1,469.52	$7,520.10	$12,989.34

*Overdraft.

STATEMENT OF RECEIPTS AND DISBURSEMENTS ON ACCOUNT OF EXECUTIVE BOARD EXPENSES

For the Year Ended June 30, 1935

Balance—July 1, 1934 .... $20,454.27

RECEIPTS

Proportion of Apportionment	$38,270.00	
Refunds a/c Convention Expense	83.97	
Funds for Transmission	300.00	
Total Receipts		38,653.97
		$59,108.24

DISBURSEMENTS

Salary—President	$6,400.00
Secretary	5,220.00
Clerks	3,392.00
Travel Expense—President	85.99
Secretary	212.71
Expense—Executive Board	954.04
General Expenses—New York City	87.45
Office Supplies, etc.—New York City	182.71
Postage—New York City	201.00
Telegrams—New York City	28.87
Telephone—New York City	158.34
Maintenance Lutheran Church House...............................	2,040.00
Auditors' Expense	235.33
Treasurer's Expense—Accounting Bond, etc.	1,401.80
Check Tax—Philadelphia and New York	6.02
United Lutheran Church—Savannah, Ga., Convention:	
Delegates Expense	24,933.00
Publicity Expenses	946.47
Bulletin and Minutes	3,700.59
Sundry Expenses	730.75
Publicity Expenses—General	147.12
Appropriation—Luther League	6,000.00
Lutheran World Convention	1,702.84
Federal Council of Churches	2,000.00
Committee—Church Papers	136.65
Women's Work	35.50
Worship	5.00

Architecture	92.88	
Adjudication	212.21	
Common Service Book	411.77	
Evangelism	230.13	
Social and Moral Welfare	17.00	
Faith and Order	66.41	
Transportation	9.98	
Necrology	388.00	
Statistics and Year Book	54.25	
Special Committees	363.19	
Transmission of Funds	300.00	

Total Disbursements in year ended June 30, 1935..   63,090.00

Deficit in United Lutheran Church—General Fund June 30, 1935 $3,981.76

STATEMENT OF RECEIPTS AND DISBURSEMENTS ON ACCOUNT OF EXECUTIVE BOARD EXPENSES

For Year Ended June 30, 1936

Deficit—July 1, 1935 $3,981.76

RECEIPTS

Proportion of Apportionment	$39,086.00	
Funds for Transmission	1,318.00	
Total Receipts		40,404.00
		$36,422.24

DISBURSEMENTS

Salary—President	$6,400.00
Secretary	5,220.00
Clerks	3,392.00
Travel Expenses—President	397.10
Secretary	293.04
Expense—Executive Board	874.72
General Expense—New York City	459.54
Office Supplies, etc.—New York City	375.38
Postage—New York City	173.91
Telegrams—New York City	28.69
Telephone—New York City	107.26
Maintenance—Lutheran Church House	2,244.00
Auditors' Expense	228.90
Treasurer's Expense	1,401.50
Appropriation—Luther League	6,000.00
Lutheran World Convention	2,302.84
Federal Council of Churches	2,000.00
World Conference Faith and Order	100.00
Committee—Architecture	121.38
Church Papers	7.20
Transportation	11.05
Statistical	41.03
Promotion	67.00
Lutheran Union and Relations	506.81

Common Service Book	88.99
Investments	121.25
Special Committees, etc.	148.88
Publicity	92.42
Legal Expense	35.00
Transmission of Funds	1,318.00

Total Disbursements 34,557.89

Balance in United Lutheran Church—General
Fund—June 30, 1936 .... $1,864.35

Trust Fund Accounts
June 30, 1936

	Equipment and Real Estate	Cash on Hand $764.75P	Investments Cost or Book Value	Investments Market Values June 30, 1936	Principal $9,656.75
Emma K. Sotter Trust:					
$1,800 Altoona and Logan Valley Electric Railway Company 1st Lien and Collateral Trust 4s, due 1/1/54					
12 shares Voting Trust Certificate common stock Altoona and Logan Valley Electric Railway Company			$2,940.00	} $1,593.00	
				840.00	
$3,000 Appalachian Electric Power 1st and Refunding 5s, 1956			2,968.50	3,176.25	
$3,000 Georgia Power Company 1st Refunding 5s, 1967			2,983.50	3,030.00	
			$8,892.00	$8,639.25	
M. S. Hottenstein Trust:					
$1,000 Certificate of Deposit Hotel Chelsea 1st 6s, 1945			$1,000.00	$180.00	1,000.00
W. P. Huffman Trust:					
$2,500 First Mortgage—5407 Vine Street, Philadelphia, Pa.			$2,500.00	$2,500.00	7,500.00
$3,000 Georgia Power Company 1st and Refunding 5s, 1967			3,000.00	3,030.00	
$2,000 American Gas and Electric 5s, 2028			2,000.00	2,142.50	
			$7,500.00	$7,672.50	
C. Pflaum, Jr., Trust:					
$5,000 Certificate of Deposit, Times Square and 46th Street Building, New York City, 1st 6s, 1953			$5,000.00	$275.00	5,000.00

Rev. R. A. Hafer Trust:				
40 shares Northern Pacific Railroad Company......	17.50I	$3,780.00	$1,105.00	
10 shares Public Service Corporation, New Jersey, 7 per cent Preferred		1,260.00	1,370.00	
		$5,040.00	$2,475.00	5,040.00
Oscar S. Grim Trust:				
$5,000 Detroit Edison General 4½s, 1961......	1,684.53P	$4,787.72	$5,787.50	6,472.25
Oscar V. Haubner Trust:				
$5,000 Pennsylvania Company 4s, due 8/1/63......	2,987.90P	$5,000.00	$5,187.50	7,987.90
General Funds:				
M. E. Smith				500.00
Estate John S. Drew				200.00
Bertha Kreugel				980.00
Naomi Smoots	7.42I*			892.71
William H. Hildebrand	1,642.71P			200.00
$1,000 New York Central Railroad C.V. 6s, 1944..		$1,130.00	$1,120.00	
Depreciation Account:				
Lutheran Church House, 39 East 35th Street, New York City	{ 460.00P			5,000.00
$4,000 New York Central Railroad, C.V. 6s, 1944..	29.87I*	$4,540.00	$4,480.00	
Lutheran Church House, 39 East 35th Street, New York City	$196,413.44			196,413.44
Real Estate at Wisner, Nebraska, held in Schmauk Trust—value not determined				
Totals	$7,520.10	$42,889.72	$35,816.75	$246,843.05
	$196,413.44			$196,413.44

Principal (P) $7,539.89, plus Income (I) $19.79* makes total uninvested cash of $7,520.10.

Respectfully submitted,
E. CLARENCE MILLER, *Treasurer.*

*Represents Deficit.

July 30, 1936.

We have audited the accounts of the Treasurer and examined the securities of the United Lutheran Church in America, for the biennium beginning July 1, 1934 and ending June 30, 1936, and we hereby certify that in our opinion the foregoing statements of:

Receipts and Disbursements on Account of Apportionment for the years ending June 30, 1935 and June 30, 1936.
Receipts and Disbursements on Account of Specials for the years ending June 30, 1935 and June 30, 1936.
Reconciliation of Cash for the years ending June 30, 1935 and June 30, 1936.
Receipts and Disbursements on Account of Executive Board Expenses for the years ending June 30, 1935 and June 30, 1936.
Trust Fund Accounts as of June 30, 1936.

are in agreement with the books of account and are true and correct.

TAIT, WELLER AND BAKER,
Accountants and Auditors.

On motion the report of the auditors was accepted.

The Convention proceeded to the election of a Treasurer under the direction of Committee of Tellers No. 2.

At eleven o'clock the presence of Governor Martin Luther Davey of Ohio was announced, and he was introduced to the Convention by Judge Charles Zimmerman. The Governor spoke especially concerning the necessity for religious influence in a healthy society. A proper response to the Governor's address was made by Mr. Edward Rinderknecht.

At this point, the Committee of Tellers reported that the Rev. F. H. Knubel had received 398 votes for President out of a total of 436 votes cast. The Secretary declared that Dr. Knubel, having received more than a three-fourths majority of the votes cast on the first ballot, was elected President of The United Lutheran Church in America.

The Committee also reported that E. Clarence Miller had received 425 votes for Treasurer out of a total of 432 votes cast. The President declared Dr. Miller elected Treasurer.

The Convention proceeded to the election of a Secretary, under Committee of Tellers No. 1.

The Secretary presented the report of the Executive Board.

REPORT OF THE EXECUTIVE BOARD

I. CONCERNING THE EXECUTIVE BOARD

1. Members:

Ex-Officio: Rev. F. H. Knubel, Rev. W. H. Greever, E. Clarence Miller.

Term Expires 1938: Rev. A. E. Bell, Rev. J. L. Morgan, Rev. R. E. Tulloss, J. K. Jensen, James C. Kinard, Claude T. Reno.

Term Expires 1936: Rev. E. B. Burgess, Rev. E. P. Pfatteicher, Rev. A. Steimle, Wm. E. Hirt, Robbin B. Wolf, John L. Zimmerman.

2. Committees of the Executive Board:

At the beginning of the biennium the following committees were appointed by the President:

Committee on Constituent Synods

Rev. E. P. Pfatteicher   Rev. J. L. Morgan
Rev. A. E. Bell   Robbin B. Wolf

Committee on Boards and Committees

Rev. E. B. Burgess   Rev. A. Steimle
Rev. R. E. Tulloss   James C. Kinard

Finance Committee

E. Clarence Miller   J. K. Jensen
John L. Zimmerman

Legal Committee

Wm. E. Hirt   Claude T. Reno
Robbin B. Wolf

Committee on Parish Education Plan

Rev. R. E. Tulloss   Rev. Paul C. White
Rev. E. B. Burgess   Rev. Franklin C. Fry
Rev. Gould Wickey   Miss Flora Prince

Committee on Mountain Work Conference

Rev. J. L. Morgan   Rev. J. L. Sieber
Rev. Z. M. Corbe   Prof. M. S. Beam
Rev. J. J. Scherer   Mrs. W. F. Morehead
Mr. H. E. Isenhour

Committee on Better Adjustment of Auxiliary Societies

Rev. A. Steimle   Rev. W. H. Greever
Rev. E. P. Pfatteicher

3. Vacancies filled:

At the meeting of the Executive Board, April 11, 1935, Mr. J. K. Jensen, of the Synod of the Northwest, was elected to membership in the Executive Board for the term ending 1938, to fill the vacancy of Mr. Henry Beisler, resigned, whose resignation was made in favor of service on the Board of American Missions.

4. Nominations to fill Vacancies:

To fill vacancies occurring at this convention, the Board places the following in nomination: Rev. E. B. Burgess, Rev. E. P. Pfatteicher, Rev. A. Steimle, Robbin B. Wolf, John L. Zimmerman, Rev. Paul H. Krauss, Rev. A. A. Zinck, Rev. M. R. Hamsher, C. W. Howe, Benjamin Apple, Carl M. Distler, A. F. Sittloh.

5. Report of the Executive Board:

The Board instructed the Secretary to prepare the report of the Board for presentation to this convention. The Secretary was also instructed to prepare the Bulletin for the convention, and to have eight hundred copies of the Bulletin printed and distributed to members of the convention.

II. MATTERS REFERRED

1. Minutes: (Minutes U. L. C. A., 1934, p. 563)

At the meeting of the Executive Board, January 10, 1935, the Minutes of the final session of the 1934 Convention were submitted by order of the Convention and approved by the Executive Board.

The Executive Board, at the same meeting, approved the order previously placed by the Secretary for the printing and distribution of four thousand four hundred copies of the Minutes of the 1934 Convention.

2. Change in Place of 1936 Convention if Necessary: (Minutes U. L. C. A., 1934, p. 559)

See XIII, 1, (a) of this report.

3. Dissolution of Immigrant Missions and Northwestern Mission Boards: (Minutes U. L. C. A., 1934, pp. 73, 114)

The matter of the dissolution of the Immigrant Missions and Northwestern Mission Boards still remains in the hands of the Board of American Missions, which Board has been instructed to notify the Executive Board when proper legal steps have been taken for the dissolution.

4. Policy concerning annuities to be reported by Commission on Investments: (Minutes U. L. C. A., 1934, p. 97)

The report by the Commission on Investments on the policy concerning annuities is still pending.

*5. Year 1938 for Board of American Missions: (Minutes U. L. C. A., 1934, pp. 51, 113) (For action on this item, see pp. 88, 184f.)

The request of the Board of American Missions for permission to use the year 1938 as a time to conduct a campaign on behalf of church extension funds, was deferred for action by this convention and is hereby presented for that purpose.

6. **Mass Meeting Preceding 1936 Convention:** (Minutes U. L. C. A., 1934, p. 175)

See XIII, 1 (b) of this report.

*7. **Better Adjustment of the Work of Auxiliaries:** (Minutes U. L. C. A., 1934, pp. 98, 114) (For action on this item, see pp. 89, 97, 261, 432.)

The Committee of the Executive Board, appointed for the further consideration of better adjustments with the auxiliaries within the Church, submitted the following report to the Executive Board, which was adopted at its meeting July 9, 1936, for presentation to the Convention:

A. Resolved, (1), That the Women's Missionary Society, the Luther League of America and the Lutheran Brotherhood, as organized groups of volunteer workers within the Church for auxiliary service to the Church and its boards and institutions, with such freedom in organization, methods and activities as is consistent with the accepted procedure of the Church, make their reports direct to the Church in the conventions of the U. L. C. A. and of the constituent synods; and in accordance herewith

Resolved, (2), That Section VII, B, 5, 6, and 7 of the By-laws of the U. L. C. A. be stricken out.

B. Resolved, That the official status of the Women's Missionary Society, the Luther League, and the Lutheran Brotherhood, between conventions, be that of recognized auxiliaries within the U. L. C. A. and constituent synods.

C. Resolved, (1), That the Women's Missionary Society, the Luther League and the Lutheran Brotherhood include in their spheres of interest the whole program of the whole Church, as formulated by the Church through its official action.

Resolved, (2), That the program of the Women's Missionary Society, the Luther League and the Lutheran Brotherhood shall include

(a) The stimulation of congregations to meet apportionments in full;

(b) The assumption of definite responsibility for designated projects, properly authorized by the Church.

(c) The exercise of freedom by these organizations in their programs of education, inspiration, method and promotion, with such co-ordination with other educational and promotional agencies of the Church as is necessary to the unity of the comprehensive program of the Church. In the selection, assignment and assumption of projects the whole work of the Church is to be considered. All administrative responsibilities in connection with these projects remain with the boards. Under the approval of the Board or institution concerned, the organizations may have such contacts with these projects as may appear necessary to the promotion of intelligent interest.

Since the justification of these group organizations within the Church is based upon practical considerations, such voice in administrative matters as their work may merit is provided for through the recognition of their members as eligible to membership on boards.

D. Resolved, (1), That in stating the budget of the United Lutheran Church, the benevolent budgets of the Women's Missionary Society, the Luther League and the Lutheran Brotherhood shall also be stated,— thus emphasizing the common interest in the one work; removing all occasion for designations, as "Men's Work," "Women's Work" or "Young People's Work";

Resolved, (2), That the preparation of the benevolent budgets of the Women's Missionary Society, of the Luther League and of the Lutheran Brotherhood shall be made in consultation and co-operation with the Finance Committee of the Executive Board and the Boards of the Church in whose financial work they share, and that the Boards in surveying their needs shall keep this arrangement in view.

NOTE: This contemplates the adoption by the Church of a budget to be presented in a two-fold form, with total, to indicate the work of the Church in its entirety and its unity.

(A.) The *Apportioned Budget*, which is the primary provision for the work of the boards and agencies of the Church. For this the Church asks the organizations to extend the service of their educational, inspirational and promotional effort to the whole membership of the Church, through individual contacts and otherwise, with the purpose to secure apportionments in full. As a first step in this direction we suggest that these organizations include in the reports which they ask from individual societies these questions: Does your congregation pay its apportionment in full? What is your society doing to educate your congregation to pay its apportionment in full?

(B.) The *Supplementary Budget*, which includes the auxiliary work done under the head of authorized designated work, for the support of which the organizations assume responsibility. These designated projects are subject to the general rule of the Church concerning all appeals: That no general appeal for their support is to be made in congregations which do not pay their apportionments in full; but the Church approves and encourages general appeals for authorized projects in congregations which meet their apportionments. In congregations which do not meet their apportionments the societies must depend upon their own members for funds for the support of their budgets. Funds contributed to the societies for designated projects ought not be diverted under any circumstances to congregational treasuries for the payment of apportionments.

(C.) The *Total Budget*.

E. With reference to the training of the children of the Church for Christian service:

Resolved, that

(1) The organizational training and leadership of children in the work of the Church, up to the age of twelve years, shall be in the hands of one agency.

(2) The merging of the two organizations now operating in this work, the Light Brigade and the Junior Luther League, and the further extension of organized work with the children as specified above, be placed in the hands of a committee of five to be constituted by the appointment of one member from the Women's Missionary Society, one from the Luther League, one from the Parish and Church School Board, one pastor and one from the Executive Board,—the last two to be

appointed by the President of the U. L. C. A., and the other members to be appointed by the organizations to be represented.

(3) This committee shall be constituted and shall meet as soon as practicable for the purpose of working out a detailed plan for the merging of the Light Brigade and the Junior Luther League, subject to the approval of the Executive Board of the U. L. C. A., and to be presented for the consideration of the Executive Board at its April, 1937, meeting. Such plan as is approved by the Executive Board shall become effective as soon after approval as may be found possible.

F. Resolved, That in the interest of efficiency, economy and co-operation, this committee call a meeting of representatives of the mission boards, Women's Missionary Society, Luther League and Lutheran Brotherhood to consider the matter of a periodical which shall serve all of the interests represented.

8. **Resolution from Inner Mission Board regarding its financial support:**
   (Minutes, U. L. C. A., 1934, pp. 355, 356)

The request of the Inner Mission Board for increased financial support was referred by the 1934 Convention to the Executive Board and by it to its Finance Committee. At the meeting of the Executive Board, April 11, 1935, the Finance Committee reported that there were no funds available for such increase, and the report of the Finance Committee was adopted by the Executive Board.

9. **Memorial from Synod of West Virginia concerning appropriation for Parish and Church School Board:** (Minutes, U. L. C. A., 1934, pp. 420, 422)
   See IV, B, 6 (a) of this report.

10. **Resolution from Commissioners to National Lutheran Council concerning its budget:** (Minutes, U. L. C. A., 1934, p. 490)
    See VII, 2, of this report.

11. **Auditors' Report for the Lutheran World Convention:** (Minutes, U. L. C. A., 1934, p. 512)
    See VIII, 1, of this report.

12. **Expense involved in Educational Survey by Committee on Moral and Social Welfare:** (Minutes, U. L. C. A., 1934, pp. 481, 482)
    The Committee on Moral and Social Welfare conducted the survey in such manner as to make it unnecessary to ask for any extra appropriation.

13. **Representation of the U. L. C. A. at the Lutheran World Convention:** (Minutes, U. L. C. A., 1934, p. 512)
    See VIII, 3 (a), of this report.

14. Merger of Statistical and Church Year Book Committee and Publicity Committee: (Minutes, U. L. C. A., 1934, pp. 82, 114)
See IV, A, 2, (c).

*15. **Restudy of procedure with reference to Nominations and Elections:**
(Minutes, U. L. C. A., 1934, p. 563) (For action on these items, see p. 20.)

(a) Concerning the restudy of procedure with reference to nominations and elections, the following is the action taken by the Executive Board at its meeting April 11, 1935, together with preliminary statements:

"At the Savannah Convention of the Church, Section V, Item 2, of the By-laws of The United Lutheran Church was amended in such manner as to provide, that the number of nominees presented to the convention by the Boards and Nominating Committees should total three times as many as are to be elected. See Minutes, U. L. C. A., 1934, page 70. At the same convention attention was called to the fact that the increased number of nominations, and the consequent lengthening of the elections, had deprived a considerable number of laymen of the privileges of several business sessions. In view of these experiences, the following action was taken during the last session of the convention:

" 'That the Executive Board be instructed to restudy the procedure with reference to the nomination and election of Board members at the convention of the United Lutheran Church, with particular attention being given to questions of methods and time required to conduct the elections, and the results of the elections as affecting the membership of the Boards at the convention—the restudy to be presented at the next convention.' (Minutes, U. L. C. A., 1934, p 563.)

"It is clear that any restudy of this method of nominations and elections must turn upon the vital question of the improvement of the personnel of the Boards. The related questions of methods of expediting business in the election rooms, and the absence of laymen from the business sessions, must be considered incidental to the main purpose, which gave the new method its birth. If the old method, with its two-fold nomination, gave stronger men to the Boards, it should be restored; if the new method gives promise of accomplishing that purpose, it should be retained long enough for a true test. Time is needed to demonstrate its possibilities in the development of alertness in nominations, keenness of interest in the electorate, and efficiency in the work of the Boards. Results cannot be adequately appraised at the close of the first convention. In view of these facts, the Committee on Boards and Committees offers the following recommendations:

"(A) That the Executive Board can find no adequate reasons for recommending a change in the method of nominations and elections at this time.

"(B) That the Secretary of the Executive Board be authorized to make such arrangements as may be necessary with the local committee of the entertaining congregations to provide local assistants for the help of the Committee of Tellers at future conventions."

The Executive Board adopted the recommendations of the Committee on Boards and Committees.

(b) The Executive Board presents the following pertaining to the second ballot:

"Resolved, That in all elections of Boards, Elective Commissions and Committees, the first ballot be considered as a nominating ballot in cases where election does not result, and that the nominees receiving the high vote be declared the nominees on the second ballot, to the number of two nominees for each vacancy, and that voting be limited to those so nominated. In cases of ties, the number of nominees for each vacancy would be increased as necessary on account of tie votes."

16. **Report of Committee on Promotion:** (Minutes, U. L. C. A., 1934, pp. 420, 421, 422, 523)

At its meeting July 9, 1936, the Executive Board requested the President to incorporate in his official report to this convention, the conclusions resulting from the various conferences and committee meetings involved in the development of a plan for general promotion in the Church.

This action followed the action taken by the Executive Board at its meeting, January 9, 1936, which action placed the whole matter of general promotion in the hands of the President until such time as further developments may indicate a different course. (See Report of President.)

17. **New Plan of Apportionment:** (Minutes, U. L. C. A., 1934, pp. 116, 418, 422)
See III, A, 2, (a), of this report.

18. **Memorial from the Synod of the Northwest concerning apportionment:** (Minutes, U. L. C. A., 1934, pp. 418, 422)
See III, A, 2, (a), of this report.

19. **Call and Location of Pastors:** (Minutes, U. L. C. A., 1934, pp. 417, 422)
See III, A, 2, (c), of this report.

20. **Monthly periodical on Church work:** (Minutes, U. L. C. A., 1934, pp. 520, 521)
The matter of a monthly periodical on Church work, by reference, is still unfinished business in the hands of the Committee on Promotion and the Committee on Better Adjustments.

21. **Triennial conventions and/or reduction of total number of delegates:** (Minutes, U. L. C. A., 1934, pp. 473, 475)
See III, 2, (b), of this report.

22. **Development of convention's decisions concerning synodical budgets:** (Minutes, U. L. C. A., 1934, pp. 62, 113, 114, 513)
Concerning the action of the 1934 Convention with reference to new items or objects for synodical budgets, the following recommendation,

viz, "that the synods make no such additions without conference with the Church" has apparently been accepted by the synods in the spirit in which it was adopted. (See III, B, 1 and 2, of this report.)

23. **Report of Committee on Women as Congregational Representatives:**
(Minutes, U. L. C. A., 1934, p. 524)

The report of the Committee on Women as Congregational Representatives will be called for in the regular order as per the convention program.

III. SYNODS

A. In General

1. Apportionment to Synods, 1936 and 1937:

The budget of $2,000,000, adopted at Savannah for the years 1936 and 1937, was apportioned among the constituent synods as follows:

Apportionment for 1936

Synod	Communing Membership	Apportionment
Ministerium of Pennsylvania	146,166	$407,007
United Synod of New York	106,148	295,575
North Carolina	19,695	54,841
Maryland	31,399	87,432
South Carolina	14,528	40,454
West Pennsylvania	34,688	96,590
Virginia	13,522	37,652
Ohio	48,236	134,316
East Pennsylvania	34,928	97,259
Alleghany	20,157	56,128
Pittsburgh	55,600	154,821
Indiana	11,655	32,454
Illinois	29,471	82,063
Texas	3,209	8,935
Wartburg	10,748	29,928
Susquehanna	25,293	70,429
Mississippi	316	879
Iowa	7,798	21,713
Michigan	4,216	11,739
Georgia–Alabama	3,055	8,506
Canada	15,638	43,544
Kansas	5,481	15,262
Nebraska	10,817	30,120
German Nebraska	10,045	27,970
California	3,824	10,648
Rocky Mountain	1,661	4,625
Northwest	27,140	75,572
Manitoba	6,226	17,336
Pacific	2,139	5,956
Nova Scotia	1,983	5,521

West Virginia	3,130	8,715
Slovak Zion	4,718	13,137
Florida	1,052	2,929
Kentucky-Tennessee	3,564	9,924
	718,246	$2,000,000

Apportionment for 1937

Synod	Communing Membership	Apportionment
Ministerium of Pennsylvania	148,215	$402,755
United Synod of New York	108,033	293,565
North Carolina	20,165	54,796
Maryland	31,716	86,184
South Carolina	14,894	40,472
West Pennsylvania	35,414	96,233
Virginia	13,368	36,326
Ohio	50,022	135,928
East Pennsylvania	34,816	94,608
Alleghany	20,741	56,361
Pittsburgh	56,953	154,762
Indiana	12,132	32,967
Illinois	31,544	85,717
Texas	3,328	9,043
Susquehanna	25,727	69,910
Mississippi	397	1,079
Iowa	8,559	23,258
Georgia-Alabama	3,010	8,179
Canada	15,958	43,364
Kansas	5,590	15,190
Nebraska	11,386	30,940
Wartburg	10,870	29,538
German Nebraska	10,411	28,290
California	4,236	11,511
Rocky Mountain	1,697	4,611
Northwest	28,949	78,665
Manitoba	6,559	17,823
Pacific	1,988	5,402
Nova Scotia	2,081	5,655
West Virginia	3,484	9,467
Slovak Zion	4,659	12,660
Michigan	4,401	11,959
Florida	1,104	3,000
Kentucky-Tennessee	3,600	9,782
	736,007	$2,000,000

2. Conference of Synod Presidents:

At the meeting of the Executive Board, September 26, 1935, the following action was taken with reference to the Conference of Synod Presidents:

"1. The holding of one conference for all synodical presidents with the President of the United Lutheran Church.

"2. The time and place of this conference to be January 7, 8, 1936, at the Deshler-Wallick Hotel at Columbus, Ohio.

"3. The Conference is to consist of five sessions, three of which are to be held on Tuesday and two on Wednesday.

"4. The subjects of the papers in thesis form are to be as follows:

"(1) The Call of a Pastor—Minutes, 1934, p. 417 (Item 2)
The congregation's right of recall. Unemployed ministers. Names of ministers disappearing from rolls of synods without any synodical action. 'Calling' across synodical lines.

"(2) Stewardship—The Proposed New Plan of Apportionment.
The Northwest Synod's Plan. The Every Member Visitation. Minutes, 1932, p. 86; 1934, p. 115; 1934, p. 418, (Item 5). Congregations and Profit Making Practices.

"(3) The Question of Authority—U. L. C. A.; synod; congregation.

"(4) Discipline—Presidential guidance of pastors. Proper use of the Sacraments. Liturgical tendencies. Washington Declaration on External Relationships.

"(5) The Question of Relationships
(a) Better Adjustment of Auxiliaries.
A survey of what the synods and their congregations are doing in this respect.
(b) Presentation of Causes at Synodical Conventions.
Discussion based on the report of the Committee on Constituent Synods to the Executive Board."

This conference was held in Columbus, Ohio, at the appointed date, and was attended by twenty-nine out of the thirty-four presidents of constituent synods, resulting in the submission of the following items for further consideration:

*(a) Basis of Apportionment: (For action on this item, see p. 89.)

On the subject of the basis of apportionment, the following resolutions were submitted to the Executive Board by the Conference of Presidents:

"Resolved, that the Executive Board of the Church be advised that it is the opinion of the Conference of Presidents that it is *not advisable to change the present basis* of apportionment in the U. L. C. A. at the present time."

"Resolved, that it is the opinion of this Conference of Presidents that no change should be made in the method of apportionment at the present time."

(b) Presentation of Causes to Synods:

The matter of presentation of the causes of the Church at meetings of constituent synods was referred by the Executive Board to the officers of the Church for conference with the committee on the same from the Conference of Secretaries.

(c) Call and Location of Pastors:

The Executive Board, having presented the matter of call and location of pastors for discussion at the Conference of Presidents of Constituent

Synods, adopted a resolution instructing the President to appoint a special committee to prepare a statement concerning this matter. At the meeting of the Executive Board, July 9, 1936, the President announced the following committee: Rev. H. F. Baughman (Chairman), Rev. C. K. Bell, Rev. E. E. Flack, Rev. E. P. Pfatteicher, and Rev. Russell D. Snyder.

At the meeting of the Executive Board, January 9, 1936, the following was adopted:

"We recommend that a roster of available pastors within the U. L. C. A. be established as the medium requested by the Alleghany Synod, and that this roster be set up in the Office of the Secretary, and that the directors of this bureau be the Secretary of the U. L. C. A., a Secretary of the Board of American Missions in the New York office of said Board, and the President of the Synod of New York."

(d) Irregularities in the filling of vacancies:

In the light of facts and practices connected with the call of pastors to vacant congregations, as the facts and practices were presented through the Conference of Presidents, the Executive Board, at its meeting January 9, 1936, adopted the following:

"Concerning certain irregularities in the filling of vacancies, we recommend that the constitutional provisions of the respective synods thereto pertaining be complied with in the interest of orderly procedure. To this end we request congregations and individuals to avail themselves of the advice of the president of the respective synod."

(e) Certificates of Ordination:

With reference to Certificates of Ordination, the Conference of Presidents requested the Executive Board to secure a ruling concerning the significance of Certificates of Ordination, including the problem of their surrender. At the meeting of the Executive Board, January 9, 1936, the recommendation was adopted that the Executive Board request the Commission of Adjudication to render an authoritative opinion on the subject stated. (For Commission's opinion, see p. 191.)

(f) Combined Confessional and Communion Service and Observance of Rubrics:

At the meeting of the Executive Board, January 9, 1936, a resolution submitted from the Conference of Presidents was adopted as a resolution of the Executive Board as follows:

"Resolved, that the Executive Board indicate through its President, in some way chosen by him, the importance of a closer observance of the rubrics of the Common Service Book concerning the administration of the Sacrament of the Altar."

The following was also adopted in answer to the request from the Conference of Presidents concerning a combined Confessional and Communion Service:

"We recommend that this matter be referred to the Common Service Book Committee, asking the Committee to report its findings to the Columbus Convention."

*3. Calendar of Special Days and Seasons: (For action on this item, see p. 89.)

For satisfactory reasons, made apparent by conference with representatives of the Boards, the Executive Board presents the following amended Calendar of Special Days and Seasons by the authority of its action taken July 9, 1936:

CALENDAR OF SPECIAL DAYS AND SEASONS OF THE UNITED LUTHERAN CHURCH IN AMERICA

1. Advent Season..........................Board of Ministerial Pensions and Relief
2. Epiphany Season..Board of Foreign Missions
3. Septuagesima Sunday...Board of Deaconess Work
4. Lenten Season...Board of American Missions
5. Post-Easter Season...Board of Education
6. Month of May...The Lutheran World Convention
7. Month of September.............................Parish and Church School Board
8. Eighteenth Sunday after Trinity.......................................Jewish Missions
9. October 15 to November 15...Inner Mission Board
10. Thanksgiving Season...Every Member Visitation

In the use of these special days and seasons the following rules shall govern the agencies concerned:

1. THE BOARD OF MINISTERIAL PENSIONS AND RELIEF shall use *Advent Season* to inform the Church of its work, continue the privilege of soliciting individuals for the work of special relief, but take no general offerings.

2. THE BOARD OF FOREIGN MISSIONS shall use *Epiphany Season* to promote the cause of Foreign Missions throughout the Church, and furnish envelopes for the gathering of offerings from the Sunday Schools on Transfiguration Sunday.

3. THE BOARD OF DEACONESS WORK shall use *Septuagesima Sunday* as a recruiting day for deaconess work throughout the Church, but shall gather no offerings.

4. THE BOARD OF AMERICAN MISSIONS shall use the *Lenten Season* to promote the cause of home missions and church extension throughout the Church, and furnish envelopes for the gathering of special offerings from the Sunday Schools on Easter Sunday.

5. THE BOARD OF EDUCATION shall use the *first four Sundays after Easter* to promote the cause of Christian education throughout the Church; and Constituent Synods may use the same season to inform their congregations concerning their educational institutions, and to gather special offerings from the congregations and Sunday Schools on Cantate Sunday for their support.

6. THE LUTHERAN WORLD CONVENTION shall use the *month of May* to inform the congregations of its work, and to gather offerings for Lutheran World Service.

7. THE PARISH AND CHURCH SCHOOL BOARD shall use the *month of September* to promote parish education, but gather no special offerings.

8. THE BOARD OF AMERICAN MISSIONS shall use the *Eighteenth Sunday after Trinity* to promote the cause of Jewish Missions, but gather no special offerings.

9. THE INNER MISSION BOARD shall use the period from *October 15 to November 15* to promote the cause of the Inner Mission throughout the Church. Constituent Synods shall have the right to gather special offerings from the congregations and Sunday Schools for the support of institutions of mercy for which they are directly responsible.

10. *The Thanksgiving Season* shall be used by the LAYMEN'S MOVEMENT and by STEWARDSHIP COMMITTEES OF CONSTITUENT SYNODS to further the cause of Christian Stewardship in all the congregations through the circulation of literature and the promotion of the Every Member Canvass.

11. All special offerings, marked special, shall be sent through the regular channels of congregational and synodical treasurers.

12. Constituent Synods are requested to print this *Calendar of Special Days and Seasons* in their annual minutes.

4. Transfer of synodical mission work to Board of American Missions:
See IV, B, 2, (b), of this report.

5. Linguistic Conferences:
(a) Upon recommendation from the Committee on German Interests, the Executive Board authorized the holding of the Ninth General German Conference of the U. L. C. A., without expense to the U. L. C. A. treasury.

(b) Permission was given to the Finnish Conference to hold a meeting on May 2 and 3, 1936.

B. In Particular

1. Michigan Synod:
The request of the Michigan Synod for approval of the proposed change in budget so as to increase the appropriation for student work, but involving no total increase, was approved at the meeting of the Executive Board, July 9, 1936.

2. United Synod of New York:
The request of the United Synod of New York for approval of the increase of its budget for student work was approved, as an act of extension of work already in progress, at the meeting of the Executive Board, April 16, 1936.

*3. Alleghany Synod: (For action on this item, see pp. 143, 306.)
With reference to a memorial from the Alleghany Synod on the subject of emergency relief, and in the light of the report of the Inner Mission Board to this convention with reference to this same subject, the Executive Board adopted the following as recommended by its Committee on Constituent Synods:

Whereas, we believe that emergencies will continue to arise which will require prompt action and,

Whereas, we believe that ordinarily the Inner Mission Board of The United Lutheran Church in America is the proper agency through which such emergencies shall be met, though this does not prevent us from recognizing the principle that there are differences in emergencies and that consequently emergencies must be met in different ways and by different agencies and,

Whereas, we believe the establishment of "a disaster emergency fund" would be detrimental rather than helpful to the fostering of Christian charity and love of the brethren in times of great need,

We would therefore suggest to the Executive Board, and to the Convention of The United Lutheran Church in America that (a) and (c) under 6, of the recommendations of the Inner Mission Board, be withdrawn, and that (b) be adopted. We believe that thereby the ends of the request made by the Alleghany Synod and the needs of the Church in times of great emergency will be fully and heartily met.

IV. BOARDS AND COMMITTEES

A. In General

*1. Amendment to Constitution: (For action on this item, see p. 20.)

From the Minutes of the meeting of the Executive Board, July 9, 1936, the following is taken, and the proposed amendment to the Constitution is presented:

Article XIII, Section 2, third sentence of the Constitution of The United Lutheran Church in America reads as follows: "No person shall be a member of more than two Boards at one and the same time."

Section V, A, Item 4, of the By-laws makes a similar provision: "No member of any Board shall be eligible for election for more than two successive terms; and no person shall be a member of more than two Boards at one and the same time."

Inasmuch as the Constitution provides the higher law, and no amendment of the By-laws would have any weight unless the restricting constitutional provision were first amended, it is not proposed to suggest any change in the By-laws at present. Our concern is with the Constitution.

An important element in the healthy development of church life is the widening of lay responsibility; and this is becoming increasingly difficult in connection with the steady decrease in the number of boards and agencies of the Church. At the present time another consolidation is before the Church which may further reduce the number of opportunities for service in general administration. A constitutional requirement, further limiting the number of boards on which any minister or laymen may serve, would strengthen the work of the Church.

The Executive Board recommends to The United Lutheran Church in America that an amendment to the Constitution be submitted to the Constituent Synods in the following form:

Amend Article XIII, Section 2, third sentence, by striking out the consecutive words "two boards," and inserting the consecutive words "one board," so that the amended sentence shall read, "No person shall be a member of more than one board at one and the same time.'

2. **Mergers of Boards and Committees:**
    *(a) **Merger of Inner Mission Board, Board of Deaconess Work, Committee on Evangelism, and Committee on Moral and Social Welfare:** (For action on this item, see pp. 89, 421.)

In continuation of attention to the special assignment of proposed mergers of boards and committees, the officers held a conference with representatives of the Inner Mission Board, the Board of Deaconess Work, the Committee on Evangelism and the Committee on Moral and Social Welfare, May 5, 1936. The following recommendations, expressing the conclusions of the conference, were adopted by the Executive Board on July 9, 1936, for presentation to this convention.

(1) That the Inner Mission Board, the Committee on Moral and Social Welfare, and the Committee on Evangelism be merged into one agency.

(2) That the Board of Deaconess Work and the Inner Mission Board, or the new agency if merger be approved, correlate their work in a practical and efficient manner under the supervision of the Executive Board of The United Lutheran Church in America.

(3) That the Executive Board be given power to arrange the details involved in the consummation of (1) and (2), consulting with the four agencies as is necessary.

(b) **Merger of Board of Publication and Parish and Church School Board:**

The proposed merger of the Board of Publication and the Parish and Church School Board is still held as a matter for further conference.

(c) **Merger of Statistical and Church Year Book Committee and Publicity Committee:**

On the matter of consolidation of the Statistical and Church Year Book Committee and the Publicity Committee, the Executive Board adopted the recommendation of its Committee on Boards and Committees that no change be made for the present in the constitution of these committees.

*3. **Transfer of Mountain Work:** (For action on this item, see p. 89.)

After extended reports and lengthy discussions, based upon the findings of the special commission on mountain work, recommendations submitted by that commission to the Executive Board, September 26, 1935, were adopted by the Executive Board at its meeting on January 9, 1936, as follows:

"(a) Without prejudice to the spheres of activity of the Inner Mission Board and the Board of American Missions as adopted in the Report of the Executive Board to the Convention in Milwaukee in the year 1930,

"We recommend, That for the purpose of practical administration the Southern Mountain Work be placed under one Board.

"(b) While recognizing the inner mission phases of the Konnarock and Iron Mountain Schools, and with full appreciation of the services that the Inner Mission Board can continue to render these institutions,

"We recommend, that for practical administration the entire Southern Mountain Work be assigned to the Board of American Missions, requesting, however, that regular reports of the Inner Mission activities at the Konnarock School and at the Iron Mountain School be sent to the Inner Mission Board."

B. In Particular

1. Board of Foreign Missions:

(a) *Location of Andhra Christian College:* The detailed plan for the location and operation of Andhra Christian College was presented to the Executive Board and was approved January 10, 1935. (See report of the Board of Foreign Missions.)

(b) *Offerings at the Columbus Convention:* See XIII, 1, (e), of this report.

(c) *Vacancies filled:* Upon nomination of the Board of Foreign Missions, elections were held by the Executive Board to fill vacancies as follows:

January 9, 1936—Ralph H. Schatz as successor to H. Torrey Walker, resigned, for the term expiring 1936; George S. Yost as successor to J. J. Bruns, resigned, for the term expiring 1938.

July 9, 1936—Rev. F. E. Reinartz as successor to the Rev. C. A. Dennig, deceased, term expiring 1938; Rev. P. O. Bersell as successor to the Rev. G. A. Brandelle, deceased, for the term expiring 1936.

2. Board of American Missions:

(a) *Co-operation with Suomi Synod:* A request from the Suomi Synod for continuation of some joint activity between the U. L. C. A. and that Synod was received by the Executive Board, July 9, 1936, and the request was referred to the Board of American Missions with instructions to confer with representatives of the Suomi Synod, and if possible submit recommendation to the Executive Board for presentation to the convention.

(b) *Transfer of Synodical Mission Work:* At the meeting of the Executive Board, April 11, 1935, it was reported that in accord with action taken at the 1934 convention, the Synod of Virginia and the United Synod of New York had placed their missions and funds in the hands of the Board of American Missions in an experimental relationship.

At the meeting of the Executive Board, July 9, 1936, the following action was proposed and was referred to the Committee on Boards and Committees:

"In view of the success of the experiment in the temporary transfer of synodical mission work to the Board of American Missions, by the Synods of Virginia and New York, and in view of the fact that items for the support of the same cannot be removed from those two synodical budgets until a similar course is followed by all synods, we recommend that all synods follow the course of the two synods referred to, pending time when all synodical mission items shall be eliminated from synodical budgets." (Amended by the Convention, see p. 89.)

*(c) *Amendment to the ruling on the plan of Operation:* (For action on this item, see p. 89.)

The Executive Board gave consideration to the following item from the Board of American Missions, as incorporated in the Minutes of that Board for April 26, 1936:

"It is recommended that the Board request the Executive Board to amplify its previous ruling (found on pp. 72, 73 of the Minutes of the Savannah Convention) to include a statement that synods shall not take steps looking toward the disbanding of congregations, when such congregations have church extension loans, without first notifying the Board of American Missions of the intention to disband the congregation."

Concerning this item, the Executive Board recommends the following amendment to the action taken at the Savannah Convention:

In the paragraph on page 73 of the Minutes of the Savannah Convention, beginning with the words "Under the plan of operation," insert this sentence after the first sentence of said paragraph:

"On the other hand, no synod shall take steps toward disbanding any congregation holding a church extension loan or loans without first notifying the Board of American Missions of an intention to disband the congregation."

(d) *Vacancies filled:* Upon nomination of the Board of American Missions, elections were held by the Executive Board to fill vacancies in the Board of American Missions and the West Indies Mission Board as follows:

January 9, 1936—Rev. John Schmieder as successor to the Rev. Jacob Maurer, resigned, for the term expiring 1936; Louis Hanson as successor to H. L. Snyder, deceased, for the term expiring 1936.

3. Board of Education:

Vacancy filled: Upon nomination of the Board of Education, an election was held by the Executive Board to fill a vacancy as follows:

April 16, 1936—H. S. Bechtolt as successor to C. J. Driever, deceased, for the term expiring 1938.

4. Board of Publication:

Vacancies filled: Upon nomination of the Board of Publication, elections were held by the Executive Board to fill vacancies as follows:

April 11, 1935—Henry Beisler as successor to Einar Schatvet, resigned, for the term expiring 1936.

September 26, 1935—Rev. H. F. Baughman as successor to the Rev. Henry Anstadt, deceased, for the term expiring 1938; H. F. Heuer as successor to Claude T. Reno, resigned, for the term expiring 1938.

April 16, 1936—Robert D. Raeder as successor to W. J. Showalter, deceased, for the term expiring 1940.

July 9, 1936—Rev. Herbert T. Weiskotten as successor to the Rev. Paul E. Scherer, resigned, for the term expiring 1938.

October 14, 1936—J. Myron Shimer, Esq., as successor to Mr. J. C. Lynch, deceased, for the term expiring 1940.

5. Board of Ministerial Pensions and Relief:

* (*a*) *Change in rules:* (For action on this item, see p. 89.)

At the meeting of the Executive Board, January 9, 1936, the following amendment to Rule 1 of the rules governing the policy of the Board of Ministerial Pensions and Relief was adopted for submission to the convention of the U. L. C. A. with recommendation of its adoption. The proposed amendment to Rule 1 is to insert the words "from full time remunerative occupation" between the words "retirement" and "be eligible" in the present rule. The rule, as amended, would be as follows:

Rule 1. Ministers of The United Lutheran Church in America, who are sixty-five years of age, or older, and who are in good and regular standing in the synods to which they belong, shall, on retirement from full time remunerative occupation, be eligible to a minimum pension of $400 per annum (provided the income of the Church for pensions be sufficient to warrant this amount) provided they shall have served at least twenty years in synods of the United Lutheran Church. Provided, further, that ministers coming into the United Lutheran Church from other evangelical churches, in order to qualify for a pension, must serve in The United Lutheran Church in America at least ten years, and must have served a sufficient number of years in the communion from which they come to aggregate a total of twenty years in all in the ministry. This pension shall not be available in case the minister shall have retired before the age of sixty-five to enter gainful secular employment.

(*b*) *Vacancy filled:* Upon nomination of the Board of Ministerial Pensions and Relief, an election was held by the Executive Board to fill a vacancy as follows:

January 10, 1935—J. C. Rovensky as successor to J. L. Clark, resigned, for the term expiring 1940.

6. Parish and Church School Board:

(*a*) *Additional Financial Support:* April 11, 1935, at the recommendation of the Finance Committee, the Executive Board answered the memorial of the West Virginia Synod concerning additional financial support for the Parish and Church School Board by saying that no funds were available at that time for such additional support.

(b) *Plan of Parish Education:* With reference to a proposal to conduct a special experimental program, in chosen congregations, by the Parish and Church School Board in connection with the comprehensive plan, report was made by the special committee of the Executive Board, at the meeting of that Board on January 10, 1935, that on account of expense involved, advice was asked. The matter was referred to the Finance Committee for report at that meeting of the Executive Board, which Committee reported that under present conditions the appropriations required could not be provided. By the approval of that report from the Finance Committee, the Executive Board accepted it as a fact that this experimental program would be abandoned automatically.

April 11, 1935, the Commission on Plan of Parish Education, after full statement of the results of its study of the comprehensive plan, submitted the following recommendations which were adopted:

(1) That the report of the Parish and Church School Board as to a Comprehensive Plan of Parish Education be received as information and filed.

(2) That the Parish and Church School Board be furnished with a copy of this report and be notified that the way is open for that Board, if it so desires, to present to the Executive Board a further report in which, through the elimination of fundamental defects in the plan as now proposed, and its general simplification, another plan may be presented, more satisfactorily adapted to the practical needs of the Church.

7. Board of Deaconess Work:

Vacancy filled: Upon nomination of the Board of Deaconess Work, an election was held by the Executive Board to fill a vacancy as follows:

January 10, 1935—F. H. Wefer as successor to James C. Kinard, resigned, for the term expiring 1940.

8. Laymen's Movement:

At the meeting of the Executive Board, April 11, 1935, Robbin B. Wolf and James C. Kinard were appointed as representatives of the Executive Board on the Administrative Committee of the Laymen's Movement to serve in connection with the Treasurer, E. Clarence Miller.

C. Standing Committees, Commissions, etc.

1. Common Service Book Committee:

* (a) *Devotional Literature:* (For action on this item, see p. 89.)

In obedience to the instruction given by the action of the 1934 Convention, the Common Service Book Committee surveyed the need for special devotional literature and recommended immediate procedure although the 1934 Convention asked that report on their survey be made to this Convention. Upon the recommendation of the Committee on Boards and Committees, the Executive Board, April 11, 1935, adopted the following and thereby authorized the Common Service Book Committee to proceed with the preparation and publication of special literature:

(1) That there be published a series of booklets every year for the guidance and development of the personal and family devotional life.

(2) That these booklets be issued under the general direction of the Common Service Book Committee, which shall appoint from its own membership an Editorial Committee, in which the active pastors shall be adequately represented.

(3) That the Editorial Committee shall confer with the representatives of the Publication House concerning details of the manufacture and distribution; and that the Board of Publication shall be responsible for publication and circulation of the booklets, receiving revenues and paying costs.

(4) That the following be approved as a general plan:
(a) That the size of the booklets be left to the decision of the Common Service Book Committee, in conference with the Board of Publication.
(b) That the first issue be prepared for the Advent Season of 1935.
(c) That these booklets be circulated at the lowest possible popular price; and that the general causes of the Church be woven into the devotional material of each season of the Church Year.

(b) *Service for Rural Life Sunday:* (For action on this item, see pp. 89, 142.)
In response to the action of the 1934 convention, with reference to literature for Rural Life Sunday, the Common Service Book Committee recommended to the Executive Board that the preparation of such an order was deemed inadvisable. Upon receipt of this report from the Common Service Book Committee, the Executive Board, April 11, 1935, reaffirmed its previous action on this matter (Minutes, U. L. C. A., 1934, p. 55) in which it also asserted the inadvisability of the observance of Rural Life Sunday by the use of a special order.

2. Publicity Committee:
Pamphlet on Church Publicity: On January 10, 1935, the Secretary reported to the Executive Board that the pamphlet on Church publicity, previously authorized and for which an appropriation of $150 had been voted, had been published and distributed at an outlay of $63.85.

3. Commission on Investments:
* (a) *Rules and Regulations:* (For action on this item, see p. 142.)
July 9, 1936, the Executive Board received a communication from the Commission on Investments and approved action as indicated in the following record:

"At a meeting of this Commission in Philadelphia, May 23, 1936, the following amendments to the Supplemental Rules and Regulations of the Commission on Investments of the United Lutheran Church, adopted at Savannah in 1934 (see Minutes, U. L. C. A., pp. 409-411), were adopted, subject to approval of the Executive Board of the Church:

"a. Add to Article VI the following new paragraph: 'The Chairman may appoint any member of the Commission to serve with the Executive Committee in the determination of investment questions as applied to any particular Board.'

"b. Strike out Article VII, and insert the following:

" 'VII. ADVICE ON SECURITIES

" 'The Commission, when requested, shall offer recommendations for the investment of endowment and/or trust funds of Church Boards and Agencies. The preparation of such recommendations shall be subject to rules and regulations adopted by the Commission from time to time.'

"Your committee recommends:

"(1) That amendment 'a' be approved.

"(2) That amendment 'b' be approved, with the addition of the words, 'and approved by the Church' inserted between the words 'Commission' and 'from' in the last line.

"(3) That the Executive Board recommend to the United Lutheran Church that the title 'Amended Rules and Regulations' be amended in the Minutes of the United Lutheran Church for 1934 to read 'Supplemental Rules and Regulations,' wherever the title appears in the business of the Commission on Investments."

(b) *Vacancies filled:* January 10, 1935, W. G. Semisch was re-elected as a member of the Commission on Investments for the term expiring 1940. July 9, 1936, W. H. Stackel was re-elected as a member of the Commission on Investments for the term expiring 1941.

4. Luther League:

(a) *Appropriation:* April 11, 1935, the Executive Board adopted a recommendation from the Finance Committee continuing the appropriation of $6,000 per annum, for the biennium, to the Luther League of America.

(b) *Amendments to Constitution and By-Laws:* The Luther League, having submitted a suggested revised Constitution and By-Laws, the Committee on Boards and Committees reported on January 9, 1936, that certain items in the proposed Constitution and By-Laws were involved in the questions under consideration by the Committee on Better Adjustments, and the following action was adopted by the Executive Board:

That action on these amendments be postponed until after the Church has taken final action on the report of the Committee on Better Adjustments.

(c) *Membership in the International Council of Religious Education:* Upon the presentation of data pertaining to membership of the Luther League of America in the International Council of Religious Education, the following recommendation was adopted:

That the Luther League of America be advised not to enter this new interdenominational relationship.

(d) *Missionary Objective:* September 26, 1935, upon the presentation by the Secretary of a request from the Luther League of America that the following action be approved by the Executive Board, the approval requested was given:

"Resolved, that the Luther League of America adopt as its special missionary objective for the coming biennium a project in China, to be known as the Tai Tung Chen project, which will include the building of a church to seat one thousand people, with a social center consisting of a kindergarten, a dispensary, and equipment for Christian education, at a total cost of $10,000.00."

5. Lutheran Brotherhood:

July 9, 1936, the President presented an official request from the Lutheran Brotherhood that permission be given that body to make an appeal for the amount needed to pay for the property for the Iron Mountain School for Boys in Virginia, and the following action was taken:

Moved and carried that permission be granted to the Brotherhood, with the limitation that appeal is to be made only to the Brotherhoods and similar men's groups.

V. FINANCE

1. Apportionment for 1936 and 1937:
See III, A, 1.

*2. Budget: (For action on this item, see p. 142.)

July 9, 1936, the following recommendation from the Finance Committee was adopted, fixing the budget of the U. L. C. A. for 1938 and 1939:

	Amount	Percentage
Board of Foreign Missions	$600,000	30.00
Board of American Missions	771,400	38.57
Board of Education	180,000	9.00
Parish and Church School Board	24,400	1.22
Inner Mission Board	34,000	1.70
Board of Ministerial Pensions and Relief	235,000	11.75
Board of Deaconess Work	40,000	2.00
Tabitha Home	2,000	.10
Lowman Home	400	.02
National Lutheran Council	23,000	1.15
American Bible Society	5,000	.25
United Lutheran Church Treasury	84,800	4.24
	$2,000,000	100.00

3. Bond of the Treasurer:

April 11, 1935, the Secretary reported that on January 24, 1935, the bond of the Treasurer was renewed with the United States Fidelity and Guaranty Company. On April 16, 1936, the Secretary reported to the Executive Board that the bond of the Treasurer had been duly renewed and executed on January 31, 1936.

*4. Uniform Rate of Annuities: (For action on this item, see pp. 142, 423.)

The matter of annuity rates, as affecting the various boards and organizations of the Church, having been under consideration by the Finance Committee, a recommendation was submitted to the Executive Board by that Committee, September 26, 1935, asking that the "Uniform Maximum Agreement Rates" as compiled by the Sub-committee on Annuities of the Committee on Financial and Fiduciary Matters of the Federal Council of Churches be adopted for the use of U. L. C. A. Boards. The recommendation was referred back to the Committee for further study and, on January 9, 1936, the recommendation was renewed and was adopted by the Executive Board for recommendation to this convention. The rates thus approved are as follows:

UNIFORM MAXIMUM ANNUITY AGREEMENT RATES
SINGLE LIFE

Calculated on Basis Adopted by Conference November 20, 1934
Basis: Combined Annuity Mortality Table—Female Interest at 4%—
Residuum 70%—Rates Modified at Younger and Older Ages

Age	Rate	Age	Rate	Age	Rate	Age	Rate
30	3.0%	43	3.8%	56	5.1%	69	6.1%
31	3.0%	44	3.9%	57	5.1%	70	6.2%
32	3.0%	45	4.0%	58	5.2%	71	6.3%
33	3.0%	46	4.1%	59	5.2%	72	6.5%
34	3.0%	47	4.2%	60	5.3%	73	6.6%
35	3.0%	48	4.3%	61	5.4%	74	6.8%
36	3.1%	49	4.4%	62	5.4%	75	7.0%
37	3.2%	50	4.5%	63	5.5%	76	7.1%
38	3.3%	51	4.6%	64	5.6%	77	7.3%
39	3.4%	52	4.7%	65	5.7%	78	7.5%
40	3.5%	53	4.8%	66	5.8%	79	7.8%
41	3.6%	54	4.9%	67	5.9%	80 & over	8.0%
42	3.7%	55	5.0%	68	6.0%		

Note: A much more elaborated table, worked out on the same principle, was approved for Uniform Maximum Annuity Agreement Rate—Two Lives—Joint and Survivor.

5. Oscar V. Haubner Bequest:

April 11, 1935, the Finance Committee reported information concerning a bequest in the estate of Mr. Oscar V. Haubner of Kew Gardens, N. Y.

Under the terms of the will, the final distribution of the bequest was made upon conditions which involved a considerable term of years. The Finance Committee was given authority by the Executive Board to make immediate settlement by division according to the actuarial basis of standard insurance companies and to accept cash settlement accordingly. September 26, 1935, the Finance Committee reported that such settlement had been made and that the amount of $7,987.90, less attorney's fee of $35.00, had been received, to be placed in a trust according to the terms of the will for the benefit equally of the Board of Foreign Missions, the Board of Home Missions, and the Inner Mission Society of Brooklyn.

*6. **Supplementary Support for Executive Board:** (For action on this item, see p. 421.)

The Executive Board recommends the following:

Resolved, that, out of the first funds of the Board of Publication available for transfer to The United Lutheran Church in America, as provided by its Charter, the Executive Board is instructed to use $25,000 on account of convention expenses.

VI. LUTHERAN CHURCH HOUSE

1. **Management and Maintenance:**

See Report of Secretary 2, (e).

2. **Auditors' Report:**

We hereby present the auditors' report for July 1, 1934 to June 30, 1936, which exhibits itemized statement of the Manager and Treasurer.

LUTHERAN CHURCH HOUSE

CASH RECEIPTS

July 1, 1934 to June 30, 1935

	Maintenance	Telephone and Telegrams	Total
Executive Board—United Lutheran Church in America	2,040.00	187.21	2,227.21
Board of American Missions	1,480.00	166.97	1,646.97
Inner Mission Board	998.41	79.83	1,078.24
National Lutheran Council	2,405.70	302.31	2,708.01
New York Synod	1,131.03	212.51	1,343.54
Miscellaneous	18.00	129.48	147.48
Totals	$8,073.14	$1,078.31	$9,151.45

CASH DISBURSEMENTS

July 1, 1934 to June 30, 1935

Salaries and Wages	$2,826.35
Telephone and Telegrams	987.54
Gas, Electric and Steam	1,907.70

Repairs, Painting, etc.	299.06
Insurance	127.81
House Supplies	125.30
Services	522.70
Miscellaneous	147.59
Total	$6,944.05

SUMMARY OF CASH IN BANK
July 1, 1934 to June 30, 1935

Balance in Bank—July 1, 1934	$5,473.14
Receipts	9,151.45
	$14,624.59
Disbursements	6,944.05
Balance in Bank—June 30, 1935	$7,680.54

CASH RECEIPTS
July 1, 1935 to June 30, 1936

	Maintenance	Telephone and Telegrams	Misc.	Total
Executive Board of the United Lutheran Church in America	$2,244.00	$135.95	....	$2,379.95
Board of American Missions	1,628.00	146.05	....	1,774.05
Inner Mission Board	704.76	76.59	....	781.35
National Lutheran Council	3,253.80	244.49	....	3,498.29
New York Synod	1,328.25	104.67	....	1,432.92
Miscellaneous	....	18.34	$34.24	52.58
Totals	$9,158.81	$726.09	$34.24	$9,919.14

CASH DISBURSEMENTS
July 1, 1935 to June 30, 1936

Salaries and Wages	$2,763.70
Telephone	784.04
Telegrams	95.28
Gas, Electric and Steam	1,651.36
Repairs, Painting, etc.	1,131.70
Services	497.12
Insurance	575.53
Supplies and Miscellaneous	509.41
Remitted to E. C. Miller for Investment as Depreciation Reserve for Lutheran Church House, 39 East 35th Street, New York City	5,000.00
Total	$13,008.14

SUMMARY OF CASH
July 1, 1935 to June 30, 1936

Balance in Bank—July 1, 1935... $7,680.54
Receipts 9,919.14

$17,599.68
Disbursements 13,008.14

Balance—June 30, 1936 .... $4,591.54

Cash in Bank $4,591.54

Respectfully submitted,
W. H. GREEVER, D.D., *Treasurer.*

July 30, 1936.

We have audited the accounts of the Lutheran Church House for the biennium beginning July 1, 1934 and ending June 30, 1936. We hereby certify that in our opinion the statements of Cash and Receipts for the two years under audit, as submitted by the Treasurer, are true and correct.

TAIT, WELLER AND BAKER,
Accountants and Auditors.

VII. NATIONAL LUTHERAN COUNCIL

1. Appeal for World Service:

April 11, 1935, upon the receipt of a communication from the National Lutheran Council, the Executive Board authorized an appeal to the U. L. C. A. congregations, designating May, 1935, as the time for the relief of Lutheran German missions. This appeal was made by the National Lutheran Council in behalf of the program of the Lutheran World Convention.

2. Budget:

April 11, 1935, the Executive Board adopted the recommendation of the Finance Committee to the effect that the National Lutheran Council be placed in the regular budget of the Church for the amount of $23,000, to be paid on the same percentage basis of receipts as other participating causes.

VIII. LUTHERAN WORLD CONVENTION

1. Auditors' Report:

April 11, 1935, the Finance Committee reported to the Executive Board that it had received no auditors' report from the Lutheran World Convention.

2. Mass Meeting for the Executive Committee:

See XIII, 1, (b) of this report.

3. Meeting of the Lutheran World Convention:

January 10, 1935, approval was given to the proposed meeting of the Lutheran World Convention, in 1935, to be constituted by heads of general bodies.

(a) *Representatives:*

The President of the United Lutheran Church was instructed to attend as our representative. At the meeting of the Executive Board, September 26, 1935, authority was given to President Knubel to appoint other advisory representatives. On January 9, 1936, President Knubel reported on the meeting of the convention, and in that connection announced his appointment of advisers.

At the meeting of the Executive Board, September 26, 1935, an appropriation of $600 was approved for the expenses of Dr. Knubel as the one voting representative and delegate to the Lutheran World Convention.

(b) *Report of President:*

At the meeting of the Executive Board, January 9, 1936, Dr. F. H. Knubel, as official delegate, submitted the following report on the Lutheran World Convention:

By your authority I attended the convention in Paris, October 13 to 20, 1935. Likewise by your authority I appointed as advisers the Rev. Drs. G. L. Kieffer, J. A. Morehead and Samuel Trexler, and Mr. S. F. Telleen. All of these were present.

A helpful view of the Paris meeting will be gained if we remember the original intention when the meeting was planned and if we also contrast this gathering with the conventions at Eisenach in 1923 and at Copenhagen in 1929. It was not intended that Paris should be like them. They were large gatherings with several hundred accredited delegates. This was planned to be primarily an assemblage of only the heads of Lutheran Churches throughout the world. It is true that this plan was modified in that these heads might have advisers with them, but the total attendance was far from one hundred, and when near the close elections were held only fifty-one ballots were cast. If it be asked how truly the heads of the churches were in attendance, the reply is that seventeen bishops, three inspectors, and four presidents were there. It must also be said that twenty-one countries had sent delegates, and that the gathering was therefore a most representative one.

All of the above relates to the personnel of the convention, considered especially in contrast with previous conventions and also in the light of the first plans for this meeting. From the same points of view we note interesting facts regarding the place of meeting. The previous conventions met in lands where the Lutheran Church is not a minority, where its influence has been powerful, where a mighty historical environment impressed the delegates. At Eisenach a great service was held within the Wartburg gates, where a multitude gathered and stood in the open, in spite of falling rain. At Copenhagen great services were held in the crowded Vor Frue Kirke, while Thorwaldsen's sculptures looked down upon us. This convention was planned to meet with one of the small Lutheran groups, in a land where Lutheran history is not so impressive. The church building where we met was a small, though beautiful one. There were no throngs at any of the services, but those services lacked nothing in devout fervor. The testimony of the French Lutherans was, however, impressive as to the good effect of this convention for French Lutheranism. They were positive that their own loyalty to our confessional faith had been strengthened, and were themselves surprised at the attention which the convention won from the French public. The President of France received the Executive Committee, and the authorities of Paris gave a reception to all delegates. The theological faculty of the university conferred honorary degrees upon Drs. Morehead and Jorgensen. We must not neglect furthermore to bear our testimony to the tireless hospitality of the small French Lutheran Church. It would be impossible even to enumerate the items wherein their welcome to us was manifested. It was indeed not merely the plans and deeds of theirs which imparted that welcome, but the brotherly spirit which counted nothing as too much if our comfort and happiness could be advanced.

The program of the convention also manifests a contrast with previous gatherings and follows the original plans for the Paris meeting. It was intended that this should be an *Arbeitstagung,* a working convention. Scholarly papers and discussions were not in mind, but rather a practical study of our present-day problems. The topics assigned dealt with Lutheranism in its relation to the religious crisis of the present day, to the crisis in the lives of the nations, to the coming generation, to the social problems, to inner and foreign mission work. In addition the organization of the Lutheran World Convention was given a place for lengthy consideration. These are all practical problems, although naturally their solution demands deep-going study.

What was the outcome of the convention? Did it have a message for the Lutheran Churches of the world? A formal message was approved and will be printed everywhere in the Lutheran press. A lengthy series of resolutions was also approved, dealing with the topics on the program and with other subjects. These will be provided to all editors. There was, however, the writer believes, an important idea which in various ways dominated the convention and which was emphasized in several forms, but which found no expression in definite language. It was the idea of our inadequacy as Lutheran Churches in the world. A consciousness of our lack of attainment seemed to prevail. It must not be supposed on that account that the convention was a discouraged one, or one of self-criticism, although on various occasions the need of changes was emphatically stressed for the meeting of our responsibilities. The idea of our inadequacy was simply inevitable in the face of the dangers that threaten today and of the problems that must be solved. It was a proper Christian consciousness that "in our own strength can nought be done, our loss were soon effected."

It was felt for instance that even our devotion to our confessions is not an adequate one. The idea of our inadequacy was emphasized also in reference to the Church's spiritual life. In at least one other respect our inadequacy was discussed again and again at this convention. It was recognized that the Lutheran World Convention must definitely become a better organization than hitherto if it is to serve the Lutheran churches adequately. Steps were planned which it is hoped will lead to this result. The purposes of the organization have been much more definitely outlined. The convention will now meet every five years, and if the Executive Committee deems it desirable in the interim, a meeting of the heads of all Lutheran churches may be called. The office of a full-time secretary has been established; he will work under direction of the Executive Committee and particularly of its president. The Executive Committee itself has been enlarged in membership from six to twelve by the simple expedient of electing six alternates. These alternates, however, have definite responsibilities and will possibly attend all meetings. Four members are chosen from each of the three major Lutheran groups—American, German, Scandinavian. The smaller Lutheran groups in the world seemed, on their own statements, not to desire representation in the committee. Each member of the Executive Committee, however, is given mandates concerning specific smaller groups and will keep in constant touch with them.

The Scandinavian members are Dr. Jorgensen of Denmark and Dr. Pehrsson of Sweden, with Prof. Moe of Norway and Bishop von Bonsdorf of Finland as alternates. The German members are Bishops Marahrens and Meiser, with Profs. Sommerlath and Ihmels as alternates. The American members are President Knubel and Dr. Long, with Drs. Wentz and Boe as alternates. Dr. Morehead was elected to an honorary presidency in view of his services. The officers of the Executive Committee are: President, Marahrens; first vice-president, Knubel; second vice-president, Pehrsson; treasurer, Jorgensen; assistant treasurer, Long; secretary, Meiser.

IX. RELATIONS WITH OTHER LUTHERAN BODIES

Suomi Synod:

(a) *Co-operation:* See IV, B, 2 (a) of this report.

(b) *Representation at Meeting:* April 16, 1936, authority was given by the Executive Board to the Finnish Conference to provide for representation at the meeting of the Suomi Synod.

X. FEDERAL COUNCIL OF CHURCHES OF CHRIST IN AMERICA

1. Appropriation:

April 11, 1935, upon the recommendation of the Finance Committee, the Executive Board authorized an appropriation of $2,000 per annum, for the current biennium, to the Federal Council of Churches of Christ in America, as a contribution to that portion of their work in which we are interested.

2. Report of Representatives:

Your representatives attended the bi-monthly meetings of the Executive Committee of the Federal Council during the biennium and endeavored to reflect in the discussions the principles and points of view of our body, as they had been commissioned to do. Among the items of interest to our churches we mention the following:

(a) The National Preaching Mission, a co-operative effort for bringing about a spiritual awakening throughout the country, has been in preparation for the greater part of the biennium and is to be conducted for three months during the coming fall. Its pronouncements have all been thoroughly evangelical in spirit, placing the emphasis upon the interpretation of the meaning of the Gospel for the personal life and seeking to strengthen the foundations of Christian faith. A group of leaders, drawn from the various communions is being assembled, who will go together to twenty-five of the major centers of population of the country, spending four days in each city. Public meetings, conferences of ministers and educational seminars for Christian workers are planned, to make a united spiritual impact upon the community. Dr. Paul Scherer, a member of the committee, and Dr. O. F. Blackwelder are included in the group of speakers, and one or the other of them will be a member of the Mission in each of the twenty-five cities. Each of these cities in turn is expected to serve as a center for an extension program reaching out into five or six other centers of that area. The holding of preaching missions in local parishes is also in the plan, and in this way the Preaching Mission hopes to become a movement in which every pastor has a share.

(b) The Decennial Census of the United States received attention, when rumors were heard that the congressional appropriations were not to include an item for the Census of Religious Bodies, which had been included in the Decennial Census since 1906. The Federal Council secured appeals for the continuation of the census from the heads of over twenty denominations and submitted them as a united request to the authorities. The congressional appropriation was not secured, but so much interest was aroused in the Department of Commerce that it has undertaken to secure the funds in another way through making a special grant from the W.P.A. funds available for this purpose. The latest information from the Secretary of Commerce is, that he believes this effort will be successful.

(c) On Social Problems the Federal Council has given attention to the matter of the family and divorce. The booklet, "Safeguarding Marriages," has been widely distributed among ministers in an effort to get them to take their relation to marriages with a greater sense of educational responsibility. A study course entitled "Building the Christian Family" has been produced. Program suggestions for local churches in the work for world peace and suggested services of worship emphasizing world understanding and peace have been issued. Better motion pictures has been a subject of increasing concern and action.

(d) Chaplains for Federal Prisons. At the request of the U. S. Bureau of Prisons, the Federal Council has assumed the responsibility for nominating and helping to train Protestant chaplains in federal prisons. The general plan which the Federal Council is following is based upon co-operation with the various denominational agencies along the lines already worked out in connection with the chaplaincy in the Army and Navy.

(e) The radio ministry, which is secured through the interdenominational approach of the Federal Council to the National Broadcasting Company, brings the influence of the Christian Gospel to hosts of people, who cannot be reached by the ordinary ministry of the Church, such as the invalids, the aged, shut-ins, and inmates of public institutions. The Lutheran period, on which the Lutheran Laymen's Radio Committee will report, is conducted as a part of the general program for which the National Broadcasting Company looks to the Federal Council.

(f) Committee on Worship, on which Dr. Luther D. Reed is our representative, is carrying on a quiet but important program. Its survey of the teaching and practice of worship in theological seminaries has called the attention of other seminaries to the almost unique place which Dr. Reed's department of instruction holds in the theological seminaries of America. Dr. Reed submits the following report:

"The Committee on Worship, Bishop Wilbur P. Thirkield, D.D. LL.D.. chairman, held four meetings during the biennium. These were well attended by the representatives of a dozen or more communions. There were important papers and discussions by the members and presentations by authorities in special fields, such as Prof. John Finley Williamson in Church Music, Dr. H. Augustine Smith in Hymns and Hymn Tunes, and Dr. Elbert M. Conover in Church Architecture.

"The committee, under the general direction of Dean Weigle of Yale, completed a survey on 'The Teaching and Practice of Worship in Theological Seminaries,' and presented its results to the Conference of Theological Seminaries of the United States and Canada, and urged greater attention to the subject of worship in the life and curricula of the seminaries. The committee compiled a bibliography of worship and laid the foundations for a library which is deposited at the Federal Council offices in New York City. It formulated a statement of 'Seven Principles of Public Worship,' which has been published. It will propose a 'Church Calendar Year' for consideration by the Protestant churches of the country. The first half of this is practically identical with the historic Church Year of the liturgical churches. In the interest of securing uniformity in the text of the Lord's Prayer, it has recommended the general use of the word 'trespasses' instead of 'debts.'

"In these and other ways the committee has sought to arouse the clergy and intelligent laity of the Protestant communions to an appreciation of the importance of public worship and to study the historic expressions of the same as a basis for at least a measure of desirable uniformity in Protestant worship throughout the country. The purposes and the spirit of the committee are altogether commendable, and its work promises to have a constantly increasing educational value."

The next meeting of the Federal Council will be held at Asbury Park, N. J., December 9-11, 1936.

A. STEIMLE,
For the representatives.

3. Visitors:

January 10, 1935, the President announced to the Executive Board that he had appointed President Joseph Sittler and Secretary Gould Wickey to serve as visitors to the Biennial Convention of the Federal Council of the Churches of Christ in America.

At the meeting of the Executive Board, September 26, 1935, the following report was submitted by the official visitors:

The biennial meeting of the Federal Council of the Churches of Christ in America was held in Dayton, Ohio, on December 4-7, 1934, with the general theme: "The Church for Such a Time as This."

Three notes predominated the sessions: *Evangelism*, seen in Dr. Buttrick's addresses, Dr. Robert's noon-day meditations, and the suggestion for a National Preaching Mission; an *Educational Approach* to social problems, with special reference to the liquor problem, although affirming the objective of its ultimate abolition; and a more *Conservative Theology,* seen in "The Message and Task of the Churches Today," and the willingness to print an address by Dr. G. W. Richards, insisting on the uniqueness of the Christian Gospel as the revelation of God.

The work of the Council was interpreted as breaking down ecclesiastical, racial and international barriers, thereby laying the basis, not of organic union, but of a church fellowship which thinks and works together. Special committees and departments are advancing the redemptive purposes of God and interpreting to the world the mind of Christ in national and world problems.

The relationship of the United Lutheran Church in America with the Federal Council of Churches offers an opportunity not to receive service but to render a conservative and constructive influence.

XI.   WORLD CONFERENCE ON FAITH AND ORDER

1. Report of Commission:

On July 9, 1936, the following report was received from the Commission on World Conference on Faith and Order, and the recommendations attached thereto were referred to the officers of the Church with power to act:

Your Commission met on May 24, 1935, immediately after a meeting of the American Section, and effected organization by electing Dr. Aberly as chairman and Dr. Steimle as secretary. It discussed the questions pertaining to its work and the forthcoming Conference, all of which are hereinafter mentioned.

The Continuation Committee of the World Conference held a meeting at Hindsgaul, Middelfart, Denmark, on August 4-7, 1935, at which the decision was made that the second World Conference shall be held at Edinburgh, Scotland, August 3-18, 1937. The program for that Conference was adopted as follows: August 3, opening service and plenary session with a statement on "The Church's Witness in the World Today."

On the succeeding days, August 4-11, the Conference will be divided, to meet in four sections for the study of the four main subjects. From August 13-17 plenary sessions for the consideration of the reports of the sections. August 18, closing sessions, question of affirmation of union in allegiance to our Lord Jesus Christ, provision for the future of the movement. August 12 is to be given to preparation and printing of the reports of the sections, and the two Sunday evenings, August 8 and 15, to statements by selected speakers, each bearing witness to what the worship and life of his Church mean to him. Each of the four sections shall consider the report of one of the four Theological Commissions to which has been assigned the task of the preparation of their respective subjects.

The Commission on the first subject, "The Grace of our Lord Jesus Christ," has completed its work and published its material in book form.

The Commission on the second subject, "The Church of Christ and the Word of God," with General Superintendent Dr. W. Zoellner as chairman, gave a very detailed outline of its study, based on the third article of the Apostles' Creed.

(1) The Spirit and the Word.
     a. The relation between the Word of God and the Bible.
     b. The inspiration of the Bible.

    c. The Bible as means of grace and source of knowledge.
    d. Word and Sacrament.
    e. The contrast between "spirit" and "letter."

(2) The Word of God and the "Una Sancta Ecclesia"
    according to the doctrine of the Orthodox, Anglican, Roman, Lutheran, Reformed and Methodist Churches.

(3) The Word of God and the Apostolicity of the Church.
    a. The relation between Scripture and tradition.
    b. The relation between the Word of God and Church Confessions.
    c. The Word of God and the Apostolic Succession.
    d. The Ministry of the Word.
    e. The Word of God and the organization of the Church as an institution.

(4) The Word of God and the Holy Church.
    a. The relation between Law and Gospel.
    b. The preaching of the Law.
    c. The Church as entrusted with the ministry of reconciliation.
    d. The Holiness of the Church—is this an attribute of the Church corporately or of its individual members?

(5) The Word of God and the Perfection of the Church.
    a. The Church and the nations of the world.
    b. The Church and the chosen people.
    c. The Church and the churches.
    d. The Church and the Kingdom of God.

Commission three, on "the Ministry and Sacraments," with Dr. A. C. Headlam, Bishop of Gloucester, as chairman, is preparing its subject under three heads:

(1) Views of Modern Churches. Under this head, among others, four papers are to be contributed as representing the Lutheran Churches, by two Germans, (Hermelink of Marburg and Brunstaed of Rostock) a Swede (Bishop Aulen of Straengnaes) and an American (Dr. C. M. Jacobs).

(2) Biblical Basis: a, Text; b, Church, Baptism and Eucharist in New Testament; c, Origin of the Christian Ministry.

(3) Historical Study—a, The Undivided Church; b, The Mediaeval Church; c, The Reformation.

The fourth Commission was originally called the Commission on the Empirical approach to Unity. This was the Theological Commission which originated in America. Dean Sperry of Boston is the chairman and Dr. C. M. Jacobs is a member. At the Commission's own suggestion, its subject was changed to read: "The Church's Unity in Life and Worship." Its material is being prepared under five heads:

(1) Progress in Church union from 1927-1937.
(2) The nature of unity.
(3) Non-theological factors in unity and disunity.
(4) The Communion of Saints.
(5) Next steps to express our existing unity.

The Executive Committee of the Continuation Committee met at Woudschoten, Zeist, Holland, on May 6, 7, 1936. It was reported there that thus far seventy-three churches of the world had appointed 265 delegates to the 1937 Conference. The committee made some recommendations in regard to procedure at Edinburgh, which will be presented for approval to the Continuation Committee. They refer to the privilege of a seat in the Conference, with voice but without vote to members of the Continuation Committee who have not been appointed delegates for 1937 by their churches, to collaborators in the work of the preparatory Commissions nominated by the Chairmen of the Commissions and to a limited number of representatives of the Youth Group (Student Christian Movement).

The committee also recommended that it be instructed to arrange for the division of the members of the Conference into its four sections, and to be prepared to present at the opening session a list of the members so divided.

The committee also expressed itself on two questions which have been discussed by the American Section. In reference to closer touch with other world movements it recommends the following resolution to the Continuation Committee: Resolved, that the committee would welcome the constitution of a Consultative Group composed of members representing the World Conference on Faith and Order, the Universal Christian Council for Life and Work, the World Alliance for Promoting International Friendship through the Churches, the International Missionary Council, and the World Student Christian Federation.

In reference to a joint Communion Service at Edinburgh the committee recommends: That the Conference itself be not responsible for the holding of any service of Holy Communion, but that the different churches represented at the Conference be asked to arrange for the holding of such services as they think best, at which services invitations to members of other churches to receive communion may be given and accepted in accordance with the principles of the Church responsible for each service and the rules of the several churches to which the members of the Conference belong.

The American Section held three other meetings during the biennium (in addition to May 24, 1935), October 4, 1935, February 14, 1936, and April 24, 1936. At the first, Dr. Jacobs opened a discussion on the meaning of the "Word of God." At the second, Canon Hodgson of Winchester, England, General Secretary of the movement, was present and spoke on the plans for Edinburgh, and at the third, reports were made on the progress of the Commission on the Church's Unity in Life and Worship, and plans were discussed for a financial campaign next fall to raise funds for the Edinburgh Conference.

Dr. Temple, Archbishop of York and Chairman of the movement, visited the United States in December, 1935, and met representatives of the five ecumenical Christian movements at an all-day session in Princeton, N. J., on December 13th.

In view of the necessity of thorough preparation for intelligent participation in the Conference at Edinburgh, your Commission would earnestly recommend

(a) That the Executive Board select the delegates who shall represent the United Lutheran Church at this Conference without delay.

(b) That the number of representatives be at least four, to insure representation in each section of the Conference.

(c) That the Executive Board express to the Secretariat of the Continuation Committee our conviction that the character of the Conference as a gathering of official representatives of the churches must be preserved for the sake of the movement itself, and that therefore we deem it unwise to give representatives of the Youth Group a voice in the Conference. As members of Christian Churches they are represented in the Conference through the delegates of their churches.

2. Universal Christian Council For Life and Work:

At the meeting of the Executive Board, September 26, 1935, the President reported that he had received a formal request that the U. L. C. A. send representatives to the Universal Christian Council for Life and Work, scheduled to meet at Oxford, England, in 1937. Also, that Drs. Steimle and Greever had served as representatives to consider and report upon the relationship of the U. L. C. A. to this Council (Minutes, U. L. C. A., 1934, page 111) and that they had been requested to make further report on this matter.

The report from these representatives was deferred from time to time on account of indefinite conditions pertaining to the Universal Christian Council for Life and Work. At the meeting of the Executive Board, July 9, 1936, the following report was submitted and received as information

(1) The representatives whom you have appointed to be unofficial observers at the meetings concerned with the Life and Work Movement would report at this time that they see no reason why the present arrangement should be changed, and recommend its continuance for the time being.

(2) On the question of appointing delegates to the Life and Work Conference, to be held in Oxford, England, in July, 1937, we submit the following considerations:

(A) The Conference in Oxford was arranged for July, 1937, in order to afford those churches which so desire, to send the same delegates to Oxford, who shall represent these churches at the Faith and Order Conference at Edinburgh, Scotland, in August, 1937, as this would entail little additional expense.

(B) The Oxford Conference will doubtless draw Lutheran delegates from many lands. The unifying influence of the United Lutheran Church representatives among the Lutherans present at the Faith and Order Conference at Lausanne in 1927, achieved a common Lutheran declaration which strongly influenced the outcome of that Conference. This gives weight to the consideration whether it is not important that the solidarity of the testimony of universal Lutheranism at the Oxford Conference be promoted by sending delegates from the United Lutheran Church.

(C) The program of the Oxford Conference centers on the subject of Church and State. The difference in relationship of the Church to the State obtaining in the Lutheran Churches of the world may give added importance to the representation of a Lutheran Church which has developed its life and confession untrammeled by any liason with the State.

The subject itself was under consideration for discussion by the Faith and Order Conference and by unofficial agreement of the officers of the two movements was assigned to the Life and Work Conference and omitted from the Faith and Order program. The preparation of papers as a basis for the discussions seems to be entirely in European hands as far as the Lutheran Church is concerned. Our participation in the discussion of this subject would possibly be necessary to a complete Lutheran testimony.

In view of these considerations we would recommend:

(a) That when the United Lutheran Church appoints delegates to the Faith and Order Conference in Edinburgh, it also appoint these representatives as delegates to the Life and Work Conference at Oxford. The American Protestant churches have been allotted eighty official delegates. The number to which the United Lutheran Church would be entitled is four.

(b) That such delegates to the Oxford Conference be appointed with the distinct understanding that we are not thereby committing ourselves to a definite participation in the movement and that our future relationship to Life and Work be decided after the report of our delegates to the Oxford Conference.

XIII. MISCELLANEOUS

1. 1936 Convention:

(a) *Arrangements:*

At the meeting of the Executive Board, September 26, 1935, information concerning hotel accommodations and other conditions at Columbus, Ohio, was submitted and the Executive Board resolved that the Convention should meet in that city, opening on October 14, 1936; and that the Deshler-Wallick Hotel should be designated as convention headquarters.

(b) *Program:*

Matters pertaining to the program of the Columbus Convention, and particularly to certain features, were provided for by the following action taken at the meeting of the Executive Board, July 9, 1936:

Moved and carried that Thursday evening be set aside for a mass meeting at which European members of the Executive Committee of the Lutheran World Convention will be presented; that Friday evening be allotted to the Board of Deaconess Work in celebration of the one hundredth anniversary of Fliedner's re-establishment of the New Testament diaconate; and that the Laymen's Movement be given the privilege of Monday evening for their usual convention banquet.

Moved and carried that we again have devotional periods at the close of the Friday and Monday morning sessions of the Convention.

*(c) *Registration of Delegates:* (For action on this item, see p. 19.)

July 9, 1936, the Executive Board passed a motion designating twelve noon of Friday, October 16, for the closing of registration of delegates, subject to the approval of the convention.

At the meeting of the Executive Board, October 14, 1936, the President announced the following as his ruling in case of the adoption of the recommendation concerning registration of delegates:

The Secretary of the Church will, in all cases, accept a written notification from the officers of a constituent synod as his only guide for the enrollment of delegates. Since, however, it has been decided that registration closes on Friday of a regular convention at twelve noon, no changes whatsoever can be made in the roll of delegates as it appears at that hour. Those who are delegates at that time continue as such to the end of that convention.

At the July 9, 1936 meeting, authority was given to the Secretary to institute a card system for the record of attendance and such other information as circumstances require.

(d) Publicity:

On January 9, 1936, the recommendation from the Finance Committee that a maximum appropriation of $1,000 for special services connected with publicity for the 1936 Convention was adopted.

(e) Offerings:

July 9, 1936, the following recommendation from the Finance Committee was adopted by the Executive Board for the Columbus Convention:

We recommend that all offerings received at the Columbus Convention services be given to the Board of Foreign Missions for further reduction of its indebtedness, except the offering at the evening service devoted to the Deaconess Cause, which offering shall be given to the Board of Deaconess Work.

(f) Memorials:

At the meeting of the Executive Board, April 16, 1936, the Secretary asked for instructions concerning the publication of memorials in the Bulletin, and the Executive Board instructed the Secretary to have all memorials mimeographed in sufficient number for circulation at the convention instead of printing in the Bulletin.

*(g) Committee on Place of Next Convention: (For action on this item, see pp. 20, 467.)

The Executive Board recommends that the Convention authorize the appointment of a Committee on Place of Next Convention, which Committee shall be composed of the chairmen of the delegations of the constituent synods.

2. Conventions:

*(a) Committee on Minutes: (For action on this item, see p. 20.)

January 9, 1936, the Executive Board approved a plan for the publication of minutes in mimeographed form from day to day in lieu of having them read in open session. As a part of this plan the Executive Board provided for the appointment of a committee to review the minutes as submitted from time to time, which committee shall be responsible for the presentation of the minutes to the convention for approval at such time as the convention may determine.

(b) Triennial Meetings:

In the fulfillment of the promise made by the President, from the chair, at the 1934 convention, the matter of triennial conventions was presented to the Executive Board, January 10, 1935, for consideration. The matter was referred to a special committee which the President appointed as follows: Rev. A. E. Bell, Rev. W. H. Greever, James C. Kinard.

This committee reported to the Executive Board September 26, 1935, as follows, and their report was adopted by the Executive Board:

Your Special Committee on Triennial Conventions having considered the merit of the change from biennial to triennial conventions from the standpoint of economy, reports:

(1) That the economy aimed at in less frequent conventions is not as great as might appear, due to the fact that less frequent conventions of the general body require more frequent meetings of boards, committees and commissions of the Church.

(2) That such proposed change from biennial to triennial conventions would require extensive changes in charters and constitutions of the Church and its agencies out of proportion to the possible benefits to be achieved by the change proposed.

(3) That the loss of efficiency entailed by less frequent conventions decidedly outweighs the benefits that might be attained by such proposed change.

Your committee therefore recommends that the present plan of biennial conventions of the Church be retained.

F. H. Knubel, *President*
E. Clarence Miller, *Treasurer.*
W. H. Greever, *Secretary*

II, 5, Year 1938 for Board of American Missions. Action was deferred on this item for consideration in connection with the report of the Board of American Missions. (See pp. 52, 184f.)

At twelve o'clock the Convention adjourned with prayer by the Rev. E. M. Morgan.

SECOND SESSION

Deshler-Wallick Hotel
Columbus, Ohio
Thursday, October 15, 1936, 2.00 P. M.
Devotions were conducted by the Rev. Conrad Wilker, and the President called the Convention to order.

The Committee of Tellers reported that the Rev. W. H. Greever had received 397 votes for Secretary out of a total of 412 votes cast. The President declared Dr. Greever elected Secretary.

Consideration of the Executive Board's report was resumed.

II, 7, Better Adjustment of the Work of Auxiliaries was considered item by item.

II, 7, A, (1) was adopted.

II, 7, A, (2) was accepted as notice, and action was deferred according to the By-laws. (See p. 97.)

II, 7, B, was adopted.

On motion, the privilege of the floor was granted, for the consideration of this item, with its sub-divisions, to official representatives of the three auxiliaries involved.

II, 7, C, was adopted.

II, 7, D, was adopted.

II, 7, E. By motion "E" was considered according to its sub-divisions, and (1), (2) and (3) were adopted.

II, 7, F. Action was deferred until the consideration of the report of the Parish and Church School Board. (See pp. 261, 432.)

III, A, 2, (a) Basis of Apportionment.   Adopted.

III, A, 3, Calendar of Special Days and Seasons.   Adopted.

The President called for items following IV, A, 2, which could be disposed of before the Special Order set for 4.30.

IV, A, 3, Transfer of Mountain Work. Adopted.

IV, B, 2, (b) Transfer of Synodical Mission Work. The third paragraph, under this item, was amended by striking out the words "of the success" in the first line.

IV, B, 2, (c) Amendment to the ruling on the Plan of Operation. Adopted.

IV, B, 5, (a) Change in Rules of Board of Ministerial Pensions and Relief. Adopted.

IV, C, 1, (a) Devotional Literature.   Adopted.

IV, C, 1, (b) Service for Rural Life Sunday. The Rev. G. H. Bechtold introduced the following motion:

Moved, that we direct the Common Service Book Committee to prepare a suitable service for the fifth Sunday after Easter, commonly known as Rural Life Sunday.

This motion was accepted by the President, who announced that it would be held as unfinished business since the hour for the Special Order had arrived. (For action on this item, see p. 142.)

The Special Order appointed for 4.30 was a brief memorial service at which the Necrologist of The United Lutheran

Church in America read the full list of ministers, laymen, deaconesses and lay women who, according to his records, have died during the biennium.

NECROLOGY REPORT

During the biennium closed for this report in July of our convention year, records have been compiled of 116 ministers, 2 deaconesses, 17 laymen, and 7 laywomen, who have entered into their heavenly reward.

Your appointee designated to attend to this business begs to thank all persons in the Church who replied promptly to his many importunities for data and dates needed to produce reliable records.

The great value of autobiographies for the writing of trustworthy memoirs cannot be overstated.

Name	Born — Where	Born — When	Ordained	Synod at Death	Died — Where	Died — When	Where Buried	Age Y.	Age M.	Age D.	Years of Service
Allen, George K.	Bedford Co., Pa.	Aug. 31, 1866	1894	O	Canton, O.	Jan. 25, 1935	Johnstown, Pa.	68	4	24	31
Anstadt, Henry, D.D.	Selinsgrove, Pa.	June 18, 1869	1894	WP	Chambersburg, Pa.	Apr. 23, 1935	Chambersburg, Pa.	65	10	5	41
Ash, Frank W., B.D.	Shannondale, Pa.	Feb. 18, 1880	1907	Pg	Penn, Pa.	Oct. 25, 1935	Nr. Barberton, O.	55	8	7	28
Baer, Daniel U., Ph.D.	Nr. Mercersburg, Pa.	Sept. 7, 1858	1886	EP	Sea Isle City, N. J.	Mar. 10, 1935	Mercersburg, Pa.	76	6	3	43
Baker, Charles W., D.D.	Bakersville, Pa.	Jan. 28, 1859	1887	WP	Gettysburg, Pa.	June 29, 1936	Gettysburg, Pa.	77	5	1	43
Barringer, Russell	Johnstown, N. Y.	Sept. 15, 1854	1871	NY	Hartwick Seminary, N. Y.	Aug. 24, 1935	Hartwick Sem'y, N. Y.	80	11	7	42
Biederbecke, Carl H.	Dappendorf, Germany	Aug. 3, 1845		NY	Paterson, N. J.	May 10, 1936	New York, N. Y.	90	9	7	6
Bell, Herbert C.	Washington Co., Md.	Jan. 14, 1868	1897	Fl	St. Petersburg, Fla.	July 12, 1935	St. Petersburg, Fla.	67	5	28	39
Benze, C. Theodore, D.D.	Warren, Pa.	Sept. 19, 1865	1885	PM	Philadelphia, Pa.	July 3, 1936	Philadelphia, Pa.	70	9	14	31
Bickel, Lewis J.	Pottstown, Pa.	July 17, 1857	1887	PM	Philadelphia, Pa.	Feb. 19, 1935	Pottstown, Pa.	77	9	2	47
Biemuller, Andreas	Masbach, Germany	Feb. 1, 1856	1887	PM	Philadelphia, Pa.	Nov. 26, 1934	Forest Hill, Pa.	78	8	25	48
Bierdemann, Gustavus A., D.D.	Seagerstown, Pa.	Nov. 15, 1859	1894	NY	Albany, N. Y.	Aug. 25, 1935	Albany, N. Y.	75	9	10	33
Bodie, Nathan D.	Saluda Co., S. C.	Jan. 25, 1862	1871	NC	High Point, N. C.	Oct. 9, 1934	Nr. Salisbury, N. C.	72	8	10	24
Bowen, Owen W.	Nr. Albion, Ind.	Mar. 6, 1841	1892	Id	Mishawaka, Ind.	Dec. 16, 1934	Albion, Ind.	93	9	10	39
Clemens, John J., B.D.	Reykjavik, Iceland	Sept. 5, 1872	1886	Il	Yorkville, Ill.	Sept. 19, 1935	Altoona, Pa.	62	10	12	43
Crissman, Frederick H.	Huntingdon Furnace, Pa.	Apr. 25, 1857	1885	Md	Macomb, Ill.	Mar. 7, 1935		77	10	12	47
Cronk, Benjamin W.	Floyd Co., Va.	Aug. 7, 1857	1907	Va	Pearisburg, Va.	Oct. 13, 1934	Pembroke, Va.	77	2	6	28
Dennig, Charles A.	Easton, Pa.	Oct. 4, 1878	1888	Pg	Pittsburgh, Pa.	Oct. 25, 1935	Warren, Pa.	57	0	21	10
Dieckhoff, W. F.	Rostock, Germany	Jan. 24, 1866	1894	O	Weston, W. Va.	June 29, 1934	Wheeling, W. Va.	68	5	5	36
Dinwiddie, Edwin C., D.D.	Springfield, O.	Sept. 29, 1867	1889	O	Washington, D. C.	May 3, 1935	Springfield, O.	67	7	6	46
Doering, Frederick H., D.D.	Gross-Gottern, Germany	Oct. 26, 1862	1879	NY	Jersey City, N. J.	Sept. 18, 1934	Middle Village, L. I.	72	10	22	47
Dornblaser, Emanuel H., D.D.	Clintondale, Pa.	Mar. 19, 1850	1896	O	Minneapolis, Minn.	Sept. 15, 1934	Springfield, O.	84	2	26	38
Ebert, Alfred O.	Nr. Lynnville, Pa.	Feb. 19, 1870	1892	PM	New Tripoli, Pa.	Nov. 14, 1934	New Tripoli, Pa.	64	9	11	43
Etter, Charles B., D.D.	Lehmasters, Pa.	Oct. 10, 1862	1885	O	Wadsworth, O.	July 21, 1935	Wadsworth, O.	72	9	6	24
Fisher, Charles L. T.	Salisbury, N. C.	Apr. 4, 1857	1887	NC	Lynchburg, Va.	Mar. 10, 1936	Lynchburg, Va.	78	11	25	48
Fogleman, David L.	Nr. Womelsdorf, Pa.	Nov. 14, 1861	1892	PM	Denver, Pa.	Dec. 19, 1935	Womelsdorf, Pa.	74	1	11	26
Fox, Clarence M.	Stroudsburg, Pa.	Aug. 11, 1870	1880	NC	Salisbury, N. C.	Mar. 10, 1936	Salisbury, N. C.	65	6	6	51
Frederick, Thomas J.	Aaronsburg, Pa.	May 2, 1846	1906	Pg	Spring Church, Pa.	Nov. 22, 1934	Spring Church, Pa.	88	6	29	29
Fuerst, Frank J.	Buchen, Germany	Jan. 26, 1860	1894	Pg	Pittsburgh, Pa.	Mar. 28, 1935	Pittsburgh, Pa.	75	11	11	29
Funk, Henry C., Ph.D.	Staunton, Ill.	Apr. 28, 1865	1897	Cf	Glendale, Calif.	Jan. 2, 1936	Glendale, Calif.	70	8	2	38
Gable, Charles J.	Seenery Hill, Pa.	Mar. 26, 1871	1889	PM	Philadelphia, Pa.	June 16, 1935		64	2	20	33
Gebhart, Horace K., D.D.	Urbana, O.	July 30, 1857	1893	NW	Kenosha, Wis.	Oct. 2, 1935	Kenosha, Wis.	78	2	2	42
Geesey, Frederick S.	Red Lion, Pa.	Feb. 15, 1862	1893	WP	Spring Grove, Pa.	Apr. 30, 1936	Spring Grove, Pa	74	2	17	40
Gehreke, Herman F. W.	Hildesheim, Germany	Oct. 15, 1863	1877	Cf	San Francisco, Calif.	Mar. 25, 1936	San Francisco, Calif.	72	5	10	43
Grau, George M., D.D.	Philadelphia, Pa.	Sept. 27, 1848	1883	O	Brookville, O.	Nov. 15, 1934	Centre Hall, Pa.	86	7	18	38
Greenhoe, Samuel F.	Beaver Springs, Pa.	May 9, 1855	1920	Sq	Jersey Shore, Pa.	Dec. 31, 1935		80	4	26	52
Haferman, Martin C. J.	Clara City, Minn.	Nov. 24, 1895	1922	Ks	Lindstrom, Minn.	Apr. 26, 1936	Lindstrom, Minn.	40	1	1	16
Hahn, Alexander F. M.	Detroit, Mich.	Aug. 11, 1884	1912	NS	Hays, Kan.	Dec. 12, 1935	Detroit, Mich.	51	0	13	23
Hartzell, Luther F.	East Bangor, Pa.	Jan. 12, 1897	1922	Pg	Lunenburg, N. S.	Feb. 25, 1935	East Bangor, Pa.	38	3	10	13
Hassinger, John E. F., B.D.	Selinsgrove, Pa.	Sept. 15, 1859	1882	NW	Jeannette, Pa.	Sept. 25, 1934		79	1	28	50
Haupt, Alexander J. D., D.D.	Greenfield, Mass.	June 1, 1876	1905	WP	Horicon, Wis.	Sept. 29, 1934	St. Paul, Minn.	75	1	22	23
Haus, Luther R.	Milton, Pa.	Jan. 8, 1851	1876	EP	Phillipsburg, N. J.	Feb. 13, 1935	Phillipsburg, N. J.	83	1	2	56
Hay, Charles E., D.D.	Harrisburg, Pa.	Oct. 29, 1851	1876	Md	Baltimore, Md.	Nov. 30, 1934	Harrisburg, Pa.	83	1	24	40
Henkel, Heinrich L.	Espol, Germany	Jan. 16, 1862	1895	Cn	Waterloo, Canada	Mar. 2, 1936	Waterloo, Canada	65	0	4	13
Herman, Harry E.	Elizabethville, Pa.	Oct. 21, 1892	1922	O	Norristown, Pa.	Nov. 23, 1935	Elizabethville, Pa.	43	1	3	35
Heuser, Wilam L.	Wytheville, Va.	Apr. 16, 1870	1895	O	Gibsonville, N. C.	May 10, 1935	Akron, O.	65	0		29
Hite, Enoch O.	Lexington Co., N. C.	Apr. 27, 1873	1906	NC	Akron, O.	Aug. 31, 1935	Gibsonville, N. C.	62	4	4	29
Houk, Aaron J.	New Middletown, O.	June 14, 1856	1888	O	Akron, O.	Apr. 17, 1935	Lima, O.	78	10	3	39

Name	Born Where	Born When	Ordained	Synod at Death	Died Where	Died When	Where Buried	Age Y	Age M	Age D	Years of Service
Houtz, Thomas C., Sc.D., D.D.	Lemont, Pa.	Sept. 28, 1853	1889	Sq	Elysburg, Pa.	Feb. 2, 1935	Selinsgrove, Pa.	81	4	4	45
Hunt, Joel R. E., D.D.	Newton, N. C.	May 14, 1876	1901	Il	Chicago, Ill.	Apr. 19, 1936	Chicago, Ill.	59	11	5	33
Hirsh, John G. M., B.S.	Nr. Hamilton, O.	Sept. 4, 1850	1874	Ks	McPherson, Kan.	Feb. 21, 1936	McPherson, Kan.	84	5	17	50
Kirsch, John A. W., D.D.	Kappeln, Germany	Aug. 5, 1865	1887	NY	Canajoharie, N. Y.	Jan. 6, 1936	Canajoharie Falls, N.Y.	70	5	1	47
Kleine, Otto, D.D.	Ohra, Germany	Nov. 12, 1871	1893	PM	Spring Mount, Pa.	June 30, 1934	Philadelphia, Pa.	62	7	18	41
Kline, Harry C., D.D.	Philadelphia, Pa.	May 27, 1868	1897	NY	Baldwin, L. I., N. Y.	Jan. 5, 1936	Allentown, Pa.	67	7	27	38
Kline, Marion J., D.D.	Frederick, Md.	Oct. 2, 1871	1896	Al	Altoona, Pa.	Sept. 29, 1934	Harrisburg, Pa.	62	11	3	38
Knabenschuh, Henry S.	New York, N. Y.	July 8, 1865		NY	New York, N. Y.	Oct. 11, 1935	Brooklyn, N. Y.	70	6	2	…
Kraeling, Hermann D.	Gemuenden, Germany	Nov. 17, 1853	1874	NY	Newburgh, N. Y.	May 19, 1936	Poughkeepsie, N. Y.	81	8	28	40
Krueger, John F., Ph.D., DD., LL.D.	Chaibassa, Bengal, E. Ind.	July 15, 1881	1904	O	Buffalo, N. Y.	Nov. 13, 1935	Springfield, O.	54	10	28	31
Kuder, Calvin F., D.D.	Laury's, Pa.	Apr. 10, 1864	1891	PM	Yeadon, Pa.	Sept. 8, 1935	Philadelphia, Pa.	71	3	10	25
Landis, Elbert E.	Nr. Plumsteadville, Pa.	Oct. 26, 1886	1913	PM	Quakertown, Pa.	July 6, 1934	Dublin, Pa.	47	10	4	21
Leonard, Charles, D.D.	Philadelphia, Pa.	Dec. 21, 1878	1904	O	Cleveland, O.	Oct. 25, 1935	Cleveland, O.	56	0	22	31
Lingle, James W.	Nr. Linglestown, Pa.	Feb. 3, 1842	1877	Al	Clarksburg, W. Va.	Jan. 27, 1935	Harrisburg, Pa.	92	8	20	36
Livingston, George A.	Nr. New Oxford, Pa.	Aug. 3, 1872	1901	WP	Dillsburg, Pa.	Apr. 23, 1936	New Oxford, Pa.	63	11	28	35
Livingston, Peter.	Nr. New Oxford, Pa.	Sept. 12, 1854	1886	WP	York, Pa.	Sept. 10, 1934	York, Pa.	79	11	28	44
Longacre, Jacob H.	Normal Square, Pa.	Aug. 10, 1865	1893	PM	Boyertown, Pa.	May 29, 1936	Slatington, Pa.	70	11	19	36
Maurer, Jacob E.	Somerset Co., Pa.	Oct. 27, 1854	1883	Md	Boonsboro, Md.	Aug. 21, 1934	Lititz, Pa.	79	9	24	45
Maxwell, David E., B.D.	Jeannette, Pa.	Mar. 17, 1894	1922	Pg	Pittsburgh, Pa.	Apr. 28, 1935	Jeannette, Pa.	41	1	16	13
Meyer, Hans E. W. R.	Muender, Germany	Jan. 17, 1872	1896	PM	Olney, Pa.	May 31, 1935	Philadelphia, Pa.	63	4	14	39
Miley, Aaron C., Ph.D., D.D.	Wabash Co., Ind.	Nov. 27, 1879	1909	Mh	Detroit, Mich.	Apr. 1, 1935	Detroit, Mich.	55	4	14	26
Miller, Curtis A.	North Lima, O.	Feb. 26, 1856	1881	KT	Ardmore, Pa.	Dec. 24, 1934	Columbiana, O.	79	3	21	40
Miller, Edwin Lunn.	Gratz, Pa.	Feb. 26, 1883	1913	PM	Allentown, Pa.	Dec. 29, 1935	Nr. Harrisburg, Pa.	52	10	3	22
Miller, John L.	Nr. Williamsford, Canada	June 7, 1861	1885	NY	Berne, Ind.	Dec. 7, 1934	Boston, Mass.	73	0	7	49
Miller, Peter L.	Nr. Harrisonburg, Va.	Aug. 29, 1902	1928	NY	Boston, Mass.	Nov. 21, 1935	Williamsford, Canada	33	2	22	7
Mock, Robert E.	Nr. Newmanstown, Pa.	June 9, 1895	1895	WV	Point Pleasant, W. Va.	Apr. 15, 1936	Point Pleasant, W. Va.	80	10	6	34
Morehead, John A., D.D., LL.D, D.Th., S.T.D.	Pulaski Co., Va.	Nov. 1, 1890	1918	Cf	Phoenix, Ariz.	June 8, 1935	Phoenix, Ariz.	44	7	7	12
Moser, Irvin O.	Norristonville, Pa.	Feb. 4, 1867	1892	Va	Salem, Va.	June 1, 1936	Salem, Va.	69	3	27	43
Myers, Charles R. D.D.	Lewisburg, Pa.	Nov. 26, 1868	1899	O	Dayton, O.	Aug. 4, 1935	Dayton, O.	66	8	8	36
Peery, Rufus B., Ph.D., D.D.	Burkes Garden, Va.	May 16, 1884	1909	NY	Yonkers, N. Y.	Feb. 28, 1935	Fountain Springs, Pa.	50	9	12	26
Pohlmann, Hugo B. J.	Rahway, N. J.	Apr. 9, 1868	1892	NC	Raleigh, N. C.	Oct. 25, 1934	Raleigh, N. C.	66	10	16	41
Possett, Otto F. W.	Berlin, Germany	Feb. 23, 1856	1904	NY	Hempstead, L. I.	Dec. 26, 1935	Hempstead, L. I.	67	6	13	27
Price, James P.	Lexington Co., S. C.	Jan. 25, 1850	1878	NC	Greenport, L. I.	July 9, 1935	Rochester, N. Y.	85	10	24	51
Rausch, John R.	Millstadt, Ill.	June 30, 1856	1888	Il	Hickory, N. C.	Sept. 8, 1935	Hickory, N. C.	79	5	13	25
Reimer, William H. W.	Stone Church, Pa.	Nov. 29, 1854	1877	EP	Metropolis, Ill.	Dec. 23, 1934	West Salem, Ill.	80	10	13	50
Reisch, John E.	State College, Pa.	Jan. 21, 1880	1905	Pg	Stone Church, Pa.	July 16, 1936	Stone Church, Pa.	55	8	9	25
Reisch, Thomas, Ph.D., D.D.	Halifax, Pa.	May 20, 1883	1913	EP	West Sunbury, Pa.	Feb. 1, 1936	Pine Grove Mills, Pa.	52	6	20	23
Renn, Ambrose, A.E., B.D., D.D.	nr Hughesville, Pa.	June 3, 1871	1902	Id	Harrisburg, Pa.	Dec. 23, 1934	Leetonia, O.	63	0	24	27
Roeder, Robert D.	Allentown, Pa.	Aug. 17, 1864	1896	PM	Indianapolis, Ind.	Aug. 29, 1935	Indianapolis, Ind.	71	6	25	36
Roth, David L., D.D.	Prospect, Pa.	Mar. 2, 1862	1885	NW	Reading, Pa.	Mar. 27, 1935	Allentown, Pa.	73	4	14	49
Schaaf, Lewis C., D.D.	Wheeling, W. Va.	Oct. 25, 1847	1876	Pg	Greenville, Pa.	Nov. 29, 1934	Prospect, Pa.	87	4	14	6
Schaeffer, George J.	Emaus, Pa.	July 15, 1903	1928	PM	Salem, O.	July 2, 1935	Wheeling, W. Va.	31	3	5	33
Schnabel, Charles W., B.D.	Madison, Ind.	Jan. 22, 1858	1887	NY	nr Pitman, Pa.	July 2, 1935	Rough & Ready, Pa.	78	4	14	9
Schroeder, Henry M.	Uehling, Neb.	June 4, 1900	1926	NY	Teaneck, N. J.	Dec. 20, 1934	Madison, Ind.	35	0	25	27
Schubarth, Ernst F.	Rodach, Germany	Dec. 29, 1861	1889	Wg	Milwaukee, Wis.	Dec. 13, 1934	Syracuse, N. Y.	72	11	14	36
Seegers, John C., D.D.	Columbia, S. C.	Oct. 6, 1867	1891	PM	Philadelphia, Pa.	June 23, 1936	Milwaukee, Wis.	68	8	17	45

Name	Born Where	Born When	Ordained	Synod at Death	Died Where	Died When	Where Buried	Age Y	Age M	Age D	Years of Service
Shupp, Floyd E., B.D.	Gilbert, Pa.	Aug. 17, 1894	1923	PM	Palmerton, Pa.	Oct. 17, 1935	Gilbert, Pa.	41	2	0	12
Sieber, Lemuel L., D.D.	McAllisterville, Pa.	Mar. 4, 1850	1876	WP	Gettysburg, Pa.	Mar. 20, 1935	Gettysburg, Pa.	85	0	16	50
Simpson, Thomas H. W.	Aberdeen, Md.	June 11, 1905	1933	Al	Baltimore, Md.	Oct. 9, 1935	Hollidaysburg, Pa.	30	3	28	2
Souder, Ivor G.	Columbus, O.	Feb. 2, 1888	1921	KT	Louisville, Ky.	Dec. 21, 1935	Louisville, Ky.	47	10	19	14
Stolz, Reinhold F.	Reading, Pa.	July 7, 1875	1906	EP	Philadelphia, Pa.	Dec. 1, 1934	Reading, Pa.	59	4	10	28
Stuckert, Edward E.	Baltimore, Md.	Nov. 19, 1870	1902	PM	Baltimore, Md.	Mar. 19, 1935	Baltimore, Md.	64	4	0	30
Stump, Joseph, D.D., LL.D., L.H.D.	Marietta, Pa.	Oct. 6, 1866	1887	NW	Minneapolis, Minn.	May 22, 1935	Minneapolis, Minn.	68	7	16	48
Taylor, Samuel J., D.D.	Newberg, Pa.	Feb. 9, 1855	1884	Al	Altoona, Pa.	Oct. 14, 1935	Altoona, Pa.	80	8	5	34
Tonsing, Paul G.	Cleveland, O.	Jan. 3, 1870	1895	Ks	Atchison, Kan.	Mar. 1, 1935	Atchison, Kan.	66	1	28	7
Tope, Homer W., D.D.	Newberg, Pa.	May 28, 1859	1888	Il	Philadelphia, Pa.	Jun. 4, 1936	Newnan, Ga.	77	0	6	48
Traeger, John, D.D.	Bernburg, Germany	May 26, 1866	1896	Wg	Chicago, Ill.	Feb. 1, 1936	Chicago, Ill.	69	8	8	38
Wagner, John, D.D.	Dell Roy, O.	Feb. 1, 1852	1874	Sq	Hazleton, Pa.	Feb. 18, 1936	Hazleton, Pa.	83	0	17	50
Waters, Mosheim S.	Stone Church, Pa.	May 4, 1866	1890	NY	Newark, N. J.	Feb. 24, 1936	Elizabeth, N. J.	69	9	23	44
Weber, Henry H., D.D.	Prospect, Pa.	Aug. 4, 1860	1885	Md	Washington, D. C.	Feb. 8, 1936	Baltimore, Md.	75	6	4	33
Weiskotten, Charles P.	Philadelphia, Pa.	Dec. 1, 1860	1894	Mh	New York, N. Y.	Apr. 17, 1935	Springfield, O.	74	4	16	38
Wenner, George U., D.D., L.H.D., LL.D.	Bethlehem, Pa.	May 17, 1844	1868	NY	New York, N. Y.	Nov. 1, 1934	New York, N. Y.	90	5	14	65
Wolfe, Harmon A.	Blair Co., Pa.	Apr. 25, 1860	1895	Il	Polo, Ill.	Sep. 23, 1934	Polo, Ill.	74	4	9	36
Yehl, Elias A., D.D.	Rockdale, Pa.	May 17, 1860	1888	PM	Allentown, Pa.	July 23, 1934	nr Guthsville, Pa.	74	2	6	44
Zimmerman, Isaac P.	Dauphin Co., Pa.	May 17, 1855	1883	EP	Lancaster, Pa.	Feb. 19, 1936	Lancaster, Pa.	80	9	2	40
Zimmerman, William, D.D.	Stuttgart, Germany			RM	Denver, Colo.	Oct. 5, 1934	Denver, Colo.	56			
Zinssmeister, Carl, D.D.	Kaiserslautern, Germany	Aug. 19, 1859	1885	NY	Arlington, Va.	Mar. 20, 1935	Syracuse, N. Y.	75	7	1	48
LAYMEN											
Albrecht, Antonius Carl	Philadelphia, Pa.	Apr. 6, 1857		PM	Philadelphia, Pa.	Nov. 16, 1934	Philadelphia, Pa.	77	7	11	
Bittner, Frank David	Lynnville, Pa.	Mar. 1, 1857		PM	Allentown, Pa.	Dec. 1, 1934	Allentown, Pa.	77	9	0	
Burkhardt, John	Philadelphia, Pa.	1868		PM	Charlotte, S. C.	Jan. 14, 1935	Philadelphia, Pa.	67			
Cromer, George Benedict, LL.D.	Newberry Co., S. C.	Oct. 3, 1857		SC	Charlotte, S. C.	Sept. 25, 1935	Newberry, S. C.	77	11	22	
Driever, Charles J.	Preston, Canada	Apr. 24, 1870		Il	Evanston, Ill.	Aug. 5, 1935	Evanston, Ill.	65	3	11	
Harter, Henry W., LL.D.	Canton, O.	May 5, 1855		O	Canton, O.	May 6, 1935	Canton, O.	80	0	1	
Henkel, Elon Osiander	New Market, Va.	Jan. 16, 1865		Va	New Market, Va.	Feb. 27, 1935	New Market, Va.	70	1	11	
Kutz, John J.	Reading, Pa.	Nov. 12, 1872		PM	Reading, Pa.	Feb. 16, 1935	Reading, Pa.	62	3	4	
Meyer, William	Hanover, Germany	Aug. 8, 1884		NW	Holland, Mich.	Aug. 14, 1935	Chicago, Ill.	51	0	6	
Miller, James W.	Edenville, Pa.	June 28, 1844		EP	nr New York, N. Y.	Aug. 6, 1934	Atlantic Ocean	90	1	8	
Mohr, William S.	Mohrsville, Pa.	Dec. 29, 1861		PM	Reading, Pa.	Aug. 22, 1934	Reading, Pa.	72	7	24	
Morehead, Wythe F., Prof.	Pulaski Co., Va.	May 20, 1855		Va	Philadelphia, Pa.	June 6, 1935	Salem, Va.	80	0	17	
Richards, Henry M. M., Capt., Litt.D.	Easton, Pa.	Aug. 16, 1848		PM	Lebanon, Pa.	Sept. 28, 1935	Reading, Pa.	87	1	12	
Riter, Frank M.	Philadelphia, Pa.	May 20, 1855		PM	Philadelphia, Pa.	Mar. 20, 1935	Philadelphia, Pa.	79	10	0	
Snyder, John E.	Lancaster, Pa.	Apr. 13, 1863		PM	Hershey, Pa.	Oct. 13, 1935	Hershey, Pa.	72	6	0	
Showalter, William J., Litt.D.	Dale Enterprise, Va.	July 10, 1878		Md	Washington, D. C.	Oct. 13, 1935	Waynesboro, Va.	57	3	3	
Strong, Ephraim Kyler, Hon.	Whitley Co., Ind.	Oct. 10, 1865		Id	Wolf Lake, Ind.	Nov. 29, 1935	Columbia City, Ind.	70	1	19	
DEACONESSES											
Aufhammer, Sister Katherine B.	Pittsburgh, Pa.	Nov. 3, 1855	1908	Md	Baltimore, Md.	Sept. 27, 1934	Baltimore, Md.	78	10	24	
Metzger, Sister Inez.	Blandburg, Pa.	Apr. 7, 1897	1928	Md	Washington, D. C.	Dec. 17, 1935	Blandburg, Pa.	38	8	10	

Name	Born		Ordained	Synod at Death	Died		Where Buried	Age			Years of Service
	Where	When			Where	When		Y.	M.	D	
LAYWOMEN											
Bell, Rena B.	Irving, Ill.	Sept. 17, 1871		F	St. Petersburg, Fla.	Sept. 1, 1935	St. Petersburg, Fla.	63	11	15	
Bornholdt, Anna Cecilia	Glen Allen, Ont., Canada.	Aug. 9, 1866		Cn	Waterloo, Ont., Can.	July 9, 1935	Waterloo, Ont., Can.	68	11	0	
Harpster, Mary Julia	Gettysburg, Pa.	Dec. 17, 1846		EP	Chambersburg, Pa.	July 1, 1935	Gettysburg, Pa.	88	6	14	
Holland, Mary McClanahan	Oakville, Texas	Jan. 16, 1859		SC	Philadelphia, Pa.	Dec. 16, 1934	Salem, Va.	75	11	0	
Kaehler, Margaret T. McNair	nr Dansville, N. Y.	June 29, 1848		NY	Buffalo, N. Y.	Aug. 14, 1934	Buffalo, N. Y.	86	1	15	
Palas, Mrs. Arthur J.	Osage, Iowa	Jan. 21, 1886		Ia	Des Moines, Ia.	Nov. 18, 1934	Des Moines, Ia.	48	9	27	
Zollikoffer, Emily Augusta	Brooklyn, N. Y.	May 29, 1849		NY	New York, N. Y.	Apr. 13, 1935	Brooklyn, N. Y.	85	10	14	

Humbly submitted,

AMES F. LAMBERT, Necrologist.

The reading of this list was followed by a service of hymns and prayer conducted by the Rev. C. J. Smith, President of Roanoke College, who delivered an impressive address in memory of Dr. J. A. Morehead, as the special feature of this Memorial Service.

Thursday Evening

At eight o'clock a mass meeting was held in the Central High School Auditorium. This meeting was largely attended. The Rev. A. R. Wentz presided. Addresses were made by Bishop August Marahrens, Dr. Hanns Lilje, and President F. H. Knubel, presenting a world view of Lutheranism and its present tasks. Delightful music was rendered by the *a capella* choir of Wittenberg College.

THIRD SESSION

DESHLER-WALLICK HOTEL
Columbus, Ohio
Friday, October 16, 1936, 8.45 A. M.

Matins were conducted by the Rev. J. A. Yount.

The Convention was called to order by the President.

Immediately after calling the Convention to order, the President made two announcements: (1) that he held in his hand a gavel, loaned by the President of the Kentucky-Tennessee Synod, the Rev. I. W. Gernert, for use in this Convention, with special reference to the use made of this gavel by the Rev. Harlan K. Fenner as President of the General Synod in 1909; (2) that the special Service of Prayer, appointed for 11.30 today, would be conducted by the Secretary, in the absence of the Rev. W. H. Traub, who was unable to attend the Convention on account of his personal illness.

In connection with this announcement, the President presented the following resolution, as a suggestion from the Executive Board, with reference to the many who are in distress:

Resolved, That the members of the Convention stand in respect to those faithful members of the Church who have been disabled by the infirmities of age or the failure of health, and especially those elected to membership in this Convention, whose presence has been prevented under the providence of God, and that all join in the following petition:

O God of love and mercy: We pray Thee to bestow special gifts of Thy grace upon all whose needs we now remember, according to Thine infinite goodness and wisdom, through Jesus Christ our Lord. Amen.

The resolution was adopted, by a standing vote, and the President led in prayer.

The President recognized the Rev. F. M. Urich, Chairman of the Committee of Reference and Counsel, who presented the following report:

REPORT OF COMMITTEE OF REFERENCE AND COUNSEL

By reason of the fact that the Rev. Alfred Haapanen, President of the Suomi Synod, is here to present the greetings of that body, and that he will be unable to stay for our afternoon session, the Committee of Reference and Counsel recommends that he be heard at once.

The recommendation was adopted, and the Rev. Alfred Haapanen was given the privilege of the floor for the presentation of the greetings of the Suomi Synod. The President called upon the Rev. E. B. Burgess to make a response, which he did in a fitting way, with cordial assurance of the very friendly feeling entertained by the United Lutheran Church for the brethren of the Suomi Synod.

The Rev. L. C. Manges, Chairman of the Nominating Committee, presented nominations as follows:

For the *Executive Board:*
Rev. E. B. Burgess, Rev. M. R. Hamsher, Rev. Paul H. Krauss, Rev. E. P. Pfatteicher, Rev. A. Steimle, Rev. A. A. Zinck, Rev. H. W. A. Hanson, Rev. J. J. Raun, Rev. J. H. Reble, Benjamin Apple, Carl M. Distler, C. W. Howe, A. F. Sittloh, Robbin B. Wolf, John L. Zimmerman, Herbert Fisher, Harry A. Fritsch, Orville Sardeson.

The President declared the nominations closed.

For the *Commission of Adjudication:*
Term expiring 1942: Rev. Stanley Billheimer, Rev. Wm. E. Frey, Rev. L. Franklin Gruber, Rev. E. E. Snyder, Rev. Carroll J. Rockey, Rev. H. B. Stock, James F. Henninger, Wm. E. Hirt, John F. Reinhardt. *Term expiring 1940:* John F. Kramer, Charles J. Tressler, Franklin Menges. *Term expiring 1938:* Rev. John Aberly, Rev. J. S. Simon, Rev. A. B. Leamer.

The President declared the nominations closed.

For the *Committee on Church Papers:*
Rev. H. C. Alleman, Rev. A. J. Holl, Rev. C. B. Foelsch, Rev. H. E. Schildroth, Rev. W. E. Wheeler, Rev. N. Willison, Charles E. Blum, O. F. H. Bert, Charles G. Shatzer.

The President declared the nominations closed.

The Rev. J. Luther Sieber, Chairman of the Nominating Committee, presented nominations for the *Executive Committee of the Laymen's Movement* as follows:

H. J. Albrecht, Henry Beisler, J. L. Clark, P. A. Elsesser, P. H. Glatfelter, W. H. Hager, J. P. Hovland, J. K. Jensen, Harold U. Landis, I. F. Mellinger, E. Clarence Miller, George E. Neff, Karl Overholt, I. A. Shaffer, Jr., Belding B. Slifer, William H. Stackel, Charles Steele, S. Frederick Telleen, Don Young, Charles B. Zimmerman, J. Milton Deck, John Havekost, Carl H. Henrich, J. E. Hirtle, Philip H. Ketterer, E. P. Miller, William H. Patrick, C. B. Patterson, P. L. Schantz, E. Harry Schirmer.

The President declared the nominations closed.

The amendment to the By-laws, striking out Section VII, B, 5, 6, and 7, presented as a part of the report of the Executive Board [II, 7, A, (2)] on October 15, was called for action and was adopted. (See pp. 53, 89.)

The Rev. S. W. Herman, President, presented the report of the Board of Foreign Missions. He requested that the Convention precede its consideration of the report by special prayer. The prayer was led by Dr. Herman.

REPORT OF THE BOARD OF FOREIGN MISSIONS

(For action on the recommendations in this report, see p. 142)

I imagine it is some time since anyone outside of those in official position has read the charter of the Board of Foreign Missions. It is worth reading—"The purpose of the Board of Foreign Missions shall be to carry on, superintend and promote the work of diffusing Christianity and charity, support and furthering Christian missions and charitable work in foreign lands or elsewhere in accordance with the constitution and purposes of The United Lutheran Church in America." Charter. This old charter is up to date in modern mission conception and ideals. It does not confine the Foreign Board to the gathering of a few called heathen, but gives it the great task of winning people for Christ and the setting up and maintaining the Church in Foreign lands. This the Board has tried to do and is doing now. In no field to which it has gone at the direction of the church has it failed and from none has it withdrawn no matter how difficult the task has been. Our church is a faith directed church and has refused to be discouraged believing that God is in the work. These last few years have been hard years for all who do mission work, yet the missionaries have never faltered and we should do them honor. The Home Church has had other appeals, real appeals that lie close to the heart, but it has helped us to carry on. We have fewer missionaries but the work has not decreased. (**Recommendation No. 1, p. 120.**)

Plans of the Biennium

Our plans for the last two years have centered about three ideas. First, to maintain as much work as our income will allow without going into debt. In other words our income must meet our spending. Second, every effort was made to reduce the debt which has continued to hamper our activities and interfere with the forward movement. Third, that replacement of missionaries be made in every field. This we followed as funds permitted. It is our purpose to follow this plan during the next biennium and advance the entire work as our income increases.

Promotion

This has been reported elsewhere, but there has been a regular plan of education. We have never had the idea of creating a new organization such as a Men's Missionary Society, but to approach the Church through the pastor and the church council, and the recognized organizations of the church. To that end we not only give special attention to the Epiphany Season, but there is a regular plan of education which has three parts to it. First, Literature; second, Deputation Service on the part of missionaries; and third, Personal visits to pastors and leading men in the congregations. During Epiphany and once again during the year we try to reach in a special manner every member in every church with information concerning Foreign Missions. (Recommendation No. 4, p. 120.)

The Home Base

Since the reduction of the number of secretaries to three and a Treasurer much of the work of the Home Base nas been carried on by the other Secretaries which has increased the work and certain things could have more emphasis, as a distinct work of the Home Base. However, two vital things have been done, first, to keep the church at home informed as to needs and progress through deputation and literature; conduct of the Epiphany Appeal and work in every way for the securing of funds. Here the work of the special department has done valiant service.   (Recommendation No. 2, p. 120.)

Candidate and Personnel

Connected with the Home Base is our Committee on Candidates and Personnel. During the biennium Rev. W. Theodore Benze and his wife have been sent as full-time missionaries to British Guiana. Rev. J. K. Donat and Rev. George Gordon Parker and their wives have been sent to Africa. Rev. and Mrs. Robert S. Oberly and Rev. and Mrs. George K. Gesler have been transferred to our India Mission. Dr. Gladys Morgan, Miss Theodora Nuedoerffer, R. N., Miss Susan Glatz, Rev. Ray L. Cunningham and family and Miss Mary Borthwick have been sent to India.

Co-operating Synods

As is known to all of us three Lutheran bodies or synods co-operate with our Board—Augustana in India; the Danish and Icelandic Synods in Japan. Their contributions have been as follows—Augustana has a full voting member on the Board and also a non-voting representative. The Danish Church has two non-voting representatives and the Icelandic Synod has one non-voting representative. We appreciate greatly not only the contributions but also the sincere interest and co-operation of these Lutheran bodies. We value their fellowship and gifts.

The Lutheran Foreign Missions Conference

This conference meets every year and brings together the Lutheran Secretaries and missionaries as no other meeting does. It is busy in surveying the Lutheran Foreign Mission Work and setting up through a committee plans that we hope will unify our work and perhaps help in unifying our church at least as far as Foreign Missions are concerned. The plan now in force for two years of gathering our missionaries at these conferences has been an important factor. An invitation to the Women's Societies to be present next year is a forward step. The meetings during the biennium have been in the west.

Andhra Christian College

Andhra Christian College under the plan of the Board is to remain at Guntur and is to be maintained under the authority of the Lutheran Mission of India, which in turn is under the authority of the Foreign Mission Board of the U. L. C. A. Four basic plans have been prepared and approved by the Executive Board of the U. L. C. A., the Foreign Mission Board and the Council of the India Mission.

(1) "Voted that the present Andhra Christian College at Guntur shall continue as a first grade College of the United Lutheran Mission in India at Guntur, under the direction of the Lutheran Mission and the Board of Foreign Missions. Its development shall be in a normal way, stressing not number but efficiency and giving due attention to the development of Christian character and leadership for the Christian Church and the nation. The money for Andhra Christian College subscribed and in hand shall be used in the maintenance and development of this institution." Approved.

(2) "Voted that in order that the idea of one College for the Andhra Country be carried out and with a desire to serve educationally the Church and people of the Andhra Country, there shall be offered by the Mission and the Foreign Board to the other missions and boards individually the opportunity to co-operate in the educational plans of this Andhra Christian College at Guntur. The conditions shall be that the missions invited shall furnish one or more professors with their salaries and maintenance and shall make a contribution of not less than 500 dollars per year for the maintenance of the College for each professor furnished. The professors shall have the same standing on College Councils as the other professors having a voice and vote in all matters belonging to the College Council." Approved.

(3) "Voted that the co-operating missions shall have the right to build and maintain for their students hostels or halls, and a chapel, if so desired, provided they are built on land belonging to the co-operating mission or board, and yet be subject to the College discipline." Approved.

(4) "Voted that these plans be put into action as soon as possible and that the acceptance or rejection of the invitation by other missions and boards shall not interfere with the conduct of Andhra Christian College plans as now approved by the mission and the Board of Foreign Missions and the Executive Board of the United Lutheran Church." Approved.

At the present time we are having some debate relating to the matters set forth in the fourfold plan but hope within the near future to have them settled, so that the College can proceed with its development.

Co-operative Auxiliaries of the U. L. C. A.

The Board of Foreign Missions has been able to carry Foreign Mission work beyond what the church in its apportionment can do, through the work of the Women's Missionary Society. It has great value as a missionary educating factor and its generous support of work in the fields which it has supported. This we appreciate more than we sometimes seem to do when questions of authority and administration are being discussed. The League has helped Foreign Missions greatly by taking each biennium a project of quite some size and carrying it through to the great blessing of the general work. Last biennium it built a new building for the Lutheran Seminary in Tokyo at a cost of $15,000. This biennium the League is building a chapel and social center at Tai Tung Chen to cost $10,000. These large projects help beyond measure when the Board can only carry the sending of missionaries and maintain the work. (Recommendation 3, p. 120.)

Recognition of Deaths

Recognition of the death of three great missionary leaders is made here. Under the report of each field proper recognition will be given to missionaries dying while in service, as for instance, our valuable missionary, J. W. Miller, who died at sea while coming home for treatment. In addition we wish to record simply the death and acknowledge the service of Rev. G. A. Brandelle, D.D., of the Augustana Synod and who up to the time of his death was a member of our Board. He had a great missionary spirit.

Another is Dr. C. T. Benze for many years a member of our Board, President from 1926-30, a great friend of Foreign Missions. We would have the Church know of our appreciation of his services to the church through the Board of Foreign Missions.

The third is that of Dr. Chas. A. Dennig, a member of our Board, who died quite suddenly October 25, 1935. He was a good and faithful member of our Board and his wise counsel and deep consecration will be missed.

DEPARTMENT OF SPECIAL GIFTS

The activities of the department of special gifts fall under three heads: support of missionaries, parishes abroad, and proteges, which include native workers and scholarships.

Missionaries.—The number of assigned missionaries at the beginning of the biennium was 46. At the close of the same period there were only 37 showing a loss of 9. In several cases death of missionary or supporter was the reason for discontinuance. But in the majority of cases congregations withdrew their support due to their inability to financially continue this type of co-operation. As a result contributions for the support of missionaries fell off by $20,000 during the biennium. There are seven missionaries available for support. This is in contrast to a decade ago when the demand for the assignment of missionaries exceeded the supply.

Parishes Abroad.—The number of assigned parishes abroad at the beginning of the biennium was 181. This has increased during the biennium by 14, making a total of 195. The total amount contributed is practically the same as during the previous two years. In a number of cases the patrons were not able to forward the full support but did what they could. This they preferred to cancellation as they remained in correspondence with the missionaries in charge of their parishes. The co-operation of missionaries and particularly of the correspondents in the several mission fields in getting information through to the patrons has been a source of much satisfaction. Sunday School scholars are learning in a very practical way how mission work is conducted and the results achieved.

Proteges.—Support of proteges has long been a practice by many devout individuals, interested Sunday School groups and others. In fact there was a time when practically all employed workers as well as many pupils in the schools of the missions were assigned. Unfortunately as the number of Christian workers has increased the number of supporters has decreased. Many of those who have carried on this type of service are no longer with us and the rising generation apparently is not inclined to work along the old lines. The number of proteges has decreased during the biennium from 350 to 326 or a loss of 24. The income under this head has remained practically the same as two years ago. The department now assigns all workers by name as well as by number and in many cases patrons receive personal letters from their proteges.

CONGREGATIONS SUPPORTING MISSIONARIES

Supporters	Pastors	Missionary	Field
Allentown, Pa. Christ's	G. H. Kinard	H. H. Moyer	India
Ashland, O. Trinity	A. H. Smith	J. M. Armbruster	Argentina
Baltimore, Md. St. Mark's	R. D. Clare	I. Cannaday	India
Baltimore, Md. Second	J. E. Grubb	L. W. Slifer	India
Baltimore, Md. St. Paul's	J. B. Rupley	J. R. Jensen, M.D.	Africa
Boyertown, Pa. St. John's	D. F. Longacre	C. E. Swavely	India

Supporters	Pastors	Missionary	Field
Brooklyn, N. Y. Redeemer..H.	T. Weiskotten......A.	F. A. Neudoerffer.....	India
Buffalo, N. Y. Holy Trinity..H.	J. Pflum................E.	Neudoerffer.................	India
Charleston, S. C. St. Andrew's...............C.	K. Derrick...........C.	K. Lippard................	Japan
Dayton, O. First................D.	H. Johnson...........V.	McCauley...................	India
Greensburg, Pa. First........C.	W. Shindler...........G.	K. Gesler.................	India
Greensburg, Pa. Zion.........J.	P. Harman...........A.	F. Schmitthenner.......	India
Hanover, Pa. St. Matthew's.................H.	H. Beidleman.......J.	C. Peery, Jr.	India
Harrisburg, Pa. Memorial...L.	C. Manges.........R.	W. Sell.................	China
Harrisburg, Pa. Zion.........S.	W. Herman..........R.	M. Dunkelberger........	India
Harrisburg, Pa. Zion.........S.	W. Herman..........J.	K. Linn...................	Japan
Harrisburg, Pa. Zion.........S.	W. Herman..........L.	Grady Cooper...........	China
Hummelstown, Pa. Zion......C.	G. Leatherman......F.	L. Coleman...............	India
Johnstown, Pa. First.........G.	W. Nicely...........A.	J. Stirewalt...............	Japan
Lititz, Pa. St. Paul's.........J.	H. Mumper..........Rajah	Manikam...............	India
Mansfield, O. First...........G.	E. Swoyer...........J.	C. Finefrock...............	India
Perkasie, Pa. Hilltown.......A.	T. Smith.............C.	H. Reinbrecht...........	China
Phila. Pa. Nativity............J.	C. Fisher.............H.	H. Sipes...................	India
Phila. Pa. Tabernacle........W.	J. Miller.............M.	L. Dolbeer................	India
Phila. Pa. Temple.............W.	G. Boomhower.......J.	K. Donat...................	Africa
Reading, Pa. Trinity..........H.	F. Miller.............E.	T. Horn.....................	Japan
Rochester, Pa. Grace.........H.	R. Shepfer...........E.	G. Wood....................	India
Rockford, Ill. Trinity.........H.	M. Bannen...........C.	W. Hepner................	Japan
Shelby, O. First................D.	B. Young.............P.	P. Anspach................	China
Shippensburg, Pa. Memorial...............W.	W. Barkley.........J.	R. Strock................	India
Toledo, O. Glenwood..........A.	E. Bell...............V.	E. Zigler, M. D..........	India
Washington, D. C., Keller Memorial...............S.	T. Nicholas...........S.	C. Burger.................	India
Wilmington, Del. Holy Trinity...................J.	F. Kelly.................J.	E. Graefe................	India
Winchester, Va. Grace........L.	A. Thomas...........L.	S. G. Miller.................	Japan
York, Pa. St. Matthew's.....J.	B. Baker..............Harry	Heilman..................	Africa
York, Pa. Zion..................W.	R. Samuel...........J.	R. Fink.....................	India

INDIVIDUALS SUPPORTING MISSIONARY

Stromsburg, Nebr............Mary and Alfred Augustine............Theo. Scholz............China

CONGREGATIONS SUPPORTING MISSIONARIES UNDER THE WOMEN'S MISSIONARY SOCIETY

Williamsport, Pa. Messiah..........................Marie Jensen................................Africa
Brooklyn, N. Y. Good Shepherd................Alice Nickel......................................India
Carlisle, Pa. St. Paul's...........................Clara Leaman....................................India
Omaha, Nebr. Kountze Mem. ....Mette Blair......................................India
Souderton, Pa. Emmanuel......................Hilda Kaercher.............................India
Milwaukee Wis. Epiphany...................Lydia Reich..................................China

LITERATURE

The Board realizes that an uninformed Church is an uninterested Church. Within its financial ability, therefore, it has done what it could to keep all our pastors, congregations, schools and societies informed concerning our mission work in all fields, districts and departments, and to urge a more adequate support of the great cause of foreign missions.

Publicity.—The monthly magazines, "The Foreign Missionary," edited by Secretary Dr. George Drach, and "Der Missionsbote," edited by Rev. Dr. Paul C. Burgdorf, are real and reliable sources of foreign missionary information and inspiration. Single subscriptions are only fifty cents and club subscriptions to one address are thirty-five cents a year. Pastors are asked to order club subscriptions for their church councils, Sunday school teachers and members of their various societies.

The Annual Report of our Foreign Missions, which is sent free to all pastors, broadcasts the voices of the missionaries in all fields speaking to the Home Church. It furnishes fine material for missionary addresses and articles.

The occasional literature, like Dr. Koller's interesting booklet "Liberia and the Mission Path," written after his visit to that field and printed in several editions totaling 20,000, keep up the Church's interest in specific fields. The mission study pamphlet "In Seven Nations" by Dr. Drach, prepared for Sunday schools and all other organizations in the church, fills a long-felt need for a comprehensive and usable course of mission study of our foreign mission effort at home and abroad, and is being widely used in Sunday schools, Luther Leagues and Women's Missionary Societies.

Included in the Epiphany season literature of 1936 was an attractive pageant "The Rainbow Star," prepared by Dr. H. W. Snyder of Washington, D. C., a member of the Board.

Stereopticon Slides and Motion Pictures.—Many pastors and others in our congregations are availing themselves of the opportunity to educate the people in foreign missions by using the Board's stereopticon slides and lectures and the motion picture reels on India, China, Japan, Africa and South America. During the months of January, February and March, an average of one set of slides and of one set of motion picture reels each day was used. During the rest of the year they are in constant demand for Sunday and Wednesday evening services and meetings of societies, schools and conventions. There is no rental charge but transportation both ways must be paid and wherever possible an offering for foreign missions is requested.

Some congregations have carried out a regular plan for the use of the Board's literature throughout the year for missionary education, including "In Seven Nations" for mission study, the magazine "The Foreign Missionary" for monthly up-to-date information, the occasional literature as it appears from time to time, the Annual Report for source material; and have used the stereopticon slides and motion pictures for a series of visible presentations of our foreign work in all our fields.

TREASURER'S STATEMENT

The Board of Foreign Missions is thankful to report that they have balanced the budget in this Biennium. The deficit, which was $166,638.11 on June 30, 1934, has been decreased to $107,637.75 as of June 30, 1936.

No reductions have been made in budgets and salaries since 1933. When one stops to consider that the receipts of the Board on General Fund for year ending June 30, 1929, were $606,602.00, and the receipts on General Fund for the fiscal year ending June 30, 1936, were $373,415.12, it is not hard to understand the problems which faced the Board in try-ing to balance the budget and decrease the deficit in view of decreasing receipts.

But since 1933 the field budgets, which include work budget, salaries and travel, have been gradually on the upward grade.

The budget of the Board passed for the fiscal year of 1933-34 was $330,383.00. The budget for the fiscal year of 1936-37 was passed at a figure of $352,500.00. Now while this increase is $22,117.00, the actual increase to the work in the fields was $25,000. The difference between the $25,000 and the $22,117.00 is in the Home Base figures, which were decreased due principally to not having to pay steady interest to banks on loans. The Board owes no money to banks and only has made short time loans in the summer months.

The problem of balancing the budget and decreasing the deficit was not the only financial problem the Board had to face.

Since Jan. 1, 1929, when the reorganization was made, endowments and trust funds were on the increase, so it was necessary to take care of these increases.

The following schedule illustrates the difference between the funds as of Jan. 1, 1929, and June 30th, 1936:

	Jan. 1, 1929	June 30, 1936
Bank Loans	$191,500.00	None
General Fund Owes Large Funds	185,458.16	107,637.75
General Fund Owes Small Funds	66,161.65	None
Total Deficit	$443,119.81	$107,637.75

It will be noted from the above schedule that the Board owes no money outside of its own organization. These figures show just where the deficit exists, but they do not show the changes made since 1929, and the hard-ships under which the Board had to work.

For illustration on Jan. 1, 1929, we only had cash on hand of $9,213.55. We owed the bank $191,500; the large funds totalled to $453,610.55, of which $185,458.16 had been spent in operation of the Board.

We now owe no money to banks, and these large funds which include Andhra Christian College, Trust Funds and Annuities, have increased to $591,163.68. So in addition to balancing our budget we have had to take care of these increases in permanent funds. These figures show that while these funds increased approximately $132,000, that the Board has taken care of the increase and at the same time lowered the indebtedness to these funds from $185,458.16 to $107,637.75.

The Board is indeed thankful to the Church for its loyal support, and thankful to present this financial statement to the Convention; but do not infer from this that the problem of the Board of Foreign Missions is solved. We still have the indebtedness of $107,637.75 and the work budgets to the fields are only one-half of what they were six years ago. Opportunities present themselves regularly, but due to shortage of funds, we must pass by. New Missionaries, church buildings, schools, native workers, new stations are appealed for regularly, but the Board must say no.

A solution to this problem would be increase in payments on apportionment. When the Board made the decreases in work budgets, it was only due to one reason, a decrease in receipts. Apportionment dropped from 66% for year ending June 1930, to 46% June 30, 1936. This 20% may look small, but in dollars and cents it represents a drop from $432,000 to $276,500, or $155,500.00. Inasmuch as apportionment represents almost 75% of our general fund receipts, any drop in it seriously hampers the work of this Board, and any increase improves working conditions. For that reason an urgent request is made to the Church to increase apportionment payments.

FOREIGN FIELDS
INDIA
MISSIONARIES

Name	Residence	Arrival
Rev. L. L. Uhl, D.D.	Emeritus	1873
Miss Agnes I. Schade	Emeritus	1890
Miss Katherine Fahs	Emeritus	1894
Miss Mary Baer, M.D.	Emeritus	1895
Miss Annie E. Sanford	Tenali	1895
Rev. Dr. S. C. Burger	Dowlaishwaram	1898
Rev. Dr. and Mrs. Victor McCauley	Repalle	1898
Rev. Dr. and Mrs. E. Neudoerffer	Luthergiri	1900
Miss Emilie L. Weiskotten	Rajahmundry	1900
Rev. Dr. and Mrs. Isaac Cannaday	Furlough	1902
Rev. Dr. and Mrs. J. Roy Strock	Guntur	1908
Miss Jessie S. Thomas	Furlough	1908
Miss Betty A. Nilsson, M.D.	Bhimawaram	1908
Rev. Dr. and Mrs. R. M. Dunkelberger	Tenali	1909
Rev. Dr. and Mrs. J. C. Finefrock	Tarlupad	1911
Rev. and Mrs. A. F. A. Neudoerffer	Furlough	1912
Miss Florence M. Welty	Furlough	1912
Rev. Dr. and Mrs. H. H. Sipes	Furlough	1913
Miss Louise A. Miller	Samulkot	1913
Rev. Dr. and Mrs. Fred L. Coleman	Luthergiri	1914
Rev. Dr. and Mrs. J. E. Graefe	Theol. Sem., Guntur	1915
Miss Charlotte B. Hollerbach	Furlough	1915
Miss Hilma Levine	Furlough	1915
Miss Agnes C. Christenson	Bhimawaram	1915
Miss Emma K. Baer	Rentichintala	1919
Rev. and Mrs. J. R. Fink	Rentichintala	1921
Rev. and Mrs. H. H. Moyer	Bhimawaram	1921
Rev. and Mrs. A. F. Schmitthenner	Peddapur	1921
Rev. and Mrs. L. A. Gotwald	Chirala	1921
Rev. and Mrs. M. L. Dolbeer	Narasaravupet	1921
Miss Lilith Schwab	Repalle	1921

Name	Residence	Arrival
Miss Alice J. Nickel	Narasaravupet	1921
Miss Mette K. Blair	Rajahmundry	1921
Miss Maida S. Meissner	Guntur	1921
Miss Edna Engle	Guntur	1921
Rev. and Mrs. Clarence H. Swavely	Guntur	1922
Rev. and Mrs. Leon L. Irschick	Tanuku	1922
Miss Clara Leaman	Furlough	1923
Miss Verna Lofgren	Furlough	1923
Miss Lottie Martin	Rentichintala	1923
Miss Edith Eykamp	Guntur	1924
Miss Emma Johnson	Chirala	1925
Rev. and Mrs. L. W. Slifer	Guntur	1925
Miss Arline Beal, M.D.	Guntur	1925
Miss Frances M. Segner	Rajahmundry	1927
Dr. and Mrs. Virgil E. Zigler	Furlough	1928
Miss Grace L. Moyer, M.D.	Rajahmundry	1928
Miss Mabel H. Meyer	Chirala	1928
Miss Hilda M. Kaercher	Rajahmundry	1928
Rev. and Mrs. E. G. Wood	Furlough	1929
Miss Christie Zimmerman	Furlough	1930
Miss Jessie Mae Cronk	Furlough	1930
Rev. and Mrs. J. C. Peery, Jr.	Sattenapalle	1931
Miss Barbara DeRemer, M.D.	Chirala	1932
Miss Amelia L. Brosius	Rajahmundry	1932
Miss Nanna Lindahl, R.N.	Guntur	1934
Miss Susan Glatz	Guntur (1929)	1935
Miss Gladys Morgan, M.D.	Guntur	1935
Rev. and Mrs. Ray L. Cunningham	Guntur (1925)	1936
Miss Theodora K. Neudoerffer, R.N.	Rajahmundry	1936
Rev. and Mrs. Robert S. Oberly	Guntur	1936
Rev. Dr. and Mrs. George K. Gesler	Guntur	1936
Miss Myrtle Onsrud, R. N.	Guntur (under appt.)	1936
Miss Mary S. Borthwick	Rajahmundry (1912)	1936

Missionaries in active service in India and on furlough number 21
ordained men, one unordained male physician, 21 wives of missionaries,
33 single women missionaries; a total of 76. There are also two retired
ordained men and three retired single women. During the biennium Rev.
G. R. Haaf severed his relation with the Board and Miss Ada Kron resigned to be married. Rev. and Mrs. Ray L. Cunningham served one
term in India from 1925 to 1932. Mr. Cunningham worked first as an
educational and then as an industrial missionary. He returns to India as
an ordained missionary and as a representative of the Augustana Synod.
Rev. and Mrs. Oberly and Rev. Dr. and Mrs. Gesler were transferred
from Liberia, Africa, to India. Miss Mary S. Borthwick who served in
India from 1912 to 1932, returns after a period of four years spent in
taking care of her parents. No death occurred during the past biennium.

A Great Mission

It is not an exaggeration to say that our India mission is one of the
most successful Christian missions in the non-Christian world. The

Church which it has organized and which is functioning with increasing efficiency, called the Andhra Evangelical Lutheran Church in India, now has over 171,000 baptized members, actively served by the missionaries, ordained Indian pastors in charge of congregations and parishes, and the other national workers in over 2,000 towns and villages in which there are Christians and inquirers. The annual net increase in baptized membership for years has been from four to six thousand men, women and children. In addition to the depressed outcasts who hitherto have been added to the Church in such large numbers, there is now a surprising and challenging mass-movement of middle class people, called Sudras, evident most conspicuously, in our own Telugu mission field along the Kistna and Godavery Rivers, as well as in the neighboring fields of the Church of England, Baptist and Methodist missions. The report of the Guntur part of the field for the year 1935 concerning the Sudra movement is as follows: Total number of baptized Sudra Christians up to December, 1934, 6,507; baptized in 1935, 821; inquirers in 1935, 1,770; confirmed in 1935, 791. The real significance of the movement lies in the large number of inquirers, who are seeking Christian baptism, which is increased to 2,471 by adding those in the Rajahmundry part of the field, where the movement as yet is less pronounced.

Confronted with the opportunities of such remarkable success our missionaries are crying out to us, their partners in the Home Church, in repeated and compelling appeals: "Our nets are breaking! Our money and our force of missionaries are utterly inadequate. Can you not see how much we need your help? Come quickly and help us!"

Andhra Evangelical Lutheran Church

The officers of the Andhra Evangelical Lutheran Church are: President, Rev. Dr. Ernst Neudoerffer; Secretary, Mr. T. S. Paul. The Joint Treasurer is Rev. C. H. Swavely. The President of the mission Council is Rev. Dr. Fred L. Coleman, the Recording Secretary is Miss Alice J. Nickel, the Corresponding Secretary is Rev. Dr. R. M. Dunkelberger. The Andhra Evangelical Lutheran Church in India is represented at this convention by two delegates with voice but no vote.

For more efficient administration the Andhra Evangelical Lutheran Church in India will be divided into five synods, three on the Guntur and two on the Rajahmundry side, which will function very much in the same manner as our synods in America, while the general convention of the Church will correspond to that of the United Lutheran Church in America as a representative body of elected synodical delegates.

The time has come for us to consider the best method of gradually transferring mission property to the Church. The Board believes that first consideration should be given self-supporting congregations which can at once assume all the obligations of upkeep and repair of the transferred property; and the property of the institutions, hospitals, high schools and college should be the last to be considered.

In The Field of Education

The outstanding developments in the field of education relate to Andhra Christian College, which is now permanently located as a first grade Lutheran College in Guntur with a full course in science as well as in arts, leading to the Bachelor of Science and Bachelor of Arts degrees. The Mission, the Board and the Executive Board of the United Lutheran Church have adopted a four point plan of co-operation for neighboring missions and Churches and their home boards, to serve as a basis for further negotiations and participation in capital expenditure, maintenance and administration.

The opening of a theological department at Andhra Christian College with nine students for the education of college graduates, is a temporary arrangement awaiting the settlement of the location and character of a joint theological seminary for all Lutherans in India by the Federation of Lutheran Missions and Churches.

Most of our Indian pastors of high school and normal school grade are still being prepared for their work in the Biblical Seminary and Training Institute at Luthergiri, Rajahmundry, where 103 men and 64 wives are under instruction. Training schools for Bible women are being continued at the Mangalamandiram, Guntur, and the Charlotte Swensson Memorial Bible Training School, Rajahmundry, attended respectively by 49 and 44 women.

In the Field of Medical Work

In the field of hospital and medical work important changes are taking place. The hospitals for women and children are beginning to receive men and boys as patients and to employ Indian male physicians and surgeons. This means that they are becoming general hospitals and that more adequate equipment for their enlarged scope soon will be needed.

The new hospital and medical work begun at Bhimawaram in one of the most densely populated parts of our field, is indebted to the Women's Missionary Society of the Augustana Synod for its fine new buildings and equipment. This hospital also is to be a general hospital for men as well as for women.

Statistics

The statistics for the year 1935 contain an interesting summary of mission finances, expressed in terms of Rupees, which shows the proportion of receipts from America and in the field. The total American subsidy was Rs. 618,786, of which Rs. 283,235 were for the support of general work, Rs. 146,891 for the women's work department, Rs. 82,346 for the salaries of men missionaries, Rs. 46,331 for the salaries of women missionaries, Rs. 30,734 for buildings and Rs. 28,249 for other purposes. Funds raised in India for general work amounted to Rs. 422,176, for women's work Rs. 104,489, for benevolence Rs. 64,206. Funds raised in India include government grants and fees from students in school and patients in the hospitals. The proportion of the funds raised in India to the funds received from America was as four to six, or forty per cent in India and sixty per cent from America. The effort at Indian self-support is about holding its own.

India Mission Statistical Summary

1. Baptized Membership Total	171,812
Increase over Previous Year	3,799
2. Communicant Membership Total	80,482
Increase over Previous Year	2,306
3. Baptisms From Christian Families	4,543
From Non-Christian Families	3,501
Total	8,044
4. Villages in which there are Christians or Inquirers	2,082
5. Congregations	1,826
6. Schools	1,044
7. Pupils, Boys and Girls	
Christians	21,687
Non-Christians	21,583
Total	43,270
8. Support of Work in Rupees	
Benevolence	68,433
Other Cash Receipts	429,820
Kind	22,591
Total	520,844
9. American Support of General Work	283,235
Women's Work	146,891
Salaries: men	82,346
women	47,331
Travel in India: men	1,384
women	5,646
Buildings	30,734
Other Purposes	21,219
Total	618,786
10. National Workers:	
Pastors	90
Other Evangelistic Workers	554
School Supervisors	1
School Teachers	1,810
Other Workers	393
Total	2,848

Centenary in 1942

In 1942 the India mission will celebrate its one hundredth anniversary. Preparations are under way in India for a worthy and wide-spread celebration. This anniversary should be observed in all the congregations, schools and societies of our United Lutheran Church in America for its manifest inspirational value and for a church-wide reconsecration to the task of world-wide Christian missionary effort with special reference to our fields abroad which God in Christ has made our Church's specific missionary obligation.

JAPAN

MISSIONARIES

Name	Residence	Arrival
Rev. and Mrs. J. M. T. Winther	Furlough	1898
Rev. Dr. and Mrs. C. K. Lippard	Moji	1900
Rev. Dr. and Mrs. A. J. Stirewalt	Furlough	1905
Rev. Dr. and Mrs. L. S. G. Miller	Kyushu Gakuin, Kumamoto	1907
Rev. Dr. and Mrs. Edward T. Horn	Furlough	1912
Rev. Dr. and Mrs. Charles W. Hepner	Furlough	1912
Miss Martha B. Akard	Kumamoto	1913
Rev. and Mrs. John K. Linn	Theological Sem., Tokyo	1915
Rev. and Mrs. S. O. Thorlaksson	Kobe	1916
Rev. and Mrs. D. G. M. Bach	Kumamoto	1916
Miss Maude O. Powlas	Furlough	1918
Miss Annie P. Powlas	Furlough	1919
Rev. Dr. and Mrs. George N. Schillinger	Furlough	1920
Miss Marion E. Potts	Furlough	1921
Miss Helen Shirk	Fukuoka	1922
Miss Faith Lippard	Tokyo	1925
Miss Mary E. Heltibridle	Ji Ai En, Kumamoto	1927
Miss Maya Winther	Ogi	1927
Miss Helene Harder	Hakata	1927

The missionaries in active service number 11 ordained men, 11 wives of missionaries, 9 single women, a total of 31. During the biennium Dr. L. S. G. Miller married one of the single women missionaries, Miss Martha B. Harder. Two single women, Miss Virginia D. Aderholdt and Miss Selma Ruth Bergner are under appointment. Rev. Arthur J. Linn, invalided home November 1933, resigned on April 12, 1935.

Difficulties of Relationships

Our second daughter church in foreign fields is the Evangelical Lutheran Church in Japan. It is passing through its initial formative period in the face of difficulties which may be summarized as difficulties of relationships between foreign missionaries and Japanese pastors, difficulties of the revival of the indigenous religions of Buddhism and Shintoism, difficulties arising from the ambitious nationalism of the Japanese nation and difficulties of economic and industrial changes.

The Lutheran Church in Japan now has thirty ordained Japanese pastors serving thirty-nine congregations, seven of which are self-supporting. In addition there are forty other workers, evangelists, teachers and Bible women. The increase in baptized membership continues to be comparatively slow, because in Japan there are no mass movements. Converts are made one by one as a result of personal work, and members of congregations frequently move to other places where it is difficult to cultivate their personal interest and co-operation. The establishment of new congregations and the vigorous development of rural evangelism are hindered by lack of money and missionaries.

Transfer of Property to the Church

In Japan also the question of the transfer of mission-owned property to the organized Church and its congregations is receiving careful consideration. It is understood, of course, that the Board of Foreign Missions through its Japan mission holds title to property in trust for the indigenous church and is willing to make the transfer as soon as conditions warrant. It believes that in Japan as in India this transfer of property should begin with congregations which are financially able to take care of the property transferred.

Developments

Two developments of major significance are the better equipment of the Theological Seminary at Tokyo by the erection of the main building and attached chapel, for which the Luther League of America contributed $15,000, and the expansion of the social service or inner mission activities at Tokyo and at Kumamoto. Government grants are being received in increasing amounts for the Kumamoto Colony of Mercy and the Bethany Home for widows and their children in Tokyo. Permission has been given to erect a new building on another site for the Old People's Home with the understanding that no expense is involved either for the Board or the mission. Inasmuch as no medical and hospital work is done or needed in Japan, such social service institutions and activities become the chief avenues of the demonstration of serving Christian love.

Officers of the Mission and Church

The Mission at its last annual convention elected Dr. L. S. G. Miller, President; Rev. J. K. Linn, Secretary; and Rev. S. O. Thorlaksson, Treasurer. The officers of the Church are Rev. I. Miura, President; Rev. K. Hirai, Secretary; and Rev. S. O. Thorlaksson, Treasurer. The mission functions ad interim through an elected Executive Committee and the Church through an elected Executive Board whose membership is composed of an equal number of missionaries and Japanese pastors and laymen. The former President of the mission, Rev. Charles W. Hepner, D.D., and the former Secretary, Rev. A. J. Stirewalt, D.D., are now on furlough in America. The Evangelical Lutheran Church as well as the Andhra Evangelical Lutheran Church in India is listed as a co-operating synod of the U. L. C. A., entitled to one delegate with voice but no vote.

Statistics

The following is a summary of the statistics of our Japan mission: Missionaries 31, national workers 70, congregations 39, baptized members 4,458, accessions 233, pupils in school 1,528, field contributions $7,052.

CHINA

MISSIONARIES

Name	Residence	Arrival
Rev. and Mrs. J. C. Voskamp	Retired	1884
Rev. and Mrs. Theodore Scholz	Tsingtao	1904
Miss Kathe Voget	Retired	1906
Miss Freda Strecker	Kiaochow	1908
Mrs. W. Matzat	Tsingtao	1922
Rev. and Mrs. P. P. Anspach	Tsingtao	1925
Miss Erva Moody	Tsingtao	1925
Miss Elvira Strunk	Tsimo	1925
Miss Lydia Reich, R.N.	Tsingtao	1927
Rev. L. Grady Cooper, Ph.D.	Tsimo	1928
Rev. and Mrs. C. H. Reinbrecht	Furlough	1928
Miss M. Clara Sullivan	Furlough	1929
Rev. and Mrs. R. W. Sell	Tsimo	1931
Miss Mae L. Rohlfs, R.N.	Tsingtao	1932

The missionaries in active service number five ordained men, four wives and seven unmarried women. During the year there were no deaths and God has enabled the force to carry on with little sickness. This has been a great blessing as the missionaries are few in number and the needs of the field are great.

Evangelism

If any one work can characterize the work in China it is evangelism. In proportion to their numbers no mission has gained more people for Christ and the church than the China Mission. Street preaching and tent services have been particularly fruitful. They also come to church. The Chinese hear and read carefully. It is said that they read more than the people of most of the fields. Our missionaries know this and make the most of their opportunities along these lines. The Mission Book Shop is unusual and is doing fine work. Nine thousand Bibles were sold last year.

Education

While we have no great schools, yet the Middle School at Tsimo for boys and girls is a model institution of its kind, and is a great feeder for the leaders in the Lutheran Church of China.

The Women's Bible Institute has been accepted by the Lutheran Church of China as the Women's School for all of the Lutheran Missions of that part of China. It is a fine institution and furnishes a great opportunity for the young women in advanced Christian education.

Lutheran Hospital, Tsingtao

In 1930 the large mission building, which was the central building of the work was turned into a hospital. The number of beds has grown until there are 35 beds. It has never had an American doctor, even though it is a general hospital. It has had some wonderful Chinese, German and Japanese doctors and has filled an important place in the mission's activities. The hospital is in charge of Miss Lydia Reich, R.N. and Miss Mae Rohlfs, R.N. China is eagerly looking forward to the coming of additional evangelical missionaries and an American doctor.

Tai Tung Chen

The mission is taking forward steps, some a bit in advance of what the Board can spend, inasmuch as it has just completed paying the Berlin Society for the mission—$185,000 gold. However, that is now paid, the Women's Board sharing in the purchase. Some of the advance steps must wait a bit. However, the mission is carrying forward with $10,000 gold given by the Luther League of America as its project for this biennium, what is known as the Tai Tung Chen Project. This will consist of a chapel seating 1,000, a dispensary, and a school and social center. It will mean great things for our China Mission.

Statistics

The following is a summary of the statistics of the Mission: Missionaries on the field 11, missionaries on furlough 5, national workers 122, congregations and preaching halls 82, baptized members 3,239, communicants 1,520, accessions 1935—553, Inquirers 479, primary schools 27, high schools 1, pupils 1,144, field contributions $3,960, Number of pupils—Women's Bible Institute 16, Hospital in-patients 287, Hospital out-patients 3,209.

LIBERIA, AFRICA
MISSIONARIES

Name	Residence	Arrival
Mrs. J. D. Curran	Furlough	1912
Miss Laura E. Gilliland, R. N.	Main Station	1915
Mrs. C. E. Buschman	Zorzor	1915
Miss Bertha Koenig	Zorzor	1916
Miss Mabel A. Dysinger	E. V. Day Girls' School	1917
Rev. and Mrs. H. J. Currens	Furlough	1927
Rev. and Mrs. Harry Heilman	Main Station	1927
Jacob R. Jensen, M.D.	Zorzor	1927
Miss K. Marie Jensen	Sanoyea	1928
Miss Irene B. Bloch	E. V. Day Girls' School	1928
George K. Gulck, M.D.	Furlough	1929
Rev. and Mrs. J. K. Donat	Sanoyea	1935

Planting the Church in the Hinterland

At the turn of the century the question of continuing work in Liberia was freely discussed on the floor of the General Church Convention. It was then resolved that the hope of our efforts in Liberia depended upon our missionaries moving into the interior and establishing the Church among the primitive people of the hinterland. At first, as was to be expected, the progress was slow and discouraging. With the passing years our missionaries have heroically pressed on with the result that today there is a very encouraging work both in the Sanoyea and Zorzor districts. It is a new note to have missionaries in Liberia write of inquirers' classes and frequent baptisms. One of the outstanding factors that has made possible this advance in the hinterland is the native trained boys and girls, trained at our Main Station, who have returned to minister to their own tribal people. For years the mission has maintained primary schools in the interior and upon graduation transferred the pupils to the Main Station, near the Coast, to complete their education. Now these young people are returning to their native tribes with both Bible and secular training. These are the evangelists who are making the contacts, inspiring confidence and influencing many to a higher and better life. In other words, the time has come, in the providence of God, when real indigenous churches are being established. In practically every letter that the missionaries write, reference is made to the progress of the work. They state that the District Commissioners and Paramount Chiefs are giving their co-operation; that not only children but older people as well who were formerly leaders in the native societies are receiving baptism; that in some instances entire families have been baptized at the same time; that regular communion services are held throughout the two districts.

Medical Work in Interior

In January 1923 the mission conference voted to open work at Zorzor, a station ten days journey from the Coast. A medical missionary joined the staff in 1925. Since that time this department of serving love has gone steadily forward, ministering to bodily ills, breaking down prejudice, and building up confidence in the white man's mission. Today after ten years of effort the results are amazing. The mission reports that one hundred patients are coming each dispensary day (three times a week) and operations are being performed every other day with a waiting list all the time. Some of the operative cases have come from distances that have required a month of travel from French country. Each patient pays something in money or produce and for operations pays in advance. The results achieved are all the more wonderful considering the poor housing conditions and equipment. The mission is preparing plans and estimates for permanent buildings for approval by the Board. It is the hope that when these plans arrive money will be available to erect these needy buildings.

Work at the Main Station

As the work in the interior develops there is no thought on the part of the Mission Board of abandoning that at the Main Station. In fact it is primarily due to the activities conducted through the years at the latter place that made the advance in the hinterland possible. Here a boys' school on one side of the river and a girls' school on the other side have flourished. Through their portals have not only passed many who are today faithfully serving their Master in communities in the interior and near the coast but also boys and girls who are active in the political and economic life of Liberia.

By the side of these two institutions of learning stand the Reed and Day Memorial Churches giving strength and grace to teachers, students and many in the communities. The Board records with sadness the death of Mr. James W. Miller, the designer and builder of the Day Memorial Church. If he had done nothing else to show his ability as a builder this Church would suffice. For he put his heart as well as his time and strength into this work, as he did in all his tasks. It is said by many that this is the finest Church building in all Liberia.

At this same station is located the Bible School which prepares young men to handle the Word of God and teaches them how to live it. The Bible School is fully justifying its worthiness in more ways than one. Several young men, graduates of this institution, are now being considered for licensure and later for ordination.

Another institution which has left an indelible impression upon the minds and hearts of many in Liberia and given to them a better conception of the constraining love of Christ is the Phebe Hospital. Here missionary doctors and nurses, national assistants and national nurses have tenderly cared for bruised and worn bodies seeking by their skill and training to restore them to health and strength. The place which this institution holds in the esteem of the officials of the Liberian government is indicated in a communication addressed to the Mission when it was proposed to transfer one of the doctors to work in the interior. They referred to the crying need of Phebe Hospital in Liberia. It is encouraging to learn that the work that our Church is doing along this line is appreciated.

Looking Forward

In view of the encouraging outlook for the Mission we regret to report a reduced missionary personnel and inadequate financial assistance. This is most unfortunate because many opportunities are being lost and responsibility for conducting the work falls upon the shoulders of so few. At the same time these few are faced with many financial worries. As we close this report Rev. and Mrs. Gordon Parker, he is a son of a former missionary of our Church in Liberia, are sailing for the field. It is our earnest hope and prayer that financial conditions will shortly permit the sending of at least two more ordained missionaries and their families. God is moving upon the hearts of the people of the hinterland. May we as a Church prepare to reap the harvest of souls.

Our loss in personnel during the biennium is due to the fact that Rev. Arnold Kaitschuk was compelled to resign due to ill health; Norman R. Sloan, M.D., resigned and accepted employment under the American Government; Rev. and Mrs. R. S. Oberly and Rev. Dr. and Mrs. G. K. Gesler, were transferred from service in Liberia to India; Mr. James W. Miller died en route to America, August 14, 1935.

Statistics

The following is a summary of the statistics of the Africa Mission on January 1, 1936: missionaries in active service, 15; national workers, 61; baptized members, 1,055; baptisms, 79; inquirers, 480; congregations, 32; pupils in schools, 425; hospitals and dispensaries, 6; patients, 1,367; field contributions, $2,227.00.

SOUTH AMERICA
ARGENTINA
MISSIONARIES

Name	Residence	Arrival
Rev. Dr. and Mrs. Paul O. Machetzki	Eldorado	1922
Rev. and Mrs. John M. Armbruster	Buenos Aires	1924
Miss Myrtle Wilke	Buenos Aires	1927

Buenos Aires and Environs

Our Argentina mission is fortunate in having four ordained Argentinian pastors in charge of the Spanish-speaking congregations in and near Buenos Aires, one of whom, Rev. Jonas Villaverde, received his theological education at Hamma Divinity School, Wittenberg College, Springfield, Ohio. Earnest efforts are being made by the congregations at Caseros and Villa Progreso to acquire their own church property and building. The Board is financially assisting them to do this, and is also making a monthly grant for the purchase of the Lohrfeldt property back of the church of the Redeemer, Villa del Parque, which is being used as a girls' dormitory and dwelling for the woman missionary, Miss Myrtle Wilke. Her return to the field in 1935, assures the development of the woman's work connected with the congregations and the middle school, called Colegio Nacional. This splendid educational institution under the direction of Mr. Piedro Viera has attained practical self-support, and is without doubt the best North American school of its kind in Argentina.

El Dorado, Misiones

In the El Dorado section of Misiones territory the work is making satisfactory progress. The congregations are expected to build their own churches. The church building at Emmaus was finished and consecrated in November, 1935. St. John's, which had a ground-breaking ceremony for their new chapel when Dr. Koller visited the field in 1934, expects to erect its edifice this year.

We regret the resignation of Rev. Dr. P. O. Machetzki who with his wife resided at El Dorado and who was assisted in the congregational and educational work by Rev. Wm. Holtz and Rev. Raquena. Another ordained man is to be secured in the person of Mr. M. E. Priebe, who has served as an evangelist and lay reader for a number of years among German and Polish people in Misiones. The schools are self-supporting and practically nothing is spent for the Misiones work by the Mission in addition to the salaries of the missionaries and pastors.

Statistics

The following is a summary of the statistics of our Argentina field: Missionaries in active service 5, national workers 27, congregations 11, baptized members 1,702, communicants 1,078, accessions 17, mission schools 6, pupils 739, field contributions $4,196.

SOUTH AMERICA

BRITISH GUIANA

MISSIONARIES

Name	Residence	Arrival
Rev. and Mrs. W. Theodore Benze	New Amsterdam	1935

This is the smallest of our foreign-mission fields. With very few exceptions it has never had more than one missionary at one time to superintend the work. During the biennium there were two missionaries on the field for a space of less than two months. The Rev. Robert H. Daube returned to the United States on furlough in August 1935 and since that time has resigned to take up pastoral work in the homeland. The Board was fortunate in securing the services of Rev. and Mrs. W. Theodore Benze to succeed Rev. Daube. He completed a term of service of seven years in our India mission field and so is well fitted by experience to direct the activities of this one-man mission.

General Situation

The condition of the work at the Main Station, New Amsterdam; among the East Indians; and at the lower and upper river stations continues much as usual. There seems to be an increase in interest particularly at the upper river stations. The congregations and schools there are in a good healthy condition. The missionary has visited all the stations regularly and held conferences frequently with evangelists and school teachers. At these conferences many practical matters have been discussed. The coming together of these national leaders assists greatly in unifying the work of the mission. The economic crisis throughout the world has made itself felt by decreased giving. With an extremely limited budget from America it has been found impossible to advance the work as one would hope. In co-operation with the Educational Department of the British Guiana Government the mission teaches special courses in aboriginal arts and crafts at two of the upper river stations. These are very helpful as many of the "red" Indian people are rapidly losing knowledge of their valuable traditions. Work at the two lower river stations, Fern and Germania is not flourishing. The latter congregation due to efforts on the part of the missionary to correct irregularities is contemplating withdrawal from the mission. It had been an independent congregation for years, formerly, and has never conformed to Lutheran ideals and practices. The missionary reports that it is a very difficult matter to correct such tendencies with the very limited supervision which he can give.

New Recruits

Seven years ago one of the outstanding young men of the mission came to the United States to study. He entered Wittenberg College. With aid from the Synod of Ohio and what support he could get from speaking engagements he worked his way through College and Seminary, and was graduated in May from Hamma Divinity School. He has been called by the mission and accepted service there with a view to being ordained after arrival on the field by the missionary, on authorization of his home Synod. Another fine young man from the same field has been studying for the last two years at the Gettysburg Seminary. He probably will remain in the United States for another year with a view to completing his college education and securing a degree. With the return of one or both of these well-equipped, young leaders the mission personnel will be greatly strengthened. There is much work for them to do.

Statistics

The following is a summary of the statistics of the British Guiana Mission on January 1, 1936. Missionaries in active service 2; national workers 12, baptized members 661, communicants 388, inquirers 21, congregations 8, pupils in school 107, field contributions $1,723.

BOARD MEETINGS, OFFICERS AND MEMBERS

During the past two years the Board of Foreign Missions has met regularly every three months, and the Executive Committee has met for ad interim business four times each year.

The list of Board officers, secretaries and members during the past biennium is as follows:

Officers

President: Rev. Stewart W. Herman, D.D., 121 State St., Harrisburg, Pa.
Vice-President: Rev. George A. Greiss, D.D., 38 S. 8th St., Allentown, Pa.
Recording Secretary: Rev. George Drach, D.D., 18 E. Mt. Vernon Place, Baltimore, Md.
Treasurer: Mr. George R. Weitzel, 18 E. Mt. Vernon Place, Balto., Md.

Secretaries

Rev. Paul W. Koller, D.D., Executive Secretary.
Rev. George Drach, D.D., Literature Secretary, Corresponding Secretary for India, Japan, Argentina.
Rev. M. Edwin Thomas, D.D., Special Gifts Secretary, Corresponding Secretary for Africa and British Guiana.

Members of the Board
Terms Expire in 1936

Rev. H. W. Snyder, D.D., 5124 Chevy Chase Pkwy., Washington, D.C.
Rev. P. E. Monroe, D.D., Lenoir Rhyne College, Hickory, N. C.
Rev. Prof. E. E. Fischer, D.D., 7300 Boyer St., Mt. Airy, Phila., Pa.
Rev. C. M. Snyder, 504 Haws Ave., Norristown, Penna.
Rev. P. O. Bersell, D.D., 415 Howard St., S. S., Minneapolis, Minn.
Mr. Frank Howard, 416 Somerset St., Johnstown, Penna.
Ralph H. Schatz, Esq., 416 Commonwealth Bldg., Allentown, Penna.

Terms Expire in 1938

Rev. S. W. Herman, D.D., 121 State St., Harrisburg, Pa.
Rev. S. T. Nicholas, D.D., 907 Maryland Ave., N. E., Washington, D. C.
Rev. C. E. Reinartz, 216 Jackson St., E. Liverpool, Ohio.
Rev. Robert D. Clare, D.D., 1900 St. Paul St., Baltimore, Md.
Mr. Charles H. Dahmer, 530 Fifth Ave., New York City, N. Y.
Mr. C. L. Peterman, 253 Springettsbury Ave., York, Pa.
George S. Yost, Esq., 1101 Longwood St., Baltimore, Md.

Terms Expire in 1940

Rev. L. C. Manges, D.D., 1431 Walnut St., Harrisburg, Pa.
Rev. George A. Greiss, D.D., 38 S. 8th St., Allentown, Pa.
Rev. H. C. Brillhart, D.D., 19 Spruce St., Leetonia, Ohio.
Rev. S. G. Trexler, D.D., 1170 Fifth Ave., New York, N. Y.
Mr. M. P. Moller, Jr., Hagerstown, Md.
Mr. W. A. Rast, Cameron, S. C.

Co-operating Members
Representing the Augustana Synod

In addition to Dr. P. O. Bersell, who is a regular voting member of the Board, Rev. R. F. Thelander, 24 Cole Ave., Jamestown, N. Y.

Representing the United Danish Church

Rev. J. P. Nielsen, D.D., Trinity Theological Seminary, Blair, Nebr.
Mr. Carl Brunn, 5019 20th St., Brooklyn, N. Y.

Representing the Icelandic Synod
Rev. N. S. Thorlaksson, Canton, South Dakota.

ADVISORY MEMBERS
Representing the Women's Missionary Society
Mrs. C. E. Gardner, 227 E. Fall Creek Parkway, Indianapolis, Ind.
Miss A. Barbara Wiegand, 465 Maryland Ave., S. W., Washington, D. C.

NOMINATIONS FOR BOARD MEMBERSHIP
The Board of Foreign Missions, at its meeting on July 23, 1936, nominated the following for election at this convention of the United Lutheran Church:

Rev. Prof. E. E. Fischer, D.D., (Eligible for re-election) 7300 Boyer Street, Mt. Airy, Philadelphia, Pa.

Rev. P. E. Monroe, D.D., (Eligible for re-election) Lenoir Rhyne College, Hickory, N. C.

Rev. C. M. Snyder (Eligible for re-election) 504 Haws Ave., Norristown, Pa.

Rev. President P. O. Bersell, D.D., (representing Augustana Synod) 415 Howard St., S. S., Minneapolis, Minn.

Rev. H. H. Beidleman, D.D., 55 Frederick St., Hanover, Penna.

Mr. Frank Howard (Eligible for re-election) 416 Somerset St., Johnstown, Pa.

Mr. Ralph H. Schatz, (Eligible for re-election) 416 Commonwealth Bldg., Allentown, Pa.

Rev. Henry W. Snyder, D.D., of Washington, D. C., who is not eligible for re-election has served faithfully as a member of the Board since July, 1926, when he was elected to fill the unexpired term of the late Rev. Prof. Dr. J. A. Singmaster.

Rev. Dr. P. O. Bersell is President of the Augustana Synod, and is nominated to succeed the late President Dr. G. A. Brandelle.

RECOMMENDATIONS
(For action, see p. 142)

1. That the Church here in convention, with the Board of Foreign Missions, devotedly gives thanks to God for His guidance and blessing in the Foreign Mission activities of our Church during this biennium.

2. That inasmuch as no Board has asked permission to make a special appeal during 1936-37, permission be given to the Board of Foreign Missions to use this period to clear the debt of the Board, appealing to congregations, individuals and Sunday schools. (Permission not granted, see p. 142.)

3. That we express to the Women's Missionary Society our appreciation of their contributions and co-operation in the work in the field which augments the regular work, and also our appreciation to the Luther League of America for its present project in Tai Tung Chen, China, and which is carried on under the direction of the Board of Foreign Missions, and also the new Seminary Building, Tokyo, Japan, which was completed last year.

4. That the magazines of the Board—The Foreign Missionary and Der Missionsbote and the other literature of the Board be commended to the churches as sources of Foreign Mission information and inspiration.

S. W. HERMAN, *President,*
GEORGE DRACH, *Recording Secretary,*
PAUL W. KOLLER, *Executive Secretary.*

REPORT OF THE TREASURER OF THE BOARD OF FOREIGN MISSIONS

BALANCE SHEET
June 30, 1935

ASSETS

Cash in Banks:

General Fund		$ 71,739.26	
Investment Fund		9,583.53	
			$ 81,322.79

Investments at Book Value:

Bonds and Stocks:

Free	$292,707.14		
Pledged as collateral to secure Notes Payable	62,544.33		
		$355,251.47	
Certificates of Participation		819.00	
Total Book Value of Bonds, Stocks, and Certificates of Participation		$356,070.47	
Ground Rents, Mortgages and Notes Receivable		15,503.55	
Real Estate		49,508.94	
			421,082.96

Other Assets:

Accounts Receivable	$ 1,462.10		
Salaries Advanced to Fields, 1934–1935 Budget	1,342.29		
Student Advances (J. R. Williams)	1,618.14		
Women's Missionary Society	1,698.55		
Travel Advances	3,518.14		
		$ 9,639.22	
Prepaid Interest on Bank Loans		96.25	
			9,735.47
Total Assets			$ 512,141.22

LIABILITIES

Notes Payable:

To Equitable Trust Company of Baltimore, secured by bonds aggregating at Book Value—$62,544.33	$ 35,000.00		
Unpaid Drafts—for June 1935	11,867.21		
Accounts Payable	2,311.44		
		$ 49,178.65	

Reserves:

for Exchange Balances—Japan	$ 3,892.35		
for Contingencies	5,000.00		
		8,892.35	
Total Liabilities			58,071.00
Net Assets, June 30, 1935			$ 454,070.22

FUNDS

Trust Funds	$208,181.66	
Annuity Funds	94,450.00	
Andhra Christian College Fund	277,483.25	
Pohlman Fund	1,600.00	
Reformation Diamond Jubilee Advance Fund	17,840.64	
Kobe Equipment Fund	2,953.69	
		$602,509.24

Less Overdraft:

General Fund	$140,423.70	
Women's Missionary Society	4,653.97	
Land and Building Fund	3,361.35	
		148,439.02
Total Funds		$454.070.22

NOTE: This Statement does not include as
Assets, investments in properties in foreign
fields, nor does it include Liabilities incurred
in the purchase of such properties.

BALANCE SHEET

June 30, 1936

ASSETS

Cash in Banks:

General Fund		$70,034.87	
Investment Fund	$ 17,030.96		
Investment Fund Savings Account..	10,066.63		
		27,097.59	
			$97,132.46

Investments at Book Value:

Bonds and Stocks	$350,351.68		
Certificates of Participation	819.00		
Total Book Value of Bonds, Stocks, and Certificates of Participation		$351,170.68*	
Ground Rents, Mortgages and Notes Receivable		13,003.55	
Real Estate		47,508.94	
			411,683.17

NOTE: This Statement does not include as
Assets, investments in properties in foreign
fields, nor does it include liabilities incurred
in the purchase of such properties.
*Market Value of Securities as of June 30, 1936—$319,224.07

Other Assets:

Accounts Receivable	$7,468.58		
Travel Advances	4,006.58		
Women's Missionary Society	10,912.61		
		22,387.77	
Total Assets		$531,203.40	

LIABILITIES

Unpaid Drafts—for June 1936	$ 12,508.57	
Accounts Payable	10,512.15	
	$23,020.72	
Reserve for Contingencies	5,000.00	
Total Liabilities		28,020.72
Net Assets—June 30, 1936		$503,182.68

FUNDS

Trust Funds	$207,430.18	
Annuity Funds	97,950.00	
Andhra Christian College Fund	285,850.13	
Pohlman Fund	1,600.00	
Reformation Diamond Jubilee Advance Fund	17,840.64	
Land and Building Fund	149,48	
		$610,820.43
Less Overdraft:		
General Fund		107,637.75
Total Funds		$503.182.68

GENERAL FUND—INCOME
For the Fiscal Year Ended June 30, 1935

Apportionment—United Lutheran Church		$270,770.00
Parishes Abroad		18,307.15
Missionaries Salaries		31,045.62
Proteges		11,852.83
Interest on Investments:		
Income from Securities, Notes and Mortgages	$7,459.54	
Rents Received on Real Estate (Net)	239.21	
		7,698.75
Co-operating Synod:		
Augustana Synod	$3,943.00	
Danish Synod	3,750.43	
		7,693.43
Contributions		12,176.32
Epiphany Appeal		11,912.83
Slides		93.26
Magazines		2,384.59
Gifts to Fields and Missionaries		1,978.86
Luther League Special for Japan		11,000.00
Profit on Sale of Securities		799.12
Total Income—General Fund		$387,712.76

GENERAL FUND DISBURSEMENTS
For the Fiscal Year Ended June 30, 1935

Fields:		
Budgets Paid to Missions		$175,940.11
Salaries Paid to Missionaries		98,114.97
Traveling Expenses of Missionaries to and from		
fields		13,344.00

Literature Department:

Annual Report	396.32
Occasional Pamphlets	500.00
Magazines and Publicity	3,916.78
Motion Pictures and Stereopticons	464.56

Finance Department:

Auditing		700.00
Interest on Loans		1,977.63
Interest Received on Andhra Christian College Endowment Fund	$2,680.00	
Less: Interest Allowed on Uninvested Funds— Andhra Christian College	2,647.10	
		32.90*
Interest on Annuities		5,968.80

Home Base:

Salaries—Secretaries and Treasurers:

Paul W. Koller, D.D.	$5,100.00	
George Drach, D.D.	3,825.00	
E. R. Thomas, D.D.	3,825.00	
George R. Weitzel	3,825.00	
		16,575.00
Office Salaries		4,878.93

Expenses—Secretaries, Treasurer and Board Members:

Secretaries and Treasurer	$1,248.01	
Board Members	1,667.09	
		2,915.10
Special Allowances and Pensions		5,722.38

Expenses of Maintaining "Baltimore Mission House" and the "Brown House:"

Repairs	460.96	
Janitor	514.80	
Insurance	54.00	
Taxes	12.76	
Interest	60.00	
Coal and Miscellaneous Expenses	326.25	
	$1,428.77	
Less: Contributed by Women's Missionary Society of Maryland Synod	100.00	
		1,328.77
Expenses—Missionaries in preparation and on Furlough		$3,842.06
Foreign Mission Conference		1,000.00

General Expenses:

Telephone and Telegraph and Cables	$ 601.92	
Postage and Express	482.36	
Gas, Electricity and Water	254.40	
Office Supplies and Expenses	1,387.98	
U. S. Government taxes on checks	20.52	
		2,747.18

Specials—General Fund:

Gifts to Fields and Missionaries	1,978.86
Luther League Special to Japan	11,000.00

Visitation to Fields 1,245.80
Contingent Fund 5,000.00
Expenses of Ephiphany Appeal 1,974.00
      Total Disbursements—General Fund $361,498.35
    *Indicates a Receipt

SUMMARY OF INCOME AND DISBURSEMENTS—VARIOUS FUNDS

For the Period from June 30, 1934 to June 30, 1935

General Fund:

Overdraft—June 30,1934	$166,638.11		
Disbursements for year ended June 30, 1935	361,498.35		
		$528,136.46	
Income for year ended June 30, 1935		387,712.76	
Overdraft—June 30, 1935			$140,423.70*

Women's Missionary Society Fund:

Overdraft—June 30, 1934		$ 2,637.26	
Disbursements:			
Budgets Paid to Mission Fields	$ 94,430.70		
Salaries Paid to Mission Fields	48,137.88		
Specials and Gifts Paid to Mission Fields	25,371.55		
Traveling Expenses of Missionaries to and from fields	1,774.18		
Final Payment on Purchase of Shantung Mission	3,500.00		
Outfit allowances for Missionaries	300.00		
Total Disbursements	$173,514.31		
Cash Receipts	171,497.60		
		2,016.71	
Overdraft—June 30,1935			4,653.97*

Trust Funds:

Balance—June 30, 1934		$205,878.09	
Gifts:			
Anna M. Roth Estate	$ 1,000.00		
Sarah J. Curran	1,302.57		
Mrs. Cecilie Cordsen—160 acre farm, Roosevelt, Oklahoma valued by Board at	1.00		
		2,303.57	
Balance—June 30, 1935			208,181.66

Annuity Funds:

Balance—June 30, 1934	$ 92,950.00		
Annuities Sold	2,800.00		
		95,750.00	
Less: Annuities cancelled by death and transferred to General Fund ..		1,300.00	
Balance—June 30, 1935			94,450.00

Andhra Christian College Fund:
Balance—June 30, 1934 .... $269,351.96
Income:
Interest on Investments .... $ 7,499.90
Donations 2,476.40
Interest on Uninvested Funds 2,647.10
Profit on Sale of Securities 357.30
                                              _____
                                              $ 12,980.70
Less: Remittances to
Fields $2,000.00
Commissions and Taxes,
etc. on Purchase and
Sale of Securities 169.41
Endowment Fund 2,680.00
                            _____
                            4,849.41
                                        _____
                                        8,131.29

Balance—June 30, 1935 .... 277,483.25

Pohlman Fund:
Balance—June 30, 1934 .... $ 1,600.00

Balance—June 30, 1935 .... 1,600.00

Reformation Diamond Jubilee:
Advance Fund:
Balance—June 30, 1934 .... $ 17,840.64

Balance—June 30, 1935 .... 17,840.64

Kobe Equipment Fund:
Balance—June 30, 1934 .... $ 7,453.69
Remittance to Japan Field 4,500.00

Balance—June 30, 1935 .... 2,953.69

Land and Building Fund:
Balance—June 30, 1934 .... $ 5,669.40
Donations 3,199.72
                                                                      _____
                                                                      $ 8,869.12
Less: Payments—China Properties:
Shantung Missions .... $ 9,625.00
Other China Property 1,200.00
                                         _____
                                         $ 10,825.00
Elderado Property 1,155.47
Buenos Aires Property 250.00
                                         _____
                                         12,230.47

Overdraft—June 30, 1935 .... 3,361.35*
Total of all Funds $454,070.22

*Overdraft

SUMMARY OF CASH RECEIPTS AND DISBURSEMENTS
For the Period from June 30, 1934 to June 30, 1935

Cash Balance—June 30, 1934		$ 93,419.13

Receipts:

General Fund	$387,712.76
Women's Missionary Society Fund	171,497.60
Trust Funds	2,302.57
Andhra Christian College Fund	17,569.77
Land and Building Fund	4,172.38
Annuity Fund	2,800.00
Sale of Securities	56,305.15
Payments on Mortgages	500.00
Accrued Interest Receivable July 1, 1934................	115.84
Bank Loans	25,000.00
Accounts Receivable	8,147.17
Accounts Payable—June 30, 1935	2,311.44

Total Receipts		678,434.68
		$771,853.81

Disbursements:

General Fund	$361,498.35	
Less: Unpaid drafts for June, 1935 charged in Disbursements but not paid until some time subsequent to June 30, 1935	11,867.21	
	$349,631.14	
Less: Contingent Fund charged as Disbursements for 1935	5,000.00	
Cash Disbursed from General Fund	$344,631.14	
Women's Missionary Society Fund	173,514.31	
Kobe Equipment Fund	4,500.00	
Purchase of Securities	80,650.62	
Andhra Christian College Fund	9,438.48	
Annuity Fund	1,300.00	
Land and Building Fund	13,203.13	
May 1934 drafts paid	25,373.82	
Bank Loans	25,000.00	
Prepaid Interest on Bank Loans	96.25	
Accounts Receivable	7,499.59	
Accounts Payable—June 30,1934	4,026.55	
Funds advanced against Reserve for Exchange Balances	1,297.13	

Total Disbursements		690,531.02
Cash in Banks—June 30, 1935		$ 81,322.79

GENERAL FUND—INCOME
For the Fiscal Year Ended June 30, 1936

Apportionment—United Lutheran Church	$276,500.00
Parishes Abroad	19,308.80

Missionaries Salaries		29,487.39
Proteges		11,540.39
Interest on Investments:		
Income from Securities, Notes and Mortgages	$4,032.92	
Rents Received on Real Estate (Net)	798.14	
		4,831.06
Co-operating Synod:		
Augustana Synod	$3,595.20	
Danish Synod	3,605.19	
Icelandic Synod	800.00	
		8,000.39
Contributions		14,726.52
Epiphany Appeal		8,255.27
Slides		84.34
Magazines		2,273.46
Gifts to Missionaries		1,300.00
Mission Study		68.74
Profit on Sale of Securities		915.63
Total Income—General Fund		$377,291.99

GENERAL FUND—DISBURSEMENTS

For the Fiscal Year Ended June 30, 1936

Fields:		
Budgets Paid to Missions		$170,524.72
Salaries Paid to Missionaries		94,634.65
Traveling Expenses of Missionaries to and from Fields		19,164.70
New Missionaries		1,396.00
Special Conference—Argentine		200.00
Literature Department:		
Annual Report		529.71
Occasional Pamphlets		445.56
Magazines and Publicity		3,715.16
Motion Pictures and Stereopticons		156.86
Finance Department:		
Auditing		700.00
Interest on Loans		214.03
Interest Received on Andhra Christian College Fund	$2,680.00	
Less: Interest Allowed on Uninvested Funds— Andhra Christian College	1,556.87	1,123.13*
Interest on Annuities		5,980.31
Home Base:		
Salaries—Secretaries and Treasurer:		
Paul W. Koller, D.D.	5,100.00	
George Drach, D.D.	3,825.00	
E. R. Thomas, D.D.	3,825.00	
George R. Weitzel	3,825.00	
		16,575.00
Office Salaries		4,871.86

Expenses: Secretaries, Treasurer and Board
Members:

Secretaries and Treasurer	$1,014.51	
Board Members	1,420.06	
		2,434.57
Special Allowances and Pensions		5,286.14

Expenses of Maintaining "Baltimore Mission
House" and the "Brown House":

Repairs	$ 206.68	
Janitor	528.80	
Miscellaneous Expense	85.00	
Taxes	24.56	
Interest	60.00	
Coal and Miscellaneous Expenses	240.00	
	$1,145.04	

Less: Contributed by Women's Missionary Society of Maryland Synod	67.37	
		1,077.67

Expenses—Missionaries in preparation and on furlough		$ 5,325.50
Foreign Mission Conference		1,020.00

General Expenses:

Telephone and Telegraph and Cables	$ 739.74	
Postage and Express	601.04	
Gas, Electricity and Water	168.57	
Office Supplies and Expenses	1,620.23	
		3,129.58

Specials—General Fund:

Gifts to Fields and Missionaries	1,300.00
Special to Fields	131.00
Africa Conference Committee	96.93
Contingent Fund	5,000.00

Expenses of Epiphany Appeal	1,719.22
Total Disbursements—General Fund	$344,506.04

* Indicates a Receipt

SUMMARY OF INCOME AND DISBURSEMENTS—VARIOUS FUNDS
For the Period from June 30, 1935 to June 30, 1936

General Fund:

Overdraft—June 30, 1935	$140,423.70	
Disbursements for year ended June 30, 1936	344,506.04	
		$484,929.74
Income for year ended June 30, 1936	377,291.99	
Overdraft—June 30, 1936		$107,637.75*

Land and Building Fund:
Overdraft—June 30, 1935		$ 3,361.35	
Disbursements:			
Shantung Missions	$ 8,125.28		
Buenos Aires Property	2,350.00		
Africa Property	300.00		
		10,775.28	
		$ 14,136.63	
Less: Donations	$ 10,393.76		
Transfer Japan Exchange Balances	3,892.35		
		14,286.11	
Balance—June 30, 1936			149.48

Trust Funds:
Balance—June 30, 1935	$208,181.66	
Gifts:		
"The Mamie Telleen Memorial India Scholarship"	625.00	
Sarah J. Curran	623.52	
	$209,430.18	
Less: Elizabeth Quist	2,000.00	
Balance—June 30, 1936		207,430.18

Annuity Funds:
Balance—June 30, 1935	94,450.00	
Annuities Sold	8,000.00	
	102,450.00	
Less: Annuities cancelled by death and transferred to General Fund	4,500.00	
Balance—June 30, 1936		97,950.00

Andhra Christian College Fund:
Balance—June 30, 1935		$277,483.25	
Income:			
Interest on Investments	$ 8,508.79		
Donations	1,104.00		
Interest on Uninvested Funds	1,623.50		
Profit on Sale of Securities	810.59		
		$ 12,046.88	
Less:			
Remittance to Field	$1,000.00		
Interest on Endowment Fund	2,680.00		
		3,680.00	
			8,366.88
Balance—June 30, 1936			$285,850.13

Pohlman Fund:
Balance—June 30, 1935	$ 1,600.00	
Balance—June 30, 1936		1,600.00

Reformation Diamond Jubilee:
Advance Fund:
Balance—June 30, 1935	$ 17,840.64	
Balance—June 30, 1936		17,840.64

Kobe Equipment Fund:
Balance—June 30, 1935	$ 2,953.69	
Donation	25.00	
	$ 2,978.69	
Remittances to Japan Field	2,978.69	
Balance—June 30, 1936		none
Total of All Funds		$503,182.68

*Overdraft

SUMMARY OF CASH RECEIPTS AND DISBURSEMENTS

For the Period from June 30, 1935 to June 30, 1936

Cash Balance—June 30, 1935		$ 81,322.79
Receipts:		
General Fund	$377,291.99	
Trust Funds	1,248.52	
Andhra Christian College Fund	12,046.88	
Land and Building Fund	10,393.76	
Annuity Funds	7,000.00	
Kobe Equipment Fund	25.00	
Sale of Securities	31,292.32	
Payments on Mortgages	1,000.00	
Payments on Notes Receivable	1,500.00	
Bank Loans	10,000.00	
Other Receipts:		
Women's Missionary Society	175,778.62	
Accounts Receivable	21,379.35	
Accounts Payable	14,001.88	
Travel Advance	3,518.14	
Interest on Bank Loans	96.25	
Total Receipts		666,572.71
		$747,895.50

Disbursements:
General Fund		$344,506.04
Less: Unpaid drafts for June 1936 charged in Disbursements but not paid until sometime subsequent to June 30, 1936	$12,508.57	

Less: Contingent Fund charged as
　　Disbursements for 1936 ....   5,000.00
　　　　　　　　　　　　　　　　　　　　　　　　　　　　―――――――   17,508.57

Cash Disbursed from General Fund	$326,997.47
Bank Loans Repaid	45,000.00
Kobe Equipment Fund	2,978.69
Purchase of Securities	25,392.53
Andhra Christian College Fund	3,680.00
Annuity Fund	4,500.00
Land and Building Fund	10,775.28
May 1935 Drafts Paid	11,867.21
Disbursements charged to Contingent Fund	5,000.00
Other Disbursements:	
Women's Missionary Society	182,037.26
Accounts Receivable	22,726.85
Accounts Payable	5,801.17
Travel Advances	4,006.58

　　　Total Disbursements 650,763.04

　　　Cash in Banks—June 30, 1936 .... $ 97,132.46

RECONCILIATION OF ACCOUNTS

June 30, 1934 and June 30, 1935

ASSETS	Balances June 30, 1934	Receipts	Disbursements	Debit	Credit	Balances June 30, 1935
Cash	$93,419.13	$678,434.68	$690,531.02			$81,322..79
Investments:						
Stocks, Bonds and Certificates of Participation	331,725.00	$56,305.15	$80,650.62			356,070.47
Ground Rents and Mortgages	9,323.55	500.00				8,823.55
Notes Receivable	6,680.00					6,680.00
Real Estate	49,507.94			$1.00		49,508.94
Accounts Receivable:						
Advances on Field Budgets and Miscellaneous Accounts Receivable	2,596.19	1,778.24	644.15			1,462.10
Salaries Advanced to Fields	1,068.43	644.97	918.83			1,342.29
Student Advances	1,518.22	645.00	744.92			1,618.14
Women's Missionary Society	389.00	364.00	1,673.55			1,698.55
Travel Advanced to Fields	4,714.96	4,714.96	3,518.14			3,518.14
Prepaid Interest	115.84	115.84	96.25			96.25
Total Assets	$501,058.26					$512,141.22
LIABILITIES						
Notes Payable to Bank	$35,000.00	25,000.00	25,000.00			35,000.00
Due on Unpaid Drafts	25,373.82		25,373.82		$11,867.21a	11,867.21
Accounts Payable	4,026.55	2,311.44	4,026.55			2,311.44
Total Liabilities	$64,400.37					$49,178.65
RESERVES						
Reserve for Exchange Balances—Japan	$5,189.48		1,297.13			3,892.35
Reserve for Contingencies					5,000.00b	5,000.00
Total Reserves	$5,189.48					$8,892.35
	$431,468.41					$454,070.22

FUNDS

Trust Funds	$205,878.09	2,302.57		1.00c $208,181.66
Annuity Funds	92,950.00	2,800.00	1,300.00	94,450.00
Andhra Christian College Fund	269,351.96	17,569.77	9,438.48	277,483.25
Land and Buildings Fund	5,669.40	4,172.38	13,203.13	3,361.35*
Reformation Diamond Jubilee Fund	17,840.64			17,840.64
Kobe Equipment Fund	7,453.69		4,500.00	2,953.69
Pohlman Fund	1,600.00			1,600.00
	$600,743.78			$599,147.89
Less: Overdrafts—General Fund	$166,638.11	387,712.76	344,631.14	$140,423.70
Women's Missionary Society	2,637.26	171,497.60	173,514.31	16,867.21	4,653.97
	$169,275.37			$145,077.67
	$431,468.41	$678,434.68	$690,531.02	$16,868.21	$454,070.22
				$16,868.21	

a—represents June, 1935 unpaid drafts of Foreign Funds; b—represents reserve set aside for contingencies; c—represents gift of farm containing 60 acres of ground located at Roosevelt, Oklahoma; *—represents deficit.

RECONCILIATION OF ACCOUNTS

June 30, 1935 to June 30, 1936

ASSETS	Balances June 30, 1935	Receipts	Cash Disbursements	Transfers Debit	Transfers Credit	Balances June 30, 1936
Cash	$81,322.79	$666,572.71	$650,763.04			$97,132.46
Investments:						
Stocks, Bonds and Certificates of Participation	356,070.47	$31,292.32	$25,392.53	$1,000.00		351,170.68
Ground Rents and Mortgages	8,823.55	1,000.00				7,823.55
Notes Receivable	6,680.00	1,500.00				5,180.00
Real Estate	49,508.94				$2,000.00	47,508.94
Other Assets:						
Accounts Receivable	6,121.08	21,379.35	22,726.85			7,468.58
Travel Advances	3,518.14	3,518.14	4,006.58			4,006.58
Women's Missionary Society	4,653.97	175,778.62	182,037.26			10,912.61
Prepaid Interest on Bank Loans	96.25	96.25				
Total Assets	$516,795.19					$531,203.40
LIABILITIES						
Notes Payable to Bank	$35,000.00	10,000.00	45,000.00			
Due on Unpaid Drafts	11,867.21		11,867.21		12,508.57	$12,508.57
Accounts Payable	2,311.44	14,001.88	5,801.17			10,512.15
Total Liabilities	$49,178.65					$23,020.72
RESERVES						
Reserve for Exchange Balances—Japan	$3,892.35			3,892.35		
Reserve for Contingencies	5,000.00		5,000.00		5,000.00	$5,000.00
Total Reserves	8,892.35					$5,000.00
Net Assets	$458,724.19					$503,182.68

FUNDS

Trust Funds	$208,181.66	1,248.52		2,000.00	$207,430.18
Annuity Funds	94,450.00	7,000.00	4,500.00	1,000.00	97,950.00
Andhra Christian College Fund	277,483.25	12,046.88	3,680.00		285,850.13
Land and Building Fund	3,361.35*	10,393.76	10,775.28	3,892.35	149.48
Reformation Diamond Jubilee Fund	17,840.64				17,840.64
Kobe Equipment Fund	2,953.69	25.00	2,978.69		
Pohlman Fund	1,600.00				1,600.00
	$599,147.89	377,291.99	326,997.47	17,508.57	$610,820.43
Less: Overdrafts—General Fund	140,423.70				107,637.75
Total Funds	$458,724.19	$666,572.71	$650,763.04	$24,400.92	$503,182.68
				$24,400.92	

* Represents a deficit.

SCHEDULE OF INVESTMENTS

June 30, 1936

Par Value	Bonds	Book Value June 30, 1936	Market Value June 30, 1936
$ 5,000	Adams Express Company, 50 years Collateral Trust 4s due 3/1/48	$ 4,658.75	$ 4,975.00
2,400	Allied Mortgage Companies, Inc. Series "M" Collateral Trust Bonds, Average 3½%—12/1/53	2,400.00	1,884.00
4,000	Allied Mortgage Companies, Inc. Series "B" Collateral Trust Bonds Average 3½%—12/1/53	3,856.00	3,160.00
900	Altoona and Logan Valley Rwy. Co. 1st Lien Collateral Trust 4s 1954	900.00	796.50
3,000	American and Foreign Power Co. Inc. Deb. 5% 2030	2,692.50	2,340.00
3,000	American Telephone and Telegraph Gold Deb. 5s 1965	3,045.00	3,390.00
10,000	Armour and Company real estate 4½s due 6/1/39	10,287.50	9,775.00
6,000	Associated E l e c t r i c Company, 4½s 1953	5,655.00	3,810.00
5,000	Atlantic Coast Line (L. & N. Div.) Coll. 4s 1952	4,293.75	4,300.00
4,000	Baltimore & Ohio R. R. Co. 1st 4s 1948 ..	3,050.00	4,240.00
3,000	Baltimore and Ohio R. R. Co. Equipment "D" 4½s due 1940	2,969.40	3,240.00
2,000	Baltimore & Ohio R. R. Co. S. W. Division 1st mtge. 5s 1950	1,985.00	2,070.00
9,500	The Baltimore Transit Company, Series A 1st 5s Deb. due 7/1/75 Reg.	9,500.00	2,945.00
9,500	The Baltimore Transit Company, Series "B" 1st 5s Deb. due 7/1/75 Reg.	9,500.00	9,405.00
4,000	The Baltimore Transit Company, Series "A" 1st 4% due 7/5/75 Reg.	4,000.00	1,080.00
3,620	British Guiana Government 5s 1946 (Church Endowment)	3,620.00	3,982.00
2,000	Brooklyn Edison Co. Inc. General Series "E" 5s 1952	1,935.00	2,080.00
5,000	Canadian Pacific Rwy. Collateral Trust 4½s 7/1/60	5,000.00	5,237.50
500	Center Court Apartment 1st and S. F. 6s 1936	500.00	175.00
4,000	Central Illinois Public Service Co. 1st 4½s due 1967 Series "F"	3,790.00	4,040.00
3,000	Central Illinois Public Service Co. 1st 5s 1968 Series "G"	2,925.00	3,090.00
1,000	Central Indiana Power Company, 1st 6s 1947	1,000.00	925.00
5,000	Central States Electric Corp. Conv. Deb. 5s 1948	4,825.00	3,500.00
1,000	Cespedes Sugar Company, 1st 7½s 1939	1,000.00	215.00

5,000	Chicago and Western Indiana R. R. Consol. 4s due 7/1/52	4,912.50	5,150.00
1,000	Cities Service Company, Conv. Deb. 5s 1950	1,000.00	830.00
5,000	Commonwealth Edison 1st mtge. 4s 1981	4,725.00	5,337.50
2,000	Consolidated Cities Light and Power Traction Co. 1st 5s 1962	1,659.90	1,730.00
2,000	Continental Investment Bond Corp. guar. and Coll. Trust Bond B. & I. Issue Average 3½s—12/1/53	2,000.00	1,560.00
3,000	Denmark (Kingdom of) 5½s 1955 30 year external	2,985.00	3,060.00
3,000	Detroit Edison Company—Series "D" General Ref. 4½s 1961	3,000.00	3,472.50
1,000	Detroit Edison Company General 4½s 1961	885.00	1,157.50
750	Duquesne Natural Gas Company, Gen'l and Ref. Mortgages 7s—7/1/48	750.00	622.50
3,000	Electric Power and Light Corp. Gold Deb. 5% 2030	2,790.00	2,670.00
1,000	Elk Horn Coal Corp. Deb. 7s 1931 (Certificate of Deposit)	1,000.00	60.00
10,000	Federal Farm Mortgage Corporation, 3s due 5/15/49 Opt. 1944	10,053.13	10,300.00
5,000	Federated Utilities, Inc. 1st Lien Collateral Trust 5½s 1957	4,737.50	3,925.00
5,000	Florida East Coast Rwy. Co. 1st 4½s 1959	3,950.00	3,000.00
4,000	Florida Power and Light Company, 1st 5s 1954	3,814.00	3,840.00
3,000	Forty Wall Street Corp. 1st mtge. Fee and Leasehold 6s 1958	2,940.00	2,100.00
3,000	Gary Electric and Gas Company Series "A" 1st Lien Collateral Gold Bonds 5s 7/1/44	2,932.50	2,932.50
2,000	Greenwich Water and Gas Company, Coll. Trust 5s Gold Bonds Series "A" due 4/1/52	1,820.00	1,970.00
68,850	Home Owners Loan Corporation, 2¾s due 8/1/49 Opt. 39	69,428.23	69,796.69
3,400	Hotel St. George Corp. 1st mtge. 4% S.F. due 10/1/50	944.00	1,768.00
21.02	Hotel St. George Corp. Scrip Certificate	1.00	
3,000	Houston Lighting and Power 1st Refunding 4½s 1981 Series "E"	2,947.50	3,157.50
5,000	Illinois Central Rwy. Co. Gold 4¾s 1966	4,825.00	3,650.00
2,000	Illinois Power and Light Corp. 1st and Ref. 5s 1956 Series "C"	1,960.00	2,000.00
2,000	Indiana Ice and Fuel Co. 1st mtge. 6½s 1947 Series "A"	2,000.00	1,380.00
4,000	Interstate Power Co. 5s 1957	3,900.00	3,120.00

1,000	Johnstown Passenger Rwy. Co. 4s 1931 (Certificate of Deposit)	1,000.00	50.00
2,000	Kansas Power and Light Company 5s due 5/1/57	2,115.00	2,100.00
3,000	Kansas City Power and Light Co. 1st 4½s 1961	3,082.50	3,345.00
3,000	Kentucky Utilities Co. Series "H" 1st mtge. 5s 1961	3,000.00	2,850.00
1,000	Lehigh Valley R. R. Co. Gen. Cons. mtge. 4s 2003	1,000.00	477.50
500	Nassau and Suffolk Lighting Co. 1st 5s 1945 30 year sinking fund	500.00	520.00
4,000	National Capital Mortgage Company 1st 6s 1939	4,000.00	3,800.00
1,000	National Power and Light Co. Deb. "B" 5s 2030	606.25	930.00
5,000	National Union Mortgage Co. Gold Bonds 3½s 1954	5,000.00	3,950.00
3,000	New England Gas and Electric Association Conv. 5s 1950	2,677.50	2,100.00
3,000	New York Central Equipment Trust 4½s 1942	2,871.36	3,300.00
3,000	New York Central R. R. Refunding Improv. 4½s 2013	2,992.50	2,595.00
3,000	North American Company, Deb. 5s 1961	2,902.50	3,195.00
1,000	North Carolina Gas Company, 1st mtge. S. F. 6s 1948 Trustees Certificate	970.00	100.00
5,000	Penn Central Light and Power Co. 1st 4½s 1977	4,725.00	5,200.00
2,000	Pennsylvania Electric Company, 1st Ref. 4s 1971	1,827.50	2,010.00
6,000	Pennsylvania R. R. Co. Series "D" General Mortgage 4¼s 1981	6,030.00	6,570.00
1,000	Pennsylvania R. R. Cons. Mtge. Bond Loan of 5/1/08 due 1948 4%	1,000.00	1,130.00
3,000	Peoples Light Gas and Coke Company Series "B" 1st & Refunding 4s 1981	2,820.00	2,850.00
8,000	Potomac Bond Corp. Guar. Col. Trust Income Average 3½% due 12/1/53	8,000.00	6,160.00
3,000	Public Service Co. of Northern Illinois 1st and Refunding 4½s 1981 Series "F"	2,925.00	3,090.00
2,000	Puget Sound Power & Light Co. 1st and Refunding 5½s 1949 Series "A"	1,340.00	1,870.00
3,000	Safe Harbour Water Power Corp. 1st Mortgage S. F. 4½s 1979	2,960.00	3,195.00
1,000	St. Louis County Gas Company, 1st 5s 1951	1,000.00	1,070.00
900	Scranton Transit Co. 1st Mortgage Sinking Fund 4s due 4/1/59	1,000.00	60.00
200	Scranton Transit Co. 2nd Mortgage and Col. Cum. 3s due 4/1/59		
3,000	Seaboard Roanoke Railroad 1st 5s 1931 (Certificate of Deposit)	3,022.50	1,560.00

		Book Value	Market Value
4,000	Seaboard Air Line 50 year 1st 4s 1950 ..	3,392.61	520.00
1,000	Seventy-Nine Realty Corp. Maximum Refund Bond due 8/1/48 Interest Paid as earned	979.00	200.00
4,000	S. W. Missouri R. R. General Refunding 5s 1931	4,080.00	40.00
5,000	Southern California Edison Co. Ltd. Ref. Mtge. 3¾s due 5/1/60	4,900.00	5,250.00
5,000	Southern Pacific R. R. Co. 1st and Re-funding 4s due 1/1/55	4,731.25	5,275.00
3,000	Southern Pacific Co. Gold 4½s 1968	2,992.50	2,715.00
1,500	Standard Power and Light Co. General Deb. 6s 1957	1,492.50	1,170.00
2,000	Texarkana and Fort Smith Rwy. Co. 1st mtge. 5½s 1950	2,010.00	2,100.00
2,300	United States Govt. Treasury 2¾ 1947-45	2,102.43	2,383.38
4,000	Unted States Gov't. 4¼s—3¼s 1943-45 ..	3,656.00	4,315.00
400	United States Gov't. Treasury Certificates 3⅛ 1949	392.38	424.00
3,100	United States Gov't. Treasury 3¼s due 4/15/45–46	2,833.74	3,332.50
	Total—Bonds	$338,278.18	$311,047.07

Shares	Stocks	Book Value June 30, 1936	Market Value June 30, 1936
6	Altoona and Logan Valley common	$	$ 420.00
1	American Telephone and Telegraph Co. ..	113.00	167.00
40	Baltimore Transit Company, pfd. Voting Trust Ceritficate	1,760.00	160.00
8½	Baltimore Transit Company, common Voting Trust Certificate	1,000.00	17.00
5	Cities Service Co. pfd.	87.50	320.00
22	Duquesne Natural Gas Co. No Par		121.00
½	Duquesne Natural Gas Co. scrip		
2,500	Electric and Peoples Traction Stock Trust Certificates Co. 4s 1945	2,500.00	325.00
30	Mutual Help Building and Loan Assn. of Baltimore	3,000.00	3,000.00
10	Seventy-Nine Realty Corporation Voting Trust Certificates		
24	W. Baltimore Building and Loan Association of Baltimore	3,120.00	3,120.00
17	Pennsylvania R. R. Co.	493.00	527.00
	Total—Stocks	$12,073.50	$8,177.00

Certificates of Participation

1,500	Federal Mortgage Company, Series "J"	$351.00	
2,000	Federal Mortgage Company, Series "J"	468.00	
	Total—Certificates of Participation	$819.00	

Ground Rents, Mortgages and Notes Receivable

Ground Rents on properties located at 924-1040 and 1042 West Fayette Street, Baltimore, Maryland	$3,323.55
First Mortgage on 2511 North Calvert Street, Baltimore, Maryland	2,000.00
First Mortgage on 5716 Hagerman Street, Phila. Penna. at 6%	2,500.00

Note of Charles R. Fisher, guaranteed by G. B. Moorehead at 6% (In hands of attorney) due:

$2,250.00 September 10, 1928 (Extended Indefinitely)
2,215.00 September 10, 1929 (Extended Indefinitely)
715.00 September 30, 1930 (Extended Indefinitely)

	5,180.00
Total—Ground Rents, Mortgages and Notes Receivable	$13,003.55

Real Estate

Equity in property located at 2900 Woodland Avenue, Baltimore, Maryland	$ 9,251.20
Property located at 18 East Mount Vernon Place, Baltimore, Maryland	16,000.00
Property located at Kodarkanal, India	13,000.00
Property located at 1019 South Randolph Street, Phila., Pa.	1,660.64
Property located at Knoxville, Tennessee	3,096.10
Property located at 5849 Woodcrest Avenue, Phila., Penna.	4,500.00
Farm located at Roosevelt, Oklahoma—160 acres	1.00
Total—Real Estate	$47,508.94

Summary of Investments:

Bonds	$338,278.18
Stocks	12,073.50
Participating Certificates	819.00
Ground Rents	3,323.55
Mortgages	4,500.00
Notes Receivable	5,180.00
Real Estate	47,508.94
	$411,683.17

Respectfully submitted,
GEORGE R. WEITZEL, *Treasurer.*

We have audited the books of account of the Treasurer, and examined the securities of the Board of Foreign Missions of the United Lutheran Church in America, for the biennium beginning July 1, 1934 and ending June 30, 1936, and we hereby certify, that in our opinion, the foregoing statements of Income and Expense, together with the Balance Sheet and other pertinent schedules, are in agreement with the books of account, and are true and correct.

TAIT, WELLER AND BAKER,
Accountants and Auditors.

Mr. George R. Weitzel, Treasurer, was introduced and explained the financial sections of the report.

The Rev. P. W. Koller, Executive Secretary, was then introduced, who, after references to particular conditions and opportunities in the fields, presented the missionaries present from the various fields.

The Rev. J. A. W. Haas moved that arrangements be made for a conference, by the officers of the Board, for a discussion of a particular problem in connection with the work in Africa.

An amendment was offered to add the words "and other matters." The amendment was adopted.

The motion as amended was adopted as follows:

"That arrangements be made for a conference, by the officers of the Board, for a discussion of a particular problem in connection with the work in Africa, and other matters."

The recommendations of the Board were presented in order.

Recommendation 1 was adopted by a rising vote.

Recommendation 2. Motion was made to adopt recommendation 2 and the motion was lost.

Recommendation 3 was adopted by a rising vote.

Recommendation 4 was adopted.

On motion the report of the auditors was accepted.

By common consent, the Treasurer of the Church was given the privilege of presenting the following resolution, which was unanimously adopted:

"That encouragement be given the Board of Foreign Missions to use its regular secretarial operations to clear the debt of the Board."

The President called for the presentation of items of unfinished business, in connection with the report of the Executive Board. (See pp. 63, 70, 72, 73, 89.)

The motion concerning a service for Rural Life Sunday, presented under IV, C, 1, (b), was adopted.

IV, C, 3, (a), Rules and Regulations of Commission on Investments, adopted.

V, 2, Budget. Adopted.

V, 4, Uniform Rate of Annuities. On motion, action on this item was deferred until the report of the Commission on Investments is before the Convention. (See p. 423.)

III, B, 3, Alleghany Synod. On motion, action on this item was deferred until the report of the Inner Mission Board is presented. (See p. 306.)

11.30 A. M., having arrived, the President announced the suspension of business for the Special Order of Prayer Service in behalf of the nations of the world. The Service was conducted by the Secretary, assisted by the Rev. A. E. Bell, the Rev. A. J. Traver, the Rev. N. R. Melhorn, and President F. H. Knubel.

FOURTH SESSION

DESHLER-WALLICK HOTEL
Columbus, Ohio
Friday, October 16, 1936, 2.00 P. M.

Devotions were conducted by the Rev. J. W. Ott, and the President called the Convention to order.

The Special Committee on Minutes reported that they had examined the Minutes of the first and second sessions and, finding them correct, moved their approval. The motion was carried and the President declared the Minutes approved.

The Rev. F. M. Urich, Chairman of the Committee of Reference and Counsel, presented the following report:

REPORT OF COMMITTEE OF REFERENCE AND COUNSEL

1. We recommend that the Rev. Ralph H. Long, Executive Director of the National Lutheran Council, who cannot be here to address the Convention in connection with the report of the Commissioners to the National Lutheran Council, scheduled for Tuesday, October 20, be heard at this time.

2. A letter of official greeting and earnest salutation, sent by T. F. Gullixon, First Vice President of the Norwegian Lutheran Church, in the absence of President Aasgaard, who is abroad, has been received.

We recommend that the Secretary send reciprocal greetings and good wishes.

3. The attention of the committee has been called to the presence at this Convention of the Rev. L. L. Uhl, who has reached the age of eighty-nine years and who spent more than fifty years in our India mission field as a faithful servant of God.

We recommend that he be heard at this time, and that the time of this presentation be limited to five minutes.

4. A telegraphic message, signed by Missionaries Miller and Linn, conveying the greetings of our Japan Mission to our Tenth Biennial Convention and urging missionary recruits, has been received.

We recommend that the Secretary make suitable acknowledgment of these cordial greetings.

5. Greetings by radiogram, from the Steamer *Republic*, addressed to the Committee on Army and Navy Chaplains, in care of the Rev. Lewis P. Speaker, and signed by Chaplain John Hall, have been received.

We recommend that this message be referred to the Committee on Army and Navy Work for suitable reply.

6. Dr. P. O. Bersell, representative and President of the Augustana Synod, will be here tomorrow to present the greetings of that body.

We recommend that he be heard at the opening of the morning session on Saturday.

Recommendations 1, 2, 3, 4, 5, and 6 were adopted.

The Rev. Ralph H. Long addressed the Convention concerning the work of the National Lutheran Council.

The Rev. L. L. Uhl was introduced and made a brief statement.

The Secretary presented the report concerning the roll of the Convention as follows:

Number of delegates elected:

Clergymen, 271; Laymen, 267. Total—538.

Number of delegates in attendance:

Clergymen, 269; Laymen, 247. Total—516.

Twenty-four synods have one hundred per cent attendance of their delegations.

Two clergymen and twenty laymen are absent. Seven synods have one delegate absent; one synod has four delegates absent; one synod has five delegates absent; and one synod has six delegates absent.

Two delegates from the Evangelical Lutheran Church in Japan are present. There are no official delegates from the Andhra Evangelical Lutheran Church, India.

The report of the Board of American Missions was called in regular order and the Rev. Z. M. Corbe, Executive Secretary, spoke with reference to particular points in the report.

REPORT OF THE BOARD OF AMERICAN MISSIONS

(For action on the recommendations in this report, see p. 184)

Napoleon's oft quoted assertion concerning the determining factor in the progress of a victorious army was again proved false by the very definite advance made by our missionary forces during the past biennium. Although the church's finances still remain at the deadly level of 1933, nevertheless through carefully arranged readjustments this Board has maintained its policy of holding its obligations within the limits of its income. Under the planned mission program reported at the Savannah convention it is now possible for the Board to begin an advance movement.

TRIBUTES

In reverent gratitude to our Heavenly Father for their lives of faithful service the Board records in this report a portion of the tributes inscribed in its Minutes in memory of two who were identified with its work for many years.

"MR. HARRY LAMBRIGHT SNYDER, loyal Churchman, has heard the call of the Heavenly Father to the Church Triumphant. After serving the Church on earth faithfully for more than half a century he has transferred his membership to the Church in Heaven. Precious in the sight of the Lord is the death of His saints."

In the death of Mr. Snyder the Board of American Missions of the United Lutheran Church in America has lost a faithful friend and an able counsellor. To the work of the Board he gave his finest energies of mind and heart. As Chairman of the Committee on Latin America he gave sacrificially of his time to this important department of the work of our Lutheran Church. Genial, courteous, always gentlemanly—we will miss his presence at the meetings of our Board.

Harry Lambright Snyder was born in Shepherdstown, W. Va., October 11, 1861. When Harry was only ten days old his father left home to join the Confederate army as a member of the famous Stonewall Brigade. He was mortally wounded in the Battle of the Wilderness. At the early age of twelve years Harry went to work. His first employment was at the "Register" office in Shepherdstown, at a salary of $5 per month and board. When Harry was about 21 years old he and his brother Will purchased "The Register" and the printing plant. For 53 years he published and edited the "Shepherdstown Register."

Primarily, Mr. Snyder was an Editor. That was his life-work. Throughout his native state he was lovingly called The Dean of Editors. He was as gentlemanly as an editor as he was as a Churchman. For a number of years he served as president of the West Virginia Newspaper Council. An outstanding honor came to him when American editors voted him highest award for the "best story" written during the year.

Mr. Snyder was a Christian gentleman. He loved his Church because he loved his Lord. To the work of the Church he gave himself sacrificially, without stint of time or effort. His home church at Shepherdstown was the pride and joy of his heart. It was largely through his untiring efforts that the beautiful Gothic builbing was erected.

But his interests in the Kingdom of God reached far beyond the Shepherdstown Church. He was a familiar figure at the conventions of the United Lutheran Church. He served faithfully as a member of the Board of Directors of the National Lutheran Home for the Aged, Washington, D. C. For seventeen years he was a member of the Board of American Missions and its predecessor Boards. Church work was not a minor consideration in his eventful life—it was a consuming passion. The love of Christ constrained him."

"REVEREND JOHN CONRAD SEEGERS, D.D. On Tuesday, June 23, 1936, our beloved brother, the Rev. Dr. John Conrad Seegers, answered the call to come Home and thus entered the portals of everlasting life. A veritable host of former parishioners, theological students and co-workers in the various branches of the church's work rise up to call him blessed. Dr. Seegers spent forty-five years in the ministry of the Word, twenty-one of these as pastor of influential congregations and nineteen as teacher in two theological seminaries. His pastorates were: First Church, Richmond, Va.; Church of the Redeemer, Albany, N. Y.; St. John's, Easton, Pa.; Trinity, Reading, Pa., and St. Paul's, Wilmington, N. C. His service as a theological professor was rendered in the Southern Seminary at Columbia, S. C., from 1914 to 1918, and in the Philadelphia Seminary from 1921 to 1936. Those who were privileged to sit under his preaching had a practical demonstration of a childlike and therefore stalwart faith; those who were privileged to sit under his teaching were impressed anew with the preciousness of God's unsearchable riches because he himself was constantly digging deeper into the mine of God's truth.

Our beloved friend spent twenty-nine years of uninterrupted service in various positions of leadership in the home mission branch of the church's work. His co-workers on the Board of American Missions were permitted to experience to the full his genial fellowship, genuine friendship, wise council, warm sympathy, deep convictions, contagious humor, keen intellect and unflinching zeal. Dr. Seegers could always be counted on to bring a cheerful spirit and a generous heart to every task awaiting his attention. As a Christian gentleman he gave himself unstintedly and became more dear with each passing year. He was faithful in promoting every effort conducive to the building of his beloved Lutheran Zion. He has carved for himself a deep niche in our heart.

Dr. Seegers was born at Columbia, S. C., on October 6, 1867. He was an alumnus of Newberry College, graduating in 1888, and of the Philadelphia Seminary, graduating in 1891. He was ordained by the Holston Synod in 1891. The funeral service was held in the Philadelphia Seminary Chapel on Friday, June 26th. He is survived by his widow, Mary Erwin Ide, to whom he was married in 1893, and by six children: Dr. John Conrad Seegers, Professor and Dean of Men at Temple University; Walter Lewis Seegers, Professor at North Carolina State College; Ernest Franklin Seegers, a student at Muhlenberg College; Virginia May Seegers, teacher at the Pennsylvania School for the Deaf, Philadelphia, Pa.; Mrs. Fred S. Habenicht, Columbia, S. C., and Mrs. George F. Hall, Philadelphia, Pa.; three sisters and one brother.

The Board records its sincere appreciation of the generous service and support given by Mr. S. Frederick Telleen, who was identified with this Board and its predecessor for twenty years and who served as Treasurer of the Board of West Indies Missions from the organization of the United Lutheran Church, and after 1933 as Treasurer of the Board of American Missions. Limitation of service, imposed by the United Lutheran Church constitution, also takes from the Board membership others who for a quarter of a century have given outstanding service to the cause of American Missions. A severe loss is experienced in the expiration of the term of our beloved and highly esteemed President, the Rev. Dr. Henry W. A. Hanson. His guiding hand as President of the West Indies Mission Board, Vice President of the Joint Commission and lastly as President of the Board of American Missions was a large factor in creating the far-reaching plans of evangelism in the program of the Board. Our Vice President, Dr. Grant Hultberg, serving for twelve years on the Immigrant Board and the Board of American Missions, has done more than any other to formulate the effective financial policy of this Board. His keen insight into economic conditions made him the ideal Chairman of the Finance Committee. His wide experience in the practical administration of a great business enabled the Board to avoid many pitfalls. The name of Mr. A. Raymond Bard, Chairman of the Divisional Committee on Church Extension, will ever be associated with the cause of home missions. Few laymen have been privileged to give so long a lifetime of service to the work of missions. Dr. Gustave A. Benze has been identified with the linguistic work of the Church, first on the Slav-Hungarian Board, then the German Board, the Northwestern Mission Board and lastly on the divisional Committee of Linguistic Interests of this Board, so that his absence will be noted by all who are in contact with this vital part of our program.

After a period of mission service extending over two generations, during which he has traveled hundreds of thousands of miles over every section of the United States and Canada, our faithful Divisional Secretary of English Missions, the Rev. Dr. John F. Seibert, because of the condition of his health, was constrained to request relief from his strenuous labors. After reviewing his lifetime service, first as a home missionary pastor, then a Field Missionary, a Synodical Superintendent of Missions, a full-time President of the Synod, a General Superintendent of Missions and the Executive Secretary of the Home Mission and Church Extension Board of the United Lutheran Church, and under the merged Board of American Missions, covering even a larger field as Divisional Secretary of English Missions, the Board could not see its way clear to accept his complete retirement. There are so many possibilities of using the results of his wide experience and long service without detriment to his health that he was asked to continue after November 1st as a General Assistant Superintendent with such duties within the limits of his strength, as might be assigned by the Executive Secretary.

ORGANIZATION

The organization of the Board for the biennium was: President—Rev. H. W. A. Hanson, D.D., LL.D.; Vice-President—Mr. Grant Hultberg, D.C.L.; Secretary—Mr. H. F. Heuer; Treasurer—Mr. S. F. Telleen, 1934-1935, Mr. H. T. Walker, 1935-1936; Executive Secretary—Rev. Zenan M. Corbe, D.D.; Asst. Executive Secretary—Rev. P. A. Kirsch; Divisional Secretary of English Missions—Rev. J. F. Seibert, D.D.; Divisional Secretary of Linguistic Interests—Rev. E. A. Tappert, D.D.; Departmental Secretary of Church Extension and Finance—Mr. H. Torrey Walker; Term Expires 1940—Rev. O. G. Beckstrand; Rev. Franklin Clark Fry; Rev. J. E. Harms, D.D.; Rev. J. J. Scherer, Jr., D.D.; Mr. Henry Beisler; Mr. A. H. Durboraw; Mr. Wm. Eck; Term Expires 1938—Rev. F. O. Evers; Rev. L. H. Larimer, D.D.; Rev. H. J. Pflum, D.D.; Rev. L. W. Steckel, D.D.; Mr. Horace W. Bikle; Mr. Henry F. Heuer; John A. Hoober, Esq.; Term Expires 1936—Rev. G. A. Benze, D.D.; Rev. H. W. A. Hanson, D.D., LL.D.; Rev. E. W. Weber; Mr. A. Raymond Bard; Grant Hultberg, D.C.L.; Mr. Louis Hanson; Rev. John Schmieder.

The readjustment of the budget not only compelled a drastic cut in the salaries of the staff but also reduced the number of men in service to such an extent that the burden of the responsibilities on those remaining threatened their physical breakdown. In November, 1934, the Committee on Staff Personnel after careful search, presented the name of the Rev. Paul Andrew Kirsch, a successful pastor of large bilingual congregations, the first full-time Secretary of the United Synod of New York, and at the time of his call, also the Superintendent of Missions, almost one hundred in number, of that Synod. At a personal sacrifice he accepted the call to the office of Assistant Executive Secretary. This valuable addition to the Staff did little to relieve the strain for before he could take office, certain Synods, desiring to carry out the Savannah plan, including the New York Synod, turned over their Synodical supervision to the Board and Secretary Kirsch was assigned to care for this additional responsibility. The sudden death of our beloved Executive Secretary, Dr. Fry, placed the duties of his office on the shoulders of the Departmental Secretary of Church Extension and Finance, a double responsibility which continued for more than a year after the election of the Departmental Secretary to the office of Executive Secretary. In the Providence of God the Committee on Staff Personnel was led to recommend calling a business man of high standing, a partner in a well-known firm of accountants and whose acceptance of the office demanded a personal sacrifice not often made. The Board issued the call being convinced that the financial experience of Mr. Walker, his large acquaintance with church work in the various Protestant bodies, taken together with his army and collegiate and post-graduate records, qualified him in unusual degree for the responsible position of Departmental

Secretary of Church Extension and Finance and the Treasurership of the Board. On June 1, 1935 Mr. H. Torrey Walker took up the duties of his office and the record of the work accomplished testifies to the wisdom of the Board's choice.

NEW DIVISION—Soon after the organization of the Board of American Missions it was found necessary to give much time to the study of mission stations already established to discover the causes for their evident lack of progress. At first these discussions took place at Board and Executive Committee meetings but the time consumed caused the appointment of a special "Committee on Review" which gave long hours to the study of our missions and proposed many constructive recommendations. New plans for more extensive surveys and canvasses were proposed and successfully put into practice. The increase in the responsibilities of this Board, resulting from the Savannah convention, added new problems, so that it was evident that the time had come to ask for the restoration of one of the Divisions which had been eliminated from the original Plan of Operation in the final conference between the Joint Commission and the Executive Board prior to the Richmond Convention in 1926.

Part of this original plan will be unnecessary since the proposed plans for promotion and publicity of the U. L. C. should provide for these items. Our Board's work, however, will be aided by the establishment of a *Division of Survey and Research*. This Division to be charged with the duty of a constant study of all mission stations under the Board's jurisdiction, seeking especially for additional methods by which missions could be more thoroughly equipped for their task and brought to an early state of self-support without endangering their spirituality. Under this Committee will be placed the surveys now being conducted and after a careful study of the results of each survey this Committee should recommend suitable actions. Under the direction of this committee there will be conducted a periodic study of trends of population and of changing social conditions which might affect the Board's work; the Committee also to keep up to date a selected list of qualified men who could be secured for the fields coming under the Board's care and arrange, as means permit, for the employment of the graduates of our seminaries.

This Committee would be given recognition as a regular Divisional Committee of the Board, and be constituted in the same manner as the other Divisional Committees.

Recommended that approval be given to the addition to the Plan of Operation adopted by the Richmond Convention of a Divisional Committee on Survey and Research with duties as outlined in the body of this report.

At the annual meeting of the Board of American Missions held soon after the Savannah convention, the President and the Treasurer of the United Lutheran Church honored the Board with their presence. They gave an interpretation of the *Savannah action* as it might be applied in the work of the Board of American Missions. The Board went on record expressing its desire to do its utmost to make a successful trial of the plan for any Synod that might request it. The first to take official action was the Synod of Virginia at its meeting in January 1935, when the Synod voted to turn over their Synodical missions. The authorities of the United Synod of New York took similar action, which was approved at their Synodical conventions both in 1935 and 1936. In assuming the supervision of the work of the New York Synod, President Hanson stated in reply to the presentation of the President of the New York Synod, who was in attendance at the meeting of the Board: "I want to make perfectly clear that this Board has had nothing to do with the inauguration of the experiment proposed. We did not ask nor did we suggest that this Board receive one ounce of authority or one added inch of field, but we intend to make this experiment just as seriously as we can." ·

The testimony of the Synodical authorities indicates thorough satisfaction with the results of the experiment. The Board, however, can only carry on the plan from year to year until either all the Synods voluntarily comply with the Savannah tendency or else the Convention itself takes action. In the meantime, the Board will continue to the best of its ability to make the experiment a success. In view of its many years of experience under the original method of operation, and in view of the very thorough test in the two Synods in whose work every type of mission congregation is included, the Board of American Missions is convinced that it can work successfully under either method.

The Commission, composed of representatives from the agencies concerned appointed to study the question whether or not the *mountain work* could best be administered by one agency, made the required report to the Executive Board, giving as its verdict that the work could best be administered by one Board. Inasmuch as the greater part of the work was already under the Board of American Missions, it was recommended that the work at Konnarock and Iron Mountain also be placed under the jurisdiction of this Board. After approval by the Executive Board this work was turned over on May 1, 1936, placing additional responsibilities on the Board of American Missions. The Board resolved to put forth a special effort to make possible the attainment of the high ideals for which the Women's Missionary Society and the Brotherhood were striving when the Schools were begun. One troublesome question has already been settled through the generous kindness of a member of the Board of American Missions, who advanced the money for the purchase of the Iron Mountain property, enabling the School to secure the advantage of a generous cash discount and giving the Brotherhood ample time to put on its campaign to raise funds to replace this loan. Readjustments are also being made which will not only keep the expenses of both Schools within their income, but will permit an extension of the work among the people who so greatly need the influence of the Schools. The statistics concerning these two Schools will be reported, as heretofore, by the Inner Mission Board.

WOMEN'S MISSIONARY SOCIETY—No report would be complete without reference to the generous and sympathetic support given to the Board of American Missions by the Women's Missionary Society of the U. L. C. There is a natural growth of interest in home missions among the consecrated members of these Societies, for none can better appreciate the dangers confronting the American home and womanhood. The financial assistance of the Women's Missionary Society enables the Board to do 10 per cent more work than its income would otherwise permit. The representatives of the Women's Missionary Society on the Board, Mrs. J. M. Cook and Mrs. Oscar Schmidt, have faithfully attended all Board and Executive Committee meetings and their counsel has been most helpful.

THE COMMITTEE ON CHURCH ARCHITECTURE, especially its efficient Secretary, Mr. Charles Scheuringer, continued to render valued assistance to our mission congregations. There are many others whose co-operation is deeply appreciated and to whom tribute would be paid were it not for the limitations of this report.

New efforts to assist the missionaries in their difficult task have been mentioned in other sections of this report, but note should be made here of the establishment of a *loan Library* for missionaries. Through the generous assistance of the Publication House, the Board has been able each year to send books to the missionaries as a Christmas remembrance. The grateful appreciation expressed in letters of acknowledgment revealed that many missionaries were unable to secure the books so greatly needed in their work. A loan library was, therefore, established, which is proving a blessing to men in the far-flung parishes who were longing for the help which comes from good books. Another form of assistance to missionaries was the experimental *school for missionary pastors* conducted in connection with the Summer School at Massanetta Springs. Lectures on meeting the false religions and isms of the day, on practical theology, on finances and the personal life of the minister were given with such success that the missionaries, present from fifteen Synods, unanimously requested the continuation of such a Summer School.

In the absence of a Home Mission magazine in which news of the field as well as helpful methods of mission work might be published, a *monthly communication paper* called "Ecclesia Plantanda" has been inaugurated. The original intention was to send it only to the missionaries of the Board and officers of the Synodical Mission Committee and those to whom the U. L. C. requires the monthly Minutes of the Board to be mailed, but interest in the paper has been so great that there is quite a demand to permit a wider circulation.

REPORT OF DIVISION OF ENGLISH MISSIONS

By Dr. John F. Seibert

This report of the Division of English Missions does not concern itself with policies or with programs. These are determined by the Board itself. It has to do with the execution of these plans in all missions using the English language. This trust has been diligently carried out and the record is herewith submitted for information and the approval of the Church.

In the retrospect of the past biennium we find evidence that our Divine Lord has set His seal of blessing upon this mission enterprise and we devoutly acknowledge His gracious guidance in the prosecution of the work. We express our sense of gratitude to the missionary pastors for their co-operation and to the Synodical Home Mission Committees and to the Superintendents and Presidents for their information and help. Experience enables us to state unhesitatingly that our Mission ary Pastors, as a whole, cannot be excelled by the missionaries of any similar group. One is thrilled to recall that in twenty-eight of our Synods, Home Mission Committees or Boards, of at least five members each, meet monthly or quarterly to direct the Home Mission Work on their territory, to counsel with the missionaries concerning their fields, and to endeavor to see that no important field for mission work is overlooked.

Missions Enrolled

At the beginning of the biennium the Division of English Missions had under its care 304 missions where the Board co-operated in the support of pastors. For many years it has been stated by Missionary Leaders and Directors of Home Mission work that a large measure of the success of the Home Mission enterprise can be determined by the number of missions that become self-supporting. If this be true it is a cause for encouragement that forty congregations in the sixteen Synods have reached that goal in the payment of pastor's salary. These missions are included in the following list of those which no longer receive aid on pastor's salary. In all but a few cases the congregations assumed the amount formerly paid by the Board. Others were made a part of a larger parish and a few were assisted by local support.

Alleghany Synod: St. John's, East Juniata; *California Synod:* St. John's Gardena; First, Sacramento; *East Pennsylvania Synod:* Calvary, West Chester; Trinity, Yeadon; *Florida Synod:* Grace, Lakeland; *Indiana Synod:* Gethsemane, Indianapolis; *Iowa Synod:* St. Paul's, Fort Madison; *Kansas Synod:* St. John's Kansas City, Mo.; *Michigan Synod:* Unity, Detroit; *Ministerium of Pennsylvania:* Calvary, Laureldale; Holy Trinity, Magnolia, N. J.; Redeemer, Vineland, N. J.; *Mississippi Synod:* Zion Pastorate, Forest; *Nebraska Synod:* Sidney-Potter Parish; *North Carolina*

Synod: Nurse, Watauga Parish; *Northwest Synod:* Our Saviour, Fond du Lac, Wis.; Redeemer, Hartford, Wis.; Faith, Winona, Minn.; First, Winnipeg, Can.; *Ohio Synod:* Holy Trinity, Salem; Redeemer, Toledo; *Pittsburgh Synod:* Mt. Lebanon, Pittsburgh; Hope-Memorial, Smithton; *United Synod of New York:* Grace, Forest Hills, L. I.; Ascension, Franklin Square; Atonement, Syracuse; Christ, Little Neck; Resurrection, Rochester; Redeemer, Dumont, N. J.; St. James, Gerrittsen Beach, Brooklyn; Grace, North Bellmore; Resurrection, St. Albans; St. John's, Mamaroneck, N. Y.; First, Jeffersonville; Immanuel, Madison, Conn.; St. John's, Long Beach, L. I.; Holy Trinity, Nutley, N. J.; *Virginia Synod:* Holy Trinity, Lynchburg; *West Pennsylvania Synod:* Augsburg, York, Pa.

The examination, too, reveals that these congregations are to be found in metropolitan sections, in suburban towns, in smaller cities, in county seats and in rural communities. The number is not as large as in some past bienniums but in view of the distressed financial situation, many of our people being still out of employment or employed at decreased incomes, the record is good. Especially so when our self-supporting congregations have had difficult times to maintain their work at the standard of other days. It is a cause for congratulation that our missions generally, have been able, not only to maintain their work, but each year to assume a larger share, amounting at times to hundreds of dollars, toward the pastor's salary and the interest and amortization of Church Extension Loans.

Thirty English missions have been taken on the funds of the Board. This by itself would be no great cause for rejoicing, in view of the many opportunities for new work that have been discovered. It does, however, reveal an encouraging growth over the number received during the preceding biennium and it justifies the expectation of what may be done when the congregations and Synods again have the means, as well as the will to meet the apportionment. The congregations that have been added to those aided by the Board are:

Canada Synod: St. Matthew's, Brantford, Ont.; Our Saviour, Owen Sound, Ont.; Bethany, Woodstock, Ont.; *California Synod:* St. Paul's Los Angeles; Holy Trinity, Tucson, Ariz.; *East Pennsylvania Synod:* Tinicum Memorial, Essington; St. John's Folcroft; *Florida Synod:* Memorial, St. Augustine; *Illinois Synod:* First, Cape Girardeau, Mo.; Gladstone Park, Chicago; *Indiana Synod:* Christ, Evansville; *Kentucky-Tennessee:* Memorial, Nashville; *Michigan Synod:* Resurrection, Detroit; *Nebraska Synod:* Messiah, Broadwater; United Lutheran, Scribner, Nebr.; *North Carolina Synod:* Fayetteville; *Northwest Synod:* Lake of the Isle, Minneapolis; First, Sheboygan; *Ohio Synod:* Gloria Dei, Cleveland; Auburn, Springfield; Christ, Euclid Village; St. John's, Mt. Vernon; *Pacific Synod:* Central, Seattle; *South Carolina Synod:* Holy Trinity, Anderson; *United Synod of New York:* Resurrection, Mount Kisco; Our Saviour, Harmon-on-Hudson; Christ, Wantagh; St. John's, Long Beach, L. I.; Old Yellow, Manheim Parish; *West Virginia Synod:* Westernport, Md.

An examination of these missions assumed by the Board will show that they are from widely scattered territories. From Arizona to Canada, from Minnesota to Florida, from New York and Philadelphia to Chicago with new missions in Ohio, Michigan, Indiana, Kentucky, Nebraska, West Virginia and South Carolina.

Representatives of the various Synods at this convention doubtless could tell of other opportunities, east and west and north and south that would challenge the finest spirit of optimism for Home Mission advance. The work of planting the church is not finished. It may be that some change in the method of conducting Mission work will have to be undertaken but with more than fifty millions of our population as yet untouched by the Gospel of Jesus Christ, there remains a tremendous challenge and the need to plant new missions in all sections of the country.

It might be well, however, to question whether the era of rapid expansion as shown in the palmiest days of this Board or of its predecessors and indeed of the Boards of other parts of the Lutheran Church, will soon come again. No longer is there an immigration in excess of a million a year. The opportunities for Home Mission advance through the expanding agricultural interests of the country likely will be very limited for many years. Our Lutheran brethren in other Synods, as recently as the date of the organization of the United Lutheran Church, did their Home Mission work largely in foreign languages or for the most part, conducted bilingual organizations. Now these groups are largely English and in the organization of new missions, with few exceptions, they do the work wholly in the English language. "The enlarged mobility made possible by the use of the automobile and the splendid net-work of good roads everywhere, has been recognized," says a well known Missouri Synod leader, "by every interest in society except the Church."

Differences do exist in the matter of the material for the growth of congregations. Whether these congregations to be organized are in sections where the ungathered people of Lutheran antecedents is large or the fact that the congregations will gain considerably from the transfer from other congregations thus saving thousands to our Church and many of them to Christ, or whether they are to be organized from the great mass of humanity, are items that must be considered. The Board is conversant with these several situations but they are not the controlling factors in the choice of mission congregations. The Board, however, does insist that each field whether in metropolitan New York or in the rural towns and country districts of Nebraska, whether in fields of rich Lutheran population in the Northwest or in the sparsely settled groups of Lutherans in the Southland, be properly surveyed and all facts be presented when it is desired to organize a congregation.

THE WORK NOW ON HAND

PRESENT WORK: Alameda, California, and St. Mark's, Seattle, Wash., were closed. Three congregations, Unity, Milwaukee, Wisconsin, Maple Shade, New Jersey, and Temple, San Francisco, were transferred from the Linguistic Division. Prince Rupert, B. C., after a thorough analysis of the field was given over to the Norwegian Lutheran Church. There were, therefore, 298 English Missions receiving assistance on Pastor's salary from the Board at the close of the biennium.

The plan adopted by the Board to limit the time of appropriations towards pastor's support to ten years is working out gradually. This is no hard and fast rule. The Board already through its recommendations from the Review Committee, after a consideration of all facts involved, has shown its entire sympathy and readiness to continue certain missions. The date of a final goal, however, has had a stimulating effect upon quite a few congregations.

The same can be said for the rule governing the submission of pledges toward the support of the church at the time applications for aid were made. We have heard from church councilmen, from missionary pastors and Mission Committees, expressions of sincere appreciation and genuine commendation and we believe, as all learn to understand the benefits that result, that there will be as general and as hearty compliance as there is in making the application itself.

ADVANCE WORK—The Board recognizes that the only way for prosecuting the mission work is to have properly qualified mission pastors to take charge of the mission congregations. However, during the years of the depression one after the other Mission Superintendents and Field Missionaries were dispensed with until there was virtually no one to serve vacant congregations in emergencies or to assume charge temporarily of newly organized missions or to make surveys. To provide this need a number of men have been called as Board Missionaries. At the time of this report they were: the Rev. H. B. Schaeffer, D.D., reviving the work at St. Augustine, the oldest city in the United States; the Rev. J. L. Sawyer, for years a successful missionary of the Board, who is at present effectively working in unifying the Central Church, Seattle, Wash.; the Rev. John Gable, released from the Board work to serve the church at The Dalles, Ore., during the illness of the Secretary of the Pacific Synod; the Rev. George A. Hagedorn, who for some years has been doing splendid work in restoring confidence in congregations that have been torn asunder and who is at present assigned to the Trinity Church, Kansas City, Kansas; Rev. Elmer E. Zieber, former missionary of the Board in Babylon, L. I., and now assigned to Resurrection Church, Halifax, Nova Scotia; the Rev. F. C. Maynard, at present assigned to the reviving of rural work in New York State with the "Old Yellow" Church at Manheim as a center; the Rev. Elwin A. Miller, at present assigned to the new work at Mount Kisco, N. Y.

On the recommendation of the Board during the present summer ten men of the Middler Class of our theological seminaries have been engaged to do survey and canvass work in the various Synods.

DEATH OF MISSIONARIES—We report the death of three of our mission staff during the biennium. The Rev. L. C. Schaaf, pastor of our mission at Sharon, Pa., was returning November 29, 1934 with his wife and child from having spent Thanksgiving with relatives when his automobile was struck by a train and he was instantly killed. Pastor Schaaf was instrumental in merging the two missions in Sharon and he became the pastor of the United Church. He was a zealous man of God. His widow and child, in his honor, presented the congregation with altar furnishings. Other deaths were: the Rev D. Upton Bair, Ph.D., of Sea Isle City, N. J., on May 10, 1935 after forty-three years service, and the Rev. Charles W. Schnable, B.D., of Teaneck, N. J., on July 2, 1935 after nine years of service. These men, one after years of faithful labor and the other just starting on his life mission as it were, did valiant service.

And now, beloved fathers and brethren, there has been presented as briefly as possible a record of the work that has been administered by the Division of English Missions during the two years that ended June 30, 1936. It does not claim that its administration of this sacred trust has been free from error but that it has earnestly endeavored to discharge the duties assigned it with sincere devotion. May I add that observation gained by actual contact with our missions in many States, convinces us that our missionaries are really hungry for a closer contact with the Board and most heartily and earnestly appreciate the visits of Secretaries or Board members. Especially is this true where the Synods are weak and the sources of contact with their brethren are limited.

DIVISION OF LINGUISTIC INTERESTS

By Dr. E. A. Tappert

At the Seamen's House at Bremen there is a Latin inscription which reads: "*Navigare necesse est; vivere non necesse est.*" This epigram may well be applied to the work of missions, for missions is the life of the Church. Home Missions, as represented by the Board of American Missions, is the prerequisite for all other missions; it means the establishment and strengthening of the base, from which all other missions operate.

The object of Home Missions is not limited by language or nationality. It is immaterial under which flag people may live, or in which tongue they prefer to worship; unless they are heathen in heathen lands, they fall under the scope of Home Missions. Inability for lack of means to cover all the territories where work is needed does not invalidate this claim.

The fact that the Lutheran Church is world-wide accounts for the cosmopolitan character of the Lutheran Church in America. The great melting-pot has received valuable contributions from Lutherans from every land on the globe; Lutherans from all lands have been amalgamated, or are still being amalgamated into a great American Lutheran Church, more solidly bound together and united by the sound teachings of Martin Luther's Catechism and the Augsburg Confession than may appear on the surface.

At the convention at Washington the United Lutheran Church laid down a Linguistic Policy, in which it recognizes its responsibility to the "stranger in our land," and in which it commts itself to conscientious and aggressive work among the linguistic groups of Lutherans in America. The duties assumed have been carried out faithfully by the Board of American Missions. Never in the history of our Church has there been more careful planning; never has more minute attention been given to this problem; and in spite of the severe handicap of limited means the results have been gratifying.

1. German Missions

Canada still offers a fertile field to German Missions, but the conditions in the United States have made mission work among Germans rather stationary. Not that there is no need for it. There are still many thousands of post-war Germans, who sorely need the Gospel, but they do not show themselves very receptive, and treat all efforts to reach them with the Gospel with the greatest indifference. Among the older Germans the process of Americanization has made rapid progress, and though we shall need German services yet for many years to come, and though the necessity of providing preachers for our German churches will cause us many a worry, the inauguration of new work in the German language at the present has small possibilities. The only exception are the Germans from Austria and other countries; there are possibilities among them in some of our large cities.

Much more compelling is the need of German missions in Canada. Here the missionary possibilities are such that they challenge the Church. The territory of the Manitoba Synod is still virgin soil; in its present form it dates back only 30 years, for Saskatchewan and Alberta were taken into the Dominion only in 1905. Our work out there began six years earlier when our first missionary, Pastor Henry C. Schmieder, was sent to Winnipeg. Though from that date our Church has been on the field, the work has never received the necessary attention and care. A small group has been trying ever since to awaken the Church to this great task, but their efforts have been like a voice crying in the wilderness. It is true that for many years the appeal was made almost exclusively to the German part of the Church. Consequently the support of the work was entirely inadequate. In spite of the frantic efforts of the men in charge, one field after the other had to be abandoned for lack of men and means. What could have been a great harvest had become an anxious effort to save and conserve what we had. A new era began when the United Lutheran Church was organized. The work received new inspiration and was conducted with renewed vigor. With the advent of the Board of American Missions it became the object of careful and systematic planning and a more liberal support. It has become more generally known in the English-speaking part of the Church, and the liberal support of special objects, which has come from readers of *The Lutheran* bears testimony to the fact that the knowledge of this field and the interest in this work is constantly growing.

But it is still far from getting the attention which it deserves. Few people realize that the territory of the Manitoba Synod covers an area equal to one third of the entire United States; that the field is 1,600 miles long and from 400 to 500 miles wide; that there are still close to 200,000 Lutherans unchurched, not indifferent ones, but people longing for the Church and hungry for the Word; that while the population of Canada has increased 18 per cent during the last decade, the increase among Lutherans has been 37 per cent. There is every evidence that Canada will open its doors to immigration again, so that we can expect great additions to the above figures. In the United States we have eight Synods at work on a territory corresponding in size to that of the Manitoba Synod on which the Church has been spending $60,000 per year. If that is taken into comparison with the $20,000 spent on the Manitoba Synod field, the inadequacy of the present support can be readily seen. Another factor is the newness of the field, and the fact that the Synod has only 24 self-supporting parishes compared to 31 mission parishes. If we consider that the Missouri Synod is putting $60,000 into this field, which in the beginning was undisputedly ours, it is evident that the greater evaluation and vision has not been ours. If we further consider that the only Lutheran Seminary in all Western Canada, that at Saskatoon, on which we must absolutely depend for the evangelization of this vast area has had to worry along for years without a president, and with only two professors in charge, we must ask: How long will the Church stand for such conditions?—how long before it will fill the hands of the Boards with the necessary means to do the work which the Lord has entrusted to our care?

During the biennium 13 German missions have become self-supporting and one was merged with a neighboring congregation. Four missions were transferred to the English department. New parishes were organized in Northmark, Alta. (German); Patience, Alta. (German); Deer Ridge, Sask. (English-Norwegian); Lipton, Sask. (German); Woodhill, Sask. (German-English); Valbrand, Sask. (English-Norwegian); Snowflake,

Man. (German-Lettish); Blind River, Ont. (German-English); and the Maritimes parish, Nova Scotia—New Brunswick (German-Danish). A number of congregations were added to existing parishes.

We are exceedingly grateful to a large number of friends who, through special contributions, have assisted in the erection of 27 churches and 15 parsonages during the past 5 years. The Women's Missionary Society has again come to our aid in many ways, particularly by providing much needed transportation for some of our missionaries. We are grateful to the many friends who have contributed clothing for the sufferers in Canada as well as to those who attended to the collection and shipping; also to St. John's Lutheran Church, Reading, Pa., Rev. Robert Ischinger, Pastor, which has again contributed part of a missionary's salary; also to *The Lutheran* and the *Lutherische Herold* for giving such splendid publicity.

2. FINNISH MISSIONS

Since taking full charge of the Finnish mission work in Canada the work has grown rapidly. This year we had the joy of seeing the first of our Finnish missions becoming self-supporting. Wuoristo Finnish Lutheran Church of Copper Cliff, Ontario, decided to make a special effort to remove whatever obstacles that stood in the way of self-support, in order that the money received as salary aid would become available for the expansion of Finnish work elsewhere. They have succeeded, and since the first of the year they manage to get along without aid. No doubt, their example will have a good effect on the other missions and stimulate their efforts. Our church in Montreal has continued in its wonderful growth; St. Mary's Sault Ste. Marie, has grown much stronger; the same is true of St. John's, New Finnland, Sask., where the pastor has succeeded in uniting divided forces and started English services for the second generation. The Kirkland Lake congregation has erected a modest house of worship. A new and vigorous mission was organized at South Porcupine, Ontario. The vacant Alberta parish has erected a parsonage. We expect to find a way in which the Finns of British Columbia can be supplied with services in their own language, and if finances permit, we will extend our work in the Thunder Bay district, the most populous Finnish district in Ontario. We have good hopes of finding a suitable pastor for the vacant Toronto congregation.—Our Finnish brethren now have their own church paper, the "Isien Usko"—"Faith of the Fathers," which is to be a bond of union among them and a valuable help in reaching the many scattered Finnish settlements.

This is the last year of our agreement with the Suomi Synod, according to which we assisted this Synod in the United States. Those who had hoped that co-operation would eventually lead to organic union with the U. L. C. A. will be disappointed. All of us who are interested in the building of our Lutheran Zion will regret that the termination of our working agreement will still more cripple the Suomi Synod in its efforts to take care of the many unchurched Finns in this country. What small means this Synod can raise is wholly inadequate to the task. In a parting resolution, adopted at the January meeting, our Board declared its readiness "at any time to relieve them of part of their responsibility by taking over the Finnish work in the East, so that the Suomi Synod could concentrate all its efforts on the great mission fields in the middle and far west." We cannot escape the conviction that our Eastern Synods could much more effectively take care of the many Finns on their territory than the Suomi Synod with its limited means and its far removed center could ever hope to do.

3. Slovak Missions

The past decade has been a time of agitation among our Slovak brethren. A movement to combine all the Slovak congregations in America into one national Synod was set on foot. Representatives of congregations connected with the United Lutheran Church, the Synodical Conference, and Independents held a number of conferences, in which the question of merger was discussed. No differences of doctrine or practice seemed to be in the way; the conferees had drawn up and adopted articles of agreement; but when the matter came up before Zion Synod, the motion to merge was rejected almost unanimously. A number of considerations brought about this decision. One of the articles of agreement was that the Slovak Pastors and congregations should sever their connections not only with the Synodical Conference and the United Lutheran Church, but also with the church of the homeland, for which every Slovak has sincere love and respect. Other considerations which decided the issue were the altar and pulpit fellowship, which the U. L. C. A. keeps with the Lutheran Church of Slovakia; the many kindnesses which the Slovaks have received from the U. L. C. A.; the impossibility of leading all Slovak congregations into this union; the warning example of other nationalistic Synods, which through isolation have been condemned to sterility and impotence; their own financial weakness and the inability to finance the ambitious program of the agreement. Since this issue has been definitely buried, the Synod seems to have taken on a new lease of life. It has had an increase in very desirable membership, and seems to be imbued with a new missionary spirit.

Our Slovak missions are gradually emerging from the slump into which the economic maelstrom had dragged them. The Philadelphia-Camden-Pottstown mission was made self-supporting by the addition of the Trenton charge. The mission at Garfield assumed self-support. The mission at Guttenberg, N. J., has added a nice parsonage to its fine church building. The congregations at Newark and the Bronx are busy paying off their Church Extension loans. There are a number of vacant fields, particularly in Ohio, which will gradually be filled as our students graduate. The present state of the Slovak work is decidedly encouraging.

4. HUNGARIAN-WENDISH MISSIONS

The Hungarian work has not fared so well. There is a reason. While in the Slovak work we have had a sufficient supply of trained workers coming from our student body, the supply for the Hungarian work has always been insufficient. We had to import an able pastor from Hungary to fill the vacancy in Pittsburgh; another pastor, for our New York field, came to us from the Presbyterians. Our work in Akron, Ohio, had to be disbanded as the people were unwilling to bear their share of the burden. The long vacancy in Buffalo, N. Y., has been filled by a graduate from Waterloo Seminary. In our Hungarian missions in Canada the state of paralysis is gradually lifting; the people begin to realize their responsibility, and take a more active part in support of the work.

5. LETTISH-ESTONIAN-LITHUANIAN MISSIONS

While our Lettish work at present is in a dormant state, due to the lack of a strong leader, our Estonian friends have approached the Board with a definite challenge. They have held a number of well-attended meetings, and they have assured us of their fullest co-operation, if we would obtain for them the kind of pastor which they need. Since there are some 5,000 Estonians in the New York area, 85 per cent of them Lutherans, there seems to be a possibility for the establishment of a representative congregation. The same possibilities exist with the Letts, if only a real leader could be found who could contact their best people and retain their respect. These Baltic nations contain some of the very best Lutheran material and it would be a pity if they were not conserved to the Lutheran Church. Another attempt has been made to revive the work among the Lithuanians in Philadelphia. Since most of these Lithuanians have become thoroughly Americanized they should have no difficulty in affiliating with our English or German churches.

6. SCANDINAVIAN MISSIONS

For years missionary Weidenhammer has made occasional use of the Norwegian language in some of the missions in Northern Saskatchewan. One of his Scandinavian fields, that at Deer Ridge, has been organized into a parish; another one at Valbrand is ready for a Scandinavian Pastor. The mission at Flin Flon is largely Norwegian. A Norwegian field at Kipling, Ontario, is being occasionally served by one of our students from Waterloo Seminary. Regular Swedish services are being held at Noral, Alberta, by Pastor Schreiber, who acquired the Swedish language so as to be able to supply his field. There is a large Swedish constituency in the Kirkland Lake district, which we hope to supply in the near future. Our new missionary in Nova Scotia serves both the German and the Danish immigrants. There is great need for work among Scandinavians in Canada, and when larger means are at our disposal we will be able to go into this branch of the work with greater dispatch and vigor.

7. ITALIAN MISSIONS

Our mission among the Italians is still a problem. The work in New York with its large Italian population is not satisfactory; the work in Chicago, which was taken up again after being suspended for two years, makes little progress. The work in Philadelphia and Erie is holding its own. The idea of a Lutheran testimony to the Italians seems good in theory, but in practice the impress which the Lutheran Church is making on the Italian problem is negligible. There is no encouraging progress; the people seem to be very apathetic. We are not antagonistic to the work, but we must admit that the lack of success has created doubts. To our mind the only permanent solution of the problem lies in an increasing consciousness on the part of the local pastors of their responsibility in bringing the Gospel to all groups of people on their field, and gathering them into their churches. That would necessitate a complete revolution in our time-honored attitudes, but it would help to solve the tragic problem of the downtown church: large church buildings empty in the midst of teeming thousands of spiritually starved souls. The Board has appointed a committee to study the problem and make suggestions for a proper solution.

8. JEWISH MISSIONS

As a wave of anti-Semitism is sweeping over the world, the need of Christian testimony to Jews and Christians alike becomes all the more apparent. Though it cannot be denied that in many countries severe offense and provocation has been given by the activities of certain Jews, the condemning of all Jews, good and bad, for the sins of the few can never be defended. The pagan philosophy of soil, race and blood has a most dangerous tendency, which in the long run will threaten all races and religions, which happen to be in the minority. It is necessary, therefore, that the Church should give assurance to the Jew that God wants all men to be saved and to come to the knowledge of the truth, that in Christ all members of the Church, no matter of what racial extraction, are members of one body. It is also necessary that the Church should bear testimony to the Christians as to Israel's place in God's plan of salvation, and as to the duty of the Christian to win rather than suppress a race, which has made so many valuable contributions to human civilization. To bear such testimony to Jew and Gentile is the object of our Jewish mission. Though resented by many Jewish leaders, our efforts to bring Israel to the fullest realization of its calling are proof that we are not blinded by race prejudice, nor discouraged by certain traits in the Jewish character, which for centuries has brought down upon them the antagonism, if not the hatred, of the nations among whom they dwell.

Our Jewish missions have carried on their work with little change. The Baltimore mission has published the collection of Gospel hymns, in English and Yiddish, a welcome addition to Jewish Christian literature.

Our Pittsburgh mission has established a medical center with clinic under direction of Dr. Bravin, the missionary's wife and co-worker. The Philadelphia mission has extended its influence into New York State, and our Toledo mission also is looking for a wider sphere of influence in neighboring states. We recommend this work to the earnest prayers of the Church.

9. Linguistic Students

The necessity of training a linguistic ministry has long been recognized. Most of our failures in this field have been due to inability to secure the proper kind of pastors. For years the Board has been training men, but for the most part this effort was confined to men for the Slovak work. With the growing need in other groups the scope had to be continually widened. At the time of this writing the Board is supporting 15 students, seven Slovaks, two Finns, two Germans, one Wend, one Hungarian, one Lithuanian and one Norwegian. Realizing the importance of this work the Board appointed a committee to study the subject and to make suggestions. On the ground of the report of this committee the Board laid down its future policy. In suggesting a solution of the problem the report says: "There are two methods which would suggest themselves. The first would be to induce capable young men with good elementary education to come over here and be trained in our American institutions. The other, and perhaps, better way is to search our American congregations for young men with a good knowledge of a foreign language, educate them in College and Seminary, and then give them at least one year's postgraduate training in a country in which they can perfect themselves in the language and acquire the background for the work in which they are engaged. Our trouble in the past has been that the imported men often lacked in things American, while the American born was handicapped because he was not sufficiently familiar with the language, customs and traditions of the groups whom he desired to serve. Both methods would require a certain amount of money, but they would not be nearly as expensive as the establishment and maintenance of an exclusively linguistic school. It is all-important that especially in work among foreigners the pastor at least should be in full sympathy with American institutions, and well versed in American methods. But on the other hand he must also have an intimate knowledge of the character of his people, and of their historical background, if he is to do effective work."—The Board made a beginning by sending Otto Reble, son of the Rev. John Reble, D.D., for a one year's study in Leipzig University, part of his expense being borne by the Gustav Adolph Verein. One of our Slovak students took advantage of a scholarship offered him by the Czecho-Slovak government, and spent a useful year of study in that country. The time will not be long in coming when we shall be faced with a strong demand for pastors who can satisfy our German American congregations. We have no institution in the United States at present where such men can be trained. We hope that under this new policy we will be able to supply the Church's needs.

> As laborers in Thy vineyard, Lord, send them out to be
> Content to bear the burden of weary days for Thee;
> To ask no other wages when Thou shalt call them home,
> But to have shared the travail which makes Thy Kingdom come.

LATIN AMERICA

The past biennium in the West Indies has been marked by a solid growth that was not anticipated since the economic and political changes taking place in the Islands were such as would discourage any expectation of development. The seed sowing by faithful missionaries for more than a quarter of a century is bearing fruit and the growing number of earnest church members, whom the turmoil of civic life cannot move from their faith, gives hope for a strong native church.

Considerable illness among the missionary staff influenced the situation to a certain degree, but the missionaries cheerfully shared the additional burdens and so the work continued without interruption. The changes in personnel were no greater than the average for a tropical country where it is difficult for missionaries from the States to stand the physical strain. The vacancy in the Christiansted parish was filled by the Rev. Viggo Mengers, from Boston, who with his wife took up the work in St. Croix. Pastor Mengers having full command of both the Danish and English language, is well qualified for the task confronting him. Clerk Carl Francis, for many years in charge of the station on the little Island of St. John, and who was looked up to as a father in things temporal as well as spiritual by the people in this primitive Island, has been compelled to give up his work because of the infirmities of advancing age. Pastor Eugene Kreider resigned the Frederiksted Parish to accept a call to the States to provide for his children's education. His place was filled by the Rev. Jens Larsen, who with his family entered upon the work December, 1935. Pastor Larsen was at one time a missionary in Africa and for several years thereafter was in charge of our mission at Brookfield, Illinois. He joyfully entered upon the work among a race to which he had originally dedicated his ministry. Pastor Larsen has an excellent command of the Danish language and a sympathetic understanding of the people's history.

The missionary staff in Puerto Rico lost one ordained minister through one of the native pastors demitting the ministry by request. The vacant congregation was provided with the means of grace by a careful readjustment of the parishes. Happily for the future of this field, two young men from the churches in Puerto Rico, graduates of the University of Puerto Rico, are now in the theological seminary at Mount Airy. During their vacation they have been giving valuable assistance on the field.

During the biennium a new plan was tried whereby a seminary graduate was given a year's practical training on the field. During this period he assists our over-burdened missionaries while gaining valuable experience for himself. The Rev. L. H. Fox was the first to act in this capacity and his labors have been so highly successful that the plan will be continued annually.

WORKS OF MERCY—The three Deaconesses in the Virgin Islands and the Registered Nurse in Puerto Rico have accomplished a blessed work of service among the poor and distressed in our mission parishes. Deaconess Sister Maren Knudsen, from the Motherhouse in Copenhagen, Denmark, has had complete charge of the work among the sick and neglected babies in St. Croix with her headquarters in the home at Christiansted. Deaconesses Sister Emma Francis and Sister Edith Prince, from the Mary J. Drexel Motherhouse at Philadelphia, have carried on the work among the children in Frederiksted, Sister Edith giving her time chiefly to the kindergarten work and Sister Emma, although hampered by her increasing illness, has been in charge of the Girls' Orphanage. Miss Frieda M. Hoh, R.N., has labored most successfully among the poor and neglected and the sick in Puerto Rico. Mrs. E. Roig, the wife of our missionary in Monteflores, has done valued service in assisting in securing emergency employment for the women, some of whose products have been sold through the Women's Missionary Society in the States. Miss Carmen Villarini, a registered teacher of the public schools of Puerto Rico, has given full-time service to the supervision of the kindergarten work in our many missions in Puerto Rico and has complete charge of the training of the teachers not only in the kindergartens, but also of those who teach in the Sunday schools.

THE SPANISH HYMNAL AND COMMON SERVICE BOOK—After years of painstaking effort the manuscript for the Common Service Book and Hymnal in Spanish was presented to the Committee on Common Service Book and arrangements are being made for the printing of the same at the earliest possible date. This book will be a greater factor in unifying our Lutheran work among Spanish-speaking people than anything yet accomplished. It is confidently expected that the book will have a large sale among all Spanish-speaking Protestants.

SPANISH WORK IN NEW YORK—While the Spanish congregation in New York City is a member of the United Synod of New York, it has been customary to report this work in this division because of its original connection with the West Indies. Missionary Soler and his capable wife have met with unusual success in developing one of the strongest and most respected Protestant Spanish congregations in New York City. The congregation is working under a very severe handicap in not having a church property of its own.

WORK AMONG THE NEGROES—This field of endeavor is also reported under the division of Latin America because the first work of this character was established through the emigration of Lutheran colored people from the Virgin Islands. Two congregations are now working successfully in Greater New York. The one, the Church of the Transfiguration, under Missionary West, is the mother church, while the new work in Jamaica, L. I., is going forward under Missionary Routte. In addition to the regular adult classes, a class of children is confirmed each Palm Sunday and the growth of the Church of the Transfiguration is shown by the regular confirmation service this year when forty-three children were confirmed. The service was held in St. Paul's German Church in the presence of almost a thousand colored people.

There is no question about the appeal of the Lutheran Church to the colored people of America nor is there any doubt about the great need that more work should be done, but it is impossible for any additional obligations to be undertaken as long as the receipts on apportionment are at so low a level that missionaries throughout North America already on the field are compelled to labor at salaries that frequently are not at the subsistence level.

AMERICAN INDIANS—The work among American Indians is for the present assigned to this division. The station at Rocky Boy Reservation, Montana, presided over by Missionary Gable and his family with the assistance of Miss Florence Buckner, has made progress. In addition to the regular Sunday services and Sunday school, the missionaries have maintained club work among the women, the boys and the girls at which meetings a Bible study is always conducted. A Light Brigade works successfully with the little children. A regular Women's Missionary Society has been organized and conducted in the same manner as in the established congregations. The Daily Vacation Bible School held for two weeks and a half during the month of July, as well as an Indian encampment on the grounds the week following have been wonderfully successful. During the past year the Rocky Boy Reservation has been enlarged by the government through the addition of some thirty thousand acres immediately to the west of our mission location. A similar addition will be made to the east in a short time. More than 120 families of homeless Indians have been established on this addition to the Reservation. This gives larger opportunity to our missionaries since this mission is the only one on the Reservation. One of the greatest needs of the present is literature in the Cree language. It is through the printed word in the language which they understand that the older Indians can best be reached.

WORK AMONG MEXICANS—Within the borders of the United States dwell more than a million Mexicans and other Latin Americans whose spiritual destitution appeals to zealous Christians. True, the laws of Mexico prohibit all but native pastors acting in the official administration of church work. However, these countless thousands are not in Mexico, but under the government of the United States where the church is still free to bring the Gospel to starving souls. This field of endeavor has been carefully surveyed by Missionary Arbaugh and although the problems of evangelization are many, the Board is ready to undertake the task whenever funds are made available.

WORK AMONG ORIENTALS—A request from the Synod of California to consider the sad condition of the thousands of Japanese on the Pacific Coast is being given serious consideration at this time. The prospects are that the way will soon be opened to do something in this neglected field of evangelization.

DEPARTMENT OF CHURCH EXTENSION AND FINANCE

By H. TORREY WALKER

The primary concern of the Department of Church Extension during the last biennium has been to conserve to the Church those congregations faced with dissolution because of the loss of their church properties through foreclosure proceedings. While many are still endangered, in view of the number of congregations involved, the number is small—only four congregations have actually suffered a loss of property thus far. Four others are now in bankruptcy having invoked Section 77B of the Bankruptcy Act. It has been the privilege of this Department to assist in refinancing and adjusting numerous financial problems during the period covered by the report.

While these measures are curative it has become necessary to take preventative care of congregations about to engage in construction programs. In addition to the standing rules requiring approval of plans by the Committee on Church Architecture and the submittal of financial information which are being rigidly enforced, the Board before granting any new Church Extension loan is asking for proof as to the ability of the congregation to carry the interest charges and amortization payments for prior liens. As a result of this the cost of mission construction is being limited to a reasonable estimate of the ability of the mission congregation to carry the indebtedness to be assumed. While not infallible it should prevent in a large measure the tragedy presented by congregations, which having assumed debts beyond their ability to pay, are compelled to center their program around "raising the interest money"—to the detriment of their primary function—seeking souls.

During this biennium it has been necessary, as in previous periods, to make some Church Extension loans in order to save missions which were endangered by foreclosure proceedings. Again and again situations have arisen indicating the fallacy of Church Councilmen and individuals endorsing congregational obligations—either promissory notes or the bond of a mortgage. This Board at its October meeting, 1935 reaffirmed its previous position as follows: "The Board has never approved endorsements by individuals for repayment of financial aid secured locally."

During the biennium the Board has adopted rules governing the amortization of Church Extension loans. These read as follows:

Group A: Standard Amortization Plan

As under the existing rule, first five years without interest, with a three year renewal at four per cent., with interest at two per cent on the outstanding balances at the end of the first five year period, and two per cent amortization, with increased interest rate after first extension.

Group B: Increased Amortization Plan

According to rule, first five years without interest, with a three year renewal upon agreement to pay ten per cent or more annually on the outstanding balance at the end of the first five year period.

Group C:

Congregations which claim to be unable to meet amortization payments under Groups A and B, and having submitted satisfactory proof of the same to the Board, may be permitted to renew Church Extension loans after the first five year period on an annual basis, and according to the circumstances, at the Board's option either—

a. Pay two per cent interest on the outstanding primary balance, or

b. If unable to pay even the interest charge, must give notes which will be so prepared as to add the same to the principal of the existing mortgage, and shall further provide that when amortization plans are elected, that payments under it shall be credited as to interest as if they had originally elected that plan, but all portions of payments which would under Groups A and B be credited to principal shall first be applied to the retirement of the interest notes.

Group D:

Into this Group will be placed all Church Extension loans in which it is useless to ask for notes as under Group C, b. That is, the financial condition of the congregation is such that it is hopelessly insolvent. These should be further classified into—

a. Those from which some portion of the principal sum can be salvaged,

b. Those which are total losses and will have to be written off in their entirety.

All congregations in this class shall regularly as requested submit full statement of their finances.

The acceptance of these plans by the congregations having Church Extension loans has been encouraging. The classifications are applied only after a full financial survey of the congregations and great care is being exercised in order not to work an undue hardship upon any congregation.

In view of the nature of the field in the Canadian Northwest, Dr. E. A. Tappert has throughout this biennium continued his splendid work of securing funds for the erection of churches in this field through interested individuals.

The total sum now invested in Church Extension loans is $1,664,108.21. There are 399 mission congregations being helped by these funds. The average loan is $4,170.69. Approximately 90 per cent of these loans are for $5,000 or less.

These funds are at work in every section of the Church—14.1 per cent in the Southern States, 26.2 per cent in the Middle Atlantic States, 22.8 per cent in the Mid-Western States, 32.5 per cent in Northwestern and Pacific Coast States and 4.4 per cent in Canada and the Maritime Provinces.

Additions to these funds are derived from three principal sources— the budget of the Women's Missionary Society, legacies and gifts, and from the Lenten Appeal. There is always a lack of sufficient money to answer the requests for loans. The response to the Lenten Appeal by the Church is limited and in view of the fact that this is the only general source of these funds, the receipts from apportionment being required for missionary support, it is extremely disheartening. Since funds derived from the Lenten Appeal are allocated to the territory of the Synod from which the funds are furnished or are reallocated to other fields at their request, it is difficult to understand the lethargy displayed.

Tribute should be paid to the consistent support of this essential part of the Home Mission enterprise by the Women's Missionary Society. The Women's Missionary Society has assisted very materially, not only by their annual budget contributions, but also by making available such balances as have remained from General Fund items for emergency funds to save desperate situations.

During this biennium the need of additional Church Extension funds has been increasingly manifest. Demands for funds to finance first mortgages particularly in areas in which interest rates of seven, eight and even nine per cent prevail are increasing. These demands can only be met by funds raised for this purpose. The 1934 Convention deferred action on the matter of an appeal for Church Extension funds in 1938 for consideration by this Convention. It is hoped that a decision will be reached which will not only enable this Board to complete its plans but also clear the way for other worthy causes of the Church desiring to make appeals of a similar nature.

Finances and Investments

The arduous labors of the Finance Committee in budget preparation have not been decreased by the nearly static condition of apportionment receipts during the biennium. To these have been added the almost impossible task of investing such trust funds as are available for investment in high grade securities which will show a fair return. Conscious of the necessity of investing these funds in a manner to safeguard the

Church from any criticism either of the character or the quality of the investment has caused many prolonged conferences and hours of careful thought.

The treasurer's report supplies a detailed statement of the financial position and progress of the Board during the biennium.

During the biennium, upon the recommendation of its Finance Committee, the Board decided to set aside, out of funds available for investment, the sum of $25,000 to be invested in First Mortgages on Mission Churches. The investments made from this fund have been used to take over First Mortgages on Mission Churches which had been held by banks or individuals, now financially embarrassed, and which banks or individuals had suggested a compromise settlement of fifty cents on the dollar or better. Practically all of this fund has been invested as of the date of this report. The Board feels gratified that the congregations borrowing these funds have strictly regarded their obligations to the Board by meeting their interest and amortization payments.

During the course of the biennium there have arisen a number of legal questions pertaining to the Church Extension loans made to congregations in the Dominion of Canada. Under the existing laws the Board is compelled to record such instruments in the name of an individual as trustee. Some now so recorded are in the names of individuals now deceased, and constant difficulty is being experienced because of this. After a careful study of the problem the Board has decided to ask the permission of the United Lutheran Church to seek a domestic charter under the same name in the Dominion of Canada.

It is, therefore, **recommended that the Board of American Missions be authorized to seek a domestic charter in the Dominion of Canada.**

Special Support

Keller Memorial, Washington, D. C., during the biennium paid the full amount of salary aid to a Home Missionary. The following congregations assisted in the support of Home Missionaries in this period—Redeemer, Buffalo, N. Y., Memorial, Harrisburg, Pa., Zion, Hummelstown, Pa., Trinity, Germantown, Pa., North Austin, Chicago, Ill., and St. John's, Reading, Pa., First Church, Richmond, Va.

RECOMMENDATIONS
(For action, see p. 184)

1. Recommended that approval be given to the addition to the Plan of Operation adopted by the Richmond Convention of a Divisional Committee on Survey and Research with duties as outlined in the body of this report.

2. Recommended that the Board of American Missions be authorized to seek a domestic charter in the Dominion of Canada.

HENRY W. A. HANSON, *President,*
HENRY F. HEUER, *Secretary,*
ZENAN M. CORBE, *Executive Secretary.*

BOARD OF AMERICAN MISSIONS
(Compiled by Board of American Missions)

Synods	No. of Parishes	No. of Congregations	No. of Missionaries and Workers	Membership — Confirmed	Membership — Sunday School	Appropriations — Salaries and Expenses	Appropriations — Interest	Appropriations — Loans Church Extension	Value of Property	Indebtedness	No. of Parsonages	Contributions — *Local Expense	Contributions — Benevolence
Alleghany				1,199	1,040	$17	$180	$15,820	$123,100	$37,395	2	$17,795	$1,444
California	11	11	11	3,101	1,217	5,768	250	23,074	199,662	65,372	10	27,051	2,280
Canada	23	29	23	3,721	3,479	14,320		46,140	594,022	292,372	12	45,560	5,643
East Pennsylvania	15	16	15	777	570	12,650		41,325	135,600	67,395	2	10,283	1,257
Florida	7	7	7	604	495	7,370	100	37,550	122,900	56,086	2	12,623	1,950
Georgia-Alabama	6	6	6	524	295	3,667		1,200	33,200	6,519	5	3,160	374
German Nebraska	5	6	5	3,756	3,262	1,021		75,816	481,760	286,113	9	38,618	4,025
Illinois	20	20	20	1,348	1,166	13,165	410	42,340	224,600	110,823	9	19,228	2,130
Indiana	10	10	10	527	352	5,384	900	5,470	45,034	12,560	1	4,442	343
Iowa	3	3	3	356	330	1,755		19,565	88,000	50,195	1	4,711	457
Kansas	3	3	3	588	537	2,978	294	12,500	57,190	24,630	1	13,112	877
Kentucky-Tennessee	5	5	5	4,068	1,504	2,195		25,193	124,425	38,579	1	10,835	1,182
Manitoba	29	56	29	2,614	2,172	18,760	4,132	36,875	437,800	187,539	22	39,015	2,335
Maryland	11	10	12	1,688	1,318	7,170	219	61,435	203,074	143,897	6	16,442	2,753
Michigan	11	11	11	681	519	7,560		2,035	46,600	6,355	3	6,317	786
Mississippi	5	11	11	748	540	3,000		5,600	38,150	6,222	4		1,163
Nebraska	6	6	5			1,727							
New York	62	72	62	10,474	7,789	34,437	2,998	99,698	978,533	464,705	17	129,493	6,922
North Carolina	18	33	20	2,614	2,816	11,493	617	23,720	378,375	58,034	13	26,036	3,160
Northwest	22	24	22	4,546	2,431	13,347	180	102,513	414,932	252,104	19	43,315	5,815
Nova Scotia	2	2	2	171	42	2,066		5,000	18,000	15,300	1	2,436	
Ohio	17	16	16	1,998	2,142	13,000		50,975	339,600	204,549	1	25,878	3,178
Pacific	17	18	16	2,546	1,748	11,338	425	54,558	224,250	110,414	7	24,915	2,277
Pennsylvania Ministerium	36	44	36	7,349	6,932	21,059		75,370	884,390	480,575	15	99,830	6,152
Pittsburgh	28	29	27	4,097	3,173	20,718		53,673	613,950	305,586	17	48,626	3,555
Rocky Mountain	7	7	7	938	774	3,644	366	5,000	177,700	101,549	3	11,915	1,408
Slovak Zion	3	6	3	593	269	1,573	750	36,950	89,500	27,122	1	11,393	1,651
South Carolina	9	15	9	1,160	1,004	5,103		5,000	103,934	9,600	3	8,904	294
Suomi	6	9	3	599	127	1,670		3,188	21,750	1,100	1	2,731	154
Susquehanna													
Texas	9	12	9	960	742	5,883	294	15,263	75,950	31,257	7	11,622	1,245
Virginia	14	26	12	2,772	2,916	8,277		20,000	220,740	35,120	8	21,340	3,455
Wartburg	6	6	6	1,262	638	4,020	150	12,250	72,875	40,003	1	11,318	829
Puerto Rico	9	14	17	872	1,934	19,513			153,002		10	3,286	159
Virgin Islands	3	5	6	1,262	747	11,781			156,700		5	4,888	1,009
West Pennsylvania	2	2	3	338	450	517			33,689		1	901	635
West Virginia	1	1	1	138	100	250			10,000			100	205
Rocky Boy Mission	1		3	30	85	3,879			13,625				
Totals	441	551	448	71,019	55,655	302,075	12,265	1,010,096	7,936,612	3,529,070	205	766,779	71,102
Loans and Interest Grants—No Salary Aid	160	147	139	46,404	30,863		1,895	655,304	7,218,663	2,880,147	93	593,128	67,338
Grand Total	601	698	587	117,423	86,518	302,075	14,160	1,665,400	15,155,275	6,409,217	298	1,359,907	138,440

*Includes both Current and Unusual Expenses.

REPORT OF THE TREASURER OF THE BOARD OF AMERICAN MISSIONS OF THE UNITED LUTHERAN CHURCH IN AMERICA

We have audited the books of account of The Board of American Missions of the United Lutheran Church in America for the fiscal year beginning July 1, 1934 and ending June 30, 1935, and we certify that in our opinion the Balance Sheet as of June 30, 1935 hereto attached correctly sets forth the fiscal position of The Board of American Missions on that date, and the Consolidated Statement of Receipts and Disbursements for the year under audit, hereto attached contains all receipts from apportionment, contributions, and other income as recorded in the books of account, the accounting for these having been duly and properly made, and that all disbursements appearing therein were supported by proper vouchers.

TAIT, WELLER, AND BAKER.

BALANCE SHEET AT June 30, 1935

ASSETS

Cash		$ 51,859.22
Securities owned at Ledger Values:		
Bonds	$319,059.64	
Stock	17,880.89	
Investment Notes	2,180.00	
Savings Bank Account	52,743.75	
		391,864.28
Advanced Expenses		525.00
Advanced a/c Estates		86.82
Loans to Churches:		
Board Loans	1,436,781.85	
Agency Loans	214,204.25	
		1,650,986.10
Real Estate and Buildings:		
Owned and Held by Board	392,137.58	
Held as Agent	25,670.00	
		417,807.58
Equipment and Furniture		5,993.86
Accounts Receivable (Synods)		8,200.00
		2,527,322.86

LIABILITIES

Loans Payable	17,200.00	
Mortgage Payable	20,000.00	
Advanced by Women's Missionary Society	7,320.13	
		44,520.13
		2,482,802.73

FUNDS

General Funds:		
Missions	139,063.03	
Church Extension	340,931.44	
		479,994.47

Endowment Funds:
Missions	45,379.93	
Church Extension	14,384.62	
		59,764.55
Permanent Loan Fund		1,289,424.90
Memorial Loan Fund		152,522.07
Restricted Funds		61,544.24
McMurray Trust Fund		23,743.29
Annuity Funds		51,801.56

Designated Gifts and Special Funds:
Missions		30,694.02
Church Extension		93,439.38

Agency Funds:
Church Extension Society New York Conference, Ministerium of New York	3,000.00	
Women's Missionary Society	211,204.25	
Sundry Churches	25,670.00	
		239,874.25
		2,482,802.73

CONSOLIDATED STATEMENT RECEIPTS AND DISBURSEMENTS

Year ended June 30, 1935

RECEIPTS

United Lutheran Church on Apportionment		342,980.00

Women's Missionary Society:
On Budget	61,168.92	
Designated Gifts	931.07	
		62,099.99

Contributions:
Synodical Missions		8,012.36
Individuals, congregations, societies		13,943.96
Bequests		8,167.35
Designated Gifts and Special Funds		1,942.04
Income on Investments		11,602.78
Real Estate and Sales Contracts		150.00
Proceeds maturity and sale of Securities		120,453.68
Withdrawals from Savings Fund account		8,500.00
Annuity		1,000.00
Repaid on Church Extension Loans		13,828.32
Repaid on Class B Securities		4,043.92
		596,724.40

DISBURSEMENTS

Loans to Churches	$ 36,380.00
Interest Grants to Churches	12,358.67
Salaries of Missionaries and Field Men	302,079.87
Expenses of Missionaries and Field Men	10,504.38
Seminary Student Aid	2,235.22
Charitable Work in the Virgin Islands	3,326.02
Payments to Annuitants	4,618.25
Interest on Loans and Mortgage	2,011.00

Designated Gifts transmitted	2,902.51
Church Buildings in Canadian Northwest	2,560.00
Purchase of Equipment	339.41
Real Estate Maintenance	3,117.68
Securities purchased	130,005.50
Invested in Savings Fund account	39,943.75
Accrued interest on securities purchased	333.60
Officers' Salaries and Expenses	6,135.88
Administrative and Office Expense	10,926.97
	569,778.71

Consolidated Summary

Balance, July 1, 1934	$ 24,913.53
Receipts for year	596,724.40
	621,637.93
Disbursements for year	569,778.71
	51,859.22

S. FREDERICK TELLEEN, *Treasurer.*

BALANCE SHEET AT June 30, 1936

ASSETS

Cash		$ 28,343.16
Securities owned at Ledger Values:		
Bonds	$359,742.57	
Stock	17,880.89	
Savings Bank Accounts	109,043.75	
		486,667.21
Advanced Expenses		525.00
Advanced a/c Estates		86.82
Loans to Churches:		
Board Loans	1,423,400.96	
First Mortgage Loans	23,963.00	
Investment Notes	1,680.00	
Agency Loans	216,744.25	
		1,665.788.21
Real Estate and Buildings:		
Owned and held by Board	384,651.75	
Held as Agent	25,670.00	
		410,321.75
Equipment and Furniture		5,609.22
Accounts Receivable		8,297.50
		2,605,638.87

LIABILITIES

Loans Payable	14,700.00	
Mortgage Payable	20,000.00	
Held for Women's Missionary Society	6,397.28	
		41,097.28
		2,564,541.59

FUNDS

General Funds:
Missions	46,183.89	
Church Extension	335,560.97	
		381,744.86

Endowment Funds:
Missions	47,052.83	
Church Extension	14,951.92	
		62,004.75

Permanent Loan Fund	1,255,376.50
Memorial Loan Fund	166,881.50
Restricted Funds	71,641.34
McMurray Fund	23,427.97
Annuity Funds	46,594.55
Designated Gifts and Special Funds:	
Missions	37,858.71
Church Extension	117,741.98
Reserve for Guaranteed Annual Synodical Budgets	145,462.11

Agency Funds:
Women's Missionary Society	230,137.32	
Sundry Churches	25,670.00	
		255,807.32
		2,564,541.59

CONSOLIDATED STATEMENT RECEIPTS AND DISBURSEMENTS
Year ended June 30, 1936
RECEIPTS

United Lutheran Church on Apportionment		$353,372.00
Women's Missionary Society:		
on Budget	$61,089.00	
Designated Gifts	6,577.75	
		67,666.75

Contributions:
Synodical Missions	13,242.31
Individuals, Congregations, Sunday Schools, etc.	17,469.26
Bequests	30,622.76
Designated Gifts and Special Funds	1,693.24
Income on Investments	13,907.33
Real Estate Sales	870.83
Proceeds maturity and sale of Securities	134,153.15
Annuity	1,000.00
Repaid on Church Extension Loans	12,417.49
Interest on Church Extension Loans	281.84
Repaid on Class B Securities	100.00
Departmental Transfers	25,547.69
	. 672,344.65

DISBURSEMENTS

Loans to Churches	62,588.00
Interest Grants to Churches	8,715.72
Salaries of Missionaries and Field Men	302,959.70
Expenses of Missionaries and Field Men	20,926.71
Seminary and Student Aid	2,947.80
Charitable Work in the Virgin Islands	3,275.00
Payments to Annuitants	3,879.00
Interest on Loans and Mortgages	1,988.08
Designated Gifts transmitted	4,232.47
Church Buildings in Canadian Northwest	2,800.00
Purchase of Equipment	319.56
Real Estate Maintenance	2,783.66
Securities purchased	175,226.68
Invested in Savings Fund accounts	56,300.00
Accrued interest on securities purchased	802.97
Repaid on Loans	2,500.00
Officers' Salaries and Expenses	6,957.40
Administrative and Office Expense	11,110.27
Departmental Transfers	25,547.69
	695,860.71

Consolidated Summary:

Balance, July 1, 1935	$ 51,859.22
Receipts for year	672,344.65
	724,203.87
Disbursements for year	695,860.71
Balance, June 30, 1936	28,343.16

H. TORREY WALKER, *Treasurer*

CERTIFICATE OF AUDIT

We have audited the books of account of The Board of American Missions of the United Lutheran Church in America for the fiscal year beginning July 1, 1935, and ending June 30, 1936, and we certify that in our opinion the Balance Sheet as of June 30, 1936, hereto attached correctly sets forth the fiscal position of The Board of American Missions on that date, and the Consolidated Statement of Receipts and Disbursements for the year under audit, hereto attached, contains all receipts from apportionment, contributions, and other income, as recorded in the books of account, the accounting for these having been duly and properly made, and that all disbursements appearing therein were supported by proper vouchers. All securities on hand at June 30, 1936, were either examined by us or otherwise properly accounted for.

TAIT, WELLER AND BAKER.

CASH RECEIPTS AND DISBURSEMENTS
July 1, 1935, to June 30, 1936
MISSIONS ACCOUNTS
RECEIPTS

United Lutheran Church on Apportionment		353,372.00
Women's Missionary Society:		
on Budget	$52,809.00	
Designated Gifts	5,152.75	
Konnarock School	1,425.00	
		59,386.75
Contributions:		
For Synodical Missions		13,242.31
Individuals, congregations, etc.		9,883.94
Interest, Dividends and Premiums		4,681.30
Designated Gifts and Specials		1,043.24
Repaid on Special Loan		500.00
Brotherhood of U. L. C. A. for Iron Mt. School		350.00
Proceeds maturity and sale of Securities		94,900.00
Total		$537,359.54

DISBURSEMENTS

Missionaries' Salaries		288,559.70
Missionaries' Expenses		
General	7,604.62	
Moving	3,175.93	
Furlough	1,550.00	
		12,330.55
Field Staff Salaries		10,400.00
Clerical Salaries		1,248.00
Field Staff Expenses		2,768.82
Canvassers' Salaries and Expenses		857.05
Seminary and Student Aid		2,947.80
Charitable Work in the Virgin Islands		3,275.00
Interest Grants		8,368.22
Special Grant		97.50
Designated Gifts transmitted		1,253.40
Konnarock School		1,425.00
Iron Mountain School		364.00
Churches and Parsonages in Canada		2,800.00
Relief and Transportation in Canada		1,147.49
Securities purchased		150,989.18
Accrued interest and commission on purchases		609.69
Invested in Savings Fund accounts		30,000.00
Departmental Transfers		25,547.69
Total		$544,989.09

CHURCH EXTENSION ACCOUNTS
RECEIPTS

Bequests	$ 30,622.76
Annuities	1,000.00

Contributions: Individuals, congregations, Sunday Schools	7,585.32
Women's Missionary Society: Budget for Loans	8,280.00
Income on Investments	9,226.03
Proceeds from sale of Real Estate	870.83
Maturity of Class B Securities	100.00
Proceeds Maturity and Sale of Securities	39,253.15
East Pennsylvania Synod: Reformation Church Fund	300.00
Interest on Church Extension Loans	281.84

Repaid on Principal of Church Extension Loans:

on Loan Funds	$11,032.49	
on Agency Funds	760.00	
on Annuity Funds	125.00	
		11,917.49
Departmental Transfers		25,547.69
Total		134,985.11

DISBURSEMENTS

Loans to Churches:

from Loan Funds	32,700.00	
from Agency Funds	6,300.00	
from Annuity Funds	21,400.00	
from Special Funds	2,188.00	
		62,588.00
Equipment purchased		319.56
Real Estate Maintenance		2,333.34
McMurray Estate Expenses		450.32
Special Grant from a/c of W. M. S.		250.00
Interest on Loans and Mortgage		1,988.08
Repaid on Principal of Loan		2,500.00
Payments to Annuitants		3,879.00
Review and Care of Securities		440.77
Legal Expenses and Bank Charges		67.48
Field Staff Salaries		4,000.00
Clerical Salaries		1,040.00
Field Staff Expenses		2,682.29
Transmission of Special Gifts		42.58
Securities purchased		24,237.50
Accrued interest and commission on purchases		193.28
Invested in Savings Fund accounts		26,300.00
		133,312.20

ADMINISTRATION

DISBURSEMENTS

Office Supplies and Expenses	$	408.26
Telephone and Telegrams		147.10
Contribution to Lutheran Church House		1,628.00
General Expenses: Postage, Insurance, Bonds, etc.		782.32
Auditing		500.00
Contributions: Interdenominational		200.00
Publicity		1,871.35
Salaries: Executive Secretary Corbe		4,000.00

Assistant Executive Secretary Kirsch	1,600.00
Clerical Help	2,768.25
Expenses of Officers	1,357.40
Expenses of Board and Committee Meetings	2,296.74
	17,559.42

SUMMARY OF CASH RECEIPTS AND DISBURSEMENTS

July 1, 1935. Balance on Hand		51,859.22
Receipts		
Missions	$537,359.54	
Church Extension	134,985.11	
		672,344.65
		724,203.87
Disbursements		
Missions	544,989.09	
Church Extension	133,312.20	
Administration	17,559.42	
		695,860.71
June 30, 1936. Balance on Hand		28,343.16

MISSIONS BALANCE SHEET, June 30, 1936

ASSETS		LIABILITIES AND FUNDS	
Cash in		Designated Gifts and	
General Fund	$ 1,682.85	Special Funds	14,837.01
Endowment Fund	1,601.95	General Funds	46,183.89
Designated Gifts	6,239.51	Reserve for Guaran-	
Harroway Fund	164.12	teed Annual Synod-	
Kaercher Fund	1,062.58	ical Budgets	145,462.11
		Endowment Fund	47,052.83
	10, 751.01	Harroway Fund	10,731.62
Bonds	207,436.68	Kaercher Fund	12,290.08
Stocks	3,520.88	Women's Missionary	
Advanced Expenses	525.00	Society	6,397.28
Savings Funds a/cs	58,943.75		
Accounts Receivable	97.50		282,954.82
Loans to Churches	1,680.00		
	282,954.82		

SECURITIES IN MISSIONS FUND ACCOUNTS

Bonds	Book Value	Market Value 6-30-36
10,000 C. R. I. and P. 1st and Ref. 4, 1934	9,900.00	1,650.00
1,500 B. and O. 1st Mtge. 4s 1948	1,500.00	1,590.00
10,000 B. and O. P. and L. E. 4s 1941	9,450.00	10,262.50
4,000 Lehigh Valley Genl. 4½s 2003	4,000.00	2,035.00
7,000 C. B. and Q. 4s 1958	6,597.50	7,910.00
1,000 Metropolitan Edison 4½s 1968	1,000.00	1,086.25

2,000 St. Louis Co. Gas 1st 5s 1951	2,000.00	2,145.00
10,000 New York City 6s 1937	10,000.00	10,225.00
2,000 Westchester County 6s 1950	2,000.00	2,067.50
5,000 U. S. Treasury Notes 4¼s—3¼ 43-45	5,000.00	5,395.31
5,000 Armour and Co. 1st Mtge. 4½s 1939	5,000.00	5,212.50
100,000 U. S. Treasury Bills 1936	100,000.00	100,000.00
5,000 Great Northern R. R. 4s 1946	5,037.50	5,762.50
5,000 Consumers Power Co. 3½s 1970	5,175.00	5,206.25
13,000 U. S. Treasury Bonds 2¾ s 48-51	13,000.00	13,227.50
5,000 Dominion of Canada 2½s 1945	4,862.50	4,962.50
5,000 Dominion of Canada 3s 1955	4,937.50	5,031.25
5,000 Penna. R. R. Co. 2¾s 1946	4,976.68	5,062.50
5,000 Chesapeake and Ohio 4s 1945	5,000.00	5,025.00
8,000 Northwestern Refrig. 5s 1939	8,000.00	8,060.00
	207,436.68	201,916.56
88 shares York Trust Co.	3,520.88	1,496.00

CHURCH EXTENSION BALANCE SHEET, June 30, 1936

ASSETS		LIABILITIES AND FUNDS	
Cash in		Mortgage Payable	20,000.00
General Fund		Loans Payable	14,700.00
Permanent Loan		General Fund	335,560.97
Fund	691.79	Permanent Loan	
Memorial Loan Fund	414.05	Fund	1,255,376.50
Endowment Fund	383.17	Memorial Loan Fund ..	166,881.50
Restricted Funds	391.15	Endowment Fund	14,951.92
McMurray Fund	250.32	Restricted Funds	71,641.34
Annuity Funds	475.95	McMurray Trust Fund.	23,427.97
Special Funds	320.70	Annuity Funds	46,594.55
Omnibus Investment		Designated Gifts	347.86
A/C	924.09	Special Funds	117,394.12
Agency A/C W. M. S.	13,393.07	*Agency Funds*	
Designated Gifts	347.86	Women's Missionary	
		Society	230,137.32
	17,592.15	St. Luke's, York, Pa. ..	25,000.00
Savings Fund a/cs	50,100.00	Harmony Grove, Pa.	500.00
Bonds	152,305.89	Cly, Pa.	170.00
Stocks	14,360.01		
Loans to Churches:			
Board Loans	1,423,400.96		
First Mtge.	23,963.00		
Agency Loans	216,744.25		
Real Estate	384,651.75		
Equipment & Furn.	5,609.22		
Due from Synods	8,200.00		
Advances a/c Estates ..	86.82		
Agency Real Estate	25,670.00		
Total	2,322,684.05	Total	2,322,684.05

SECURITIES IN CHURCH EXTENSION FUND ACCOUNTS

Bonds	Book Value	Market Value 6-30-36
10,000 New York City 6s 1937	10,000.00	10,225.00
11,000 Westchester County 6s 1950	11,000.00	14,341.25
2,000 Westchester County 6s 1953	2,000.00	2,677.50
15,000 Nassau County 6s 1937	15,000.00	15,450.00
5,000 N. O. Tex. and Mex. 1st 5s 1954	5,005.00	1,825.00
5,000 L. and N. 1st and Ref. 4½s 2003	5,100.00	5,375.00
15,000 L. and N Unified 4s 1940	14,580.00	16,218.75
5,000 Illinois Central 4s 1955	4,743.75	4,243.75
3,000 El and Peoples Tract 4s 1945	1,875.00	375.00
2,000 St. Louis Spr. and P. 5s 1939	2,000.00	1,935.00
1,000 Howard Gas and Coal 6s 1937	1,000.00	
4,000 Metropolitan Edison 4½s 1968	4,000.00	4,345.00
10,000 Canadian Pacific Eq. 4½s 1941	9,892.00	10,950.00
500 B and O. 1st Mtge. 4s 1948	500.00	530.00
5,000 B. and O. 1st Mtge. 4s 1948	5,285.00	5,631.25
6,000 Southern Pacific 4s 1955	5,692.50	6,337.50
1,000 Jeff. and Placq. Dr. Dist. 5s 1949	1,000.00	160.00
5,000 C. and N. W. 1st and Ref. 5s 2037	5,303.75	1,050.00
2,000 City of Cincinnati Con. 3½ s 1952	1,970.00	2,000.00
1,000 City of Cincinnati Ref. 4s 1960	1,000.00	1,085.00
5,000 Ala. Prd. Co. 1st Mtge. 5s 1956	5,131.25	4,950.00
5,000 Pa. R. R. Genl. Mtge. 4½s 1965	5,043.75	5,625.00
1,000 L. V. R. R. Genl. Cons. 4s 2003	1,000.00	477.50
5,000 Phila. Electric Co. 4s 1971	4,946.39	5,262.50
5,000 Armour and Co. R. E. Mtge. 4½s 1939	5,000.00	5,212.50
10,000 Pa. R. R. Genl. 3¾s 1970	9,887.50	10,125.00
5,000 York Ice Mach. Corp. 6s 1947	4,575.00	4,937.50
5,000 Dominion of Canada 2½s 1945	4,775.00	4,962.50
5,000 Penn Central Lt. and Pr. 4½s 1977	5,000.00	5,212.50
	152,305.89	151,520.00

Stocks		
18 Integrity Trust Co., Phila	3,520.01	117.00
40 Fidelity T. and T., Pittsburgh	3,250.00	3,400.00
45 Cincinnati G and El. 5% A. Pref.	4,140.00	4,770.00
6 Dayton and Michigan Ry. 8% Pref.	390.00	603.00
14 First National Bank of Cincinnati	1,960.00	2,128.00
11 Little Miami R. R. Par 50	737.00	1,122.00
11 Little Miami Spec. Guar. Bet. Par. 50	363.00	539.00
	14,360.01	12,679.00

REAL ESTATE OWNED
June 30, 1936
In United States and Canada

Property, 74 West 126th Street, New York, N. Y.	$43,000.00
McMurray Estate, Commercial Street, Waterloo, Ia.	20,000.00
Aspen, Colorado	50.00

David City, Nebraska	50.00
Martindale, Nebraska	10.00
Colorado City, Colorado	10.00
Lewisburg, Pennsylvania	3,700.00
York Haven, Pennsylvania	150.00
Sylvan Lake, Alberta, Canada	540.00
	67,510.00

In the Virgin Islands

* Church at St. Thomas	$37,000.00
* Parsonage at St. Thomas	7,600.00
* Parish House at St. Thomas	3,600.00
* Church at Christiansted, St. Croix	37,000.00
* Parsonage at Christiansted,	7,600.00
* Administration Bldgs. and Cottages, Christiansted	1,600.00
† Children's Home, Christiansted	7,000.00
* Church at Frederiksted, St. Croix	22,600.00
* Parsonage at Frederiksted	3,600.00
* Parish House at Frederiksted	3,200.00
† Children's Home, at Frederiksted	5,000.00
† Ebenezer Orphanage at Frederiksted	13,000.00
* Church at St. John's	1,400.00
* Church at Kingshill, St. Croix	3,600.00
	153,800.00

* Property held under protection of Treaty between the
United States and Denmark
† Title held by the West Indies Mission Board

* In Puerto Rico

Church, Puerta de Tierra	$26,600.00
Property, 14 Lutz Street, Santurce	3,700.00
Parsonage, Gertrudis Street, Santurce	5,300.00
Chapel, Dorado	2,700.00
Parsonage, Dorado	1,250.00
Church, Bayamon	9,600.00
Sunday School Building, Bayamon	6,200.00
Parsonage, Bayamon	7,250.00
Villa Betania, Bayamon	8,700.00
Church, Comerio Street, Bayamon	8,700.00
Sunday School Building, Comerio Street, Bayamon	2,500.00
Church, Catano	7,100.00
Sunday School Building, Catano	4,500.00
Parsonage, Catano	1,150.00
Church, Parsonage and Lot, Palo Seco	3,300.00
Lot, Palo Seco	56.75
Training School, Parsonage and Chapel, Monte Flores	34,800.00
Church, Monacillo	3,600.00
Chapel, Maracayo	450.00
Chapel and Parsonage, Gandul	3,100.00
Chapel, Juan Domingo	270.00

Church, Toa Baja	5,600.00
Parsonage and Lot, Toa Baja	3,100.00
Chapel, Higuillar	450.00
	149,976.75

* All titles held by West Indies Mission Board

Rocky Boy, Montana

Indian Help House	400.00
Light Plant	800.00
Mission House	5,300.00
Chapel	965.00
Barn and Livestock	500.00
Parsonage	5,400.00
	13,365.00

Buildings at Rocky Boy Indian Reservation, erected by Board, revert to the United States Government should work be abandoned.

Total Real Estate

In United States and Canada	$ 67,510.00
In the Virgin Islands	153,800.00
In Puerto Rico	149,976.75
In Rocky Boy Indian Reservation	13,365.00
	384,651.75

Equipment Owned
June 30, 1936

Philadelphia Office	265.17
New York Office	1,117.50
Chicago Office	848.25
Harlem, New York City	30.00
Puerto Rico Parsonages	1,450.34
Virgin Islands Parsonages and Homes	997.96
Rocky Boy Indian Reservation, Montana	900.00
	5,609.22

LOANS TO CHURCHES

Synod	Amount
California	$ 40,922.00
Canada	28,423.72
North Carolina	32,720.75
South Carolina	3,244.75
Florida	56,325.00
Georgia-Alabama	37,550.00
Illinois	155,693.12
Indiana	49,015.00
Iowa	41,394.82
Kansas	35,300.00
Kentucky-Tennessee	12,500.00
Manitoba	37,705.00
Maryland	46,790.25

Michigan	95,521.68
Mississippi	2,122.35
Nebraska	31,236.32
German Nebraska	3,700.00
New York	183,712.50
Northwest	216,729.13
Nova Scotia	5,000.00
Ohio	96,458.33
Pacific	82,457.50
East Pennsylvania	70,800.37
Ministerium of Pennsylvania	97,095.50
Susquehanna	1,000.00
Pittsburgh	72,395.00
Rocky Mountain	46,962.42
Slovak Zion	16,475.00
Texas	15,262.70
Virginia	25,300.00
West Virginia	6,000.00
Wartburg	19,975.00
	1,665,788.21

Board Loans:

In Permanent Loan Fund	1,254,684.71	
In Memorial Loan Fund	140,367.45	
In Annuity Funds	8,650.00	
In Restricted Funds	18,698.80	
In Concordia Loan Fund	1,000.00	
In Fund for Missions (Kaercher)	300.00	
In General Fund for Missions	1,380.00	
In Annuity Funds (interest at 5%)	21,775.00	
In Special Funds	2,188.00	
		1,449,043.96

Agency Loans:

Women's Missionary Society	216,744.25
	1,665,788.21

The Rev. J. F. Seibert was introduced as one who had served more than forty-four years in the home mission work and whose retirement from active service in the field had been announced. Dr. Seibert spoke feelingly with reference both to the past and to the future.

In conclusion, the Rev. H. W. A. Hanson spoke as the retiring president of the Board of American Missions.

The recommendations were presented in order.

Recommendation 1 was adopted.

Recommendation 2 was adopted.

II, 5, of the report of the Executive Board, referring to the request of the Board of American Missions, for the privilege of a campaign on behalf of church extension, was presented, and after lengthy discussion, and after special prayer led by the Rev. J. A. W. Haas, the following motion was adopted:

That the Board of American Missions be given permission to make a special effort, during the year 1938, for church extension funds.

On motion the report of the auditors was accepted.

The Rev. Franklin Clark Fry, Secretary, presented the report of the Committee on Evangelism.

REPORT OF THE COMMITTEE ON EVANGELISM

I.

No Evangelical Lutheran Church can ever disavow or neglect Evangelism without denying itself. Severed from it, having a name to live— and an honored name!—it will be dead. Evangelism is nothing superfluous, no counsel of perfection which dare be slurred over in any preoccupation with more transient interests or eclipsed in years of stress. In the anatomy of religion, it is the lips which correspond to faith as the heart, the mouth by which confession is made to salvation. Evangelism, with its vital witnessing to Christ, can no more be waived by a Christian in transference to another, whoever he may be, than any man can depute someone else to love his wife for him or to be a true father to his children. As for a church, the cessation of Evangelism is a functional disorder which never fails to be fatal, while its sluggishness is a symptom which can only excite the gravest alarm.

Wholesomely, this cardinal Christian spirit has never been so pronounced or pervasive in its ascendancy in the United Lutheran Church in America as it is now. The stimulus to vitality and constructive zeal in all that it implies which the Committee on Evangelism has insistently furthered, ever since its original appointment at the Washington Convention of 1920, goes constructively forward. Its contagion has spread into the far reaches of the church and an exuberance is manifesting itself which bodes well for a constant, vigorous advance. With that aspiration, your committee, although still handicapped by the total absence of funds specifically designated for it and the wide dispersion of its membership, has prosecuted all of its projects in deep conviction and in prayerful hope.

II.

On February 5, 1935, in conjunction with the first and only session sanctioned for the committee during the biennium, the Open Conference on Evangelism which the Savannah Convention directed by special resolution occurred at the Lutheran Church House, New York. A general call in *The Lutheran*, supplementing direct notices to all synodical committees, invited all responsive pastors and laymen to attend,—fewer of whom appeared, however, than had been anticipated. Definite objectives for 1935 and 1936 were crystallized for the sake of the most efficient operation and the various committeemen were deployed to promote their achievement, with each one allotted a concrete task.

With the keenest gratification, the committee heard from its chairman that his impending retirement from the successful pastorate in which he had exemplified Evangelism for many years would release all of his virile energies into a wider ministry of itinerating for this cause, especially in weeks of special services, wherever he might be called. Immediately, he was designated as pre-eminently the committee's "special representative" and was most cordially commended to the church for the fullest employment of his talents. The almost incessant journeys which have carried him into many synods and into scores of appreciative parishes between that time and this have eloquently testified to the enthusiastic reception which both he and the evangelistic fervor which he personifies have everywhere been accorded.

Round-tables for pastors and Church Councilmen, in addition to the Preaching Missions which have increasingly become the vogue, have added substantially to the diffusion of the spirit of Evangelism as well as of the most effective techniques for its incorporation in normal church life. Special Conference assemblies have been convened, notably in the West Pennsylvania Synod, with a syllabus of problems submitted by the pastors themselves as their agenda. The Alleghany Synod divided itself into two sections, in Altoona and Johnstown, on September 17-18, 1935, for an animated survey, led by the secretary of the committee, of valid evangelistic methods which have proved themselves in practice, a procedure which it has resolved shall be an annual event. More than three hundred intent pastors and key laymen thronged a series of institutes in the Central Conference of the Synod of Ohio in January, 1936, which are to be extended throughout that synod. These few instances are cited without any pretense that they are exhaustive. They could readily be duplicated in the recent past and are destined to be so more and more in an expanding future.

Many Summer Schools, at the instance of this committee, have introduced studies in Evangelism as a permanent element in their curricula and have extended its impact among literally thousands of our most intelligent and earnest leaders. Among the many which have responded with admirable cooperation have been those at Massanetta Springs for the Virginia Synod, at Lake Wawasee, Ind., for the Synods of Indiana and Michigan, at Lakeside for the Ohio Synod, on the Thiel College campus for the Pittsburgh Synod, at Paradise Falls for the Pennsylvania

Ministerium, at Silver Bay for the United Synod of New York, and at Hendersonville, N. C., for the synods of the deeper south.

The publications of the Committee on Evangelism have again been restricted by financial compulsion to occasional contributions to which *The Lutheran* has graciously opened its columns. A sequence of nine such articles appeared during 1935 alone. As what we hope will be a foreglimpse into a better future, a quarter-year length course on Evangelism is now being prepared by the committee's secretary for adult and young people's classes in the Sunday Schools at the solicitation of the Parish and Church School Board. Synodical bulletins, meanwhile, have manifested the same generous liberality in elevating this cause to its deserved prominence with all of the growing facilities at their command, reaching a notable climax in the Ministerium of Pennsylvania's comprehensive Manual which was distributed broadcast in every one of its congregations during last winter. The issuing of select lists of tracts by the Committee on Evangelism of the United Synod of New York and the Publicity Committee of the Synod of Ohio has also abundantly demonstrated its worth. Compiled with critical care from a diversity of sources, including our own United Lutheran Publication House, such lists have elicited hundreds of inquiries and samples have been furnished to all who desire them.

Currently, no forward stride in Evangelism is more salutary or more widespread through the church than the determination to reintroduce the evangelical custom of family worship. Your committee delegated two of its pastors to indicate its readiness to edit a calendar of devotions for that purpose, preferably in tabular form, and when conference with the authorities of the Publication House disclosed that this task had already been ably assumed by the Common Service Book Committee, its sincere gratification at the excellent monthly booklet which was assured and which has since become a reality as "Light for Today" was unbounded. Heartiest acknowledgment is due, too, to the Laymen's Movement for Stewardship for the convincing brochure, "Christ in the Home: The What, the How, and the Why of The Family Altar," coping as it did with most of the chronic objections and presenting many salient benefits, of which one hundred thousand copies were circulated to the farthest frontiers of United Lutheranism in the first week in Lent, 1935. The tremendous volume of it equalled inter-nationally, piece by piece, the even more significant, because more concentrated, achievement in the Illinois and Wartburg Synods, in which another hundred thousand pieces of literature on this theme found their way in two years into Lutheran homes.

Without the slightest intention of incurring the fault with which the modern church has been plausibly charged, of "doing again what the

Reformation undid, re-professionalizing religion," a candid recognition that the most crucial responsibility for Evangelism, as for all else in church life, devolves upon a congregation's pastor simply cannot be evaded. Impelled by that knowledge, your committee communicated to the Board of Education an abstract of replies which it had received from all theological seminaries late in the preceding biennium and requested it to confer with the seminaries on the basis of those findings with a view to inculcating Evangelism more prominently in their curricula. This survey, which the Committee on Evangelism had thus initiated, was later amplified by further research conducted by the Board of Education itself among an aggregate of fifty-five seminaries of numerous denominations. Curiously enough, that investigation had as its most immediate effect the stimulation of a divinity school of another church to do precisely what this committee, at least, has had a fervent desire to accomplish within our own. At the annual conference of United Lutheran theological professors in June, 1936, at the Philadelphia Seminary, the perennial issue of a more adequate instruction in Evangelism which had consequently come to a vivid focus was met with clarity and resolute intelligence. Constructive effects should promptly appear.

Another fond ambition prompted a respectful request to the Executive Board for an Evangelism evening at the Columbus Convention when all administrative mechanics could be submerged and souls would be attuned alone to the vibrant heart of the Gospel.

III.

The Committee on Evangelism is constantly perplexed, and almost distraught, at how it can conceivably be expected to acquit itself worthily in the momentous responsibilities reposed in it with the paucity of the resources at its disposal. Devoutly persuaded as it is of the primacy of its sphere of activity in our common Christian life, it has never renounced its vision that the day will come for its emergence into a Board of Evangelism with ampler prestige, not for itself but for its task, and with commensurate means. Above all, it is impatiently eager for the action of the Richmond Convention ten years ago empowering it "to employ a full-time secretary" to be fulfilled.

Meanwhile, although invariably ready to counsel individual pastors directly by correspondence, your committee deems it obvious that the objectives which cry out to be attained become most accessible only when the synods, which have the primary contact with all congregations, exert themselves to their ardent utmost. To that end, the policy of assigning its entire personnel among neighboring synodical committees to stimulate their alertness and vigor has been consistently pursued again in the past biennium. In addition, a corresponding secretary was elected to whom the synodical committees, of which incidentally a substantial majority of the church-wide committeemen were themselves chairmen, were invited to report and to assess the success of their projects and from whom, consequently, they could obtain recommendations of procedures derived from the experience of others.

Conscious that the church's prior resolutions confer upon the Committee on Evangelism or its successor a wholly adequate commission, we submit no recommendations. In their stead, we lift up our hearts in incessant prayer that the church may grow not only in stature, numerically, nor in wisdom, by education, but in favor with God and man, that by His compassion, despite all human frailties, it may merit our Saviour's approbation as a faithful steward of the manifold grace of God.

Respectfully submitted,
A. POHLMAN, *Chairman*.
FRANKLIN CLARK FRY, *Secretary*.

Pastor Fry introduced the Rev. W. C. Davis who spoke concerning the Family Altar, and Dr. Davis was followed by the Rev. O. F. Blackwelder who spoke concerning the preaching mission.

The Rev. W. F. Rangeler, Vice President, presented the report of the Commission of Adjudication.

REPORT OF THE COMMISSION OF ADJUDICATION

At the conclusion of the Convention at Savannah, Georgia, October, 1934, the Commission was constituted as follows:

MEMBERS

Term expiring 1940—Rev. George J. Gongaware, D.D., LL.D., Rev. John A. Haas, D.D., LL.D., and Hon. E. K. Strong.

Term expiring 1938—Rev. Luther Kuhlman, D.D., Rev. W. F. Rangeler, D.D., and Hon. C. M. Efird.

Term expiring 1936—Rev. Wm. E. Frey, D.D., Rev. H. C. Roehner, D.D., and Hon. James F. Henninger.

ORGANIZATION

President—Luther Kuhlman, D.D., 166 Carlisle St., Gettysburg, Pa.
Vice President—Rev. W. F. Rangeler, D.D., Fremont, Nebraska.
Secretary—Rev. George J. Gongaware, D.D., 31 Pitt St., Charleston, S. C.
Clerk—Hon. E. K. Strong, Columbia City, Indiana.

Early in December, 1936, the president of the Commission was advised that one of our members, Hon. E. K. Strong, was with us no longer. A letter of warm sympathy was addressed to the family of Judge Strong, while the pastor of the local church was requested to assure the congregation and the community of the high esteem in which Mr. Strong was held by his colleagues and how greatly they appreciated his valuable services. A little later *The Lutheran* carried a suitable article. The notice which appears in this report, and also in the Minutes of the Commission, was kindly prepared by Rev. William F. Rangeler, D.D.

DEATH OF HON. EPHRIAM K. STRONG

The Commission of Adjudication has been called upon within this biennium to mourn the loss by death of one of its most capable and faithful members in the passing of Judge E. K. Strong of Columbia City, Ind.

His death occurred November 29, 1935, at Columbia City, and the funeral services were held December 2, in charge of his pastor, the Rev. Wm. E. Bradley, assisted by the Rev. R. D. Wheadon, D.D., of Logansport, Indiana, who represented the Synod and Wittenberg College.

Judge Strong was born in Whitley County, Indiana, on October 10, 1865, to Ephriam and Elenor Kyler Strong. On February 12, 1891, he was united in marriage to Miss Jessie Adair, whose father, Judge Adair, was later associated with Judge Strong in the practice of law. Mrs. Strong and two sons, Robin Adair Strong and Donald Adair Strong, survive to mourn his death.

Judge Strong, as a layman, served his church in many different capacities. In the local congregation he served on the church council, and for many years was teacher of the Bible Classes in the Sunday school. He was a faithful attendant at the worship service, and a loyal supporter of the Brotherhood.

In his Synod he was also active, being a trustee for years and on its Board of Ministerial Education. He was always present at the meetings of his Synod. In the United Lutheran Church he was widely known. He served two terms on the Board of Directors of Wittenberg College. For thirty years he attended the general meetings of the Church, first of the old General Synod and at, and since the merger, he has regularly attended the meetings of the United Lutheran Church in America.

At the merger convention in New York City in 1918, Judge Strong was made a member of the Commission of Adjudication, and with the exception of two years he has served continuously on this Commission. The two years off the Commission were made necessary by the constitutional provisions of the Commission disallowing more than two consecutive terms.

Judge Strong brought to bear upon the initiatory organization and work of the Commission his judicial knowledge and experience as well as his experience in ecclesiastical affairs and the Church's conception of the judicial functions of this important Commission and procedures of it as an ecclesiastical court. In fact, Judge Strong did most of the work in preparing the forms of procedure adopted by the United Lutheran Church to govern the work of this Commission. In fact, the synopsis of the constitutional provisions creating and governing the Commission of Adjudication of the United Lutheran Church in America, together with its Rules of Practice and Procedure as they are now in printed form and holding is largely the work of his hand in association with Rev. Holmes Dysinger, D.D., LL.D., another charter member of the Commission who, with Judge Strong, made up the committee appointed to prepare this synopsis and formulate the Rules of Procedure.

From the beginning Judge Strong most freely contributed his time and counsel in all the judgments of the Commission. In the matters of the Commission his judgment was usually sound and his counsel wise. And while this applies particularly to the Commission of Adjudication of which he was so long a member, it applies in a most general sense to his relation to all the affairs of the Church in which he was interested as a member of the United Lutheran Church in America. He was also greatly appreciated by all of us who were members of the Commission of Adjudication because of what he added to the happy fellowship that obtains among us.

We hereby record our deep sense of loss at his departure, and express our heartfelt sympathy with his beloved family in their bereavement, and to his local church and pastor in their sorrow.

For the Commission of Adjudication,
By W. F. RANGELER.

Owing to the fact that Dr. Luther Kuhlman has sent in his resignation from the Commission of Adjudication to the President of the U. L. C., stating as his reason his ill health, it becomes necessary to nominate an additional member to take his place.

Dr. Kuhlman was president of the Commission, and served long as a member with fidelity and high distinction. It is therefore fitting that this Convention should express appreciation of his service in the Church, and that the Secretary of the U. L. C. be instructed to convey to Dr. Kuhlman the gratitude of the Church for his notable service.

We regret to report that Rev. H. C. Roehner, by reason of his continued serious ill health, has not been able to participate in any activity of the Commission during the biennium. Under these circumstances we have not renominated him for further membership on the Commission.

To keep expenses at a minimum no meetings of the Commission were held during the biennium, except at the Conventions of the U. L. C. A.

RESOLUTIONS REFERRED BY THE EXECUTIVE BOARD

In January, 1936, at the instance of the Conference of the Presidents of the Constituent Synods, the Executive Board requested the Commission "to give a ruling concerning the significance of Certificates of Ordination, including the problem of their (the certificates) surrender."

The resolution of the Executive Board came to the Commission in the following form:

"This is to notify you officially of the following action taken by the Executive Board at its meeting on January 9th:

" 'The Conference of Presidents asks the Executive Board to arrange to secure a ruling concerning the significance of certificates of ordination, including the problem of their surrender.

" 'Your Committee or Constituent Synods would recommend that the Executive Board request the Commission of Adjudication for an opinion on the subject stated.

" 'This is recorded as Item 6 on page 77 of the Minutes.' "

THE COMMISSION'S REPLY

In replying to these resolutions from the Executive Board your Commission would respectfully call attention to the requirements of our Rules of Procedure regarding the definite manner in which questions are to come before us. This question as here presented to the Commission scarcely meets these requirements. The Commission, however, has given them consideration in spite of their indefiniteness.

The Commission finds two questions here involved: namely, first, the significance of a Certificate of Ordination, and second, the question of the surrender of an Ordination Certificate.

As to the first question, the Commission of Adjudication does not consider it to involve the question of the significance of the act of ordination, but only the significance of the certificate of that act which we commonly call the Ordination Paper.

The Commission, after a study of such different forms of Certificates of Ordination as were available, finds that the pertinent portions of these certificates substantially agree in providing as follows:

"Be it known that Rev. .... has been set apart and ordained .... to the ministry of the Gospel of Our Lord and Saviour Jesus Christ."

This is the single central truth or fact that the certificates are intended to convey. Now, what *is* the fact to which they certify? Clearly, to the fact that an action of Synod has been taken which confers upon Rev. .... the office of the ministry. It is not a question of what our conception of the office of the ministry is, but of what the relation of this certificate is to the act to which it certifies, namely, the act of a Synod in conferring upon said person authority to perform the functions of the office of the ministry.

The real proof of the ordination is to be ascertained in the records of Synod, that is, in the official minutes of its proceedings, and the certificate has no value apart from the action of a Synod to which it certifies. The certificate might be lost entirely but the action of Synod would still be holding and the person's ministerial authority still intact.

And, on the other hand, if, for any reason, voluntary or otherwise, so far as the person holding the certificate is concerned, the Synod takes subsequent action relieving him of, or suspending, or expelling him from, the office of the ministry, then, a certificate of *this* fact would invalidate any certificate of the former action and the certificate, or any number of certificates, of the former act of Synod becomes worthless.

In the practical phases of the matter, however, because it is possible for unscrupulous persons to impose by means of a worthless ordination certificate, it might become morally desirable that such an annulled certificate should either be destroyed or turned in to the Synod by whose action it has become of no further official significance.

This brings us to a consideration of the second part of the Executive Board's question, namely, the question of the surrender of ordination certificates.

As to the property rights involved in the certificate of ordination, that would be a question for civil courts to determine and the Commission of Adjudication would be acting out of the sphere of an ecclesiastical court should it attempt to pass judgment here.

But from purely a moral and ethical standpoint, and to prevent unscrupulous persons from imposing upon the public in the name of the Church, a Synod, because it has the right to annul the ministerial authority of the person, also has the right, when it deems it advisable, to request the deliverance to it of such a worthless certificate of ordination and the person possessing such a certificate should feel morally bound to comply with such a request.

Respectfully submitted for the
Commission of Adjudication by
W. F. RANGELER, *Vice President.*

The President declared that the report as presented is the pronouncement of the Church.

At the suggestion of the Commission of Adjudication, the Convention instructed the Secretary to express the appreciation of the United Lutheran Church to the Rev. Luther Kuhlman for his valuable service to the Church.

At 5.10 P. M. the Convention adjourned with prayer by the Rev. S. W. Herman.

Friday Evening

At 8.30 o'clock the celebration of the Centennial Anniversary of the Protestant Diaconate was observed by a pageant presenting history, present work, and a glimpse of the future of the Deaconess, in the Music Hall of Capital University. The interest in this event was made manifest by the large attendance for the presentation of the pageant and by subsequent comments. Special commendation was given to the book published in connection with this anniversary, "Fliedner the Faithful," by the Rev. Abdel Ross Wentz.

FIFTH SESSION

DESHLER-WALLICK HOTEL
Columbus, Ohio
Saturday, October 17, 1936, 8.45 A. M.

Matins were conducted by the Rev. Earl S. Rudisill.

The Convention was called to order by the President.

The Rev. A. J. Traver, Chairman of the Nominating Committee, reported nominations as follows:

For the *Board of Foreign Missions:*

Rev. H. H. Beidleman; Rev. P. O. Bersell; Rev. E. E. Fischer; Rev. P. E. Monroe; Rev. C. M. Snyder; Rev. W. F. Bacher; Rev. D. P. Bair; Rev. J. Frederick Bermon; Rev. H. Brueckner; Rev. Voigt R. Cromer; Rev. W. C. Davis; Rev. John L. Deaton; Rev. S. L. Hench; Rev. George S. Kressley; Rev. Earnest A. Trabert; Frank Howard; Ralph H. Schatz; A. Raymond Bard; W. H. Menges; Mrs. H. C. Michael; Mrs. C. F. Weaver.

The President declared the nominations closed.

For the *Board of American Missions* and the *West Indies Mission Board:*

Rev. A. J. Holl; Rev. John Schmieder; Rev. Chester S. Simonton; Rev. Emil W. Weber; Rev. C. G. Aurand; Rev. T. K. Finck; Rev. Elmer W. Harner; Rev. William J. Miller; Rev. K. P. Otten; Rev. T. F. Suber; Rev. Charles Trexler; Rev. H. E. Turney; A. S. Bauer; Louis Hanson; Heiby W. Ungerer; Warren M. Koons; John George Kurzenknabe; Jesse Martsolf; Mrs. G. W. McClanahan; E. H. Rights; Mrs. P. M. Rossman.

The President declared the nominations closed.

For the *Board of Education:*

Rev. Stanley Billheimer; Rev. H. J. Black; Rev. F. K. Fretz; Rev. G. Franklin Gehr; Rev. H. R. Gold; Rev. Simon Snyder; Rev. E. F. Sterz;

Rev. H. T. Weiskotten; Rev. A. M. Huffman; Rev. B. R. Lantz; Rev. Armin G. Weng; Rev. Norman S. Wolf; O. F. H. Bert; Windsor Cousins; Samuel Fausold; Frederick Henrich; R. J. Seeger; Heiby W. Ungerer; Hiram H. Keller; Harold U. Landis; Jacob Wagner.

The President declared the nominations closed.

For the *Inner Mission Board:*

Rev. G. H. Bechtold; Rev. Herman Brezing; Rev. P. D. Brown; Rev. George Englar; Rev. Charles B. Foelsch; Rev. H. D. Hoover; Rev. J. B. Baker; Rev. B. Mehrtens; Rev. Conrad Wilker; Carl M. Distler; James Gear; J. A. Geidel; Jacob Umlauf; P. P. Hagan; C. H. C. Muller.

The President declared the nominations closed.

For the *Board of Publication:*

Rev. Oscar F. Blackwelder; Rev. S. W. Herman; Rev. J. J. Scherer; Rev. F. B. Clausen; Rev. G. K. Rubrecht; Rev. L. W. Rupp; Rev. Corson C. Snyder; Rev. Ross Stover; Rev. Wm. F. Sunday; L. Russel Alden; Henry Beisler; James L. Fisher; E. G. Hoover; D. P. Deatrick; Charles W. Fuhr; Earle C. Greiner; George W. Hafer; E. H. Schirmer; Luther C. Schmehl; A. F. Sittloh; W. H. Steinkamp.

The President declared the nominations closed.

For the *Board of Ministerial Pensions and Relief:*

Rev. J. H. Reble; Rev. Frank M. Urich; Rev. Frederick J. Weertz; William H. Emhardt; William A. Granville; H. J. Herbst; W. T. Stauffer; H. E. Cope; S. M. Goodyear; E. B. Graeber; A. B. Greiner; John Greiner; Austin W. Howard; Dorner L. Keyser; A. J. Nauman.

The President declared the nominations closed.

For the *Parish and Church School Board:*

Rev. R. Homer Anderson; Rev. W. G. Boomhower; Rev. Paul H. Heisey; Rev. C. Franklin Koch; Rev. Wm. C. Schaeffer; Rev. Albert W. Steinfurth; Rev. John F. Fedders; Rev. Ira S. Fritz; Rev. E. Martin Grove; Mrs. H. S. Bechtolt; Clarence C. Dittmer; Mrs. Charles A. Davis.

The President declared the nominations closed.

For the *Board of Deaconess Work:*

Rev. P. S. Baringer; Rev. H. F. Baughman; Rev. Allen L. Benner; Rev. William C. Lauer; Rev. J. J. Schindel; Rev. L. A. Thomas; Rev. Paul Kuehner; Rev. J. A. McCulloch; Rev. W. M. Weaver; E. S. Gerberich; Albert B. Hardwick; Harry S. Myers; Frederick J. Singley; Mrs. Theo. Kemnitz; Mrs. W. P. M. Braun.

The President declared the nominations closed.

Committee of Tellers No. 1 reported elections as follows:

For the *Executive Board* each of the following received a majority of the votes cast:

Rev. E. B. Burgess   Robbin B. Wolf
Rev. E. P. Pfatteicher   John L. Zimmerman

The President declared them elected and stated that one clergyman and one layman were yet to be elected.

For the *Commission of Adjudication* each of the following received a majority of the votes cast:

Term Expiring 1940: John F. Kramer
Term Expiring 1938: Rev. John Aberly

The President declared them elected and stated that two clergymen and one layman were yet to be elected for the term expiring 1942.

For the *Committee on Church Papers* the Rev. H. C. Alleman received a majority of the votes cast.

The President declared Dr. Alleman elected and stated that one clergyman and one layman were yet to be elected.

For the *Executive Committee of the Laymen's Movement* each of the following received a majority of the votes cast:

H. J. Albrecht	W. H. Hager
J. L. Clark	E. Clarence Miller
P. H. Glatfelter	George E. Neff

Charles B. Zimmerman

The President declared them elected and stated that three laymen were yet to be elected.

The President stated that ballots had been prepared for the completion of elections to these Boards.

At this time the Special Order, adopted at the recommendation of the Committee of Reference and Counsel on Friday, was announced.

The Rev. Dr. P. O. Bersell, President of the Augustana Synod was presented and the President invited him to address the Convention. Dr. Bersell spoke at length of past relationships between the Augustana Synod and The United Lutheran Church in America, but dwelt with force and feeling upon the close present relationship of the two bodies, and of their mutual interests. The Convention received many of Dr. Bersell's statements with evident satisfaction.

The response to the greetings of President Bersell was made by the Rev. Paul H. Roth, President of the Lutheran Theological Seminary, Minneapolis, Minn. This response was made in a most happy vein, with assurance of cordial agreement between the two bodies in what constitutes sound, conservative Lutheranism.

The Rev. H. R. Gold, President, presented the report of the Board of Education.

REPORT OF THE BOARD OF EDUCATION

(For action on the recommendations in this report, see p. 247)

FORWARD WITH CHRISTIAN HIGHER EDUCATION

"If Christianity is to survive it must survive in an environment made by Christian leaders. It cannot survive in the atmosphere that is thickening with modern paganism. Out of that paganism come the crass ideals of tyrants . . . And don't think America is free of that atmosphere. We are still the land of liberty, 'the land of the free and the home of the brave.' But unless the free are brave, they will no longer be free."

Education without religion is defective and incomplete. Education without Christ is sterile. Education with Christ makes men free and brave.

The Board of Education of The United Lutheran Church in America was formed "to promote the general educational interests of the Church," and to keep Christ in education.

In the fulfilment of this function during the biennium the staff visited 51 Lutheran and 155 non-Lutheran institutions, attended 1,430 sessions of 200 different groups, committees, conferences, and conventions, delivered 1,158 addresses and talks, and had 9,090 personal interviews. In addition, the Service Bulletin and two News Bulletins were edited regularly, articles and pamphlets were written, and a book was prepared for the printer.

For discharging its responsibility in Christian higher education, the Board received from the Church in this biennium $164,175, as over against $224,200 for the biennium of 1930-32.

Conscious of its inheritance, its responsibility, and its opportunities for leading the Church forward through Christian higher education, the Board of Education presents this biennial report.

I. COOPERATING WITH THE INSTITUTIONS

"Unless those who believe in a Christian civilization are willing to sacrifice of their good, hard-earned cash to educate Christian leaders, they will find in a few generations that their dream has vanished, that tyranny with its hard and fast, ruthless rules of life will be substituted for the good life . . . It is not a question so much of churches and preachers as it is of colleges that will make leaders who will create a world in which churches can thrive, leaders in all walks of life, in all callings and professions. If American churchmen fail to support the kind of colleges that turn out Christian leaders, American life under another leadership soon will close the churches." This challenge from a layman demands the consideration of the Church. (See Recommendation 1, p. 239.)

1. The Service of the Board

Secretaries Consulted

From the college administrative point of view the visit of a secretary means more than an address before the student body and private conferences with students. The secretary takes opportunities for extended conferences with the president and members of the faculty, round-table discussion with the faculty, visits to the classes, and examinations of buildings and grounds. The type of advice sought by the institutions and offered by the secretary covers general administrative problems, curriculum changes, teaching staff, student welfare, advertising and publications, and relations to the alumni and church constituency.

During the biennium the round table discussions with the college faculties concerned primarily: what it means to be designated a Christian college, and the objectives of a church college. As a direct result of these conferences faculty committees have been selected to make college self-surveys and to prepare statements of the purposes of the college. Also during the past two years the executive secretary rendered special service to three colleges in the rewriting of their constitutions.

Grants-in-Aid

Notwithstanding the increased appreciation of the Board's service through the secretaries, the Board is quite anxious that a large percentage be distributed to the colleges and seminaries. During the past biennium the grants amounted to 55 per cent of the total disbursements. To these sums should be added the cost of promotion through addresses and printing. During the biennium the colleges and seminaries received the sum total of $94,000, which is an increase of about $3,000 over the previous biennium.

Financial Advisory Service

For a few years the Board has given consideration to the necessity of more uniform and adequate financial reports from our institutions. Recently the American Council on Education has established a financial advisory service to the colleges and universities. It takes the form of examination of the chart of accounts, the accounting books, and the general bookkeeping system. This service is rendered gratis but payment of expenses is required. The Board believed the matter of sufficient importance to enter into an arrangement with the American Council on Education whereby this service will be given to our colleges during the next biennium. There will be no expense to the institutions.

Contacts and Publicity

During May, 1936, each secretary, upon invitation of the presidents, visited the territories of Hartwick, Susquehanna, Thiel, Wagner and

Wittenberg Colleges. Meetings were set up by the college officials at which the secretary spoke. In addition the folder entitled "After High School—?" was distributed widely through the colleges to prospective college students. A special letter, prepared for each college, was sent to the parents of prospective Lutheran students in those colleges which cooperated with the Board in this matter.

Educational News Bulletin

During the past year the Board published, in mimeographed form, an Educational News Bulletin to fulfil the following purposes: to keep the colleges and seminaries informed of what the others are doing, to present summaries of educational projects being carried on by both Lutheran and non-Lutheran institutions, to give ideas for more effective and efficient administrative policies, and to bring the Board and the institutions into closer cooperative relationship. This Bulletin is mailed to the administrative officers of all colleges and seminaries, to pastors working with students, to synodical presidents, to the members of the Executive Board and the Board of Education, and to selected individuals both within and without the Lutheran Church.

Cooperation with Church Educational Groups

Conference of Theological Professors. The proceedings of the meetings held in June, 1935 and 1936, were mimeographed by the office of the Board and distributed to all seminary faculty members, as well as to other interested individuals. This service is greatly appreciated by the seminaries.

National Lutheran Educational Conference. Through the staff the Board continues a cooperation that has been uninterrupted since the formation of the Conference. Mr. Wickey is on the executive committee and Miss Markley is the vice-president. In January, 1935, when Mr. Wickey resigned as secretary, having served for six years, Miss Markley was appointed editor of the News Bulletin of the Conference. This News Bulletin is circulated once a month except June, July, and August, through the News Bureau of the National Lutheran Council.

Council of Church Boards of Education. During the biennium our Church was honored by the Council of Church Boards of Education, of which Dr. F. G. Gotwald was one of the founders, in their request for the service of Mr. Wickey to become their General Secretary. Since 1930 he has been active as an official of the Council, being president, treasurer, and a member of the executive committee. It was agreed to share his time provided it be "without prejudice to the work of the Board of Education." The Council of Church Boards in return shares his travel expenses, grants him an honorarium, and pays for the salary of an office secretary. Mr. Wickey has returned to the Board of Education a sum at the rate of $600 per year. A year of this arrangement has passed. Monthly reports show that the work of the Board has not suffered, and that the services of an additional office secretary make our work more effective. As editor of the Journal of Christian Higher Education and in his larger contacts, Mr. Wickey is exerting an important influence in a most vital phase of American culture.

2. The Institutions Report

In accordance with the by-laws of The United Lutheran Church, our colleges and seminaries report to the Church through the Board of Education. Statistics on finances and enrolments are secured on blanks especially prepared for that purpose. Statements of important events and facts are received from time to time, and are herewith summarized for the information of the Church.

Changes in Presidents

Northwestern Seminary: On May 24, 1935, President Joseph Stump passed to the Church Triumphant. The Board of Directors elected Dr. Paul H. Roth, Professor of Church History, president.

Carthage College: The Rev. Rudolph G. Schulz, Jr., D.D., pastor of Hope Lutheran Church, Toledo, Ohio, was called as president and took office October, 1935. The Rev. I. W. Bingaman, D.D., president of the Board of Trustees, acted as president since July, 1933.

Muhlenberg College: President John A. W. Haas concluded a service of 31 years as president June, 1936. The Board of Trustees elected Dean Robert C. Horn as acting president.

Wagner College: In the spring of 1935 the Trustees announced the election of Clarence C. Stoughton to the presidency. Mr. Stoughton was serving as dean during that year, and had been connected with the institution for several years.

The Enrolment Situation

On October 1, 1935, the colleges reported a total enrolment of 4,619, an increase of .8 per cent over the figure of 4,582, reported March 1, 1935. The picture does not change when the grand total enrolments, including summer schools, extension schools, and special schools, are considered. In 1934 the colleges reported 7,833, while this year the report totals 7,900.

At the seminaries in the regular undergraduate courses there was reported 396 in 1932, 378 in 1934, and 334 in 1936. While graduates of our seminaries are still unplaced, nevertheless this decline in the number of young men studying for the ministry needs the prayerful consideration of the whole Church.

The percentage of college graduates continues to increase in the enrolment at the seminaries. In 1932 only 79.5 per cent of the students registered in the regular courses were college graduates. In 1934, 90 per cent had received the Bachelor degree before entering the seminary. In 1936 more than 91 per cent are graduates of colleges.

The Church Affiliation of Students at the Colleges

Two years ago the figures for the church distribution of the students at our colleges showed a continued decline in the number of Lutheran students, namely, 2,069 or 45.8 per cent in 1932, and 1,832 or 40.3 per cent in 1934. It is heartening to note that the number of Lutheran students is again on the increase, there being 1,923 or 41.6 per cent in 1936, as indicated in the first table below.

This table shows the church affiliation or preference of students enrolled at the thirteen senior colleges and one junior college for the past two academic years. All denominations and sects having less than one per cent enrolled are placed in the miscellaneous list, which includes twenty-four groups. The number of different religious groups registered at the colleges amounts to thirty-four. Ten church groups account for more than 93 per cent of the students.

Denomination	1934-35		1935-36	
	No.	%	No.	%
Lutheran	1,888	41.	1,923	41.6
Methodist	778	17.	754	16.3
Presbyterian	462	10.1	476	10.5
Baptist	293	6.4	288	6.2
Catholic	278	6.	258	5.5
Reformed	168	3.7	144	3.1
Episcopal	165	3.7	162	3.5
Cong.-Christian	127	2.8	116	2.5
Evangelical	71	1.6	106	2.3
Jewish	82	1.8	83	1.8
Miscellaneous	172	3.8	213	4.6
No Affiliation	98	2.1	96	2.1
Totals	4,582	100.0	4,619	100.0

Of special interest is the exhibit indicating the number and percentage of Lutheran students at each of the colleges, not including special schools, during the past two years.

Colleges	1934-35		1935-36	
	No.	%	No.	%
Carthage	152	52.	154	51.2
Gettysburg	266	52.8	290	54.5
Hartwick	47	14.	44	13.3
Lenoir Rhyne	166	44.3	160	45.7
Marion	39	29.	37	36.2
Midland	125	42.2	138	44.3
Muhlenberg	190	44.6	214	50.3
Newberry	143	46.7	143	44.9

Roanoke	55	14.8	48	13.8
Susquehanna	120	49.8	104	43.8
Thiel	115	41.6	110	41.8
Wagner	72	39.3	76	42.6
Waterloo	35	44.2	29	31.2
Wittenberg	363	45.3	376	45.4
Totals	1,888	41.	1,923	41.6

Gifts and Bequests

Chicago Seminary: Notice was received of a bequest of $5,000, and $2,000 was paid on previous bequests.

Gettysburg Seminary: The executors of the Cronhardt Estate paid the sum of $224,722. A bequest of approximately $25,000 by Dr. Henry G. Ulrich was announced.

Hartwick Seminary: Valuable books from the extensive liturgical library of the late Dr. G. U. Wenner.

Philadelphia Seminary: Notices were received of bequests amounting to $61,756, on which several thousand dollars have been paid. From the estate of Mrs. Ada Norton Jamison $40,000 has been bequested.

Saskatoon Seminary: Gifts of several hundred dollars were received to assist in paying interest, towards the Students' Aid Fund, and to inaugurate a Revolving Text Book Fund. From the libraries of the late Rev. E. C. Dinwiddie, D.D., and the late Rev. H. E. Berkey, D.D., contributed by their widows, several thousand valuable volumes were received. These books cover all phases of the theological curriculum, many of which are much to be desired Latin and German works.

Southern Seminary: The campaign for $50,000 for the Voigt Memorial Professorship will be completed, it is hoped, during 1936.

Waterloo Seminary: Three bequests amounting to $1,300 and a $10,000 offering in commemoration of the silver jubilee of the seminary were received.

Hartwick College: From the estates of Arnold E. Potter and Mrs. Ada Stillson the sum of $10,000. Books from the library of Hartwick Academy.

Lenoir Rhyne College: From the estate of Dr. J. S. Armentrout $2,300. To the college was willed by the late George W. Rabb all his property, real and personal.

Midland College: A bequest to the amount of $1,620.

Muhlenberg College: Gifts and bequests to the endowment and building funds to the amount of about $5,000, and $23,000 from the estate of Mrs. Annie D. T. Fondersmith.

Newberry College: From the estate of Mrs. Sophie Magel the sum of $3,000.

Roanoke College: A bequest of $5,000 from Mrs. Ada Norton Jamison and $10,665 in gifts from friends. A $2,000 scholarship was endowed.

Susquehanna University: Two bequests amounting to $4,000 and for the new gymnasium and women's recreational field the sum of $51,000.

Thiel College: From the Samuel Livingston estate valuable properties, and from the estates of Mrs. Anna Rink, Miss Julia Wattles, and Carl N. Conrad bequests to the amount of $11,000. A local campaign amounted to about $7,500.

Wagner College: From the estates of Mrs. Josephine Nicum and others $10,350; and bequests by the Reverend Herman D. Kraeling, Miss Elizabeth Müller, and others amounting to $16,300.

Wittenberg College: From Clarence L. and Grace S. Catherman, $75,000; from Charles C. Patterson, $50,000; other gifts and bequests amounting to $13,540.

Financial Needs

In direct answer to questions regarding the immediate financial needs, the colleges request $1,000,000 for buildings and $2,000,000 for permanent funds. To balance current budgets the colleges need $40,000 and the seminaries $25,000. These needs are not the result of desire to expand; they arise out of the demands and needs of efficient educational programs.

A Four Year Theological Course

At meetings of Theological Professors held at Gettysburg in June, 1935, and in Philadelphia, June, 1936, the consensus of opinion was "that both class room work and clinical work of students should be extended as rapidly as the Church, through its gifts, its officers, and its congregations, manifests a readiness to make such an extension possible." There are professors who believe the time has long been here when the seminaries of The United Lutheran Church should establish a year of field work, as has been done by Concordia, Augustana, and Luther seminaries.

The Board of Directors of Saskatoon Seminary have approved the plan of a year of field work, and the Manitoba Synod has directed the faculty and the president of the synod to cooperate in effecting the project. This fourth year will be required for graduation.

Significant Events and Occasions

Carthage College: On October 26, 1935, in connection with the Annual Homecoming Festival, the Reverend Rudolph G. Schulz, Jr., D.D., was inaugurated president. President Schulz is the first alumnus to become the administrative head of Carthage College.

Gettysburg College: In June, 1935, Gettysburg Academy held its last commencement, after operating continuously for 108 years. To use the buildings vacated by the Academy, the Board of Trustees voted to make the college coeducational. In September, 1935, young women were admitted and the Woman's Division was established.

Lenoir Rhyne College: On April 30, 1935, the inaugural ceremonies were held for the installation of the Reverend P. E. Monroe, D.D.

Susquehanna University: As part of the commencement exercises of June, 1935, the first unit of the new Alumni Gymnasium was dedicated. This new building was made necessary through the destruction by fire of the old gymnasium during the previous year.

Saskatoon Seminary: March 3, 1935, witnessed a unique program of broadcasting in Saskatoon when the seminary presented a program in English and German.

Thiel College: Under the direction of President E. S. Rudisill an Institute on Parenthood and Home Relations was inaugurated November 15-17, 1934. This institute is to be an annual event and is unique among American colleges.

Wagner College: After twenty-nine years of service Professor William Ludwig retired in June, 1936, and was honored with the title of Professor Emeritus. The previous year he was titled Dean Emeritus. In 1936 the Middle States Association of Colleges and Secondary Schools placed Wagner on its list of approved colleges.

Wittenberg College: On April 26-28, 1935, the Second Lutheran Youth Conference was held with 500 delegates in attendance, coming from the states of Ohio, Indiana, Michigan, Tennessee, West Virginia, and Kentucky.

3. Persistent Problems

The Arrangements for Training of Ministers

The 1932 Convention of the Church adopted a program regarding the Church's arrangements for the training of ministers and teachers. In addition, the Church requested "the Board of Education to approach the constituent synods and the theological seminaries with reference to the question of approving the program indicated." Within two years Susquehanna, Pacific, and Martin Luther seminaries suspended operation. At the 1934 Convention, the Board of Education reported the resolutions of synods and seminary boards, the appointment of negotiating committees, and the results of the negotiations.

During the past biennium conversations and conferences were held with the representatives of Chicago Theological Seminary and Hamma Divinity School. This procedure was in response to the report of the Board of Wittenberg College to the supporting synods that *coordination* "offers the only practical solution of our seminary difficulties at the present time." Both schools agreed to recognize any one year of the curriculum of the other as requirement for graduation. This action was taken to allow students, who desire, to study for a year at the other institution.

The United Synod of New York asked its Board of Education to continue efforts for the merger of Hartwick and Philadelphia seminaries. At its 1936 meeting the United Synod of New York expressed the conviction that there should be one seminary in the east and memorialized the Church to change its constitution to the effect that the establishment, control, and maintenance of seminaries for theological education may be vested in The United Lutheran Church in America.

The service of the Board of Education in carrying out the program adopted by the Church is limited by the responsiveness of synods and seminary boards. **(See Recommendation 2, p. 239.)**

The Training of Men for Bilingual Ministry

The Church has placed upon the Board of Education the responsibility for the adequate and effective training of students preparing for bilingual ministry. To supply the Church with pastors who can minister in more than one language has always been a problem with the Lutheran Church in America. The problem arises because of the principle of the Reformation that the Church must preach the Gospel in the language of the people. Today the problem concerns more than the training of men to serve German-English parishes. Accordingly the Board at its June, 1931, meeting took action favoring the establishment of a professorship at one of our seminaries to train men for the Slovak and Hungarian ministry. After consultation with the secretary for linguistic matters of the American Board of Missions, it was deemed inopportune to proceed with this matter

The solution of this problem involves encouraging an adequate number of young men to prepare for the bilingual ministry, designating a college and a seminary where such candidates will be adequately trained. In addition it may be desirable in some cases to send students to Germany for a year of practical experience in German life and culture. Also it would be helpful for bilingual students to spend their summers in bilingual parishes. But back of all institutional training lies the influence and spirit of the home and local parish. Here our youth will catch the spirit and the vision of this field of special service in the Kingdom of God.

The Placement of Seminary Graduates

On October 1, 1935, from the graduating classes of 1932, 1933, 1934, and 1935, 26 were still unplaced. Of the 95 graduates in 1936 less than one-fourth were placed on July 1. According to figures released from the office of the Church, in 1935 there were 183 unemployed pastors and 100 vacant parishes. Again we say to the Church, *God calls, our youth answer, but our Church has no plan for placement.*

The Purposes of the Church in a Church-Related College

Convinced that the time has long been here when there should be some understanding of just what are the purposes of the Church in her colleges, the Board adopted the following statement which has been transmitted to the colleges:

A. *The General Purpose*

The general purpose of the church in a church-related college is to help discover and apply truth, and to help develop Christian personality under the best educational standards and procedures.

B. *The Specific Purposes*

The specific purposes of the church in a church-related college are:
1. To furnish college training.
    a. To those who will exercise an intelligent Christian influence. whatever their occupation.
    b. To those who will render special Christian service in the church, the school, and the community.
    c. To those who plan to enter the church's theological seminaries.
2. To present the relationship of Christian principles to our social and economic life.
3. To offer extension courses especially in the Bible, Church History, Christian Education, and other subjects directly related to the life of the church.
4. To conduct research in fields directly related to the church and her work.

C. *The Means for Achieving These Purposes*

1. *The policy* of the church college will be positively Christian, in business administration, in academic standards, and in the supervision of student life.
2. *The activities of the students* will correspond to the principles of Christian culture and will be planned to develop Christian personality in the students.
3. *The teachers* will be Christians. Such teachers, having Christian consciousness, Christian convictions, and Christian courage, are essential to the development of Christian personality. Their example and their varied activities, apart from their teaching, will be instruments to that end.
4. *The correlated curriculum,* in the hands of these Christian teachers, will afford the student a comprehensive knowledge of the Bible, an adequate understanding of Christian truth, and right techniques of Christian living.

4. The Story of Numbers

While statistics may be variously interpreted, nevertheless they tell a story. That story indicates that the total assets of ten seminaries and fourteen colleges is $650,000 less than four years ago but about $400,000 more than two years ago. Likewise, the total indebtedness is $59,000 more than four years ago but $191,000 less than two years ago. The combined current deficits are $2,614 more than two years ago, but $67,993 less than four years ago. Of special interest is the declining deficits of the seminaries. In 1932 the seminaries reported deficits amounting to $49,330; in 1934, $27,877; and in 1936, $23,245. The fact that in 1932 there were thirteen seminaries to operate while today there are only ten is an important factor in the situation.

The statistical tables will answer questions of detail concerning the stewardship of the fourteen colleges and ten seminaries. Although totals are not given in connection with the tables, the following tabulation of summaries of certain items presents an interesting story.

SUMMARY OF STATISTICS FOR INSTITUTIONS

	10 Seminaries	14 Colleges	Grand Total
Value of all Property	$2,445,723	$12,128,298	$14,574,021
Value of Fund Assets	2,284,353	7,815,395	10,099,748
Total Value of all Assets	$4,730,076	$19,943,693	$24,673,769
Total Indebtedness	$367,956	$2,705,268	$3,073,224
Current Funds			
Income	$192,205	$1,730,270	$1,922,475
Expenditures	215,450	1,742,803	1,958,253
Total Current Deficits	$23,245	$12,533	$35,778
Total Volumes in Libraries	134,150	325,428	459,578
Total Faculties	67	439	506
Total Student Enrolment	334	7,900	8,234
Total Alumni	5,247	21,503	26,750

STATISTICAL TABLES—I. THEOLOGICAL SEMINARIES

THE PROPERTY

Index No.	Founded	Institution	Location	President or Dean	Plant — Campus Acres	Plant — Campus Value	Plant — Buildings No.	Plant — Buildings Value	Value of Real Property	Equipment — Library Vol.	Equipment — Library Value	Equipment — Furn. and Fixtures	Value of Equipment	Total Value of Property
1	1797	Hartwick Theo. Seminary	Brooklyn, N. Y.	Rev. S. M. Paulson, D.D.	40	$47627	10	$202987	$250614	2000	$50000	$18505	$68505	$319119
2	1826	Luth. Theo. Seminary	Gettysburg, Pa.	Rev. J. Aberly, D.D., LL.D.	6	15000	5	145000	160000	43500	12000	3000	15000	175000
3	1830	Luth. Theo. Southern Sem.	Columbia, S. C.	Rev. C. A. Freed, D.D.										
4	1845	Hamma Divinity School	Springfield, Ohio	Rev. R. E. Tulloss, Ph.D., D.D., LL.D.					See Wittenberg College	10000	College			
5	1864	Luth. Theo. Seminary	Philadelphia, Pa.	Rev. C. M. Jacobs, D.D., L.H.D., LL.D.	10	350000	15	745000	1095000	43000	52800	25000	77800	1172800
6	1891	Chicago Luth. Theo. Sem.	Maywood, Ill.	Rev. L. F. Gruber, D.D., LL.D.	15	218250	11	199076	417326	20000	17143	24287	41430	458756
7	1893	Western Theo. Seminary	Fremont, Nebr.	Rev. H. F. Martin, Ph.D., D.D.					20045	4000	3000			23045
8	1911	Luth. Sem. of Canada	Waterloo, Ont., Can.	Rev. F. B. Clausen, D.D.	16	10000	6	165000	175000	3650	3000		4000	179000
9	1919	Lutheran Seminary	Saskatoon, Sask., Can.	Rev. W. Magnus, Acting	16	4050	7	56558	60608	4000	2100	1900	4000	64608
10	1921	Northwtn. Luth. Theo. Sem.	Minneapolis, Minn.	Rev. Paul H. Roth, D.D.	16		1	34456	34456	4000	14418	4721	19139	53395

NOTE: Cents are omitted. Blanks indicate no report or nothing to report. Desirable totals are given on previous page.

THE FUNDS—PERMANENT

Index No.	Productive — Restricted	Productive — Unrestricted	Unproductive — Annuities	Unproductive — Other	Scholarships	Total Endowment	Other Assets — Interest Bearing	Other Assets — Non-Interest Bearing	Total Funds	Total All Assets Property and Funds	Additions to Capital 1934-35	Additions to Capital 1935-36	Total Indebtedness
1						$40113			$40113	$40113			$32185
2	$256591	$480520	$37750		$69028	843889	$14846		858735	1177854	$5000	$210000	8983
3	61000		7600	$14245		82845	2000	$8000	92845	267845		14245	8694
4	77000	588346				665346		See	Wittenberg 665346	College 1838146	400	7500	48344
5	39000	232414			12500	283914						22478	106998
6		203436	133516		37050	374002		5151	379153	837909			84365
7	1575	36394			6000	43969		395	44364	67409			9500
8	26000					26000			26000	205000			49525
9												130	19362
10	500	77724	300	40		78564		99233	177797	231391			

I. THEOLOGICAL SEMINARIES—Continued

THE FUNDS: CURRENT INCOME

Index No.	Endowment	Students	U.L.C.A.	Synods	Parishes	Total	Special Gifts	Miscellaneous	Total Current Income
1	$24894	$2041		$9053		$9053	$2613	$338	$6822
2	2844	585	$3300	3974		7474	515	429	38939
3	12047	1020		6677		6677		793	11847
4	17884	1340	2400	21404	$7885	29289	1935	6215	20537
5	17163	932		3868		6268	2913	96	56663
6	1177	475		1312	31	1343		50	27372
7		15	7529						3045
8				1583	369	9481	201	847	10328
9	3448			12858		12858		145	16652
10									

CURRENT EXPENDITURES

Index No.	Administration	Instruction	Books Equipment	Operating	Maintenance	Interest	Loss on Annuities	Miscellaneous	Total Expenditures	Surplus or Deficit
1	$575	$22043		$10043	$9521	$671			$6809	$13 s
2	115	9265		3048		2675	$850	$498	43032	4093 d
3	600	12232	$399	4340	4046	4187			13597	1750 d
4	6238	29635		14040	1114	5030		5505	24292	3755 d
5		20177		1135	551	728	6044		59605	2942 d
6	598	4118	20					61	32365	4993 d
7	See Waterloo Collage								7211	4166 d
8	1330	4589	47	1577	473	714		1436	9663	635 s
9	427	15325		1664		6		950	18846	2194 d
10										

THE STUDENTS

Index No.	Alumni	Non-Lutheran	Total Col. Grad.	Grad. in Corresp.	Grad. in Residence	Special	3rd Year	2nd Year	1st Year	Total Enrolled	Grad. Total	Grad. In Correspondence	Grad. In Residence	U-Grad. Total	Specials	3rd Year	2nd Year	1st Year
1	314		40		19	1	4	4	12	41	19		19	22	2	4	4	12
2	1597	10	91		15	8	17	28	23	99	15		15	84	16	17	28	23
3	321		27				10	8	9	27				27		10	8	9
4	683		49		12		14	13	10	52	12		12	40		15	15	10
5	1400	9	147	45	76	2	21	20	30	150	76	45	76	74	2	22	21	31
6	500	7	76				9	10	10	76	45			31	1	9	10	10
7	218	4	11				5	2	4	15				15	3	7	3	4
8	70		10				3	3	4	13				13	0	0	3	3
9	31				4	2	5	2	6	9	4		4	9	2	6	3	8
10	113		19							23				19				

THE FACULTY

Index No.	Doctor	S.T.M.	B.D.	A.M.	A.B.	No Degree	Part Time	Full Time
1	4			1	2		4	3
2	4		1	3	3		1	6
3	1		3					4
4	8		3		5		3	4
5	11		4	2			2	9
6	2		5	1	3		2	5
7	1		1				6	3
8	1							2
9		1	3	2			2	4
10							2	

STATISTICAL TABLES—II. COLLEGES

THE PROPERTY

Index No.	Institution	Location	Founded	President	Type	Accredited by	Campus Acres	Campus Value	Buildings No.	Buildings Value	Value of Real Property	Library Vols.	Library Value	Laboratory and Museum	Furniture, Fixtures, Etc.	Value of Equipment	Total Value of Property
1	Gettysburg	Gettysburg, Pa.	1832	Rev. H. W. A. Hanson, D.D., LL.D.	C	1,2,3,4	100	$150000	15	$1500000	$1650000	55000	$100000	$45000	$125000	$270000	$1920000
2	Wittenberg	Springfield, O.	1845	Rev. R. E. Tulloss, Ph.D., D.D., LL.D.	C	1,2,3,4	54	334592	17	1606941	1941533	57537	46960	125500	125187	297647	2239180
3	Roanoke	Salem, Va.	1853	Rev. C. J. Smith, D.D., LL.D.	C	2,3,4	20	62448	9	473988	536436	18000	91276	26020	31025	148321	684757
4	Newberry	Newberry, S. C.	1856	Rev. J. C. Kinard, Litt.D., LL.D.	C	2,3,4	47	12587	11	350000	362587	22000	35000	10000	28644	73644	436231
5	Susquehanna	Selinsgrove, Pa.	1858	Rev. G. M. Smith, D.D.	C	3,4	62	141553	11	533513	675066	13385	23000		103830	126830	801896
6	Thiel	Greenville, Pa.	1866	Rev. E. S. Rudisill, Ph.D., D.D.	C	2,3,4	35	35000	8	353500	388500	17000	15000	17000	38250	70250	458750
7	Muhlenburg	Allentown, Pa.	1867	Rev. J. A. W. Haas, D.D., LL.D.	M	1,2,3,4	75	570344	10	1547894	2118238	51000	51000	32489	61987	145476	2263714
8	Carthage	Carthage, Ill.	1870	Rev. R. G. Schulz, D.D.	C	2,4	38	27808	10	364884	392692	25000	24335	19671	48373	92459	485161
9	Wagner	Staten Is., N. Y.	1885	C. C. Stoughton, A.M.	C	2,4	50	350000	10	724839	1074839	11000	19145	46776		65921	1140760
10	Midland	Fremont, Nebr.	1887	Rev. H. F. Martin, Ph.D., D.D.	C	3	15		6		335542	14000				27877	363419
11	Lenoir Rhyne	Hickory, N. C.	1891	Rev. P. E. Monroe, D.D.	C	2,3,4	37	149835	6	461224	611059	9300	15000	12000	52405	79405	690464
12	Waterloo	Waterloo, Ont. Can.	1911	Rev. F. B. Clausen, D.D.	C	2,3	See	Waterloo Seminary				10206	15000	6000	9792	30792	30792
13	Hartwick (Junior)	Oneonta, N. Y.	1928	Rev. C. W. Leitzell, D. D.	C	4	90	39000	4	287500	326500	7000	20000	68500	22000	110500	437000
14	Marion (Junior)	Marion, Va.	1873	Rev. E. H. Copenhaver, D.D.	W	5	5	25000	5	125000	150000		10000	1500	14674	26174	176174

Note: Blanks indicate no report or nothing to report.
Cents are omitted. Certain totals are on previous page.

Code: M—Men.
W—Women.
C—Coeducational.

Code:
1. Association of American Universities.
2. Regional Accrediting Association.
3. State University.
4. The Regents (New York).
5. Virginia State Board of Education.

THE FUNDS: PERMANENT — OTHER ASSETS

Index No.	Productive Restricted	Productive Unrestricted	Unproductive Annuities	Unproductive Other	Total Endowment	Loan Funds	Scholarships	Notes Interest Bearing	Notes Non-Int. Bearing	Other Property and Funds	Total Other Assets	Total Funds and Assets	Total Value of All Assets	Inc. Plant and Equip.	Inc. Endowment	Inc. Indebtedness	Indebt. Bldgs, Equip, Etc.	Indebt. Cur. Accumulated	Indebt. Total
1	$62008	$648265	$45500		$755773	$10000	$9066	$5795	$63941		$15795	$771568	$2691568		$68424	$37151			$73300
2	103527	1315881	298345		1808753	76662	21506	21506		12412	171174	1979928	4219108	$714	1000		$704450		704450
3		652506	3000		655506	8480		6379	289086		27271	682777	1367534	2500	6472	1000	71600	$32606	104206
4		347211			347211		5782		289086		289086	636297	1072528	72742			30000	28000	58000
5		353802	34300		388102			5308		16841	22623	410725	1212621						
6		131000		37000	168000				18200	5600	23800	191800	650550				98500		98500
7	106700	808122		14438	929260		1000				42039	971299	3235013				160000	62000	222000
8	233997	625577	16400		875974	713	949			36731	1713	877687	1362848				600500	87420	687920
9		368449			368449			713			18720	387169	1527929				153190		
10	32500	103626	5500		141626	1568		949			1568	143194	506613				250000	115014	365014
11	330132		1750	85702	417584		300		101661	17771	101661	519245	1209709				83240	13962	97202
12	28296				28296								643770					29440	29440
13		71000	3700		74700	2800		129270			132070	206770					68514		6851
14							4000	2920	1420		8340	8340	184514				37850	5682	4353

STATISTICAL TABLES—II. COLLEGES—Contin ued

THE CURRENT FUNDS—INCOME

Index No.	Students	Endowment	The Church U.L.C.A.	The Church Synods	The Church Parishes and Individuals	The Church Total	Sales and Services	Miscellaneous Sources	Educational and General Total	Aux. Dormitories	Aux. Dining Halls	Aux. Other	Aux. Total	Non-Ed. Invested Funds	Non-Ed. Current Gifts	Non-Ed. Other	Non-Ed. Total	Total Annual Income
1	$168125	$16998		$13857		$13857		$9882	$195005	$10715	$1749	$21	$10715	$4632		$9996	$13628	$205720 d
2	278529	82980	$1800		$11379	13179		7832	383208		2394	546	1770	180			180	398606 s
3	77638	25539	4500	1664	345	6509		1198	117554		3362		2940					120674
4	40644	9877	1805	7300	426	9531	$7419		57030		3317	8716	2362					60392
5	62725	20555	3000	10600	750	14350		7000	100231	12511	1200	4300	24544			5151	5151	129926
6	58700	5500		18000	131	18131			85550				5500					91050
7	158056		3000	1693	189	4882		3751	176187	5656	10922	1128	5656	41080		4342	45422	227265
8	56506	9723	1500	8325	1935	11760		2448	107497	3067	4684	4728	15118					89978
9	39529	12814	9000	7456	213	16669		416	65551	4843	958	506	8312					73363
10	49852	6477	2400	150		2550			73414	2846	4455	799	6307					82993
11	68505	7396	5000	15640	324	20964		11825	78454				8100			3272	3272	92655
12	7120								29900					6101			6101	29909
13	82212	4948	750	6500	98	7348		1197	94809		10		10					104819
14	6504		600	300	470	1370	124	676	8500		12420		12420		$10000		10000	20920

EXPENDITURES

Index No.	Gen. Admin.	Instruction	Organ. Research	Extension Activities	Library	Operation and Maintenance	Ed. & Gen. Total	Aux. Dorm. and Res.	Aux. Dining Halls	Aux. Other	Aux. Total	Annuities (Net Loss)	Interest on Loans	Scholarship Student Aid	Non-Ed. Other	Non-Ed. Total	Plant and Equipment	Indebtedness	Cap. Other	Cap. Total	Total Expenditures	Surplus or Deficit
1	$44913	$94553			$6884	$30873	$177223	$1089		$2012	$3101	$1460	$36164	$33924	$32037	$33497	$5168		$5095	$10263	$210720	$5000 d
2	83731	171374		$11225	8513	48504	323347	4388		3110	7498	1961	5511	13821	4972	7049	2376	$1000		$10263	398498	108 s
3	24554	54946			2367	8492	90360					180	3666			24484	5769	1000		6769	132605	11931 d
4	9615	33250			2124	8992	53981						8482	6792		3666				3376	61024	632 s
5	18092	56631			3678	20191	98592			7056	7056		9200		13000	15274					127692	2234 s
6	16400	32100			1800	20400	70700			3900	3900			4025		22200					96800	5750 s
7	26473	77464		28087	783	17270	151681			773			33950	5895		74207					227538	273 d
8	21966	23839			850	8960	55549		$877		1650			777		13520	1787	15406	1332	18525	87854	2124 s
9	10077	27556			1596	14284	52767			260	260		7625		4220	18213	375	267		642	70980	4388 s
10	19657	40154		2146	4087	11117	74670						17231	9133	250	4220					83438	444 d
11	10967	38754		5000	550	4000	62808			3905	3905			850		26602	2225	3226		5451	89410	3245 d
12		22895			3400	1504	24949								18531	850					31250	1341 s
13	12632			6298	967	6502	84360						3225	5751	2908	11884		4500		4500	100868	3951 s
14	14698	55528				6815	22480	124			124			1347		1347		300		300	24127	3207 d

STATISTICAL TABLES—II. COLLEGES—Continued

THE FACULTY

Index No.	Lutheran M	Lutheran W	Lutheran T	Total M	Total W	Total T	No Degree	A.B. Only	A.M. Only	Doctor
1	30		30	46	28	46	3	3	22	18
2	46	7	53	62	28	90	7	21	20	42
3	6	0	6	23	2	25	0	4	15	6
4	13	5	18	16	8	24	1	16	5	2
5	13	4	17	22	12	34		9	12	11
6	23	3	26	33	0	33		5	12	3
7	23	0	23	37	1	33		2	10	21
8	18	5	23	27	0	27		9	22	5
9	11		11	28	1	29	1	4	11	13
10	11	5	16	31	9	31		14	11	6
11	6	4	10	17	6	23	2	2	8	6
12	8	3	11	14	9	29	2	4	6	2
13	2	4	6	20	11	13	1	7	9	12
14		7	9	2			3	4	6	

THE STUDENTS — College of Liberal Arts

Index No.	Fresh M	Fresh W	Fresh T	Soph M	Soph W	Soph T	Jun M	Jun W	Jun T	Sen M	Sen W	Sen T	Spec M	Spec W	Spec T	Grad M	Grad W	Grad T
1	150	44	194	128	11	139	104	8	112	90		90	11	3	14		2	
2	178	160	338	111	109	220	57	51	108	53	52	105	15	10	25	5	1	7
3	112	25	137	87	26	113	47	21	68	33	14	47	1	0	1			1
4	64	40	104	30	30	60	40	21	61	25	23	48	26	27	53			
5	30	27	57	35	18	53	25	14	39	36	17	53	5	1	6			
6	47	41	88	55	25	80	21	29	50	20	25	45	5	3	8			
7	135	0	135	98	0	98	85		85	75		75	20	0	20			
8	66	36	102	42	47	89	25	22	47	40	19	59	2	12	14			
9	60	23	83	28	17	45	31	4	35	19	9	28	3	2	5			
10	76	81	157	55	28	83	20	17	37	16	13	29	10	9	19			
11	67	50	117	48	32	80	23	27	50	38	27	65	14	38	52			
12	11	7	18	35	31	66	11	9	20	5	6	11	13	26	39	1	1	2
13	66	53	119	5	19	24	25	38	63	7	66	73	8	9	17	3	3	3
14	5	40	45															

THE STUDENTS — Continued

Index No.	Lutheran M	Lutheran W	Lutheran T	Total M	Total W	Total T	Acad M	Acad W	Acad T	Spec Sch M	Spec Sch W	Spec Sch T	Summer M	Summer W	Summer T	Ext M	Ext W	Ext T	Grand Total No Dup. M	W	T	Alumni Graduates	Alumni Ex-Students
1	260	41	301	483	66	549				85	41	126	71	10	81	203	338	541	532	51	583	3525	1211
2	186	184	370	428	384	812							147	222	369				780	875	1655	4784	
3	44	4	48	280	87	367				14	18	32	53	55	108	9	12	21	310	121	431	1056	3698
4	77	70	147	185	141	326				28	45	73	47	103	150				246	272	518	1548	1700
5	60	44	104	131	77	208							43	47	90				203	178	381	3000	800
6	57	54	111	148	123	271				40	41	81	35	33	68	119	286	405	170	153	323	1042	4000
7	211		211	413		413				182	234	416	134	120	254				591	406	997	2605	
8	83	76	159	175	136	311				14	38	52	15	15	30	46	38	84	185	150	335	1207	4414
9	67	16	83	145	46	191							21	12	33				192	89	281	446	79
10	86	63	149	177	148	325							72	190	262	10	55	65	292	396	688	646	6000
11	80	87	167	190	147	337							50	296	346	60	365	425	314	821	1135	660	
12	18	12	30	47	51	98							13	19	32				59	66	125	101	818
13	19	25	44	174	167	341		17	17	1	20	21							174	167	341	327	818
14	2	28	30	10	59	69													11	96	107	556	2101

II. SERVING OUR STUDENTS

"The object of the Board shall be . . . to conserve the religious life of the students in the educational institutions of the Church, in the State Universities, and in other schools." The Constitution of the Board of Education, Article II.

The *Student Division* carries on its work of serving the students of the Church in the institutions of the Church, in tax-supported institutions of higher learning, in privately endowed colleges and universities, in professional and technical colleges and schools.

1. Visits of Secretaries

To Lutheran Colleges and Seminaries

Meaning of a Visit

A secretary visiting a campus interviews the administrative officers and those members of the faculty who are especially concerned with the religious life and activities of students. Upon invitation, a secretary visits classes in religious education, Bible, or in other fields in which a general class discussion may be carried on. Meetings of organized groups, like the Christian Association and Lutheran Student Association, are attended. Interviews with students individually and in groups become an opportunity for Christian guidance. Through the pastors of the local churches attended by students, the secretary will get into touch with church groups. In the seminaries, the secretary explains in detail the work of the Board, especially as it relates to the responsibility a future pastor faces with youth preparing for or attending college. A secretary may be invited to speak at convocation, in chapel, or before other academic, church or civic groups.

Lutheran Institutions Visited

United Lutheran Colleges: Carthage, Gettysburg, Hartwick, Lenoir Rhyne, Marion, Midland, Muhlenberg, Newberry, Roanoke, Saskatoon, Susquehanna, Thiel, Wagner, Waterloo, Wittenberg. *Seminaries:* Chicago, Gettysburg, Hamma, Hartwick, Northwestern, Philadelphia, Saskatoon, Southern, Waterloo, Western. *Secondary Schools:* Allentown Preparatory School, Lankenau School for Girls. *Motherhouses:* Baltimore, Mary J. Drexel. *Hospitals:* Manhattan, Lankenau.

Other Lutheran Institutions: Colleges: Augustana, Capital, Dana, Hebron, Jon Bjarnason, Luther, St. Olaf, Suomi; *Seminaries:* Augustana, Concordia, Suomi, Trinity, Immanuel Motherhouse. *Hospitals:* Augustana (Chicago), Immanuel, Lutheran (Moline), Norwegian Lutheran Deaconess (Chicago).

To Non-Lutheran Institutions

Meaning of a Visit

In places where a pastor is working with students, he sets up a visit for a secretary. Opportunity is given, if the visit occurs over a week-end, to speak to the Luther League or Student Association, to the Sunday School, and to the congregation on the work of the Board and of its own privileges and opportunities. Sometimes a secretary meets with church council, congregational committee on student work, or missionary societies. Interviews with individual Lutheran students and faculty are held, at least one group meeting of students, and a conference with student officers or cabinet is arranged. Through the pastor an invitation from the college administration to speak in convocation or chapel is often received. The president, and especially the dean, of an institution is visited, as are faculty members who are directly in contact with the religious courses or activities of students. Secretaries of the Christian Associations offer cooperation in meeting students, and church secretaries occasionally speak at their group meetings. Where pastors of other churches are working with students, calls are made in order to understand better the part the Lutheran Church has in the whole program of Christian activities of students. In places where there is no student pastor or Lutheran congregation, the visit by a secretary is arranged for in advance by a student, a Christian Association secretary, or an interested dean. In other cases, the secretary must arrange after arrival for the best possible contacts and future follow-up of work.

Non-Lutheran Institutions Visited

Alabama: Birmingham, Howard.

California: University: Berkeley and Los Angeles, Southern California, Stamford, Los Angeles Junior, Glendale Junior, San Jose Teachers.

Colorado: University, Colorado, Denver.

Connecticut: Hartford Seminary.

Georgia: Agnes Scott, Atlanta, Spelman, Georgia Industrial School for Negroes.

Illinois: University, Chicago, Northwestern, Bradley, Macomb.

Indiana: University, Butler, Notre Dame, Purdue.

Iowa: University, State, Coe, Drake.

Kansas: University, Manhattan, Ottawa.

Maryland and the District of Columbia: University, Western Maryland, Hood, Western Maryland Theological Seminary, Johns Hopkins Hospital, George Washington.

Massachusetts: Boston, Harvard, Radcliffe, Simmons, Mt. Holyoke, Smith, Wellesley.

Michigan: University, Hope, Kalamazoo; *State Teachers' Colleges:* Kalamazoo, Ypsilanti.

Minnesota: University.

Nebraska: University; *State Teachers' Colleges:* Peru, Wayne.

New Jersey: Princeton; *State Teachers' Colleges:* Trenton, Glassboro; Rider.

New York: West Point, Buffalo, Syracuse, Union, Elmira, Russell Sage, Skidmore, Vassar; *State Teachers' Colleges:* Albany, Buffalo, Fredonia; *Metropolitan New York:* Columbia, New York, College of the City of New York, Hunter, Barnard, Teachers College, New, Brooklyn, Brooklyn Law, Pratt, Packer, St. Joseph, College of Fine and Applied Arts, Julliard, Cooper Union, Savage, Gramercy Park, Union Theological Seminary, Biblical Seminary, New York School of Social Work, Bellevue Medical, International House; *Hospitals:* Bellevue, Booth, Cornell, Fifth Avenue, Flower, Lenox Hill, Metropolitan, Mt. Sinai, Saint Lukes, Stuyvesant.

North Carolina: University, State, Woman's College of University, Duke.

Oklahama: University.

Ohio: State University, Akron, Marietta, State Teachers College at Kent.

Oregon: University, Reed, State College at Corvallis, Willamette.

Pennsylvania: University, Temple, Pittsburgh, Lehigh, Bucknell, State, Albright, Carnegie Institute of Technology, Franklin and Marshall, Grove City, Juniata, Lafayette, Lebanon Valley, Margaret Morrison, Moravian College for Women, Moravian College for Men, Penn Hall, Pennsylvania College for Women, Swarthmore, Tenent, Ursinus, Wilson, Reformed Episcopal Seminary; *State Teachers Colleges:* Bloomsburg, California, East Stroudsburg, Kutztown, Lock Haven, Mansfield, Millersville, Shippensburg, Slippery Rock, West Chester.

South Carolina: University, Winthrop.

Virginia: University, Bridgewater, Staunton; State Teachers College at Harrisonburg.

Washington: University; State Teachers at Bellingham.

Wyoming: University.

Canada: University of Western Ontario, London.

2. Pastors for Students

It has been a principle in the work of the Board among students that the congregation in the college community is responsible for the Christian welfare of Lutheran students. The pastors of 236 congregations in educational centers in the United States and Canada have been listed. Most of these pastors are rendering service to students in universities, colleges, or professional schools. To these pastors the Board gives guidance by the Service Bulletin and through printed material for students. By correspondence and visits, the secretaries of the Board offer such personal assistance as is sought and needed by pastors. To twenty-three pastors or congregations in which the financial situation is such that work with students cannot be carried on without some assistance, the Board makes annual grants. To eight pastors or secretaries in as many metropolitan centers grants are made for student work. The vast majority of pastors and congregations work with students as one of their Christian privileges.

The following facts are of importance: Twenty-seven congregations that should be or are doing student work have church extension loans from the Board of American Missions. Thirty-five additional congregations doing some work among students get a salary or other grants from the Board of American Missions. To twenty of these sixty-two congregations or pastors the Board of Education makes some grant for student work. Two of these congregations are at independent universities, eighteen of these congregations are in cities or towns in which are located great state universities or colleges. The Church has never yet adequately faced the challenge of maintaining adequate parishes in strategic educational centers. **(See Recommendation 3, p. 239.)**

DIRECTORY OF PASTORS IN EDUCATIONAL CENTERS:

Alabama
G. H. C. Park ....Birmingham ....Birmingham Southern

California
E. A. Trabert ....Berkeley ....University of California
Muriel Bixby (Sec.) ....Los Angeles ....All Institutions
J. G. Dorn ....Los Angeles ....Junior College
R. D. Lechleitner (Am) ....Los Angeles ....University of California
                                                               at Los Angeles
H. I. Kohler ....Los Angeles ....University of Southern
                                                               California
P. L. Miller ....Glendale ....Junior College
D. L. Dyreson ....San Diego ....Teachers College
G. P. Kabele ....Fresno ....State Teachers College
G. H. Hillerman ....Pasadena ....Institute of Technology
W. C. Miller ....Redlands ....University of Redlands
E. T. May ....Santa Barbara ....State Teachers College
J. J. Raun ....San Francisco ....Teachers College
W. E. Crouser ....San Jose ....State Teachers College

Colorado
L. A. Swan ....Boulder ....University of Colorado
R. B. Wolf ....Colorado Springs ....Colorado College
E. W. Harner ....Denver ....Denver University

Connecticut
G. R. Seltzer ....Hartford ....Hartford Foundation
F. W Schaefer ....New Britain ....State Teachers College
Behrend Mehrtens ....New Haven ....Yale University

District of Columbia
Frances Dysinger (Sec.)..Washington ....All Institutions
O. F. Blackwelder ....Washington ....George Washington
                                                               University

Florida
B. D. Wessinger ....Lakeland ....Southern College
G. F. Snyder ....Tampa ....University of Tampa

Georgia

J. L. Yost ....Atlanta ....All Institutions
W. J. Ducker ....Macon ....All Institutions

Illinois

C. A. Piel ....Carthage ....Carthage College
D. P. Bair ....Champaign ....University of Illinois
I. O. Miller ....Aurora ....Aurora College
C. W. Kegley (Sec.) ....Chicago ....All Institutions
C. E. Paulus ....Chicago ....University of Chicago
C. A. Naumann ....Evanston ....Northwestern University
C. I. Empson ....Decatur ....Millikan University
R. R. Frobenius ....Elmhurst ....Elmhurst College
W. E. Koepf ....Macomb ....State Teachers College
W. L. Wilson ....Peoria ....Bradley Polytechnic
O. G. Beckstrand ....Rockford ....Rockford College
G. J. Curran ....Wheaton ....Wheaton College
D. R. Kabele ....Wilmette ....National College of Education

Indiana

L. T. Riley ....Evansville ....Evansville College
P. H. Krauss ....Ft. Wayne ....All Institutions
A. K. Trout ....Indianapolis ....Butler University
H. C. Stolldorf ....Lafayette ....Purdue University
H. R. Ogle ....North Manchester ....Manchester College
L. C. Westenbarger ....Muncie ....State Teachers College
J. L. Cauble ....Terre Haute ....Rose Polytechnic
C. F. Koch ....Richmond ....Earlham College
G. F. Schutes ....Valparaiso ....Valparaiso University

Iowa

W. S. Dysinger ....Iowa City ....Iowa State University
Henry Scherer ....Cedar Rapids ....Coe College
J. A. Miller ....Davenport ....All Institutions
A. J. Beil ....Des Moines ....All Institutions
G. B. Arbaugh ....Dubuque ....Dubuque University
W. F. Rex ....Fairfield ....Parsons College
A. B. Schwertz ....Sioux City ....Morningside College

Kansas

C. A. Puls ....Lawrence ....Kansas University
W. E. Wheeler ....Atchison ....St. Benedict's College
O. W. Ebright ....Emporia ....State Teachers and Emporia Colleges
W. H. Moeller ....Hays ....State Teachers College
B. R. Lantz ....Salina ....Wesleyan College
C. L. Stager ....Topeka ....Washburn College
E. E. Stauffer ....Wichita ....Wichita and Friends Universities

Kentucky

H. C. Lindsay ....Louisville ....University of Louisville

Maryland

R. D. Clare ....Baltimore ....Goucher College and Johns Hopkins University
W. A. Wade ....Baltimore ....State Teachers College
A. J. Traver ....Frederick ....Hood College
W. V. Simon ....Frostburg ....State Teachers College
H. R. Spangler ....Lutherville ....Maryland College
S. H. Kornmann ....Washington, D. C. ....University of Maryland and College Park
P. W. Quay ....Westminster ....Western Maryland College

Massachusetts

N. D. Goehring ....Boston ....Harvard University and Other Institutions

Michigan

H. O. Yoder	Ann Arbor	University of Michigan
H. J. Fennig	Battle Creek	Battle Creek College
T. F. Weiskotten	Detroit	All Institutions
R. J. White	Grand Rapids	Calvin College
C. E. Jensen	Kalamazoo	State Teachers and Kalamazoo Colleges

Minnesota

C. A. Wendell (Aug.)	Minneapolis	University of Minnesota
G. C. Koehler	St. Paul	Hamline University and Macalester College
H. E. Reinhardt	Duluth	State Teachers College

Mississippi

J. W. Mangum	Jackson	All Institutions

Missouri

R. G. Riechmann	Cape Girardeau	State Teachers College
F. F. Mueller	St. Louis	Washington University

Montana

L. G. Cloninger	Billings	Polytechnic Institute

Nebraska

F. C. Pryor	Fremont	Midland College
R. E. Rangeler G. K. Rubrecht M. Koolen	Lincoln	University of Nebraska
F. C. Schuldt	Hastings	Hastings College
W. H. Traub	Omaha	All Institutions
W. C. Heidenreich	Wayne	State Teachers College
H. A. Coder	York	York College

New Jersey

A. H. Holthusen	New Brunswick	Rutgers and New Jersey College for Women
E. A. Steimle	Jersey City	All Institutions
M. F. Walz	Newark	All Institutions
P. T. Warfield	Trenton	State Teachers and Rider Colleges

New Mexico

W. F. Martin	Albuquerque	University of New Mexico

New York

F. L. Gollnick	Oneonta	Hartwick College and State Normal School
Frederic Sutter	Staten Island	Wagner College
C. E. Frontz	Albany	State Teachers College
P. E. Schmidt	Brooklyn	Pratt Institute
H. J. Pflum	Buffalo	All Institutions
C. E. Eichner	Elmira	Elmira College
E. T. Horn	Ithaca	Cornell University
A. Steimle	New York City	Columbia University
Charles Trexler	New York City	Hunter College
P. E. Scherer	New York City	New York University
C. C. Hine	New York City	N. Y. U. (Heights)
F. J. Baum	Poughkeepsie	Vassar College
F. R. Knubel	Rochester	All Institutions
H. D. Shimer	Schenectady	Union College
E. L. Keller	Syracuse	Syracuse University
L. H. Grandy	Troy	All Institutions

North Carolina

J. D. Mauney	Hickory	Lenoir Rhyne College
H. A. Schroder	Chapel Hill	University of North Carolina
A. J. Yount	Boone	State Teachers College
J. F. Crigler	Charlotte	Queens-Chicora College

H. A. Schroder ....Durham ....Duke University
C. E. Fritz ....Greensboro ....Woman's College of University of North Carolina
F. L. Conrad ....High Point ....High Point College
C. E. Norman ....Raleigh ....State College
M. L. Stirewalt ....Salisbury ....Catawba College
S. W. Hahn ....Winston-Salem ....Salem College

Ohio

E. G. Howard ....⎱ Springfield ....Wittenberg College
E. C. Xander ....⎰
L. A. Sittler ....Columbus ....State University of Ohio
G. D. Busch ....Athens ....University of Ohio
C. S. Hayner ....Ada ....Ohio Northern University
F. C. Fry ....Akron ....Akron University
S. D. Meyers ....Alliance ....Mt. Union College
A. H. Smith ....Ashland ....Ashland College
E. R. Walborn ....Bowling Green ....B. G. State University
H. L. Meister ....Cincinnati ....All Institutions
A. M. Lutton ....Cincinnati ....All Institutions
Joseph Sittler, Jr. ....Cleveland ....Western Reserve and Case
Dana Johnson ....Dayton ....Dayton University
B. F. Hofer ....Defiance ....Defiance College
                         Delaware ....Ohio Wesleyan
J. L. Urich ....Elyria ....Oberlin
H. Ward Grieb ....Findlay ....Findlay College
M. W. Wappner ....Kent ....State Teachers College
W. L. Spielman ....Marietta ....Marietta College
P. J. Renz ....Oxford ....Miami University
W. O. Kantner ....Tiffin ....Heidelberg College
W. W. Larson ....Toledo ....Toledo University
P. S. Kelly ....Wooster ....College of Wooster
W. M. Brandt ....Newark ....Denison University (Granville)

Oklahoma

                         Stillwater ....State College
C. N. Swihart ....Oklahoma City ....Oklahoma City University
E. V. Roland ....Tulsa ....University of Tulsa

Oregon

F. S. Beistel ....Eugene ....University of Oregon
L. R. Nielsen ....LaGrande ....State Normal School
W. E. Brinkman ....Portland ....Reed College
P. W. Eriksen ....Salem ....Wilamette University

PENNSYLVANIA

Alleghany Synod

J. O. Krueger ....Huntingdon ....Juniata College

East Pennsylvania Synod

W. E. McHale ....Annville ....Lebanon Valley College
A. C. Kanzinger ....Ardmore ....Haverford College
W. L. Wolf ....Easton ....Lafayette College
R. H. Gearhart ....Philadelphia ....University of Pennsylvania and Other Institutions

Ministerium of Pennsylvania

H. P. C. Cressman ......Allentown ....Muhlenberg College
W. C. Schaeffer, Jr. ......Allentown ....Cedar Crest College
G. F. Gehr ....Bethlehem ....Lehigh University and Moravian College
M. A. Kurtz ....Bethlehem ....Lehigh University
H. A. Weaver ....Chester ....Pennsylvania Military College
W. O. Fegeley ....Collegeville ....Ursinus College
Frank Croman ....Elizabethtown ....Elizabethtown College
K. P. Otten ....Jenkintown ....Beaver College
C. F. Brobst ....Kutztown ....State Teachers College
E. J. Hoh ....Lancaster ....Franklin and Marshall College

Millersville ....State Teachers College
L. S. Sweitzer ....Reading ....Albright College
J. S. Kistler ....Stroudsburg ....State Teachers College
J. H. K. Miller ....West Chester ....State Teachers College

Pittsburgh Synod
W. E. Eisenberg ....Greenville ....Thiel College
J. R. Booth ....Beaver Falls ....Geneva College
F. C. Snyder ....Clarion ....State Teachers College
A. J. Pfohl ....Indiana ....State Teachers College
R. A. Kline ....Meadville ....Allegheny College
Pittsburgh ....All Institutions
R. C. Lauffenberger ....Slippery Rock ....State Teachers College
H. B. Ernest ....Washington ....Washington and Jefferson

Susquehanna Synod
D. C. Baer ....Selinsgrove ....Susquehanna University
N. S. Wolf ....Bloomsburg ....State Teachers College
Lewisburg ....Bucknell University
C. H. Stein ....Lock Haven ....State Teachers College
J. F. Harkins ....State College ....Pennsylvania State College

West Pennsylvania Synod
D. F. Putman ....Gettysburg ....Gettysburg College
H. B. Stock ....Carlisle ....Dickinson College
C. A. Neal ....Chambersburg ....Wilson College and Penn
Hall
W. W. Barkley ....Shippensburg ....State Teachers College

South Carolina
E. B. Keisler ....Newberry ....Newberry College
P. D. Brown ....Columbia ....University of South Caro-
lina
K. W. Kinard ....Columbia ....Columbia College
G. J. Gongaware ....Charleston ....Citadel and College of
Charleston
J. E. Stockman ....Greenville ....Furman and Greenville
Colleges
W. J. Roof ....Rock Hill ....Winthrop College
D. B. Werts ....Spartanburg ....Converse and Wofford
Colleges
B. M. Clark ....Walhalla ....Clemson College

Tennessee
A. M. Huffman ....Knoxville ....University of Tennessee
S. C. Ballentine ....Bristol ....All Institutions
H. A. McCullough ....Chattanooga ....University of Chattanooga
L. A. Wertz ....Greeneville ....Tusculum College
V. D. Derrick ....Memphis ....Teachers College and
Southwest College
I. W. Gernert ....Nashville ....All Colleges

Texas
F. W. Kern ....Austin ....Texas University
N. H. Kern ....Dallas ....Southern Methodist College
Houston ....Rice Institute
J. F. Vorkoper ....San Antonio ....Westmoreland College

Virginia
C. A. Honeycutt ....Marion ....Marion College
H. J. Rhyne ....Salem ....Roanoke College
D. W. Zipperer ....Blacksburg ....Virginia Polytechnic
M. L. Minnich ....Harrisonburg ....State Teachers College
R. T. Troutman ....Lexington ....All Institutions
R. L. Markley ....Lynchburg ....All Colleges
Radford ....State Teachers College
J. J. Scherer ....Richmond ....All Colleges
J. L. Sieber ....Roanoke ....Hollins College
C. M. Teufel ....Staunton ....Staunton Military and
Mary Baldwin

Washington

O. A. Bremer	Seattle	University of Washington
V. J. Eylands	Bellingham	State Teachers College
A. K. Walborn	Spokane	Whitworth and Gonzaga Colleges

West Virginia

W. R. Hashinger	Morgantown	University of West Virginia
W. P. Cline	Charleston	All Institutions
A. F. Richardson	Davis	Davis and Elkins College
H. L. Hann	Fairmont	State Teachers College
A. B. Leamer	Huntington	Marshall College
F. G. Robinson	Keyser	State Teachers College
J. H. Fray	Shepherdstown	Shepherd College

Wisconsin

C. J. Rockey	Madison	University of Wisconsin
D. E. Bosserman	Appleton	Lawrence College
F. A. Berg	Beloit	Beloit College
H. N. Stoffel	LaCrosse	State Teachers College
A. A. Zinck	Milwaukee	Marquette University
J. F. Fedders	Milwaukee	State Teachers and Milwaukee Downer Colleges
E. R. Wicklund	Oshkosh	State Teachers College
R. R. Doering	Platteville	State Teachers College
A. G. Riggle	Superior	State Teachers College
A. A. Hahn	Waukesha	Carroll College

Wyoming

H. S. Lawrence	Laramie	University of Wyoming

Canada

C. S. Roberts	Waterloo, Ont.	Waterloo College and Seminary
H. Hodel	Saskatoon, Sask.	Lutheran Seminary
C. Kleimer	Edmonton, Alta.	University of Alberta
N. Willison	Hamilton, Ont.	McMaster University
T. S. Rees	Winnipeg, Man.	University of Manitoba

Other Lutheran Pastors Who Work with Students

In student centers where there are no United Lutheran pastors, the staff cooperates, as far as possible, with student pastors of other Lutheran Synods.

3. Work in Student Centers

Philadelphia

Concerted work among students goes back to the formation in 1908 by the late Frank M. Riter, Esq., of a student work committee of laymen and clergy which has perpetuated itself in influence and financial support to the present day. In 1922 the Rev. Robert Gearhart, D.D., succeeded the Rev. C. P. Harry, D.D., who from 1917 had been university pastor in Philadelphia called by the committee on university work of the General Council. Dr. Gearhart has been longest in continuous service as a pastor of students in the United Lutheran Church and he is the only pastor for students who has no responsibilities as the pastor of a parish. He conducts a Bible class for students at Holy Communion Church and cooperates closely with about ten city congregations.

The Ministerium of Pennsylvania and the East Pennsylvania Synod have purchased an admirable and well located Student House which is used for student groups and for a residence by the pastor.

The Lutheran students of Philadelphia number about 1,250, half of whom Dr. Gearhart knows personally and 350 of whom are definitely connected with his campus or church centered work. At least one half of the whole number of students live in their own homes. Students from nine major and five smaller institutions and from four schools of nursing are served.

At the University of Pennsylvania Dr. Gearhart is associated with the appointees of five other Protestant bodies in heading up the Christian Association. Each pastor has definite duties in a cooperative program as well as to his own church students. The Christian Association building built by contributions of Philadelphia church men including Lutherans, provides an excellent office and headquarters. In it was held the conference for pastors in February, 1936, and the annual conference of the North Atlantic region of the L. S. A. A. in 1935. The third and fourth annual metropolitan conferences of Lutheran students gathered here in December, 1934 and 1935.

Student luncheon groups conducted on six campuses provide opportunity for serious study. During the biennium the groups have used Dr. Gearhart's material, *The Application of the Teaching of Jesus to the Needs of the World Today* and *The Meaning and Value of the Creeds of the Church*. The 275 study groups at the luncheon hour had an aggregate attendance of 2,854.

Student deputations, in which fifty-eight students took part, presented programs in fifty-eight different metropolitan or suburban congregations. Through these engagements students receive actual training in presenting the message of the Church, make valuable congregational contacts, and interest congregations in student work.

Interviews with 2,806 students and calls on 791, hospitality to 786, attendance at 14 conferences, and 101 addresses, s h o w s o m e of the procedures.

Thirty-five students made definite personal commitment to Christ. Dr. Gearhart has noted "a much deeper appreciation of life, its meaning and value, and the necessity of a vital religious experience in order to meet the problem it thrusts upon us."

Greater Boston

The United Lutheran Synod of New York in convention in Albany in June, 1936, voted a campaign for $110,000 to build a chapel for the University Lutheran Association of Greater Boston. The chapel will be erected on the desirable property near Harvard Yard, owned for a number of years by the Association. A committee with which Mr. Wickey has been called in consultation was appointed to procure this money. The synod and the Board of Education each have continued giving $2,500 a year toward the budget of the Boston work.

For eleven years Mr. Goehring has been pastor for the University Lutheran Association and Church. The congregation is composed of 81 members, largely professional people. More than 100 Lutheran students are closely associated with the congregation in working among 250 students from the ten major and numerous minor institutions in Greater Boston. These students represent more states and countries and a greater variety of synodical bodies proportionately than any other one student center An unusually large proportion of students do graduate work.

A large number of students regularly attend the service of worship held for a number of years at Phillips Brooks House, then in a rented hall, and now in their own temporary chapel. The Church Board and the Lutheran Student Council of twenty members from seven different institutions this biennium cooperate closely. This makes the administrative aspect of the association an important part of student life. It has resulted in generous financial contributions from the students for the maintenance of the Boston work. A well balanced social program has helped create an esprit de corps that continues in close relationships between Mr. Goehring and the alumni. The weekly discussion meetings and much of the social program is held in the parsonage. During the past year financial adjustments were made so that the parsonage could again be opened in Cambridge. This has increased the effectiveness of the work.

Mr. Goehring each year accepts invitations from the administrations to speak in the various institutions in Greater Boston. He has been active in the Student Christian Movement. This has resulted in making the Lutheran Church a strong factor in the policies of the Movement in New England. Through it Mr. Goehring has spoken on many campuses in New England. He has also been active in the Ministerial Association of the City and has gained for the University Lutheran Student Association a place of importance in the religious and educational life of Boston.

New York City

For the past five years the Board of Education has given to New York City a greater proportion of its resources than in previous years. In addition to the regularly allotted budget, the Board has asked Miss Winston to give as much time as possible to the metropolitan area. This has amounted to about five months out of each year. The services of the Washington office and generous use of printed matter have added to the effectiveness of the work.

During the first year of the biennium the Reverend C. B. Holand continued his work among the men students on the Columbia campus. The second year, the Reverend R. F. Auman made that particular contact. The Lutheran work at Columbia is done cooperatively by Dr. Steimle, Sister Pearle Lyerly, Rev. Auman and Miss Winston. Relationship with the chaplain's office coordinates the Lutheran interests with the religious activities of the campus. Weekday and Sunday Chapel speakers are arranged for through Miss Winston. The Columbia Lutheran Student Association has general meetings throughout the year. The various colleges of the University have frequent meetings of their units of the Association. Personal visiting is the most important phase of the campus work. The Church of the Advent is the specifically designated church for Columbia. Through the annual reception, the services of worship and the weekly twilight hour the students here find a church home. A brief but intensive period of activity is carried on during each summer session. The students are largely doing graduate work. Many teach on other campuses where they promote the relationship of the Church with the student.

The New York University Lutheran Student Association has monthly meetings at Holy Trinity Church. At other times the students use the facilities of the church for their social activities. Students from a number of institutions in the city attend the services of worship. Through the cooperation of Dr. Paul E. Scherer, the Reverend W. H. Davies and Sister Bessie Engstrom, the New York University Lutheran Student Association has become one of the most vital religious groups on the campus. The official contact with the University and most of the personal calling is done by Miss Winston.

The unique and continuous activities of the Hunter Lutheran Student Association are due to faculty members, Miss Dorothea Hess, Dr. Helene Hartung and Miss Henrietta Tichy. St. James Church, Dr. Charles Trexler, pastor, offers its facilities for worship, meetings and social functions of the Association.

The Lutheran Nurses Association, with units in the larger training schools for nurses, is under the immediate direction of Sister Pearle Lyerly. Through monthly meetings and personal calls several hundred nurses annually have contact with the Church. Each year there is a special communion for nurses on Ash Wednesday in the Church of the Advent.

Wagner College is an important factor in the life of the Lutheran Student Association in New York City. Students from the college have been leaders in the Metropolitan Association. Faculty members have accepted invitations to speak to various campus associations.

A very large proportion of students are in the smaller professional and vocational schools in the city. Contact with them is possible through personal visiting, publicity and the services of worship.

The Lutheran Student Association of Greater New York is the organizing factor, from the student angle, of the New York City work. On the council of the association are two representatives from each organized campus, including the nurses Association and three representatives at large. Miss Winston is the official adviser. Council meetings are held at least three times each semester. Plans are formed and carried out for the metropolitan association. These include one social function and one conference a semester. The general annual conference the first semester had Dr. H. D. Hoover and Dr. M. Hadwin Fischer as speakers during the biennium. The international meeting held each second semester has had Dr. Conrad Hoffmann and Dr. R. H. Long as the speakers. Students from other countries and young people from the non-English speaking congregations of New York City were special guests. The metropolitan association is active in the area, regional, and national work of the Lutheran Student Association

The Lutheran Student Association not only helps the student from distant communities adjust himself to his metropolitan campus life. It also offers the New York City student opportunities for fellowship and spiritual guidance in company with other students from his own church. The disconcerting influences of academic, social, economic, and commuting life in New York make work with all types of Lutheran students an important integrating factor in their personal lives and their church relationships.

Cooperation from the Women's Missionary Society of New York Synod has made available through the student census a large number of names of students which otherwise could not be obtained. The financial and general promotional contributions of the women have been invaluable. The Lutheran Woman's League of New York has also assisted financially in specific New York City work.

The outstanding need of New York City is a student pastor. In this project the Board of Education of the United Lutheran Synod of New York has expressed an interest for several years. A pastor doing full time work among the 2,000 Lutheran students in 76 different institutions would complement, from the campus angle, the influence of the home church. He would help conserve for the Church the students whom he directly touches and those students who would be reached in all parts of the country where New York City alumni enter professional life.

West Chester

The State Teachers College at West Chester is one of the most influential of the thirteen institutions of this type in Pennsylvania. Of an approximate enrollment of 1,100, 150 are Lutheran students of whom 135 live on campus. Two-thirds of these students come from congregations which belong to the Ministerium of Pennsylvania.

It was not until 1926 that a regular pastor was provided for Calvary Church, a mission organized in 1923 by the East Pennsylvania Synod. The last regular pastor resigned in 1934 and the Board of American Missions withdrew its support. Later the East Pennsylvania Synod discontinued Calvary Church as a mission. Because of the value of the congregation as a necessary basis for work with students, the Board of Education took over the responsibility of holding together the few members. Mr. Harry was directed to care for the congregation as well as for the students and the East Pennsylvania Synod agreed to contribute $300 annually to the Board of Education in consideration of this service.

Mr. Harry has been in charge of the work since July, 1934. During the biennium the communing membership of Calvary has increased from 54 to 87. The congregation has paid its apportionment in full. The average church attendance of students has been 15. Students have helped in ushering, with the music, and in Sunday School. They have also contributed to the budget.

Calvary Church asked to be transferred to the Ministerium of Pennsylvania and the transfer was effected on Ascension Day, 1936. The Ministerium and the Board are working out plans for the development of this strategic field. These include the acquiring of an adequate church building which the congregation has never had and without which no permanent advance among townspeople or students can be made. Church services have been held in the New Century Club and Mr. Harry has been compelled to use a rented room as a study and for group meetings and Luther League.

Chicago

For more than a decade the Board has been actively interested in work among students in the Chicago area. It promoted such efforts as the pastors of congregations nearest the great educational institutions could carry on by giving them modest annual grants-in-aid.

In the fall of 1934 the Board entered into an arrangement with Mr. Charles W. Kegley, then a middler at Maywood Seminary and a graduate student at Northwestern University at Evanston, to work with the students on that campus. Mr. Kegley's interest spread from that campus to the McKinlock campus of Northwestern in Chicago. Earlier contacts gave him entrance into professional schools of the city. As a consequence of student interest Mr. Kegley with the cooperation of Mr. Carl Lundquist, a former president of the L. S. A. A. doing his practical year of the Augustana Seminary work in a Chicago parish, conducted two successful conferences for students in November, 1934, and March, 1935.

In October, 1935, a Metropolitan Lutheran Student Council was elected by students and Mr. Kegley was elected active adviser. This council in November, 1935, acted as host to students from Augustana, Carthage, the Universities of Illinois, Iowa, Nebraska, and Wisconsin, who voted to form a new Region of the L. S. A. A. to be called The Hub. Another metropolitan conference in February, 1936, indicated growing interest and need.

The Board has arranged with Mr. Kegley to continue his work as student secretary for the Chicago metropolitan area on approximately a half time basis. Individuals of various Lutheran bodies are keenly interested and the Chicago Conference of the Women's Missionary Society of the United Lutheran Church are definitely cooperating. The Illinois Synod has enthusiastically voted its cooperation and financial support.

The importance for the Church of establishing a real work among the students in the many varied types of institutions in the Chicago area cannot be over-emphasized. This field offers a magnificent challenge to all Lutheran bodies for a cooperative project.

4. Cooperative Activities and Contacts

Only with the cooperation of the synods, boards, and organizations of the Church can the work with the students of the Church be well done.

With the Synods

Some years ago the Board requested every synod to appoint a standing committee on student work. With such a committee, the staff tries to keep in close touch, through correspondence and visits on the territory and by occasional meetings. Only ten synods have functioned in the student field through a duly appointed committee.

The sense of responsibility toward the student youth of the Church can be noted, however, in the fact that fourteen synods have made grants for work among students on their territory: Illinois, Indiana, Iowa, Nebraska, German Nebraska, New York, North Carolina, Ohio, Pacific, Ministerium of Pennsylvania, East Pennsylvania, Susquehanna, S. Carolina, Virginia.

With the Augustana Synod

The staff continues to render every possible service to students and pastors of the Augustana Synod. No attempt has been made to separate the service given to Augustana students: they are found on many campuses in all parts of the United States. Many Augustana students are leaders of the Lutheran Student Association groups on campuses, in the regions, and in the national organization. Secretaries have served predominantly Augustana groups of students in Manhattan, Kansas, Minneapolis, Seattle. Our pastors serve many Augustana students at Purdue University, University of Illinois, in the universities and colleges of Boston and New York City. Pastors of the Augustana Synod are designated as Lutheran pastors for students in twenty-one centers in thirteen states. Our secretaries serve them by correspondence and personal visits as the occasion may warrant. All of our Board's printed material is available to them without charge, and is largely used. The Board appreciates the fine spirit of cooperation on the part of the Augustana Synod, both personal and financial, and trusts that it may continue.

With the Luther League

Reports from student pastors show that in a number of places the Luther League is the organization through which work with students is carried on. Much printed material in the field of Christian guidance published by the Board has been used by the Luther League. Mr. Harry continues as chairman of the literature committee and editor of the *Topics Quarterly* of the Luther League.

With the Women's Missionary Society

Because the Women's Missionary Society in 1918 saw the advantage of doing its promotional and recruiting work among college women through a secretary for women students on the staff of the Board of Education, The United Lutheran Church has the distinction of being the first Church which has brought to college women, through one staff agency, the complete challenge of the Church.

In 1922 Miss Markley became a member of the candidate committee, and in 1924, the chairman. She is the chairman of the enlarged personnel committee which is charged with finding young women qualified for specific positions. This personnel committee presents to the executive board of the Women's Missionary Society young women who are recommended for appointments by the Board of American Missions and by the Board of Foreign Missions.

Miss Markley and Miss Winston, through official membership or special appointment in the educational department and sub-committees, and through constant contacts, keep in touch with the executive board of the Women's Missionary Society. As guest speakers at missionary conventions and conferences they emphasize the inherent relation of Christian higher education and the progress of the Church at home and abroad.

The direct contact of the Board with the Women's Missionary Society is through the two women who are named as advisory members to the Board of Education and who are voting members of its committee on student work. To the Board of Education the Women's Missionary Society has been making a generous annual grant since 1920. The W. M. S. of the Synod of New York and of the Ministerium of Pennsylvania provide a share of this grant, because of the large number of women students in their areas.

Through a student secretary in every conference and synodical Women's Missionary Society since 1919 an annual census of students has been taken by the Board. For the academic year 1935-36, 7,707 students were reported from forty-five per cent of the congregations of our Church. These names are valuable to the student pastors and the staff in making contact with students. By far the most valuable service rendered by the seventy women who act as student secretaries is their part in presenting the important work of the Board, and in creating an educational consciousness not only in the home congregation but in student centers.

The Board has published three pamphlets with the joint imprint of the Education Department of the Women's Missionary Society: *Students Going and Coming, Does It Make Sense, Like a Mighty Army,* a reprint from the *Christian Herald.*

With the Inner Mission Board

The Board has always considered student nurses as part of the general student group and pastors have included them in their work. Inner Mission pastors in a number of metropolitan centers have done most successful work with student and graduate nurses as they meet them in institutional activities. A joint committee of the Board of Education and of the Inner Mission Board is working on the responsibility of the Church in this field. Two pieces of printed material in editions of 20,000 have been issued with the joint imprint of the two Boards.

A Guild for Lutheran Nurses,—nation-wide, to be open to all nurses of the Lutheran Church,—somewhat on the lines of the Lutheran Student Association of America, is in the forming. Such Guilds are now in existence in a number of metropolitan centers.

In Educational Centers

At the *University of Michigan* a joint committee consisting of members of the United Lutheran congregation and of the American Lutheran congregation oversees the student work. By agreement, the parish house of the American Lutheran congregation is the student center, and the pastor of the United Lutheran congregation directs the student work.

At the *University of Nebraska* a joint committee, composed of pastors and laymen, uses a local pastor on part time to make initial contacts with students, to link them with the local congregations, and to direct the activities of the Lutheran Student Association. The budget of the committee is balanced by grants from the Nebraska Synods of the United Lutheran Church, from our Board, from the Danish Synod, and from the Augustana Synod.

In *Oregon* pastors and laymen form the Oregon Lutheran Student Service Association which provides for individual and group membership. A pastor of the American Lutheran Church is the secretary, and directs valuable work at the State University in Eugene, at the State College in Corvallis, and at the State Teachers College in Monmouth. The Pacific Synod cooperates in this work.

In *Los Angeles* pastors and laymen form the Luther Associates. This organization gathers funds, cooperates with the university religious conference, and through an executive committee carries on work among students. Students and pastors representing different campuses, congregations, and synods, coordinate their activities through a capable part time secretary, a young woman who is a member of a United Lutheran congregation.

With the Lutheran Student Association of America

This association is nation-wide, with a membership of students from practically every general Lutheran body, but with no official affiliation to any synod. The work of the L. S. A. A. is directed by the Lutheran Student Council of America, made up of delegates from the various regions. Mr. Harry, who has been annually elected by the Council as one of its advisers, was in 1935 elected an adviser for life. By invitation, all members of the staff have been guest speakers and leaders at various regional conferences during the past biennium. (Mr. Harry helped organize and conduct the national conference or *Ashram* held in Oconomowoc, Wisconsin, August, 1936, and limited to 100 delegates.)

The Association continues its annual grant for graduate study to a student in India. It also continues to assist the National Lutheran Council in its overseas work.

No Lutheran fellowship is doing more to bring about a better understanding of the Lutheran Church and of its present and future responsibility.

With the Student Commission of the American Lutheran Conference

By invitation Miss Markley and Mr. Harry met with the Commission in Chicago on May 7, 1935, to explore possible areas of cooperation and coordination. The obvious fields are in the publishing of literature for students and in the counselling and encouraging of the L. S. A. A. Further opportunities are seen in joint work in undeveloped student centers and in defining general areas of supervision of work among Lutheran students.

5. Items of Interest

Conferences for Pastors Working with Students

The Board invited pastors for students and representative faculty members from Lutheran colleges and seminaries to two-day conferences in February, 1936, for a frank study of the work that is being done for students. The conference for the east was held in Philadelphia, February 4 and 5 and for the middle west in Chicago, February 18 and 19, with a registration of about fifty guests at the former and thirty-five at the latter conference. (Work with students of all types of institutions was represented by the pastors present: liberal arts colleges, some of them church-related, some of them Lutheran; universities, state, metropolitan, and independent; state teachers colleges and technical and professional schools.) Those attending the two conferences knew student problems on the campuses of eleven state universities, ten metropolitan or independent universities, nineteen Lutheran institutions, ten state colleges, and technical and professional schools and liberal arts colleges numbering well up in the thirties. These workers with students in the name of the Church came from Canada and from states as far separated as Washington, South Carolina, and Massachusetts.

The program was the same for both conferences. It was built up on the seminar plan so as to provide well prepared direction as well as free discussion. The five planned sessions, the luncheons, and the dinner which the guests enjoyed together, gave ample opportunity for expressing points of view and sharing practical experiences. The following is an outline of the program: *The Student Mind*—seminar leaders, the Rev. R. H. Gearhart, D.D., Philadelphia; the Rev. Wendell S. Dysinger, Ph.D., Iowa City. *The Message of the Church*—seminar leaders, the Rev. N. D. Goehring, Cambridge; the Rev. Carroll J. Rockey, D.D., Madison. *The Program and Method of Work*—seminar leaders, the Rev. Howard R. Gold, D.D., New Rochelle, N. Y.; the Rev. Henry O. Yoder, Ann Arbor. *The Personal Problems and Privileges of the Pastor:* An Evaluation of the Conference —seminar leaders, the Rev. Gould Wickey, Ph.D., Washington; the Rev. Ross Miller, Ph.D., Wittenberg College.

Points of value stressed at the conferences included the following: The challenge to our student pastors and faculty to compile the results of their experience in case studies, as examples of the need of sanctified psychiatry, by brief accounts of successful techniques. The tremendous need of articles, essays, books, by Lutheran writers on the problems pertinent to thinking Christian students or laity who face uncertain futures. A renewed call to the Church to bring to students or laity alienated or unwon by legalism or dogmatism, through fellowship, worship, and sacraments, its message of love as well as of authority.

These two conferences, like the similar conferences of 1930 and previous years, were of tremendous value both to the staff of the Board and to all guests who returned to their fields inspired to work more earnestly for the upbuilding of the Christian life of students.

Publications

Going to College. From parents, pastors, and professors came requests for a little book which would help the prospective college student to make the transition from the life at home to the life at college, and to direct him in his college activity in accordance with Christian principles. To satisfy this need the Board of Education authorized its staff to prepare such a book. *Going to College* is the name of the book and is now available at fifty cents the copy. It may be ordered through the United Lutheran Publication House or the Board of Education. Sunday school teachers, pastors, and friends will find this a worth while volume to place in the hands of every prospective college student.

Service Bulletin. For pastors and others interested in working with students the Board published four issues of this paper during each of the academic years of 1934-35 and 1935-36. The various issues have carried articles written by student pastors, by Lutheran college administrators, and by faculty in Lutheran and in non-Lutheran colleges and universities.

New Folders. For use by students and pastors the following have been printed: *Students Going and Coming, Going to College, Introduction Card, Card of Application for Guest Membership, Guest Membership Card, Lutheran Nurses Guild, So You Are a Nurse, Does It Make Sense?, the Church and Social Problems, Like a Mighty Army.*

Reprints. Much of the material printed in previous years has been re-issued in answer to repeated demands.

Finding the Way. This study book written by the Rev. Robert Harris Gearhart, D.D., and published by the Association Press, has been commended by the staff for student discussion groups.

Self-Measurement for College Students. This booklet by the Rev. Wendell S. Dysinger, Ph.D., printed and distributed by the Extension Division of the State University of Iowa, has been distributed by the staff among pastors and students.

Service to Students through Scholarships

Many Church Boards of Education have large funds for scholarships and loans to students. Our Board has two slowly growing small funds.

Ministerial Education Fund. By agreement with the California and Pacific Synods the Board assists their students studying for the ministry by paying part of their travel expense to an eastern college and seminary. For this purpose four hundred and twenty-five dollars was given to seven different students during the biennium. In addition, since the temporary suspension of Martin Luther Seminary, the Board aids the students from the German Nebraska Synod pursuing a bilingual curriculum at the Chicago Seminary. Six hundred dollars was contributed during the past two years.

Scholarship and Loan Fund for Women. Three young women doing under-graduate work at three Lutheran colleges received small grants-in-aid.

6. A Concern of the Church

With the increasing numbers of young men and women who are enjoying higher education, the whole Church is called upon to give especial attention to this group. This group exemplifies in a startling way what one religious leader phrases as follows: "The richest assets, greatest problems, sternest perils, mightiest forces, costliest offenders, strongest defenders, highest hopes of the church, are her young men and young women." Upon the home congregation of the prospective student rests the obligation to prepare the student for his later spiritual development on the campus. And the home congregation in its educational program must foster an understanding and loyalty which is broader and deeper than that of the local parish. Without such preparation a student whether at a Lutheran or a non-Lutheran college or university will find unwarranted difficulties, for which he cannot be solely blamed, in maintaining an intelligent interest in the Church or in developing Christian character and faith. Upon the congregation in the college or university community there rests the equally important obligation to offer to students opportunities for worship, for service, for fellowship, and for study, which will make church life a continuous experience and Christian growth a natural process. Pastors, parents, congregations, Synods, Boards, and the Church itself are all directly concerned in the procedures of Christian education as they parallel—in time at least—present-day secular education. And the whole Church is vitally concerned in the product of this education in terms of Christian personality. (See **Recommendation 3, p. 239.**)

III. INFORMING THE CHURCH

Practically all the work of the Board and of its staff has some promotional value in the field of Christian higher education: in the individual parishes; among students in all kinds of institutions of higher learning; for our own colleges and seminaries; and in behalf of The United Lutheran Church to the general public. A few avenues of influence not previously referred to may properly be mentioned here.

1. The Season for Christian Higher Education

The four Sundays after Easter are assigned for the consideration of the Board's work and prayer for seminaries, colleges, universities, students, and faculties. During this period in 1936, the Board issued a folder two pages of which parishes could use for the announcement of their Sunday services and notices, and colleges could use for their own advertisement. Three hundred fifty-eight thousand of these folders were distributed to 888 parishes and ten colleges. A large number of requests could not be filled, and many orders had to be limited. The amount of such promotional activity is limited by the income of the Board.

The comments received from all sections of the Church and from a large number of pastors were very enthusiastic and might be summarized as follows: "The folders were most attractive and brought forth many favorable comments from our people. More of our Church promotion media should display such artistry. I believe that only through such presentation of the work of the Church can real results be secured."

While we appreciate the responses of the more than 900 pastors who requested literature, we are compelled to ask: what of the other 2,200? Their members desire and deserve information about the educational work of the Church. (See Recommendation 1, p. 239.)

2. Articles and Addresses

An informed church is generally a responsive church. Definite efforts are made to keep the church aware of the educational situation in our institutions and of educational problems confronting the Church. The many articles prepared by the staff have appeared in *The Lutheran, The Parish School, Lutheran Woman's Work, Luther League Review,* the *News Bulletin of the National Lutheran Council, The American Lutheran Student,* and *Christian Education.* In addition the staff is active in securing others to write desirable articles for the various papers.

While the printed word is a valuable medium for the transmission of information, the spoken word is generally more effective. During the biennium the staff has been in about 200 different parishes, speaking at church services, Sunday Schools, Luther Leagues, and other groups. In addition, synods, synodical conferences, missionary conventions, Luther League conventions, summer schools, student conferences, and educational conferences have been attended. In fact, wherever opportunity presents itself, the staff endeavor to tell the story of the forward march of the Church through Christian higher education, showing how the work of the Board of Education is coordinated with the work of other boards and agencies.

IV. FINDING THE FACTS

"It shall have authority to prepare general surveys of educational standards; to investigate any phase of educational work, and make recommendations to institutions and synods."—(Constitution—Article VIII.)

The projects for special study this biennium are the result of the authorization of the Church and have grown out of the recurring problems of importance in the very life of the Church.

1. A Study of Beneficiary Ministerial Education

The Church at the 1934 Convention resolved,

That the Church direct the Board of Education to make contact with each synod or proper committee thereof, during the present biennium, for consultation, coordination, and cooperation in the problems of beneficiary ministerial education, and that during the biennium one or more regional conferences of synodical chairmen of committees on ministerial education be called to further assist this committee in the formation of its plans and for the personal aid and benefit of such synodical chairmen.

In compliance with that resolution conferences of the chairmen of synodical committees on ministerial education were called at Columbia, S. C., Harrisburg, Pa., Ft. Wayne, Ind., and Omaha, Nebr. All synods, except five, were represented and several other interested individuals were present, making a total of seventy. The Board paid the expenses of the official representatives of the synodical committees.

The situation as it exists in each synod was described, and the problems raised by the Board's report two years ago were discussed. The consensus of opinion was that each synod should have one committee which deals with the whole problem of men for the ministry, that financial aid should not be given too early in the college course, that committees should be more faithful in their investigations before aid is given and in their interviews while the students are in college and seminary. The idea prevailed that the money given should be considered a loan conditioned by a period of years of service, of which seven was deemed sufficient. Uniformity of requirement on this point throughout the Church is urgent. Rules and regulations should be reduced to a minimum.

The Board of Education was asked to prepare record forms for synodical committees to keep the data regarding beneficiaries, and series of questions to guide individuals in their interviews of students, and forms of report—other than scholastic—for use of colleges and seminaries. These blanks are in the process of preparation. The American Association of Theological Colleges and Seminaries is giving extensive consideration to problems in this general field. We hope to use some of their suggestions.

One of the most interesting developments at these meetings was the conviction that students should be allowed to attend more than one Lutheran seminary, taking two years at one school and one year at another, the choice of institution and plan of study being made with the consent of the synodical committee. The students at the seminaries are very anxious for this privilege. Some synods allow this privilege, two having taken such action during the biennium.

In addition the Board has authorized, and the conferences heartily approved, the preparation of folders covering such subjects as: What a minister does; why be a minister; preparing to be a minister; and the call to the ministry. These will be prepared and distributed for wise use by pastors and committees.

Plans also have been approved to use the services of the secretaries of the Board for addresses and interviews throughout the Church on the vital subject of *Men for the Ministry*.

2. The Place of Evangelism in the Seminaries

Recently to the office of the Board came an inquiry regarding the place of evangelism in the curriculum and the life of the seminaries. Some communications from seminaries submitted in connection with the inquiry seemed to indicate that evangelism, as a definite problem in the work of the minister, did not have the place in the seminaries which it merited. In fact, the church officials making the inquiry expressed their concern "about the obvious inadequacy of particular instruction on evangelism. The helplessness of most of our ministers in teaching the art of witnessing and evangelizing declares their own incompetence."

The question was of sufficient importance to justify an investigation, especially since the inquiry came from a member of the Committee on Evangelism. In addition to the 19 Lutheran seminaries in America, 36 others were selected. A letter was sent to the seminaries asking the following questions: (1) Does your seminary have a course or courses on Evangelism? If so, what are the names? Amount of time allowed? (2) If you do not have any such courses, in what courses is the subject specifically treated?

Of the 55 seminaries studied, less than half, 26, appear to offer a definite course on evangelism. The course averages 34 hours, the minimum number of hours being 15 and the maximum 64. It is generally an elective subject. In only four institutions does it appear that a course in evangelism is required for graduation. One outstanding seminary does not require evangelism of all students for graduation, but offers an excellent course which is part of a vocational group requirement. Probably a similar situation exists in other institutions.

Of the 19 Lutheran seminaries, seven offer courses in evangelism with an average number of hours of 33. The hours range from 17 to 48. Two institutions require the course for graduation.

Where a definite course is offered it appears under 15 different titles. The titles most frequently mentioned are Evangelism (7), Personal Evangelism (4), Pastoral Evangelism (2), Work with Individuals (2), Evangelistics (2), Evangelistic Preaching (2), and Home Missions and Evangelism (2).

The Lutherans use five titles to name their courses: Evangelism (2), Evangelistics (2), Case Evangelism (1), Home Missions and Evangelism (1), and Stewardship and Evangelism (1).

It must not be assumed, however, that an institution's interest in evangelism is revealed by the number of hours of instruction in a definite course. Most seminaries give considerable attention to the subject in the various courses. It is stressed especially in Practical Theology, Religious Education, Missions, Psychology of Religion, Homiletics, Catechetics, and Pastoral Care.

The replies of the seminaries indicated (1) an apparent indifference to their full responsibility in this field; (2) a belief that evangelism concerns all departments of a seminary, and not only one course; and (3) an attempt to meet the seminary's responsibility by definite courses.

Considering evangelism as "the direct and urgent endeavor to lead a soul to a personal decision for Christ," this investigation leads to the conclusion that (1) the spirit of evangelism should penetrate the whole seminary; (2) effective evangelism requires an understanding of principles and methods; (3) these principles and methods should be gathered together in a definite course. Assuming an adequate understanding of the Christian message and of human nature, such a course should include a sketch of evangelism during New Testament times and the history of the Church, the types and forms of evangelism; a description of proper motives; a study of effective methods; an application to and a study of concrete cases; and a program for the local church.

These times challenge the seminaries to make the ministers more effective in the work of evangelism. **(See Recommendation 4, p. 239.)**

3. Influences in Higher Education

The 1934 Convention of the Church requested the Board of Education to study the facts and influences in modern education in relation to morals and religion in the colleges and universities, both church and secular. The Board after careful consideration approved the object of this study but believed it would require "an expenditure of money and effort beyond anything reasonably obtainable at this time." The suggestion was made that the boards and agencies involved in this whole study should limit it to a scope and sphere within the means and time available. Accordingly there was common agreement that our study of this problem should be limited to the summarization of the results of certain investigations already made in this field. This study will be reported to the Church through the report of the Committee on Moral and Social Welfare.

V. ADMINISTERING THE WORK

As laborers together with God, the Board of Education endeavors to administer the work economically, efficiently, and effectively.

1. Board Personnel

The following constituted the officers and membership of the Board for the biennium:

Officers:
President—Rev. H. R. Gold, D.D.
Vice-President—Rev. H. H. Bagger, D.D.
Secretary—Rev. Gould Wickey, Ph.D., D.D.
Treasurer—Thomas P. Hickman.

Staff:
Executive Secretary—Rev. Gould Wickey, Ph.D., D.D.
Secretaries—Mary E. Markley, Litt.D.
            Rev. C. P. Harry, D.D.
            Mildred E. Winston, A.M.

Members:
Terms expiring 1936—Henry W. Bikle, LL.D., Rev. H. J. Black, D.D., Rev. H. R. Gold, D.D., Rev. F. K. Fretz, Ph.D., D.D., Rev. N. Willison, Litt.D., Mr. Frederick Henrich, Prof. R. S. Saby, Ph.D.

Terms expiring 1938—Rev. G. M. Diffenderfer, D.D., Mr. C. J. Driever,* Mr. L. C. Hassinger, Rev. Paul Krauss, D.D., Prof. Ralph D. Owen, Ph.D., Rev. W. H. Traub, D.D., Rev. Abdel R. Wentz, Ph.D., D.D.

Terms expiring 1940—Rev. H. H. Bagger, D.D., Dean Adelaide Le S. Burge, Rev. E. C. Herman, D.D., Miss Flora Prince, Hon. Charles Steele, Rev. M. L. Stirewalt, D.D., Rev. A. A. Zinck, D.D., S.T.D.

Advisory Members:
Rev. P. O. Bersell, D.D.—Representing the Augustana Synod of North America.
Mrs. E. H. Copenhaver, Mrs. L. H. Waring—Representing the Women's Missionary Society of The United Lutheran Church.

Committees:
Executive—The officers, together with Rev. E. C. Herman, Prof. Ralph D. Owen, Hon. Charles Steele.
Institutions—Rev. A. A. Zinck, Rev. H. H. Bagger, Rev. M. L. Stirewalt, Rev. W. H. Traub, Rev. A. R. Wentz.
Student Work—Prof. Ralph D. Owen, Rev. F. K. Fretz, Miss Flora Prince, Rev. N. Willison, Mrs. E. H. Copenhaver, Mrs. L. H. Waring, Rev. P. O. Bersell.
Public Relations—Rev. G. M. Diffenderfer, Rev. H. J. Black, Dean Adelaide Le S. Burge, L. C. Hassinger.

---

* Mr. Howard S. Bechtolt, Chicago, was elected by the Executive Board to fill the unexpired term of Mr. C. J. Driever, who died August 5, 1935.

Research—Rev. F. K. Fretz, Prof. R. S. Saby, Rev. P. H. Krauss.
Investments—H. W. Bikle, Esq., C. J. Driever, Frederick Henrich, Hon. Charles Steele, Thomas P. Hickman.

2. Board Nominations

The nominations of the Board for the terms which expire at this Convention are the following:

Clergy	Residence	Synod	Occupation
Rev. Stanley Billheimer, D.D....	Palmyra, Pa.	East Penn	Ministry
Rev. H. J. Black, D.D.	Savannah, Ga.	Ga-Ala.	Ministry
Rev. F. K. Fretz, Ph.D.	Easton, Pa.	Min. of Penn.	Ministry
Rev. G. Franklin Gehr, D.D.	Bethlehem, Pa.	Min. of Penn.	Ministry
Rev. H. R. Gold, D.D.	New Rochelle, N. Y.	New York	Ministry
Rev. Simon Snyder, D.D.	Wheeling, W. Va.	West Virginia	Ministry
Rev. E. F. Sterz.	Hanover, Ont., Can.	Canada	Ministry
Rev. H. T. Weiskotten, Ph.D.	Brooklyn, N. Y.	New York	Ministry

Lay	Residence	Synod	Occupation
Prof. O. F. H. Bert, Sc.D.	Washington, Pa.	Pittsburgh	Education
Windsor Cousins, Esq.	Philadelphia, Pa.	Min. of Penn.	Law
Samuel Fausold, Ph.D.	Harrisburg, Pa.	Pittsburgh	Education
Frederick Henrich	Buffalo, N. Y.	New York	Business
Prof. R. J. Seeger, Ph.D.	Washington, D. C.	Maryland	Education
Heiby Ungerer, Esq.	Rochester, N. Y.	New York	Law

3. Change in Annuity Rates

During recent years serious consideration has been given the problem of annuity rates. In keeping with sound financial advice, the Board adopted the rule of accepting annuity gifts on the following scale:

49 years and under	4	per cent
50 to 54 years	4¼	per cent
55 to 59 years	4½	per cent
60 to 69 years	5	per cent
70 to 74 years	5½	per cent
75 years and over	6	per cent

4. Unwise Limitation of Service

The amount of money received from the Church limits the service which the Board of Education is allowed to render. The colleges and seminaries and student centers are constantly requesting larger grants and greater assistance. The sum of $100,000 ought to be available each year for emergency situations and for carrying on special projects.

On the assumption that there will be available from all sources the sum of $90,000 during the next year, a budget has been prepared allotting fifty-five per cent for grants to colleges and seminaries, fifteen per cent for grants-in-aid to student centers, and thirty per cent to cover the service of the secretaries to the institutions and student centers, the cost of promotion including addresses, travel, and printing, and the general administrative expenses.

With inadequate income through the ordinary channel of the apportionment the Board of Education can only hope that friends who see the vital importance of Christian higher education will come to the aid of this cause by gifts and bequests. (See Recommendation 1, p. 239.)

VI. CONCLUSIONS AND RECOMMENDATIONS

(For action, see p. 247)

The unfailing vitality of organizations and institutions lies in their devotion to ideas and ideals. The significance of the work of the Board of Education is in the fact that it is carried on by and for men and women who are interested in Christian ideas and ideals.

Christian higher education offers the Church a basic means for directing and molding youth in a constructive leadership. Our colleges and seminaries are mighty instruments for the accomplishment of the Church's task and program. The Christian service to the thousands of students in non-church schools is an important part of the Church's task and program.

The Board of Education is the representative of the Church before the colleges, the seminaries, the universities, and the educational world. To direct and develop Christian higher education is the constitutional purpose of the Board. To this end all effort and time is spent. For this cause we plead.

Gratefully acknowledging the help and guidance of the great Head of the Church, we submit the following recommendations for prayerful consideration:

Forward with Christian Higher Education

1. Resolved, That The United Lutheran Church call upon its pastors and members to promote the cause of Christian higher education as a vital part of the whole program of the whole Church.

The Church's Arrangements for the Training of Ministers and Teachers

2. Resolved, That The United Lutheran Church direct the Board of Education to continue to work with synods and seminaries in the furtherance of the program adopted by the 1932 Convention with reference to the Church's arrangements for the training of ministers and teachers.

An Endowment Fund for the Christian Work with Students

3. Resolved, That The United Lutheran Church authorize the Board of Education to assist financially in the necessary building programs of parishes doing student work.

Evangelism in the Seminaries

4. Resolved, That, in view of the widespread indifference among church members and the large numbers of unevangelized people within the reach of the Church, The United Lutheran Church in America request the theological seminaries in their t r a i n i n g of the Christian ministers of the future to emphasize the aggressive character of genuine Christian faith and, by special teaching in course and by the entire spirit of the institutions, to cultivate a zeal for souls and a technique for personal work with the unchurched and lapsed.

GOULD WICKEY, *Secretary.*
HOWARD R. GOLD, *President.*

REPORT OF THE TREASURER OF THE BOARD OF EDUCATION

RECEIPTS AND DISBURSEMENTS
GENERAL FUND

July 1, 1934, *to June* 30, 1935

Cash in General Fund—July 1, 1934 .... $13,593.09

RECEIPTS

Apportionment—United Lutheran Church in
  America $81,232.00
Contributions:
  Women's Missionary Society $2,250.00
  Augustana Synod 500.00
  East Pennsylvania Synod, through Board
    of American Missions 300.00
  Others 61.77
                                       3,111.77
Refunds, Transfers and Miscellaneous 198.46

    Total Receipts 84,542.23

                                       $98,135.32

DISBURSEMENTS

Seminaries and Colleges $47,299.84
Student Centers 12,522.49
Salaries—Secretaries 12,425.00
           Stenographers 1,506.88
Service 102.81
Travel—Secretaries 3,256.31
      Board Members 529.66
Rent—Office 1,200.00
    House 1,200.00
Furniture and Fixtures 58.50
Supplies and Stationery 385.89
Telephone and Telegrams 305.05
Postage and Mailing 1,389.53
Printing and Publication 2,290.44
Books and Magazines 180.65
Insurance 86.83
Dues and Fees 444.99
Auditing 194.23
Transfers to Other Funds 175.54

    Total Disbursements... 85,554.64

Cash in General Fund—June 30, 1935............................... $12,580.68

RECEIPTS AND DISBURSEMENTS BY FUNDS
INCOME ACCOUNT

July 1, 1934, *to June* 30, 1935

	Annuity Fund	Endowment Fund	Permanent Ministerial Education Fund	Scholarship and Loan Fund for Women
Balance—July 1, 1934			$ 96.80	$ 499.77
Contributions			199.30	
Income on Securities	$2,852.49	$60.00	444.15	286.77
Repayments of Loans				270.00
Transfer from General Fund			231.23	
Transfer from Principal	1,296.70			
	$4,149.19	$60.00	$971.48	$1,056.54
Paid to Annuitants	$4,092.01			
Paid to Students			$971.48	$ 325.00
Transfer to General Fund		$55.69		
Accrued Interest on Bonds Purchased	57.18	4.31		4.30
	$4,149.19	$60.00	$971.48	$ 329.30
Balance—June 30, 1935				$ 727.24

ANALYSIS OF FUNDS

July 1, 1934, *to June* 30, 1935

	General Fund	Annuity Fund	Endowment Fund	Permanent Ministerial Education Fund	Scholarship and Loan Fund for Women
Balance—July 1, 1934	$13,593.09	$64,428.59	$5,118.67	$13,299.04	$6,914.45
Receipts	84,542.23	2,901.22	60.00	874.68	587.09
	$98,135.32	$67,329.81	$5,178.67	$14,173.72	$7,501.54
Disbursements	85,554.64	4,149.19	60.00	971.48	329.30
Balance—June 30, 1935	$12,580.68	$63,180.62	$5,118.67	$13,202.24	$7,172.24

RECEIPTS AND DISBURSEMENTS—GENERAL FUND

July 1, 1935, *to June* 30, 1936

Cash in General Fund—July 1, 1935 .... $ 12,580.68

RECEIPTS

Apportionment—United Lutheran Church in
America $82,948.00
Contributions:
Women's Missionary Society $2,250.00
Augustana Synod 1,475.00
East Pennsylvania Synod 300.00
Other Synods 31.14

For Special Work 1,000.00
                                                              ————
                                                          5,056.14
Refunds 57.66
Sale of "Survey" 8.00
                                                                        ————
                                                                      88,069.80

        Total Receipts $100,650.48

DISBURSEMENTS

Seminaries and Colleges—Regular	$47,050.00
—Special College	32.27
Student Centers	13,756.80
Salaries—Secretaries	12,125.00
Stenographers	1,633.00
Service	76.51
Travel—Secretaries	3,408.21
Board Members	545.59
Committees	301.49
Rent—Office	1,200.00
House	1,200.00
Furniture and Fixtures	105.30
Supplies and Stationery	448.31
Telephone and Telegrams	230.17
Postage and Mailing	1,308.32
Printing and Publications	2,772.57
Books and Magazines	112.30
Insurance	29.60
Dues and Fees	546.05
Auditing	185.80
Refunds	20.75

        Total Disbursements 87,088.04

Cash in General Fund—June 30, 1936 .... $13,562.44

RECEIPTS AND DISBURSEMENTS
OTHER FUNDS—INCOME ACCOUNT

July 1, 1935, to June 30, 1936

	Annuity Fund	Endowment Fund	Permanent Ministerial Education Fund	Scholarship and Loan Fund for Women
Balance—July 1, 1935				$ 727.24
RECEIPTS:				
Contributions			$238.06	50.00
Income on Securities	$2,707.29	$61.63	483.42	267.97
Repayments of Loans				315.00
Transfers	1,119.18			
Totals	$3,826.47	$61.63	$721.48	$1,360.21

PAYMENTS:

Paid to Annuitants $3,757.40				
Paid to Students			$636.75	$ 650.00
Transfers		$54.10		
Accrued Interest and Charges				
on Securities Purchases, etc.	69.07	7.53	11.59	4.11
Totals $3,826.47		$61.63	$648.34	$ 654.11
Balance—June 30, 1936			$ 73.14	$ 706.10

RECEIPTS AND DISBURSEMENTS BY FUNDS

July 1, 1935, to June 30, 1936

	Annuity Fund	Endowment Fund	Permanent Ministerial Education Fund	Scholarship and Loan Fund for Women
Balance, July 1, 1935........$63,180.62		$5,118.67	$13,202.24	$7,172.24
Receipts 5,890.74		1,811.63	768.65	675.47
	$69,071.36	$6,930.30	$13,970.89	$7,847.71
Disbursements 5,576.47		61.63	648.34	654.11
Balance, June 30, 1936......$63,494.89		$6,868.67	$13,322.55	$7,193.60

GRANTS TO STUDENT CENTERS

July 1, 1934, to June 30, 1936

	1934-35	1935-36
University of California ....$	200.00	$ 200.00
University of Colorado	83.33	100.00
Washington, D. C.	75.00	75.00
University of Illinois	800.00	800.00
Chicago Metropolitan, Illinois	200.00	200.00
Purdue University, Indiana	150.00	150.00
University of Iowa	400.00	400.00
University of Kansas		50.00
State College, Manhattan, Kansas*	50.00	25.00
Boston Metropolitan, Massachusetts	2,500.00	2,500.00
University of Michigan	475.00	475.00
University of Minnesota*	150.00	200.00
University of Nebraska	400.00	400.00
New York Metropolitan	416.23	438.82
State College of North Carolina	250.00	250.00
Duke University, Durham, North Carolina	400.00	400.00
Ohio Synod Student Work	170.69	200.00
Philadelphia Metropolitan, Penna.	2,500.00	2,500.00
Pennsylvania State College	500.00	500.00
State Teachers College, West Chester, Penna................	1,052.24	814.62
Clemson College, South Carolina	75.00	150.00
Winthrop College, South Carolina	225.00	225.00
Virginia Polytechnic Institute	100.00	100.00
University of Washington	250.00	250.00

University of West Virginia	200.00	200.00
University of Wisconsin	200.00	200.00
Miscellaneous Points	700.00	575.00
Student Pastors Conferences		1,378.36
Total	$12,522.49	$13,756.80

* To Augustana Pastor.

GRANTS TO COLLEGES AND SEMINARIES
July 1, 1934, to June 30, 1936

	1934-35	1935-36
Colleges:		
Carthage	$ 3,000.00	$ 3,000.00
Hartwick	750.00	750.00
Lenoir Rhyne	2,400.00	2,400.00
Marion	600.00	600.00
Midland	9,000.00	9,000.00
Newberry	4,500.00	4,500.00
Roanoke	1,800.00	1,800.00
Susquehanna	1,800.00	1,800.00
Thiel	3,000.00	3,000.00
Wagner	1,500.00	1,500.00
	$28,350.00	$28,350.00
Seminaries:		
Chicago	$ 2,400.00	$ 2,400.00
Southern	3,499.92	3,500.00
Saskatoon	7,800.00	7,800.00
Waterloo	4,999.92	5,000.00
Martin Luther	250.00	
	$18,949.84	$18,700.00
Total Colleges and Seminaries	$47,299.84	$47,050.00

SALARIES OF SECRETARIES AND RENT ALLOWANCES
July 1, 1934, to June 30, 1936

	1934-35	1935-36
Gould Wickey	$ 4,200.00	$ 3,900.00
Mary E. Markley	3,000.00	3,000.00
C. P. Harry	3,000.00	3,000.00
Mildred E. Winston	2,225.00	2,225.00
Gould Wickey—Rent	1,200.00	1,200.00
	$13,625.00	$13,325.00
Salaries as Shown	$12,425.00	$12,125.00
Rent as Shown	1,200.00	1,200.00
	$13,625.00	$13,325.00

BALANCE SHEET
June 30, 1936
ASSETS

Cash in Bank:
General Account $11,042.28
Office Account 1,000.00
                                                                                $12,042.28
Stocks, Bonds, Notes and Other Investments at Ledger Values   92,399.87*
Office Furniture and Equipment 1,846.39

Total Assets $106,288.54

FUNDS

General Fund $15,408.83
Annuity Fund 63,494.89
Endowment Fund 6,868.67
Permanent Ministerial Education Fund 13,322.55
Scholarship and Loan Fund for Women 7,193.60

Total Funds $106,288.54

* Market Value—$90,405.23.

INVESTMENTS
June 30, 1936

Par Value	Annuity Fund	Book Value	Market Value June 30, 1936
$4,800 Altoona and Logan Valley Electric Rwy. 4s, 1954		$ 4,800.00	$ 4,272.00
5,000 Appalachian Electric Power Co. 5s 1956.......		4,950.00	5,262.50
1,000 Associated Gas and Electric Co. 5½s, 1973....		1,000.00	880.00
2,000 Atchison, Topeka and Sante Fe 4s, 1995........		2,036.83	2,300.00
4,000 Baltimore and Ohio R. R. 5s, 1950.....................		4,055.00	4,130.00
2,000 Baltimore and Ohio R. R. 5s, 1948...................		1,975.00	2,252.50
6,500 Bell Telephone Company of Pa. 5s, 1948...........		6,395.00	7,840.63
1,000 Burlington Realty Trust, Boston Parcel Post Station 5½s, 1935		980.00	160.00
3,000 Georgia Power Company, 5s, 1967..................		2,943.75	2,988.75
2,000 Lackawanna & Wyoming Valley R. R. 5s, 1951		1,935.00	540.00
1,000 Minnesota Power & Light Co. 5s, 1955...........		1,000.00	1,050.00
3,000 N. Y. Central R. R. 6s, 1944		3,397.95	3,360.00
3,000 Oregon Washington R. R. 4s, 1961...................		2,909.00	3,210.00
1,000 Potomac Edison, 5s, 1956		1,055.21	1,060.00
3,000 Pennsylvania R. R. 4¼s, 1981		2,075.30	3,281.25
1,500 Pacific Gas and Electric 4s, 1936		1,616.48	1,500.00
2,000 Pennsylvania R. R. 4¼s, 1984		1,955.00	2,180.00
3,000 Pennsylvania R. R. Equipment 5s, 1938		2,974.80	3,273.75
3,000 Pacific Gas and Electric 4s, 1964		3,082.95	3,255.00
4,600 Philadelphia Electric Co. 5s, 1966		4,574.37	5,060.00
3,500 Philadelphia Electric and Power Company, 5½s, 1972		3,631.25	3,832.50
1,000 West Pennsylvania Power Company, 1st 5s, 1956		1,080.21	1,050.00
4,000 U. S. Post Office Corporation 5½s, 1955		4,000.00	1,160.00
		$64,423.10	$63,898.88

Shares

13	Western Union Telegraph Company	1,560.00	1,098.50
32	Altoona and Logan Valley R. R.	320.00	2,140.00
	Total—Annuity Fund	$66,303.10	$67,137.38

INVESTMENTS

June 30, 1936

SCHOLARSHIP AND LOAN FUND FOR WOMEN

Par Value	Book Value	Market Value June 30, 1936
$ 500 Associated Gas and Electric Company, temp. certificates 5½s, 1973	$ 500.00	$ 440.00
1,000 Lackawanna & Wyoming Valley R. R. Company 5s, 1951	967.50	270.00
3,000 Westmoreland Water Company 5s, 1952	2,970.00	3,090.00
1,000 United Biscuit 5s, 1950	1,056.40	1,080.00
1,000 U. S. Treasury Note 3%, 1946-48	1,034.53	1,051.00
Total—Scholarship and Loan Fund for Women	$ 6,528.43	$ 5,931.00

PERMANENT MINISTERIAL EDUCATION FUND

	Book Value	Market Value
$1,000 Appalachian Electric Power Company, 5s, 1956	$ 990.00	$ 1,052.50
1,000 Illinois Post Office Building Corp., Chicago, Ill. Station P. O. 5½s, 1932	1,000.00	250.00
2,000 Lackawanna and Wyoming Valley R. R. 5s, 1951	1,935.00	540.00
1,000 Philadelphia Electric Power Co. 5½s, 1972	1,022.50	1,110.00
4,000 Washington Gas Light, General Mortgage 5s, 1960	4,283.75	4,800.00
1,000 Chelsea Hotel Company, 6s, 1945	1,000.00	180.00
1,000 U. S. Treasury 3¼s, 1946	1,000.00	1,071.90
500 Pacific Gas and Electric Co. 4s, 1936	538.82	500.00
1,000 N. Y. Central R. R. 6s, 1944	1,132.65	1,120.00
Total—Permanent Ministerial Education Fund	$12,902.72	$10,624.40

ENDOWMENT FUND

	Book Value	Market Value
$1,000 United Biscuit 5s, 1950	$ 1,056.40	$ 1,080.00
Franklin National Bank—Impounded Bonds	3,089.00	3,089.00
1,000 N. Y. Central R. R. Co. 3¾s, 1946	982.71	970.00
1,000 Scranton Electric Co. 5s, 1937	1,000.00	1,037.50
500 U. S. Treasury Certificates 3¼s, 1946	537.51	535.95
Total—Endowment Fund	$ 6,665.62	$ 6,712.45

Respectfully submitted,

THOMAS P. HICKMAN, *Treasurer.*

July 30, 1936.

We have audited the books of account of the Treasurer and examined the securities of the Board of Education of the United Lutheran Church in America, for the biennium beginning July 1, 1934, and ending June 30, 1936, and we hereby certify that, in our opinion, the foregoing statements of Cash Receipts and Disbursements for the years ending June 30, 1935, and June 30, 1936, the Balance Sheet as of June 30, 1936, and pertinent schedules, are in accordance with the books of account and are true and correct.

TAIT, WELLER AND BAKER,
Accountants and Auditors.

Dr. Gold introduced Miss Mary E. Markley, one of the Secretaries, who addressed the Convention. The Rev. Gould Wickey was then introduced and addressed the Convention. Terse, clear statements outlined the purposes and activities of the Board and emphasized anew the present importance of Christian education.

The recommendations were presented in order.

Recommendations 1, 2, 3, and 4 were adopted.

On motion the report of the auditors was accepted.

Dr. Gold was granted the privilege of introducing the other two secretaries of the Board, Miss Mildred Winston and the Rev. C. P. Harry.

In connection with the report of the Board of Education, it was requested that the report of the Committee on German Interests be taken up. The request was granted.

The Rev. R. H. Ischinger, Secretary, presented the report of the Committee on German Interests.

REPORT OF COMMITTEE ON
GERMAN INTERESTS

(For action on the recommendations in this report, see p. 249)

In accordance with the action of the Executive Board the Committee on German Interests called the biennial session of the General German Conference of the U. L. C. A. to meet in St. John's Church, Buffalo, the Rev. Martin J. Hoeppner, pastor, on October 8th and 9th, 1935. The deliberations of this Body were fruitful in many ways. The chief concern, however, was preeminently the future supply of pastors adequately prepared to serve German and German-English congregations. A Committee was appointed to draft and submit to the U. L. C. A. recommendations for securing a more adequate supply of pastors for bi-lingual congregations. This Committee met in the Muhlenberg Building at Philadelphia on July 24th, 1936. It submits the following for serious consideration and proper action:

The Situation

At present there are approximately 500 congregations within the U. L. C. A. in which preaching, teaching, and "Seelsorge" in the German language are required. Not a few of these congregations are entirely German, while many may be called bi-lingual, and then of course there are those that are almost entirely English, German services being required only occasionally, the care of the older folks particularly requiring a knowedge of the German tongue.

In former years the supply of German pastors was filled most satisfactorily through a special arrangement with the seminaries at Kropp and Breklum. This however was terminated some years ago because it was felt that the need for men from these institutions was no longer pressing and that if necessary other sources of supply might be found. Institutions in our own country, which formerly supplied us with German-speaking pastors no longer prepare men for efficient work in this tongue. Nor are our seminaries, as they are constituted at present, able to fill any specific demand for pastors who might be thoroughly prepared for German or German-English work. As a result the German element in our churches is sorely neglected. It is not unusual for a man who has a barely elementary knowledge of the German language to be given charge of a congregation with a large German constituency. Frequently the men placed in charge of German congregations have no real appreciation of the cultural and spiritual background of those whom they are to serve, and as a consequence no sympathy with the desires and inner needs of the people given into their care. It would not be difficult to quote specific instances in which the very founders of congregations, and those who have been the main stay of their life, have been betrayed when the church which they helped to found and maintain with their sacrifices and prayers became estranged to them because of an only too often premature change to English, while the language of their hearts and of their devotion still remained the tongue of the Fatherland, or much more expressively "die Muttersprache."

There is still a very evident need of men, whose acquaintance with German is not merely of the head but also of the heart, to supply many of the most fruitful fields in the U. L. C. A. The older generation of pastors is passing away. We need well prepared men to take their place.

It is also very evident to those who are not constitutionally adverse to German and German-English work, that there are many opportunities for German home mission work, especially in our larger cities. Other denominations and sects are doing such work and winning the recent immigrant away from his mother church.

RECOMMENDATIONS

(For action, see below)

In recognition of this dire and desperate need of the German and German-English congregations for a continued adequate supply of well trained bi-lingual pastors we recommend:

1. That young men specifically interested, and through their home background as well as their scholastic preparation specially adapted to future work in our German and German-English congregations, be referred to the Board of Education on the recommendation of the Committee on German Interests for a special course of training to fit them for such work.

2. That arrangements be made through the Board of Education in consultation with the proper authorities of the Lutheran Church in Germany for a course of training of such men in carefully selected schools and institutions in Germany after they have been graduated from a seminary of the U. L. C. A.

3. That the Board of Education be requested to appoint a standing Committee on Conference with the Committee on German Interests to carry out the above resolutions.

Respectfully submitted,

E. C. J. KRAELING, *Chairman.*

R. H. ISCHINGER, *Secretary.*

Recommendations 1, 2, and 3 were adopted.

The Rev. F. R. Knubel, President, presented the report of the Parish and Church School Board.

REPORT OF THE PARISH AND CHURCH SCHOOL BOARD

(For action on the recommendations in this report, see pp. 261, 432)

The Parish and Church School Board herewith submits its regular biennial report to the United Lutheran Church in America.

In His Great Commission to the Church, Jesus said, "Go—teach." In one of its efforts to carry out this Great Commission, the United Lutheran Church in America, in creating the Parish and Church School Board, said:

"The object of this Board shall be to develop and execute under the direction of the Executive Board a system or systems of literature for use in the home, the parish and the Church schools; to organize schools for weekday Christian training; to plan methods of school administration; to recommend books for the library; to outline programs for Summer Assemblies, Sunday School Conventions and Normals, and all festival occasions of the Church; to prepare hymnals; to have oversight over and control of whatever pertains to the best interests of the parish and the Church school. It shall carry on its work in the name of The United Lutheran Church in America, and in accordance with the Doctrinal Basis, Constitution, Acts and Rulings of said United Lutheran Church in America.

"Section 1. The Board shall have power to prosecute the work entrusted to it. It shall prepare a system or systems of lessons for the religious training of the young in the Sunday Bible School, Weekday Bible Training School, Catechetical Class, Christian Kindergartens, Daily Vacation Bible School, Teacher Training, Young People's Societies, Boys' and Girls' Organizations, Home Studies in the Christian Religion for parents and children, and such other efforts by which the members of the Church will be confirmed in their holy faith. The system or systems shall be known as the Christian Training Series of The United Lutheran Church in America, and shall be under its control. It shall supply material necessary for the thorough development of all these agencies.

"Section 2. The Board shall keep itself informed concerning the best methods in parish and Church school work and administration, and shall publish literature, tracts, magazines and books for the information and assistance of parents, pastors and teachers. It shall recommend suitable books for libraries and the home, and encourage and stimulate Lutheran writers in the preparation of such literature. After consultation with the Common Service Book Committee it shall prepare hymnals for Church school use.

"Section 3. It shall have oversight and control of the Church school. It shall prepare plans, methods of operation, and programs for Summer Assemblies, Sunday School Conventions and Normals, and other festival occasions of the Church." (Charter and Constitution of The Parish and Church School Board.)

The Parish and Church School Board is conscious of the trust which the Church has placed in it and is earnestly striving to fulfil its responsibilities.

In carrying out its operations, the Board functions through four departments of work. This report is therefore presented under the following headings:

I. Executive and Administrative
II. Literature
III. Field Work
IV. Finance
V. Recommendations

I. EXECUTIVE AND ADMINISTRATIVE:

   A. *Organization of the Board:*
      1. The officers of the Board are as follows:
         President—Rev. F. R. Knubel, Rochester, N. Y.
         Vice-President—Rev. W. C. Schaeffer, D.D., Allentown, Pa.
         Secretary—Rev. D. Burt Smith, D.D., Philadelphia, Pa.
         Treasurer—Rev. M. Hadwin Fischer, Ph.D., Gettysburg, Pa.

      2. The members of the committees of the Board are as follows:
         Executive Committee:
            Rev. F. R. Knubel, Rochester, N. Y.
            Rev. W. C. Schaeffer, D.D., Allentown, Pa.
            Rev. M. Hadwin Fischer, Ph.D., Gettysburg, Pa.
            Rev. A. J. Traver, D.D., Frederick, Md.
            Rev. P. D. Brown, D.D., Columbia, S. C.

Committee on Field Work:
Rev. P. D. Brown, D.D., Columbia, S. C.
Rev. C. C. Rasmussen, D.D., Washington, D. C.
Rev. J. D. M. Brown, Litt.D., Allentown, Pa.
Mr. C. C. Dittmer, Brooklyn, N. Y.

Committee on Literature:
Rev. A. J. Traver, D.D., Frederick, Md.
Rev. Paul H. Heisey, Ph.D., Springfield, Ohio.
Rev. W. C. Schaeffer, D.D., Allentown, Pa.
Mrs. Virgil B. Sease, New Brunswick, N. J.

Committee on Finance:
Rev. M. Hadwin Fischer, Ph.D., Gettysburg, Pa.
Rev. George H. Rhodes, Albemarle, N. C.
Mr. George M. Jones, Reading, Pa.

3. The present employed personnel of the Board is
Executive Secretary—Rev. S. White Rhyne.
Field Secretary—Rev. Chas. H. B. Lewis, D.D.
Editors—Rev. Chas. P. Wiles, D.D., Rev. D. Burt Smith, D.D.,
Rev. Paul J. Hoh.
Assistant Editor—Miss Mabel Elsie Locker.
Rev. Paul E. Keyser, formerly assistant editor, resigned his
position on the staff to accept a call to become pastor of
the First Evangelical Lutheran Church, Ridgway, Pa.,
effective June 1, 1936.

B. *Nominations:*
The four members of the Board whose terms expire at this
convention are:
Rev. Paul H. Heisey, D.D., Ph.D., Springfield, Ohio.
Rev. Wm. C. Schaeffer, Jr., D.D., Allentown, Pa.
Rev. George H. Rhodes, Albemarle, N. C.
Mr. Clarence C. Dittmer, Brooklyn, N. Y.
According to the recommendation of the Executive Board, the
Board offers the following two sets of nominees for membership
on the Board:
Rev. Paul H. Heisey, D.D., Ph.D., Springfield, Ohio.
Rev. Wm. C. Schaeffer, D.D., Allentown, Pa.
Rev. R. Homer Anderson, D.D., Lynchburg, Va.
Mr. Clarence C. Dittmer, Brooklyn, N. Y.
Rev. W. G. Boomhower, D.D., Philadelphia, Pa.
Rev. C. Franklin Koch, Richmond, Ind.
Rev. A. W. Steinfurth, D.D., Wilkinsburg, Pa.
Mrs. H. S. Bechtolt, Chicago, Ill.

C. *General Conferences:*
Two meetings of the Intersynodical Conference on Elementary
Education were held in Chicago, Ill., during the biennium. Drs.
Wiles and Smith attended and participated in these meetings.
Each member of the staff had the privilege of attending at
least one of the two meetings of the International Council of
Religious Education, held in Chicago, Ill., during the biennium.
Dr. Wiles was our representative at the meeting of the World's
Sunday School Association Convention, held at Oslo, Norway.

D. *Action on the Comprehensive Plan of Parish Education:*
The action of the Executive Board on the Comprehensive Plan of Parish Education was reported to our Board and the following action was taken: "That the Executive Committee of the Parish and Church School Board study the action of the Executive Board (United Lutheran Church in America) on a Comprehensive Plan of Parish Education and bring some recommendation to a future meeting of the Parish and Church School Board."

E. *A Three-Year Program:*
During the biennium the Board has been working on an outline of a three-year program of activity. This program is to include the organization for parish education which the Board will promote in the Church and the literature which the Board will prepare. Considerable progress has been made in this outline, and the program for literature will be presented in the section of this report on literature.

F. *Memorial from the Evangelical Lutheran Synod of East Pennsylvania:*
The memorial from the Evangelical Lutheran Synod of East Pennsylvania, concerning Sunday school literature being furnished with the Bible text printed in the American Revised Version, having been referred to our Board for report, we offer the following:

(1) Present practice of our Board:
    A. In the Augsburg Uniform Series:
        1. In the pupils' books and leaflets, the Bible text is always printed from the authorized version.
        2. In the teacher's book, the Bible text is printed as a whole from the authorized version and is printed verse by verse in the lesson exposition from the American Standard Edition of the Revised Bible.
        3. In the Lesson Commentary, the Bible text used is that from the American Standard Edition of the Revised Bible.

    B. In the Christian Life Course:
        1. All quotations are given from the authorized version; however, most Bible passages are given by references, in which case the teachers and the pupils may use any version which they may have.

(2) Reasons for this practice:
    A. This practice gives a common text for reading in Sunday school sessions, where such practice is followed.
    B. This practice gives a common text for reading which conforms with the text used in the Common Service Book, the Parish School Hymnal, the Children's Hymnal and Service Book, and most hymnals in use in schools.
    C. This practice gives a text for pupils that conforms with the texts which most of them have memorized.
    D. This practice gives a text that conforms with the texts used in most manuals on the catechism.
    E. This practice gives the teachers the use of the American Standard Edition of the Revised Bible in their study both in the *Augsburg Teacher* and *Lesson Commentary.*
    (For Recommendation, see V. A., p. 259.)

G. *Memorial from the Ohio Synod:*

The memorial from the Ohio Synod concerning the preparation of a Sunday School Standard having been referred to our Board, the Board took the following action:

"That a progressive standard, plus a guide, be prepared;

"That this standard deal with a somewhat larger aspect of the program of parish education than that of the Sunday school;

"That the executive secretary and the field secretary be authorized to prepare such a standard and guide, and submit the same to the staff for further consideration."

Considerable work has been done toward the preparation of this guide, but it is still not in a form for presentation to the Church.

H. *Resolution concerning Children without the Church:*

The resolution concerning children without the Church having been referred to our Board by the last convention of the Church, our Board has verified the finding from several recent surveys and studies and has made its findings known through the periodicals of the Church. A program to reach the unreached was suggested in Parish Education Month in 1935. Since this is a condition which will continue to be with us for many years, the Board is making this a part of its regular program.

II. LITERATURE:

A. *Curriculum Materials continued in their former form:*

1. The Christian Life Course
2. The Religious Education Texts for Vacation Church Schools
3. The Religious Education Texts for Weekday Church Schools
4. The Parish School magazine
5. Lutheran Boys and Girls
6. Lutheran Young Folks
7. The Parish School Hymnal
8. The Children's Hymnal and Service Book
9. Special Services for Christmas, Easter, and Children's Day

B. *The Augsburg International Uniform Lesson Series being revised:*

This series of Sunday school lessons has been undergoing a gradual revision for the past two years. The revision has been confined almost entirely to the method of presentation. Beginning with the last quarter of 1936 the quarterlies will appear with new cover pages, making the lesson books more attractive.

C. *The New Lutheran Leadership Course:*

At the last convention of the Church, this new course was announced. Since that time seven textbooks on the first level and four on the second level have appeared. Other texts will be prepared as rapidly as possible. One on the first level—*My Progress*—and one on the second level—*Our Congregation and Its Work*—are in manuscript form at present. The texts which have appeared are:

First Series: *My Life; My Pupils; My Bible; My Work; My Preparation; My Materials;* and *My Group Sessions.*

Second Series: *The Old Testament—A Study; The New Testament—A Study; Human Nature;* and *Improving Our Leadership.*

D. *New Literature:*

1. A Nursery Packet—This new product comprises the following: Twelve letters to be mailed to the parents of nursery children, the first letter to go at the birth of the child and the other letters to be sent, one at the end of each quarter of the first three years of the child's life; four cards—one for each of the child's first three birthdays; an envelope for each letter; a large envelope for all the materials; and a sheet of instructions with a place for a record of all materials mailed. This new literature will be ready for use in the fall of this year.

2. A Catechetical Course for Adults—This text is in course of preparation and should be ready for distribution some time in the next year.

3. Elective Courses for Young People—A series of elective courses for young people is being prepared. The first of this series, *The Gospel According to St. Luke—A Study,* has just appeared. This particular course is a study of a single book of the Bible. About five other studies of books of the Bible will be included in the series. Authors have been selected for twelve of these elective courses and other authors will be selected as soon as several of these texts have appeared and have been tried. Each of these courses will include twelve chapters and will furnish materials for one quarter of the year. Pupils' and teachers' books are being prepared for each course.

4. A Beginner-Primary Hymnal—Work has been started on the preparation of a hymnal for the beginner and primary departments of the Church School.

5. A Handbook for Service Organizations—A handbook for those service organizations of the Church which now have no educational materials is being prepared.

E. *A New Literature Program Projected:*

During the biennium the Board gave its attention to a study of the literature needs of our congregations. This study involved an evaluation of all literature being prepared for the congregation at present as well as a study of untouched areas. As a result of this study the Board has launched a program of literature production which will occupy the time of the staff and other writers at least for the next three years. Some of the literature proposed is already prepared, some is in course of preparation, and the rest is projected for the future literature. This program embraces the following:

1. Continued preparation and publication of *The Augsburg International Uniform Course,* including the *Lesson Commentary.* (See item II, B, above.)

2. Continued publication of *The Christian Life Course.*

3. Continued preparation and publication of the *Elective Courses for Young People,* already planned. (See item II, D, 3, above.)

4. Careful study of the whole field of *Elective Courses for Adults,* and, possibly, the planning and preparation of a number of such courses.

5. Continued preparation and publication of the *Nursery Letters.* (See item II, D, 1, above.)

6. Continued preparation and publication of *The Lutheran Leadership Course,* including necessary blanks, course cards and certificates; and continued study of the needs in this area with a view to possible expansion of our leadership curriculum. (See item II, C, above.)

7. Continued preparation and publication of *The Parish School,* with the continuation of its department on Workers' Conferences.

8. Continued preparation and publication of *Lutheran Boys and Girls* and *Lutheran Young Folks.*

9. Continued preparation and publication of the *Beginner-Primary Hymnal.* (See item II, D, 4, above.)

10. Continued preparation and publication of *Christmas, Easter,* and *Children's Day Services.*

11. Continued preparation and publication of a *Catechetical Course for Adults.* (See item II, D, 2, above.)

12. Continued preparation and publication of a *Handbook for Service Organizations.* (See item II, D, 5, above.)

13. Continued preparation and publication of *Standards and Guides* for the direction of the congregation's educational program and for the measurement of this program's effectiveness. (See item I, G, above.)

14. Collaboration with the auxiliary agencies of the Church in the annual preparation of a series of *Reading Courses* (Book Lists).

15. Preparation and partial publication of a series of *Courses for Weekday Sessions,* including one course on catechetical instruction.

   a. This course to be planned so as to be *usable also in vacation schools of the Church.*

   b. To be planned *for persons three to seventeen years of age, inclusive*—Nursery through Senior.

   c. To be *group-graded.*

   d. To be relatively *complete in itself.*

   e. To be *correlated in a general way with The Christian Life Course.*

   f. To be *sufficiently different from The Christian Life Course, in content and form, to avoid the feeling of sameness on the part of the pupils.*

   g. To be *sufficiently flexible to be usable in schools of varying length.*

   h. To be constructed upon a policy of *no homework.*

16. Preparation and publication of *Publicity and Promotional Materials.*

17. Informal and unofficial consultation with the auxiliary agencies of the Church, with a view to securing a more thoroughly integrated literature for our local churches. This study included a study of the periodical literature of the Church. On the basis of the findings in this study, the Board feels that there is need for a thorough study of our program of periodical literature by an impartial commission. (**For Recommendation see V. B., p. 259.**)

III. FIELD WORK:

   A. *Parish Education Month:*

   According to the action of the Church, September has been used as a month for a special emphasis on parish education.

During September, 1935, the special emphasis was upon leadership education; during September, 1936, the emphasis was upon co-operation in parish education. Each year the emphasis is changed to give freshness to the program. The response to our efforts has been exceedingly gratifying. Pastors and their congregations have co-operated splendidly. Synodical committees on parish education and officers of synods have given their heartiest support. Every agency within the Board is directed toward the promotion of parish education during September: The staff is in the field a large part of the time; *The Parish School* magazine publishes articles and programs; *The Lutheran* is very gracious in offering space which is used; other periodicals are used; and this year twenty pages of folders and leaflets were prepared and samples were distributed to all pastors, and to other leaders upon request.

B. *Engagements in the field:*

During the biennium the members of the staff were exceedingly active in field work. Group meetings of various types were attended. The following summary will give an idea of the contacts made:

The total number of group meetings attended—422.

The total number of congregations represented in these meetings (some duplication)—3,034.

The total number of individuals in attendance (some duplication)—34,776.

The different synods and other Church bodies touched:

Alleghany	10
East Pennsylvania	39
Florida	1
German Nebraska	3
Georgia-Alabama	4
Illinois	10
Indiana	9
Iowa	3
Kansas	4
Kentucky-Tennessee	5
Manitoba	11
Maryland	16
Michigan	16
Ministerium of Pennsylvania	53
Nebraska	25
New York	24
North Carolina	19
Northwest	4
Ohio	23
Pittsburgh	30
Rocky Mountain	8
South Carolina	20
Susquehanna	15
Virginia	15
Wartburg	3
West Pennsylvania	20
West Virginia	8
Other Lutheran Bodies	10
Interdenominational	14
Total	**422**

During the biennium the field secretary was able to give considerable time to the Manitoba, Canada, and Nova Scotia Synods. It is not possible to give a report on the work in the latter two synods at this time as the trip is not yet completed.

C. *Co-operation with Synods:*

Announcing, at the last convention of the Church, its policy to develop fuller co-operation with synods, the Board has directed its efforts in that direction with very encouraging response from all synods. At the present time, every synod in the Church has a committee or an individual leader charged with the responsibility of developing parish education. The Board offers to send a representative to meet with these committees or leaders to confer on the developmnt of synodical programs. Many synodical committees have invited our representatives.

Six regional conferences on parish education have been held during the biennium: Two in the middle west at Chicago, Ill., two in the south at Charlotte and Concord, N. C., and two in the east at Philadelphia and Nawakwa Leadership Camp, Pa. To these conferences are invited the presidents and the members of the synodical committees on parish education of the territory in which the conference is held and representatives of the Parish and Church School Board. Nine synods sent representatives to the mid-west conference, six sent to the southern, and nine sent to the eastern. Through these conferences a synodical program of parish education is being gradually developed. The finest spirit of co-operation has been manifested in these conferences.

D. *Sunday School Conventions and Institutes:*

The Board assists synodical and conference groups to develop Sunday School Conventions and Institutes. Suggested programs are prepared and sent out to these groups each year. Copies of the programs for 1937 may be had on request.

E. *Summer Schools for Church Workers:*

The Board offers its services in developing programs for Summer Schools for Church Workers. At present there are fifteen such schools in the Church under the auspices of synods or conferences. These schools are rendering an invaluable service. During the past biennium the Board has had representatives at eleven of these schools each year.

F. *Nawakwa Leadership Camp:*

The past two years have been the most successful seasons in the history of Camp Nawakwa. The camp is now rated A National Red Cross Camp by Red Cross Headquarters in Washington, D. C. Reports for 1936 have not been received, but during 1935 there were 1,140 pupils and leaders in attendance at the various camps. During the summer 1,449 enrichment credits and 480 standard course cards were earned, and 4,130 hours of club work in fifteen areas of interest were completed.

G. *The Parish School Magazine:*

This magazine is a splendid promotional agency of the Board. It is increasing in popularity and deserves a place in the library of every Church worker. Many congregations are subscribing to the magazine for all workers in the Church school.

H. *Visual Education:*
This department of the work of the Board has been referred to the Committee on Field Work, but developments have had to await increased financial appropriations.

I. *Survey of Parish Education:*
In the early part of 1936, a general survey of conditions in parish education throughout the Church was started. Survey blanks were sent to all pastors. At the time this report is being made, approximately fifty per cent of the reports have been returned. The information on the blanks returned has been tabulated, but summaries have not been made and conclusions have not been drawn. As soon as these findings are available they will be broadcast throughout the Church. The information will be used by the Board in the development of future programs and literature.

J. *A New System of Recognition in Leadership Education:*
Very gratifying interest is being manifested in leadership education in all parts of the Church. For the first six months in 1936 course cards were issued as follows:

> First series courses—1,242
> Second series courses (Lutheran)—1,196
> International Certificates—1,188

In an attempt to correlate our system of recognition in leadership education with that of the International Council of Religious Education, our Board has adopted the International Council of Religious Education's requirements for an experimental period of two years. A new booklet, *The Lutheran Leadership Course Bulletin*, has recently been prepared and is available on request. This bulletin describes the course and the system of requirements. The following is a digest of these requirements:

First Series	*Second Series*
Completion of four courses, properly distributed	Completion of ten courses, properly distributed
Participation in worship, service, budget, and fellowship of a church; and reading of a church periodical	
Some plan of personal religious growth	Some plan of personal religious growth for two years
One year's experience as church worker, and regularity of attendance	Two year's experience as church worker, and this successful
Regular reading of religious education magazine or reading of one book on religious education	Regular reading of religious education magazine and reading of one book on religious education
Attendance at workers' conferences in local church or at a religious education convention or institute	Attendance at workers' conferences in local church and at a religious education convention or institute

IV. FINANCE:
During the biennium, the Board received approximately $20,000 on apportionment, or approximately $10,000 a year. With these funds the Board must finance all of its executive, field work, and general Board expenses. The work of the Board is limited considerably because of a lack of funds. At the present time, the following projects are being delayed on this account:

A department of visual education
A department of promotion and administration of leadership education
The study of the facts and influences in primary and secondary education in reference to morals
An aggressive promotion of weekday and vacation Church schools
The Guides and Standards in Parish Education
A program for reaching the unreached

In 1935, the Board of Publication very graciously granted our Board the sum of $2,000 to help meet our necessary expenditures.

The Board renews its pledge to the Church. Christ has said to His Church, "Go—teach." The Church has said to the Parish and Church School Board, "Plan—Prepare—Promote." The Board is at work. Much has been accomplished. More needs to be done. Soliciting the continued support of all units of the Church and praying for wisdom and strength, the Board promises a continuation of its efforts.

V. RECOMMENDATIONS: (For action, see pp. 261, 432.)
A. That no action be taken concerning Sunday school literature being furnished with the Bible text printed from the American Revised Version in order that the Parish and Church School Board may be permitted to continue to use its discretion, in the selection of the text to be used in the various publications, as new situations arise. (See section I, F, above.)
B. That a Commission be appointed to study the whole field of the Church's periodical literature with a view to formulating a policy and an adequate program of periodical literature for the whole Church. (See section II, E, above.)

F. R. KNUBEL, *President,*
S. WHITE RHYNE, *Executive Secretary.*

REPORT OF THE TREASURER OF THE PARISH AND CHURCH SCHOOL BOARD

CASH RECEIPTS AND DISBURSEMENTS
July 1, 1934 to June 30, 1935

Balance in Bank—July 1, 1934	$2,064.46

RECEIPTS:

United Lutheran Church Apportionment	9,790.00
Total	$11,854.46

DISBURSEMENTS:

Salary—Executive Secretary	$3,780.00
Salary—Field Secretary	3,240.00

Executive Secretary's Expenses (Office Secretary's salary, travel and office expenses)	1,703.08
Field Secretary—Expenses	684.40
Travel and Expenses—Board Meetings	423.86
Committee Meetings	108.86
Editors	86.06
Publicity	278.46
Auditing	25.00
Dues	2.00
Contributions for Maintenance of Muhlenberg Building	660.00
Premium on Treasurer's Bond	12.50
Insurance	41.25
Tax on Checks	1.24
Nawakwa Leadership Camp	200.00
Furniture and Fixtures	42.50
Rental—Safe Deposit Box	5.50
Office Supplies	15.70

Total Disbursements	11,310.41
Balance in Bank—June 30, 1935	$544.05

CASH RECEIPTS AND DISBURSEMENTS
July 1, 1935 to June 30, 1936

Balance in Bank July 1, 1935		$544.05

RECEIPTS:

United Lutheran Church on Apportionment	$10,279.00	
Board of Publication of the United Lutheran Church in America, (Grant)	2,000.00	
		12,279.00
Total		$12,823.05

DISBURSEMENTS:

Salary—Executive Secretary	$3,780.00
Salary—Field Secretary	3,240.00
Executive Secretary's Expense (Office Secretary's salary, travel and office expense)	1,613.48
Field Secretary's Expense	403.51
Travel and Expenses—Board Meetings	340.00
Committee Meetings	252.59
Editors	135.24
Publicity	334.65
Auditing	25.00
Dues	8.00
Contribution for Maintenance of Muhlenberg Building	660.00
Premium on Treasurer's Bond	12.50
Insurance	36.00
Nawakwa Leadership Camp	200.00

Furniture and Fixtures 22.50
Rental—Safe Deposit Box 5.50

Total Disbursements 11,068.97

Balance in Bank—June 30, 1936 .... $1,754.08

Respectfully submitted,

DR. M. HADWIN FISCHER, *Treasurer.*

July 17, 1936.

We have audited the books of account of The Parish and Church
School Board of the United Lutheran Church in America, for the
biennium beginning July 1, 1934 and ending June 30, 1936, and we
hereby certify that, in our opinion, the foregoing statements of Cash
Receipts and Disbursements are in accordance with the books of account,
and are true and correct.

TAIT, WELLER AND BAKER,

Accountants and Auditors.

Pastor Knubel introduced Miss Mabel Elsie Locker, who is
in charge of children's work; the Rev. D. Burt Smith, editor;
the Rev. C. P. Wiles, editor; the Rev. Paul J. Hoh, editor; the
Rev. C. H. B. Lewis, Field Secretary; and the Rev. S. White
Rhyne, Executive Secretary.

The Rev. S. White Rhyne, the Rev. Paul J. Hoh, and the Rev.
C. P. Wiles addressed the Convention. Through these several
addresses the Convention received full explanation of the aims,
plans and procedures of this Board.

The recommendations were presented.

Recommendation V, A, was adopted.

Recommendation V, B, was deferred until the consideration
of the report of the Committee on President's Report.(See p. 432.)

Item II, 7, F, of the report of the Executive Board, which had
been deferred until the time of this report, was also deferred
until the consideration of the report of the Committee on President's Report. (See p. 432.)

On motion the report of the auditors was accepted.

At 11 : 50 A. M. the Convention adjourned with prayer by the
Rev. E. C. Xander.

Saturday Afternoon and Evening

The convention members responded in large numbers to the
invitation from Wittenberg College to visit that institution. By
the courtesy of the Local Committee in Columbus, transporta-

tion to and from Springfield by automobile was provided. Wittenberg College extended a cordial welcome and made the visit interesting by admission to a football game, and by provision of a buffet supper, and a tour of the grounds and buildings of the College.

The evening entertainment was given in the form of a pageant presenting the history of Wittenberg College, said by many to have equalled any other pageant they ever witnessed. Many delegates visited the Oesterlen Home in connection with the visit to Springfield.

Sunday

The Sunday Services were conducted according to the program of the Local Committee. A number of local Lutheran churches heard guest preachers from the membership of the Convention.

On Sunday evening, the delegates and visitors were guests of Capital University and they filled the auditorium to enjoy an evening of rare music and to hear a very able address delivered by Prof. Luther D. Reed concerning the place of music in the history of the Lutheran Church. A very cordial address of welcome was given to the delegates and visitors by President Otto Mees.

SIXTH SESSION

DESHLER-WALLICK HOTEL
Columbus, Ohio
Monday, October 19, 1936, 8.45 A. M.

Matins were conducted by the Rev. Harold S. Miller.

The Convention was called to order by the President.

On account of special conditions, the President suggested to the Convention a slight change in the hours of intermission and announced, by the consent of the Convention, that the adjournment would be at 11 : 30 A. M., the Seventh Session to begin at 1 : 45 P. M. and to extend until 5 : 15 P. M.

Committee of Tellers No. 1 reported elections as follows:

For the *Executive Board* each of the following received a majority of the votes cast:

Rev. H. W. A. Hanson   Carl M. Distler

The President declared them elected.

For the *Commission of Adjudication,* term expiring 1942, each of the following received a majority of the votes cast:

Rev. Wm. E. Frey James F. Henninger
Rev. L. Franklin Gruber

The President declared them elected.

For the *Committee on Church Papers* each of the following received a majority of the votes cast:

Rev. A. J. Holl Chas. G. Shatzer

The President declared them elected.

For the *Executive Committee of the Laymen's Movement* each of the following received a majority of the votes cast:

J. K. Jensen W. H. Stackel
S. F. Telleen

The President declared them elected.

Committee of Tellers No. 2 reported elections as follows:

For the *Board of Foreign Missions* each of the following received a majority of the votes cast:

Rev. P. O. Bersell Ralph H. Schatz
Rev. E. E. Fisher
Rev. P. E. Monroe

The President declared them elected and stated that two clergymen and one layman were yet to be elected.

For the *Board of American Missions* and the *West Indies Mission Board* each of the following received a majority of the votes cast:

Rev. A. J. Holl A. S. Bauer
Rev. John Schmieder Louis Hanson
Rev. Emil W. Weber

The President declared them elected and stated that one clergyman and one layman were yet to be elected.

For the *Board of Education* each of the following received a majority of the votes cast:

Rev. Stanley Billheimer O. F. H. Bert
Rev. H. J. Black Frederick Henrich
Rev. H. R. Gold

The President declared them elected and stated that one clergyman and one layman were yet to be elected.

For the *Inner Mission Board* each of the following received a majority of the votes cast:

Rev. G. H. Bechtold Carl M. Distler

The President declared them elected and stated that two clergymen and one layman were yet to be elected.

For the *Board of Publication* each of the following received a majority of the votes cast:

Rev. O. F. Blackwelder   L. Russell Alden
Rev. J. J. Scherer   Henry Beisler
                                E. G. Hoover

The President declared them elected and stated that one clergyman and one layman were yet to be elected.

For the *Board of Ministerial Pensions and Relief* each of the following received a majority of the votes cast:

Wm. H. Emhardt   Wm. A. Granville
              W. T. Stauffer

The President declared them elected and stated that one clergyman and one layman were yet to be elected.

For the *Parish and Church School Board* each of the following received a majority of the votes cast:

Rev. Paul H. Heisey   C. C. Dittmer
Rev. W. C. Schaeffer

The President declared them elected and stated that one clergyman was yet to be elected.

For the *Board of Deaconess Work* each of the following received a majority of the votes cast:

Rev. A. L. Benner   E. S. Gerberich

The President declared them elected and stated that two clergymen and one layman were yet to be elected.

The President announced that ballots had been prepared and distributed for the completion of all elections.

The Rev. S. W. Herman, President, presented the report of the Board of Publication.

REPORT OF THE BOARD OF PUBLICATION

The Board has labored diligently during the biennium to furnish good and wholesome Christian literature and necessary church and parish school supplies to our pastors, congregations, Sunday schools and other organizations, as well as members in general. In doing this, we have been encouraged by the consistent and generous support of our constituency. The department of ecclesiastical ware and vestments instituted some years ago has been further developed and has met with an encouraging response from our pastors and congregations.

The study of the needs of devotional literature committed by the Savannah Convention to the Common Service Book Committee was promptly taken up by this committee, and after a report to the Executive Board and the latter's approval of the committee's action, our Board was requested to undertake the publication of a devotional monthly under the title "Light for Today." This publication was begun with devotions for the month of December, last year, and has been continued regularly every month since then. The response was at once most encouraging, and the issues particularly for February, March and April were in good demand as they covered the Lenten season. The monthly was accorded second-class privileges for the April issue, and has since then enjoyed a steady increase in circulation until now the demands exceed 20,000 copies a month. As it appeared that there was a real need for a devotional booklet covering the entire Lenten season, the Board has decided to undertake the publication of such a booklet for the next Lenten season, and it will be available in January, next year.

The "Collects and Prayers" mentioned by the Common Service Book Committee in its report to the Savannah Convention, was published early in May, 1935, and made available in a neatly bound cloth edition at $1.00, with de luxe editions in red and black morocco. This book has been in great demand and appears to fill a long felt need.

In response to expressed desires for a one volume commentary on the New Testament, the Board decided several years ago to undertake the publication of such a work. Professor Dr. H. C. Alleman of the Gettysburg Seminary, was elected as editor, and under his guidance writers were selected from among the Bible scholars of the Church. The preparation of copy for a book of this character necessarily required time by the various writers, as they had to do their writing at spare moments as permitted by their other arduous duties. The copy was, however, all in early in 1935, and we expected to have the Commentary ready for distribution early this year. But as is usual with a work of this magnitude, delays were encountered in publication that compelled the advancement of the publication date to October of this year.

OTHER NEW BOOKS

Several new books have been published during the biennium in addition to "Collects and Prayers," of which we wish to call particular attention to the following: Second volume of "Epistle Messages," edited by Rev. Hermann F. Miller; "Children of God," a collection of story sermons for children, by Rev. W. R. Siegart; "Sacred Song," by Dr. John W. Horine; "The Translated Bible," published under the editorship of Dr. O. M. Norlie and sponsored by the National Lutheran Council for the 400th Anniversary of Luther's translation of the Bible; "A Lutheran Handbook," by Dr. Amos J. Traver; The United Lutheran Church "Year Books" for 1935 and 1936, edited by the Secretary of The United Lutheran Church; and Der Lutherische Kalender for 1936, edited by Dr. C. R. Tappert.

In the Lutheran Leadership Training Course, prepared under the auspices of the Parish and Church School Board, eleven volumes have thus far been published and others are in course of preparation. The first in a series of electives for the adult classes has been issued, entitled, "The Gospel According to St. Luke, A Study." The Lesson Commentary has been issued for both years of the biennium, and has been in such demand that the volume for 1935 was sold out early in last year, and the volume for 1936 is also sold out, though an increased number of copies were printed.

A new Confirmation booklet entitled "Confirmation Candles," by Rev. Paul J. Hoh; a Reformation pageant entitled "The Voice of Faith," by Leona E. Becker; and a Christmas pageant entitled "The Spirit of Christmas," by Sarah E. Bitner, have also come from our presses.

An edition of the popular Baptismal booklet, "The Order for Baptism of Infants," has been available for those desiring a special edition for girls.

In all, a total of 182,203 new books have been published during the biennium.

Books Reprinted

Among books coming under this classification may be mentioned the Common Service Book, Large Word, Small Word and Music Editions; the Parish School Hymnal; The Children's Hymnal and Service Book; various editions of the catechism; At the Altar and After; Upon This Rock; Little Visits with Jesus; Bible Facts and Scenes; How to Teach in Sunday School; Bible Teachings; and Hymns and Prayers. The reprinted books total 290,438.

Pamphlets and Tracts

During the biennium, 337,720 new pamphlets and tracts have been published, and of those previously issued, a total of 104,050 have been reprinted. During each year of the biennium children's services for Christmas, Easter and Children's Day have been issued and the Church Year Calendar has been continued each year, the edition for 1935 being entirely sold out, and the one for 1936 almost exhausted, though a greatly increased number were printed for this year.

Periodicals

As was probably to be expected, the distribution of the Christian Life Course did not run as high as it did during the beginning of the course, but the distribution for the first year of the biennium averaged 255,205 for each quarter, and for the second year of the biennium, the average was 241,451, with a sale of 257,777 for the quarter beginning April 1,

1936. The Parish School Magazine has slowly increased its circulation during the biennium, and the two Sunday school weeklies have maintained an even distribution during the two years. Recently a slight gain has been noticeable. Of the Augsburg Uniform Lesson Series, a total of 435,700 copies has been provided of each issue, the Augsburg Sunday School Teacher easily maintaining its leadership position, and the Augsburg Adult Lessons having reached a distribution of 165,000 copies for the second quarter of the current calendar year.

The Lutheran has slowly been gaining ground, so that its circulation at the end of the biennium exceeded the low water mark by approximately 3,000 copies. With the vigorous support being given The Lutheran by a number of synodical presidents and other leaders in the Church, it is to be hoped that this increase in circulation of our common church paper will be accelerated during the coming biennium. As stated by one synodical president, "Through it the facts and activities, the principles, the policies, and the personalities of the whole church may become known as through no other agency open to the average man or woman. Well edited, well printed, well priced—it is well worth while, if not well nigh essential." To meet the expressed wishes of a good many subscribers, The Lutheran is at the present printed on a less glossy paper than formerly, which makes it more readable, especially with artificial light.

While Lutherischer Herold has not made any gains during the biennium, its subscription list nevertheless appears to be stationary at least. This paper is ably edited and deserves and should receive the vigorous and active support of the German constituency of The United Lutheran Church. The editor deserves the encouragement of the German brethren of the Church, and it goes without saying, that if the Herold is to wield its full measure of influence and impart Church information to the German readers of our United Lutheran Church, it should have a much larger list of subscribers.

MECHANICAL EQUIPMENT

During the biennium, the Board has disposed of three old presses, one folding machine, and a Ludlow type caster, and has replaced this equipment with a new high speed Miehle press, a new Miehle perfecting press, a new Cleveland folder, and a modern and up-to-date Ludlow type caster, at a total net cost of around $28,000. With these changes in the composing room, pressroom and bindery, our printing equipment has been brought to a high degree of efficiency.

GENERAL BUSINESS

The financial reports attached hereto give figures in detail of the business done by the Board during the biennium and its financial standing at the present time. While we regret that the net sales do not show the anticipated increase for the biennium, we are nevertheless happy to report that the sales closely approach the figures of the previous two years.

ORGANIZATION

The organization meeting of the Board was held on October 30, 1934, when Dr. S. W. Herman was elected president; Mr. E. G. Hoover, vice-president; Dr. J. Henry Harms, secretary; and Mr. Grant Hultberg, treasurer. Regular meetings of the Board have been held quarterly, and the Executive Committee has met monthly, except during the month of August. These meetings have been well attended, and the utmost harmony and good spirit have prevailed. The business of the Board has been thoroughly discussed and necessary actions taken as found proper.

During the biennium, the Board has lost three members through death. Dr. Henry Anstadt died on April 23, 1935; Dr. W. J. Showalter on October 13, 1935; and Mr. J. C. Lynch on May 12, 1936. Dr. Anstadt and Mr. Lynch had both been members of the Board for a number of years, and attended its meetings with regularity, and their wise counsel and uniform courtesy were highly regarded by all the members. Dr. Showalter was not able to attend more than one meeting after his election at Savannah, but was highly respected and well thought of by the Board.

Mr. Schatvet found it necessary to tender his resignation on account of pressing duties, and this was accepted at the January meeting in 1935. Judge Reno, having been elected to the Executive Board by the Savannah Convention, submitted his resignation, which was accepted at the April meeting in 1935, and Dr. Paul Scherer found it necessary on account of other pressing duties to offer his resignation, which was accepted at the April meeting in 1936.

The Board will greatly miss all these fine Christian gentlemen who have either been taken away from us by death or found it necessary to resign their membership on the Board.

On nomination of the Board, the Executive Board has elected Mr. Henry Beisler to fill the vacancy caused by the resignation of Mr. Schatvet; Dr. H. F. Baughman to fill the vacancy caused by the death of Dr. Anstadt; Mr. H. F. Heuer to fill the vacancy caused by the resignation of Judge Reno; Mr. Robert D. Raeder to fill the vacancy caused by the death of Dr. Showalter; and the Rev. H. T. Weiskotten to fill the vacancy caused by the resignation of Dr. Paul Scherer.

TERMS EXPIRING WITH THIS CONVENTION

The men whose terms expire at this time are: Rev. Oscar F. Blackwelder, D.D.; Rev. S. W. Herman, D.D.; Rev. J. J. Scherer, Jr., D.D.; L. Russel Alden, Esq.; F. Wm. Cappelmann, Esq.; Mr. E. G. Hoover; Mr. Henry Beisler.

The Board's nominations are: Rev. Oscar F. Blackwelder, D.D., Rev. S. W. Herman, D.D., Rev. J. J. Scherer, Jr., D.D., L. Russel Alden, Esq., Mr. E. G. Hoover, Mr. Henry Beisler, Mr. James L. Fisher.

Respectfully submitted,

S. W. HERMAN, President,
J. HENRY HARMS, Secretary.

REPORT OF THE BUSINESS MANAGER AND TREASURER OF THE BOARD OF PUBLICATION

CONSOLIDATED STATEMENT OF PROFIT AND LOSS
July 1, 1934 to June 30, 1935

SALES AND INCOME—Books, Periodicals, etc............................$620,803.79
Less: Returns and Allowances 11,785.95

Net Sales $609,017.84

COST OF SALES 320,042.54
Gross Profit on Sales...$288,975.30

LESS:
Shipping and Delivery Expenses:
Shipping Department Salaries.................................... $8,232.50
Shipping and Delivery Expense, Postage, Freight,
etc. 26,711.47

Total Shipping and Delivery Expense.............. $34,943.97

EDITORIAL EXPENSES:
Salaries—Editors and Office Assistants.................... $52,257.02
Manuscripts and Contributors 11,960.87

Total Editorial Expenses...................................... $64,217.89

ADMINISTRATIVE AND GENERAL EXPENSES, INCLUDING APPROPRIATION TO UNITED LUTHERAN CHURCH:
Executive and Office Salaries...................................... $64,435.49
Expense of Board Meetings... 863.00
Telephone and Telegraph 984.35
Advertising 9,250.65
Legal and Auditing 2,728.26
Lighting 1,220.34
Bad Debts 2,221.18
General Expense 3,644.68
Stationery and Supplies 4,986.91
Rent 22,570.00
Depreciation, Furniture and Fixtures....................... 2,273.16
Appropriations:
United Lutheran Church (Apportionment)........ 40,000.00

Lutheran Historical Society 500.00

Total Administrative Expenses..........................$155,678.02

Total Expenses 254,839.88

Net Profit from Operations $34,135.42

OTHER INCOME:
Interest and Dividends Received $8,937.02
Profit from Sale of Securities 303.53
Interest Earned on Notes Receivable 20.95
Bad Debts Recovered 69.58
Cash Received on Balances in Closed Banks........... 1,155.59
Miscellaneous 103.16
Gain from Operation of Buildings................................ 1,246.30

Total Other Income 11,836.13

$45,971.55

OTHER DEDUCTIONS:
Adjustment of Notes Receivable $125.00
Reduction in Value of Land and Buildings................. 150,000.00
Miscellaneous Adjustments 92.05

Total Other Deductions 150,217.05

Net Loss Carried to Surplus $104,245.50

CONSOLIDATED STATEMENT OF PROFIT AND LOSS
July 1, 1935 to June 30, 1936

SALES $604,042.81
Less: Returns and Allowances....................................... 7,318.79

Net Sales $596,724.02

COST OF SALES 330,629.64

Gross Profit $266,094.38

SHIPPING AND DELIVERY EXPENSES:
Salaries and Wages $8,345.94
Postage and Supplies 21,614.57
Freight and Hauling (Outbound) 2,665.65

Total Shipping and Delivery Expenses.................... $32,626.16

EDITORIAL EXPENSES:
Salaries—Editors and Office Assistants........................ $48,724.07
Illustrations 1,292.00
Dues and Subscriptions 235.00
Miscellaneous Expense 766.60

Contributors 7,016.20

Total Editorial Expenses $58,033.87

ADMINISTRATIVE AND GENERAL EXPENSES:

Insurance	$542.34
Telephone	966.62
Light and Power	1,243.61
Expenses—Board Meetings	935.90
Advertising	5,678.10
Salaries	65,911.39
Legal Expense	5.00
Pensions	1,200.00
Provision for Retirement Pensions	6,062.71
Library	52.59
Office and Showroom Rent	22,570.00
Provision for Depreciation—Furniture, etc.	1,691.81
Auditing	855.94
Stationery and Supplies	7,689.71
Miscellaneous Expenses	2,253.63
Appropriations—Apportionment	30,000.00
The Parish and Church School Board of the United Lutheran Church in America	2,000.00

Total Administrative Expenses $149,659.35

Total Expenses 240,319.38

Net Profit from Operations $25,775.00

OTHER INCOME:

Interest Earned on Notes Receivable	$16.95
Bad Debts Recovered	357.79
Cash Received on Balances in Closed Banks	136.70

Total Other Income 511.44

26,286.44

OTHER DEDUCTIONS:

Bad Accounts Charged Off	$2,178.26
Loss from Disposal of Fixed Assets	2,504.82
Loss from Sale of Securities	83.28

Total Other Deductions 4,766.36

Net Profit before Loss from Building Operations $21,520.08
Loss from Operation of Building 1,142.99

Net Profit Carried to Surplus $20,377.09

CONSOLIDATED BALANCE SHEET
June 30, 1936

ASSETS

CURRENT ASSETS:
Cash in Banks and on Hand		$198,165.44
Notes Receivable	$2,094.69	

Accounts Receivable:		
Merchandise	138,338.94	
Advertising	1,023.67	
Unpaid Subscriptions	565.16	
	$142,022.46	
Less: Reserve for Doubtful Accounts	25,000.00	
Net Accounts and Notes Receivable	117,022.46	
Accrued Interest on Investments	2,755.36	
Inventories on Books, Publications, Paper Stock, etc.	223,032.14	
Total Current Assets		$540,975.40

FIXED ASSETS:
Land	$211,859.50	
Buildings	629,679.81	
Machinery and Equipment	183,423.73	
	$1,024,963.04	
Less: Reserve for Depreciation	333,763.35	
Net Book Value—Fixed Assets	691,199.69	

DEPRECIATION RESERVE FUNDS:
Uninvested Cash Balances	$50,851.44	
Bonds at Market Value	278,157.87	
Total Depreciation Reserve Funds	329,009.31	

OTHER ASSETS:
Permanent Funds		9,225.96
Prepaid Accounts:		
Taxes and Water Rent	2,289.53	
Insurance	3,130.40	
Total Prepaid Accounts		5,419.93
Total Assets		$1,575,830.29

LIABILITIES

CURRENT LIABILITIES:
Accounts Payable		$11,012.47
Accrued Royalties Payable		1,006.83
Accrued Payroll		631.40
Total Current Liabilities		$12,650.70

DEFERRED INCOME:
Subscription to:
"The Lutheran" $11,306.28
"Der Lutherischer Herold" 2,261.46
Periodicals 50,004.00

Total Deferred Income 63,571.74

PERMANENT FUNDS:
John Rung Legacy $3,000.00
David Beidle Bequest 200.00
Accumulated Profits, Appreciation of Securities
and Income 6,025.96

Total Permanent Funds 9,225.96

RESERVE FOR RETIREMENT PENSIONS 6,062.71

NET WORTH 1,484,319.18

Total Liabilities and Net Worth $1,575,830.29

SCHEDULE OF DEPRECIATION RESERVE FUND SECURITIES
June 30, 1936

Par Value	Description	Market Value as of June 29, 1935	Market Value as of June 30, 1936
$5,000	Baltimore and Ohio R. R., 1st Mortgage, 4s, due 1948	$5,206.25	$5,300.00
4,600	Electric and Peoples Traction Certificates, 4s, due 1945	603.75	609.50
6,000	Lehigh Coal and Navigation, 4½s, due 1954	6,330.00	6,150.00
5,000	Lehigh Valley R. R., 4s, due 2003	1,975.00	2,387.50
3,000	United Traction of Pittsburgh, 5s, due 1997	900.00**	
5,000	Reading Company General, 4½s, due 1997	5,314.75	5,350.00
10,000	Baltimore and Ohio Southwestern, 1st Mortgage, 5s, due 1950	9,662.50	10,325.00
5,000	Reading Jersey Central, 4s, due 1951	4,987.50	5,000.00
5,000	Pennsylvania R. R. Co., 5s, due 1964	5,362.50**	
10,000	Philadelphia Company, 5s, due 1964	9,787.50	10,575.00
5,000	Metropolitan Edison, 4½s, due 1968	5,362.50	5,431.25
10,000	Penn Central Light and Power, 1st Mort, 4½s, due 1977	9,900.00	10,425.00
5,000	Missouri Pacific, 1st Series "F," 1977, 5s	1,356.25	1,587.50
5,000	Illinois Central, 4¾s, due 1966	2,672.50	3,706.25
8,000	Philadelphia Electric, 5s, due 1948	8,120.00	8,160.00
5,000	New Orleans, Texas and Mexico, 1st Mortgage, 5s, due 1954	1,400.00	1,825.00
8,000	American Gas and Electric deb., 5s, due 2028	8,460.00	8,560.00

5,000	Central Illinois Public Service, 5s, due 1968	4,762.50	5,187.75
5,000	Public Service Company of Northern Illinois, 4½s, due 1978	5,100.00	5,175.00
5,000	Pennsylvania Company, 4¾s, due 1963..	5,325.00**	
5,000	Chesapeake and Ohio, 4½s, due 1993......	5,531.25	5,537.50
5,000	Railway Express Agency, 5s, due 1938....	5,387.50	5,250.00
10,000	Pennsylvania Power and Light, 1st Mortgage, 4½s, due 1981	10,562.50	10,725.00
5,000	Commonwealth Edison, Series "F," 4s, due 1981	5,187.50	5,350.00
5,000	Ohio Edison, 1st and Consol Mtge., 5s, due 1960	5,300.00	5,268.75
5,000	Consolidated Gas Company of New York, 4½s, due 1951	5,406.25	5,331.25
10,000	Philadelphia Electric, 1st and Refunding, 4s, due 1971	10,687.50	10,525.00
10,000	City of Philadelphia, Reg., 4s, due 1945..	10,575.00	10,750.00
30,000	United States Treasury, 3⅛s, due 1949-52	31,481.25	31,790.62
20,000	United States Treasury, 3s, due 1951-55..	20,775.00	20,856.25
10,000	Pennsylvania Company, 4s, due 1963....		*10,375.00
20,000	Commonwealth of Pennsylvania Tax Anticipation Note, 1½s, due 1937............		*20,050.00
5,000	Republic Steel Company, 4½s, due 1961.		*4,831.25
10,000	Pennsylvania R. R. Company, 3¾s, due 1970		*10,125.00
5,000	United States Treasury, 2¾s, due 1948-51		*5,087.50
10,000	Chesapeake and Ohio R. R. Co., 3½s, due 1996		*10,100.00
10,000	National Dairy Products, 3¾s, due 1951, w. w.		*10,450.00
		$213,482.25	$278,157.87

**Sold since last audit report.
*Purchased since last audit report.

PERMANENT FUNDS
SUMMARY OF CASH ACCOUNT

July 1, 1935 to June 30, 1936

Cash in Bank July 1, 1935.. $1,857.58

RECEIPTS:

Income from Investments	$278.25	
Interest on Balance on Deposit......................................	51.69	
		329.94

Cash in Bank June 30, 1936... $2,187.52

PERMANENT FUND SURPLUS ANALYSIS

Balance—Permanent Fund Surplus, July 1, 1935		$4,200.20
Add: Income from Investment	$278.25	
Interest on Balance on Deposit	51.69	
Increase in Market Value of Securities	1,495.82	
		1,825.76
Balance—Permanent Fund Surplus, June 30, 1936		$6,025.96

PERMANENT FUNDS
BALANCE SHEET
June 30, 1936

ASSETS

Cash in Bank		$2,187.52

Investments (at market value):

Par Value

$1,000	U. S. Treasury 3⅛s, due 1949-52	$1,059.69	
1,000	Lehigh Valley R. R., 4½s, due 2003	508.75	
1,000	Penna. Power and Light, 4½s, due 1981	1,072.50	
1,000	Detroit Edison, Series "D," 4½s, due 1961	1,157,50	
2,400	Altoona and Logan Valley R. R., 4s, due 1954	2,232.00	

Shares

16	Altoona and Logan Valley R. R., common	1,008.00	
			7,038.44

Total Permanent Fund Assets	$9,225.96

FUNDS

Principal:

John Rung Legacy	$3,000.00
David W. Beidle Bequest	200.00

Surplus:

Accumulated Interest and Adjustment of Value of Securities to Current Market Value	6,025.96
Total Permanent Fund Liabilities	$9,225.96

Respectfully submitted,
GRANT HULTBERG,
Business Manager and Treasurer.

July 24, 1936.

We have audited the books of account and examined the securities of the Board of Publication of the United Lutheran Church in America, for the biennium beginning July 1, 1934 and ending June 30, 1936, and we hereby certify that the foregoing Profit and Loss Statements, setting forth the result of the operations for the biennium under audit, together with the Balance Sheet as of June 30, 1936, setting forth the financial condition at that date, and the Statements of Permanent Funds, are in our opinion, true and correct.

TAIT, WELLER & BAKER,
Accountants and Auditors.

Dr. Herman introduced Mr. Grant Hultberg who announced the principal new publications for the biennium and assured the Convention of the desire of the Board of Publication to serve in every possible way.

On motion the report of the auditors was accepted.

Mr. Carl M. Distler, President, presented the report of the Inner Mission Board.

REPORT OF THE INNER MISSION BOARD

(For action on the recommendations in this report, see p. 306)

In presenting its report to the Tenth Biennial Convention of the Church, the Inner Mission Board does so with mingled feelings of humility before and gratitude to Almighty God. The responsibility of promoting adequately the Inner Mission in the Church and arousing and quickening the interest of our people in this glorious work of mercy, consecration and love rests heavily upon us. We feel our human insufficiency to cope with the many problems that are ever arising, and to solve them in the name and in accordance with the teachings of Christ. We realize our helplessness to tear the blinding veil from the eyes of the Church, and make it see and feel, as we see and feel, imperfectly and dimly though it may be—the importance of the Inner Mission and the glorious opportunities and grave responsibilities offered by it.

Its field is suffering humanity—in all of its needs—spiritual and material, temporal and eternal. It would redeem society through the salvation that is in Christ Jesus only. It recognizes sin as the cause of all social need and offers Christ as the only solution of social problems. It reclaims bodies that it might save souls. It would establish a social order founded upon and governed by the laws of God. It deals with those both within and without the Church. It seeks through the Church and those consecrated to God therein to release the power of God for the spiritual and social redemption of mankind. It would inspire each Church member so to give his life to God, that through him the works of Christ shall be made daily manifest to a world of sin and need. It seeks to make Christ real and His teachings the basic rule of life to all men. Its magnitude is so great, its possibilities so unlimited, its aims so Christlike—that only the Spirit of the living God can achieve the results that we so ardently desire to accomplish in the life and the thinking of the Church concerning it. May He send that Spirit to work His will!

The past biennium has been one of unusual handicaps and difficulties for the Board, yet not without real growth and achievement. In spite of additional obstacles it has had to cope with, the Board can report a steady growth and development of the Inner Mission throughout the Church. To God be the glory!

During most of the past two years the Board has been without the services of an Executive Secretary, a condition which has grievously hampered it in its work.

On January 10, 1935, the Reverend William Freas, D.D., who had been the Secretary of the Board since its organization in 1918, and its Executive Secretary since May 1, 1919, being the first person to hold that office, and who had done much in the intervening years to develop and spread the Inner Mission throughout the Church, was stricken with a serious incapacitating illness, which confined him to his home and prevented him from performing the duties of his office. Due to his physical condition and the uncertainty of the time of his recovery, Dr. Freas tendered his resignation as Executive Secretary to the Board at its May meeting in 1935. Loathe to believe that his services would no longer be available to its work, and beseeching God for guidance and Dr. Freas' recovery, no action was taken on his resignation until the December meeting following.

Dr. Freas not having recovered sufficiently to permit him to assume his active duties by that time, at his insistance and believing it for the best interests of the work, the Board with much regret accepted his resignation and thereby terminated a relationship which had continued uninterruptedly for sixteen years. During these years, the Inner Mission had steadily grown in the Church; and to this growth Dr. Freas through his insight, labors and Christian spirit had contributed much. We are grateful to God for the work done by His servant, as Executive Secretary of the Board. We rejoice that his health has now sufficiently improved to permit him to continue his labors for the advancement of the Kingdom of God on earth in other capacities in the Church, even though this Board will no longer have the benefit of his services.

Through a special committee of the Board, an immediate and careful survey was made for a suitable successor to Dr. Freas. After a most careful study, and ever seeking Divine guidance, the committee finally recommended to the Board that the Reverend Clarence E. Krumbholz, D.D., then serving as Superintendent of the Lutheran Inner Mission Society of Pittsburgh, be elected to the office of Executive Secretary of the Board, and that a call be extended to him. After due and prayerful consideration, the Board at its meeting in May, 1936, unanimously elected

Dr. Krumbholz as its Executive Secretary; and the call sent was accepted by him, he to assume the duties of his office on September 1, 1936.

Dr. Krumbholz comes to this position with rich experiences both as a pastor and an Inner Mission worker. His many years of labor in the Inner Mission field, particularly in New York and Pittsburgh, and the knowledge and experience thus gained, as well as his devout consecrated life, his genial personality and his recognized ability, well fit him for the duties and responsibilities of his new office. We ask for him the loyal support and aid of the Church in his work. And so we face the future confident that God has great things in store for the Board and the Church.

In this connection it is but fitting to record an expression of appreciation for the extra services rendered by many of the members and the staff of the Board, especially the chairmen of the various committees and Miss Frances Knoob, the office secretary, in these trying times. Needless to say that heavier responsibilities and duties were their lot during these many months in order to carry on as effectively as possible the work committed to the Board. In this they have not failed, but have gladly and freely given of themselves; the tasks, in some instances, often requiring and receiving an unusual amount of time and effort.

MEETINGS, OFFICERS AND MEMBERS

During the past biennium, the Board met regularly twice each year in New York City on the first Thursdays in May and December. In the interim between Board meetings, the work was supervised by the Executive Committee, which met frequently as occasion required.

The officers and the personnel of the Board during the last two years were as follows:

Officers:
President: Carl M. Distler, Esq., 402 American Bldg., Baltimore, Md.
Vice-President: The Reverend Gustavus H. Bechtold, D.D., 1228 Spruce Street, Philadelphia, Pa.
Secretary (until January 10, 1935): The Reverend William Freas, D.D., D.D., 39 East 35th Street, New York, N. Y.
Secretary pro tem: Miss Frances Knoob, 39 East 35th Street, New York, N. Y.
Treasurer: Mr. L. Henry Lund, 39 East 35th Street, New York, N. Y.
Executive Secretary (until December 5, 1935): Rev. William Freas, D.D.
Secretary for Immigrant and Seamen's Work (part-time only): Rev. E. A. Sievert, 218 Seventh Avenue, New York, N. Y.

Board Members:
Terms Expire in 1936
The Rev. Gustavus H. Bechtold, D.D., 1228 Spruce Street, Philadelphia, Pa.
The Rev. Herman Brezing, D.D., Wartburg Orphans' Farm School, Mt. Vernon, N. Y.

The Rev. P. D. Brown, D.D., 1330 Laurel Street, Columbia, S. C.
Carl M. Distler, Esq., 402 American Building, Baltimore, Md.
Mr. T. C. Rohrbaugh, Roanoke, Va.

Terms Expire in 1938
The Rev. Harvey E. Crowell, D.D., Grand Ave. and Xenia Drive,
Osborne, Ohio.
The Rev. Harold S. Miller, 5313 Fourth Avenue, Brooklyn, N. Y.
The Rev. J. Luther Sieber, D.D., 352 Church Ave., S. W., Roanoke, Va.
Dr. Harry C. Hoffman, 146 East Church Street, Somerset, Pa.
Mr. L. Henry Lund, 95 Cranford Avenue, Cranford, N. J.

Terms Expire in 1940
The Rev. Franklin K. Fretz, D.D., Ph.D., 330 Ferry Street, Easton, Pa.
The Rev. A. H. Keck, D.D., 1348 West Fifth Avenue, Gary, Ind.
The Rev. Rufus E. Kern, 135 East Third Street, Hamburg, Pa.
Mr. Thomas P. Hickman, 10th Street and Pennsylvania Ave., N. W.,
Washington, D. C.
Mr. Harry E. Isenhour, Salisbury, N. C.

Advisory Members (appointed by the Women's Missionary Society):
Mrs. Philip M. Rossman, 318 West 84th Street, New York, N. Y.
Mrs. William A. Snyder, 476 Clinton Avenue, Brooklyn, N. Y.

Of the above Board members, whose terms expire in 1936, all are
eligible for re-election, having served continuously but one term of six
years. Mr. Rohrbaugh, however, finds that he will not be able to give
the requisite time to the work expected of a Board member, and has
requested that his name be not considered for re-election.

CONGREGATIONAL ACTIVITY
The Board emphasizes again the importance of the local congregation
as a center from which the Inner Mission activity of the Church must
radiate. To meet its opportunities and wisely to administer its resources
of life, compassion, mercy and love, and to distribute effectively the
wealth at its disposal, demands an efficient properly selected Inner
Mission Committee in *each* congregation; a committee able to study the
needs that exist both in the congregation and in the community or
the parish of which it is a part, and to determine the best means of
satisfying them. The necessity of such a committee is primary; its value
beyond question.

During the biennium we stressed the importance of such committees;
and while responses received from Synodical Inner Mission Committees
for information in this respect were by no means complete, yet they
indicated a growing appreciation on the part of the Church of the value
of the Congregational Inner Mission Committee, and a determination
on the part of some Synods to urge the use of such committees in each
congregation. As illustrative of this we can say that the Synod of South
Carolina reported that fifty-three of its congregations had appointed

such committees; the Susquehanna Synod adopted the Congregational Inner Mission Committee as a Synodical project, furnished all its congregations with pertinent questionnaires and is working toward the goal of an Inner Mission Committee in each congregation; the Alleghany Synod, through its Synodical Inner Mission Committee, has recommended such Congregational Committees for several years; and in some Synods the matter of the Congregational Inner Mission either has been or will be the topic of discussion at Synodical Conferences.

In order to assist the local congregation in the proper prosecution of its Inner Mission opportunities and responsibilities, the Board, through its Congregational Committee, of which the Reverend G. H. Bechtold, D.D., was Chairman, revised its "Congregational Inner Mission Program," and a copy of the same was sent to all Synodical Inner Mission Committees for transmission by them to each pastor of their respective Synods. This program, which was adopted after careful study, is capable of use by a congregation of any size or type. It is suggestive as well as comprehensive. It may be adopted by a particular congregation in its entirety or only a portion or even a single feature thereof may be utilized in developing the Congregational Inner Mission activity. The program presented a three-fold departmental division of the Inner Mission into Evangelism, Social Action, and Merciful Service; briefly developed each in outline with helpful suggestion; discussed the organization required and the local program to be adopted; and gave suggestions as to a survey to be made by each congregation, and the information to be sought; and concluded with an outline of the prosecution of the work.

The Board, through its said committee, also prepared and distributed to Synodical Inner Mission Committees a "Program for Synodical Inner Mission Committees or Boards" and a "Program for an Inner Mission Society."

It is felt that these three programs, properly used, are capable of much good, and it is urged that a ready use be made of them by the Church.

Preaching Mission. The Preaching Mission was also stressed during the biennium. Wherever properly used, it has proved of great value in deepening the spiritual life of the congregation, in reclaiming some who have drifted from the Church, and in winning other souls for Christ. It is well to recognize the fact that the Preaching Mission is a *Congregational* enterprise and not a vehicle for the exploitation of a preacher. Its success rests in the whole-hearted co-operation of the membership in hearing and doing the Word of God. It should be repeated every year. A program for the Preaching Mission, explaining just how it should be carried out, was distributed widely. A revised edition of this program is now being prepared and will be ready for distribution in the late fall.

Child Welfare. The matter of the welfare of the child is receiving more and more consideration both on the part of social agencies and on the part of the State. New legislation, both State and National, is being constantly passed. Child Welfare has developed far beyond the institutional program of child care. It is essential that the Church keep pace with the most recent developments in this field, ever scrutinize the effect upon the Church and its work among children of any and all legislation passed or to be passed in this respect, and be alert to safeguard and preserve its rights. Thus the Federal Security Act has as one of its major objectives security for children. Many states are amending their laws to meet the requirements of the Federal Act. The assistance of the Government is given under four classifications.

1. Grants to States to assist in meeting the costs of aid to dependent children (mother's aid).
2. Grants to States to assist in meeting the costs of maternal and child-health services.
3. Grants to States to assist in meeting the costs of services for crippled children.
4. Grants to States to assist in meeting the costs of child-welfare services.

Under 4 the Rural Extension Unit has been devised for the development of public child welfare services in rural areas, and surveys have been made by the Federal Children's Bureau on the care of dependent children in rural areas. What effect this legislation and governmental activity will have on the service already rendered by Church institutions and agencies cannot be foreseen. However, since the United Lutheran Church is largely rural in character, the Board urges the various Synods to keep themselves informed in these matters and to be vigilant to protect their interests. **(See Recommendation No. 1, p. 302.)** The Board further suggests the creation of Lutheran child placing agencies in all our Synods. **(See Recommendation No. 2, p. 302.)**

Lutheran Nurses Guild. The Board, in co-operation with the Board of Education, has been actively pushing the matter of Nurses Guilds. There has been an increasing interest in this work. Many Lutheran nurses have expressed their appreciation of this concern for their spiritual welfare. There are no tabulated reports, but in a number of communities special Communion Services are being held for nurses, and there is a growing movement for the organization of chapters of the Nurses Guilds in the larger hospitals. During the biennium, two pieces of literature—"So You Are a Nurse" and "Lutheran Nurses Guild" —were published by the two Boards jointly. The first of these is a folder to be given to girls entering training as nurses, and should be sent to them either by their pastor or by the institutional chaplain in the community where they are beginning their training. The second is a card with the seal of the Guild and its six-point program.

INSTITUTIONAL ACTIVITY

The Board exercises an advisory relationship only to the various Inner Mission Institutions and Agencies in the Church. It does not own, operate, manage or control any of them. While it may suggest the initiation of new work, where needed, it has no financial resources with which to aid, but must rely on local support for such projects. However, even though there is no official relation between the Board, or even the Church, as such, and the many Inner Mission institutions and agencies on the territory of the Church, yet it is with joy that we give due recognition to the magnitude and far-reaching effects of the work accomplished by them. During the past biennium approximately $2,500,000 were expended each year in the maintenance of these institutions and agencies, which ministered in Christian love to an approximate average of 850,000 persons each year. Nor does this tell the whole story. For, undoubtedly, the members of the Church are constantly making gifts to other charitable and philanthropic causes and as individuals are giving aid in many ways to many persons of which no record is possible. Where is there any benevolent activity of the Church that can compare in magnitude and support with that of this work of merciful love? The seed has indeed grown into the mightiest of trees!

However, it is the duty of the Board each year to gather together, collate and systematize the statistics of these various institutions and agencies, and list the same for publication in the Year Book. This was diligently done each year of the biennium through its Institutional Committee, of which the Reverend F. K. Fretz, D.D., Ph.D., was chairman. It is worthy of comment that out of 132 institutions and agencies from whom a statistical report was requested responses were received from all but six. This spirit of co-operation was most gratifying and exceedingly helpful in enabling us to furnish nearly accurate statistics for each year. The response was greatly appreciated. Many of our institutions also sent their official annual reports of the work done by them. This was helpful in that it placed at our disposal much information, frequently sought by other agencies, concerning various phases of institutional work and methods of administration. We were thus the better enabled to act as a clearing house in such matters.

The Inner Mission survey conducted by the National Lutheran Council has been completed as far as the field work and collection and tabulation of data is concerned. It now remains for a careful study and interpretation of the results to be made. Part of this will be undertaken as project work by Lutheran candidates for higher degrees in various universities. The final results will undoubtedly be illuminating and exceedingly helpful to the Church.

New Organizations. During the biennium, two new societies—the Lutheran Welfare Society at Stapleton, Staten Island, New York, and the Inner Mission Society at Springfield, Ohio, both under capable leadership, were organized. In addition, the Laura Reiss Memorial Fresh Air Camp, at Red Hook, Dutchess County, New York, under the control of the Inner Mission and Rescue Society of Brooklyn, was opened; and the U. L. C. A. Home for the Aged, at Chicago, Illinois, was founded by the Inner Mission Society of Chicago. Moreover, several other cities have sought information as to the organization of an Inner Mission Society in their midst, some of which inquiries will undoubtedly bear fruit in the near future.

Civilian Conservation Camps. We were glad to learn of the response that was made to the appeal for service by Lutheran pastors in the Civilian Conservation Camps throughout the country. We rejoice that so many of our pastors have ministered to young men enlisted in these camps. In a number of the camps, preaching services have been held, and hours for Bible Study and Sunday schools conducted. These pastors, through their services, have given material help not only in conserving the spiritual morale of these youth, but also in building it up and strengthening it, and in developing manly character.

The Williams-Henson Home. The Board continued its contacts with this home for problem boys, located near Knoxville, Tennessee, making a contribution each month for its maintenance, and receiving reports as to the work being done there. The Home ministered to twenty-one boys during the last year, and continued its work of developing Christian character. Religious instruction was given both at the Home and at St. John's Lutheran Church, as heretofore.

The Board, through its committee, also investigated and made valuable recommendations to a number of inquiries asking guidance as to the advisability of establishing new institutions. In one instance, in which a hospital was contemplated being taken over under Lutheran support and ownership, the committee caused a rather thorough study of the entire situation to be made, involving the population of the city and surrounding territory, the present hospital facilities there and the normal needs of the community. Contacts were also made with the American Medical Association and the American Hospital Association, and their advice requested and given. As a result of this study the committee was prepared to recommend that the project was not feasible. This is but illustrative of a type of service that can be and gladly is given by the Board.

EDUCATIONAL ACTIVITY

This activity of the Board was carried on through its Educational Committee, of which the Reverend Harold S. Miller was chairman. During the biennium, three pamphlets, two of them in furtherance of temperance education, were published, eight issues of "Inner Mission Work" were edited and distributed, special promotional activities carried on particularly during the month of June in each year, a Youth's Temperance Promotion Essay Contest conducted, and preparation made for the issuance of a new series of "A Message for the Day."

Believing that the resolutions and pronouncements of the Church should not be lost in the formal records of the proceedings of its Conventions, but should be brought to the attention of the Church in a concise and practical way for observance and guidance, the Board prepared and distributed 17,500 copies of a pamphlet entitled "The Church Speaks on Modern Problems." In this pamphlet there were set forth in an attractive and readable style, with pertinent introductory comments, four of the resolutions adopted at the Convention of the Church in 1934. These resolutions were those expressing the thought of the Church on Motion Pictures, the Liquor Problem, the Church and State, and the Spiritual Life. Two editions of this pamphlet were printed and distributed to churches in thirty-two states, the District of Columbia, and Canada. In this connection, it is the belief of the Board that more publicity should be given to official pronouncements of the Church, and the laity, as well as the clergy be made acquainted in a practical way with them.

Temperance. In accordance with the authority given at the Savannah Convention, the Board gave serious consideration to the matter of temperance education.

As a first step, at the request of its Educational Committee, the Reverend W. H. Greever, D.D., wrote a pamphlet on "The Bible Speaks on the Liquor Problem," presenting three distinct ideas; first, what the Bible teaches; second, the responsibility of the Church; and third, the responsibility of the State. This pamphlet was printed and distributed to the extent of 10,000 copies.

In order to stimulate the thought of the young people of the Church in the matter of temperance, the Board conducted a "Youth's Temperance Promotion Essay Contest," open to all the young people of the Church who had not passed their twenty-first birthday. The essay was written on the subject "Why I Believe in Temperance," and limited to 1,000 words. The rules and requirements were set forth in advertisements and communications appearing in "The Lutheran" and the "Luther League Review," and in posters and notices sent to each pastor for display in their respective churches. The contest was conducted from July to December 15, 1935. The merits of the essays were passed upon by five judges, namely, Miss Mary E. Markley, Litt.D., Prof. James C. Kinard, LL.D., Litt.D., the Reverend Paul M. Kinports, the Reverend Paul C. White, Ph.D., and the Reverend Franklin C. Fry, whose task it was to determine the best two. The winning essay, written by Alfred

K. Beck, a student at Wagner College, was published in "The Lutheran," issue of April 2, 1936, and was also printed in pamphlet form by the Board and distributed free of charge through the Church, 50,000 copies being printed. The two essays (there being a tie in this respect) which were adjudged second best were printed in the "Luther League Review," issue of May, 1936. The Board expresses its appreciation of the services given by the judges.

Other literature on the subject of temperance is under consideration by the Board.

The Parish and Church School Board, the Luther League, the Women's Missionary Society, and the Brotherhood, were also asked to have suitable articles on temperance appear in their official organs or publications from time to time.

Eight issues of "Inner Mission Work"—the quarterly publication of the Board—were prepared and distributed to the 600 names on the mailing list. The first two were edited by the Executive Secretary, the remainder by the Chairman of the Educational Committee. Through this quarterly, the Board hopes to render valuable service to Inner Mission workers and other interested persons, through the dissemination of information on Inner Mission subjects and the exchange of ideas. By action of the Board, no subscription charge is at present being made for "Inner Mission Work."

In addition to other promotional activities, the Board also sought to concentrate the thought of the Church on Inner Mission work during the month of June in each year. Accordingly, in 1935 four articles and in 1936 five articles on various phases of the Board's work were prepared and printed in "The Lutheran." Other articles also appeared from time to time in "The Lutheran" and in the "Luther League Review." We are appreciative of the courtesy thus extended by the editors of these publications.

In 1936, in connection with its June publicity, the Board also prepared a special leaflet with pertinent facts pertaining to the Inner Mission work of the Church printed on the back page, the inside pages being left blank for use by local congregations. Over 133,000 copies were printed and distributed throughout the Church, free of charge, requests for the same having been received from churches in thirty-eight States, the District of Columbia, and Canada.

A new series of "A Message for the Day" is now in preparation. This message is in the form of a four-page folder. It contains a brief service and a short sermon for each Sunday and Festival of the Church year, and is intended for distribution among those who are prevented from attending Church services by reason of illness, disability or occupation, generally termed "shut-ins" and "shut-outs." It has proved of much value and has been greatly appreciated. During the past biennium over

8,000 copies were distributed each week. The Board also continued to supply "Der Kranken Trost," a publication similar to "A Message for the Day," but published in Germany, to those desiring such a leaflet in the German language.

WORK FOR THE DEAF AND BLIND

This phase of the Board's work during the biennium was in charge of a Committee on Work for the Deaf and Blind, of which the Reverend Rufus E. Kern was chairman.

Work for the Deaf. The Board continued its monthly contribution to the salary of the Reverend E. F. Kaercher, pastor to the deaf, who worked under the supervision of the Board of Inner Missions of the Ministerium of Pennsylvania. Pastor Kaercher rendered an effective service to a large number of the deaf of our Church during the past two years, thus continuing his helpful and fruitful ministry. Reports received of his activities show an ever widening sphere of work, both as to the number of places visited and the variety of pastoral acts performed. His parish extended from New York City on the north through the larger cities of Eastern Pennsylvania to Baltimore and Washington on the south. Among the cities served were New York, Philadelphia, Lancaster, Wilkes-Barre, Hazleton, Pottsville, Scranton, Reading, Allentown, Carbondale, York, Baltimore, Washington and others. During the past biennium he held 204 services, with an attendance of more than 5,700. Frequent visits were made to hospitals and other institutions. Communion services were conducted, catechetical classes taught and confirmed, and instruction in the sign language given to a number of young people. A variety of other pastoral acts were also performed. An important work was done by him through his regular visits at Gallaudet College in Washington, D. C. As a result of his instruction and influence, one of the students of that college, who was graduated with the Class of 1936, offered himself for service among the deaf of our Church through the ministry of the Gospel. He is planning to enter the Lutheran Theological Seminary at Mt. Airy, Philadelphia, Pa., this year, and begin his training for the Christian ministry. The Board is making arrangements toward his support during the coming year. There is a real need for properly trained ministers for the deaf. The activities of the Board in this field of work are limited by the meager funds at its disposal.

Work for the Blind. A new impetus was given during the past biennium to the work for the blind through the receipt by the Board from the Women's Missionary Society of the sum of $1,000, to be expended in the purchase of "Talking Book" machines for use among the blind, and in the purchase of certain subscriptions to the "John Milton Magazine," a magazine for the blind.

The "Talking Book" machine is similar to a Victrola, and can be secured in two types, one operated by spring and the other by electricity. Special records of various books are made and used on this machine. It is intended primarily for the blind. For a fuller understanding of the machine and its use, reference is made to an article entitled "Talking Books for the Blind," written by Mrs. William A. Snyder, an advisory member of the Board, and published in "The Lutheran," issue of June 18, 1936.

The Board, through its committee, immediately contacted various Inner Mission societies and agencies through the Church, seeking to place a machine with those who had use for the same. A special agreement to be entered into between the Board and the agencies to whom a machine is loaned was also prepared. As a result of requests received, eleven machines were purchased and distributed among the following Inner Mission agencies of the Church:

The Lutheran Inner Mission Society of Trenton, N. J.,
The Inner Mission Society of the Lutheran Church in New York City (two machines),
The Board of Inner Missions of the Ministerium of Pennsylvania, Philadelphia, Pa.,
The Inner Mission Society of North Dakota,
The Lutheran Charities of Detroit, Michigan,
The Lutheran Inner Mission League of Miami Valley, Dayton, Ohio,
The Lutheran Welfare Society of Tacoma, Washington,
The Lutheran Inner Mission Society of Pittsburgh, Pa.,
The Inner Mission Society of Philadelphia, Pa., and
The Lutheran Inner Mission Society of Reading and Vicinity.

Until its funds for this purpose are exhausted, the Board, upon proper application, will furnish a machine to other Lutheran agencies having use for the same. According to the terms of the agreement under which these machines are loaned, semi-annual reports must be made to the Board by the agencies receiving them. All of the reports received thus far express the appreciation of the persons served.

The Board is looking into the matter of having "Talking Books," that is, records, of Lutheran literature made for use on these machines, with the view of building up a library of distinctively Lutheran records. While the making of such a "book" entails considerable expense, we are hopeful that something along this line can be accomplished in the near future.

The Board made a contribution to the John Milton Foundation, which sends the "John Milton Magazine" to those requesting it for the use of the blind, and had all requests for the magazine which had come to it filled.

IMMIGRANT AND SEAMEN'S WORK

Immigrant Work. When the Board actively undertook immigrant port work, more than eleven years ago, a five-fold program was laid down as a basis for the execution of this work, namely,

1. Port entry work at New York
2. Work at other ports in this country
3. Work at Canadian ports of entry
4. Follow-up work
5. Contacts with foreign ports.

This program is still generally followed. A decided curtailment of immigration and an increased emigration, both voluntary and compulsory, have brought some changes and restrictions. Nevertheless, the demands for our assistance were such that it was found necessary to continue our full force of workers, although our Secretary for Immigrant and Seamen's Work, and our two immigrant pastors in Canada, gave only part-time to this work.

The necessity for our services can be better appreciated by the fact that in the last biennium over 17,396 contacts were made. These contacts represent persons to whom help in some form or other was given. This embraced services rendered to passengers at steamship piers and railroad stations, to persons repatriated or deported to foreign countries, to immigrants and emigrants at Ellis Island, and to callers at the offices of our Secretary for Immigrant Work and our immigrant pastors in Canada, seeking information, advice, employment, charity and the like, and follow-up work both at home and abroad. It did not include a large correspondence, telegrams and other services, which accounted for another 3,000 contacts, thereby making over 20,000 in all. In addition, an extensive distribution of clothing, Bibles and New Testaments, various German and Scandinavian publications and other literature, was made. Considerable sums of money for wages due them by employers, etc., were also collected for persons to be deported from Ellis Island.

We are happy to record that co-operation with other Lutheran agencies engaged in similar work was not only possible, but was pleasant and helpful to all concerned.

As heretofore, the Board labored principally in the port of New York in this country and in Montreal and Winnipeg in Canada. At Montreal, our immigrant pastor was the Reverend O. C. D. Klaehn, D.D., and at Winnipeg, the Reverend G. O. Juettner. The Ministerium of Pennsylvania, through its Board of Inner Missions, continued doing its own immigrant work.

In New York City the work was carried on in close co-operation with the Lutheran Emigrants' House Association, which maintained an office at 218 Seventh Avenue, where were located the headquarters of our Secretary for Immigrant and Seamen's Work. This association engaged the services of two full-time workers, while the Inner Mission Board had an additional full-time worker at Ellis Island. All three were under the direction of our Secretary for Immigrant and Seamen's Work, the Reverend E. A. Sievert, who by special arrangement was also the pastor of the Lutheran Emigrants' House Association.

Through the said association's membership in the Lutheran Welfare Council, co-operation therein on the part of our Board with the Lutheran Immigrant Society of New York was made possible. We also co-operated with the German Society of New York in the matter of representation granted it at Ellis Island.

Our worker at Ellis Island did a fine piece of work in looking after those of the Lutheran faith who had to pass through it. The character of the services rendered was exceedingly diverse and had many ramifications, including contacts in Washington, D. C., and in Europe. In addition to our regular activities at the island, we secured for its library about 300 books and a large number of magazines, printed in German, for the use of those detained there. Two months each year were assigned to us for the purpose of holding divine services on the island. In these services the Lutheran Emigrants' House Association and the Lutheran Immigrant Society participated with us.

In Canada, we worked through the Inner Mission Committees of the Canada and the Manitoba Synods, making a contribution each year to the respective Synods towards the salaries of our immigrant pastors located on their territory. Housing and feeding the stranger were a problem every winter, especially in Montreal. Co-operation of our immigrant pastor with other agencies made it possible to do much in this respect. In Winnipeg, an extensive visitation of hospitals, asylums and other institutions, both merciful and penal, was also made by our immigrant pastor. The Canadian immigration laws require each immigrant to state his church preference. From the records thus compiled, more than 2,300 Lutherans entered Canada the last biennium. The prospects for increased immigration to that country are encouraging. Certain movements now under way, such as the "Back to the land movement," and the "Continental Movement," as well as the need for certain classes of labor, indicate a steady growth of immigration to Canada.

Our European contacts have not only been kept intact, but have grown even closer. This was due partly to the fact that we have been regularly reporting the sailings of those who were deported from this country or returned to their native land for repatriation, so that they might be met and cared for upon their arrival in their mother country;

but even more because of our work in Canada, where the possibilities for settlement have evoked a lively interest in our European contacts.

Seamen's Work. The need for a real work on the part of the Church among seamen in the ports along the Atlantic and Pacific coasts, as well as along the Gulf of Mexico and the shores of the Great Lakes remains unabated. With the renewal of shipping and increased activities in this form of transportation, it is growing more urgent.

The Board, through its Committee on Immigrant and Seamen's Work, of which the Reverend Herman Brezing, D.D., was chairman, could do nothing in a financial way to alleviate these needs. The customary work heretofore established by various agencies of the Church was carried on; but lack of employment for seamen, causing many of them to become destitute, added heavily to the burden. The committee gave considerable thought to a review of past endeavors and the status of projects in course of development, studied possibilities, and surveyed the situation in the field in its relationship to work abroad, to other church bodies and to government attitudes, and also considered new undertakings. It found that the spirit among seamen was better and more courageously Christian, that Bible study groups and devotional meetings were being organized with some success on boats; but that a great need existed in most of the chief ports along the sea, gulf and lake shores of the country for reading rooms and recreation centers for seamen, for seamen's missions conducting a real Christian home for the men, and for Christian workers among seamen.

We urge our Synods, especially those along the coastal regions, to study the needs of seamen in their respective territories and to do all possible to meet those needs. **(See Recommendation No. 3, p. 302.)**

MOUNTAIN WORK

As a result of the action of the Executive Board, in approving the recommendations of the Commission on Survey of Mountain Work, that all mountain work be consolidated under the jurisdiction of one Board, and designating the Board of American Missions as such board, the Inner Mission activities heretofore carried on among mountain folk, as reported by the Inner Mission Board, have now been officially placed under the administration of the said Board of American Missions. This action became effective as of May 1, 1936, and except for a few legal details yet awaiting adjustment, the Inner Mission Board now has no further jurisdiction in the matter.

This Board, however, submits the following on the mountain work done during the biennium at and around Konnarock, Virginia.

The Konnarock Training School for Girls. The work at this school, near Konnarock, was supported by the Women's Missionary Society. The school completed a decade of service in 1935. It was managed by a board of nine persons, consisting of Mrs. S. R. Kepner, Mrs. Fred Schmidt, Mr. Everett B. Bonham, Mrs. W. F. Morehead, Rev. J. J. Scherer, Jr., D.D., Mr. L. C. Hassinger, Mrs. Theodor Kemnitz, Rev. R. H. Anderson, and Mr. E. F. Schmidt.

The members of this Board have been heretofore elected for the term of six years each by the Inner Mission Board, the terms of three expiring each two years. Four of the members were selected from nominations made by the Women's Missionary Society, four for the Church at large from nominations made by the Inner Mission Board, and one from a nomination made by the Lutheran Synod of Virginia.

The officers of the Board were: The Reverend J. J. Scherer, Jr., D.D., Chairman; Mrs. W. F. Morehead, Vice-Chairman; Mrs. Sydney R. Kepner, Secretary; and Mr. L. C. Hassinger, Treasurer.

The school, which is well equipped, had a regular staff of from seven to nine teachers, including a nurse and an assistant nurse. Miss Helen Dyer was principal, having now served on the staff for seven years. The number of boarding students enrolled ran from thirty-one to thirty-five girls, the latter number being the maximum that could be adequately taken care of. Wherever possible the boarding pupils were required to pay at least one-tenth of their cost each year. Where this payment could not be made in cash or produce the girls generally gave the equivalent by working extra hours on household or farm projects, such as laundering, cleaning, sewing, milking, butter-making, dairying, poultry care, preserving, and the like. During the past biennium, most of the payments were made by these extra services. Approximately two-thirds of the girls were Lutherans. In addition to the boarding students, the school also had an enrollment of day pupils, ranging in number from thirty-five to fifty-five. These came primarily from Smyth County, which paid the salary of one member of the staff in exchange for the school having accepted them as day pupils. Primary, intermediate and upper grades and high school were conducted. In addition to the regular studies, instruction was also given in home economics, cooking, sewing, housekeeping, gardening, home nursing and care of the sick, health work, personal hygiene, music, and corrective gymnasium. A ground improvement project was conducted, which included the planting of trees, shrubs, flowers, and the laying and repair of walks, thereby making the grounds more attractive as well as teaching valuable lessons to the girls. The health work, done both at the school and in the neighborhood, largely increased. A new health center was built and opened, clinics and health institutes were held, homes in the territory visited by the nurses, and helpful instruction and services given. A valuable piece of library work was also done. A Mother's club group and a Men's club group, for health and community betterments, were active and progressive. The school raised large quantities of fruits, vegetables, farm products, and some livestock for its own consumption. Much of the vegetables and fruits were canned. Repairs and improvements on the buildings kept them in good shape. Chief of all, since the school ever seeks the development of Christian ideals in character and conduct, and the deepening of the spiritual life, many religious activities were carried on. These included preaching services, catechetical instruction, Bible study, Sunday school, Luther League, Light Brigade, morning chapel, evening prayers, religious education, and Daily Vacation Bible Schools. There were also troops of Boy Scouts and Girl Scouts. After more than ten years of growth and service, the school has made and continues to make its impress for Christ and good upon the community to which it so earnestly ministers. It fills a much needed want.

The Iron Mountain Lutheran School for Boys. This school, located at Konnarock, Virginia, has now been in operation for nearly five years. It has been seriously handicapped from its beginning by a lack of proper financial support, which was undertaken by the Brotherhood, yet withal has labored for good among the boys of the mountain region. During the past year, due to financial conditions, it became necessary to reduce the number of students from twenty to twelve. Its first student to graduate from the high school in 1935 has since entered college. The Reverend C. L. Miller continued to serve as superintendent of the school. No progress was made by the Brotherhood in raising enough money to pay for the property acquired by the school, liquidate all outstanding indebtedness, and establish the school on a solid financial basis, although a campaign for such purposes had been contemplated from the beginning of the biennium.

The property of the school is located in Smyth and Washington Counties, Virginia. It consists of approximately 420 acres of land, more than one-half of which is timber and brush land, and the balance is partly in orchards, partly in pasture, and partly under cultivation, to which it responds well. The land is improved by a number of buildings. One of them, a well constructed frame hotel building of thirty-one rooms, heated with steam, was used as the dormitory of the school as well as for class rooms. A considerable amount of livestock was kept on hand.

Religious as well as academic instruction was given. In addition, vocational training in farm, stock and dairy work, fruit growing and the like, was received. The spiritual life of the students was nurtured by their attendance at Church services, Sunday school, Bible classes, Luther League, and Catechetical classes. There are great possibilities for good in this school, provided it is properly supported.

The school was duly incorporated under the laws of the State of Virginia in February, 1932. It is controlled by a self-perpetuating Board of eleven trustees. The elections heretofore were made for a term of six years each from nominations submitted by the Inner Mission Board; which received five nominations from the Brotherhood, one from the Lutheran Synod of Virginia, and made five additional nominations itself. The Board, during the past biennium, consisted of Mr. L. C. Hassinger, the Reverend J. J. Scherer, Jr., D.D., Harry C. Hoffman, M.D., Mr. T. C Rohrbaugh, Mr. H. E. Isenhour, Mr. Thomas P. Hickman, the Reverend R. Homer Anderson, the Reverend Samuel J. McDowell, D.D., Mr. Fred Wessels, Mr. Charles E. Miller, and Mr. Everett B. Bonham. Its officers were: Mr. H. E. Isenhour, President; Mr. L. C. Hassinger, Vice-President; Dr. H. C. Hoffman, Secretary; and Mr. T. P. Hickman, Treasurer.

We express our appreciation to the men and the women who have labored so faithfully and conscientiously during these years on the Boards of the above schools for girls and boys, and thank them for the time given and services rendered.

The Reverend Martin L. Zirkle succeeded the Reverend C. W. Cassel as pastor in charge of the congregation at Konnarock. The Board continued its monthly payments to the Lutheran Synod of Virginia to such pastor's support until May 1, 1936.

The committee of the Board on Mountain Work had Mr. H. E. Isenhour as chairman during the biennium.

GENERAL MATTERS

Conference with Other Lutheran Bodies. Pursuant to the action of the Church at its Savannah Convention, and the authority thereby given the Inner Mission Board, repeated attempts were made during the biennium to secure a meeting of officially designated Inner Mission representatives of other General Lutheran Bodies in America in order to discuss the desirability and feasibility of co-ordinating the Inner Mission work of the Lutheran Church in America, and, if possible, to take some definite steps towards the accomplishment of that purpose. After considerable correspondence, the presidents of the American Lutheran Church, the Augustana Synod and the Norwegian Lutheran Church advised that the Inner Mission Commission of the American Lutheran Conference represented them in negotiations with other bodies in problems concerning Inner Missions, and designated that commission as the agency which should act for them "in any dealings of this kind"— "inasmuch as they have more or less merged their Inner Mission interests with those of the Conference."

Interviews were had with a member of the Commission on Unity of the Synodical Conference, at which the subject of co-operation in Inner Missions was discussed, and subsequently with representatives from the American Lutheran Conference, and also with the Vice-President of the Associated Lutheran Charities. As a result it was agreed that as soon as representatives from all the bodies could be appointed a meeting was to be called in Chicago. Correspondence was then had with the chairman of the Special Committee of the Missouri Synod. The Synodical Conference, through its Committee on Lutheran Church Union, through a copy of a letter sent to the president of the American Lutheran Charities, informed us that "we hold that before the Synods co-operate in Inner Mission work, the necessary doctrinal basis for Church fellowship should be established."

Consequently, it was then decided to proceed with a meeting with the American Lutheran Conference alone. However, for various reasons, this meeting has not yet been held. Present plans are to hold it some time in the fall of 1936.

Prison Chaplains. There is an increasing interest in many places in the spiritual welfare of prisoners confined in the numerous penal institutions throughout the land. The desirability of holding regular religious services in these institutions, and the need for the ministrations of the Christian pastor are apparent. Not that this is something new. Religious services have been held in a number of prisons for years past. Some do have duly appointed chaplains, either paid or volunteer. Christian ministers and organizations have been serving in many such places for many years. Thus, the Pennsylvania Prison Society of Philadelphia, which in 1937 will observe its 150th anniversary, was organized in the schoolhouse of St. Michael-Zion's Lutheran Church. Among its founders were the Reverend Doctors Helmuth and Demme, pastors of the church. Dr. Demme was the first regular prison visitor recorded in America. Our Lutheran Church has therefore a good beginning from which to proceed. Today, this type of work is receiving renewed attention. The United States Bureau of Prisons has recently made arrangements with the Federal Council of Churches for the training and furnishing of Protestant chaplains for federal prisons and correctional institutions. Many states already have such chaplains, either paid or volunteer, for their penal institutions. In order to ascertain what, if anything, was being done by our Lutheran Church in this respect, the Board, through its sub-committee on Prison Welfare, of which the Reverend G. H. Bechtold, D.D., was chairman, sent a letter, requesting information, to the chairmen of the Synodical Inner Mission Committees. From the replies received, it appears that in but a very few Synods are any Lutheran ministers the official chaplains at such institutions, although in a number of Synods much volunteer work is done by Lutheran pastors and others. This is particularly true in those Synods which have Inner Mission societies in their midst. One of the activities of these societies is the preaching of the Word to those in prisons and reformatories, the holding of religious services, and in some instances the conducting of catechetical classes. So it can be seen that a great field for much intensive work exists. During the next biennium, efforts will be made to secure full-time men or volunteer Lutheran chaplains for all penal institutions and the like, wherever possible. In this we seek the co-operation of the Church and its constituent synods. (**See Recommendation No. 4, p. 302.**)

The National Lutheran Inner Mission Conference. A meeting of this organization of Inner Mission workers was held in the month of June, 1935, at Toledo, Ohio. Helpful and interesting discussions and presentations were made. The study groups covered the following subjects, family, children, institutional, health, recruiting, and training. Papers on Evangelism and Inner Missions, a Congregational Program, Building Life with Christ through Relief, and Social Action, were ably presented by qualified speakers and earnestly discussed.

The 1936 meeting of the Conference will be held at Omaha, Nebraska, from September 30 to October 2. The Conference is proving of value to Inner Mission workers.

Synodical Inner Mission Committees. Shortly after the last Convention, letters were sent to the presidents of all constituent Synods, advising of the action taken by the Church in the matter of Synodical Inner Mission Committees. Most of our Synods now have such committees. The need for them and the possibilities of a far-reaching service by them are greater than ever. Many of these committees are doing what they can in their Synods, sometimes at personal expense to themselves. But to do an effective work, ample financial provision must be given them so as to enable them to contact pastors, visit congregations, institutions, etc., hold meetings, institutes and conferences, make necessary surveys, and generally promote the Inner Mission cause in their respective Synods. It is to be regretted that so many Synods make little or no financial provision for the work of these committees. We would urge a change of policy in this respect, and request that a proper and adequate support be given them. (**See Recommendation No. 5, p. 302.**)

These committees form the vital connecting link between the Board and the local congregation. Too much importance cannot be placed upon their personnel. The Board again calls to the attention of all Synods and their officers the resolutions passed by the Church at its Savannah Convention in this respect, and urges a full compliance on their part with the same. A number of matters of importance were sent by the Board to Synodical Committees during the past biennium, many of them for transmission to the local congregations. Upon these committees rest to a large extent the development and prosecution of the Inner Mission in each Synod.

We would especially call upon them to study all social legislation that may be passed from time to time, and its effect upon the activities of the Church; to urge the creation of Lutheran Child Placing Agencies in each Synod, in order to keep abreast of recent developments in Child

Welfare, (See Recommendation No. 2, p. 302); and wherever possible to secure the appointment of Lutheran chaplains or provide for voluntary pastoral ministrations in all penal institutions on the territory of their Synods. (See Recommendation No. 4, p. 302.)

Synodical reports indicate that the Church is becoming more conscious of the greatness of the task presented through the Inner Mission, and is growing more active in its services of mercy to suffering humanity.

Finances. During the past biennium the Board has liquidated all of its outstanding indebtedness, paid all its bills, and closed the period with a modest balance to its credit. This was accomplished through a strict curtailment of expenses and by necessity the doing of an extremely limited amount of field visitation.

It does not mean, however, that the Board has received an adequate financial support by the Church. There is so much need that awaits fulfillment; so many avenues of progress that remain closed because of financial want. There is in contemplation a campaign of promotional work, including conferences with Synodical officers and Inner Mission Committees, the holding of institutes and similar meetings in various parts of the country, the visitation of our Inner Mission institutions and agencies for the purpose of study and good-will, and of our Theological Seminaries for a practical presentation of the Inner Mission cause, and the like.

As has been already indicated, the Board in addition to its regular expenditures, continued its contributions to the Board of Inner Missions of the Ministerium of Pennsylvania towards the support of its pastor for the deaf; to the Canada and Manitoba Synods toward the support of our immigrant pastors at Montreal and Winnipeg; to the Lutheran Synod of Virginia toward the support of the pastor of the mountain congregation at Konnarock, Virginia; and to the Williams-Henson Home.

Disaster Emergency Relief. The disastrous floods that swept through so many sections of the country this spring, leaving death, destruction and suffering in their wake, focused the attention of the Church, especially of Inner Mission workers, upon the need of having some agency in the Church with authority and resources sufficient to meet such emergencies promptly and adequately. Not only were many of our Lutheran people the victims of these disasters, but a number of our churches suffered as well through damage to or destruction of their properties. A number of our Inner Mission agencies did a magnificent piece of work in gathering money, food, clothing, and other material supplies for those stricken, and in sending their workers to the scenes of disaster to distribute these supplies and to minister to those so suddenly in need. Nor, when these agencies appealed to the Church for aid, did their appeals, localized and limited though they necessarily were, fall on deaf ears. The response was prompt and generous. Too much cannot be said in praise of all who in any way helped to meet a great emergency and to overcome the effects of a drastic catastrophe. But these efforts and responses necessarily came from but a part of the Church. The Church at large was not prepared for such an emergency. Yet here was an opportunity for service which should have been met by the entire Church.

In times of great disasters, often wide spread in their scope, local organizations with limited means cannot cope properly with the demands. A disaster which affects Lutherans should be met by the Lutheran Church—promptly, effectively, surely. Promptness and dispatch are primary requisites in cases of disaster emergencies. Time is of the very essence of the relief. There is a pressing need that an agency of the Church be given the authority and power to issue to the Church at large immediate appeals for aid in such emergencies, to build up and have ready for instant use an organization sufficiently equipped to deal promptly with such situations, to throw necessary workers and resources speedily into affected areas, and to undertake the immediate relief of those in distress. The Church should also establish and maintain a sufficiently large emergency relief fund upon which the said agency would have authority to draw for such purposes.

This Board urges therefore that the Church give careful consideration to this matter and take definite action thereon. It suggests that disaster emergency relief be made a part of the Inner Mission activities of the Church under its Inner Mission Board; that the said Board be designated and empowered as the agency of the Church to issue appeals for and to receive and distribute relief in disaster emergencies, and to work out the details of a suitable disaster emergency relief organization; and further that a disaster emergency relief fund of sufficient size be authorized and maintained by the Church, to be available for the giving of immediate relief in times of emergencies, and to be disbursed at those times as the Inner Mission Board shall direct. (See Recommendation No. 6, p. 303.)

Reports for Institutions

For the sake of brevity and in the economy of space, the Board, in reporting for the various Inner Mission institutions and agencies of the Church, which under the requirements of its constitution it is charged with doing, submits herewith only a list of the same, and a general summary of the work done by them. The tabulated results are for the year 1935. The figures given are a minimum, as in some cases complete reports were not received. Of the 132 agencies listed below, reports, though not always as full and complete as might have been desired. were returned by all but six.

Classification and List of Inner Mission Institutions and Agencies. Unless otherwise noted, the institutions and agencies listed below were owned, controlled and supported entirely by the United Lutheran Church in America, one or more of its constituent synods, one or more of its congregations, or by associations of its members. Those marked "Inter-synodical" indicate that other Lutheran bodies, or the members thereof, co-operated in their management, support and control. Those marked "Extra-Synodical" had independent self-perpetuating boards of managers, majority Lutheran, with full control.

Children's Homes

††1. Emaus Orphan House, R.D., Middletown, Pa.
2. Orphans' Home and Farm School, Zelienople, Pa.
3. Lutheran Orphans' Home, 6950 Germantown Ave., Philadelphia, Pa.
4. St. John Orphans' Home, Mineral Spring Road, Buffalo, N. Y.
††5. Wartburg Orphans' Farm School, Bradley Ave., Mt. Vernon, N. Y.
6. Tressler Orphans' Home, Loysville, Pa.
7. Tabitha Home, 48th and Randolph, Lincoln, Nebr.
8. Orphan Home of the South, Salem, Virginia.
9. Lutheran Orphans' Home, Topton, Berks Co., Pa.
10. Oesterlen Orphans' Home, State Route 4, Springfield, Ohio.
11. Kinderfreund Orphans' Home, 93 Nelson Avenue, Jersey City N. J.
12. Nachusa Lutheran Orphanage, Nachusa, Ill.
**13. Ebenezer Orphanage, Frederiksted, St. Croix, V. I.
14. Good Shepherd Home, 6th and St. John Sts., Allentown, Pa.
††15. Tabor Home for Children, Doylestown, Pa.
†16. Children's Home, 564 2nd St., Brooklyn, N. Y.
†17. Tiding Over Home, 525 Clinton Ave., Brooklyn, N. Y.
†18. Children's Receiving Home, 809 Madison St., Maywood, Ill.
††19. Children's Receiving Home, 1245 N. Hamline, St. Paul, Minn.
20. Bethesda Home, N. Main ext., Meadville, Pa.
21. Williams-Henson Home (Boys), Route 3, Knoxville, Tenn.

Fresh Air Camps

†1. Lutheran Summer Camp, Zelienople, Pa.
†2. Lutheran Children's Camp, Pike Lake, Amery, Wis.
†3. Girls' Camp, Lake Independence, Minn.
†4. Camp Wilbur Herrlich, Towners, Putnam County, N. Y.
††5. Camp Miller, Shawnee-on-Delaware, Pa.
6. Camp Wa-Shun-Ga, R.F.D., Junction City, Kan.
7. Camp Susquehanna, Selinsgrove, Pa.
†8. Jolly Acres, Annapolis Junction, Md.
9. Camp Luboca, Marblehead, Ohio.
††10. Camp Trexler, Southfields, N. Y.
††11. Camp Arewa, Fredericksburg, Pa.
††12. Paradise Falls Girls' Camp, Paradise Falls, Monroe County, Pa.
13. Laura Reiss Memorial, Red Hook, Dutchess County, N. Y.

Homes for the Aged

1. Asylum for Aged and Infirm, 6940 Germantown Ave., Philadelphia, Pa.
2. Tabitha Home, 48th and Randolph, Lincoln, Nebr.

3. Mary J. Drexel Home, 2100 S. College Ave., Philadelphia, Pa.
4. National Lutheran Home, 18th and Douglass, N. E., Washington, D. C.
†5. Luth. Church Home for Aged, 217 E. Delavan Ave., Buffalo, N. Y.
††6. Marie Louise Heins Home, Bradley Ave., Mt. Verson, N. Y.
7. Luth. Home for the Aged, 2201 Sassafras St., Erie, Pa.
8. Feghtly Lutheran Home, 300 W. Main St., Tippecanoe City, Ohio.
9. O. P. H. of Pittsburgh Synod, Zelienople, Pa.
††10. Franke Home, 261 Calhoun, Charleston, S. C.
11. Good Shepherd Home, 6th and St. John Sts., Allentown, Pa.
12. Lowman Home, White Rock, S. C.
††13. Artman Home for Lutherans, Ambler, Pa.
14. Lutheran Home for the Aged, Main Street, Southbury, Conn.
15. Lutheran Home for the Aged, Clinton, N. Y.
16. Kinderfreund O. P. H., 93 Nelson Ave., Jersey City, N. J.
17. Louisville Lutheran Home, Jeffersontown, Ky.
18. Mulberry Lutheran Home, Mulberry, Ind.
††19. Lutheran Home for Aged, 688 Madison Ave., Albany, N. Y.
20. U. L. C. A. Home for Aged, 212 S. Ashland Blvd., Chicago, Ill.

General Hospitals

††1. The Passavant Hospital, Reed and Roberts Sts., Pittsburgh, Pa.
2. Children's Hospital of Mary Drexel Home, 2100 S. College Ave., Philadelphia, Pa.
†3. The Robinwood Hospital, 2517 Robinwood Ave., Toledo, Ohio.
***4. Kugler Hospital, Guntur, India.
***5. Mission Hospital, Chirala, India.
***6. Lutheran Hospital, Rajahmundry, India.
††7. Lutheran Hospital of Manhattan, 343 Convent Ave., New York, N. Y.
***8. General Hospital, Rentichintala, India.
***9. Lutheran Hospital, Tarlupad, India.
†10. The California Hospital, 1414 S. Hope St., Los Angeles, Calif.
***11. Phoebe Hospital, Muhlenberg, Liberia, Africa.
***12. Lutheran Hospital, Nidadavole, India.
***13. Mission Hospital, Zorzor, Liberia, Africa.
14. Lutheran Hospital Reuss Memorial, Cuero, Texas.
15. St. Luke's Lutheran Hospital, 230 W. Madison St., Milwaukee, Wis.
***16. Augustana Hospital, Bhimawaram, India.
***17. Lutheran Hospital, Tsingtao, Shantung, China.

Sanatoria, Special Hospitals and Homes

1. Passavant Memorial Homes for Epileptics, Rochester, Pa.
**2. Queen Louise Home for Sick and Neglected Babies, Christiansted, St. Croix, V. I.
††3. Kensington Dispensary for Treatment of Tuberculosis, Hancock and Susquehanna Ave., Philadelphia, Pa.
4. Good Shepherd Home for Crippled Children and Old People, Allentown, Pa.
5. Lowman Home for the Aged and Helpless, White Rock, S. C.
††6. River Crest Preventorium, Mont Clare, Pa.
***7. Tuberculosis Hospital, Vishrantipuram (near Rajahmundry), India.

Hospices

1. The Luther Hospice, 1932 Race St., Philadelphia, Pa.
††2. The Luther House, 828 S. 6th St., Minneapolis, Minn.
†3. Lutheran Hospice for Girls, 509 Park Ave., Baltimore, Md.
††4. Cotta Hall (for Women), 330 E. North, N. S., Pittsburgh, Pa.
†5. Trabert Hall, 625 E. 14th, Minneapolis, Minn.
6. Tryon Hall, 29th and Glenwood Ave., Philadelphia, Pa.
†7. Lutheran Hospice for Girls, 1104 N. 12th St., Milwaukee, Wis.
8. U. L. C. Girls' Club, 5402 Magnolia Ave., Chicago, Ill.
9. Luther Hall for Women, 210 9th St., N., Fargo, N. D.
††10. Lutheran Hospice, 1520 Mineral Spring Road, Reading, Pa.

Seamen's and Immigrants' Missions and Homes

††1. Lutheran Emigrants' House Association, 218 Seventh Ave., New York, N. Y.
2. Seamen's and Immigrant Mission, 1402 E. Moyamensing Ave., Philadelphia, Pa.
†3. Lutheran Seamen's Mission, 64 Hudson St., Hoboken, N. J.

Settlement Houses

1. Lutheran Settlement House, 1340 Frankford Ave., Philadelphia, Pa.
2. Martin Luther Neighborhood House, 1333 S. 9th St., Philadelphia, Pa.

Child Placement Agencies

1. Lutheran Children's Bureau, 1228 Spruce St., Philadelphia, Pa.

Industrial Missions

†1. The Inner Mission, 23rd and Sidney Sts., S. S., Pittsburgh, Pa.

Missions for the Deaf and Blind

1. Lutheran Mission for the Deaf, 1228 Spruce St., Philadelphia, Pa.
2. Lutheran Mission for the Blind, 1228 Spruce St., Philadelphia, Pa.

Mountain Missions and Schools

1. Konnarock Training School (Girls), Konnarock, Virginia.
2. Iron Mountain Lutheran Boys' School, Konnarock, Virginia.

Deaconess Motherhouses

1. Philadelphia Motherhouse of Deaconesses and Mary J. Drexel Home, 2100 S. College Ave., Philadelphia, Pa.
2. Lutheran Deaconess Motherhouse and Training School, 2500 W North Ave., Baltimore, Md.

Inner Mission Societies and Agencies

†1. Baltimore, Md.—Lutheran Inner Mission Society, 509 Park Ave
††2. Bridgeport, Ohio—Lutheran Women's League, 446 Main St.
†3. Brooklyn, N. Y.—Lutheran Inner Mission Society, 525 Clinton Ave
†4. Brooklyn, N. Y.—Society of Inner Mission and Rescue Work, 564 Second St.

††5. Charleston, S. C.—Ev. Luth. Charities, 261 Calhoun St.
  6. Chicago, Ill.—In. Mis Soc. of Chicago Area, 212 S. Ashland Blvd.
†††7. Dayton, Ohio—Luth. In. Mis. League of Miami Valley, Montana
      and McLain Sts.
††8. Detroit, Mich.—The Lutheran Charities, 2900 Benson St.
  †9. Fargo, N. D.—Lutheran Mission Society, P. O. Box 42.
†10. Minneapolis, Minn.—Lutheran Welfare Society, 404 S. Eighth St.
††11. New York, N. Y.—In. Mis. Soc. of Evan. Luth. Ch., 105 East
      22nd St.
††12. New York, N. Y.—Lutheran Welfare Council, 105 East 22nd St.
†13. New York (Jamaica), N. Y.—Luth. Wel. Center for Queens,
      92-53 165th St.
†14. New York (Stapleton, S. I.), N. Y.—Luth. Wel. Soc., 309 St.
      Paul's Ave.
  15. Philadelphia, Pa.—Lutheran City Mission, 1228 Spruce St.
  16. Philadelphia, Pa.—The Inner Mission Soc., 1932 Race St.
  17. Philadelphia, Pa.—Lutheran Bureau, 1228 Spruce St.
  18. Philadelphia, Pa.—Board of Inner Missions, 1228 Spruce St.
††19. Pittsburgh, Pa.—Luth. Inner Mission Soc., 533 Wabash Building.
†20. Portland, Oregon—Luth. Welfare Soc., 727 N. E. Grand Ave.
††21. Reading, Pa.—Luth. In. Mis. Soc., 25 S. Fifth St.
  22. Rochester, N. Y.—Luth. In. Mis. Soc., 546 N. Clinton Ave.
†23. Saginaw, Michigan—Luth. In. Mis. Soc., 1608 Tuscola St.
†24. Seattle, Washington—Luth. Welfare Society, 779 Lakeview Blvd.
  25. Southbury, Conn.—Inner Mission Society, Main St.
  26. Springfield, Ohio—Inner Mission Society, 27 West Ward St.
†27. Tacoma, Washington—Luth. Welfare Society, 1525 Pacific Ave.
†28. Toledo, Ohio—Luth. In. Mis. Soc., 538 N. Erie St.
††29. Trenton, N. J.—Luth. Inner Mission Society, 1742 S. Clinton Ave.
†30. Washington, D. C.—Luth. Inner Mission Society, 1225 New York
      Ave., N. W.

---

  †Inter-Synodical.
  ††Extra-Synodical.
  **Supported and operated by Board of American Missions.
  ***Supported and operated by Board of Foreign Missions.

Summary of work of Inner Mission Institutions and Agencies

Children's Homes. 2,088 children were cared for in our twenty-one children's homes. These included orphans, half-orphans and those who had both parents incapacitated. Some were permanent, others temporary shelters.

Summer Camps. 3,011 boys and girls were given an outing in the country for at least two weeks during the summer, with training.

Old People's Homes. 671 aged persons were ministered to by our Church in these homes.

Hospitals. 67,005 patients received treatment in our seventeen hospitals.

Sanatoria and Special Homes. 1,025 patients were looked after in these institutions.

Hospices. 1,562 young men and young women made their homes in our hospices.

Seamen's Missions. 25,169 seamen visited and were helped through our seamen's missions.

Settlements. 75,624 people were given aid in some way in our settlements located in the poorer sections of a few of our great cities.

Child Placement. Fifty children were newly placed in private homes through this agency during the year, making a total thus looked after of 499.

Missions to the Deaf and Blind. 5,215 deaf and blind folk were reached by these missions.

Industrial Mission. Nearly 50,000 men received assistance through this instrumentality.

Mountain Schools. 110 boys and girls received education and hundreds of mountain folk were benefited by the work of these schools.

Deaconess Motherhouses. 154 deaconesses connected with the two motherhouses at Philadelphia and Baltimore served the Church in their ministry of love.

Inner Mission Societies. The U. L. C. A. participated in the work of thirty Inner Mission Societies. In the many forms of activities of these organizations 726,546 persons were served in the name of the Church.

U. L. C. A. Institutional Work. The U. L. C. A., in 132 institutions and agencies used 3,922 workers and ministered to 865,554 people at an outlay of $2,480,389.

RECOMMENDATIONS

(For action, see p. 306)

The Inner Mission Board submits for adoption by the United Lutheran Church in America the following recommendations:

1. That the Church urge all Synodical Inner Mission Committees and Boards of its constituent Synods and all members of managing Boards of Inner Mission Institutions and Agencies to study carefully all social legislation that may be passed, and its effect upon the merciful work of the Church, and particularly the possible effect of all Federal Security legislation upon the work being done by Lutheran Institutions and Agencies on the territory of their respective Synods, or to whose support they contribute or whose affairs they manage; and to take such proper steps as may be necessary to safeguard the interests of the work and the rights of the Church therein.

2. That the Church recommend to its constituent Synods and their officers and Inner Mission Committees and Boards the study of the need of Lutheran Child Placing Agencies in each Synod.

3. That the Church urge its constituent Synods situated along the Atlantic and the Pacific Oceans, the Gulf of Mexico and the Great Lakes to study the needs of Lutheran seamen entering ports in their respective territories; and to undertake constructive work for their welfare.

4. That the Church recommend to its constituent Synods and their officers and Inner Mission Committees that a survey be made of all penal institutions and reformatories on their respective territories; and that they seek to place full-time or volunteer Lutheran chaplains in each such institution.

5. That the Church request its Constituent Synods to give sufficient financial support to the work of Synodical Inner Mission Committees, so

as to enable them to render a more effective service to the Church and its Inner Mission cause.

6. (a) That the Inner Mission Board be charged with the duty of studying and developing an adequate organization to cope with disaster emergencies that may affect the Church on any part of its territory from time to time; and that the matter of Disaster Emergency Relief be made a part of the Inner Mission activities of the Church under the jurisdiction of its said Board.

(b) That, as disasters occur, the Inner Mission Board, with the approval of the officers of the Church, be authorized to make such appeals for funds and other contributions for disaster emergency relief as circumstances may require, and to receive, administer and distribute the same.

(c) That the Church provide for the raising and the maintenance of a Disaster Emergency Reserve Fund sufficient to meet first aid requirements; and that the same shall be immediately available in times of emergency to the Inner Mission Board for distribution, subject to the approval of the officers of the Church. (Not adopted, see p. 306.)

Respectfully submitted,

For the Inner Mission Board,

Carl M. Distler, *President.*

REPORT OF THE TREASURER OF THE INNER MISSION BOARD

RECEIPTS AND DISBURSEMENTS BY FUNDS

July 1, 1934 to June 30, 1935

RECEIPTS

	General Fund	Mountain Work	Immigrant Work	Deaf Work
Apportionment	$11,008.41	$306.88	$3,102.46	$926.25
Women's Missionary Society		8,550.00		1,000.00
The Brotherhood of the United Lutheran Church in America..		1,010.00		
Literature Sales and Subscriptions	1,060.76			
Contributions	877.83	2.00	24.50	
Bank Loans	700.00			
Travel Refunds by Churches	210.00			
Total Receipts	$13,857.00	$9,868.88	$3,126.96	$1,926.25

DISBURSEMENTS

	General Fund	Mountain Work	Immigrant Work	Deaf Work
Salaries—				
Secretary	$3,466.58		$600.00	
Office and Church	1,536.00		1,478.00	
Pastors'		$400.00	1,096.62	$900.00
Travel—Executive Secretary	22.72			

Board—Travel and Expense	862.14			
Literature and Printing	1,638.59			
Office Expense	302.73		120.80	
Office Supplies	177.91			
Office Postage	473.95			
Office Printing	76.20			
Office Maintenance	939.68			
Williams - Henson H o m e and School for Boys	437.40			
Contributions	12.50		20.00	
Konnarock Training School		10,687.50		
Iron Mountain Lutheran School.		1,010.00		
Bank Loans Repaid	600.00			
Total Disbursements	$10,546.40	$12,097.50	$3,315.41	$900.00

SUMMARY OF CASH IN BANK

July 1, 1934 to June 30, 1935

	General Fund	Mountain Work	Immigrant Work	Deaf Work	Total
Balance, July 1, 1934	$1,654.90*	$2,281.04	$661.95	$130.30	$1,418.39
Receipts	13,857.00	9,868.88	3,126.96	1,926.25	28,779.09
	$12,202.10	$12,149.92	$3,788.91	$2,056.55	$30,197.48
Disbursements	10,546.40	12,097.50	3,315.42	900.00	26,859.32
Balance, June 30, 1935	$1,655.70	$52.42	$473.49	$156.55	$3,338.16
Women's Missionary Society				1,000.00	
				$1,156.55	

*Deficit.

SUMMARY OF CASH IN FUNDS

July 1, 1935 to June 30, 1936

	General Fund	Mountain Work	Immigrant Work	Deaf Work
Balance—July 1, 1935.....................	$1,655.70	$52.42	$473.49	$1,156.55
Receipts	12,678.43	7,623.18	3,145.80	964.54
	$14,334.13	$7,675.60	$3,619.29	$2,121.09
Disbursements	9,843.39	8,158.00	3,164.67	1,276.63
	$4,490.74	$482.40*	$454.62	$844.46
Transfer	482.40	482.40		
Balance—June 30, 1936..................	$4,008.34		$454.62	$844.46

*Deficit.

RECEIPTS AND DISBURSEMENTS BY FUNDS

July 1, 1935 to June 30, 1936

RECEIPTS

	General Fund	Mountain Work	Immigrant Work	Deaf Work
Apportionment	$11,342.88	$252.18	$3,133.80	$940.14
Women's Missionary Society		7,125.00		
The Brotherhood of the United Lutheran Church in America		220.00		
Literature Sales and Subscriptions	1,035.06			
Contributions	109.16	26.00	12.00	10.00
Refunds and Miscellaneous	191.33			14.40
Totals	$12,678.43	$7,623.18	$3,145.80	$964.54

DISBURSEMENTS

	General Fund	Mountain Work	Immigrant Work	Deaf Work
Salaries—				
Dr. Freas	$2,399.94			
Dr. Sievert			$600.00	
Office and Clerical	1,637.40		1,314.50	
Pastors		$175.00	939.96	$900.00
Travel—Board	1,236.36			
Literature and Printing	767.56			
Office—				
Expense	125.65		110.21	
Supplies	205.86			
Postage	682.03			
Printing	58.91			
Maintenance	704.76			
Williams-Henson Home for Boys	349.92			
Contributions		13.00		5.00
Konnarock Training School		7,125.00		
Iron Mountain Lutheran School		220.00		
Bank Loans Repaid	700.00			
Talking Book Machines				371.63
Accounts Payable—Old	975.00	625.00	200.00	
Totals	$9,843.39	$8,158.00	$3,164.67	$1,276.63

BALANCE SHEET

June 30, 1936

ASSETS

Cash in Bank	$4,664.65
Women's Missionary Society Fund	642.77

Petty Cash and Stamps	60.00
Furniture and Fixtures	100.00
Talking Book Machines	371.63
Total Assets	$5,839.05

Funds

General Fund	$4,143.34
Immigrant Work	479.62
Deaf Work	1,216.09
Total Funds	$5,839.05

Respectfully submitted,

L. HENRY LUND, *Treasurer.*

July 30, 1936.

We have audited the books of account of the Treasurer of the Inner Mission Board of the United Lutheran Church in America, for the biennium beginning July 1, 1934 and ending June 30, 1936, and we hereby certify that, in our opinion, the foregoing statements of Cash Receipts and Disbursements for the years ended June 30, 1935 and June 30, 1936, and the Balance Sheet as of June 30, 1936, are in accordance with the books of account, and are true and correct.

TAIT, WELLER AND BAKER,

Accountants and Auditors.

Mr. Distler introduced the Rev. C. E. Krumbholz, Executive Secretary, the Rev. Harold S. Miller, and the Rev. G. H. Bechtold, who spoke in their order on different phases of the Inner Mission work.

The recommendations were presented.

Recommendations 1, 2, 3, 4, and 5 were adopted.

Recommendation 6. Under this recommendation the President called up the deferred item of the report of the Executive Board, III, B, 3, page 63, which was considered in this connection. Action on recommendation 6 was as follows:

Recommendation 6, (a) adopted.
(b) adopted.
(c) not adopted.

On motion the report of the auditors was accepted.

At 11:00 o'clock the President called for the Special Order appointed for prayer in behalf of the pastors of the Church. The service was conducted by the Rev. A. M. Knudsen who, after reading a suitable scripture lesson, presented important points connected with the work of the ministry, and then special prayer was offered by the Revs. J. C. Mattes and C. A. Linn. The Rev. Mr. Knudsen led the Convention in the Lord's Prayer and the benediction was pronounced by President Knubel.

SEVENTH SESSION

DESHLER-WALLICK HOTEL
Columbus, Ohio
Monday, October 19, 1936, 1.50 P. M.

Devotions were conducted by the Rev. D. P. Putman, and the President called the Convention to order.

The Special Committee on Minutes reported that they had examined the Minutes of the third, fourth and fifth sessions, and, finding them correct, moved their approval. The motion was carried and the President declared the Minutes approved.

The Rev. F. M. Urich, Chairman of the Committee of Reference and Counsel, presented the following report:

REPORT OF COMMITTEE OF REFERENCE AND COUNSEL

1. A telegram addressed to President Knubel by Dr. T. O. Burntvedt, President of the Lutheran Free Church, conveying fraternal greetings, has been received.

We recommend that the President extend the cordial greetings of the Convention to President Burntvedt.

2. A telegram sent to our President by the Andhra Lutheran Convention in session at Rajahmundry, and praying God's blessing upon the Convention of the Mother Church, has been received.

We recommend that President Knubel convey to President Neudoerffer the reciprocal greetings of the Convention.

3. The National Preaching Mission, in a telegraphic message to Secretary Greever, expressed a feeling of kinship with the historic reliance of the Lutheran Church on the promise of God and the preaching of His Divine Word, and adds heartfelt appreciation of the generous service given by a number of pastors of the United Lutheran Church in this spiritual enterprise.

We recommend that Secretary Greever be authorized to make suitable reply.

4. The Rev. J. C. Mattes has appeared before your Committee requesting the privilege of presenting an amendment to the Constitution of the

United Lutheran Church relative to the tenure of office of the officials of the United Lutheran Church. ·

We recommend that he be granted time to present his resolution immediately after the report of the Committee on Memorials from Constituent Synods. (See p. 360.)

5. The Rev. G. H. Bechtold submitted the following resolution to your Committee: Resolved, That the United Lutheran Church, through its President, extend to Bishop Fuglsang, Damgaard, Primate of the Lutheran Church in Denmark, the hearty greetings and good wishes of the Convention on the occasion of the 400th Anniversary of the Reformation of the Church in Denmark.

We recommend the adoption of this resolution.

6. The Rev. C. W. Hepner, of the Japan Lutheran Theological Seminary, an official delegate of the Lutheran Church in Japan, is present.

We recommend that he be heard at once and that eight minutes be granted for this presentation.

7. We recommend that President Mees of Capital University be presented to the Convention.

8. A telegram of fraternal greetings received by Secretary Greever from the Federal Council of the Churches of Christ in America, and signed by the officers of the Federation, has been referred to this Committee.

We recommend that Secretary Greever be authorized to make suitable reply.

9. The Rev. Dr. R. E. Golladay, representing the American Lutheran Church, in the absence of President Hein, is here to present greetings from that body.

We recommend that he be heard at once.

10. The following resolution of the Michigan Synod delegation has been submitted to your Committee:

Whereas, the whole program of the whole United Lutheran Church is seriously hampered and restricted as a result of the failure to meet the apportioned budget in full, and,

Whereas, this failure is due to inadequate training in Christian stewardship on the part of a large percentage of the membership of the Church, and,

Whereas, this serious condition must be remedied if the Church is to carry out faithfully her Divine Commission,

Be it therefore resolved, that the United Lutheran Church in convention assembled instruct the Executive Board to provide for the preparation and promotion, through the synods, of an intensive and thorough evangelistic and inspirational program, in the year 1937, for the purpose of meeting the apportioned budget in full. ·

The Michigan Synod delegation,

Herbert E. Schildroth, President of Synod

F. P. Madsen, Secretary of Synod.

We recommend that this resolution be submitted to the Committee on President's report. (For action, see pp. 419, 431.)

11. The Rev. A. A. Hahn, a regularly elected delegate from the Synod of the Northwest, while on his way to this convention, was called back by the sudden death of his father, a pastor in the American Lutheran Church. The Rev. Mr. Hahn is now in attendance here.

We recommend that, in view of the circumstances, he be permitted to register as of Friday morning last.

12. Word has come to us that Dr. Luther Kuhlman, faithful pastor and professor in Gettysburg Seminary, passed away Sunday morning, October 18, on the eve of his eighty-fifth birthday.

Dr. Kuhlman was, for many years, President of the Board of Foreign Missions in the General Synod. He occupied various positions of trust and responsibility in our Church. He was Vice-President of the Commission of Adjudication, and during the last biennium served as its President.

We recommend that the Convention stand in silent prayer as a tribute to his memory.

Recommendations 1, 2, 3, 4, and 5 were adopted.

Recommendation 6 was adopted and the Rev. C. W. Hepner and the Rev. Kyoshi Watanabe addressed the Convention.

Recommendations 7 and 8 were adopted.

Recommendation 9 was adopted, and the Rev. R. E. Golladay was introduced.

Dr. Golladay explained that he carried a dual commission from the President of the American Lutheran Church, first to extend a special greeting from the congregations of the American Lutheran Church in Columbus and vicinity, and the official greetings of the American Lutheran Church, authorized in its recent convention. Dr. Golladay spoke in most cordial terms concerning the oneness of the American Lutheran Church with the United Lutheran Church in fundamental tasks and purposes, and then enlarged upon the same by saying that he was speaking without official authority but in expression of his own sentiments. His address was received with decided approval.

Response to the greetings of Dr. Golladay was made by the Rev. E. P. Pfatteicher. The remarks of Dr. Pfatteicher constituted a genuine response to the cordial greetings extended by Dr. Golladay.

In this same connection, the Rev. Otto Mees, President of Capital University, was introduced and addressed the Convention very cordially, from the standpoint of his position as a church educator.

Recommendation 10 was adopted.

Recommendation 11 was unanimously adopted.

Recommendation 12 was adopted, and the Convention stood in silent tribute.

The Rev. W. A. Wade, President, presented the report of the Board of Deaconess Work.

REPORT OF THE BOARD OF DEACONESS WORK
(For action on the recommendations in this report, see p. 326)

The Board of Deaconess Work herewith presents its tenth biennial report to the United Lutheran Church in America.

DEACONESS WORK CENTENNIAL

It so happens that the opening of this Convention of the United Lutheran Church in America occurs one day later than the centennial of the founding of Lutheran Deaconess Work, October 13, 1836. The Board of Deaconess Work has, therefore, arranged for a fitting commemoration of the restoration of the Apostolic office of the Female Diaconate by Pastor Theodore Fliedner, who, under God, revived the ancient office. One hundred years of Lutheran Deaconess work are of sufficient importance to merit a worthy commemoration. From the modest beginning of Deaconess work by Pastor Fliedner, who was practically without means, but with unbounded trust in God, modern deaconess work spread throughout all Protestant countries, and today there are more than 50,000 sisters serving in hospital, institutional, congregational, educational, Inner Mission and Foreign Mission work. **(See Recommendation No. 1, p. 314.)**

"FLIEDNER THE FAITHFUL"

The Board of Deaconess Work is happy to announce the publication of an English biography of Fliedner, *"Fliedner the Faithful,"* giving a brief outline of the establishment of the work in Germany, featuring the need which Fliedner recognized and endeavored to meet by enlisting and training young women as deaconesses. The book has been written by the Rev. Prof. Abdel Ross Wentz, Ph.D., D.D., and we trust that it will enlist the interest of the whole Church and be the means of interesting many young women in the service of the Diaconate. Thus we may be able to meet the present and future needs of the Lutheran Church of America for Christian trained young women.

PROMOTIONAL WORK

Realizing the imperative need of a second full-time man for the Baltimore Motherhouse and general deaconess work, the Board of Deaconess

Work, at its June meeting, this year, authorized a special committee to consider this matter seriously and to report at the October meeting. We were led to this action in order that we might be able to more adequately present the cause and inform the Church of the value and needs of deaconess service. Since the retirement of the late Dr. Charles E. Hay, the burden of the work has been carried largely by one full-time man.

In view of the many needs and opportunities for trained Christian services in various sections of the Church, which we believe might be served with good results by our sisters, in loving service and works of mercy, thus fulfilling the primary purpose of the Female Diaconate, the Board of Deaconess Work, at the June meeting this year, unanimously adopted the following recommendation, presented by the Executive Committee:

"That the plans be made for one or more sisters to be assigned to congregations, parishes, Conferences, Synods and church institutions in which their services may be desirable; that they be assigned for such periods of time as the cases may need, under the direction of pastors and Conference, Synodical and institutional officials, who will be expected to provide room, board and travelling expenses for the sisters while in service. Such arrangement shall in no way change, or interfere with, our plan for full-time deaconess service." (**See Recommendation No. 5, p. 315.**)

Possible Plans and Goals

Recognizing the fact that the Church will and must grow and meet her opportunities in a larger and more efficient way in the future, and appreciating the faithful, efficient and noble service of those engaged in training and directing deaconesses, the Board approved an outline of possible aims and goals for future consideration and development.

Believing the congregation to be the fundamental unit of the church, and recognizing two objectives in our Deaconess Work, (1) the objective of the preparation and direction of trained workers for congregations and other agencies of the church; and (2) the rendering of some service in the preparation of Christians engaged in public service—in social or educational service, not under the direction of the church, the following outline of Possible Plans or Goals is presented.

I. *Goals of Works of Mercy and Christian Service.*

1. *Evangelism.* The church should assume a larger measure of the responsibility and have a larger trained force of workers for bringing the *least*, the *last* and the *lost* to Christ. Much of the present work of volunteer missions, the Salvation Army and similar agencies should be done by the church.

2. The ministry within the parish: the deaconess, the parish worker, shepherdess, etc.

3. Christian nurses.

4. Missionaries of the church at home and abroad.

5. Institutional workers, rendering a merciful ministry to the aged, the orphaned, the disabled, the defective, the delinquent and the unfortunate.

6. The ministry of leadership of worship and church music.

7. The educational ministry: (a) Religious Education,—Bible schools, camps and training schools, church schools. (b) Administrative—advisers of youth, personal directors, deans of women. (c) Teachers of Bible for colleges and other educational institutions. (d) Leaders in the general work of the church.

8. Social workers: (a) Rescue, (b) Relief, (c) Rehabilitation, (d) Administrative, survey, research, direction, etc.

9. Inner Mission workers: (a) Congregational service, (b) General or community work.

10. Constructive Human Welfare Work: (a) Child Guidance, (b) Psychiatrists, (c) Counselors, (d) Clinicians.

11. Prepared workers of the church for other works of mercy made necessary by changing social conditions.

II. *Consequent Functions in the Work of Education and Training.*

1. Deaconesses adequately equipped and trained.

2. Parish Workers with a training equal to that of the clergy.

3. Preparation of missionaries, *e. g.*, in Bible, in specific training for special fields and in general preparation for Christian work.

4. The preparation of persons for secretarial and administrative work of the congregation.

5. Technically trained Inner Mission Workers.

6. Choristers, organists and teachers of the Art of Worship.

7. Trained makers of vestments and church goods, including the illumination of Service and Prayer Books, etc.

8. Bible teachers and catechists.

9. The preparation of secretaries and executives for the general work of the church.

10. Instruction of many others by means of "Short Courses." For example, (a) Teachers in the public schools, (b) Parish school workers and teachers, (c) Home builders, (d) Church members, (e) Leaders of youth, (f) Seekers after the Truth.

11. Co-operation with special schools and institutions of advanced learning for the training of deaconesses in special fields in which they may have aptitude or in which there may be a call to serve. Such co-operation would be especially helpful now and during the period of the development of the work toward more adequate equipment and support.

III. *Faculties and Working Force.*

1. The Administrative Division.

2. Division of Instruction. A skeleton Outline: Bible, Methods of Church Work, Institutional Work, The Way of Salvation, Art of Worship, Church History, Religious Education, Missions, Music, Literature and Science, History, Philosophy, Sociology and Economics, Civics, Psychology, Education, Ethics, Clinical and Field Work.

3. Direction and Supervision and Contact Service.

4. Extension Service.

IV. *The Plant.*

1. Motherhouses, strategically located.

2. Sanctuaries (Houses of Prayer).

3. Educational Buildings, *e. g.* Bible School, School of Social Work, School of Music, School of Missions, Schools of Church Workers, etc.

4. Libraries.

5. Recreational Buildings.

6. Clinics and Laboratories.

7. Auditoriums.

8. Institutions contiguous, if the Motherhouse cannot co-operate with institutions of Mercy, Medicine, etc., in the community and elsewhere.

The above aims and goals will necessitate a larger financial appropriation.

CONFERENCE ON DEACONESS WORK

In carrying out the action of the Savannah Convention (see Minutes, page 368), a conference of parish deaconesses and the pastors of the congregations in which they serve was held on June 28, 1935. The conference was attended by pastors, members of the Board, the Baltimore Motherhouse staff and a large number of Sisters from various sections of the church. Many helpful suggestions were made and we believe that good resulted from it.

BOARD OFFICERS AND MEMBERS

Following is the list of Board Officers and members during the past biennium:

Officers

President: Rev. William A. Wade, D.D., 505 Harwood Ave., Baltimore, Md.

Vice-President: Rev. U. S. G. Rupp. D.D., 1501 Bolton St., Baltimore, Md.

Recording Secretary: Rev. Foster U. Gift, D.D., 1901 Thomas Ave., Baltimore, Md.

Treasurer, Frederick J. Singley, Esq., 215 N. Charles St., Baltimore, Md.

Members of the Board
Terms Expire 1936
Rev. Allen L. Benner, D.D., 21 E. James St., Lancaster, Pa.
Rev. J. J. Schindel, D.D., 19 W. Southampton Ave., Philadelphia, Pa.
Rev. L. A. Thomas, D.D., 605 S. Stewart St., Winchester, Va.
Mr. E. S. Gerberich, 2403 N. Front St., Harrisburg, Pa.
Frederick J. Singley, Esq., 215 N. Charles St., Baltimore, Md.

Terms Expire 1938
Rev. George N. Lauffer, D.D. 220 N. Jefferson St., Kittanning, Pa.
Rev. William A. Wade, D.D., 505 Harwood Ave., Baltimore, Md.
Mr. Harry R. Hagerty, 2707 Queen Anne Road, Baltimore, Md.
Mr. I. Searles Runyon, 601 W. 156th St., New York City.
Edgar W. Young, Esq., 3309 Carlisle Ave., Baltimore, Md.

Terms Expire 1940
Rev. H. D. Hoover, Ph.D., D.D., S.T.D., 321 Springs Ave., Gettysburg, Pa.
Rev. U. S. G. Rupp, D.D., 1501 Bolton St., Baltimore, Md.
Rev. W. C. Schaeffer, Jr. D.D., 18 S. 14th St., Allentown, Pa.
Mrs. Elsie Singmaster Lewars, Litt.D., Seminary Ave., Gettysburg, Pa.
Mr. Frederick H. Wefer, 115 Liberty St., New York City.

Advisory Members
Representing Women's Missionary Society
Mrs. W. P. M. Braum, 250 Pelham Road, Philadelphia, Pa.
Mrs. J. L. Morgan, 612 S. Main St., Salisbury, N. C.

NOMINATIONS FOR BOARD MEMBERSHIP

The Board of Deaconess Work, at its meeting on June 25, 1936, nominated the following for election at this convention of the United Lutheran Church:
Rev. Allen L. Benner, D.D., (eligible for re-election), Ministerium of Pennsylvania.
Rev. J. J. Schindel, D.D. (eligible for re-election), Ministerium of Pennsylvania.
Rev. L. A. Thomas, D.D., (eligible for re-election), Virginia Synod.
Mr. E. S. Gerberich (eligible for re-election), East Pennsylvania Synod.
Frederick J. Singley, Esq., (eligible for re-election), Maryland Synod.

RECOMMENDATIONS
(For action, see p. 326)

1. That the United Lutheran Church in America give thanks to Almighty God for the prayers, faith and perseverance of Pastor Theodore Fliedner, which enabled him to revive the ancient order of the Female

Diaconate, and that we are permitted this month to celebrate the centennial of the restoration of this Apostolic office.

2. That we record our sincere appreciation of the faithful service rendered by the many deaconesses during the past century, and especially those who have labored so whole-heartedly and unselfishly in the Lutheran Church of America for more than a half century in congregations, institutions and other agencies of the church at home and abroad.

3. That we express to the Women's Missionary Society, the Luther League of America, and to all other agencies, groups and individuals our gratitude for their interest and co-operation in the deaconess work.

4. That we commend to the Church the value and importance of deaconess service in the parish and also the institutions of the church; and that we earnestly urge our pastors to present the deaconess cause to their people on *Septuagesima Sunday,* and that through their church schools and young women's groups reference be made to the opportunities for Christian life-service in the ministry of the deaconess.

5. That we commend the promotional efforts and aims of the Board of Deaconess Work, looking to the future development and enlargement of the work, in order that we may be able to meet the opportunities for larger and more helpful service in the name of our Lord and Saviour.

THE BALTIMORE MOTHERHOUSE

The total number of deaconesses and probationers at present connected with the Baltimore Motherhouse is 68. On December 17, 1935, the Sisterhood suffered a sad loss in the death of Sister Inez Metzger, one of our younger Sisters who, while directing the rehearsal of a Christmas pageant at the Home for the Aged, Washington, was suddenly overtaken with illness and although she was rushed to the hospital, in less than three hours her earthly life came to its end. Services were held in the Chapel of the Washington Home on Wednesday evening, December 18th, and the next day the body was taken to the home of her parents in Blandburg. Funeral services were held in the church on Saturday afternoon, December 21, after which the body was laid to rest in the family burial plot.

Sister Inez entered the Motherhouse as a candidate on October 2, 1923 and was consecrated in June, 1928. In a quiet and unassuming manner she faithfully served her Master in the fields of labor to which she was assigned. In humility of spirit she went about doing good until our Heavenly Father called her home to dwell with her Saviour to Whose service she had consecrated her life.

FIELDS OF LABOR

Of the total number of Sisters now in service, twenty-six are serving as parish deaconesses in Akron, Ohio; Baltimore, Md.; Canton, Ohio;

Detroit, Mich.; Frederick, Md.; Hagerstown, Md.; Lewistown, Pa.; Miamisburg, Ohio; New York, N. Y.; Philadelphia, Pa.; Richmond, Va.; Rochester, N. Y.; Syracuse, N. Y.; Toledo, Ohio; Washington, D. C.; Williamsport, Pa.; Wilmington, Del.

Among the other fields in which Baltimore deaconesses are serving are the following: Inner Mission Society and Girls Hospice, Baltimore; Tabitha Home, Lincoln, Nebr.; Lutheran Settlement and Martin Luther Neighborhood House, Philadelphia, Pa.; Good Shepherd Home, Allentown, Pa.; Bethany Home, Milwaukee, Wis.; Home for the Aged, Washington, D. C.; Franke Home, Charleston, S. C.; Tiding Over Home, Brooklyn, N. Y.; Inner Mission Society and Home for Aged, Chicago, Ill; Artman Home, Ambler, Pa.; St. Johns Orphan Home, Buffalo, N. Y.; Gettysburg College (Women's Division), Gettysburg, Pa.; Norwegian Lutheran Hospital, Brooklyn, N. Y.

In addition to all this the Motherhouse conducts a Christian kindergarten and a flourishing weekday church school. Some private nursing is being done and during the school year the students of the Training School engage in numerous welfare activities in Baltimore.

CONSECRATION SERVICE

At a special service held in the Motherhouse Chapel on June 25, 1936, the following probationers were set apart as deaconesses by the sacred rite of consecration.

> Sister Clara Bailey, Warren, Ohio.
> Sister Frieda Buerger, Chicago, Ill.
> Sister Elaine Dunlap, New York, N. Y.
> Sister Lucille Lyerly, Granite Quarry, N. C.

THE FORTIETH ANNIVERSARY

The 40th anniversary celebration in June, 1935, revealed a surprising interest in the Baltimore Motherhouse. Letters received from every part of the Church and the fine local interest manifested, are clearly indicative of a growing interest in the training of young women for full time life service.

The first service was held on Sunday, June 23d, at 3 P. M. in the tent erected on the Motherhouse grounds for the occasion. On account of illness, Dr. Knubel was prevented from being present. Dr. A. Steimle, as his official representative, therefore, preached the anniversary sermon.

The historical pageant, especially prepared for the anniversary, was given in St. Mark's Church, and the church auditorium was not nearly large enough to accommodate all who came to see it.

At the service held in the tent on Tuesday evening, the 25th, official greetings were extended by representatives from the Maryland Synod, the Deaconess Conference, the Women's Missionary Society and the Luther League of America.

One of the outstanding features of "Baltimore Night" (Wednesday evening, June 26th) was the rendition of two anthems by a massed choir of nearly 150 voices.

The anniversary festivities were brought to a close with a banquet on Thursday evening, the 27th.

THE TRAINING SCHOOL

During the biennium 41 young women were enrolled as students of the Training School. Of this number 9 came as candidates for the diaconate. The others came to pursue the one and two year courses of training offered by the Motherhouse to young women who do not wish to become deaconesses or cannot qualify. Among this splendid group of students were some who had college and university training, some who have had teaching and other practical experience, and several with nurses' training. Eleven states were represented.

A new department designed to familiarize the students with the field of social service has been added to the training courses. It includes weekly class periods under the leadership of one of our own Lutheran young women, who is a graduate of a Lutheran college and has done graduate work in several well known universities. During the second semester one-half day each week is devoted to practical work consisting chiefly in observation tours to various merciful institutions for the purpose of correlation with the social service course.

Plans have been completed for the extension of the curriculum by the addition of courses in Sacred Music. The need for such training has been felt for some time and at the Triennial Homecoming in June, 1935, the Sisters expressed the hope that definite efforts would be made to meet this need. Among the subjects to be included will be hymnology and liturgics.

In accordance with the action of the Board a third year has been added to the deaconess training course, by providing opportunities for practical experience and office training.

The practical work under the direction of the Training Sister has been reorganized and more effectively developed during the biennium. The work done by the seniors in various local parishes is more closely supervised and the juniors are more definitely trained for such service. Students are carefully trained before they are sent out to do "case work," to visit weekday church school children, to conduct teachers' training classes and group meetings, and to engage in other practical activities.

THE PHILADELPHIA MOTHERHOUSE
(By Rev. E. F. Bachmann, D.D.)

The Mary J. Drexel Home and Philadelphia Motherhouse of Deaconesses has been privileged for fully half a century to have a share in this

important service of the Church. Begun with 7 deaconesses from abroad
to take charge of a small hospital, in June 1884, the Sisterhood has grown
to 124 members serving in 20 different fields. During 1935 they gave hospital or institutional care to fully 5,700 persons, besides almost 7,500
dispensary patients, and contacted about 20,000 other persons. Recognized
by their garb as representatives of the Church rendering service from
a religious motive, these deaconesses were observed at their work by
thousands of persons during the year, many of whom were impressed
with the reality and the power of the religion of Jesus Christ. The
Sisters meet thousands every year who are beyond the reach of the
regular ministrations of congregational pastors. They are in the front
ranks of the workers for Christ.

THE WORK

1. HOSPITAL. The credit for having introduced deaconess work in
Philadelphia belongs to a secular corporation, the Lankenau Hospital. Its
president, John D. Lankenau, advised by leaders of the former General
Council, soon recognized the need of a Lutheran Motherhouse and
founded it in connection with the Mary J. Drexel Home for the Aged, so
named in memory of his departed wife. At his personal expense a large
and beautiful building on the grounds of the hospital was erected to
serve both purposes and both, the hospital and the Home, were pledged to
work together. As a result, the Lankenau Hospital is still our largest
field. The Directing Sister of the Motherhouse was appointed Superintendent of the Hospital and since July 1, 1935, has borne this double responsibility. Here 4,423 patients were admitted in 1935 and 8,086 were treated
by the dispensary. The Children's Hospital, however, is a department of
the Motherhouse, with 857 patients during the year; 4,064 others made
14,951 visits to the dispensary. At the Kensington Dispensary, founded
30 years ago under the leadership of the deaconess who is still in charge,
390 patients were treated for tuberculosis. Preventive work of outstanding merit is done by "River Crest," the Preventorium of this Dispensary
near Phoenixville, Pa. Here our Sisters are in charge of 75-100 under-
nourished young children in danger of tuberculosis.

2. HOMES. Three Homes for the Aged with a total of 165 men and
women, are under the supervision of our Sisters, the Mary J. Drexel, the
Lutheran Home in Germantown, and the Lutheran Home in Erie, Pa.
Two Homes for Children, the Lutheran Orphans' Home in Germantown
with 134 children and the Tabor Home near Doylestown, Pa., with 84,
have deaconesses as Matrons who are assisted by other Sisters. To this
group belongs also the small Ebenezer Orphanage at Frederiksted, St.
Croix, whose two native deaconesses are associated with our Motherhouse.

3. INNER MISSION. The Inner Mission Society of Berks County, Pa.,
has a deaconess as Executive Secretary and another as Matron of the

Hospice for Women in Reading, Pa. Two of our deaconesses are accredited visitors to Moyamensing Prison, Philadelphia. The Inner Mission Society of Dayton, Ohio, has been granted a deaconess to begin her work in September as assistant to the Superintendent.

4. PARISHES. Ever since a Sister was granted to a Philadelphia congregation in 1887, our Sisters have been engaged in Parish Work; but yielding to insistent calls from other fields, this work has so far found only a limited development. The congregations served at present are Zion and Tabor in Philadelphia; St. Paul's, New York; St. John's, Easton, Pa.; St. John's, Erie, Pa.; and Trinity, New Haven, Conn. Numerous calls for Sisters had to be refused, because we had no trained Sisters to send.

5. SCHOOL. A school for girls was opened in 1890 and, having outgrown its quarters in the Motherhouse, was transferred in 1910 to spacious buildings and grounds directly west of the Drexel Home. It was reorganized with a full twelve-year course and re-named The Lankenau School for Girls. It is the only school in this country conducted by deaconesses, admits resident and day pupils to all grades, and is accredited by the Pennsylvania State Council of Education. The High School is a member of the Middle States Association of Colleges and Secondary Schools. Girls have come from as far as Maine and Florida, British Columbia and Mexico. A reunion held last September gave ample evidence of the gratitude and love cherished for their Alma Mater because the thorough instruction and Christian training received here proved their value in meeting life's problems. Of the 19 members of the faculty eight are deaconesses; four of these are in the High School department.

THE TRAINING

Training in practical work is as important as teaching. It involves the spiritual life no less than ability and character. It is not limited to a definite time, differs with each individual and requires expert guidance, patience, perseverance, and definite aims. The Motherhouse endeavors to prepare every Sister for her special work. After the two-year fundamental course for candidates, each Sister is assigned to practical work, as far as possible with full consideration of her talents. She may go to one of the Homes for children, or enter the Training School for Nurses or in exceptional cases, take a college course in preparation for a position requiring a college degree. In June 1935 one Sister received from the Philadelphia College of Pharmacy her B.S. degree in Sciences; she teaches at the Lankenau School. This year another Sister was awarded a B.S. by Temple University qualifying her as instructress in the Nurses Training School; a third Sister expects this degree from Temple, in order to take over the Kindergarten. Besides these, five Sisters have been given a college course at the expense of the Motherhouse; and one other Sister had her degree when she entered the work.

In teaching and nursing our Sisters meet prescribed educational standards, but not yet in all other fields. One Sister, a college graduate, is taking courses in the Philadelphia School for Social Service while already actually engaged in this work at the Lankenau Hospital. Sending a Sister to a standard school for Religious Education to help in training Sisters for Parish and institutional work, has for some years remained an unfulfilled hope.

At the same time, however, neither the Church nor the Motherhouse dare lose sight of the fact that the deciding factor in successful work of a deaconess is not her scholarship, but her spirit, the spirit of Jesus Christ Who has set up for all His servants standards infinitely higher than those of any secular profession. For this reason a thoroughly consecrated young woman with good intelligence, sound judgment and practical ability is as welcome in the diaconate as a college graduate. "The Lord looketh on the heart."

THE SUPPORT

The support needed is twofold, moral and financial. The Philadelphia Motherhouse is grateful for having received both during the past biennium.

MORAL SUPPORT. This was expressed by the good will shown by many pastors and other leaders of the Church, foremost among these the Women's Missionary Society of the United Lutheran Church and its various Synodical organizations; likewise by the Luther League. Their programs have brought the deaconess work to the attention of local groups throughout the Church. Without such help this would not have been possible. Pastors within an easy radius of Philadelphia have brought catechetical classes, Luther Leagues and other groups to visit the Motherhouse and have testified of the inspiration received by their people.

The most important support is, of course, co-operation in enlisting qualified candidates. We are deeply grateful to God for having inclined the hearts of young women to enter this service, so that we are able to report an increase of eight Sisters for the biennium, 124 instead of 116 reported two years ago. Seven Sisters were consecrated last Pentecost, so that on July 1, 1936 we have 97 deaconesses and 27 probationers. It is interesting to note that 31 of our Sisters came from the territory of the Synod of New York and 54 from that of the Ministerium of Pennsylvania, about one half of these from the Philadelphia area. Of our Sisters 72 entered during the past twenty years, and of these 48 during the past decade. These facts are certainly encouraging, not only because of the increasing numbers, but also because of the larger proportion of younger Sisters for responsible positions and for the relief of Sisters who have been in the service for forty years or more. We will need many more trained Sisters to meet the increasing needs of our present stations and to answer some of the calls we must now refuse.

FINANCES. The Philadelphia Motherhouse is training and maintaining Sisters for service in the Church at a cost to her which is only nominal. While the actual cash expenses for the Sisters amounted to $40,596.66 during the biennium, the amount allotted to the Philadelphia Mother-house from the appropriation of the U. L. C. A. for the Board of Deaconess Work is $5,000 annually on the basis of the full apportionment. But the proportionate amount of the appropriation received for the past two years was only $4,704.25. This means an annual amount of $18.97 per Sister toward their cash allowance and nothing for their maintenance. Including the latter, the Motherhouse spent approximately $266.00 for each Sister last year and, carrying this cost with that of the other departments of the corporation, found its current income in 1934 $17,063.91 short of its current expenses; in 1935 $17,898.15.

Fortunately the income from the endowment left by Mr. Lankenau, from "Founder's Day" observed in March, and from the "Friends of Children" who conduct a "Children's Hospital Day" early in November, together with the support from the United Lutheran Church for which we are sincerely grateful, did help to reduce the annual deficits materially, to $11,189.25 in 1934 and to $10,231.73 in 1935.

SUMMARY OF THE TREASURER'S REPORT

Receipts	1934	1935
From Stations served by Sisters	$11,696.43	$15,469.80
Entrance fees to Drexel Home	6,257.62	2,860.04
Children's Hospital	11,148.95	15,162.90
Income from investments	31,926.17	30,219.41
Miscellaneous	5,409.98	2,864.61
	$66,439.15	$66,576.76

Expenses	1934	1935
Deaconess Account	$18,869.10	$21,727.56
Salaries	8,605.00	8,570.00
Wages	17,330.84	17,187.30
Household Supplies	20,695.39	21,618.12
Repairs and improvements	3,546.13	2,658.34
Insurance	1,293.32	519.04
Miscellaneous	13,163.28	12,194.55
	$83,503.06	$84,474.91

Special Income	1934	1935
United Lutheran Church	$ 2,000.00	$ 2,704.25
"Friends of Children"	1,582.88	1,092.28
Founder's Day Fund	1,741.78	2,533.64
Donations	550.00	1,336.25
	$ 5,874.66	$ 7,666.42

A more detailed report for the year 1935 appears in the "Deaconess Messenger" and will be sent on request.

W. A. WADE, *President,*
FOSTER U. GIFT, *Secretary.*

REPORT OF TREASURER OF THE BOARD OF DEACONESS WORK
CASH RECEIPTS AND DISBURSEMENTS
July 1, 1934 to June 30, 1935
GENERAL FUND

Cash Balance—July 1, 1934 .... $ 5,443.57

RECEIPTS

United Lutheran Church in America—Apportionment	$18,050.00
United Synod of New York	10.16
Ministerium of Pennsylvania	10.00
Tuition	1,835.67
Kindergarten	477.50
Nursing	254.00
Stations	9,882.01
Miscellaneous	968.98
Contributions—General	1,286.78
Contributions—Elevator Fund	3,036.00
United States Treasury Notes Sold	1,590.94
Interest on Treasury Notes	127.76
Annuity Fund—Ground Rents Collected	1,237.82
Discounts	117.52

Total Receipts 38,885.14

(Forwarded) $44,328.71

DISBURSEMENTS

Books	343.19
Lectures	731.90
Board Meeting Expense	203.85
Salaries—Dr. Foster U. Gift	2,200.00
—Rev. Chas. E. Hay	600.00
Pastors' Travel	258.89
Office Expense	67.48
Clerical Expense	525.60
Sisters' Quarterly Allowances	5,085.00
Sisters' Vacation Allowances	1,650.00
Sisters' Travel Allowances	695.80
Sisters' Hospital and Medical Care	1,475.23
Sisters' Wearing Apparel	2,606.56
Sisters' Permits	150.00
Telephone	221.25
Printing and Stationery	915.54
Postage	195.84
Audit	125.00
1901 Thomas Avenue, Maintenance	175.48
1905 Thomas Avenue, Maintenance	435.59
Incidentals	1,096.67
House Wages	1,965.05
House Food	3,626.79
House Furnishings	552.97
Gas, Electric and Water	690.89
Coal	1,093.52
Engineer and Helper	865.60

Grounds Maintenance	285.76
Insurance	429.39
Improvements and Repairs	892.06
Elevator Installation (not complete)	2,923.15
Mary J. Drexel Home and Philadelphia Motherhouse of Deaconesses	2,704.25
Annuity Interest	1,482.70
Funeral Expenses	280.00

Total Disbursements	37,553.00
Cash Balance—June 30, 1935	$ 6,775.71

CASH RECEIPTS AND DISBURSEMENTS

July 1, 1934 to June 30, 1935

OTHER FUNDS

	New Building Fund	Endowment Fund	Annuity Fund
Cash Balance—July 1, 1934	$797.19	$1,641.55	$325.03
RECEIPTS			
Interest on Deposits	24.97	50.10	10.80
Distribution in Bank Reorganization	98.97	203.80	
Subscriptions	35.10		
Legacy	89.98		
Annuity Purchased			300.00
No DISBURSEMENTS			
Cash Balance—June 30, 1935	$1,046.21	$1,895.45	$635.83

ANALYSIS OF FUNDS
June 30, 1935

	General Fund	New Building Fund	Endowment Fund	Annuity Fund	Totals
Cash	$ 6,775.71	$1,046.21	$1,895.45	$ 635.83	$ 10,353.20
Ground Rents				22,833.33	22,833.33
United States Treasury Notes				2,060.13	2,060.13
Due from General Fund	12,136.38*	6,137.23	2,500.00	3,499.15	
Real Estate	313,835.27				313,835.27
Burial Plot	600.00				600.00
Totals	$309,074.60	$7,183.44	$4,395.45	$29,028.44	$349,681.93

*Represents Deficit

CASH RECEIPTS AND DISBURSEMENTS
July 1, 1935 to June 30, 1936
GENERAL FUND

Cash Balance—July 1, 1935	$ 6,775.71

RECEIPTS

United Lutheran Church in America—Apportionment	$18,431.00
United Synod of New York	14.73
Book Fund	124.00
Tuition	4,510.00
Kindergarten	319.00
Nursing	247.00
Stations	10,745.53
Miscellaneous	743.72
Contributions—General	680.57
Interest on Treasury Notes	57.50
Annuity Ground Rents Collected	1,517.78
Discounts	115.38
Rents—1905 Thomas Avenue	148.90

Total Receipts	$37,655.11
(Forwarded)	$44,430.82

DISBURSEMENTS

Books	$ 557.46
Lectures	795.76
Board Meeting Expense	67.67
Salary—Dr. Foster U. Gift	2,200.00
Pastors' Travel	158.02
Office Expense	72.88
Clerical Expense	548.40
Sisters' Quarterly Allowances	3,803.75
Sisters' Vacation Allowances	1,600.00
Sisters' Travel Allowances	361.05
Sisters' Hospital and Medical Care	1,577.39
Sisters' Wearing Apparel	2,958.72
Telephone	248.59
Printing and Stationery	691.24
Postage	235.65
Audit	115.50
Maintenance—1901 Thomas Avenue	24.00
Maintenance—1905 Thomas Avenue	24.00
Incidentals	1,529.41
House Wages	2,226.85
House Food	5,073.97
House Furnishings	641.63
Gas, Electric and Water	791.21
Coal	1,420.14
Engineer and Helper	1,027.30
Grounds Maintenance	271.85
Insurance	335.00
Improvements and Repairs	368.75
Elevator Installation	3,980.88
Mary J. Drexel Home and Philadelphia Motherhouse	2,303.90
Annuity Interest	1,725.85

Total Disbursements	37,736.82
Balance—June 30, 1936	$ 6,694.00

CASH RECEIPTS AND DISBURSEMENTS

July 1, 1935 to June 30, 1936

OTHER FUNDS

	New Building Fund	Endowment Fund	Annuity Fund
Cash Balances—July 1, 1935	$1,046.21	$1,895.44	$ 635.83

RECEIPTS

Interest on Deposits	22.40	43.66	48.30
Distribution in Bank Reorganization	39.58	81.52	
Legacy	10.00	500.00	
Annuities Purchased			7,100.00

DISBURSEMENTS—None

Balance—June 30, 1936	$1,118.19	$2,520.63	$7,784.13

BALANCE SHEET

June 30, 1936

ASSETS

Cash in Banks and on Hand	$ 18,116.95
Ground Rents Owned	22,833.33
Treasury Notes 1955-60—$2,000.Par	2,060.13
Real Estate and Equipment	317,816.15
Lorraine Park Burial Plot	600.00
Total Assets	$361,426.56

FUNDS

General Fund	$312,973.77
New Building Fund	7,255.42
Endowment Fund	5,020.63
Annuity Fund	36,176.74
Total Funds	$361,426.56

GROUND RENTS OWNED

June 30, 1936

	Principal	Interest Received During Year
2003 East 30th Street	$ 2,000.00	$ 120.00
3007 Wayne Avenue	1,300.00	78.00
2430 Liberty Heights Avenue	1,500.00	135.00
5301 Midwood Avenue	1,000.00	60.00
247 North Payson Street	1,000.00	65.00
3810 Plateau Avenue	1,400.00	84.00
819 South Elwood Avenue	600.00	43.50
2019 West North Avenue	1,333.33	80.00

4504 Wakefield Road	1,500.00	90.00
4506 Wakefield Road	1,500.00	90.00
4508 Wakefield Road	1,500.00	90.00
38 South Calverton Road	1,200.00	72.00
40 South Calverton Road	1,400.00	126.63
46 Prospect Avenue	1,500.00	137.65
53 Prospect Avenue	1,500.00	90.00
20 Prospect Avenue	1,400.00	84.00
1413 Longwood Street	1,200.00	72.00
Totals	$22,833.33	$1,517.78

Respectfully submitted,
FREDERICK J. SINGLEY, *Treasurer.*

July 31, 1936

We have audited the books of account of the Board of Deaconess Work of the United Lutheran Church in America for the biennium beginning July 1, 1934 and ending June 30, 1936, and we hereby certify that the foregoing statements of Cash Receipts and Disbursements for the two years under audit, the Balance Sheet as of June 30, 1936 and the Schedule of Ground Rents Owned as of June 30, 1936 are in agreement with the books of account of that Board, and, in our opinion, are true and correct.

TAIT, WELLER AND BAKER.
Accountants and Auditors.

After suitable introductory remarks, Dr. Wade introduced the Rev. F. U. Gift as pastor of the Motherhouse at Baltimore, and the Rev. E. F. Bachmann as pastor of the Motherhouse at Philadelphia. These two pastors addressed the Convention presenting certain phases of deaconess work and also emphasizing the place of the cause of the deaconess service in the program of the Church.

Recommendations 1, 2, 3, 4, and 5 were adopted.

On motion the President was requested to convey recommendations 1 and 2 to the Motherhouse at Kaiserswerth.

On motion the report of the auditors was accepted.

Mr. Belding B. Slifer, President, introduced the work of the Board of Ministerial Pensions and Relief and made extensive explanation of the financial statements, in the place of the treasurer who was unavoidably absent.

Mr. Harry Hodges, the Executive Secretary of the Board, presented the report and spoke concerning the recommendations of the Board.

REPORT OF THE BOARD OF MINISTERIAL PENSIONS AND RELIEF

(For action on the recommendations in this report, see p. 355)

This Board declares that it is not one of the benevolent boards of the Church. Pensions are not benevolence; they are justice; deferred salary. The Standard Dictionary says: "A pension is an allowance paid to an individual or those who represent him for some past service or some meritorious work done by him."

The idea of a pension for a retired minister, his widow and dependent children is not to make a gift in order that they can have easier lives. Rather it is to pay the promised part due him from the Church in obligation to him for putting in his life for a mere "support." The retired minister is the Church's graduated leader, not its pauper dependent. These men have been faithful to all tasks assigned to them and have earned the appreciation of the Church.

It is not unreasonable to suppose that the movements to protect old age, which is the loneliest and most distressing period of life, have come out of the Christian gospel of good will and justice, set forth by the Church from the beginning of American history. It brings forward boldly the question of the care and comfort of those gospel ministers whose message taught the whole country to "deal justly and love mercy."

THE HONORABLE HENRY W. HARTER

We announce with sorrow the death of our venerable and much beloved Vice-President, the Honorable Henry W. Harter of Canton, Ohio. Judge Harter, though an octogenarian, never missed a meeting of the Board when in health and was keenly interested in its tasks.

THE CAMPAIGN FUND

The total subscription was $4,175,065.00. At this date (June 30, 1936) there has been paid $3,227,449.66 or 77 per cent. Of this amount there has been paid during the past biennium $9,773.85. 665 Churches have paid their subscriptions in full. 421 Churches paid nothing.

While not going after delinquent subscriptions at present for obvious reasons, it is the purpose of the Board to do so in the future and it asks that churches with unpaid subscriptions regard them as future obligations.

STATISTICS

Since the last report the following additions and deductions have been made in the roll:

Additions

Retired and Disabled Ministers, 67; Widows, 73; Children, 35; Missionaries, 2.

Deductions

Retired and Disabled Ministers, 64; Widows, 53; Children, 35; Missionaries, 0.

During the biennium 83 special grants were made amounting to $3,690.

The roll by Synods is as follows:

Synod	Retired	Disabled	Widows	Children	Missionaries	Pension	Relief
Alleghany	9		10	1		$ 4,750	$ 100
California	17	1	13	1		8,050	200
Canada	11	2	15	2		7,000	160
East Pennsylvania	15	2	40*	2		13,200	160
Florida	2	1	1	3		1,250	
Georgia-Alabama	1		7*			1,700	60
German Nebraska	14	1	13	4		7,300	60
Illinois	11	2	24****	12		9,300	600
Indiana	6		13			4,400	60
Iowa		1	4	2		1,200	
Kansas	1	1	10	4		2,800	100
Kentucky-Tennessee			7*	1		1,450	80
Manitoba	3	5	4	9		3,650	470
Maryland	16	1	28*			10,700	600
Michigan	2		7	1		2,050	
Mississippi		1		1		350	
Nebraska	4		10			3,200	100
New York	25	5	84**	20		26,800	870
North Carolina	13		26	2		9,200	340
Northwest	1		10	7		2,650	
Nova Scotia		2	1	3		950	
Ohio	29	2	45	11	1	19,150	760
Pacific	5	1	5	1		2,850	160
Pennsylvania Min.	27	7	64	12		23,600	860
Pittsburgh	23	3	44	9	2	17,650	540
Rocky Mountain	4	1	5	1		2,550	200
Slovak Zion	1	3	1	8		1,800	
South Carolina	2	3	15	4		4,700	520
Susquehanna	7	1	15	2		5,500	200
Texas	4		4	2		2,100	220
Virginia	15	2	15	7		8,450	
Wartburg	2	3	6			2,700	100
West Pennsylvania	18		31	9		12,050	310
West Virginia	2		5	4		1,800	
Specials	2				2	1,200	
TOTAL 1936	292	51	582	145	5	$228,050	$7,830
TOTAL 1934	278	55	558	142	3	$219,500	$9,710

NOTE: * Includes Unmarried Daughter of Clergyman.

ANNUITY BONDS AND BEQUESTS

During the biennium ten annuity bonds have been sold amounting to $20,200.

Eight Annuitants have died releasing to the Board $16,100.00.

Five Bequests have been reported amounting to $12,500 and the Board is a residuary legatee in three others. Nine Bequests have been paid amounting to $5,167.63 and $5,000.00 York Ice Machinery Corporation First Mortgage 6 per cent Bonds.

Women's Missionary Society

The Board voices its high appreciation of their appropriation of $7,980.00 during the past biennium. The Board is now pensioning five women missionaries.

Pension Problems

The Pension Family today numbers 1,075 persons and the annual budget is $235,880.00.

The Board derives its income from two sources, the income from its endowment, and its income from the Church's apportionment, of which it is assigned eleven and three-quarter cents of the apportionment dollar. But only about 45% of the apportionment has been paid during the past few years.

The endowment income pays about 50% of our budget, therefore we must depend on the apportionment for the other 50% with the result that the Board is operating temporarily at a deficit believing that the Church would not countenance a further reduction in our pitifully small pensions. **It will continue so to do unless the church rules otherwise.**

It has been stated that at the beginning of the Campaign a pension of $600.00 was promised but not paid.

In the light of the 1928 earning power of money a pension of $600.00 was promised if the Church raised $4,000,000 and maintained the apportionment. In 1928 money could be safely invested at 6%; today, at 4% at the most. $3,227,449.66 was paid by the Church and the apportionment has been reduced $50,000 per annum Q. E. D.

The economic cataclysm has disabled the present pension plan and it is past time to put faith and dependence in it for adequate pensions.

The Reserve Pension Plan is sound and correct and if it were in operation throughout the Church it would do for our ministry what similar plans have done for other communions.

Unemployment

The Savannah Convention requested the Board "to study the problem of relief for unemployed ministers and report to the next biennial convention."

The Synodical Presidents were communicated with relative to unemployed "employable" ministers within their synods. Fifty-nine were reported.

Several of these Presidents have relief funds from which these men have been temporarily aided.

The Board felt that it could not use its regular funds for this purpose. It makes a Christmas appeal, however, from which is derived about $2,500 which is not designated. It has accordingly been helping unemployed ministers from this fund upon recommendation of the Synodical President. **And unless the Church instructs it otherwise, the Board will continue this practice.**

RESERVE PENSION PLAN

The Savannah Convention instructed the Board to report to this Convention a Reserve Pension Plan.

The idea of pensions is in the air. It is in the daily newspapers, the church papers, the secular magazines and on the radio. It is also before the National Congress and every State Legislature in America. It has become a part of the fixed purpose of the nation to help provide old age security through pensions to thirty million salaried people, who work all of their lives for somebody else.

The Social Security Act is now a law of the nation. Its contributory pension plan goes into operation January 1, 1937. About thirty million employees and employers will begin their payments on that date. Automatically these millions of workers, whether one or a hundred, or a thousand, and those for whom they work, will become a part of the national contributory pension plan.

Not included are all employees of religious, charitable, educational, scientific and other organizations not operated for profit. That means definitely that all ministers are excluded. And that means that all State governments and the National government expect the Churches to care for their own. That means Church Pension Systems. Therefore our concern is the men and women who are omitted from the government plan.

Some years ago the Federation of Lutheran Brotherhoods, through a well qualified committee, compiled a reserve pension plan which it submitted to all the American Lutheran Bodies, believing that a joint pension system would be another stepping stone to Lutheran unity.

The Augustana Synod and the United Norwegian Church adapted and adopted it. The American Lutheran Church and the Missouri Synod have it under consideration.

Your Board, in consultation with the Actuary, who has built most of the Church Pension Systems, have adapted it and submit it herewith:

THE PROPOSED NEW PENSION PLAN

WHY A NEW PLAN?

It is now one hundred years since our Church began its pension work. Up to 1920 only relief work was done and consequently comparatively little interest was taken by either the congregations or the pastors in this important work. That year our pension work was reorganized on a regular basis and eleven and three-quarter cents of the apportionment dollar assigned to it. This income plus the income from the endowment has been used for the Board's operations.

The pension plan under which the Board has been operating during the past sixteen years has been successful, so why change? Why not leave well enough alone? The answer is not far to seek. During the depression years the falling off in income both from apportionment and endowment compelled the Board to reduce pensions.

The new plan has been worked out under expert actuarial guidance. The experience of other pension boards has been utilized and the conditions peculiar to our church have been taken into consideration. It now appears very difficult, if not impossible, to carry out the original plan of increasing the permanent endowment fund to such an amount that it will yield sufficient revenue for pensions to a steadily increasing number of pensioners. Because the amount paid out in pensions and aid has increased each year, it is necessary to increase the endowment fund or the apportionment, or both, or to create a new source of income, in order to provide sufficient funds for the payment of these pensions from year to year.

The apparent impossibility of increasing the endowment fund for pension purposes so as to keep pace with the growing pension roll is not peculiar to our present pension plan; it is common to all pension plans, which, like ours, are on the endowment basis. Hence practically all other communions and other pension paying organizations have been compelled to change their original endowment plans into reserve plans.

The reserve plan does not require a large permanent fund. It is a "pay as you go" plan in that it provides for annual payments by the minister himself and by his congregation or other salary paying organization to the minister's future pension. Because these payments and the interest from the endowment can be used, it requires only between one-third to one-half of the amount of endowment that would be necessary under the present plan. There will be no need of other funds or collections for pensions and it will remove the necessity for future drives. It will save future generations from the burden of inheriting from the present generation the heavy pension load of hundreds of retired church servants for whose pensions sufficient provision has not been made. It will save the church from the unpleasant experience of incurring large future pension obligations for which sufficient provision for their ultimate payment has not been made.

Promoting ministerial efficiency is the basic principle and fundamental purpose of our ministerial pension work. Our present pension plan was not established simply for the purpose of providing food, clothing and shelter for retired and disabled servants of the Church and their dependents. Some seem to think that the pension plan of our Church is simply a charitable arrangement for the benefit of retired and disabled ministers and missionaries. A pension is simply deferred salary; there is really just as much charity in the salary check that the pastor received from his congregation from time to time as there is in the pension check. If the latter implies charity, then the former is charity also.

We must get away as soon as possible from the notion that our Pension Plan is established on the principle of charity; instead we must realize that every pension system is based on service. Perhaps the most effective service of our Pension Plan is what it is doing to encourage those now in the active ministry and thus make their work more fruitful because they know that, on their retirement, they are assured of a steady income.

One of the main objectives of ministerial pensions is, therefore, to encourage the men who are now in active service to throw themselves wholeheartedly and unstintingly into the work of the Church with every ounce of their energy, every moment of their time, and every dollar at their disposal, because of the assurance that, when they have given their life and all to the Church, the Church will see to it that they and their dependents will be provided for, not only as long as they are able to work, but as long as they live. They must be made to feel that when they no longer, because of disability or old age, are able to serve, they shall not be looked upon as objects of charity, but as pensioners, that is, as having earned what the Church is granting them in pensions.

THE PENSION PLAN

ARTICLE I
Definitions

(a). The word "salary" as herein used means fixed salary. In case a member receives free house rent the same shall be considered as equivalent to fifteen (15) per cent of his fixed salary and added thereto in order to determine his salary basis.

(b). The words "prior pension plan" shall be held to mean and refer to the pension plan provided by the United Lutheran Church just prior to the adoption of this new plan.

(c). The words "the Plan" shall be held to mean and refer to the pension plan as provided herein, being the plan following and subsequent to the "prior pension plan" as above defined.

(d). The word "his" when used herein shall be construed to mean either "his or her", and the word "he" shall be construed to mean either "he or she" as the context may require.

(e). The words "minor children" when used herein shall be construed to mean the children of a deceased member of the Plan who have not attained the age of eighteen years.

(f). The words "contributions by a member" shall be held to mean the regular monthly payments of the member as provided in Article II. The words "contributions by a congregation" shall mean the regular monthly payments by a church or other salary paying organization enjoying the services of a member, as provided in Article IV.

(g). The word "allocations" shall be construed to mean the amounts credited annually to the account of the member as provided in Article V, Section 6.

ARTICLE II
Contributions by a Member

Each member of the Plan shall contribute each year an amount equivalent to two and one-half (2½) per cent of his salary. The total of the accumulations, including the interest additions, shall be referred to herein as the accumulated contributions.

ARTICLE III
Application of the Contributions of a Member

These accumulated contributions shall be applied towards providing an age annuity upon retirement or in the event of prior death, towards providing a widow's annuity or other specified benefits, or to be paid as hereinafter provided.

If, in the case of the death of the member, or his widow, or his minor children, individually or all together have not been paid in annuities and other benefits a total of payments equal to the accumulations of his contributions, any excess of such accumulated contributions over such payments shall be paid to such beneficiary as may have been designated by the member, or if no such designation has been made, to the legal representative of the deceased member.

ARTICLE IV
Contributions by a Congregation

Each congregation shall contribute each year an amount equivalent to eight (8) per cent of the salary of the member serving it.

ARTICLE V
Application of the Contributions by Congregations

The contributions received from congregations during the year shall be applied as follows:

(1). To set aside on a reserve basis an amount sufficient, first, to waive the payment of contributions by disabled members and by their congregations and, second, to provide annuities payable during disability to such members as have retired on account of disability under the minimum retirement age of sixty-five (65) years, having become totally and presumably permanently disabled within the year and compelled to give up ministerial work and to terminate any salary relationship. Should the disabled member attain the minimum retirement age of sixty-five (65) years, the total of the accumulations and the allocations shall be applied toward providing an age retirement annuity, but in no case shall the annuity payable thereafter be less than the disability annuity being paid. The amount of the disability annuity shall be forty (40) per cent of the average salary during the preceding years of service under this Plan, but not to exceed $400.00 at the outset. The Board shall have the right to increase or decrease the scale of disability annuities to be granted thereafter, as the actual experience and the resources of the Plan may justify. Disability must be certified to by a competent physician as well as by the member and shall be subject to the approval of the Board, with the right on the part of the Board to call for proof of continued disability from time to time. If a disabled member recovers sufficiently to enable him to resume work for the Church or engage in any business or other occupation for compensation or profit, his disability annuity may be reduced or terminated by the Board at its discretion. If the disability has been terminated and the member has again entered into a salary relationship with the Church, he shall resume his contributions to the Plan.

(2). To set aside on a reserve basis an amount sufficient to build up an annuity for the widow, if any, of a member in the event of the member's death prior to drawing an age retirement annuity. Such widow's annuity shall be a minimum of $200.00. The basic annuity for the widow and minor children, if any, shall be the amount of annuity provided by the accumulated contributions and the allocations calculated on the basis of the tables adopted by the Board for that purpose. If the widow marries or leaves the United Lutheran Church, her annuity shall terminate when the sum of the payments to her deceased husband, the minor children and herself, equal his accumulated contributions as provided in Articles II and III. If, at the time of his marriage, the member has attained the age of fifty-five (55) years, the amount applied to provide the widow's and children's annuities shall be limited to his accumulations and his allocations; or if at the time of his marriage, the member is receiving an age retirement annuity or a disability annuity, the amount of the widow's annuity shall be one-half of the amount of the member's annuity, but her annuity shall cease if and when the sum of the payments to her deceased husband, the minor children and herself shall have equaled the member's accumulated contributions. If the accumulations and the allocations to the credit of the member will give the widow a basic annuity of more than $200.00, then she shall not participate in the benefits provided for in this Section. Subject to the above provisions, the annuity to the widow of a member who has entered upon an age retirement annuity shall be one-half of her husband's age retirement annuity, provided, however, that until changed by the Board, such annuity shall be at least $200.00.

(3). To set aside on a reserve basis an amount sufficient to provide annuities of $50.00 to each of the minor children of a member, whether such member was in active relationship or receiving an age retirement or disability annuity. The total amount of the widow's $200.00 annuity and the minor children's annuities shall not exceed $400.00, except when the accumulations for the deceased member would provide a larger amount, in which case the larger amount shall be paid.

(4). If necessary, to bring up to and maintain the reserves at such amounts as may be required according to the tables adopted from time to time by the Board as standards, together with such additional amount as may be deemed wise to hold as surplus for contingencies.

(5). To pay administrative expenses not otherwise provided for.

(6). The balance available after providing for the items set forth in Sections (1), (2), (3), (4), and (5) shall be so allocated that all the members who have qualified shall receive therefrom equal benefits in so far as provided by the amount contributed to the Plan by the congregations for the purpose of providing age retirement annuities as provided in Article XIII, provided that in no case shall such benefits be less than three and one-half (3½) per cent of the average salary of the participating members for the current year even though it be necessary to reduce correspondingly the minimum benefits hereinbefore otherwise provided. The above benefits are referred to as the allocations.

ARTICLE VI
Age Retirement Annuities

(1). Upon retirement after attaining the age of sixty-five (65) years, all the accumulations referred to in the next Section shall be applied to provide an age retirement annuity for a member upon the basis of the tables adopted by the Board for that purpose, with the further provision that one-half (½) of such annuity shall be continued to the widow of the member if their marriage took place before the member entered upon such age retirement annuity, subject to the conditions set forth in Article V. Retirement is understood to mean the giving up of active work and the termination of salary relationship.

(2). Such accumulations shall include:
- (a). The accumulations from the member's own contributions as provided in Articles II and III, and
- (b). The accumulations from the allocations as provided in Articles IV and V.

(3). If the member receiving such age retirement annuity has become a member of the Plan through the merging of the prior pension plan and the new pension plan, and if the annuity provided through the accumulations referred to in paragraph (b) Section (2) of this Article is less than the minimum annuity of $300.00 now being provided members of the prior pension plan, the Contingent Fund shall be drawn upon as provided in Article XIII and in so far as the resources of the Contingent Fund justify, to provide an annuity, supplemental to that provided by the accumulations in paragraph (b), so that the combined annuity from those two sources in so far as possible shall not be less than the above minimum annuity of $300.00 based upon thirty-five (35) years of service. For periods of service less than thirty-five (35) years, the combined annuity shall be reduced proportionately. Provided, however, that a member of the prior pension plan having served the Church as minister or missionary for at least twenty (20) years and having attained the age of sixty-five (65) years shall upon retirement be entitled to an age retirement annuity of at least $300.00. The amount to be drawn from the Contingent Fund shall be the reserve required to provide the supplemental annuity thus granted.

ARTICLE VII
Right of Member to Participate in Allocations and Other Benefits

(1). The right of a member to participate in the full yearly allocations and the full disability and other benefits shall be contingent upon both the member and his congregation having made their contributions in full.

(2). If the member or his congregation shall fail to make the required contributions in full, the participation in the yearly allocations and the benefits provided under Articles V and VI shall be reduced in the same proportion as the contributions have been reduced.

(3). In any case when the member or his congregation shall have failed to make contributions in full, the minimum age retirement annuity and disability annuity payable to such member and other minimum benefits payable to his widow and children shall be reduced in the same proportion.

(4). If for any reason a congregation ceases to make its contributions on account of the service of a member who has continued his two and one-half (2½) per cent contributions, the Board shall have the right to deduct, with the consent of the member, from his accumulated allocations in so far as his accumulated allocations will permit, amounts equivalent to the contributions from his congregation, so as to provide the member with the full benefits of the Plan in the event of disability or death. It is understood that at any time the congregation may resume its contributions.

ARTICLE VIII
Withdrawal Benefits

In the event of the termination of ministerial relationship of a member with the United Lutheran Church no further contribution shall be received from such a member; but in such event the member may withdraw his accumulated contributions referred to in Articles II and III, or at the discretion of the Board he may let them remain in the Fund to be applied towards providing annuity benefits as outlined in the Plan, but without further claim against the Plan for benefits provided out of its other funds.

ARTICLE IX
Time of Payment of Contributions

The contributions by the member and his congregation shall be due on the first day of each month in advance. In case of any change in salary during a period for which remittance has been made, adjustment shall be made in the succeeding remittance. In case the contribution of the member or the congregation is not paid within the current month, interest at the rate of five (5) per cent shall accrue from the due date to the date of payment.

ARTICLE X
Annuity Payments

All annuity payments shall be made in monthly installments at the end of the month.

ARTICLE XI
Additional Optional Payments

The member may pay into the Plan such additional amounts as he may elect, to be increased by interest additions, for the purpose of providing annuity benefits additional to those otherwise herein provided, with the right on the part of the member or the Board to apply the same to the payment of the member's contributions.

ARTICLE XII
Interest

Interest shall be added on amounts credited to or accumulated for a member out of the earnings on investments at a rate to be determined by the Board.

ARTICLE XIII
Contingent Fund

The Contingent Fund shall consist of all assets and property accumulated during the administration of the prior pension plan, and all gifts, contributions, legacies and other income, not specifically designated for other purposes.

The Contingent Fund shall be used as follows:

(1). To continue the payment of pensions granted under the prior pension plan to retired or disabled members, to their widows and to their minor children.

(2). (a). To provide annuities exclusive of those provided from the members' accumulations (Article III), not less in amounts than those provided in Section (1) above for the active members of the prior pension plan (as well as for their widows and their minor children) who after the merging of the prior pension plan into the new Plan shall retire or become disabled or die and by whom and on whose account all requirements have been met, but for whom there do not remain before retirement or death, years of future service under the Plan sufficient to build up the accumulations necessary to provide adequate annuities as outlined in the Plan.

(b). If the contributions of the member and his congregations have not been made in full, and if his period of service has been less than thirty-five (35) years, then these minimum annuities shall be reduced proportionately in accordance with the provisions of the Plan.

(c). Such pensions and annuities shall be increased as the Contingent Fund shall justify.

(3). To provide pensions under the prior plan to those who are in active service on the date of the inauguration of the Plan and who are fifty-five years of age and over, and who do not participate in the Plan.

ARTICLE XIV
Relief Fund

The Board shall have and maintain a Relief Fund out of which aid may be given to ministers, missionaries and their families in instances of extraordinary need.

ARTICLE XV
Right to Alter or Amend the New Pension Plan

The right is reserved to the United Lutheran Church by a majority vote of those present and voting at any convention, to alter and amend this pension plan as may be required and justified by experience and the available resources, and as may be found to be to the general advantage of the Church; provided, however, that the proposed amendment has been recommended by the Pension Board and has been submitted to the Executive Board in writing at least forty days before such Convention and published in the official organ of the Church at least thirty days before said Convention.

EXPLANATORY NOTES

The purpose of the proposed plan is to establish the pension fund on a reserve basis so that it may be sound actuarially and financially, and be able at all times to meet its obligations as they fall due.

Out of the funds received from the current contributions of members and congregations, there will be set aside accumulated reserve funds to provide retirement annuities payable when the members cease their active service through age or disability. Further than this, provision will be made for annuities to the widow and minor children in the event of the death of the member.

Sixty-five years is the minimum set for retirement on account of age, but disability annuities are payable in the event of total and permanent disability prior to age sixty-five.

Provision is made for the creation of a Contingent Fund to which will be credited special gifts, legacies and other funds available for the following purpose: To increase the regular retirement annuities available to those who retire during the earlier years following the establishment of the new plan with a view to providing an annuity to each retired member who has met the requirements as to the minimum age (65 years) and the period of service (35 years). For members of the prior pension plan the service requirement is thirty (30) years.

The Contingent Fund will be available also for continuing the pensions to the existing beneficiaries under the present pension plan because the funds of both the prior and the new plan will be merged. All the assets and properties accumulated under the prior plan will be credited to this Contingent Fund.

A Relief Fund will be maintained to meet causes of extraordinary need, supplementing regular benefits provided through the Plan.

The classes of persons eligible to membership in the Plan will be the same as those who were eligible for membership under the prior plan.

In the event of the termination of his ministerial relationship with a synod of the United Lutheran Church in America, a member will receive benefits equivalent to his own accumulations.

There is one very valuable provision: namely, that members may make additional deposits over and above the required contribution so as to increase with their own savings the benefits regularly provided.

The plan is submitted with these recommendations (For action, see p. 355.)

1. That the plan be referred to a special committee, to be appointed by the President, with the advice of the Executive Board, for consideration and report to the next convention; and

2. That the officers of the constituent synods be asked to ascertain meanwhile, what proportion of their churches would cooperate in this or some similar plan.

It is obvious that unless 75% of the Churches cooperate it will be ineffective.

It is to be understood that the 8% payable by the Church is to be a current expense item and not deducted from the benevolence or the pastor's salary.

Of course the present plan must be continued concurrently with the new pension plan as long as there are any living beneficiaries in the former.

At this convention the terms of the following members expire:

William H. Emhardt, Esq.
William A. Granville, Ph.D., LL.D.
H. J. Herbst
Rev. J. H. Reble, D.D.
W. T. Stauffer, Esq.

The Board places in nomination the following:

William H. Emhardt, Esq.
William A. Granville, Ph.D., LL.D.
H. J. Herbst
Rev. J. H. Reble, D.D.
W. T. Stauffer, Esq.

·   Respectfully submitted,
HARRY HODGES, *Executive Secretary.*

REPORT OF THE TREASURER OF THE BOARD OF MINISTERIAL PENSIONS AND RELIEF

BALANCE SHEET
June 30, 1936

ASSETS

Cash on Hand and in Bank	$ 33,376.22	
Cash Investment Fund	8,942.00	
		$ 42,318.22
Investments, Stocks and Bonds at Ledger Values, Market Value—July 11, 1936—$1,348,700.81		1,310.661.17
Accounts Receivable:		
Bankers Trust Company	$ 60,319.13	
Adjusted War Service Certificate	1.00	
Participating Trust Certificate, Park County, Montana	1.00	
Advance on Real Estate Foreclosure	7.50	
		60,328.63
Mortgages		806,050.15
Real Estate at Ledger Values		1,242,455.84
Note Receivable, York Machinery Corporation		1,091.32
Advances Receivable		785.28
Furniture and Fixtures		773.20
Equipment, Buery Building, 3701 North Broad Street, Philadelphia, Penna.		27.85
Total Assets		$3,464,491.66

LIABILITIES AND FUNDS

Accounts Payable, Sundries	$	65.06
Reserve for Repairs and Replacements, Buery Building		9,474.89
Funds:		
Annuities	$ 103,150.00	

Endowment 3,431,008.39
General Fund Deficit 79,206.68*
                                                   3,454,951.71

      Total Liabilities and Funds $3,464,491.66

* Deficit.

STATEMENT OF CASH RECEIPTS AND DISBURSEMENTS
July 1, 1934, to June 30, 1935

	Endowment Fund	General Fund
Balances on Hand—July 1, 1934	$ 77,080.66	$ 39,633.06*
RECEIPTS		
Campaign for Endowment Fund ....$	6,969.13	
United Lutheran Church Apportionment		$106,054.00
Women's Missionary Society		3,990.00
Bequests	1,861.63	
Donations—General Relief..		4,726.93
Interest and Dividends:		
Interest on Mortgages		45,784.16
Interest on Bonds		60,478.01
Dividends on Stocks		367.00
Annuity Contracts Sold	11,200.00	
Mortgages Paid in full or on account	3,160.24	
Rents Collected and Miscellaneous Income:		
Beury Building		45,530.60
Other Real Estate		49,523.71
Sale of Securities	10,315.78	
Bank Loan Received— Chase National Bank	20,000.00	
Fifteen per cent distribution received on monies on deposit with Bankers Trust Company, Phila., Penna. (In Liquidation)..	18,095.75	
Discount Earned on payment of Real Estate Taxes		900.88
Proceeds—Sale of Real Estate	1,562.40	
Collected on Account Receivable	22.60	
Amortization—Mrs. Hoppe pension	233.34	
Total Receipts ....—	73,420.87	317,355.29
	$150,501.53	$277,722.23

DISBURSEMENTS

Pensions		
Retired Ministers	$ 84,100.00	
Disabled Ministers	16,475.00	
Widows of Ministers	112,212.39	
Children of Ministers	7,013.38	
Missionaries	1,225.00	
		$221,025.77
Relief		
Ministers	$ 7,240.00	
Widows of Ministers	4,645.02	
		11,885.02
Annuity Interest		6,637.40
Salaries		
Executive Secretary	$ 3,600.00	
Office Salaries	3,600.00	
		7,200.00
Traveling Expenses of		
Executive Secretary	$ 511.65	
Expenses of Board Mem-		
bers	321.44	
Promotion Expense	261.41	
		1,094.50
Treasurer's Fidelity Bond....		62.50
Auditing		904.38
Postage		710.09
Office Supplies and Expense		478.39
Rental of Office		701.25
Federal Tax on Bank		
Checks		143.12
Legal Fees		2,000.00
Fees paid for Collection of		
Bond Interest and Divi-		
dends on Stock		1,209.47
Real Estate Expenses		
(Properties other than		
Beury Building):		
Real Estate Agent's Fee..	$ 4,000.00	
Real Estate Agents'		
Fidelity Bonds	200.00	
		4,200.00
Other Expenses		
Repairs—		
Plumbing and Heating	$ 3,027.37	
Papering	1,156.75	
Painting	1,679.15	
Roofing	1,440.25	
General	2,652.64	
Total Repairs	9,956.16	
Taxes	$ 15,317.75	
Water Rents	1,103.53	
Total Taxes and Water		
Rents	$ 16,421.28	

Insurance

Fire	$ 1,173.83	
Vandalism	229.47	
Plate Glass	246.67	
Public Liability and Compensation	367.45	
Total Insurance	$ 2,017.42	

Heat, Light and Power

Electric Current	$ 179.99	
Gas	209.97	
Coal	824.86	
Total Heat, Light and Power	$ 1,214.82	

Janitor Service	$ 1,068.00	
Miscellaneous Expense	286.55	
Total Expense of Real Estate other than Beury Building		30,964.23

Real Estate Expenses
Beury Building:

Insurance	$ 2,278.57	
Taxes and Water Rents	17,721.78	
Repairs	1,655.75	
Labor	16,705.95	
Elevator Service	1,584.00	
Heat, Light and Power	7,124.64	
Commissions paid on rent collections	1,372.05	
Miscellaneous Expenses	2,573.17	
Interest Paid on Borrowed Money		51,015.91
		96.66
Office Equipment Purchased		367.30
State of Pennsylvania Documentary Stamps		25.00
Deposits on Electric Coolers		66.00
Taxes Advanced for account of mortgagors		678.69

Real Estate Foreclosure Costs	$ 4,897.87	
Improvement to Buildings	75.00	
Mortgage Satisfaction Fees	1.00	
Legal Expenses paid for collection of Bequest Money	50.11	
Securities Purchased	29,635.88	
Payment on account of loan —Chase National Bank	10,000.00	
Postage re: Sale of Securities	1.26	

Improvements to Beury
Building — t w o electric
transformers 1,200.00

Total Disbursements	$ 45,861.12	$341,465.68
Balance—June 30, 1935 ..	104,640.41	
Overdraft—June 30, 1935		63,743.45*
	$150,501.53	$277,722.23

SUMMARY OF CASH RECEIPTS AND DISBURSEMENTS

Cash Balance—Endowment Fund—June 30, 1935		$104,640.41
Cash Overdraft—General Fund—June 30, 1935		63,743.45
Cash Balance — June 30, 1935		$ 40,896.96
Cash on Hand in office— Muhlenberg Building ......$	25.00	
Cash in Checking Account —Fidelity-Phila. T r u s t Company	30,357.44	
Cash in Investment Fund— Fidelity - P h i l a. Trust Company	10,314.52	
Cash in hands of Lehman and Snyder	200.00	
	$ 40,896.96	

STATEMENT OF CASH RECEIPTS AND DISBURSEMENTS

July 1, 1935 to June 30, 1936

	Endowment Fund	General Fund
Balance on Hand—June 30, 1935	$104,640.41	$ 63,743.45*

RECEIPTS

Campaign for Endowment Fund ....$	3,700.72	
Bequests	2,637.94	
Donations—General Relief..	1,678.81	
Annuity Contracts Sold	13,100.00	
Mortgages Paid in Full or on Account	7,096.27	
Securities Called or Sold....	166,413.84	
Bank Loan—Chase National Bank	10,000.00	
Proceeds from Sale of Real Estate ....:........	12,757.66	
Tax Refund	300.00	

Amortization, Mrs. Hoppe Pension	200.00		
United Lutheran Church— Apportionment		$108,296.00	
Women's Missionary Society		3,990.00	
Donations—General Relief		6,442.28	
Interest and Dividends			
Interest on Mortgages		43,981.54	
Interest on Bonds Dividends on Stocks		60,889.08	
Rents Collected:			
Beury Building		45,573.44	
Other Real Estate		53,903.33	
Discount Earned on Payment of Real Estate Taxes		798.40	
Collected on Accounts Receivable		2,614.23	
Total Receipts		217,885.24	326,488.30
		$322,525.65	$262,744.85

DISBURSEMENTS

Expense in connection with Real Estate Sales	$ 1,099.76		
Real Estate Foreclosure Costs	2,216.77		
Improvements to Buildings	9,498.10		
Securities Purchased	157,272.77		
Mortgages Purchased	8,300.00		
Payment on Bank Loan— Chase National Bank	20,000.00		
Telegram	.76		
Pensions			
Retired Ministers		$ 85,375.00	
Disabled Ministers		14,400.00	
Widows of Ministers		114,533.63	
Children of Ministers		7,088.30	
Missionaries		1,500.00	
Relief			$222,896.93
Ministers		$ 7,270.00	
Widows of Ministers		3,745.00	
			11,015.00
Annuity Interest			6,505.94
Salaries			
Executive Secretary		$ 3,600.00	
Office Salaries		3,600.00	
Traveling Expenses of Executive Secretary			7,200.00
		$ 549.20	
Expenses of Board Members		322.85	
Promotion Expense		184.93	
			1,056.98

Treasurer's Fidelity Bond...		62.50
Auditing		700.00
Postage		682.77
Office Supplies and Expense		588.04
Rental of Office		701.25
Legal Fees		2,000.00
Fees Paid for Collection of Bond Interest and Dividends on Stock		1,206.59

Real Estate Expenses
(Properties o t h e r than Beury Building):

Real Estate Agents' Fees..	$ 4,000.00	
Real Estate Agents' Fidelity Bond	200.00	
Other Real Estate Agents' Expense	216.97	
	————	4,416.97

Real Estate Property Expenses

Plumbing and Heating..	$ 3,075.07	
Papering	1,259.75	
Painting	3,560.91	
Roofing	953.70	
General Repairs	4,784.40	
Total Repairs	$ 13,633.83	
Taxes	$ 14,539.43	
Water Rent	1,280.50	
Total Taxes and Water Rents	$ 15,819.93	

Insurance:

Fire Insurance	1,358.87	
Vandalism	168.84	
Plate Glass	225.36	
Public Liability and Compensation	315.00	
Total Insurance	$ 2,068.07	

Heat, Light and Power:

Electric Power	120.22	
Gas	232.17	
Coal	836.10	
Total Heat, Light and Power	$ 1,188.49	
Janitor Service	$ 1,036.00	
Miscellaneous Expense	400.13	
Total Expenses of Real Estate o t h e r t h a n Beury Building	————	34,146.45

Real Estate Expenses
Beury Building:

Repairs	$ 3,269.36	

Taxes and Water Rent....	14,762.31	
Insurance	1,357.61	
Heat, Light and Power....	5,623.18	
Janitor and Lamp Supplies	909.75	
Labor	18,034.20	
Elevator Service	1,664.00	
Commissions Paid on Rent Collections	1,367.22	
Miscellaneous Expenses....	1,765.58	
		48,753.21
Deposits on Water Coolers..		66.00
Office Equipment Purchased		30.90
Interest Paid on Borrowed Money		63.33
Taxes Advanced for Account of Mortgagors		2,471.26
Total Disbursements	$198,388.16	$344,564.12
Balance—June 30, 1936	124,137.49	
Overdraft—June 30, 1936		81,819.27*
	$322,525.65	$262,744.85

Summary of Cash Receipts and Disbursements

Cash Balance—Endowment Fund, June 30, 1936	$124,137.49
Cash Overdraft—General Fund, June 30, 1936	81,819.27*
	$ 42,318.22
Cash on Hand in Office	$ 25.00
Cash in Checking Account, Fidelity-Philadelphia Trust Company	33,151.22
Cash in Investments Fund, Fidelity-Philadelphia Trust Company	8,942.00
Cash in Hands of Lehman and Snyder	200.00
	$ 42,318.22

* Overdraft.

INVESTMENTS
June 30, 1936

Par Value	Railroad Bonds	Value As Carried on Books	Market Value as of July 11, 1936
$ 50,000.00	Atchison, Topeka and Santa Fe Railway, General Mortgage 4s, due 1995	$ 48,321.25 @ 115	$ 57,500.00

25,000.00	Baltimore and Ohio Railroad Co., Series "A" 5s, due 1995	25,515.00	@ 87	21,750.00
50,000.00	Buffalo, Rochester and Pittsburgh Cons. Mortgage 4½s, due 1957	47,250.00	@ 81	40,500.00
25,000.00	Canadian Pacific Railway Co. Equipment Trust 5s, due 1944	25,375.00	@ 115	28,750.00
10,000.00	Canadian Pacific Railway Co., Perpetual 4s Cons. Debentures	9,427.25	@ 96	9,600.00
25,000.00	Chesapeake and Ohio Railway Equipment Trust 4½s, due 1940	24,900.33	@ 109	27,250.00
25,000.00	Chesapeake and Ohio General Mort. 4½s, due 1992....	26,312.50	@ 125	31,250.00
6,000.00	Chicago, Indianapolis and Louisville First Gen. Mort. Series "A," due 1966, 5s....	6,000.00	@ 21	1,260.00
25,000.00	Chicago and Northwestern Railway Co. Convertible Series "A" 4¾s, due 1949..	24,925.00	@ 12	3,000.00
10,000.00	Chicago and Western Indiana Railroad Co., First and Refunding 4¼s, due 1962	10,162.50	@ 102	10,200.00
10,000.00	Great Northern Rwy. Series "E" General 4½s, due 1977	10,122.51	@ 102	10,200.00
25,000.00	Kansas City Terminal Rwy. Co., First Mortgage 4s, due 1960	22,156.25	@ 108	27,000.00
5,000.00	Lehigh Valley Railroad Co., Cons. Mort. 5s, due 2003....	5,110.00	@ 63	3,150.00
5,000.00	Lehigh Valley Terminal Railway Co., First 5s, due 1941	5,313.13	@ 105	5,250.00
50,000.00	New York Central Railroad Co., 4½s, due 2013	49,531.25	@ 89	44,500.00
50,000.00	New York, Chicago and St. Louis Railroad Co., Series "C" 4½s, due 1978	48,870.00	@ 90	45,000.00
10,000.00	New York, Lackawanna and Western Rwy. First Series "B" 4½s, due 1973	10,594.65	@ 104	10,400.00
35,000.00	Pennsylvania Company, Secured 4s, due 1963	35,000.00	@ 104	36,400.00
25,000.00	Pennsylvania Railroad Co., 4½s, due 1970	23,812.50	@ 103	25,750.00
5,000.00	Pennsylvania Railroad Co., Gen. Mort. 4½s, due 1965..	5,000.00	@ 112	5,600.00
25,000.00	Pere Marquette Rwy. Equip. Trust 4½s, due 1942	24,885.22	@ 100	25,000.00
25,000.00	Pere Marquette Rwy. First Mortgage 4½s, due 1980....	24,937.50	@ 110	27,500.00
5,000.00	Pittsburgh, Cincinnati, Chicago and St. Louis Railroad Series "B" 5s, due 1975....	4,985.00	@ 119	5,950.00

25,000.00	Southern Pacific Co., 4½s, due 1969	24,281.25 @ 91	22,750.00
25,000.00	Southern Pacific Co., Oregon Lines First Mortgage 4½s, due 1977	24,375.00 @ 97	24,250.00
$576,000.00		$567,163.09	$549,760.00

Public Utility Bonds

$ 25,000.00	American Telephone and Telegraph Co., Sinking Fund Deb. 5½s, due 1943..$	27,312.50 @ 113	$ 28,250.00
25,000.00	American Telephone and Telegraph Co., Debenture 5s, due 1965	25,175.00 @ 113	28,250.00
50,000.00	Appalachian Electric Power, First Mortgage 5s, due 1956	49,987.50 @ 106	53,000.00
10,000.00	Bell Telephone Co., Series "C" 5s, due 1960	10,373.13 @ 128	12,800.00
25,000.00	Carolina Power and Light Co., First and Refunding 5s, due 1956	25,175.00 @ 103	25,750.00
1,000.00	Des Moines City Rwy. Co., Income Bond 5s, due 1955..	950.00 @ 23	230.00
25,000.00	Detroit Edison Co., Series "D" General Mortgage 4½s, due 1961	23,997.50 @ 116	29,000.00
50,000.00	Georgia Power Co., First Mortgage 5s, due 1967	49,987.50 @ 101	50,500.00
10,000.00	Kansas Power and Light Co., First Mort. 4½s, due 1965..	10,301.65 @ 108	10,800.00
25,000.00	Monongahela West Penn Public Service Company, 4½s, due 1960	25,000.00 @ 105	26,250.00
15,000.00	New York Steam Corporation, 5s, due 1951	15,872.25 @ 107	16,050.00
5,000.00	New York Water Service Corporation, 5s, due 1951..	5,062.50 @ 97	4,850.00
10,000.00	Pacific Gas and Electric Co., 4s, due 1964	10,200.00 @ 109	10,900.00
1,000.00	Pacific Telephone and Telegraph Co., 5s, due 1937	1,000.00 @ 101	1,010.00
25,000.00	Philadelphia Co., Series "A," 5s, due 1967	24,675.00 @ 105	26,250.00
50,000.00	Philadelphia Electric Power Co., First Mortgage 5½s, due 1972	51,547.77 @ 112	56,000.00
24,500.00	Philadelphia Rapid Transit, First Mort. 6s, due 1944....	24,500.00 @ 91	22,295.00
2,000.00	Tennessee Power Co., First Mortgage 5s, due 1962	1,600.00 @ 95	1,900.00

25,000.00	Virginia Power Co., First and Collateral Trust 5s, due 1942	25,515.00 @ 106	26,500.00
5,000.00	West Virginia Water Service, 5s, due 1961	5,175.00 @ 102¾	5,137.50
$408,500.00		**$413,407.30**	**$435,722.50**

Government and Municipal Bonds

$ 20,000.00	Alberta, Province of Canada, Debenture 5s, due 1959......$	19,775.00 @ 67	$ 13,400.00
25,000.00	Boston, City of, Metropolitan Dist., Series "B" 4¾s, due 1965	25,906.25 @ 132	33,000.00
10,000.00	Manitoba, Province of, Debenture 5s, due 1959............	9,937.50 @ 104	10,400.00
10,000.00	Montreal Metropolitan Commission Sinking Fund, 4½s, due 1953.......................	9,262.50 @ 99	9,900.00
25,000.00	Montreal Harbour Commission First 5s, due 1969........	25,412.50 @ 120	30,000.00
25,000.00	New York, City of N. Y., Corporate Stock Issue 4¼s, due 1960	23,250.00 @ 115	28,750.00
25,000.00	Ontario, Province of, Debenture 5s, 1960	25,750.00 @ 121	30,250.00
10,000.00	Ottawa, City of, Canada, 4½s, due 1954	9,309.96 @ 113	11,300.00
10,000.00	Philadelphia, City of, Pennsylvania 4s, due 1947	8,456.81 @ 109	10,900.00
15,000.00	Philadelphia, City of, Pennsylvania 4s, due 1953	12,174.90 @ 113	16,950.00
75,000.00	Philadelphia, City of, Pennsylvania 4¼s, due 1977-47	67,296.87 @ 112	84,000.00
25,000.00	Philadelphia, City of, Pennsylvania 4¼s, due 1978-48	20,112.71 @ 113	28,250.00
25,000.00	Saskatchewan, Province of, Debenture, 5s, due 1959....	25,112.50 @ 89	22,250.00
$300,000.00		**$281,757.50**	**$329,350.00**

Industrial and Miscellaneous Bonds

$ 1,000.00	Howard Gas and Coal, First 6s, due 1937 ....$	1,000.00 @ 20	$ 200.00
10,000.00	National Dairy Products, Debenture 3¾s, due 1951 (with Warrants)	10,413.58 @ 106	10,600.00
16,000.00	Texas Corporation, Conv. 5s, due 1944	16,200.00 @ 101	16,160.00
7,984.20	Walnut Street Trust Building, First 6s, due 1932........	7,984.20 @ 17	1,357.31
5,000.00	York Ice Machinery Corporation, 1st 6s, due 1947....	5,000.00 @ 99	4,950.00
$ 39,984.20		**$ 40,597.78**	**$ 33,267.31**

INVESTMENTS
June 30, 1936

Shares	Miscellaneous Stocks	Value As Carried on Books	Market Value as of July 11, 1936
50	Fred W. Albrecht Grocery Company, 7% Preferred ....$	5,000.00	No Market
12	Baltimore Feed and Grain Company, 8% Preferred	1,200.00	No Quotation Available
17	Pennsylvania Railroad Company, Common	535.50	$ 561.00
10	Philadelphia Dairy Products $4.00 non-cumulative second pre-ferred stock	1,000.00	40.00
		$ 7,735.50	$ 601.00

Par Value	Summary		
$576,000.00	Railroad Bonds ....$	567,163.09	$ 549,760.00
408,500.00	Public Utility Bonds	413,407.30	435,722.50
300,000.00	Government and Municipal Bonds	281,757.50	329,350.00
39,984.20	Industrial and Misc. Bonds..	40,597.78	33,267.31
	Miscellaneous Stocks	7,735.50	601.00
	Totals ....$	$1,310,661.17	$1,348,700.81

MORTGAGES
June 30, 1936.

Fund	Property	Net Amount of Mortgage June 30, 1936	Rate of In-terest	Classifica-tion of Mort-gage	Appraised Value June 30, 1936	Assessed Value
189	5901 Belden St., Phila., Pa.....$	9,400.00	5½%	AY	$ 9,500.00	$ 8,000.00
109	5345 Belfield Ave., Phila., Pa.	3,000.00	6%	B	2,500.00	3,300.00
307	5917 North Bingham Street, Phila., Pa.	3,000.00	5%	A	3,100.00	3,500.00
306	5923 North Bingham Street, Phila., Pa.	3,000.00	5%	A	3,100.00	3,500.00
305	5949 North Bingham Street, Phila., Pa.	3,500.00	5%	A	3,100.00	3,500.00
334	5961 North Bingham Street, Phila., Pa.	2,925.00	6%	A	3,100.00	3,500.00
294	3470 Bowman St., Phila., Pa..	843.20*	6%	C	3,000.00	3,600.00
297	614 Boyer Rd., Rowland Park, Cheltenham Township	5,000.00	6%	AS	5,500.00	2,600.00
253	616 E. Brill St., Phila., Pa......	3,000.00	6%	A	2,800.00	3,200.00
227	622 E. Brill St., Phila., Pa......	3,000.00	6%	A	2,800.00	3,200.00
263	626 E. Brill St., Phila., Pa......	2,500.00	6%	A	2,800.00	3,200.00
285	656 E. Brill St., Phila., Pa......	3,000.00	6%	A	2,800.00	3,200.00
328	1310 Butler St., Phila., Pa......	4,000.00	6%	C	3,200.00	4,800.00
316	N. W. Cor. Buxmont St. and Overhill Road, Somerton Gardens, Phila., Pa..............	6,000.00	6%	A	6,000.00	7,000.00
72	8130 Cadwallader Ave., El-kins Park, Pa.	12,000.00	6%	AS	17,000.00	7,000.00
261	3228 N. Carlisle St., Phila., Pa.	3,000.00	6%	B	3,000.00	3,600.00
53	312 Chandler St., Phila., Pa..	4,000.00	6%	A	4,200.00	5,000.00
37	1407 W. Chelten Ave., Phila., Pa.	4,850.00	6%	BY	5,500.00	5,500.00

Fund	Property	Net Amount of Mortgage June 30, 1936	Rate of Interest	Classifica-tion of Mortgage	Appraised Value June 30, 1936	Assessed Value
63	514 Cheltena Ave., Jenkintown, Pa.	15,000.00	5%	AS	12,000.00	6,000.00
12	599 East Cheltenham Ave., Phila., Pa.	3,900.00	6%	A	4,200.00	5,500.00
342	4614 Chester Ave., Phila., Pa.	5,000.00	5%	A	7,500.00	8,500.00
271	6633 Chew St., Phila., Pa.	4,400.00	6%	BY	6,200.00	6,200.00
336	213 Church Rd., Elkins Park, Pa.	5,500.00	5%	BS	6,000.00	3,000.00
289	535 East Church Rd., Elkins Park, Pa.	8,550.00	6%	AS	10,000.00	4,500.00
290	537 East Church Rd., Elkins Park, Pa.	9,250.00	6%	AS	10,000.00	4,500.00
22	7530 Claridge St., Phila., Pa.	3,500.00	6%	A	3,800.00	4,000.00
96	305 Corinthian Ave., Willow Grove, Pa.	3,000.00	6%	AS	4,500.00	3,200.00
331	4221 Cottman St., Phila., Pa.	3,412.50	6%	A	4,600.00	5,000.00
326	4225 Cottman St., Phila., Pa.	3,500.00	6%	A	4,600.00	5,000.00
304	4235 Cottman St., Phila., Pa.	3,900.00	6%	A	4,600.00	5,000.00
303	4237 Cottman St., Phila., Pa.	4,000.00	6%	A	4,600.00	5,000.00
302	4239 Cottman St., Phila., Pa.	3,500.00	6%	A	4,600.00	5,000.00
329	231-33 Coulter St., Phila., Pa.	12,000.00	5%	CY	10,000.00	17,000.00
29	104 Cypress Ave., Jenkintown Manor, Pa.	9,000.00	5%	AS	7,500.00	4,500.00
226	2605 N. Douglas St., Phila., Pa.	2,150.00	6%	C	1,800.00	1,900.00
192	2505 N. 18th St., Phila., Pa.	3,000.00	6%	C	2,400.00	4,300.00
218	5952 Elsinore St., Phila., Pa.	3,000.00	5%	B	2,700.00	3,000.00
344	6524 Elmwood Ave., Phila., Pa.	1,300.00	6%	A	2,600.00	3,800.00
129	1622 W. Erie Ave., Phila., Pa.	9,950.00	6%	BY	9,500.00	10,600.00
310	213 Evergreen Rd., Jenkintown Manor, Pa.	10,500.00	6%	AS	10,500.00	5,800.00
324	532 Fanshaw St., Phila., Pa.	3,300.00	6%	B	2,800.00	4,500.00
32	1133 Faunce St., Phila., Pa.	2,222.00	6%	B	2,500.00	4,000.00
92	6053-55 N 5th St., Phila., Pa.	9,700.00	6%	AY	22,000.00	18,700.00
130	184 W. Fern St., Phila., Pa.	3,000.00	5%	A	2,400.00	2,700.00
332	4630 N. 5th St., Phila., Pa.	9,000.00	6%	BY	9,000.00	9,000.00
105	6041 N. 5th St., Phila., Pa.	14,000.00	6%	AY	11,000.00	11,200.00
102	7214 Frankford Ave., Phila., Pa.	8,000.00	6%	AY	9,000.00	10,000.00
235	2642 Germantown Avenue, Phila., Pa.	15,000.00	6%	BY	15,000.00	12,600.00
309	5340 Germantown Avenue, Phila., Pa.	17,910.00	4%	CY	10,000.00	13,800.00
104	148-150 West Girard Avenue, Phila., Pa.	11,000.00	6%	BY	8,500.00	10,000.00
279	461-63 E. Girard Ave., Phila., Pa.	2,600.00	6%	CY	2,700.00	4,500.00
1	522 E. Godfrey Ave., Phila., Pa.	1,800.00	6%	A	3,200.00	4,000.00
2	528 E. Godfrey Ave., Phila., Pa.	2,500.00	6%	A	3,200.00	4,000.00
162	531 E. Godfrey Ave., Phila., Pa.	3,000.00	6%	A	4,700.00	5,700.00
4	538 E. Godfrey Ave., Phila., Pa.	2,975.00	6%	A	3,200.00	4,000.00
5	542 E. Godfrey Ave., Phila., Pa.	1,800.00	6%	A	3,200.00	4,000.00
134	609 E. Godfrey Ave., Phila., Pa.	3,000.00	5%	A	3,000.00	3,900.00
136	613 E. Godfrey Ave., Phila., Pa.	3,205.00	6%	A	3,000.00	3,700.00
137	615 E. Godfrey Ave., Phila., Pa.	3,000.00	5%	A	3,000.00	3,900.00
139	619 E. Godfrey Ave., Phila., Pa.	3,400.00	6%	A	3,000.00	3,900.00

Fund	Property	Net Amount of Mortgage June 30, 1936	Rate of Interest	Classification of Mortgage	Appraised Value June 30, 1936	Assessed Value
145	631 E. Godfrey Ave., Phila., Pa.	3,100.00	6%	A	3,000.00	3,900.00
106	2111 Eastburn Ave., Phila., Pa.	25,500.00	5%	BY	20,000.00	20,000.00
81	6221 Hasbrook St., Phila., Pa.	2,850.00	6%	A	4,000.00	4,200.00
313	6236 Hasbrook St., Phila., Pa.	7,600.00	5%	AY	6,700.00	9,500.00
337	755 E. Herkness St., Phila., Pa.	4,000.00	6%	A	3,800.00	4,000.00
34	8317 High School Rd., Elkins Park, Pa.	9,000.00	5%	AS	11,000.00	4,500.00
54	8431 High School Rd., Elkins Park, Pa.	3,000.00	6%	AS	3,200.00	1,900.00
55	8435 High School Rd., Elkins Park, Pa.	436.20**	6%	AS	3,200.00	1,900.00
333	2208-10 Hunting Park Ave., Phila., Pa.	8,000.00	6%	BY	7,000.00	8,000.00
280	2248 W. Huntingdon Street, Phila., Pa.	2,000.00	5%	B	1,800.00	2,700.00
97	S. W. Cor. Jenkintown and Evergreen Roads, Jenkintown Manor, Pa.	12,000.00	6%	AS	13,000.00	6,500.00
312	5900-02-04 Kemble Avenue, Phila., Pa.	9,000.00	6%	BY	7,500.00	8,100.00
278	3300-02 Kensington Avenue, Phila., Pa.	15,000.00	3%	CY	11,000.00	12,900.00
229	6429 Lawndale Ave., Phila., Pa.	1,481.25	6%	A	4,200.00	5,200.00
91	7531 Lawndale Ave., Phila., Pa.	2,350.00	6%	A	3,600.00	4,000.00
180	7404 N. Lawrence St., Phila., Pa.	3,000.00	6%	A	3,200.00	3,500.00
194	2612 W. Lehigh Ave., Phila., Pa.	10,000.00	4%	BY	8,000.00	8,000.00
186	622 Levick St., Phila., Pa.	5,000.00	6%	AY	5,200.00	6,000.00
185	208 W. Linton St., Phila., Pa.	2,500.00	6%	A	2,700.00	2,900.00
167	218 W. Linton St., Phila., Pa.	3,000.00	6%	A	2,700.00	2,900.00
168	230 W. Linton St., Phila., Pa.	1,500.00	6%	A	2,700.00	2,900.00
295	3430 Midvale Ave., Phila., Pa.	5,200.00	6%	A	5,200.00	6,300.00
291	308 Marvin Rd., Phila., Pa.	12,000.00	6%	AS	12,500.00	5,000.00
338	1551 McKean St., Phila., Pa.	7,500.00	6%	CY	5,000.00	6,800.00
220	2009 Norris St., Phila., Pa.	2,500.00	6%	C	2,000.00	3,900.00
107	7215 Oak St., Phila., Pa.	2,500.00	6%	C	2,200.00	1,800.00
314	2853-55 W. Oakdale Street, Phila., Pa.	6,780.00	6%	CY	6,000.00	9,600.00
293	6167 Oakley St., Phila., Pa.	4,000.00	6%	A	6,200.00	5,500.00
311	8240 Ogontz Ave. (Brookside Ave.), Phila., Pa.	9,000.00	6%	AS	7,100.00	3,200.00
18	7308 Palmetto St., Phila., Pa.	670.00	6%	A	1,500.00	2,800.00
179	22 and 24 Park Ave., Upper Darby, Pa.	20,000.00	4%	CYS	12,000.00	8,500.00
47	423 Passmore Ave., Phila., Pa.	2,500.00	6%	A	2,700.00	4,000.00
48	425 Passmore Ave., Phila., Pa.	3,000.00	6%	A	2,700.00	4,000.00
49	427 Passmore Ave., Phila., Pa.	3,000.00	6%	A	2,700.00	4,000.00
181	6032 N. Phillip St., Phila., Pa.	3,000.00	6%	A	2,800.00	3,200.00
256	1031 Pleasant St., Phila., Pa.	550.00	6%	AS	1,600.00	1,500.00
259	3425 Princeton Ave., Phila., Pa.	3,625.00	6%	A	3,900.00	4,600.00
257	3427 Princeton Ave., Phila., Pa.	3,900.00	6%	A	3,900.00	4,600.00
282	3435 Princeton Ave., Phila., Pa.	3,700.00	6%	A	3,900.00	4,600.00
320	3443 Princeton Ave., Phila., Pa.	3,465.00	6%	A	3,900.00	4,600.00
283	3445 Princeton Ave., Phila., Pa.	2,675.00	6%	A	3,900.00	4,600.00
276	3451 Princeton Ave., Phila., Pa.	4,000.00	6%	A	3,900.00	4,600.00

		Net Amount of Mortgage June 30, 1936	Rate of Interest	Classification of Mortgage	Appraised Value June 30, 1936	Assessed Value
101	3459 Princeton Ave., Phila., Pa.	425.00	6%	A	3,900.00	4,600.00
251	Rhawn and Ridgeway Sts., Phila., Pa.	4,850.00	6%	A	5,400.00	5,200.00
165	6529 Rising Sun Ave., Phila., Pa.	7,500.00	5%	AY	8,000.00	9,500.00
260	36 Robbins Ave., Rockledge, Pa.	3,500.00	6%	BS	3,500.00	4,000.00
233	924 West Rockland St., Phila., Pa.	4,000.00	6%	B	3,400.00	4,300.00
59	3310 St. Vincent St., Phila., Pa.	2,850.00	6%	A	4,400.00	4,400.00
343	1623 Ruscomb St., Phila., Pa.	1,950.00	5½%	A	4,000.00	5,300.00
95	3337 St. Vincent St., Phila., Pa.	3,800.00	5%	A	3,900.00	4,400.00
188	3353 St. Vincent St., Phila., Pa.	3,600.00	6%	A	3,900.00	4,400.00
35	3357 St. Vincent St., Phila., Pa.	4,000.00	6%	A	3,900.00	4,400.00
274	5127 Sheldon St., Phila., Pa.	1,975.00	6%	C	1,900.00	2,700.00
90	3401 N. 16th St., Phila., Pa.	18,950.00	6%	BY	15,000.00	14,000.00
292	6520 N. 16th St., Phila., Pa.	5,500.00	5%	A	4,800.00	5,200.00
16	1329 65th Ave., N. Phila., Pa.	6,500.00	6%	B	7,200.00	9,300.00
173	2514 W. Somerset St., Phila., Pa.	3,000.00	6%	C	2,800.00	3,400.00
224	2862 N. Stillman St., Phila., Pa.	1,400.00	6%	C	2,000.00	2,200.00
341	4209 Stirling St., Phila., Pa.	1,900.00	6%	A	3,400.00	3,500.00
339	4217 Stirling St., Phila., Pa.	3,000.00	6%	A	3,400.00	3,600.00
69	7248 Tabor St., Phila., Pa.	3,500.00	6%	A	3,400.00	4,200.00
275	7526 Tabor Rd., Phila., Pa.	2,500.00	6%	A	7,200.00	7,500.00
174	5415 Tacoma St., Phila., Pa.	4,000.00	6%	CY	3,000.00	6,500.00
197	4010 E. Teesdale St., Phila., Pa.	3,200.00	5%	A	3,000.00	3,800.00
199	4014 E. Teesdale St., Phila., Pa.	3,000.00	6%	A	3,000.00	3,600.00
112	4015 E. Teesdale St., Phila., Pa.	3,200.00	6%	A	3,000.00	3,600.00
113	4017 E. Teesdale St., Phila., Pa.	3,200.00	6%	A	3,000.00	3,600.00
115	4035 E. Teesdale St., Phila., Pa.	3,200.00	6%	A	3,000.00	3,600.00
116	4037 E. Teesdale St., Phila., Pa.	3,200.00	5%	A	3,000.00	3,600.00
205	4044 E. Teesdale St., Phila., Pa.	3,200.00	5%	A	3,000.00	3,600.00
121	4045 E. Teesdale St., Phila., Pa.	3,200.00	6%	A	3,000.00	3,600.00
122	4047 E. Teesdale St., Phila., Pa.	3,200.00	5%	A	3,000.00	3,600.00
207	4048 E. Teesdale St., Phila., Pa.	3,200.00	5%	A	3,000.00	3,600.00
123	4049 E. Teesdale St., Phila., Pa.	3,200.00	5%	A	3,000.00	3,600.00
208	4050 E. Teesdale St., Phila., Pa.	3,200.00	5%	A	3,000.00	3,600.00
211	4054 E. Teesdale St., Phila., Pa.	2,950.00	6%	A	3,000.00	3,600.00
124	4051 E. Teesdale St., Phila., Pa.	3,200.00	5%	A	3,000.00	3,600.00
126	4055 E. Teesdale St., Phila., Pa.	3,200.00	6%	A	3,000.00	3,600.00
127	4057 E. Teesdale St., Phila., Pa.	3,200.00	5%	A	3,000.00	3,600.00
195	4058 E. Teesdale St., Phila., Pa.	3,200.00	6%	A	3,000.00	3,300.00
120	4061 E. Teesdale St., Phila., Pa.	3,200.00	6%	A	3,000.00	3,300.00
128	4063 E. Teesdale St., Phila., Pa.	3,600.00	6%	A	3,400.00	3,900.00
330	2226 N. 13th St., Phila., Pa.	4,500.00	6%	CY	3,500.00	5,700.00
335	5900 N. 21st St., Phila., Pa.	7,500.00	5½%	AY	6,500.00	6,000.00
277	2764 N. 22nd St., Phila., Pa.	2,000.00	6%	C	2,800.00	4,800.00
175	2915 N. 22nd St., Phila., Pa.	7,625.00	6%	AY	8,000.00	7,900.00
272	2404 N. 26th St., Phila., Pa.	2,000.00	5%	C	1,800.00	2,500.00
50	2836 N. 27th St., Phila., Pa.	1,000.00	6%	A	3,000.00	4,000.00
178	7611 Verree Ave., Phila., Pa.	3,600.00	6%	A	3,900.00	4,500.00
28	5708 Virginian Rd., Phila., Pa.	6,000.00	6%	A	5,500.00	6,000.00
234	5300 Wayne Ave., Phila., Pa.	18,000.00	6%	BY	12,000.00	15,000.00
79	6908 Weisel Rd., Warrington Township, Pa.	6,000.00	6%	CYS	5,500.00	5,600.00
65	1421 W. Westmoreland St., Phila., Pa.	8,000.00	6%	BY	8,200.00	8,600.00
111	206 W. Widener St., Phila., Pa.	3,000.00	6%	A	2,800.00	3,100.00
132	223 W. Widener St., Phila., Pa.	3,000.00	6%	A	2,600.00	2,900.00
183	240 W. Widener St., Phila., Pa.	3,000.00	6%	A	2,800.00	3,400.00

Fund	Property	Net Amount of Mortgage June 30, 1936	Rate of Interest	Classification of Mortgage	Appraised Value June 30, 1936	Assessed Value
169	243 W. Widener St., Phila., Pa.	3,000.00	6%	A	2,600.00	2,900.00
315	600 E. Woodlawn Ave., Phila., Pa.	4,750.00	6%	BY	5,000.00	5,500.00
75	115 York Rd., Hatboro, Pa.	8,000.00	4%	CYS	6,500.00	4,500.00
74	117 York Rd., Hatboro, Pa.	8,000.00	4%	CYS	7,000.00	5,000.00
		$806,050.15				$836,600.00

MORTGAGES
June 30, 1936

Summary:	Total Number of Mortgages	Total Amount of Mortgages	Assessed Value	Appraised Value	Appraisals Over Mortgage Investment	Under Mortgage Investment
A	104	$399,644.95	$430,700.00	$444,700.00	$61,160.05	$16,105.00
AY	9	76,325.00	86,800.00	85,900.00	14,475.00	4,900.00
B	10	36,022.00	41,700.00	35,400.00	1,478.00	2,100.00
BY	14	156,400.00	141,100.00	136,400.00	2,900.00	22,900.00
C	11	25,368.20	35,900.00	25,900.00	3,556.80	2,825.00
CY	12	112,290.00	100,400.00	82,200.00	100.00	30,390.00
	160	$806,050.15	$836,600.00	$810,500.00	$83,669.85	$79,220.00

* Under and Subject to First Mortgage of $3,372.80.
** Under and Subject to First Mortgage of $2,944.80.

SUMMARY OF REAL ESTATE OWNED
June 30, 1936

Number of Properties	Book Value	Assessed Value	Appraised Value
121	$ 740,960.17	$ 557,450.00	$ 550,000.00
Beury Building	501,495.67	527,000.00	615,000.00
122	$1,242,455.84	$1,084,450.00	$1,165,000.00

Respectfully submitted,
WILLIAM G. SEMISCH, *Treasurer.*

August 5, 1936.

We have audited the books of account of the Treasurer of the Board of Ministerial Pensions and Relief of the United Lutheran Church in America, for the biennium beginning July 1, 1934, and ending June 30, 1936; we have examined the Mortgages, Deeds and Securities held by this Board as of June 30, 1936, and we hereby certify that the foregoing statements:

Balance Sheet, June 30, 1936
Statement of Receipts and Disbursements for the year ending June 30, 1935
Statement of Receipts and Disbursements for the year ending June 30, 1936
Investments, June 30, 1936
Mortgages Owned, June 30, 1936
Summary of Real Estate Owned, June 30, 1936

are in accordance with the books of account and, in our opinion, are true and correct.

TAIT, WELLER AND BAKER,
Accountants and Auditors.

Recommendations 1 and 2 were adopted.

On motion the report of the auditors was accepted.

The Rev. P. W. Roth, Chairman, presented the report of the Committee on Memorials from Constituent Synods.

REPORT OF COMMITTEE ON MEMORIALS FROM CONSTITUENT SYNODS

(For action on the recommendations in this report, see pp. 359, 432)

1. BOARD MEMBERSHIP: *From the Ministerium of Pennsylvania.*

"Believing that the interests of the Church are served by the distribution of the board membership of The United Lutheran Church in America among a large number of individuals; the Ministerium of Pennsylvania petitions The United Lutheran Church in America to adopt a rule providing that no person shall serve on more than one board at one and the same time."

> Reply: The subject matter of this memorial has been dealt with by the action of the Convention on Thursday morning when it adopted, for submission to the synods for action, the proposed amendment to the Constitution as submitted by the Executive Board. (Item IV, A, 1, of Executive Board Report.)

2. PRESENTATION OF GENERAL CAUSES TO CONGREGATIONS: *From the Synod of Iowa.*

"Whereas, in former years immeasurable good was done for the great causes of the Church at large by the personal appearance of representatives of boards and institutions in our several congregations;

"And whereas, in these days we believe that our congregations are losing interest in the great causes of the Church at large in spite of the best efforts of consecrated pastors and workers, and the distribution of such printed matter as we have now available;

"Therefore, be it resolved, That the United Lutheran Synod in Iowa in convention assembled in Sioux City, Iowa, on May 13, 1936, memorialize The United Lutheran Church in America to direct the various boards and institutions of our Church to make possible the personal appearance of representatives of boards and institutions in the congregations of The United Lutheran Church in America, bearing information and inspiration regarding the specific and general work of the Church.

"It is our belief that these personal appearances will be most helpful in arousing our people to a new sense of loyalty and responsibility in these most vital fields of endeavor."

> Reply: Since this matter is dealt with in substance from the report of the President, we recommend that it be further considered in connection with that report. (See p. 432.)

3. (a) CHANGE IN PRESENT PENSION SYSTEM: *From the United Synod of New York.*

"Whereas, the guaranteed pension for a minister, retired at age 65, should be $600; and $400 for a minister's widow, and

"Whereas, under the present pension system, such pensions are impossible,

"Be it resolved, That a plan be devised by which every ordained active minister should contribute yearly a certain percentage of his salary to the pension fund and that the congregation which he serves should pay a like amount yearly to the pension fund."

(b) MINISTERIAL RELIEF: *From the United Synod of New York.*

"Be it resolved, That the United Lutheran Church seek to arrange the rules and regulations of the Board of Ministerial Pensions and Relief so as to enable the Board to care for all cases of necessary ministerial relief on the territory of The United Lutheran Church in America."

Reply: These items are dealt with in the report of the Board of Ministerial Pensions and Relief. We therefore recommend that they be referred to the special committee to be appointed under the recommendations of the Board of Ministerial Pensions and Relief.

4. AGE RETIREMENT LIMIT FOR PASTORS: *From the Ministerium of Pennsylvania.*

"Resolved, That we petition the United Lutheran Church to consider the subject of an advanced age retirement limit for pastors, with a view to recommending to constituent synods a uniform practice to be observed in the matter of such age retirement."

Reply: Your Committee recommends that this memorial be referred to the Executive Board of The United Lutheran Church in America for study and report at the next convention.

5. (a) U. L. C. A. CONTROL OF THEOLOGICAL EDUCATION: *From the United Synod of New York.*

"Be it resolved, That The United Lutheran Church in America amend its Constitution in the following particulars:

"A. To amend Article VI, Section 4, item (a), by adding the words 'through the establishment, control and maintenance of theological seminaries' so that the amended Section shall read; 'To awaken, coordinate, and effectively direct the energies of the Church in such operations as the following:

"'(a) The training of ministers and teachers to be witnesses of the Word through the establishment, control and maintenance of theological seminaries.'

"B. To amend Article VIII, by adding Section 10, to read: 'As to Theological Seminaries for the Training of Ministers. The United Lutheran

Church in America, in accordance with the objects stated in Article VI of this Constitution, shall have power to establish, maintain, own and control such theological seminaries as it may deem necessary for the training of an adequate ministry for all its constituent synods.'"

(b) U. L. C. A. CONTROL OF THEOLOGICAL EDUCATION:
From the German Synod of Nebraska.

"Whereas, the following memorial of Synod, to the Ninth Biennial Convention of The United Lutheran Church in America, was declared unconstitutional at the said convention: 'It is the judgment of the German Evangelical Lutheran Synod of Nebraska that ministerial education should be controlled by the Church at large, and we memorialize The United Lutheran Church in America to take steps in this direction';

"Therefore, be it resolved, That the German Evangelical Lutheran Synod of Nebraska memorialize the Tenth Biennial Convention of The United Lutheran Church in America to change her Constitution to the effect of placing theological education under the control of the Church at large."

Reply: Your Committee recommends that these memorials dealing with U. L. C. A. control of theological education be referred to the Executive Board of the U. L. C. A. for study and report at the next convention.

6. CONSOLIDATION OF OFFICIAL PERIODICALS: *From the German Synod of Nebraska.*

"We memorialize the United Lutheran Church, convening in convention in Columbus, Ohio, to order final action on the consolidation of official periodicals by the auxiliaries of the Church, according to a previous memorial submitted in Philadelphia, 1932." (Cf. U. L. C. A. Minutes, 1932, pp. 444, 447, 449.)

Reply: Your Committee finds that the substance of this memorial is dealt with in the recommendations of
    (1) the Executive Board, Item II, 7, F
    (2) the Parish and Church School Board, recommendation V, B
We therefore recommend that it be submitted to the convention and considered in connection with the report of the Committee on President's Report. (See p. 432.)

7. LITERATURE ON MARRIAGE RELATIONS: *From the Ministerium of Pennsylvania.*

"Resolved, That we request the United Lutheran Church to secure the publication of literature setting forth the attitude of the Church toward the marriage relation in all its phases."

Reply: Your Committee recommends that this memorial be approved and referred to the Committee on Moral and Social Welfare, with instructions to prepare the desired literature.

8. USE OF THE TITLE "BISHOP": *From the Texas Synod.*

"Whereas, the title 'president' is a secular term and is neither found in God's Word nor has any historical basis;

"Therefore, be it resolved, That the Texas Synod memorialize The United Lutheran Church in America to recommend to its constituent synods that they change the title of their executive officer from 'president' to 'bishop,' in accordance with Biblical usage."

> Reply: In regard to the memorial from the Texas Synod "Use of the title 'Bishop,'" your Committee reports this memorial as impracticable of execution, and therefore recommends that it be disapproved. (Referred, see p. 359.)

9. MISSION WORK AMONG NEGROES IN THE SOUTH: *From the Georgia-Alabama Synod.*

"Whereas, among the large Negro population of the South, by reason of circumstances that have been beyond the control of the Negro race, the Gospel is still preached by many ministers whose ignorance and superstition, and whose crass methods of evangelism hinder its effectiveness;

"Whereas, with the enlightenment growing out of improved educational advantages, large numbers of Negroes are growing restless in their religious life and are eager for Christian training and worship of a more edifying and dignified character;

"Whereas, it is within the power of The United Lutheran Church in America to satisfy the desire of many earnest souls by establishing, in the South, Lutheran Churches, with well-trained ministers proclaiming the pure Word of God and promoting worship and Christian living in accordance with Lutheran forms and standards;

"Whereas, in view of the fact that the Southern territory is, for the Lutheran Church, distinctly the territory of The United Lutheran Church in America, it is the sincere opinion of the Georgia-Alabama Synod that no other Lutheran body can serve effectively the Southern Negro population; and

"Whereas, in the opinion of the aforesaid Synod, there are those who would willingly contribute, in addition to their present benevolences, sufficient sums to make possible the establishment of Lutheran work among Southern Negroes;

"Therefore, be it resolved, That the Georgia-Alabama Synod memorialize The United Lutheran Church in America:

"A. To acknowledge its due share of responsibility for the effective administration of the Gospel and all its benefits to the Negroes of the South.

"B. To begin, as soon as an adequate program can be initiated, the establishment of the Lutheran Church among Southern Negroes, with the ultimate object in view of establishing for them a Synod or Synods to be enrolled among the Synods of The United Lutheran Church in America.

"C. To effect, before beginning work, plans of such comprehensive character as to meet the conditions of possible Negro work in any part of the Church.

"D. To give consideration, if work is begun, to a plan which the proper officials of the Georgia-Alabama Synod will be prepared to submit."

Reply: Your Committee recommends

(1) That paragraph "A" be adopted.

(2) That paragraphs "B", "C", and "D" be referred to a special commission to be appointed by the President of the U. L. C. A., composed of representatives of the Board of American Missions, the Board of Education, the Inner Mission Board, and the memorializing synod, whose findings and recommendations shall be subject to the approval of the Executive Board of The United Lutheran Church in America, and upon such approval by said Executive Board, said commission shall be authorized forthwith to put said plan into operation. (Amended by Convention, see below.)

PAUL WAGNER ROTH, *Chairman,*
C. FRANKLIN KOCH, *Secretary.*

Recommendation 1 was received as information.

Recommendation 2 was adopted.

Recommendation 3 was adopted.

Recommendation 4 was adopted.

Recommendation 5. Question was raised concerning the propriety of the motion to refer, and the President ruled that such a motion was entirely in order. The recommendation was adopted.

Recommendation 6 was adopted.

Recommendation 7 was adopted.

Recommendation 8. In connection with this recommendation, the following resolution was presented and adopted:

Resolved, That a special commission of seven be appointed by the President of the Church to study the whole matter of the title "Bishop" in The United Lutheran Church in America and to report to the next convention of the Church concerning its consonance with Scripture, its historical implications, its desirability and feasibility among us, and the changes in constitution and practice that would be necessitated by its introduction among us.

Recommendation 9, (1) was adopted.

Recommendation 9, (2). By motion this paragraph was amended by striking out the words following "The United Lutheran Church in America." The item as amended was adopted as follows:

"(2) That paragraphs "B", "C", and "D", be referred to a special commission to be appointed by the President of the U. L. C. A., composed of representatives of the Board of American Missions, the Board of Education, the Inner Mission Board, and the memorializing synod, whose findings and recommendations shall be subject to the approval of the Executive Board of The United Lutheran Church in America."

The Rev. J. C. Mattes was given the privilege of the floor, in accordance with recommendation 4 of the Committee of Reference and Counsel, and presented the following which was adopted: (See p. 307.)

"Be it resolved, that the Executive Board be instructed to prepare the necessary amendments to the Constitution and By-laws of the U. L. C. A. so as to provide that the term of office for the President, the Treasurer and the Secretary be for six years instead of two years as at present; and that such proposed amendment be presented to the 1938 convention."

The Rev. C. B. Foelsch, Chairman, presented the report of the Committee on Moral and Social Welfare, and made such comments as seemed necessary to him to give the basic background for the recommendations of the report.

REPORT OF THE COMMITTEE ON MORAL AND SOCIAL WELFARE

(For action on the recommendations in this report, see pp. 375, 376, 377)

PRESENT-DAY EDUCATIONAL AGENCIES AND THE CHRISTIAN LIFE

INTRODUCTION

The Savannah Convention instructed the committee to continue the study of facts and influences in modern education in relation to morals. Because of the specialized character of certain aspects of the task, the Church requested the Board of Education to carry on this study in the field of higher education, the Parish and Church School Board in the field of primary and secondary education, and this committee in those non-scholastic fields which have a wide influence—e. g., the radio, the motion picture, the public press, etc.

Upon the basis of work done in these several fields, the following findings are reported.

I. THE GENERAL PICTURE

Christian Education, in all its branches, must be a primary interest of the Church, because it is the vital factor in developing an individual and corporate Christian life.

Theoretically, the state, in its scheme of education, must not encroach upon the sphere of religion. Practically, however, government-controlled education works to the detriment of the Christian life, for however well the state may guard against the teaching of positive religion in its schools, it does not, and cannot effectively, eliminate the opposite tendency.

A multitude of subtle influences which tend to discredit religion and the Church, has crept into state schools. This is true because many teachers (even some who are careful not to make direct attacks upon religion) do indirectly, often stealthily, seek to undermine the faith of their students, and alienate them from their loyalty to the Church.

This is true, not only in institutions of higher education, but also in many primary and secondary schools. The credulity of youth is exploited. The theories of science are paraded as finally authenticated conclusions. Teachers go out of their way to belittle the idea and the ideals of theistic religion. The fountain-head of this vicious anti- and irreligious propaganda is all too frequently the school which specializes in the training of teachers.

Thoroughly indoctrinated, only too often with the negatives of life, its graduates take teaching posts in public schools and colleges, and, in large numbers, become propagandists for materialism, rather than trustworthy teachers of truth.

These statements are based on facts discovered in the course of our investigations two years ago in selected institutions of higher education, especially those which emphasize special courses for the teaching profession, and on the results of studies made, during this biennium, of the basic spirit of certain self-constituted, but widely reverenced, authorities in the field of education.

Books revealing their underlying principles have been read, as well as articles in general and specialized journals. Curricula have been studied. Prescribed reading courses have been examined. The work of other investigators in this field has been evaluated. Concerning the religious and moral influences of secular education the conclusion is inevitable, "Weighed in the balances, and found wanting."

Materialistic concepts of the universe menace the whole system. In consequence, as must necessarily be the result if man be persuaded that he has no nobler parentage than the dust and to the dust must return forever, the noble ideals of truth and beauty and goodness, in the genuine Christian sense, are in danger of being relegated to the rubbish heap.

And morals? How shall there be morality, in any adequate sense, if tomorrow we die? The best one may hope for is a lame espousal of the proposition, that even though man is an unimpressive creature, the chance by-product of unintelligent might and doomed to the oblivion from which he came, "It is still better to be brave than a coward, and well-informed than a dolt."

The Church's program of education has also been critically scrutinized. Offering, we believe, the only effective antidote to the insidious poison of secularism and non-morality and immorality, at an hour when atheistic communism is attacking the very citadels of our civilization, it is imperative that we know just where we stand in our educational efforts.

Certain fears, often expressed, are now proved to be well-grounded. Generally speaking, it is clear that neither our efforts at education in the local parish nor our programs of higher education, are at all adequate.

Religious education in the home, despite the solemn covenants made by parents and sponsors at the baptismal font, is often, from the first, a puny, sickly thing, and in many a home virtually non-existent. (See Recommendation 1, p. 372.)

So it comes about, that at six years of age, the average child enters the public school, with its spiritual life hardly at the embryonic stage, when it might well, with proper home conditions, be expected to possess the rudiments of a divinely-awakened soul life, well enough instructed to discriminate definitely, if unconsciously, between the true and the false that falls upon its ears in the school room—in matters of morals and religion.

The years spent in the public school are usually likewise years of inadequate, desultory instruction in the field of religious faith. Even today, with all our widely-heralded advances, the church school is usually hardly more than a pedagogically anemic Sunday school, meeting for an hour a week often with woefully ill-equipped and frequently listless and careless teachers and officers in charge, and with the average pupil absent at least one session in three. Here and there only, do we reinforce the work of the Sunday school with a short-term daily vacation Bible school, or a week-day session of the church school.

At junior high school age, our boys and girls usually enroll in the catechetical class, for instruction preparatory to confirmation. Many pastors use this opportunity profitably. All in all, we are giving more time and effort to this phase of our educational work than ever before in the story of American Lutheranism. But even forty hours of systematic instruction—in distressingly few cases are there more (often many fewer)—are inadequate, as a written or oral examination of the average confirmation class might easily (and often does) reveal. (The practice of conducting catechetical classes in connection with Sunday school sessions is bad, both from the standpoint of the class and of the school.)

With the day of confirmation past, too many pupils and parents count the child's religious education completed. Our average boy or girl has had a smattering of home training, a half hour a week (some weeks!)

in the church school and from twenty to forty hours (?) of catechetical instruction. To hold his interest in the Sunday school from then on is a difficult problem, but offers fruitful possibilities, for until now, the high school years, very largely, have been blanks in the youth's religious training. (See Recommendation 2, p. 372.)

When he enters college, if it be a Christian institution, the situation is much improved. He is expected to attend chapel services and, in more than ninety per cent of the colleges, to take courses in the department of Bible and religion. He comes daily into contact with teachers, who consciously and unconsciously inculcate the ideals of true religion. (A teacher in a Christian college who is not a practising Christian himself is an anomaly—as investigation of the facts has demonstrated.) His school environment is (one speaks generally!) more definitely conducive to growth in Christian character than any he has had before. If his personality has not been malformed during his pre-college years, there is a fine likelihood that he will one day issue forth from the institution with stalwart Christian character, well-calculated to be a positive force for good and for God wherever he takes up his abode. (See Recommendations 3, 4 and 5, pp. 372, 373.)

II. THE FIELD OF PRIMARY AND SECONDARY EDUCATION
(To be prepared by the Parish and Church School Board.)

The Parish and Church School Board was asked:
1—To make a study of the stated objectives of primary and secondary education; 2—To make an evaluation of certain movements in primary and secondary education, such as the character education movement, and the new week-day education movement.

These projects, together with a survey of parish education in the U. L. C. A., are definitely under way, but because of limitation of time it is not possible to present findings at this time. The Board will complete these studies and report to the Church as early as possible.

III. THE FIELD OF HIGHER EDUCATION
(Prepared by the Executive Secretary of the Board of Education.)

The Board of Education was authorized "to carry on this study in the field of higher education in colleges and universities, both church and secular." This request of the Church was given careful and extended consideration by the Board of Education. At the January, 1935, meeting, the ultimate purpose of the study was approved but the Board believed this would require "an expenditure of money and effort beyond anything reasonably obtainable at the present time." The suggestion was made that representatives of the boards and agencies involved confer "with a view to limiting the study (a) to a scope within our means, and (b) to a sphere of study where there may be co-operation." Accordingly, there was mutual agreement that this phase of the study be limited to the summarization of some of the results of certain investigations already made in this field.

For the sake of information the studies on which this report is based are listed here. Economy of space makes future reference only by number desirable. Naturally such facts are noted as may be directly related to our problem. It must not be thought that this report is a summary of the whole of these books and articles. Data regarding the status of Lutheran colleges on file in the office of the Board were consulted.

1. Anderson, O. V.—The Place of Religion in the Life of Freshmen at the Colleges of the Augustana Synod.
   The Augustana Quarterly, Vol. XIII, 1934, pp. 126-152; 233-256; 348-374.
2. Beam, Lura—Classroom Instruction in Two Hundred and Fifty Colleges.
   Christian Education, Vol. VIII. (March, 1925.)
3. Blough, W. H.—The Unique Contribution of the Denominational College in our National System of Liberal Arts Education.
   A Master of Arts Thesis, submitted at Ohio University, 1930. (Unpub.)
4. Coons, J. E.—Religious Trends in Methodist Colleges.
   The Proceedings of the Educational Association of the Methodist Church, 1935, pp. 33-40.
5. Edwards, Artman and Fisher—Undergraduates.
   Doubleday, Doran and Co., Inc. New York, 1928. Pp. 366.
6. Gilbert, Dan—Crucifying Christ in our Colleges.
   The Danielle Publishers, Cal. 234 pp.
7. Hartshorne, Stearns, and Uphaus—Standards and Trends in Religious Education.
   The Yale University Press, New Haven. 1933. Pp. 230.
8. Katz and Allport—Students' Attitudes.
   The Craftsman Press, Inc., Syracuse. 1931. Pp. 408.
9. Parsons, P. A.—Report on The Survey of Religious and Character Influences on State University and College Campuses in the Area West of the Rocky Mountains.
   Eugene, Oregon, 1933 (Mimeographed).
10. Wickey and Eckhart—A Study of Courses in Bible, Religion, Religious Education and Related Subjects in American Universities and Colleges.
    Christian Education, Vol. XX (October, 1936).

A. *Religious Instruction*

During 1935-36 the Council of Church Boards of Education carried on an extensive inquiry into the status of instruction in Bible, religion, and related subjects in all the colleges and universities in America, including state, private, Protestant and Roman Catholic (10). Of 858 institutions solicited 826 sent replies. More than fifty per cent (421) of those replying have some requirement in this field for graduation. Naturally state schools do not include this requirement. The average for all non-tax-supported schools is 91 per cent; for the Protestant colleges 81 per cent; for the Catholic colleges 95 per cent. Of the Protestant schools 70 per cent offer a major in this field. From 765 institutions came information showing that they gave 3,817 courses in this field of which 29 per cent were in the Bible. State schools give four semester hours, while the church-related colleges give twenty-two semester hours. The colleges of the United Lutheran Church give an average of twenty semester hours. The 765 institutions reported an enrolment of 539,225 of whom 147,884 were enrolled in religious courses. The church-related colleges reported an enrolment of 198,652 with 130,352 taking courses in religion. Of the 279,802 enrolled at state schools, 10,295 took courses in this field. The average number of semester hours in this field required for graduation is eight, which is an increase of one in comparison with a study made of 100 colleges in 1930-31 (7). The requirements range from two to twenty-four. The United Lutheran colleges have an average requirement of eight, and their range is from four to twelve.

The establishment of schools of religion or chairs of religion, privately supported, at state colleges and universities is an important factor in the number of students taking these courses at these institutions.

There has been a great increase in the number of state schools offering courses in this field. For example, in 1922-23 fifty per cent of these schools offered such courses; in 1931-32, eighty per cent; in 1934-35, ninety-one per cent. While Bible courses are given as literary subjects, and ethics and other subjects may not be closely related to Christian principles, it is encouraging to note the increased attention given to this field of study.

However, more important is the emergence of religion in other courses as reported in the study made of ten state colleges and universities west of the Mississippi river (9). The most frequent emergence was found in English, including literature, history, education, and sociology. The instructors in English and other languages and literature are, according to student judgment, the most sympathetic towards religion, with instructors in history and education ranking very high in sympathetic interest. The teachers of sociology and anthropology appeared to be sympathetic but were disturbing although helpful.

The significance of this emergence is that in these non-religious courses the student's faith is likely to be disturbed. Studies indicate that both in high school and in colleges and universities, the most disturbing courses are in the biological and physical sciences. Others named are literature, the social sciences, psychology and philosophy. Dan Gilbert in "Crucifying Christ in our Colleges," gives evidence to the same effect (6).

B. *Religious Agencies and Provisions*

The institutions provide a convocation and/or chapel exercise. In state institutions these operate more for the social unification of the student body than for the development of their moral and religious lives. Some universities have chaplains and directors of religious activities. Church colleges give more emphasis to the place of chapel service in the lives of students, but do not give sufficient attention and thought to making the services inspiring and effective. The atmosphere of worship is too often missing, and the addresses are often boresome. It is the judgment of students that the administrations and faculties are not doing what they should in the direction of developing the religious life of the students.

Several denominations are quite active on the campuses of the larger state and private universities in developing the spiritual life of their students, in giving religious counsel, and in conserving for their churches this potential lay leadership. The pastors working with these students have been able in considerable degree to awaken them to the moral and religious issues of the day and to show them the adequacy of the Christian faith. Accurate figures are not available, but it is the judgment of these student pastors that there is an increase of recruits for the ministry and foreign missions from the state universities.

The students themselves are often active in forming organizations and agencies which will help satisfy their religious desires. The Ys have experienced a decline in influence over the student mind. Some denominations have their own student organizations. The effectiveness of these varies with institutions, with regions, and with student generations.

Inquiring as to the helpfulness of the university or college experience in solving the moral and spiritual problems of students one study (9) found that forty per cent of the students at certain state institutions were not helped. A study of fifteen Methodist colleges indicates that the religious experience of their students is made definitely more real and vital (4). For example, in comparing their status with that before entering college, for seventy-one per cent God was more real; seventy per cent were more influenced by the life and teachings of Jesus; sixty-seven per cent were more resolved to do God's will; sixty-eight per cent prayed the same or more.

C. *Religious Attitudes*

In considering the reglious attitudes of students much weight must be given to the experiences of the students while at home and in the high schools. It can be safely stated that most students come from religious homes. This has been found to be true in sections of the country where the percentage of church membership is even lower than forty.

It was found that eighty per cent of the students who joined church before going to college retained their membership. Facts also show that most of the students who do not go to church or Sunday school while in college stopped before they went to college.

Several studies concur in their conclusion that students become less religious as they go through college. Only one study (3) is available comparing the religious attitudes of students at church and state colleges. Professor Blough of Wittenberg College, found that the students at both institutions tend to grow away from the church during the first two years. In the state college this tendency continues in the last two years; in the church college there is a tendency to return during the last two years. This seems to indicate a very positive and constructive religious influence on the part of the church college, as it should be.

Various factors determine this change of religious attitudes. All youth go through a period of change of ideas and ideals at that time; college youth are not peculiar in this respect. Perhaps the degree of adjustment is greater in college students than in non-college youth. Subjects studied and books read are important factors. Teachers and fellow students are probably the most important influences. At state schools some teachers are actively Christian and exert a great influence; some teachers are lukewarm and indifferent; and some are definitely negative and antagonistic. Of the faculties of church colleges the same might be said, although the proportion of the three groups would vary greatly with the negative and antagonistic group practically absent. However, we dare not close our eyes to the fact that sometimes a teacher gets on the faculty of a church college and exerts a definitely negative influence. Lutheran colleges are not excepted.

D. *Some Observations*

1. It is encouraging to note that the requirement of credits in Bible, religion, and related subjects for graduation is not decreasing. All Lutheran colleges should require at least eight credits in this field.

2. It is hopeful to find so many courses in religion being offered at state colleges and universities, but students need to be warned that religion and Christianity are not the same.

3. Religious homes and religious instruction prior to college experience are positive factors in assisting students in the necessary adjustments which must be made during those important years.

4. The atmosphere of the institution, created by the example and ideas of faculty and students, is pre-eminent in determining the type of changes which a student experiences. It becomes highly important that youth be directed and encouraged in their selection of educational institutions where the atmosphere is most likely to be Christian.

5. Church colleges should be encouraged in their efforts to develop and maintain a Christian atmosphere on their campuses. Too often these efforts are counteracted by pressure from parents, alumni and even some of the church constituency.

6. The Church should be encouraged in its efforts to serve the religious needs of students at state colleges and universities. The students of America constitute the greatest mission field in the world. Here are potentialities of leadership which the Church must capture for the cause of Christianity and the Kingdom of God.

III—NON-ACADEMIC AGENCIES

From among the several non-academic agencies which play an important part in molding character, this committee chose the motion picture for particular evaluation, both because of its wide influence and because it has recently been so much in the public eye.

Investigation reveals that more than half the population of the United States and Canada attends the motion picture theatre, on the average, once a week. More than one-third of those who attend are minors, and at least one-seventh are under fourteen. It requires no prophet, as one looks at these figures, to see how gigantic are the possibilities, for good or for evil, of the motion picture. All who attend are affected, positively or negatively, especially the children.

A few years ago, the motion picture was at its lowest, as regards quality and moral tone. The Motion Picture Research Council reports that in 115 pictures that followed one another across the screen of a mid-western theatre during an early year of this decade, 408 crimes were actually committed (including fifty-four murders) and forty-three additional ones attempted.

This, of course, was typical. And usually, the feature film of that day mixed in much cheap eroticism and plain lewdness. It was thought that such sex-appeal would assure the constant clicking of the turn-stiles. At least the producers suggested that was the purpose of their scheme. "We must give the public *what it wants*."—how often one heard this apology for vileness.

In the light of the last biennium's developments, such talk is proved twaddle. For investigation reveals that (with increased patronage!) there has been improvement in the quality of pictures produced and shown, during the last two years.

This has been due, not to a spirit of repentance and resulting good works on the part of the producers, but to the effective public crusade for decency launched almost simultaneously by many Christian bodies in 1934. The threat of empty tills in the box offices was strong enough to free the screen from much of its sordidness.

One fears, however, that with a lessening of the public clamor against the "immorality, irreverence, and untruthful glamor" of the screen, the unclean spirit may presently return to the motion picture house and fill it with vileness worse than before. The program which proved so effective during the past two years must be continued. **(See Recommendation 6, p. 373.)**

The most dangerous injury done by the still far too frequently exhibited unworthy motion picture is to the character of the millions of young children and adolescents who attend them. On the other hand, those films which measure up to the highest canons of Christian good taste, and artistic excellence, often make a happy and worthy contribution to the developing mind. Wise parents will carefully guide their children in choosing excellent pictures only. Further, because investigation seems to show that too frequent "movie going," no matter how fine the films, is hurtful to the child's mental equilibrium, wise parents will definitely limit the frequency of their children's going to the movies. **(See Recommendation 7, p. 373.)**

Making full allowance for the progress that has been made, there are still many pictures below decent standards, both as regards artistic excellence and good taste, to say nothing about indecency and positive lewdness. At present our people have no adequate helps to make possible choosing the good and avoiding the bad, among the pictures scheduled for exhibition. It would be at least a beginning in remedying this situation, if our official church papers, without assuming responsibility for the accuracy of the reviews, were to publish the findings, from week to week and month to month, of a reliable agency making such evaluations. **(See Recommendation 8, p. 373.)**

Finally, investigation disclosed that the chief difficulty faced by the theatre owner in meeting his public's demands for quality and good taste in pictures lies in the trade practises known as "block booking" and "blind selling."

Block booking is that trade arrangement which compels the exhibitor to take all, or none, of the entire year's output of a motion picture producer-distributor. He may not buy a few selected pictures from each of the eight major producers (who are a virtual monopoly) and build up his year's program by selection.

Blind selling is the practice, also followed by the "Big Eight," of selling pictures to local exhibitors in advance of production and without any adequate information as to the proposed content of the film.

With these practises in vogue, it is quite impossible for the local community to be sure of getting the kind of pictures it wants or to enforce the moral standards it believes in. To do it under present conditions, either the exhibitor must purchase the complete output of a half dozen producers and choose from that great bulk the pictures the community wants on his screen, and discard the rest (but paying the producer for all) or he may buy the "block" of only one or two exhibitors, which as far as number of films is concerned, would be just right for his house, show those he discovers to measure up to his standards, and leave his theatre dark on other evenings! In either case quick bankruptcy would overtake him.

Mere boycotting of bad pictures will not cure the ills of the cinema. It will help, but must be reinforced by another remedy: an act of the government to prevent block booking and blind selling. Until these practices are discontinued, there will be no practicable way for any community to be sure of getting the pictures that meet its standards of quality and morality.

An article in a metropolitan daily, some months ago, makes this pointed observation in behalf of community freedom of picture selection: (If there were no block booking or blind selling) "each exhibitor would have to take the business risk of estimating correctly the tastes of his customers, and educators, dramatic critics, and moral leaders in each community would be able to exert effectively whatever influence they can command."

Judging from the progress made by interested legislators in behalf of an act to prohibit block-booking and blind-selling, there is reason for hope that the next Congress of the United States will enact such a bill, to the great benefit of the cause of clean pictures. There will, however, be no easy victory. The motion picture interests are powerful and influential, and will continue vigorously to oppose such legislation. Now is the time for action on our part also. Let all who believe in this cause promote it by urgent pleas in its behalf to the legislators who represent their states and congressional districts. Let us have community freedom in the selection of motion pictures! (See Recommendation 9, p. 373.)

MATTERS OF GENERAL SOCIAL INTEREST

Although, since the last convention, there has been significant improvement in the motion picture situation, in other spheres of interest, the opposite has been true. (See Recommendation 10, p. 373.) (Notable exception: the desperado type of lawlessness in the United States is being effectively and summarily dealt with by agents of the Federal Department of Justice.)

Gambling of all kinds is more flagrant than ever. In an increased number of states, it has legislative sanction. In others, clever schemes are being used to bring thinly-disguised lotteries (e.g., Theatre "Bank Nights") within the letter of the law. Devices to catch the pennies and nickels of youth, trickily catering to the sin of greed, are found in increasing numbers in every community, and even when cleaned out through a flare-up of civic righteousness, soon return because they are profitable to the professed Christians and others, who make place for them on their sales-counters. In the United States, and in Canada, the present gambling mania is imperilling integrity of character and putting a premium upon laziness, shiftlessness and positive dishonesty. (See Recommendation 11, p. 373.)

The program of peace has been flouted. Wars of conquest have been waged and the rights of minority populations have been trampled by militaristic powers, with the shedding of much innocent blood. Increasingly, armaments have been built up, and the fear of another world orgy of blood and death has seized the nations. The United States has voted the largest peace-time budget in its history for the maintenance and expansion of its fighting establishment and is now reported to be spending more money for military and naval purposes than any other nation of the world. (See Recommendations 12 and 13, pp. 373, 374.)

Open vice and drunkenness continue to be major problems. From all quarters come reports of the growing brazenness of the liquor traffic. The old saloon, which, it was promised by those who advocated repeal of the prohibition amendment was never again to be known in the land, is back with a vengeance in many of the states. The Dominion of Canada has its problem with this evil also, as witness the reports concerning the great menace to morals the "Beer Parlor" in Ontario has become. Alcohol, up to its old tricks and more, e.g., the intemperate "cocktail habit" is debauching youth, making highways dangerous, breaking up homes, and, behind screened doors and windows of saloons, is making game of Christian standards of decency and sobriety. (See Recommendation 14, p. 374.)

Divorce has continued a scandal in the United States. Progressive polygamy raises its lewd head in almost every state, with South Carolina the only commonwealth in the union that has no provision for divorce. In states that have laws designed to prevent unduly hasty marriages, the law is frequently circumvented by the issuing of quick licenses in neighboring states, with lax regulations. Folk marrying hastily, repent at leisure and soon after are prone to turn up in the divorce court. (See Recommendations 15 and 16, p. 374.)

Problems of social reconstruction, including re-employment, proper housing, relief from abject poverty, the abolition of class feeling and all measures conducive to the realization of Christian brotherhood, are urgently important today.

Christian business men, like all followers of our Lord, are solemnly obligated to act as God's stewards. Capital and labor are meant to work together co-operatively in public service rather than in opposition to each other for selfish ends. The earnings and profits of a business should be justly distributed among all parties to the business. The exploitation of wage earners ought not to be tolerated in civilized society. Ruthless, predatory competition among business enterprises should be halted. The looting of small investors through the low practices of "corporation sharks" should be regarded as a crime drastically to be dealt with by society. Investors, managers, workers, and the community should be partners in the effort to bring about an increasingly Christian economic order, able to solve our present distressing social problems, in harmony with the brotherly spirit of the Gospel. Unless it has the character to conduct its affairs equitably in freedom, the time may come when business will be under a strong-armed dictatorship, un-christian in ideal and in practice. (See Recommendation 17, p. 374.)

The ills considered in this report, and whatever other social ills plague society today, have their common origin in unregenerate human nature. The root cause is sin.

The social order can never be made good, until the individuals who compose it have become regenerate men and women. It is proper that the Church should speak out with prophetic voice against rampant social evil, boldly exposing hidden or open subversive forces, and summoning good men and true to hold fast the noble things of life. But this is not sufficient.

Our primary concern must be the winning of individual souls, by the power of the holy Spirit through the faithful proclamation of the Word. For the Gospel, lived truly in individual lives—and only the Gospel—is the effective cure for society's sorrows.

When men and women have been born anew and have been taught to love the true and the beautiful and the good, they will no longer give themselves to works of darkness. When the mass of humanity shall have learned to follow our Lord's way of life, as individuals, the moral order of society will become increasingly beautiful and brotherly. Here is our only hope for a Christian social order. (See Recommendation 18, p. 374.)

RECOMMENDATIONS
(For action, see pp. 375, 376, 377.)

1. We urge our pastors, church school leaders, and parents to give special emphasis to Christian education by the home, and commend to them our new literature in this field, especially "The Nursery Packet," and the manual, "In the Nursery."

2. To help compensate for the absence of religious training in the public schools, we call upon our congregations to find and develop more consecrated and more efficient workers for places of leadership in the educational program of the parish, especially for the senior and young peoples' age groups.

3. To meet conditions in the circles of higher education, we commend every effort made by our Board of Education and by our colleges to offer such educational advantages under definite Christian influences as will attract our young people to our Church institutions.

4. We advise parents to obtain the help of their pastors in careful investigation of courses, teachers, and general environment before they choose an institution of higher learning for their children, with especial concern about the place given the Christian religion in the colleges under consideration, and we call attention, with earnest emphasis, to the new book of the Board of Education, "Going to College," which issued from the press last month.

5. We recommend hearty co-operation on the part of parents and pastors with those agencies of the Church which are serving Lutheran students in non-church institutions with pastoral care and Christian instruction.

6. We challenge our people to attend only wholesome, decent, worthy pictures since degraded films work havoc with their own moral well-being and make them accomplices in a conspiracy to enrich motion picture producers at the expense of society's moral order.

7. We urge upon all parents the wisdom of making it a rule that their minor children shall not attend a motion picture until they shall have satisfied themselves that the films to be shown are of wholesome character for juveniles, and that their children shall not normally have permission to attend the theatre more than once a week.

8. We request the editors of our several publications, if feasible, to secure the service of a reliable film estimate agency, and publish its evaluation of current films regularly for the information of our constituency.

9. We challenge our people to further the cause of free community selection of motion pictures, by using their influence in every legitimate way in behalf of the abolition of the motion picture trade practices known as "block booking" and "blind selling."

10. We call attention to the flood of indecent literature, especially magazines, vile beyond belief, freely and contrary to law on sale at news stands and other public places in many communities, and recommend that pastors and other leaders investigate this matter in their own communities and co-operate with local law enforcement officers and others for the elimination of this evil, as has been done in Lancaster, Harrisburg and other places. (Amended by the Convention, see p. 377.)

11. We request pastors and church leaders to urge upon Christians the need for conscientious avoidance of everything that bears any taint of the gambling spirit; to be scrupulously careful that all money-raising efforts of their respective congregations or auxiliary organizations be above reproach in this respect; to seek the repeal of all legislation that legalizes gambling; and to use every Christian means within their power to destroy this foe, so destructive of the moral fibre of our civilization. (Amended by the Convention, see p. 377.)

12. We reaffirm our devotion to the cause of peace, and urge upon our people their full co-operation in the adoption of measures designed

(a) to create the will to peace; (b) to assure our country's neutrality, if war should come; and (c) to limit our seemingly extravagant expenditures on the military establishment of the United States. (Amended by the Convention, see p. 377.)

13. We deprecate the growing militaristic spirit of many nations and call upon our constituency, to be often in penitent prayer to the Prince of Peace to have mercy upon the world's erring peoples and to lead them in paths of peace and world brotherhood.

14. Having due regard to the growing menace of the liquor traffic, we request the Executive Board to direct the proper agencies of the church to publish and distribute educational literature dealing with this evil; and we admonish our pastors, our other church leaders, and the parents in our homes to use every effort to enlighten our youth on the meaning of temperance.

15. We request our pastors, wherever possible, to hold conferences with couples planning to marry, with the purpose of emphasizing the sacredness and enduring character of the married state, according to the plan of God.

16. We reaffirm our position, holding that no Lutheran minister should perform a marriage ceremony for a divorced person, until he is convinced that the individual is the innocent party in a divorce occasioned by grounds recognized by the Church as valid. (See U. L. C. Minutes 1930, page 112, Item 6.)

17. We affirm the evangelical principle, for the conduct of all business, that Christian brotherhood must afford the spirit, and Christian stewardship must determine the practices by which injustice is removed and mutual good will and brotherly fair-play are established, as between employers and employees, and between producers and consumers, and by which a truly moral and sound economic order must be secured.

18. We reaffirm our conviction that it is the task of the Church to proclaim principle, and to be concerned about root causes, rather than symptoms of moral evil in society, and request our pastors and lay-leaders to give further study to Dr. Greever's "Facts and Forces in the Social Order," so that we may not be tempted to substitute the legalistic regulation of life for the power of the Gospel in our efforts to make society Christian.

STANLEY BILLHEIMER
F. A. DRESSEL
N. WILLISON
G. MORRIS SMITH
PAUL H. HEISEY
W. A. SADTLER
J. HENRY HARMS
WILLIAM C. ZIMMANN
E. E. FLACK
CHARLES B. FOELSCH
Committee

Mr. W. H. Hager, a member of the Committee, expressed his dissent from the positions stated by the chairman, and upon request was granted the privilege of having his name removed as a signer of the report. Accordingly the name of Mr. Hager was removed from the signers of the report.

The time for adjournment having arrived, the President announced that the recommendations of the Committee would be placed in the list of unfinished business. Upon motion the further consideration of the report was made a special order for the opening of business immediately after the devotions Tuesday morning.

At 5 : 20 P. M., the Convention adjourned with prayer by the Rev. R. L. Lang.

MONDAY EVENING

The banquet of the Laymen's Movement was held in the assembly hall of the hotel, opening at 6 : 45. The attendance was probably the best in the history of that agency. Mr. W. H. Hager presided in an able manner. Banquet music was furnished in the lighter vein by banquet songs led by the Rev. Ross Stover. Instrumental and vocal numbers of classical music were rendered most acceptably by members of the Department of Music from Wittenberg College.

The speakers for the occasion were President F. H. Knubel, Secretary Arthur P. Black, and the Rev. Ross Stover. Dr. Knubel spoke of the essentials of true religion; Mr. Black presented the purposes and plans of the Laymen's Movement; and Dr. Stover paid fitting tribute to Mr. Harvey C. Miller, deceased. Mr. J. L. Clark, President of the Laymen's Movement, was introduced and received a very cordial response to his words of greeting.

EIGHTH SESSION

DESHLER-WALLICK HOTEL
Columbus, Ohio
Tuesday, October 20, 1936, 8 : 45 A. M.

Matins were conducted by the Rev. R. Homer Anderson.

The Convention was called to order by the President.

By unanimous consent the report of Tellers Commitee No. 2 was heard before the Special Order for the day.

For the *Board of Foreign Missions* each of the following received a majority of the votes cast:

Rev. H. H. Beidleman   Frank Howard
Rev. C. M. Snyder

The President declared them elected.

For the *Board of American Missions* and the *West Indies Mission Board* each of the following received a majority of the votes cast:

Rev. Chester S. Simonton   H. W. Ungerer

The President declared them elected.

For the *Board of Education* each of the following received a majority of the votes cast:

Rev. F. K. Fretz   R. J. Seeger

The President declared them elected.

For the *Inner Mission Board* each of the following received a majority of the votes cast:

Rev. Herman Brezing
Rev. P. D. Brown   P. P. Hagan

The President declared them elected.

For the *Board of Publication* each of the following received a majority of the votes cast:

Rev. S. W. Herman   James L. Fisher

The President declared them elected.

For the *Board of Ministerial Pensions and Relief* each of the following received a majority of the votes cast:

Rev. J. H. Reble   H. J. Herbst

The President declared them elected.

For the *Parish and Church School Board,* the Rev. R. Homer Anderson received a majority of the votes cast. The President declared him elected.

For the *Board of Deaconess Work* each of the following received a majority of the votes cast:

Rev. H. F. Baughman   F. J. Singley

The President declared them elected and stated that one clergyman was yet to be elected. The Tellers passed ballots on the floor of the Convention to complete the election.

The Special Order for the morning was called.

The Rev. C. B. Foelsch, Chairman, presented the recommendations of the Committee on Moral and Social Welfare.
(See p. 372.)

On motion the recommendations were considered seriatim.

Recommendations 1, 2, 3, 4, 5, 6, 7, 8, and 9 were adopted.

Recommendation 10. An amendment was presented to strike out the words "call attention to" after the word "we" and insert the word "condemn." The amendment was adopted and the recommendation as amended was adopted as follows:

"We condemn the flood of indecent literature, especially magazines, vile beyond belief, freely and contrary to law on sale at news stands and other public places in many communities, and recommend that pastors and other leaders investigate this matter in their own communities and co-operate with local law enforcement officers and others for the elimination of this evil, as has been done in Lancaster, Harrisburg and other places."

Recommendation 11. An amendment was presented to insert the words "scriptural and therefore" after the word "be" and before the words "above reproach in this respect." The amendment was adopted and the recommendation as amended was adopted as follows:

"We request pastors and church leaders to urge upon Christians the need for conscientious avoidance of everything that bears any taint of the gambling spirit; to be scrupulously careful that all money-raising efforts of their respective congregations or auxiliary organizations be scriptural and therefore above reproach in this respect; to seek the repeal of all legislation that legalizes gambling; and to use every Christian means within their power to destroy this foe, so destructive of the moral fibre of our civilization."

Recommendation 12. An amendment, to strike out " (a) " after the word "designed" and before the words "to create" and to strike out all following the word "peace" to the end of the paragraph and to insert the following in its stead, was presented:

"and to this end we recommend to our people the thoughtful and prayerful consideration of the following possible methods of avoiding war, and request the educational agencies of our Church to provide material on these and kindred themes in their treatment of the cause of peace,
  (1) mandatory neutrality legislation
  (2) removal of munition manufacture from private industry
  (3) limitation of military expenditure
  (4) popular referendum before our country can enter war, except in case of invasion."

The amendment was adopted and the recommendation as amended was adopted as follows:

"We reaffirm our devotion to the cause of peace, and urge upon our people their full co-operation in the adoption of measures designed to create the will to peace; and to this end we recommend to our people the thoughtful and prayerful consideration of the following possible methods of avoiding war, and request the educational agencies of our Church to provide material on these and kindred themes in their treatment of the cause of peace,

(1) mandatory neutrality legislation
(2) removal of munition manufacture from private industry
(3) limitation of military expenditure
(4) popular referendum before our country can enter war, except in case of invasion."

Recommendations 13, 14, 15, 16, 17, and 18 were adopted.

The President announced that such recommendations as had been offered by individuals for addition to the above report, by general consent, would be presented through the Committee of Reference and Counsel, and if adopted would be regarded as a part of this report.

The Chairman of the Committee of Reference and Counsel presented Dr. George W. Brown, representing the American Bible Society. Dr. Brown, after brief references to special features of the American Bible Society, expressed warm appreciation of the support given to the Society by The United Lutheran Church in America.

Mr. Milton J. Deck, President of the Lutheran Brotherhood, presented the report of the Committee on Lutheran Brotherhoods, in place of the chairman of the Committee who was not in attendance upon the Convention.

REPORT OF THE COMMITTEE ON LUTHERAN BROTHERHOODS

(For recommendations and action, see pp. 381, 382, 419, 431.)

During another biennium the men of the United Lutheran Church in America, full of faith, obedient to the Word, loyal to the truth, manifesting love, radiating hope, through their Congregational Brotherhoods and in varied capacities within the Church, have held high the banner of His cross, and have unselfishly promoted and advanced Jesus' Kingdom of Love and of Righteousness. Your committee, through its chairman, is happy to present herewith the biennial report of the Executives of the Brotherhood of the United Lutheran Church in America. It tells the story of the Brotherhood's part in the triumphant program of the Church of our living and never failing God.

The Brotherhood of the United Lutheran Church desires to report, as follows, concerning its activities during the past biennium:

1. The purpose of the Brotherhood and its relationship to the Church has been dealt with at length in previous reports. Any further elaboration of these fundamental principles would be costly repetition and unduly burden the printed records.

2. The Five Objectives have been published in numerous forms with full explanation of their import and value to the Brotherhood and its work for the Church. The Brotherhood has continued to make these objectives the ideal by which to guide its activities. Common acceptance and practice of the Objectives has not become universal by any means. In an encouragingly large number of instances, one or more of the Objectives have been "majored" by a Brotherhood to a very definite strengthening of the congregation. Many others are catching the vision of service offered and will join the aggressive forces of the Master as the years pass. The Fifth Objective offers a wide field for service of a constructive nature and should receive continued emphasis.

3. The Brotherhood is considerably better organized than ever before in its history. During the biennium, many of the so-called inactive organizations have been revived; new congregational Brotherhoods have been organized and affiliated; Conference or District Brotherhoods have been organized in a majority of the Synods. As this work makes progress, the Brotherhood becomes better prepared to do effective work for the Church. Almost without exception, where the pastors are interested in developing the man-power of his charge, Brotherhoods are doing valuable work for the Kingdom. In a few instances, Brotherhoods exist without the active interest of the pastor. Few of such are productive of much service. The Brotherhood would urge the pastors to make more extensive use of the services of the organization.

4. Dr. J. W. Kapp resigned as Executive Secretary during the biennium. The Executive Committee secured the services of Mr. Earle W. Bader of Bethlehem, Pa., as Executive Secretary. Mr. Bader has been spending considerable time in basic organization work. Improved office records and methods have been instituted, giving a more comprehensive contact with the Brotherhood units throughout the Church. A more compact and workable organization will result in due time.

5. The services of Dr. J. W. Kapp have been retained as editor of Lutheran Men, thereby retaining for the Brotherhood his valuable experience. The influence of Lutheran Men is very great in stimulating men throughout the Church to definite service for the Kingdom. The topic for the monthly meetings has proved popular and of wide acceptance and use. The topics are prepared by prominent pastors and laymen. Around them the congregational Brotherhoods build their monthly meetings, and through them a consciousness is being developed that must eventually help mould the thinking and activities of the men of the Church.

6. Closer contact with the Brotherhood groups in a number of the other General Lutheran Bodies, especially those that are members of the American Federation of Lutheran Brotherhoods, has resulted in a special section of Lutheran Men edited by an editor selected by the

Federation. It is of peculiar interest to us that Rev. J. Allen Leas, D.D., of Chicago, a pastor of the U. L. C. A., was selected for this important service. Contacts and friendships that are being made through the Federated Brotherhoods will have a great influence in the coming of a real United American Lutheran Church.

7. The Iron Mountain Lutheran School, at Konnarock, Va., has been a special project of the Brotherhood for five years. The joint Commission on Southern Mountain Work, authorized by the Savannah Convention of the U. L. C. A., recommended to the Executive Board that this project, along with the whole Southern Mountain work, be placed under the supervision of the Board of American Missions. This was done as of May 1, 1936. The Brotherhood is pleased to have the Board of American Missions work out many needed co-ordinations of the school and mountain work. The Atlanta Convention of the Brotherhood authorized a campaign for funds with which to liquidate the purchase debit of the school and provide necessary improvements and equipment. This effort was deferred until the status of the work had been determined by the Joint Commission. As a result the school has had a very precarious existence during the biennium. Only faith and a small amount of money has enabled the school to survive. No expansion has been possible.

Under approval of the Executive Board of the U. L. C. A. and the Board of American Missions, and under the supervision of the latter Board, the Brotherhood is conducting a campaign to free the school of debit and expand its activities into a more potent factor in the mountain work. Certain reductions in purchase price were obtained, some property that had been reserved has been added to the school property, and work has been started on the reconditioning of the buildings. Needed equipment is being added, and the staff and student body greatly expanded. This work will have an ever increasing appeal to the hearts and means of the men of the Brotherhood, and an important place in the development of the Lutheran Church in the Southern Mountains.

8. The Brotherhood is glad to have a part in the work of the Lutheran Church. It hopes to be of more assistance, as the years pass, in the development of the Church-wide consciousness and desire to carry out the whole program of the Church. To this end, it offers its services to the Church. It solicits the nurture and admonition of the Church. It prays for the growth of the Master's Kingdom in the hearts of men.

Respectfully,

H. E. Isenhour, *President,*

Earle W. Bader, *Executive Secretary.*

Respectfully presented by your Committee on Lutheran Brotherhood.

David A. Davy, *Chairman.*

Mr. Deck introduced Mr. Earl W. Bader, Executive Secretary of the Brotherhood, who spoke especially upon the "objectives" of the Brotherhood and of the undeveloped man-power of the Church.

Mr. Bader introduced the Rev. Kenneth Killinger who addressed the Convention concerning the character of the work in the Southern Mountain area, with special reference to the Iron Mountain School for Boys.

Mr. Harry E. Fritsch, Treasurer, was presented and explained that the Brotherhood has adopted a financial program on the basis of which it expects to project a constructive service.

Mr. Lawrence F. Speckman, Second Vice President, was introduced and brought the following recommendations, adopted at the convention of the Brotherhood in Springfield, Ohio, October 11-13, 1936, to the Convention: (For action, see pp. 382, 419, 431.)

1. Whereas, the President of the United Lutheran Church in his report to the Columbus Convention defines plans for the promotion activities of the Church; and

Whereas, the Brotherhood of the United Lutheran Church is one of the auxiliary organizations designated by the President in his report to assist in presenting the whole program of the whole Church to individuals and congregations; and

Whereas, the Brotherhood gladly offers the co-operation of the synodical, conference and local Brotherhoods now organized; and

Whereas, it will assist materially in the furthering of these promotional activities if the Brotherhood is a vigorous and well-organized body in every Synod of the United Lutheran Church;

Therefore, the Brotherhood of the United Lutheran Church in America, in convention assembled, herewith respectfully requests that in any plan adopted by the United Lutheran Church for the promotion of the whole work of the whole Church that provision be made for the further development and organization of synodical Brotherhoods as a step toward providing additional means for the dissemination of information and providing a body of workers to carry out the larger aspects of such a plan.

2. Whereas, the Brotherhood accepts its full responsibility as the strong right arm of the Church and is committed to the whole program of the whole Church and is desirous of contributing its full share to that program and to the program of promotion of The United Lutheran Church in America, and

Whereas, the Brotherhood at its Springfield Convention has adopted measures for its more effective operation both as to constituency and in the field of finances, and

Whereas the Brotherhood senses a lack of appreciation on the part of many pastors throughout the United Lutheran Church, who have failed to co-operate in the organization of local Brotherhoods and failed to stimulate the organization of conference and synodical Brotherhoods, to recognize the Brotherhood movement and organization as officially sponsored by the Church at large and have failed to recognize the call of the Church to this field; now therefore,

Be it resolved, That the Brotherhood of the United Lutheran Church hereby request The United Lutheran Church in America to approve the

Brotherhood's efforts to bring about a stronger organized set-up and earnestly request The United Lutheran Church in America to call upon every pastor in The United Lutheran Church in America to support and promote Brotherhood work and Brotherhood organizations in their respective congregations and in their conferences and synods.

3.   Resolved, that the United Lutheran Church Brotherhood, assembled at Springfield, Ohio, request The United Lutheran Church in America to earnestly commend to its pastors each of the six objectives of the Brotherhood as essential parts of our church program and request its pastors throughout the coming biennium to give a positive and stimulating leadership to the program of each objective.

Recommendation 1. On motion this recommendation was referred to the Committee on President's Report. (See pp. 419, 431.)

Recommendations 2 and 3 adopted.

In connection with recommendation 3, the Sixth Objective of the Lutheran Brotherhood, which was adopted by the Brotherhood at its Convention in Springfield, Ohio, was presented. The Convention approved the Sixth Objective as follows:

Whereas, each member of every congregation belonging to The United Lutheran Church in America has a personal responsibility toward the raising of the apportionment in accordance with the Scriptural teaching, "as God hath prospered him," and

Whereas, "giving" is the fruit of faith in lives rooted in a knowledge of the Word, cultivated by the Holy Spirit and used for God's work through the Church only in proportion to a knowledge of the Church's mission and opportunity, and

Whereas, the Brotherhood has the consecrated man power to assist in the promulgation of facts regarding our Church and her mission, and a better understanding of her program,

Therefore, we the Brotherhood of the United Lutheran Church, in convention assembled, at Springfield, Ohio, do hereby resolve to add a sixth objective to the five already adopted, and now so effectively working among our Brotherhoods, as follows:

"The stimulation of the congregation, through educational, inspirational, and promotional efforts, to meet *as a minimum* the apportionment of the Church in full."

And, whereas, the former objectives were approved by the United Lutheran Church, we respectfully submit this Sixth Objective to the Church for its approval by this Convention.

We desire to add further that in the adoption of the Sixth Objective by the Brotherhood, it was interpreted among other things to mean:

(A)   That it shall be an integral part of the program of each local congregational Brotherhood to assist the other auxiliary organizations of that congregation in an effective program of distributing information on and generally promoting the program of the congregation, the synod, and the United Lutheran Church.

(B)   That each local Brotherhood shall include in conjunction with the regular topics assigned for monthly meetings at least four periods a year devoted to some phase of the work of the Church at large.

(C) That committees planning district or regional rallies shall so plan their program as to afford from time to time effective presentation of the causes of the Church.

(D) That synodical, conference, and local Brotherhoods be requested to assist in setting up general meetings sponsored by the United Lutheran Church, as a part of its promotional program, and/or the Lutheran Laymen's Movement for instruction and disseminating of information on its stewardship program, with special emphasis on "The Calendar of Special Days and Seasons."

The Rev. F. M. Urich, Chairman, presented the report of the Committee on Women's Work with the report of the Women's Missionary Society.

REPORT OF THE COMMITTEE ON WOMEN'S WORK

It is a source of genuine satisfaction to report that during the biennium the women of the Church have given a splendid account of themselves in the prosecution of every phase of the missionary task.

They have most graciously accepted in principle and in practice the aim to develop the whole program of the whole Church in all their activities. They have displayed a commendable readiness to co-operate in the general effort now under way to secure greater effectiveness in the Church's program of work by adjustments in relationships among the various boards and agencies of the Church to prevent overlapping of activities, duplication of effort, competitive programs and the resultant confusion arising therefrom.

The women of the Church have enriched our appreciation of the fundamental missionary task implied in the Gospel. They have made the entire Church conscious of the missionary imperative. To their devotion, zeal and consecration is due in generous measure the enlarged conception of the theory and practice of missions that prevails among us.

The Chairman of the Committee on Women's Work has attended numerous meetings of the Executive Board of the Women's Missionary Society since the last Convention of the United Lutheran Church, and is prompted by these contacts to call attention to the fact that the various details of executive management are handled with efficiency and dispatch, and that our women are steadily keeping in mind the interests of the whole Church and seeking to co-ordinate their work with that of our Mission Boards.

The supreme work of Christian missions is "nothing less than the effort to produce Christ-like character in individuals, societies, organizations and nations through faith in true fellowship with Jesus Christ, Our Saviour." To this task our women have committed themselves with unreserved enthusiasm and power.

The vital necessity for greater effectiveness in the general work of the Church is a unified educational approach to our congregations. The literature published by the Women's Missionary Society and the care which is being exercised to integrate its educational and promotional activities with the work of the Church as a whole, reveal the earnest purpose and helpful attitude of our women in achieving this desirable goal.

The report which the Women's Missionary Society submits to the Church shows the large measure of material support which it is giving to the work of our Mission Boards. Mere statistics, however, fail to tell the full story of the earnest prayers, the passionate interest and the warm-hearted devotion of the women of our Church to the cause of missions.

The glory of their work lies in the courageous and prayerful spirit of loving service that characterizes their plans and inspires their work.

Respectfully submitted,

THE COMMITTEE ON WOMEN'S WORK,

FRANK M. URICH, *Chairman.*

REPORT OF THE WOMEN'S MISSIONARY SOCIETY OF THE UNITED LUTHERAN CHURCH IN AMERICA

THE WHOLE PROGRAM OF THE WHOLE CHURCH

The Women's Missionary Society presents this report to the Church with the prayer that the record of the work of the Society may show in some small measure the accomplishment of that for which especial efforts have been made during the past two years—October, 1934 to October, 1936, namely: a thoroughgoing concern for "the whole program of the whole Church." In the plans adopted for Missionary Advance this concern for the whole program of the whole Church has been emphasized by individual and group approach to missions, as the challenge to every member of the Church to claim his rightful privilege of participation in maintenance of missions at the home base, where opportunities for the spread of the Kingdom are ever widening, and likewise that every member of the Church may have a loyal interest in that same spread of the Kingdom in the United Lutheran Church fields in Asia, Africa and South America. These special efforts are in direct accord with the establishment of the Society "under the constitution of the United Lutheran Church." These efforts are also in harmony with Article II, Section 2, of the Society's constitution: "To promote and stimulate the interest of the whole Church in the work of missions." Further, the Society's constitution provides that "loyal support of the regular apportionments of the Church by every member of a congregational society shall be a recognized policy of the Society." This has been true from the very beginning.

PARALLEL SYNODICAL ORGANIZATIONS

The Synodical organizations parallel thirty-two of the thirty-four synods which make up the United Lutheran Church:

Alleghany	Kansas	Ohio
California	Kentucky-Tennessee	Pacific
Canada	Maryland	Pittsburgh
East Pennsylvania	Michigan	Rocky Mountain
English Nebraska	Ministerium of	South Carolina
Florida	Pennsylvania	Susquehanna
Georgia-Alabama	Mississippi	Texas
German Nebraska	New York	Virginia
Illinois	North Carolina	Wartburg
Indiana	Northwest	West Pennsylvania
Iowa	Nova Scotia	West Virginia

In sixteen of these Synodical Societies there are also Conferences which parallel the Synod Conferences. An easy atmosphere of co-operation is thus gained.

REVISED CONSTITUTION

At the biennial convention held in Dayton, Ohio, October, 1934, two conspicuous changes were made in our constitution: first, that our general convention shall be held every three years instead of two; second, the Executive Board shall consist of representatives from the Synodical Societies—one thousand members and more entitling the Society to have a Board representative continuously, and for those of less than a thousand members there shall be alternation of representation. Representatives are elected for three years by their Synodical societies and shall be eligible to one re-election. Hence for this year 1936 there is no general convention being held. The first Triennial Convention will come October, 1937, in Buffalo, New York.

Officers and members of the Board are: President, Mrs. C. E. Gardner; Vice-President, Mrs. Philip M. Rossman; Recording Secretary, Miss A. Barbara Wiegand; Statistical Secretary, Mrs. Oscar C. Schmidt; Treasurer, Mrs. John M. Cook.

Alleghany	Mrs. Joseph Biddle
East Pennsylvania	Mrs. D. Burt Smith
Georgia-Alabama	Mrs. J. A. Linn
Illinois	Mrs. O. A. Sardeson
Indiana	Mrs. A. H. Keck
Iowa	Mrs. E. M. Redeen
Kentucky-Tennessee	Mrs. Fred S. Schmidt
Maryland	Mrs. L. H. Waring
Ministerium of Pennsylvania	Mrs. W. K. Hauser

Nebraska (English)..................................Mrs. Claude DeWald
Nebraska (German)..................................Mrs. H. O. Rhode
New York ....Mrs. Wm. A. Snyder
North Carolina ....Mrs. J. L. Morgan
Northwest ....Mrs. N. K. Feddersen
Nova Scotia ....Miss Minna Liechti
Ohio ....Mrs. C. S. Stroup
Pacific ....Mrs. T. A. Jansen
Pittsburgh ....Mrs. H. C. Reller
Rocky Mountain ....Mrs. O. F. Weaver
South Carolina ....Mrs. J. H. Summer
Susquehanna ....Mrs. Walter C. Hanning
Virginia ....Mrs. Eldridge Copenhaver
West Pennsylvania ....Mrs. H. D. Hoover
West Virginia ....Mrs. B. F. Becker
Treasurer of the Board of Trustees............Miss Flora Prince

The Board and Administrative Committee have held meetings as provided for in the constitution for the transaction of the regular business
of the Society between conventions. All meetings, except October, 1936,
have been held at headquarters, seventh floor, Muhlenberg Building, Philadelphia. There is satisfaction in renting our offices from the Publication
House. The work is facilitated by using the Muhlenberg Building.

CO-OPERATION WITH THE CHURCH BOARDS

The Women's Missionary Society maintains close co-operation with
the Boards of the Church in several ways—appointed advisors meet with
the Board of Foreign Missions, the Board of American Missions, the
Inner Mission Board, Board of Deaconess Work, Board of Ministerial
Pensions and Relief and the Board of Education. Single women missionaries are recommended by the Society, but called and commissioned
by the Board of Foreign Missions or the Board of American Missions.
Appropriations to the Boards are sent to the Treasurer of the United
Lutheran Church for distribution. These appropriations provide for
salaries of single women missionaries under Board of American Missions
and Board of Foreign Missions, the travel to and from the fields, and
maintenance of the work of women missionaries. These salaries, travel
and work maintenance are not provided by the Church in any other way.

In addition to the single women missionaries and their work, the
Women's Missionary Society supports entirely the only work done by
the United Lutheran Church among North American Indians at Rocky
Boy, Montana. The Society also appropriates to the Board of American
Missions money for part or whole salary of forty Home Mission pastors,
loans to churches and interest on loans. The Society receives no subsidy
from the United Lutheran Church apportionment.

An excellent co-operative service with the Board of Education has been developed through the years. The Board of Education Secretaries for Women are considered members of the Staff of the Women's Missionary Society. Dr. Mary E. Markley served formerly as chairman of the Candidate Committee and serves now as chairman of the Personnel Committee.

Representatives of the Women's Missionary Society at the request of the Executive Board of the Church have been appointed to serve on Committees: Miss Flora Prince on the Investment Commission; Mrs. C. E. Gardner, Mrs. Philip M. Rossman, Mrs. Eldridge Copenhaver, Dr. Mary E. Markley and Miss Amelia D. Kemp on the Committee on Better Adjustment.

In recognition of the Centennial of Deaconess Work the Executive Board requested that wherever possible a Deaconess feature be included in Conference and Convention programs. This has been done quite faithfully, and with real profit to the constituency. The Deaconesses have themselves made presentations when called upon.

EDUCATION AND PROMOTION

The Education Department publications have to a marked degree brought the constituency clear cut information concerning the program of the whole Church, and an insistence on co-operation on the part of every local and synodical society.

Two staff members, also members of the Education Department, Miss Nona M. Diehl and Mrs. A. J. Fenner, continue to make contacts as opportunity affords to promote missionary education through the whole program of the whole Church.

The Missionary Advance literature has been made easily available for the large demand. Increasing response in every direction to the call for Missionary Advance deserves notice. No financial aim or goal is included in this challenge—simply a wider understanding of Christian Missions as the United Lutheran Church maintains the enterprise. Knitted into all the plans is the call to advance individual lives spiritually through closer acquaintance with the progress of the Kingdom, through methods of work and through individual study and gifts.

CRONK MEMORIAL SCHOLARSHIPS

The following communication was sent out June 5, 1935:

"To the United Lutheran Church colleges admitting women students: Carthage, Gettysburg, Hartwick, Lenoir-Rhyne, Marion, Midland, Newberry, Roanoke, Susquehanna, Thiel, Wagner, Waterloo, Wittenberg.

"The Women's Missionary Society of the United Lutheran Church in America holds in trust a fund contributed in honor of Mrs. E. C. Cronk, the interest on which is now available for distribution, in accordance with actions taken at the meeting, April 24, 25, 1935, of its Executive Board. The first award to Marion College, Mrs. Cronk's Alma Mater, for the academic year 1934-1935 will be retroactive.

"The formal actions of the Executive Board of the Women's Missionary Society, April 24, 25, 1935, are:

"Beginning January 1, 1935, annual scholarships of at least $300 shall be awarded to United Lutheran Church Colleges, the recipients of such scholarships to be chosen by the college authorities with the right of approval by the committee in charge of the fund.

1. One annual scholarship of $300 shall be awarded to Marion College for the academic year 1934-1935 and for the academic year 1935-1936.

2. One annual scholarship of $300 shall be awarded for two successive years (after June, 1936) to United Lutheran Church Colleges in alphabetic order.

3. One annual scholarship of $300 shall be reserved by the Board for award to a United Lutheran Church College for an emergency scholarship.

    (a) An emergency scholarship shall not be awarded to a college holding another Cronk Memorial Scholarship.

    (b) An emergency scholarship may be assigned no more than two years in succession in the same college."

In accordance with these actions the first awards were made to Marion College. The first Emergency Scholarship was awarded to Wittenberg College for the academic year 1935-1936. Carthage College has received an award for 1936-1937.

MISSIONARIES

There is only one loss to report in the missionary staff—Miss Ada Kron was married immediately upon her return to the United States in the fall of 1935. Miss Kron went to India in 1929, representing the Augustana Women's Missionary Society, who paid her salary through their children's funds.

There is one addition to be reported for the year 1935—Miss Theodore K. Neudoerffer, Wittenberg A.B., 1932, and R. N. Toronto, Canada, General Hospital, 1935. From October, 1935 to March, 1936, Miss Neudoerffer was enrolled for special midwifery course at the Elsie Inglise Maternity Hospital, Edinburgh, Scotland, and she went to India in May, 1936.

Under appointment are:

Miss Virginia Dare Aderholdt, Kansas City, Kansas
    Bethany A.B. and Mus. Bac., 1932

Miss Myrtle A. Onsrud of Milwaukee, Wisconsin
    R.N., Whitehall, Wis., 1927

Miss Selma R. Bergner of Lancaster, Pa.
    Wittenberg A.B., 1930.

Miss Aderholdt will go to Japan in the fall of 1936.

Miss Onsrud will go in the fall of 1936, too, to India, after being commissioned in her own home congregation, the Church of the Redeemer, Milwaukee, Wis. It is most interesting to note that at the height of the Epiphany Season of 1936 this congregation, under the able guidance of Pastor A. A. Zinck, pledged the full support of Miss Onsrud, including six months at the Biblical Seminary in New York.

Miss Selma Bergner will have a scholarship from the Women's Missionary Society for study at the Biblical Seminary in New York, October, 1936 to May, 1937, and be commissioned to sail to Japan in 1937.

Miss Mary Borthwick, who had been teaching in India, 1912 to 1932, when she came home on furlough, found family conditions which made it necessary for her to resign in 1934. We are happy to report that she is able to return to India in August, 1936, thus meeting an emergency on the field.

Our roster of women missionaries under the Board of Foreign Missions, (including the additions in the fall of 1936), is:

Africa—3 teachers, 2 nurses, 2 evangelists..............................Total 7
China—3 teachers, 2 nurses, 2 evangelists............................... "   7
India—13 teachers, 10 nurses, 5 evangelists, 5 doctors,
     3 industrial .... "   36
Japan—3 teachers, 5 evangelists, 2 kindergartners............. "   10
Argentine—1 evangelist .... "   1
                                                         —

Grand total of women missionaries on foreign fields............ 61

Our missionaries under the Board of American Missions are:

At Jewish Mission, Baltimore, Md........................... 1 Parish Worker
At Rocky Boy, Montana .... 1 Parish Worker
At Watauga, N. C.. 1 Parish Worker
In the Virgin Islands... 3 Deaconesses
In Puerto Rico.. 1 Nurse
At Konnarock Training School.............................. 1 Teacher
(6 members of Faculty, not missionaries)
Grand total of women missionaries on home —
    field 8

CHANGES IN ADMINISTRATION

The Konnarock Training School at Konnarock, Va., maintained entirely by the Women's Missionary Society, has been functioning under the Inner Mission Board since the school was opened in 1926. By action of the Executive Board of the Church, the school functions now beginning May 1, 1936, under the Board of American Missions. This will simplify greatly the administration of the mountain work done by the Church both in the Watauga Mission, N. C., and in Konnarock.

MEMBERSHIP

The membership of the Women's Missionary Society for June 30, 1935, was as follows:

Women's Societies..............................	2,127	55,793	members
Young Women's Societies.................	667	12,261	"
Light Brigade Societies.....................	1,162	44,833	"
Total for the whole Society......	3,956	112,887	"

CONTRIBUTIONS

Total receipts of the Women's Missionary Society from July 1, 1934 to June 30, 1935, were $335,151.56.

Of this amount, $244,598.05 was sent to the Treasurer of the United Lutheran Church for distribution to the Boards of the Church as designated.

It is interesting to note that this total was contributed:

From Women's Societies	$249,056.38
From Young Women's Societies	35,190.21
From Light Brigades	20,500.83
Income Trust Funds and Annuities	22,142.53
From all other sources	8,261.61
Total	$335,151.56

BUDGET

The budget of the Society is that which was presented for one year adoption at the 1934 general convention, to remain in force until 1937 at the time of the next general convention, subject to yearly review by the Executive Board of the Society. The budget was published on page 449 of the minutes of the United Lutheran Church Convention of 1934. With minor internal adjustments the appropriations are the same as published in 1934.

IN CONCLUSION

The report is presented to the Church without any recommendations. The Women's Missionary Society has resolved to work more earnestly than ever before in gratitude to Him who is the great Head of the Church. The coming year will be faced with fresh zeal to continue that close co-operation with the Church which will fulfill the requirements of our common task—the whole program of the whole Church

AMELIA D. KEMP, *Executive Secretary.*

Dr. Urich introduced Mrs. C. E. Gardner, President of the Women's Missionary Society, who spoke of the ideals and principles by which the life of the Women's Missionary Society is guided.

Miss Amelia Kemp, Executive Secretary of the Society, was introduced, and gave assuring information concerning the work of the Society, as contained in the official report.

The Rev. H. A. Bosch replied to the greetings, expressing admiration and appreciation of the work of this great auxiliary in the Church.

The Rev. O. F. Blackwelder, Chairman of the Committee on Associations of Young People, presented Mr. John George Kurzenknabe, President of the Luther League, who in turn presented the Rev. Paul M. Kinports, Executive Secretary of the Luther League. The Rev. Mr. Kinports presented his report and spoke of the work of the great army of young people of the Church, declaring that they wait eagerly for leadership.

REPORT OF THE EXECUTIVE SECRETARY OF THE LUTHER LEAGUE OF AMERICA

Youth is vital to the Church's life. The Church needs the idealism, heroism, energies and sacrificial devotion of youth.

In this day growing young people are finding many of their experiences of living in groups outside the family circle. These groups vary greatly in size, personnel and influence. There is the social clique, play group, study group, Boy Scouts, Girl Scouts and other groups of young people that meet anywhere from the roadhouse to the young people's room in the Church.

In these groups young people find themselves suddenly confronted with many new and conflicting ideas and are often subject to direct and indirect propaganda.

Out of these group experiences come opinions and convictions on all questions—opinions that may modify or change the opinions and convictions that have been developed in the home and the Church.

This it is that makes the Church group so important. By intelligent Christian methods it seeks to build a type of group experience which will develop the individual and help him evaluate as a Christian the various issues and proposals he may meet in other groups.

The church group like the Luther League provides for its members also an opportunity to develop and state convictions and to gain such skill in organizing and managing a group that he can later play his part in the other groups in the church and the life of the community.

There is great need today for us to show our young people what our Lutheran Church stands for and why she thus stands. We need to give our youth a clearer, more definite conception of the foundation truths and principles upon which our church has been builded and by which she has wrought. There are today forces of confusion which have an insatiable passion for the destruction of all consistent and persistent institutions. They are using every method at their disposal to destroy the loyalty of our youth for their church and her principles. It is not necessary to spend much time in quarreling with them. We need to untangle the misconceptions they create and let light shine in to dispel the mists so that the young people may see their church in her true colors and she will retain their affection.

The Luther League of America through her program for youth groups is endeavoring to actually keep young people with Christ and the church. It supplies personal stimulation to faith and life; it builds Christian fellowship and valued friendships; it increases opportunities for Christian service and gives experience in church work.

The leaders within the League see today an opportunity unprecedented in its timeliness and unparalleled in its proportions, that the spirit, the genius and potential leadership of the Luther League are required, even imperatively required, by the Church herself. They are convinced that as a youth organization within the Church, the League under God and the Great Head of the Church, they have the wisdom and courage, the unselfishness, the sacrificial devotion to sustain and strengthen a program that stimulates interest and loyalty to the whole work of the Church.

Encouraging Comments

Expressions regarding the activities of the local Leagues indicate the spirit of the work. Comments from Pastors such as these: "Both material and spiritual progress", "Renewed interest and enthusiasm", "A growing attendance at devotional meetings", "Large increase in membership", "Sunday evening meetings particularly well attended", "The League is in a flourishing condition, there is a fine spirit of a fellowship and the young people are all active in the work of the congregation."

These particulars do not exhaust the record of the Christian activities of the Leagues. They are simply striking examples of the helpful agency of the Luther League in its legitimate sphere.

Personnel

Officers and Executive Committee for 1935-1937 are as follows: Honorary Members: Rev. L. M. Kuhns, D.D., Litt.D.; Hon. E. F. Eilert, C.S.D.; Mr. Harry Hodges; Rev. A. J. Traver, D.D.; Officers: President, Mr. John

George Kurzenknabe; Vice-President, Mr. Alvin H. Schaediger; Second Vice-President, Mr. Alfred J. Gorsky; Recording Secretary, Miss Irene Schaefer; Treasurer, Mr. Charles W. Fuhr; Executive Secretary, Rev. Paul M. Kinports; Intermediate Secretary, Rev. R. J. Wolf; Junior Secretary, Miss Brenda L. Mehlhouse; Educational Secretary, Rev. C. P. Harry, D.D.; Missionary Secretary, Miss Winnie Butt; Life Service Secretary, Rev. Chester S. Simonton, D.D. Members at Large: Mr. Harold Sundberg, Mr. Austin W. Howard, Rev. J. W. Frease, Mr. Ray Anderson, Miss Mildred Gartelmann, Mr. John Lauman, Rev. Alfred J. Beil, Rev. William J. Ducker, Mr. Herbert W. Fischer, and Chairman of the Committee on Associations of Young People, Rev. O. F. Blackwelder, D.D.

AGE DEPARTMENTS

The Luther League is divided into three departments: Junior (8-12 years) with supplementary program for Little Leaguers under 8; Intermediate (13-16), and Senior (17 plus). Throughout these three departments the program of Education, Missions and Life Service has a unique place and value.

The Intermediate Department is seeking to satisfy some of the many interests and activities peculiar to the teen age. Rev. R. J. Wolf, Secretary of this department says: "The Intermediate Luther League is the 'Take and give' unit of the Church's youth organization. Into it is 'taken' the graduated members from the Junior unit, and from it is 'given', four years later, these same boys and girls to the Senior unit. That is, at least, idealistically the place we would like to hold in each and every congregation of our Church with respect to her youth.

"Occupying as we do this middle ground the business of the Intermediate Department is to conserve the results accomplished by the Junior Luther League, build higher thereon, and prepare for still more intelligent and resourceful leadership in the Senior division.

"But this 'middle ground' denotes the 'riddle age' in youth's mental, physical and spiritual growth. Of all ages it is by far the most difficult to 'hold at attention' long enough to interest in any sustained endeavor. To keep a program fresh and vigorous and a leadership quickened to the task, is ever a problem.

"Teen age youth is energy and action over-Websterized. The Intermediate Luther League has more than 800 such units, numbering 24,000 boys and girls; plus thousands of others who are less directly touched in organizations, such as the Boy Scouts of America, Girl Scouts, and through a ready service at Headquarters and frequent visitation afield."

The Junior Department in caring for the children under the direction of Miss Brenda Mehlhouse reports that, "The Junior Department of the Luther League of America, caring for the children twelve years old and under, during the past two years has consistently followed its program of education, service activities, and training for leadership.

"It is comprised of 1,034 registered Junior Luther Leagues in the United States, Canada, South America, Puerto Rico and India, with a membership of 21,522. In addition, there are about 150 groups of 'Little Leaguers,' the children under eight, with over 1,800 members, and their own special programs.

"Education. Junior Topics are prepared for weekly meetings in the form of units of study, covering the Bible, the Church, Luther, Play, Worship, Christmas, Lent and Easter, Prayer, Life Service, Outdoor Devotions, Books, etc., with Topics Booklets for each unit.

"A Junior Reading Course, selected Daily Bible Readings, Study classes on Life Service, Luther, Stewardship, etc. are additional phases of the educational program.

"The missionary program of study consists of the missionary meeting the last of each month when the Light Brigade topic is used, and the use of Junior Mission Study books, about 500 Mission Study classes among the Juniors being reported during the two years.

"Service Activities. There is a saying that no lesson is perfectly learned until 'something is done about it,' and the Junior Leaguers prove this. There is time and opportunity in the Junior League to help the various causes studied, and there is no form of activity in the United Lutheran Church in which the Juniors are not interested and have not helped in some way. If the activities could all be accurately tabulated, their variety and their sum total value would indeed be surprising.

"For their own church they have been busy in many ways, with financial gifts, and with service, helping with special services and programs, serving as Junior choirs, and activities of all sorts too numerous to mention.

"In Inner Missions they have helped in the work of our homes and orphanages, our hospitals, and with the sick and shut-ins, shared with others less fortunate, and contributed to all the regular Inner Mission activities.

"For Home Missions, they have aided in all the various phases of this work, and for their special activity have been helping the work in Puerto Rico, through our 'Good Neighbor Club.'

"In the foreign field, they have contributed to China, India, Africa, Japan and South America, sending boxes and gifts, and sharing in many of the Light Brigade projects as well.

"$706.62 was contributed by the Juniors to the Luther League's missionary objective—the building at the Seminary in Japan.

"In all the Juniors have supported the work financially with contributions amounting to over $11,000 in the past two years.

"Leadership. The specific function of the Junior Department is to train for leadership. The boys and girls are here trained for the work of the Luther League and the Church. From their ranks must come the future leaders in our local congregations, our church leaders in all branches of the church, our future pastors, deaconesses and missionaries. They are the Hope of the Church. We believe this is the Junior League's distinct contribution to the program for the training of our children.

"A REAL responsibility! A REAL opportunity! To the program of the Junior Department we direct your attention, and bespeak your study, interest and co-operation."

MEMBERSHIP

The steady growth of the League membership indicates the larger interest of our youth in the League and its program. Comparative statistics reveal a decided increase in organizations and membership.

	1934	1935	1934	1935
	Organizations		Membership	
Senior	1,502	2,142	33,296	48,696
Intermediate	489	535	8,093	10,381
Junior	816	834	20,723	24,332
Total	2,807	3,511	62,112	83,409

PUBLICATIONS AND CORRESPONDENCE

The monthly Review in view of reports of the decrease in subscriptions to other Church publications, has but a slight decrease in subscribers. The Topics Quarterly, edited by Rev. C. P. Harry, D.D., is distributed in quantities of 11,000 per quarter. These publications are practically self-supporting, due to the fact that there is no expense for editorial service.

The Intermediate Quarterly Helps and the Junior Topics Booklets have a distribution of 6,000. Thousands of separate pieces of literature as aids to program building and organization work were printed and distributed by the six departments in the last biennium. This literature is sold at a minimum cost or provided for in the budget for free distribution.

During the biennium 32,351 pieces of mail were sent out from the national office, this figure excludes the regular mailing of all publications.

FINANCES

The League continues to function under a greatly reduced income. There has been a slight increase in the income from dues, but a decrease in the Sustaining Membership Fund. The current accounts for the year 1935 showed a deficit of $434.70. This was due to the increased activity of the League demanding increased service, travel, postage and publications. Only 80 per cent of the budget of the League is raised through dues and the appropriation from the United Lutheran Church. The other 20 per cent is contributed through Sustaining Membership Fund. This Fund is contributed by members and friends of the League who have a deep interest in the work of the League and the promotion of the program for youth.

MISSIONARY OBJECTIVES

The Luther League is decidedly interested in the Missionary program of the Church. It has manifested this interest by establishing special funds in the support of this work. While the Leaguers have been contributing to these mission projects they have also been greatly informed regarding the whole mission program of the Church.

In 1935 the League completed its Japan project and contributed $15,312.53 to the Board of Foreign Missions for the erection of the Administration Building at the Theological Seminary in Tokyo, Japan.

The League in convention assembled in Charleston, S. C., July 1935 decided with the approval of the Executive Board of the United Lutheran Church to raise a missionary objective during the biennium as a gift to the church and administered through the Board of Foreign Missions the sum of $10,000.00. This project is in China to be known as the T'ai Tung Chen Project, which will include the building of a church with a social center consisting of a kindergarten, dispensary and equipment for Christian education. This project has been approved by the Executive Board of the Church and a considerable sum of money already contributed to this project.

A NEW PROJECT

At the Charleston Convention in 1935, the Luther League of America voted to promote the Pocket Testament League among its members.

The original Pocket Testament League was founded by Mrs. Charles M. Alexander when she was a school girl in England, as a means of helping to win her friends to Christ. It was officially launched as a worldwide movement in Philadelphia, Pa., in 1908. It has spread throughout the world. There are more than seven million members.

It is a means of binding human lives and the Word of God together. It unites those who agree to carry a Testament or Bible with them and to read a portion of it every day. It aims to exalt God's Word as a daily Companion and Guide and as a means of winning souls. (Titus 1 : 9 and Philippians 2 :16.)

The enrollment as of July 28, 1936 is 3,860.

CONVENTIONS

The Twentieth Biennial Convention was held in Charleston, S. C., July 8-11, 1935. This occasion marked the fortieth anniversary of the Luther League of America. It was a great convention in a hospitable city and in a memorable year. The total registration of delegates and visitors was 1,008.

The twenty-first Biennal Convention will be held in Sprinfield, Ohio, in July 1937. Plans for the convention are under way and a wide-spread interest is being manifested in the next general convention of the League.

ACKNOWLEDGMENT

The Luther League expresses its deep appreciation and hearty thanks to the United Lutheran Church for the support given during the past biennium to carry on an enlarged program in an ever extending field of service.

Pastors and Church workers, the Luther League has proven its practical value in the local congregation and Church at large. What the League shall be and do in the future depends in no small measure upon us. The League needs your help, guidance, co-operation and prayers.

Respectfully submitted,
PAUL M. KINPORTS, Executive Secretary.

Dr. Blackwelder introduced Miss Brenda Mehlhouse who spoke concerning the work of the Junior Luther League. The Rev. J. Wolf was also introduced to the Convention.

The time for adjournment having come, the President announced that the report of the Committee on Women as Congregational Representatives would be made the item of business following the report of the Executive Committee of the Lutheran World Convention. This was made the special order by general consent.

The President announced that it seemed necessary to provide for an evening session, in case of which the unfinished business would be made the order, so as to clear the way for the regular order on Wednesday morning. The Convention voted to hold such a session beginning at 7 : 30 P. M.

At twelve o'clock the Convention adjourned with prayer by the Rev. Guy E. McCarney.

NINTH SESSION

DESHLER-WALLICK HOTEL
Columbus, Ohio
Tuesday, October 20, 1936, 2 : 00 P. M.

Devotions were conducted by the Rev. D. G. Jaxheimer, and the President called the Convention to order.

The Special Committee on Minutes reported that they had examined the Minutes of the sixth and seventh sessions and, finding them correct, moved their approval. The motion was carried and the President declared the Minutes approved.

Tellers Committee No. 2 reported on the remaining election for one position in the *Board of Deaconess Work*. The Rev. L. A. Thomas, having received a majority of the votes cast, was declared elected by the President.

The Rev. F. M. Urich, Chairman of the Committee of Reference and Counsel, presented the following report:

REPORT OF COMMITTEE OF REFERENCE AND COUNSEL

1. The convention receives with sorrow the news of the death, on October 18th, of Mr. Frederick C. Hassold. Mr. Hassold was a frequent delegate of the Ministerium of Pennsylvania to the General Council and of earlier conventions of the United Lutheran Church. He was a former member of the Board of Deaconess Work, and served for many years as a member of the Board of the Philadelphia Seminary and of the Board of the Philadelphia Motherhouse of Deaconesses and the Mary J. Drexel Home.

2. Dr. Virgil E. Zigler, medical missionary to India and a lay delegate from the Ohio Synod, appeared before your Committee on behalf of the following resolution:

Resolved, that a Committee of Five be appointed by the President to consider and to report at the next convention, concerning the feasibility of planning a tour to India in 1942 to attend the centennial celebration of the founding of our mission work in India.

We recommend the adoption of this resolution.

Item 1 was received as information.

Item 2. The resolution was adopted.

The Rev. C. M. Jacobs, Secretary, presented the report of the Commission on Relations to American Lutheran Church Bodies.

REPORT OF THE SPECIAL COMMISSION ON RELATIONSHIPS TO AMERICAN LUTHERAN CHURCH BODIES

I. Membership

The Commission consists of the following members,—the Revs. H. H. Bagger, Charles M. Jacobs, P. H. Krauss, and H. Offermann and Messrs. E. F. Eilert, J. K. Jensen, E. Clarence Miller and E. Rinderknecht. By resolution of the Savannah Convention, of 1934, President F. H. Knubel is chairman of the Commission. The Rev. J. F. Krueger was a member of the Commission and its Secretary until his death.

II. Meetings

The Commission has held three meetings, Sept. 25, 1935, in Philadelphia; Feb. 6 and 7, 1936, at Pittsburgh, Pa.; and April 2 and 3, 1936, at Columbus, Ohio.

At the first meeting the President reported that he had received a number of replies to the invitation authorized by the Savannah Convention. The only declinations of the invitation had come from the Wisconsin Synod and the Norwegian Synod. Their replies are herewith transmitted.

THE EVANGELICAL LUTHERAN JOINT SYNOD OF WISCONSIN AND OTHER STATES
Lansing, Mich., Sept. 16, 1935.

Honorable Sir:
The Evangelical Lutheran Joint Synod of Wisconsin and other States, in convention assembled at New Ulm, Minn., has taken notice of an invitation issuing from the United Lutheran Church in America and proposing "the establishment of closer relationships between them and ourselves," and now desires that answer be made to this invitation with the following statement:

We fully agree as to the desirability of establishing complete fellowship with all Lutheran bodies of America if that can be effected without sacrifice of principle and confession. We further hold that to refuse such recognition of fellowship where there is actual agreement in all essential points would be equivalent to perpetuating a most serious offense against the truth of the Gospel.

We feel constrained to say, however, that in our opinion such required unity does not as yet exist between the United Lutheran Church in America and our own body.

Although the doctrinal statement in which the United Lutheran Church takes its stand on Scripture and the Lutheran Confessions is one with which, as far as it goes, no Lutheran can find fault, it nevertheless fails to take into consideration two facts:

(1) That doctrinal issues may arise which did not exist and were not even foreseen at the time these confessions came into being.

(2) That confessional writings, even as Scripture itself, may meet with varying and often contrary interpretations.

Since both of these possibilities have actually occurred among the various Lutheran bodies of our land, we hold that the doctrinal criterion set up in the "Savannah Resolutions," while stating the first essentials toward Lutheran unity, cannot take the place of an exhaustive study of the doctrinal differences that have arisen among Lutherans. We hold agreement on these questions to be an absolute pre-requisite to true fellowship. "That ye all speak the same thing, and that there be no divisions among you; but that ye be perfectly joined together in the same mind and in the same judgment." I Cor. 1, 10.

Practical considerations which preclude any approach between the United Lutheran Church and our own body at the present time are:

(a) A disturbing tolerance that the United Lutheran Church has shown toward doctrinal statements arising out of its own midst and patently not in agreement with Scripture and the Lutheran Confessions. We hold that this more than weakens the doctrinal platform proposed in the "Savannah Resolutions."

(b) A treatment of the question of lodge-membership on the part of congregation members and even pastors which is not consistent with the principles laid down by the United Lutheran Church itself on this question in its "Washington Declaration."

(c) A disquieting tendency toward Unionism, as shown by the increasing practice of pulpit fellowship with non-Lutherans.

While some of these questions are often relegated to the realm of church practice, we hold that it is dangerous thus to segregate practice from doctrine. On the contrary, the practice followed by a church in such matters is the clearest manifestation of the doctrine which it holds. Tolerance here becomes synonymous with liberalism, indifference, and denial. "A little leaven leaveneth the whole lump." I Cor. 5, 6. Gal. 5, 9.

These last-named conditions constitute obstacles to an early establishing of fellowship between the United Lutheran Church and our own body, which obstacles only the former itself can remove. Until this is done we must regretfully decline this invitation.

We ask that this statement be taken not as captious criticism or willful faultfinding on our part, but as offered in a sincere spirit of good will and out of an earnest concern that fellowship between Lutheran bodies of our land, if and when it comes about, may be based upon a true unity of the Spirit, and thus be a God-pleasing union.

Respectfully yours,

(Signed) Karl F. Krauss, *Secretary.*

The Norwegian Synod of the American Evangelical Lutheran Church
Minneapolis, Minn. Jan. 21, 1935

Dear President Knubel:

Your letter of Jan. 10th addressed to President Madson, has been turned over to me as acting President of Synod. We acknowledge the receipt of same with thanks and appreciate your good intentions. However, we have no reason to hope for much blessing from the contemplated move, in view of the fact that the official organs of the various Lutheran Church bodies afford sufficient evidence to prove that they are not in all essentials one in doctrine. We enclose a copy of resolutions passed at our last convention in June 1934, addressed to Mr. Paulus List of Chicago. This will indicate the stand of our Synod in this Union Movement. With kind greetings,

C. A. Moldstad, *Acting President.*

Plans were soon consummated for conferences with the American Lutheran Church. The second and third meetings of your Commission were held in connection with joint sessions with the commission of that body. Since the third meeting the President has been in conference with the President and other representatives of the Missouri Synod and a joint-meeting with a commission of that Synod was pending when this report was prepared.

III. Meetings with the American Lutheran Church

The two meetings with the commission of the American Lutheran Church were marked by free and frank discussion of the matters that seem, at the present time, to be obstacles to closer relationships.

An initial difficulty arose from the fact that the commissions of the two bodies were working under different instructions. Your Commission was definitely charged to work for the organic union of the Lutheran Church bodies in America, on the basis of the Lutheran Confessions, while the commission of the American Lutheran Church was instructed only to seek the establishment of pulpit and altar fellowship between the two bodies, a matter which presents no problem at all to the United Lutheran Church, inasmuch as it already grants full and free pulpit and altar fellowship to the members of the American Lutheran Church.

This difference in objectives did not, however, prevent the discussion of differences, as it is self-evident that things which would prevent pulpit and altar fellowship would also prevent organic union. Nevertheless, your Commission has endeavored constantly to make it clear that organic union is the objective which the United Lutheran Church desires to obtain.

The commissioners of the American Lutheran Church expressed it as their belief that there were just three matters holding the two church-bodies apart. These were the different attitudes of the two bodies toward secret societies, the difference in practice concerning pulpit and altar fellowship with non-Lutherans, and a difference of view concerning the Scriptures. No fault was found with the official utterances of the United Lutheran Church on any of these subjects. The doctrinal basis of our Church and the Washington Declaration of 1920 were declared to be satisfactory, but it was objected that the practice of the United Lutheran Church was not in harmony with these official statements, and new statements on these three points were asked.

The statements on the first two points, unanimously adopted by the two commissions are as follows,—

1. That all persons affiliated with any of the Societies or Organizations designated in the Washington Declaration of the U. L. C. A. as "Organizations injurious to the Christian faith," should sever their connections with such society or organization and shall be so admonished; and members of our churches not now affiliated with such Organizations shall be warned against such affiliation. Especially shall the shepherds of the flock be admonished to refuse adherence and support to such organizations.

2. That Pastors and Congregations shall not practice indiscriminate pulpit and altar fellowship with Pastors and churches of other denominations, whereby doctrinal differences are ignored or virtually made matters of indifference. Especially shall no religious fellowship whatsoever be practiced with such individuals and groups as are not basically evangelical.

Agreement has not yet been reached upon the third point. When attained the agreements on all points will be submitted for approval.

(Signed for the committee)

CHARLES M. JACOBS, *Secretary.*

The report of the Commissioners to the National Lutheran Council was presented.

REPORT OF THE COMMISSIONERS TO THE NATIONAL LUTHERAN COUNCIL

The report herewith submitted is concerned chiefly with the major activities engaging the attention of the National Lutheran Council during the past biennium. The common interests of the churches were represented at the national conventions of the co-operating bodies and before other church agencies and governmental bureaus. The scope of representation included, world Lutheranism, foreign missions, church finance, inner missions, Lutheran co-operation, World Sunday School Convention, radio service, chaplaincy, statistics, and relief for refugees.

Opportunities for more extensive representation of Lutheran interests, especially in organizations outside of our own Church, have not been wanting. In an ever wider circle of religious organizations and activities, the Lutheran voice is being heard and the Lutheran cause is being represented.

The Publicity and News Bureau under the direction of Pastor C. K. Fegley has developed its service to new high standards. Through the weekly NEWS BULLETIN which is mailed to 600 editors and officials, Lutheran events have been released regularly. The news is gathered from over 200 periodicals from all parts of the world, and from many correspondents who have been enlisted in supplying first hand information. The third issue of each month is given over to a special EDUCATIONAL BULLETIN in behalf of the National Lutheran Educational Association, of which Dr. Mary E. Markley is the editor. Regional Conferences on Publicity were conducted by Secretary Fegley in 1935 in the interest of a greater efficiency and coverage of Lutheran news, in Baltimore, Columbus, Chicago and Minneapolis. As a result the Chicago Lutheran Council has organized a Publicity Bureau which gathers and releases the news of Chicago Lutherans regularly. In recognition of Secretary Fegley's services, the World Sunday School Association requested his service to cover the Convention which was held in Oslo in July 1936.

The Council granted permission to Secretary Fegley to undertake this project.

The Reference Library and Statistical Department under the direction of Dr. G. L. Kieffer continues to render a most valuable service to the entire Lutheran Church of the world, but more particularly to the Lutheran Church of America. Dr. Kieffer is the President of the Association of Religious Statisticians also, and prepares the article and statistical tables of the religious bodies in America annually for the CHRISTIAN HERALD. As specified in the governing regulations of the National Lutheran Council, the statistical department has gathered and compiled statistics of Lutheran Church bodies in America which in turn have been released to all Lutheran editors and to the religious editors of other denominational papers, and of the secular press. Through his connection with the Association of Religious Statisticians, Dr. Kieffer was able to enlist the interest and activity of practically all the large religious bodies in America, in behalf of the United States Census of Religious Bodies. A united and conservative appeal was made to the Committee on Appropriations and to Secretary of Commerce Roper, on the basis of which the President of the United States finally allocated W. P. A. funds to provide for the decennial religious census for which Congress failed to make an appropriation.

During the past biennium the Council co-operated with an inter-synodical committee of Texas in arranging and providing a Lutheran Exhibit at the Texas Centennial at Dallas during the summer of 1936. Efforts have also been made looking toward a United Lutheran Exhibit at the World's Fair which is to be held in New York City in 1939. Present prospects are that the American Lutheran Publicity Bureau of the Missouri Synod will co-operate with the National Lutheran Council in setting up a single unified Lutheran Exhibit in 1939.

The translation and publication of Professor Koeberle's, RECHTFERTIGUNG UND HEILIGUNG, was completed in the last biennium. The translation is by Dr. John C. Mattes, and the book is published in English under the title, THE QUEST FOR HOLINESS, by Harper and Bros., New York. The selection of another book for translation and publication has not yet been made, pending the results of this first venture. If this initial effort succeeds other English editions of outstanding theological books by foreign authors will follow.

After a delay of several years, due to financial inability, the publication of the 8th edition of the Lutheran World Almanac was authorized, and the Executive Director instructed to proceed with the preparation and publication as soon as possible. It is proposed to publish it by means of the off-set process. The preparation of the manuscript is now in process. The date of publication has been delayed somewhat on account of the continued illness of Dr. Kieffer, chief editor, during the summer of this year. A new feature in the forthcoming edition of the Lutheran World Almanac is a complete directory of all Lutheran congregations and institutions in the United States and Canada. This will take the place of the geographical directory of ministers and will not be printed again for a number of years since there is very little change in the name and address of congregations.

At the request of the original committee, three additional members were appointed on the Committee on Social Trends. The present Committee consists of:

Dr. Martin Anderson	Oak Park, Ill.
Dr. H. E. Sandstedt	Chicago, Ill.
Rev. N. P. Lang	Chicago, Ill.

Dr. L. H. Schuh	Toledo, Ohio
Dr. C. E. Krumbholz	New York, N. Y.
Prof. H. F. Schersten	Rock Island, Ill.
Dr. Ernest Correll	Washington, D. C.
Dr. G. M. Bruce	St. Paul, Minn.
Dr. R. H. Long	New York, N. Y.

The Committee has made a number of studies including a study of, The Relation of Church and State, Moving Pictures, Family and Divorce, Crime and Lawlessness, The Sunday Question, Economic and Social Security in Relation to the Life of the Church, Communism in its relation and effects upon the Church, Gambling, and Work among Boys. An effort is also being made to collect all resolutions and pronouncements of the co-operating Lutheran bodies in America on the burning questions of the day. Some of the studies are not yet completed, others have been released for discussion and criticism. The facts and findings of these studies are to be made available to the Churches through the Church Press, pamphlets, and other media. To awaken and arouse the great body of Christians in the Lutheran Church to a realization of their responsibility as God-fearing people, to live soberly and walk uprightly, and to use their influence in the promotion of the principles given to mankind 1900 years ago by our Lord Jesus Christ, that is the ultimate object of the work that is being done by the Committee on Social Trends.

Another project which has been carried through to completion is the Inner Mission Survey. In co-operation with the Associated Lutheran Charities of the Synodical Conference it has been possible to gather the factual material of all phases of Inner Mission Work done by the Lutherans in America in this survey. Tabulations of all the reports have been made and have been assigned to various members of the Committee for further study and evaluation. Some of this material will be released as information. The more intimate details of the report will be used only for a deeper study of this branch of the Church's work. Some of the members of the Committee will endeavor to enlist the co-operation of post-graduate students in making a careful and comprehensive study of a particular phase of social service, as the basis for a Masters or Doctors thesis. The Committee is composed of the following:

Rev. G. H. Bechtold, D.D.	Rev. S. C. Michelfelder
Rev. C. O. Pedersen	Rev. G. L. Kieffer, D.D.
Rev. R. H. Long, D.D.	Rev. C. E. Krumbholz, D.D.

Rev. E. P. Pfatteicher, D.D.

The National Lutheran Council has acted as the final clearing agency of all Lutheran applications for appointment as Chaplains in the Army and Navy, except those coming from bodies having a Committee on

Chaplaincy in their own organization. This is done in co-operation with the General Committee on Army and Navy Chaplains. At present there are twelve Lutheran Chaplains serving in the regular Army and four in the Navy. An additional Lutheran Chaplain is to be appointed in the Navy soon. From twenty to thirty Reserve Chaplains have been engaged in the Civilian Conservation Camps during the past biennium. An effort was made to ascertain how many Lutheran pastors are giving voluntary service in the C. C. C. camps, but there seems to be no source from which this information could be obtained except to inquire of all the Reserve and Regular Chaplains engaged in this service. In 1935, the number of camps was increased from 300 to 600 with a double capacity making it necessary to engage many more chaplains in order to care for the spiritual needs of the men in the camps. The question of spiritual ministry in federal and state penal institutions and hospitals was referred to the Committee on Inner Mission Survey for study. The Council resolved to request the participating Church bodies to make contributions for the publication of literature and the supplying of other needs for the Lutheran Army and Navy Chaplains serving in the Army and Navy and in the Civilian Conservation Camps.

In continuation of its original policy, the Columbia Broadcasting System has looked to the National Lutheran Council to secure speakers for the Lutheran Church of the Air. The period of the broadcast has been extended to include the summer months, thus giving eight services to the Lutherans. The schedule for 1936-37 will present the following speakers:

Dr. Hanns Lilje	Berlin, Germany
Dr. N. M. Ylvisaker	Minneapolis, Minn.
Dr. O. F. Blackwelder	Washington, D. C.
Dr. E. Poppen	Columbus, Ohio
Dr G. Wickey	Washington, D. C.
Dr. C. Bergendorf	Rock Island, Ill.
Dr. J. W. Behnken	Oak Park, Ill.
Rev. Norman A. Menter	Detroit, Mich.

It is the policy of the Council to secure different speakers for each year and to distribute them among the various Lutheran Church bodies in America.

At the annual meeting of the Council, held January 17, 1935, the recommendation of the special Committee on the Relationship of the National Lutheran Council and the Lutheran World Convention was received and adopted as follows:

1. The National Lutheran Council and the Lutheran World Convention are and should continue to be two distinctly different and independent entities.
2. There is a definite place for both in the life of the Lutheran Church.

3. Problems of emergency aid arising in and through the agency of the World Convention, should be transmitted by the Executive Committee of the World Convention directly to the General Bodies in America and should be undertaken by them in such manner as they shall deem fit.

4. The Executive Committee of the World Convention should do more than it has in the past to inform its world constitutency of the common life, common interests, and the common needs of World Lutherans. The National Lutheran Council offers its services in an effort to carry out this policy in the United States and Canada.

5. It is the opinion of the National Lutheran Council that emergency appeals for definite causes continuing indefinitely lose their character as emergency appeals and become "causes" to be listed as such and provided for as such through regular agencies of the participating bodies.

Due to the special emergency which had arisen in the German Foreign Missions, the provisions of these resolutions were not put into effect until the beginning of 1936.

The matter of a National Lutheran Institute which was proposed by the Executive Director was referred to the participating bodies for approval before being undertaken.

The Rev. R. Dunkelberger, D.D. of the United Lutheran Mission in India was appointed to succeed Dr. Isaac Cannaday as a trustee of the Gossner Mission property for the Council.

Greetings and congratulations were extended to the United Lutheran Synod of New York, Lutheran Deaconess Motherhouse in Kaiserswerth, Germany, Lutheran Deaconess Motherhouses in America, The Gossner Mission, The Leipzig Mission, North German Mission, and the Neuendettelsau Mission, on their anniversaries which are being celebrated in 1936.

By unanimous vote, Article 9 of its constitution and governing regulations was amended, changing the time of the Annual Meeting of the National Lutheran Council from the 3rd Thursday in January of each year to the 4th Wednesday in January of each year.

Dr. E. F. Eilert, Treasurer since the organization of the Council, reported that for the calendar year 1934, the total income, including balance was:

Balance	$25,928.83
Total Expenses	$24,671.85
Balance Dec. 31, 1934	$1,256.98

For the calendar year 1935, he reported

Total income, including balance	$27,202.73
Total Expenses	$25,297.73
Balance Dec. 31, 1935	$2,005.00

The contribution of the United Lutheran Church was: $10,350.00 in 1934 and $10,857.00 in 1935. The budget allowed by the commissioners for 1936, is $24,880.00.

Officers of the Council

President, Dr. C. C. Hein
Vice President, Dr. N. C. Carlsen
Secretary, Dr. M. R. Hamsher
Treasurer, Hon. E. F. Eilert, C.S.D.

The above officers together with the following members constitute the Executive Committee:

Dr. J. A. Aasgaard
Dr. P. O. Bersell
Dr. E. B. Burgess
Dr. T. O. Burntvedt
Dr. E. H. Rausch

The Commissioners of the co-operating bodies are:

Norwegian Lutheran Church
Rev. J. A. Aasgaard, D.D.
Rev. L. W. Boe, D.D., LL.D.
Rev. J. A. O. Stub, D.D.

Augustana Synod
Rev. P. O. Bersell, D.D.
Rev. Peter Peterson, D.D.
Mr. Karl J. Olson

American Lutheran Church
Rev. C. C. Hein, D.D.
Rev. E. H. Rausch, D.D., LL.D.
Rev. M. P. F. Doermann
Rev. E. Poppen, D.D.

United Danish Church
Rev. N. C. Carlsen, D.D.

Lutheran Free Church
Rev. T. O. Burntvedt, D.D.

Icelandic Synod
Rev. K. K. Olafson

United Lutheran Church
Rev. P. W. Koller, D.D.
Rev. L. W. Steckel, D.D.
Rev. C. A. Freed, D.D.
Rev. M. R. Hamsher, D.D.
Rev. John A. W. Haas, D.D., LL.D.
Rev. C. E. Krumbholz, D.D
Rev. E. P. Pfatteicher, D.D.
Mr. G. F. Greiner
Hon. E. F. Eilert
Rev. E. B. Burgess, D.D.

Submitted for the Commission

The President, as the representative of the United Lutheran Church in the Lutheran World Convention, announced that no additional report would be made to that which was made by him through the Executive Board. He called attention to the previous presence of European members of the Executive Committee of the Lutheran World Convention and to the special information which had come in a personal way to the Convention.

The Rev. Henry H. Bagger, Chairman, presented the report of the Committee on Women as Congregational Representatives. It was explained that the report presented to this Convention is the same as the report presented to the convention at Savannah and postponed for action until this Convention.

REPORT OF THE COMMITTEE ON WOMEN AS CONGREGATIONAL REPRESENTATIVES

(For action on the recommendations in this report, see pp. 418, 432f)

The matter with which this committee has had to deal was presented to the United Lutheran Church in America in 1930 through two memorials from the Texas Synod. They read as follows (Minutes, 1930, pp. 142f)—

(a) "That we memorialize the United Lutheran Church in America in the matter of women delegates to synod, to determine whether or not such procedure is unscriptural."

(b) "Dass wir, die Texas Synode, die Vereinigte Lutherische Kirche von Amerika, ersuchen, ein Gutachten ueber diese Frage zu geben: Ist die Gemeindevertretung seitens der Frauen der Gemeinde Schriftwidrig?"

These memorials were referred in 1930 to a special committee, which presented to the last biennial convention both a majority and a minority report (Minutes, 1932, pp. 427-30). The action of the convention was to authorize the appointment of a new committee to which both of these reports were referred for further study. This committee respectfully presents the following report.

I. The Question

While the two memorials differ somewhat in their wording, the intent of both is the same. They raise the question whether the election and seating of women as delegates in synodical conventions is a practice that can be followed without violating the teaching of Holy Scripture concerning women's place in the Church.

The committee recognizes that this question has certain broader implications, including the right of women to serve as members of church councils, as delegates to general conventions, and as members of boards and committees of the Church. It does not involve their right to receive ordination or to serve as ministers of the Word and Sacraments.

The committee, therefore, conceives this question to be a part of a larger question, viz.,

Whether women can be granted all the rights of lay-members in our Churches without violation of the teaching of Holy Scripture: or whether the teachings of the Scriptures compel to withhold from them certain rights that are enjoyed by laymen.

II. The Argument against the Election and Admission of Women

The argument against the election and admission of women is presented in the minority report of 1932. (Minutes, pp. 429f.) It is based on I Tim. 2:11, 12, which reads, "Let the woman learn in silence, with all subjection; but I suffer not a woman to teach or to usurp authority over the man but to be in silence." The word rendered in the Authorized Version as "usurp authority over" (authentein) is translated in the Revised Version as "have dominion over;" by Moffatt, "dictate to."

It is argued that "under all normal conditions, the election of women delegates to synodical meetings and to membership in Church councils is unscriptural, because the placing of women in positions of authority over men in the official direction and ruling of the Church or in the conduct of its public worship is expressly forbidden by St. Paul in I Tim. 2:11, 12. That this passage is to be so understood is the opinion of nearly all learned commentators and has been the unanimous understanding of the universal Church for almost nineteen hundred years."

The committee has had to determine whether this is a correct interpretation of the passage cited, and to endeavor to discover whether there are other passages, elsewhere in the New Testament, which support this interpretation.

The only additional passage which we have been able to find is I Cor. 14:34, 35. It reads, "Let your women keep silence in the Churches; for it is not permitted unto them to speak, but to be under obedience; as also saith the law. And if they will learn anything, let them ask their husbands at home; for it is a shame for women to speak in the Church." The passage in I Cor. 11: 3-16 is obscure. In so far as it bears on woman's place in the Church, it should be interpreted by the passage just quoted.

III. The Interpretation of the Scripture Passages.

In the interpretation of these passages, the committee has sought to follow the principle that the Scriptures are always to be understood in the light of the circumstances in which they arose. This principle is of especial importance in the interpretation of the New Testament Epistles, which deal so extensively with specific situations that had arisen in the early congregations. Even definite prescriptions of the kind contained in the statements quoted are not to be taken as laws, applicable to different situations, unless they contain a principle of universal application.

The passage I Cor. 14:34, 35 is taken from a section of that letter in which Paul is dealing with abuses that have grown up at Corinth in connection with the Church's services of worship. They had become disorderly because everyone claimed the right to speak whenever he felt himself moved by the Spirit to do so. Paul attempts to correct this. He says, "Let all things be done unto edifying" (v. 26). That is the principle. It is applicable to Christian worship in all times and places, but he applies it in three specific ways. He applies it, first, to those who "speak with tongues." They are to restrain themselves. Not more than two or three are to speak at any one service, and then only when some one is there to interpret what they say. His second application is to the "prophets." Not more than two or three of them are to speak and they are to speak in turn. His third application is to the women. They are not to speak at all. The congregation would not be edified. "Let your women keep silence in the churches" should be more accurately rendered "in the meetings" or "in the assemblies." In 11 : 5 he had declared that "a woman who prayeth or prophesieth with her head uncovered dishonoreth her head." Here he goes still further. A woman is not to "pray or prophesy" at all in the public worship of the Church.

In I Tim. 2 : 11, 12, on which the argument of the minority report mainly rests, we find that it is the public appearance of women which is again in the writer's mind. "I will therefore that the men pray everywhere" (v. 8) refers obviously to public prayer. Then follows the reference to the women; and, first of all, to their dress. They are to "adorn themselves in modest apparel," "not with braided hair or gold or pearls or costly array" (vs. 9, 10). This has plainly to do with the conduct of women in the public meetings. Then, with no break in the thought, "Let the women learn in silence, with all subjection." She is to be a listener in the services. "But I suffer not a woman to teach or to dictate to the man, but to be in silence." The whole passage has to do with woman's place in the public worship of the Church.

If the question before us were that of ordaining women to the ministry and placing them in charge of the public worship of the Church, the committee would have to agree with the minority report of 1932, that such a practice is "expressly forbidden," and that "this has been the understanding of the universal Church for almost nineteen hundred years." That, however, is not the matter under discussion. We have rather to inquire whether a different kind of official activity in the Church can be interpreted as "teaching" or "dictating to men" in the sense of I Tim. 2 : 11, 12.

IV. The Nature of the Office under Discussion.

Official activities in the Church may be described broadly as of two kinds, spiritual and administrative. There is no sharp line of division between the two. Some of them, to be sure, are definitely spiritual, concerned directly with the application of the Gospel to the lives of men. Others are clearly administrative, concerned with the government of an institution. But even the most clearly administrative activities have a spiritual aspect and are directed toward ultimate spiritual aims.

The spiritual aims of the Church are constant, as are also the means to their attainment. They have not changed in nineteen centuries, and they cannot change. But the forms of its administrative activity have changed greatly from time to time. They are created to meet the needs of the time in which they are produced. The Church has created them and the Church can alter them or abandon them and create new forms, as the need arises. There is no divinely given order of Church government and administration.

The first important development in the organization of early Christianity was the division between clergy and laity. The beginning of the process of cleavage can be found in the New Testament and it was completed by about the year 150. The government of the Church was in the hands of the clergy, who also performed all the spiritual functions of the Church. They managed the affairs of the Church, administered its discipline, preached, taught and administered the sacraments. For a time the laity did have a voice in the choice of bishops, but even this right eventually disappeared. The clergy were the institution and the laity were its subjects. Neither the ancient nor the medieval Church had any institution corresponding in any way to the modern church council, or congregational governing board of laity, and the synods were assemblies of the clergy. This form of organization is perpetuated in Roman Catholicism, where it is buttressed by a theory of the priesthood and of an indelible mark conferred in ordination.

The Reformation denied the whole Roman theory of the Church. It asserted that the Church is "the assembly of saints and true believers" and that all Christians are spiritual priests. In accordance with this doctrine, it gave the laity such rights in the government of the Church as they had never possessed since the line between clergy and laity had been sharply drawn. It was in the Protestant Churches that the theory of democratic government was first declared, not as a political creed, but as a principle inherent in the nature of the Church. The right to organize the Church, to control its property, to make rules for its administration, to call and dismiss ministers and teachers, and even to determine doctrine on the basis of the word of God—all these rights were declared to belong to the laity as well as to the clergy. The clergy became "ministers," or "pastors," who held the office of Word and Sacraments. They were not to be rulers of their congregations, but office-holders in them, set apart for a particular form of spiritual service.

The application of this democratic principle lagged far behind its assertion, and the lag was somewhat more marked in the Lutheran Churches than in some others. The rights that were declared in theory to belong to the whole body of the laity, were exercised, in practice, by the political rulers or by those classes of the laity that possessed political standing. It was in America that Lutheranism secured for the first time a representative form of government, in harmony with the idea of the Church that Luther had proclaimed as early as 1520.

In this form of government, the administration of the Church is placed in the hands of groups of individuals who are chosen to represent the whole body from which they are drawn and by which they are chosen. The acts of the group are therefore regarded as acts of the whole body. The group has "authority," but the individuals who compose the group have none. Moreover the authority which it possesses is delegated to such a group by those over whom it is exercised and is therefore the authority of the whole body. It is difficult to see how the authority of a church council or a synod or a board of the Church can be called "dominion" or "dictation," in the sense of I Tim. 2:12. It is still more difficult to see how membership in such a body can be construed as conferring such "dominion."

Moreover, it may be questioned whether the administration of the Church ought to be regarded at all from the point of view of authority. In the highest and truest conception of it, it is a form of service, for which certain individuals are designated by the Church, of which they are a part. When it is so regarded, the question of "dominion" does not arise, and when the individuals are regularly chosen for this service, there can be no "usurpation."

V. The Opinion of the Committee. (For action, see pp. 418, 432f.)

In view of these facts, the committee believes that the question raised by the Texas Synod is really whether we may allow the principle of representative government in the Church, based on the priesthood of all Christian believers, to be universally applied, or whether we are compelled by Holy Scripture to exclude women from the right to represent us all.

The opinion of the committee is that we are not so compelled. We therefore concur in the recommendation of the majority report of 1932,

1. "That the reply of the United Lutheran Church in America to the Texas Synod be as follows, That the election of women delegates to meetings of synod is not unscriptural" (Cf. Minutes, 1932, p. 428), in the sense that it is not contrary to or forbidden by the Scriptures.

We also recommend

2. That this action shall be understood as applying to any similar question that may hereafter arise concerning the eligibility of women for membership in church councils, or in general conventions, boards or committees of the Church.

In order to prevent any misunderstanding that may arise out of these recommendations, we desire to point out that not all things that are lawful are also expedient. We therefore recommend

3. The adoption of the following statement from the majority report of 1932: "The conception of spiritual equality in Christ does not alter the fact that, by divine appointment, certain spheres of Christian service are more natural or normal to men, while other types of service can best be performed by women. Since the Church deeply deplores those social,

industrial, and economic conditions which oppose the Christian home, the glory of motherhood, and the rearing of children in the nurture and admonition of the Lord, it should encourage the fulfillment of those duties by the exercising of care in the organization and assignment of its work."

We also approve the statement of the minority report of 1932, as follows,— "The Lutheran Church has welcomed women to all phases of the ministry of serving love, in which they not only excel men, but in which, due to the different qualifications conferred on the sexes by the order of creation, they are able to render services for which men are not normally qualified. It is in such ministrations, and in the divinely given task of motherhood and the care of the young, that the New Testament finds the highest crown of womanly glory. Here is a mission just as vital, honorable, and glorious as the government of the Church, and one for which women are pre-eminently fitted by their God-given endowments."

Signed:

> H. F. BAUGHMAN
> J. W. HORINE
> MRS. H. C. MICHAEL
> CHARLES M. JACOBS, *Secretary.*
> H. H. BAGGER, *Chairman.*

MINORITY STATEMENT

Preliminary Remarks

The ideal of the true Church at the present time (or at any time) must not necessarily consist of an exact repristination of all external forms, organizations, offices, and other features of the primitive Church. Some or even many of these were probably never intended to be permanent. They were most suitable and adapted to the conditions of the Church in the various localities at that time. Changing conditions would naturally affect the usefulness of many of them.

The New Testament is not a rigid codex of laws, rules, and regulations to cover every possible occasion and exigency that has arisen or may yet arise in the course of the Church's growth and development. It is not a complete collection of casuistic decisions from which we might pick the one needed for any given case. Some regulations which were required in the earliest period of the Church may have become obsolete; others, new ones, may be needed under changed conditions.

There are, however, certain principles and fundamental ideas which influenced and governed the actions and rulings of the apostles in their dealings even with the more external affairs of the Church and concerning which we ought to inquire whether they do not apply also to present conditions, similar to, even though perhaps not identical with, those of the apostolic Church. We should do this so much the more reverently and carefully since the guidance of the Holy Spirit was never more apparent than in those early days of the Church. Indeed it would be impious lightly to pass over or haughtily to disregard the lessons which we may learn from the way the apostles disposed of questionable practices. It is right and proper to ask and, in the Light of New Testament examples, to answer the question: How would the apostles act and rule in similar cases today?

The Scripture text which bears most directly on the question at issue is I Tim. 2:11-14: "Let the woman learn in silence with all subjection. But I suffer not a woman to teach, nor to usurp authority over the man, but to be in silence. For Adam was first formed, then Eve. And Adam was not deceived, but the woman, being deceived, was in the transgression."

What was the Situation?

It may be assumed that there was a special occasion for the rulings here reported. Probably similar tendencies became noticeable and similar disturbances were impending here as had caused trouble in the Corinthian congregation. There, so it seems at least, women, *had* already attempted to set themselves on a level with the men in public speaking, praying, raising questions, and so on (I Cor. 14:34-36; 11:5). *Doubtless they considered their actions justified on the basis of the equality of all believers in the possession of all spiritual blessings in Christ.* (Gal. 3:28).

The Attitude of the Apostle

Evidently it was the conception of the apostle that equality in the possession of grace does not imply equality in every respect. It does not justify the claim that every member of the Church has on these grounds equal part in all the functions and activities of the congregation, irrespective, for instance, of age, sex or qualification. He refuses to countenance the active participation of women in the conduct of public meetings of the Church. They should not teach nor pray nor even speak in public (when men, capable of such service, were available).

What Reasons does the Apostle give for such Rulings?

He gives two reasons.

1. Let the woman learn—with all subjection. He wishes the divine order of creation upheld. He says: "Adam was first formed, then Eve." In I Cor. 11:8, 9 we read: "The man is not of the woman, but the woman is of the man. Neither was the man created for the woman, but the woman for the man." In the parallel text, I Cor. 14:34, the apostle writes: "It is not permitted unto them (the women) to speak, but they are commanded to be under obedience, as also saith the law." Here he evidently refers to the Thora, Genesis 3:16: "He (the husband) shall

rule over thee." In Ephesians 5:22 he writes: "Wives submit yourselves unto your own husbands, as unto the Lord."

The original order which gives man a position of superiority has not been changed by the Gospel. Therefore the apostle does not wish woman to, "authentein andros." What does that mean? Luther translates: "Das sie des Mannes Herr sei;" the Revised Version of the English Bible has; "Have dominion over man;" the Authorized Version: "Nor to usurp authority over the man." As the etymology of the word and the connection indicates, the meaning seems to be: to act independently of man, to assert herself over against man, setting herself on a level with him. The apostle does not wish woman to do anything that looks like an affectation of changing the divine order in the relation between the two sexes. Because of the original order of creation woman should not "authentein andros," but learn and listen with all subjection.

2. The other reason is given in the 14th verse: "Adam was not deceived, but the woman, having been utterly deceived, was in the transgression." Eve herself admitted that she had been deceived, saying: "The serpent beguiled me, and I did eat" (cf also II Cor. 11:3). Adam was not deceived or beguiled, but persuaded. The Lord said: "Because thou hast hearkened unto the voice of thy wife, etc." She was last in creation, but first in transgression.

It seems that woman is psychologically more liable than man to fall victim to deception. She is more emotional, more easily impressed. At the same time she has an alluring way of making man yield to her persuasion. For that reason it would not seem safe to entrust her with the teaching and preaching of the Church independently of man. The apostle will not permit it. Albert Bengel says "Facilius decepta, facilius decipit."

Conclusions

It can be admitted that today greater freedom is granted to women in public opinion and that their appearing and speaking in mixed assemblies would not in itself give offense as in the days of the apostles. For that reason there would not be any objection to women presenting reports of their own activities or requests from their Societies to the Church in its public conventions. But the apostle does not give the customs and social prejudices of his time as reasons for his forbidding women to set themselves on a level with men by teaching, praying, and raising questions in the meetings of the Church. His reasons are still valid and we cannot ignore them without disobeying clear and well-founded precepts of the Scriptures. We should also keep in mind the rather solemn words with which the apostle introduces his remarks concerning the conduct of women in public meetings: "As in all Churches of the saints" (I Cor. 14:34). What is observed in all Churches of the saints is more than a common usage of the time, it is a higher, a divinely appointed order. This is corroborated by the concluding words: "If any man think himself to be a prophet or spiritual let him acknowledge that the things that I write unto you are the commandments of the Lord" (I Cor. 14:37).

It cannot be claimed that the injunctions of the apostle referring to teaching, preaching, and praying in public worship have no bearing on ecclesiastical assemblies which deal also with more secular concerns, such as Church councils, synods, conventions of the U. L. C. A., etc. All these meetings are not or should not be entirely, not even predominantly, secular. Very probably external affairs affecting the maintenance and administration of the congregation were also prayerfully discussed in the meetings referred to in the before-mentioned texts. And the reasons for which the apostle forbids the active participation of women have a bearing also, *and even more so,* on their taking part in debating with men about resolutions concerning and determining doctrine, forms of worship, discipline, and organization for the guidance, sometimes, even of a great number of pastors and congregations.

Our text and the parallel texts, the entire complex of the apostle's admonitions and argumentations, are opposed to the admittance of women as delegates to, or members of, organizations which in the Church of Christ were hitherto exclusively reserved to men. We certainly do not find in them, or elsewhere in the Scriptures, any approval of or encouragement for the introduction of such a practice.

We must be careful, that we as a Church do not become guilty of the sin of usurping authority, not only over man, not only over an apostle, but even over the Holy Ghost himself.

If there are congregations which think that they are at liberty to go their own way and disregard the rulings of the apostle and the almost universal order of the Church in all ages and countries, they should be reminded of the words with which St. Paul concludes his admonitions to the Corinthians with regard to the conduct of their women: "What? Came the word of God out from you? Or came it unto you alone?" (I Cor. 14:36-37) *i. e.:* Are you the only Church favored with divine revelation, that you will depart from the usages of all the other Churches?

It ought to be taken into consideration also that great changes are taking place in the trends of the time, a return from the artificial conditions of modern civilization to the more natural orders of the past. *Naturam expellas furca, tamen usque recurret!* Also in the emancipation-movement of woman which has led to flapperism, free love, trial-marriages, polyandry, dissolution of family-life, race suicide, etc., the turning of the tide seems to be at hand. A weak yielding to a passing fad, (Rom. 12:2), a concession prompted perhaps by a misdirected chivalry, may prove a step backwards rather than forward. It would not work for the benefit, but to the detriment, of woman.

Counter-Arguments

To the undersigned the arguments that have been advanced to the contrary do not seem convincing. The practice of having women serve as delegates to synods, etc. is, of course, not "expressly" forbidden in the New Testament simply because there was no occasion for such an inhibition at that time.

The interpretation of the word "authentein" (I Tim. 2:12) as "dominion" or "dictation" can hardly be upheld. If that thought had been in the apostle's mind he could have found quite a number of adequate and familiar words in the Greek vocabulary of his time to express it. He must have had a special reason for choosing the unusual word "authentein." All deductions, therefore, from the meaning of this word as "dominion" or "dictation" do not prove anything.

The assertion that in our form of Church administration the group has authority but the individuals who compose the group have none, must be questioned. According to this way of thinking the individuals would not have any responsibility either. Practically a group of delegates is not an abstractum. The individuals certainly share the authority of the group not only in proportion of their number, but also in accordance to their influence. One vote often decides the issue, when a measure is resolved that may become the law of the Church.

It is said that when individuals are regularly chosen for the service there can be no usurpation. If, however, as the undersigned believe, it is contrary to the will of the Lord (I Cor. 14, 37) to have women function in the capacity of delegates etc., it would be a usurpation on the part of the Church to overrule the rulings of the apostle and of the electors to place women in such positions. And since the word of God in the Scriptures is the supreme authority in our Church the women would still have to satisfy themselves whether their functioning in such positions is really a service rendered to God. To accept such a position with any doubts in their consciences whether their election is in accordance with good order, as approved by the Scriptures, would be also usurpation on their part.

Reservation

The deductions which the undersigned draw from the principles underlying the rulings of the apostle would not prevent women from teaching classes of women or children or from conducting services for them, of course, as in all cases, under the supervision of the pastor. It would not prohibit their private testimony of Christ as in the case of the Samaritan woman (St. John 4:29), nor a motherly or sisterly private instruction of an individual under proper conditions, as in the case of Priscilla (Acts 18:26). There may even be cases of emergency in times of war or persecution when women under the force of necessity have to take the places of men, and all honor is due to them when in such situations they bravely step into the gap. Luther says: "If it should come to pass that there were no man, a woman might get up and well preach to the others, if she had the ability to do so." But under normal conditions it would in most cases be a testimonium paupertatis for congregations or synods to admit that they had no capable man available.

In fine the undersigned would not omit to emphasize their most hearty consent to the last two paragraphs in the majority report beginning with the words: "In order to prevent any misunderstanding, etc." If the sentiments expressed in these two paragraphs could be made to prevail in our synods and congregations the question at issue would solve itself. The undersigned do not question for a moment the sincerity and honesty of the signers of the majority report. They could not, however, conscientiously agree with their conclusions and, since a compromise was not possible, both sides being set in their convictions, they considered it their duty to present again a minority report.

C. R. TAPPERT,
CARL M. DISTLER.

Recommendation 1 was adopted. Upon the announcement of the vote on this item, the Rev. John C. Mattes exercised his personal privilege by asking that his name be recorded as having voted against the recommendation and proposed an appeal to the Commission of Adjudication. The right of an individual to make such appeal was ruled out of order and attention was called to the fact that such an appeal could be made by the Convention only. (See p. 432f.)

Recommendation 2 was adopted.

Recommendation 3 was adopted.

The President ordered that the statement of the Minority be printed in the Minutes.

The Rev. J. Schmieder, Chairman, presented the report of the Committee on President's Report.

REPORT OF COMMITTEE ON PRESIDENT'S REPORT

(For action on this report, see pp. 420, 431)

I. Your Committee submits its report with hearty commendation for all that the honored President of The United Lutheran Church in America has achieved in the past biennium, as in those that preceded it, for the health and advancement of the Church. Especially do we appreciate and concur in his thoughtful concern, which he has so cogently expressed in his report to this Convention, for promotional activities in the future which will be increasingly effective. As he has presented that concern, it is so clearly a valid judgment and is in such manifest agreement with the temper of the Church that we transmit the following recommendations:

1. The Board of Publication is instructed to collaborate with the President of the Church and the Boards in the preparatiton of a promotional medium which it shall issue for distribution among all the families of our congregations with such frequency and in such manner as may be found practicable. (Amended by the Convention, see p. 420.)

2. The Boards of Foreign Missions, American Missions, Education, Parish and Church School, Inner Mission, Deaconess Work, and Ministerial Pensions, and the Laymen's Movement are instructed to arrange for a promotional activity, during their special seasons, in general (not in detail) as explained in this report, and also to appoint their executive secretaries as members of a joint committee for the special purposes assigned to the committee in this report.

3. This Convention commends the loyalty of the Lutheran Brotherhood, the Women's Missionary Society, and the Luther League, and instructs them to further their present purposes whereby their congregational units will be vigorous promotional agents for the interest of the entire congregation in the whole work of the whole Church.

4. The three groups of agencies mentioned in recommendations 1, 2, and 3 are instructed to carry out these plans in cooperation with the President of the Church. If agreement cannot be cooperatively reached in any important matter, the point of difference is to be decided by the Executive Board of the Church.

5. The Executive Board is instructed to consider the feasibility and desirability of an arrangement whereby it will send (at the expense of its own treasury) to each meeting of each constituent synod an authoritative representative of the Church as a whole. If its decision is favorable, it is instructed to proceed. It is in that event also hereby authorized to declare as rescinded all previous actions of the Church concerning the presentation of causes at the meetings of constituent synods.

6. The Executive Board is instructed to consider the second supplementary item in this report (concerning pastors) and is authorized to act in accordance with its decisions and arrangements.

7. All constituent synods are asked to cooperate whole-heartedly in all efforts to make these plans effective, including the use of the delegates to this convention, since they hold office as delegates for the biennium.

II. In response to the petition of the Michigan Synod delegation concerning an evangelistic and inspirational program for the raising of the apportionment which was referred to the Committee on President's Report, it is the conviction of this Committee that the purposes contemplated in the request should be accomplished through the operation of the plan of promotion hereinbefore recommended by this Committee.

III. In response to recommendation 1 of the Brotherhood of The United Lutheran Church in America requesting aid from the Church in organizing synodical units of that auxiliary, also referred to the Committee on President's Report, your Committee recommends that this Convention express its judgment that the Brotherhood itself is and inevitably must be responsible for the extension of its own organization and approves any efforts that the Brotherhood may make to that end.

The recommendations were considered in order.

Motion was made to adopt Recommendation 1, under I.

In connection with the consideration of Recommendation 1, the President called the Rev. E. B. Burgess to the Chair and asked the privilege of addressing the Convention. The President made a very full statement concerning the development of this item, and the proposed plan of promotion. Representatives of the Board of Publication and members of the Committee on President's Report presented different aspects of the policy involved.

A motion was made to substitute the original recommendation made by the President.

A motion to amend the original recommendation by inserting the words "or equivalent" after the words "The Lutheran," was lost.

The motion to substitute the original recommendation of the President was lost.

An amendment was offered to the recommendation of the Committee to strike out the words "and the Boards" between the words "the Church" and "in the preparation of."

The amendment was adopted and recommendation 1 as amended was adopted as follows:

"1. The Board of Publication is instructed to collaborate with the President of the Church in the preparation of a promotional medium which it shall issue for distribution among all the families of our congregations with such frequency and in such manner as may be found practicable."

The hour for adjournment having arrived, the President announced that this report would be resumed at the end of the schedule for unfinished business at the evening session. (See p. 431.)

At 5 : 00 P. M. the Convention adjourned with prayer by the Rev. V. D. Naugle.

TENTH SESSION

DESHLER-WALLICK HOTEL
Columbus, Ohio
Tuesday, October 20, 1936, 7 : 30 P. M.

Devotions were conducted by the Rev. E. V. Roland, and the President called the Convention to order.

In the order of unfinished business, items from the report of the Executive Board were considered. (See pp. 65, 74.)

Item IV, A, 2, (a) of the Executive Board's Report, concerning the Merger of the Inner Mission Board, the Committee on Evangelism, and the Committee on Moral and Social Welfare, was considered.

Recommendations (1), (2), and (3) were adopted.

Item V, 6 of the Executive Board's Report, concerning Supplementary Support for the Executive Board, was considered and adopted.

Mr. W. H. Stackel, Chairman, presented the report of the Commission on Investments.

REPORT OF COMMISSION ON INVESTMENTS

(For action on the recommendations in this report, see p. 423.)

The past biennium has witnessed a sharp rise in the market values of bonds and a corresponding drop in yields and income. Consequently, endowment trustees have been faced with an increasingly difficult problem in selecting suitable investments.

Where the Commission has been consulted concerning the investment of funds, it has advised against committing too large a portion of any endowment in long term bonds at prevailing low yields, believing that a board should be in position to benefit from better rates of income if eventually obtainable.

The scarcity of good investments offering fair yields has at times slowed down the Commission's operations and not infrequently funds have been held awaiting new offerings. The favorable outcome of such a procedure is best illustrated in the case of the Women's Missionary Society whose Administrative Committee, shortly after the last biennial convention, turned to the Investment Commission for advice on the investment of its funds. In the past biennium the Commission has approved $65,000.00 in sound bond purchases which net the Missionary Society 4 per cent.

Realizing that the careful supervision of investments is as important over a period of years as is the original selection, the Commission has authorized its chairman to render an investment review service to those boards and agencies desiring it. This service is intended primarily as a periodic check on investments which the Commission itself has approved for purchase and is likely to grow in importance from year to year.

The Commission recognizes its status as a purely advisory body. It has no authority nor does it seek to interfere with the investment operations of any board. It offers recommendations only upon the express request of a board or of its officers. In the case of two of the boards, the Commission has at no time had any official contact concerning investment operations because those boards engage the supervisory investment services of a bank which specializes in such services. On the other hand, the Commission through its membership does have contact with all boards. There has happened to be at least one member of the Commission on the Finance Committee of every board controlling endowments. Also members of the Commission have often been consulted as individuals concerning investment matters.

In order to clarify the Commission's procedure for the benefit of the boards, it should be noted that the Commission deems its judgment to have been given only in those cases where the machinery outlined in Article VI of its Supplemental Rules and Regulations are employed, that is to say, only where the Chairman of the Commission's Executive Committee certifies to any given recommendation as evidence of its approval by at least three of its members.

A careful reading of the Supplemental Rules and Regulations (pages 409-411 of the 1934 Minutes, as amended, pages 70, 71 of these Minutes) reveals important respects wherein the procedure followed by the boards is out of harmony with these Rules and Regulations. The experience gained by the boards and by the Commission during the period of nearly four years that these Rules and Regulations have been in force, should be sufficient to enable adjustments in Rules and/or practical procedure that would harmonize the two. Therefore,

1. We recommend that each of the boards and agencies holding endowment and/or trust funds be requested to re-examine the existing Rules and Regulations of the Commission with a view to conforming its investment procedure therewith or proposing to the Commission such amendments to the Rules and Regulations as seem to it desirable and that the Commission be instructed to make full report at the next biennial convention.

A sub-committee of the Commission, composed of Mr. S. F. Telleen and Mr. B. B. Slifer, has made an exhaustive study of the whole subject of annuities. Their report contains much valuable data which should be of genuine assistance to boards and agencies in the formulation of sound policies with respect to annuities. Among the conclusions reached by this committee, is the following:

"Any organization which now issues or proposes to issue annuity agreements should regard them as an important phase of its money raising activities and solicit them actively through articles in its publications, by means of special literature and through personal interviews with likely prospects."

This conclusion is significant when viewed in the light of questions which have been raised concerning the wisdom of accepting annuities under present day conditions. However, the committee recommends many important safeguards as to procedure, accounting and legal advice without which annuity contracts might well become a liability rather than an asset. This suggests a re-study of the whole subject of annuities by all of the boards and agencies of the Church which may be concerned.

The Commission has taken definite steps in that direction,—(a) by adopting the report of its annuity committee after careful consideration; (b) by appointing a standing advisory committee on annuities composed of Messrs. S. F. Telleen, B. B. Slifer and Robbin B. Wolf; and (c) by adopting the following recommendation to the Church:

2. We recommend that the Commission on Investments be instructed to make its report on annuities available to all boards and agencies of the Church so that it may be studied carefully by those most directly concerned; that the Commission be authorized to arrange an early conference between its own committee on annuities and fiscal representatives of the several boards and agencies, for the purpose of reviewing thoroughly all phases of the annuity question; that the Commission present to the Executive Board, for its approval, the recommendations of

such joint conference and make full report at the next biennial convention; that the annuity rates on single lives recommended by the Executive Board, being the same as those recommended by the annuity committee of the Commission, be adopted by this Convention as the maximum rates that should be used by any board or agency of the Church; and that the annuity rates on two lives, submitted by our annuity committee, be adopted by this Convention. (Amended by the Convention, see below).

Finally, it seems fitting that this report should stress the imperative need for growth in the Church's endowments through gifts and legacies. The Finance Committees of the several boards are safeguarding with meticulous care the funds entrusted to their respective boards. Has the membership of the Church done its part in remembering the Church's endowments when choosing the objects of their bounty? There is no more profitable investment than one which goes on in perpetuity doing the Lord's work. There is genuine need for substantially greater endowments. This applies to every board and agency of the Church.

Respectfully submitted,
WILLIAM H. STACKEL, *Chairman.*

Recommendation 1 was adopted.

Recommendation 2. In connection with this recommendation, the item on annuities (V, 4 of the Report of the Executive Board, page 73), deferred until this time, was called up. The recommendation was amended by striking out the word "should" between the words "maximum rates that" and "be used by" and inserting the word "shall." The recommendation as amended was adopted as follows:

2. We recommend that the Commission on Investments be instructed to make its report on annuities available to all boards and agencies of the Church so that it may be studied carefully by those most directly concerned; that the Commission be authorized to arrange an early conference between its own committee on annuities and fiscal representatives of the several boards and agencies, for the purpose of reviewing thoroughly all phases of the annuity question; that the Commission present to the Executive Board, for its approval, the recommendations of such joint conference and make full report at the next biennial convention; that the annuity rates on single lives recommended by the Executive Board, being the same as those recommended by the annuity committee of the Commission, be adopted by this Convention as the maximum rates that shall be used by any board or agency of the Church; and that the annuity rates on two lives, submitted by our annuity committee, be adopted by this Convention.

The Rev. H. F. Baughman, Secretary, presented the report of the Committee on Church Papers.

REPORT OF COMMITTEE ON CHURCH PAPERS
(For action on this report, see p. 425.)

The Committee on Church Papers held one meeting during the biennium, on April 30, 1935. The purpose of this meeting was to give effect to the resolutions of the Savannah Convention,—minutes, page 520.

Further meetings of the entire committee were obviated by authorizing the Executive Committee to carry into effect the proposals adopted.

Organization of the committee was effected by electing the following officers: Chairman, Dr. John Aberly; Secretary, Dr. H. F. Baughman; member of the Executive Committee, the Rev. M. R. Hamsher.

After a discussion, resolutions were adopted recognizing the merit of *The Lutheran* and the appeal it makes to its number of select readers, and expressing the judgment of the committee that the appeal could be made wider through changes in the publication and the addition to the staff of an Associate Editor. This was referred to the Board of Publication with the request that sufficient appropriation be made to carry it into effect. The Executive Committee of the Church Papers Committee, with Dr. Hermann Miller were empowered to act in consultation with the Board of Publication, and to nominate an Associate Editor should the necessary funds be provided. Changes in the publication suggested by the Committee included:—Use of the cover page for announcements of special articles, a department of news from foreign Church bodies, special articles requiring research, a greater opportunity for opinion on controversial matters than the open letter column affords, editorials by others in addition to the Editor-in-Chief of *The Lutheran,* a different division of Departments and a different mechanical layout.

These matters were discussed in a conference with the Editors of *The Lutheran* and *the Lutherischer Herold,* and provision was made for continuing their consideration and applying them as conclusions reached.

The question of an Associate Editor referred to in Report to Savannah Convention of the U. L. C. A. is involved with promotion plans of the Board of Publication and therefore remains an item of unfinished business. Other outcomes of the colloquy between the Editor of *The Lutheran* and the Committee have been: The addition of the Rev. Julius Seebach to the staff as a contributor of a weekly resume of world news; the enlargement of the news letter staff to forty-five clergymen; the holding of semi-monthly conferences of editorial and business staffs together with invited clergymen or laymen to formulate schedules for special articles; and the enlistment of faculty members of our Theological Seminaries as special contributors. The response to these measures is indicated in an increase of subscriptions to *The Lutheran* from 17,000 in July, 1934, to 20,000 in June, 1936, and in an increasing number of positive expressions of approval received.

The Committee hereby nominates Dr. Nathan R. Melhorn, as Editor of *The Lutheran,* and Dr. C. R. Tappert as Editor of the *Lutherischer Herold.*

The terms of office of Drs. John Aberly, A. J. Holl and William J. Showalter, deceased, expire in 1936. The nominees of the Committee are as follows: Dr. Herbert C. Alleman, Gettysburg, Pa., to succeed Dr. John Aberly, ineligible for re-election; Dr. A. J. Holl to succeed himself; and Mr. Charles E. Blum, Philadelphia, Pa., to succeed Dr. W. J. Showalter, deceased.

JOHN ABERLY, *Chairman.*

H. F. BAUGHMAN, *Secretary.*

The Rev. Mr. Baughman introduced the Rev. N. R. Melhorn, Editor of *The Lutheran,* who spoke briefly to the delegates.

Upon nomination of the Committee on Church Papers, the Convention elected the Rev. N. R. Melhorn editor of *The Lutheran,* and the Rev. C. R. Tappert editor of the *Lutherischer Herold.*

Mr. Arthur P. Black, Secretary, presented the report of the Laymen's Movement, and emphasized its various activities.

REPORT OF LUTHERAN LAYMEN'S MOVEMENT
· FOR STEWARDSHIP

(For action on the recommendations in this report, see p. 430.)

During the biennium 1934-1936 the Laymen's Movement in its efforts to render an acceptable account of its stewardship has been witnessing for Christ in the promotion of:

1. Christian Stewardship Fundamentals.
2. The Every Member Visitation throughout our Church.
3. More Useful Literature.
4. A Church-wide movement to establish the Family Altar in every home.
5. The Calendar of Special Days and Seasons as part of permanent program in every Congregation.
6. Regional Meetings for Pastors and Laymen in every Synod.
7. A Circulating Library.
8. Student Aid.
9. Visits to Seminaries.

Our labors in these various fields represent our impartial contribution to the Congregation, the Synod, and the United Lutheran Church in America, along educational and spiritual lines. The following paragraphs summarize our activities during the biennium.

CHRISTIAN STEWARDSHIP FUNDAMENTALS

In our correspondence, our literature, our contacts with seminarians, pastors and laymen, in summer schools, and in congregations, we have continued to emphasize the vital importance of basing all congregational, synodical, and Church work on these three Scriptural teachings: (1) that God is the Owner; (2) that Man is a Steward; and (3) that our acknowledgment of divine ownership and man's stewardship must be translated into active *Christian* service. More requests for information and literature on stewardship were addressed to our office this biennium than during any preceding biennium. More synodical stewardship secretaries and committees are taking their office seriously. More attention is being given the subject of *Christian* stewardship by pastors, Church and synodical officials, and the different boards and agencies, generally. *"Render an account of thy stewardship"* is coming to have a deeper meaning for all of us.

THE EVERY MEMBER VISITATION

More pastors ordered Every Member Visitation literature than in any preceding biennium—1,932 in 1934, and 1,997 in 1935. In five of the twenty-nine English speaking synods in the United States proper every pastor ordered. Five synods were in the 90 per cent class; eight in the 80 per cent class; six in the 70 per cent class; four in the 60 per cent class; and only one below 60 per cent. In these twenty-nine synods eight out of every ten pastors ordered. Of the 199 pastors in the German Nebraska Synod and the three Canada Synods 51, or approximately 26 per cent ordered. In the Fall of 1935 we revised and enlarged our outline for the set-up of a real Every Member Visitation, and forwarded copy to every pastor with our annual letter the first week in September. Copy accompanied annual Every Member Visitation letter to pastors this year, also. We urge the merits of our suggested set-up, as it is based upon the experience of pastors who have made the Every Member Visitation a success over a period of years. There is not a word of theory in it. Our only claim for it is that it works. Official proof that it works was given in a series of eight articles in *The Lutheran* during September and October, 1935. The series gave the official records of seventeen congregations in ten different synods. The congregations were representative of about every type. The synods were well distributed geographically. Those official records prove the claim of the Laymen's Movement that a real Every Member Visitation will work in any congregation.

MORE USEFUL LITERATURE

The demand for our literature has shown a healthy increase. During 1935 we were required to print 2,650,000 copies of literature, to compare with 2,289,000 copies in 1934. It has been necessary to have reprints made of Nos. 1, 2, and 3 of the series of "First Steps in Christian Stewardship" folders. We now have six strictly Christian Stewardship folders. This year's folder, "The Stewardship of Tithing," is our answer to requests for something on tithing from a growing number of pastors this biennium. The steadily increasing demand for stewardship literature is one of the most cheering facts it is our joy to record. We shall aim to make our literature more useful every year.

CHURCH-WIDE FAMILY ALTAR MOVEMENT

During the Lenten Season in 1935 the Laymen's Movement printed 200,000 copies of "Christ in the Home," a six-page folder explaining "The What, the How, and the Why," of the Family Altar, and mailed copy to 3,021 pastors. The response was immediate, and so many encouraging letters from pastors were received that the folder was made one of the regular pieces of literature in the 1935 Every Member Visitation. All told, 500,000 copies of this folder were printed, of which 490,000 have been distributed upon request. For several years different synods have been promoting the Family Altar within their respective synodical boundaries. The wide circulation of "Christ in the Home" put the movement on a Church-wide basis, and paved the way for the monthly booklet for daily devotional use, "Light for Today," the initial number of which appeared in December, 1935. This booklet was authorized by the Savannah Convention, and is published by our United Lutheran Publication House, under the direction of our Common Service Book Committee. The Laymen's Movement regards it a high privilege to co-operate in the promotion of "Light for Today," believing it to be an invaluable aid in the development of individual Christian character in the home.

THE CALENDAR OF SPECIAL DAYS AND SEASONS

During the biennium we have been urging the use of the Calendar of Special Days and Seasons as a permanent feature of the annual congregational program. This is a spiritually educational program suggested by the United Lutheran Church in America. Its outline appears regularly in the annual Year Book. Details of the program are left with the individual congregations. Briefly, it assigns regular periods each year for the special presentation of the program and work of eight Boards and Agencies as follows:

1. The month of September: The Parish and Church School Board.
2. The Advent Season: The Board of Ministerial Pensions and Relief.
3. The Epiphany Season: The Board of Foreign Missions.
4. Septuagesima Sunday: The Board of Deaconess Work.
5. The Lenten Season: The Board of American Missions.
6. Four Weeks following Easter: The Board of Education.
7. The third Sunday in May: National Lutheran Council.
8. The month of June: Inner Mission Board.

The program embraced in this outline is designed to place the interests of (1) the local parish, (2) the synod, and (3) the United Lutheran Church in America, on a co-operative basis, and to make clear that no one of the three can be built up permanently at the expense of the other two. This for the reason all three are interdependent—always have been, and always will be. Those who would like to know more about the what, the why, and the how of the Calendar of Special Days and Seasons program are invited to consult the article on that subject in the September (1936) issue of *The Parish School* Magazine by the Secretary of the Laymen's Movement.

Regional Meetings for Pastors and Laymen

Regional meetings for pastors and laymen, either under the direct supervision of Synodical officials, or with their consent, were worked out in a systematic manner in a number of synods and conferences during the biennium. Our aim is to have such meetings become a part of the regular program in all synods, and to have them conducted as informal round table discussions rather than occasions for long "set" speeches. The purpose of such regional meetings is to bring about better understanding and more fruitful co-operation between the clergy and the laity, and to serve as clearing houses for reaching mutual agreement on disputed points. In a series of five regional meetings in the South Carolina Synod the attendance was 565; in ten such meetings in the Nebraska Synod the attendance was 620; in six meetings in the Knoxville Conference of the Virginia Synod the attendance was 334; in four meetings in the York Conference of the West Pennsylvania Synod (with zero weather and icy roads) the attendance was 190. These figures indicate interest in regional meetings by both pastors and laymen. Whether the meetings should be synod-wide, conference-wide, city-wide, or made up of representatives from three, four or more congregations, is a question of detail rather than a problem. The Laymen's Movement stands ready to do what it can to promote regional meetings throughout the Church during the coming biennium.

The Circulating Library

Our circulating library which has been a feature of our program since 1933 is meeting a real need for many pastors. The number of users has increased steadily during the biennium. Our prize patron is Rev. Douglas Conrad of Bridgewater, Nova Scotia, who has read twenty of our books since October, 1935. We have increased the number of available books from 150 to 251. A folder carrying a revised list went to all pastors the first week in September, along with our annual letter carrying samples of Every Member Visitation literature. The books are classified as follows: (a) Stewardship, Evangelism, Missions, 74; (b) Church Administration and Finance, 27; (c) Biographical, 27; (d) Religious Book Club, 23; (e) Miscellaneous, 57; (f) Oxford Group Books, 7. There is no rental charge. We pay the postage when mailing the books to borrowers. They pay the postage when they return the books. Books are loaned for a maximum period of two months. We are happy to share our select list of books with pastors and laymen and laywomen throughout our United Lutheran Church in America, and invite them to make free use of our offer.

STUDENT AID

During the biennium eight seminarians who received financial aid from our Laymen's Movement were graduated. Seven of the eight were placed as regular pastors before the end of 1935. Since then the eighth has been placed as assistant pastor in a large congregation. The total number of our beneficiaries graduated into the ministry since 1922 is 163, practically all of whom are giving our Church full-time service. A survey of congregations in the United States and Canada, served by ministers who were on our Student Aid rolls, reveals that they are serving more than 40,000 people daily. We have continued to co-operate with the Church officials and Synodical officials in curtailing our Student Aid. No new students have been added to our rolls during the biennium. On the other hand, no students have been dropped from our rolls. Our Student Aid budget for the biennium was $2,757.78. For the year 1936-37 it will be $852.50, for six seminarians three of whom will be graduated in May, 1937. Our Student Aid will reach the vanishing point in 1938.

VISITS TO SEMINARIES

The Secretary of the Laymen's Movement visited the following seminaries in 1934 and 1935: Southern, Mt. Airy, Gettysburg, Hamma Divinity, Chicago, Northwestern and Western. In every instance the reception by both the faculty and the student body left nothing to be desired. The cordial relations between the Laymen's Movement and our seminaries through the years is one of our greatest joys. The purpose of our annual visits to seminaries is to discuss with the seminarians problems of Church administration which all pastors face from the day they enter the ministry. Seminarians are being graduated with a much clearer knowledge of what is expected of pastors than in former years. Our literature is used regularly in the seven seminaries here listed, also in Waterloo and Saskatoon.

ENCOURAGING ANSWERS TO QUESTIONNAIRE

Early in 1936 the Laymen's Movement addressed a letter to pastors who ordered Every Member Visitation literature in 1935, asking them a number of questions directly related to the working out of the Visitation in their congregations. The hundreds of answers, representing every geographical section of the Church, and every type of congregation, contained a wealth of information and suggestions that will be an invaluable guide in our work. A summary of the first 400 answers showed: (a) a decided increase in interest, (b) gratifying increases in the number of pledges, as compared with the decreases, (c) numerous increased amounts in pledges to compare with relatively few decreased amounts, (d) a wider use of the Duplex envelope.

Other facts in the summary revealed (a) that an increasing number of pastors are using women as well as men to make the Every Member Visitation; (b) that while councilmen generally are more active in their support of the Every Member Visitation program, there still remain altogether too many who are lukewarm, or give it no support at all; (c) that there is no unanimity of opinion among pastors regarding the number of pieces of literature that can be used to advantage in the promotional work leading up to the Every Member Visitation: some favor four, some three, some two, some one; (d) that there is a growing demand for literature on tithing; and (e) that many pastors are highly appreciative of the help given them every year by the Laymen's Movement. We never before received so many complimentary references to our literature, and such enthusiastic approval of our efforts to serve the Church. Naturally, such expressions of the stewardship of appreciation make pleasant reading. Our constant aim will be to merit the continued good will of friends everywhere by rendering a more acceptable account of our stewardship year by year.

RECOMMENDATIONS
(For action, see below)

1. That in working out all Church programs through the year added emphasis be placed on Christian stewardship fundamentals as explained in the Scriptures.

2. That in the preparatory work leading up to the annual Every Member Visitation, the spiritual, educational, social and financial objectives be stressed in the order named, and that visitors be trained to talk causes rather than money.

3. That all teachers, leaders, and officials, throughout the Church, be urged to co-operate actively in a year around Church-wide movement to establish the Family Altar in every U. L. C. A. home, and to encourage daily reading of "Light for Today" as part of the family devotionals.

4. That the Calendar of Special Days and Seasons be recommended to all congregations as a permanent spiritual and educational feature of their annual program, September to June, inclusive.

5. That in the interest of better understanding and more fruitful co-operation between pulpit and pew, and among the various auxiliary organizations, regional meetings along the lines of those held this biennium be given every encouragement during the coming biennium.

Respectfully submitted,

J. L. CLARK, *President,*

ARTHUR P. BLACK, *Executive Secretary.*

Recommendations 1, 2, 3, 4, and 5 were adopted.

It was moved and carried that this Convention express its appreciation to the Laymen's Movement, and Mr. Black its Secretary, for providing such fine literature for our Every Member Visitation.

The Report of the Committee on President's Report was taken up as unfinished business and the Chairman presented item **2 under I.** (See p. 419.)

Recommendations 2, 3, 4, 5, 6, and 7 under I were adopted.

Recommendation II was adopted.

Recommendation III. On motion recommendation 1 from the Lutheran Brotherhood was referred to the Executive Board of the Church.

The President called for the reading of the deferred items.

The President granted the privilege for the presentation of one item by the Rev. F. M. Urich, Chairman of the Committee of Reference and Counsel.

REPORT OF COMMITTEE OF REFERENCE AND COUNSEL

Dr. E. Clarence Miller appeared before your committee to present the following recommendations:

The treasurers of synods, present at this Convention, held their usual meeting to discuss matters of special interest to them in the administration of the duties of their office. All present were strong in the belief that their attendance at the Conventions of the Church were of great benefit to them officially, and so to the Church. They respectfully ask this Convention to approve the following recommendations:

1. That we suggest to synods the election of their treasurers as delegates to biennial conventions, or of sending them at the expense of the synod.
2. That inasmuch as the value of a treasurer grows with experience and length of tenure of office, we suggest to synods that no limit be set to the term of his service.

E. CLARENCE MILLER,
Acting Chairman, Meeting of Treasurers.

We recommend the adoption of these recommendations.

The recommendations were adopted.

At 10 : 20 P. M. the Convention adjourned with prayer by the Rev. W. I. Guss.

ELEVENTH SESSION

DESHLER-WALLICK HOTEL
Columbus, Ohio
Wednesday, October 21, 1936, 8 : 45 A. M.

Matins were conducted by the Rev. Paul R. Clouser.

The President called the Convention to order.

The Special Committee on Minutes reported that they had examined the Minutes of the eighth, ninth and tenth sessions, and, finding them correct, moved their approval. The motion was carried and the President declared the Minutes approved.

By general consent, various items of unfinished business were given attention before the regular order of business for Wednesday morning was taken up.

On motion Item II, 7, F, of the Report of the Executive Board (page 53), Recommendation V, B, of the Report of the Parish and Church School Board (page 259), and Item 6 of the Report of the Committee on Memorials from Constituent Synods (page 357), all dealing with the matter of consolidation of periodicals, were referred to the Executive Board with power.

The President stated that Item 2 of the Report of the Committee on Memorials from Constituent Synods (page 355) was sufficiently covered in the President's Report.

The President called attention to the fact that at the Tuesday afternoon's session, (page 418) after the adoption of the report of the Committee on Women as Congregational Representatives, an effort had been made on the part of an individual to present an appeal on grounds of conscience to the Commission of Adjudication. This had been properly ruled out of order because appeals to the said Commission may be made only by a convention of the Church or by a constituent synod. The appeal was based on Article VIII, Section 5 of the Constitution and especially on this sentence therein: "If, on grounds of doctrine or conscience, the question be raised as to the binding character of any action, the said question shall be referred to the Commission of Adjudication." The President now stated that the Convention itself might make an appeal and indeed, on a strict construction of the sentence quoted, is obligated to do so.

On the basis of this constitutional obligation, it was moved and carried that the Convention instruct the Executive Board to be its agent in formulating an appeal to the Commission of

Adjudication concerning the binding character of the action which adopted the recommendations of the Committee on Women as Congregational Representatives.   (Reconsidered and lost—again presented and adopted, see below.)

After several motions had been made and lost, a motion was made and carried to reconsider the action instructing the Executive Board to formulate an appeal to the Commission of Adjudication. Upon reconsideration the motion instructing the Exectuive Board was lost.

It was moved and carried that the three actions taken at the Ninth Session, on the recommendations of the Committee on Women as Congregational Representatives, be reconsidered.

The President stated that the three recommendations were before the Convention.

A motion to adopt recommendation 1 was made.

A motion to postpone the question indefinitely was lost.

The motion to adopt recommendation 1 of the report of the Committee on Women as Congregational Representatives was carried.

Recommendations 2 and 3 were adopted.

It was moved and carried that the Convention instruct the Executive Board to be its agent in formulating an appeal to the Commission of Adjudication concerning the binding character of the action which adopted the recommendations of the Committee on Women as Congregational Representatives.

Taking up the regular order of business, recognition was given to the centennial of the Ohio Synod, and the event was emphasized by an address by the Rev. A. H. Smith, of Ashland, Ohio.

The Rev. L. D. Reed, Chairman, presented the report of the Common Service Book Committee.

REPORT OF THE COMMON SERVICE BOOK COMMITTEE

(For action on the recommendations in this report, see p. 444)

Because of the expense involved, the Committee held only one general meeting during the biennium. At this meeting January 16-17, 1935, Dr. L. D. Reed was elected Chairman and Dr. H. D. Hoover, Secretary. Much work was done by sub-committees, some of which met frequently and reported the results of their activities to the entire membership for comment and final approval.

The death of Prof. John F. Krueger, Ph.D., D.D., LL.D., removed one of the able members of the Committee and brought a deep sense of personal loss to all his colleagues. His character and attainments won for him the highest regard and affection of all who knew him.

DEVOTIONAL LITERATURE IN PAMPHLET FORM

At the Savannah Convention the Church directed the Common Service Book Committee "to study the needs of devotional literature," and to report to this convention with recommendations. (Minutes U. L. C. A., 1934, p. 529.)

A sub-committee of the Common Service Book Committee made a careful survey and discovered a very general demand for devotional literature in pamphlet form. The Committee expected to recommend to this Convention that such pamphlet literature be issued.

When the officers of the Church and the Executive Board learned the results of the survey and the proposed action of the Committee, they expressed the opinion that, in view of the strong demand for such literature, the Committee should proceed to provide it and not wait for the next convention of the Church.

The sub-committee thereupon presented a complete report based on its findings, with a plan of publication. This was transmitted to the Executive Board of the Church. The Board amended and then adopted the proposed plan.

The Common Service Book Committee accordingly appointed an Editorial Committee which arranged with the Publication Board for the the publication of a monthly devotional Magazine which was named "Light for Today." The first issue appeared in December, 1935. The members of the Editorial Committee are Drs. Clare, Fischer, Stirewalt, Steimle, Strodach and Hoover, chairman.

THE DAILY OFFICE BOOK

Another type of devotional literature has also received very careful study by the Committee, which has discussed from time to time both the desirability and possibility of an evangelical "Breviary" for the use of pastors and lay folk. It has felt that it *is* desirable, also that it is possible; and that nothing finer could be provided for the fostering of private devotion than such a guide and help.

Private devotion beside being one of our holiest privileges is one of our most fruitful inspirations. That this should be a matter of daily, devout, and careful, even methodical, practice is realized by all who are spiritually minded, though their lives are busily engaged. A book of daily, private prayer, would be a blessed help not only in offering a vehicle of devotion, but also in building up the life of worship, adoration, thanksgiving, and intercession, without which the believer is as barren as the fig tree from which our Lord expected fruit!

In order to provide for such a sacred use, and that it may be the authorized publication of the Church, the Committee appointed a sub-committee to undertake the preparation of material. It is devoutly hoped that this work when completed will be a book of *private* prayer not unworthy to be placed side by side with the Church's book of *public* prayer, The Common Service Book. This sub-committee consists of the following: Drs. Fischer, Hoover, Keever, Krueger, Mattes, Reed, Seltzer, and Strodach, chairman.

The sub-committee, after extended consideration, submitted a general plan or working basis which the general Committee approved. Realizing that our pastorate and laity will need to be led to the use of such a book, the first principles laid down are simplicity, moderation, practicability. While the liturgical uses of the Western Church are to be employed as model, the development of the work is to be strictly upon the evangelical principles which obtained in the purification of the Mass and other Uses at the time of the Reformation. The structure of the services is to be liturgical (and historical), but simplicity is to be of primary consideration. As the Calendar is fundamental to the preparation and use of such a book, that of the Common Service Book, with such evangelical additions as may be deemed acceptable, is to be used. The Word as Lection, in Psalter, Canticle, etc., is to rule the spirit of the book and inspire the devotions.

With these principles in view it has been determined to confine the scope of the book to one service for each day of the Church Year. This is to be complete in all details and appear as such, thus obviating reference to any other part of the book. While liturgical in structure and containing historic elements, this service is to meet the needs of today and speak the language we employ today. The advantage of one service lies in the fact that it may be used at any period of the day, that is, at the convenience of the user.

However, the committee determined to include two other very brief invariable services, for the use of those who may desire a three-fold daily observance. These will appear but once in the book; be simplicity and brevity itself; and will be provided with Lesson and Collect as season uses during the progress of the Church Year. The primary service is named, The Daily Office; the others, The Mid-day Office, The Night Office.

Thus far the three Offices have been prepared and all material required for the Daily Office for each day from Advent Sunday to the Saturday after the Transfiguration.

Variety and richness will be secured throughout by employing different Versicles, Hymns, Lessons, Prayers, etc.,and by differences in structure of the Office for different days of the week. A Canticle will be used on Sunday; A Psalm on three other days; and a homily on two days. The prayer will consist of Preces on Monday and Wednesday; a series of Collects on four days, and various types of Litanies every Friday. Much of the material will be composed for the book and a great many hymns new to our collections will be introduced.

By way of illustration the outline and material of the Daily Office for the First Sunday in Advent is given as follows:

INVOCATION
THE LORD'S PRAYER
THE CREED
VERSICLES
Behold, the King cometh:
R—O come, let us worship Him.
Rejoice greatly, O daughter of Zion; behold thy King cometh unto Thee:
R—He is just, and having salvation.
Lift up your heads, O ye gates, even lift them up ye everlasting doors:
R—And the King of glory shall come in.
Thou art the King of glory, O Christ.
R—Thou art the everlasting Son of the Father.
Glory be to the Father, and to the Son, and to the Holy Ghost; as it was in the beginning, is now, and ever shall be, world without end. Amen. Alleluia.
THE CANTICLE—*Benedictus*
Blessed be the Lord God of Israel: for He hath, etc.
THE LESSSON—Deut. 18:15-19.
The Lord thy God will raise up unto thee a Prophet from the midst of thee, of thy brethren, like unto me; unto him ye shall hearken; according to all that thou desiredst of the Lord thy God in Horeb in the day of the assembly, saying, Let me not hear again the voice of the LORD my God, neither let me see this great fire any more, that I die not. And the Lord said unto me, They have well spoken. I will raise them up a Prophet from among their brethren, like unto Thee, and will put my words in his mouth; and he shall speak unto them all that I shall command him. And it shall come to pass, that whosoever will not hearken unto my words which he shall speak in my name, I will require it of him.
O Lord, have mercy upon us.
R—Thanks be to God.

THE HOMILY
Behold, thy King cometh unto thee. Mat. 21:5
"Behold!" With this word the evangelist at once rouses us from sleep and unbelief, as though he had something great or remarkable to offer, something we have long wished for and now receive with joy. Such waking up is necessary, because everything that concerns faith is against reason. But the nature of faith is that it does not judge or reason by

what it sees, but by what it hears. It depends upon the Word alone
and not on vision or sight. Christ is received as King only by the followers of the word of the prophet, by the believers in Christ: these are
the true daughters of Zion.

This King is *thy* King, Who was promised to you; Whose own you are.
For Him you have yearned from the beginning; Him the fathers have
desired to see. He will deliver you from all that has hitherto burdened,
troubled, and held you captive. This is a comforting word to a believing
heart.

Where the heart receives the King in steadfast faith, it is secure and
does not fear sin, death, nor any other evil. For it well knows and in
no wise doubts that this King is the Lord of life and death, of sin and
grace, of hell and heaven, and that all things are in His hands.

Thus He became our King, and came down to us that he might deliver us; and such are the boundless gifts brought by this poor, despised
King. All this, reason does not understand, nor nature comprehend; but
it is comprehended by faith alone. (Luther)

HYMN

The Advent of our God
  Our prayers must now employ,
And we must meet Him on His road
  With hymns of holy joy.

The Everlasting Son
  Incarnate deigns to be;
Himself a servant's form puts on,
  To set his people free.

Daughter of Zion, rise
  To meet Thy lowly King,
Nor let thy faithless heart despise
  The peace He comes to bring.

All glory to the Son,
  Who comes to set us free,
With Father, Spirit, ever One,
  Through all eternity.
            Charles Coffin, 1736
            Tr. John Chandler, 1837. a.

THE PRAYER

V—My voice shalt Thou hear in the morning, O Lord:

R—In the morning will I direct my prayer unto Thee, and will look up.

O God, the Father in heaven:

R—Have mercy upon us.

O God, The Son, Redeemer of the world:

R—Have mercy upon us.

O God, the Holy Ghost, the Comforter:

R—Grant us Thy peace.

Blessed be God, Who hath called me from the rest of night to this day:
R—Thanks be to God.
Blessed be God, Who hath sent His son to redeem me:
R—Thanks be to God.
Blessed be God, Whose love surroundeth me:
R—Thanks be to God.
Blessed be God, Whose peace enfoldeth me:
R—Thanks be to God.
Vouchsafe to direct my goings in Thy way, and to use my life to Thy
service.
R—Praise be to God.

Stir up, we beseech Thee, Thy power, O Lord, and come; that by thy
protection we may be rescued from the threatening perils of our sins, and
saved by Thy mighty deliverance; Who livest and reignest with the
Father and the Holy Ghost, ever One God, world without end. Amen.
O Jesus, Sun of Righteousness, rise in our hearts and enlighten us with
the brightness of Thy coming, that we, who rejoice in the sure word of
Thy promise, may not be confounded at Thy coming in glory; through
Thy mercy, O our God, Who, with the Father and the Holy Ghost, livest
and dost govern all things now and evermore. Amen.

Bless we the Lord.
R—Thanks be to God.

The Mid-day Office, an invariable form, contains an Ascription,
Versicles with the Gloria Patri, Collects, and Benedicamus and a concluding Aspiration. The Night Office, also an invariable form, contains
opening Versicles, the Lord's Prayer, a brief Confession and Absolution,
a very brief Lesson, varying with the season, the ancient hymn "Hail,
Gladdening Light," the Preces of the Evening Suffrages, a series of Collects and the Benediction and Commendation.

THE SPANISH LITURGY AND HYMNAL

At the Philadelphia Convention, 1932, the Church adopted the recommendations of the Board of American Missions and authorized the publication of a Spanish Service Book and Hymnal. (Minutes, pp. 339 and
371). A sub-committee of the Common Service Book Committee (Drs.
Strodach, Fischer, Pflum, Swank, Hoover and Reed) was appointed to
confer with the editorial committee of the Spanish Mission and review
the manuscript. With the assistance of Prof. C. T. Benze, D.D., and the
Rev. Jaime Soler, the sub-committee spent several days early in 1933 in
critical examination of the first draft.
A number of suggestions were made in the interest of balance and
unity. These included the consistent use of one version of the Scriptures;

the unification of all rubrics; the preparation of a special preface to the book; items in the Collect translations and the selection of Psalms; the inclusion of material from "Collects and Prayers for Use in Church," etc. Permission was granted for minor changes in the General Prayers to meet local national conditions. The Spanish Committee was advised to seek the aid of a competent Spanish scholar familiar with the liturgical as well as the literary niceties of the language in a final revision of the work.

The editorial committee in Puerto Rico completed a thorough revision of the manuscript conferring from time to time by correspondence with the sub-committee of the Common Service Book Committee. A final conference was held May 27th, 1936 at the Seminary, Mt. Airy, between the sub-committee and the Rev. Wm. G. Arbaugh and Miss Frieda Hoh of the Mission, at which all remaining details were agreed upon.

The Committee is pleased to express its approbation of the earnest and scholarly work of the Spanish editors and of their consistent endeavor to attain the standards desired by the Common Service Book Committee and the Board. Building upon work begun by the Rev. Alfred Ostrum many years ago, the latter Committee consisting of the Rev. Wm. G. Arbaugh, the Rev. Eduardo Roig and Miss Frieda Hoh, has labored diligently to produce a Spanish Liturgy and Hymnal which will creditably represent the United Lutheran Church and be a valuable instrument in the Church's work in all Spanish fields.

Because of financial considerations the book has been compressed so as to include all that is necessary, rather than all that is desirable. The Liturgy is a faithful translation of the essential portions of the Common Service Book. The Hymnal required more than mere translation, and contains considerable original work. It includes 323 hymns. More than one-third of these and about 200 tunes are from the Common Service Book. 140 hymns are original Spanish productions. The collection has been built up to meet the peculiar conditions and requirements of the Spanish fields.

The Common Service Book Committee has given final approval to the manuscript which it is assured can be prepared for publication within a few months. The Committee sincerely hopes that it may be published very soon.

AN ORDER FOR THE BURIAL OF THOSE WHO DIE WITHOUT THE SIGN OF FAITH

The Savannah Convention instructed the Common Service Book Committee to prepare an Order for Burial to be used at the discretion of ministers when it does not seem proper to use the regular Order. The Committee therefore reports the following Order:

Inasmuch as the regular *Order for the Burial of the Dead* is provided only for those "who depart this life in the Christian Faith," the following order may be used at the discretion of the minister in the case of one who has died without giving any evidence of this faith.

The Minister shall say:

In the Name of the Father, and of the Son, and of the Holy Ghost. Amen.

Then shall be said the following:

Turn Thee unto Me, and have mercy upon me.

R—O bring Thou me out of my distresses.

Enter not into judgment with Thy servants.

R—For in Thy sight shall no man living be justified.

O Lord, hear my prayer.

R—And let my cry come unto Thee.

Lord, have mercy upon us.

R—Lord, have mercy upon us.

Christ, have mercy upon us.

R—Christ, have mercy upon us.

Lord, have mercy upon us.

R—Lord, have mercy upon us.

Then shall be said one or more of the Psalms here following:

Psalm 38 *Domine, ne in furore*

O Lord, rebuke me not in Thy wrath. Neither chasten me in Thy hot displeasure.

For Thine arrows stick fast in me: and Thy hand presseth me sore.

There is no soundness in my flesh because of Thine anger: neither is there any rest in my bones because of my sin.

For mine iniquities are gone over mine head:

as an heavy burden they are too heavy for me.

For in Thee, O Lord, do I hope:

Thou wilt hear, O Lord, my God.

For I am ready to halt:

And my sorrow is continually before me.

For I will declare mine iniquity:

I will be sorry for my sin.

Forsake me not, O Lord:

O my God, be not far from me.

Make haste to help me:

O Lord my Salvation.

Glory be to the Father, and to the Son, and to the Holy Ghost:

As it was in the beginning, is now, and ever shall be,

World without end. Amen.

Instead of this, Psalm 1, 61, 6, 36, or 51 may be used.

Then shall be read one or more of the following lessons of Holy Scripture:

For God so loved the world, that he gave his only begotten Son, that whosoever believeth in him should not perish, but have everlasting life. For God sent not his Son into the world to condemn the world, but that the world through him might be saved. He that believeth on him is not condemned; but he that believeth not is condemned already, because he hath not believed in the name of the only begotten Son of God. And this is the condemnation, that light is come into the world, and men loved darkness rather than light, because their deeds were evil. For everyone that doeth evil hateth the light, neither cometh to the light; lest his deeds should be reproved. But he that doeth truth cometh to the light, that his deeds may be made manifest, that they are wrought in God.

John 3:16-21

Instead of this: Lamentations 3:22-33; Luke 12:32-40; John 5:19-29; Romans 6:12-23; I Thessalonians 5:1-11; I Corinthians 4:2-5 may be read.

Then shall the minister say one or more of the following Collects:

Almighty God, Who hast granted us Thy Holy Word and revealed Thyself to us therein, and through it dost teach us the way of righteous living: Grant us ever to reverence, love, and treasure the Holy Scriptures; implant within us the desire and purpose constantly to read and study them; and as Thou has promised wisdom to all who seek it, teach us by Thy Holy Spirit wisdom for this earthly life, so that we may grow in grace and in the knowledge of Jesus, our Lord, and be made wise unto salvation; through the same Jesus Christ, our Lord. Amen.

O Lord God, Heavenly Father, we pray Thee, lead and direct us by Thy Holy Spirit, so that we may not regard our sins lightly or lose ourselves in over-confidence, but by His grace continually bring forth the fruits of repentance, and endeavor to amend our lives from day to day, always finding sure comfort in that Thou art ever gracious to us, and dost forgive our sins and save us eternally; through Jesus Christ, our Lord. Amen.

O most Loving Father, Who willest us to give thanks for all things, to dread nothing but the loss of Thee, and to cast all our care on Thee, Who carest for us: Preserve us from faithless fears and worldly anxieties, and grant that no clouds of this mortal life may hide us from the light of that love which is immortal, and which Thou hast manifested to us in Thy Son, Jesus Christ, our Lord. Amen.

O Heavenly Father, Who through Thy Son, Jesus Christ, hast brought us to sonship with Thyself: Send, we beseech Thee, the Spirit of Thy Son continually into our hearts, that amid all our striving to know and do Thy will, we may not lose the consciousness that Thou art ever near to support our weakness, to increase our strength, and to satisfy our need; and grant that by Thy Spirit we may have grace ever to call Thee by Thy Name, crying, Abba, Father; through the same, Jesus Christ, our Lord. Amen.

O Lord, Who didst pray amidst the shadows of the olive trees, teach us to pray, lest we enter into temptation. Teach us the patience of unanswered prayer, and such an abiding trust in Thy good will that no impatience, no foolish fear, no suffering of the mind or body shall break our faith in Thee. Teach us to say: Thy will be done; to accept Thy will in all things; and to do it as we know it; and out of our shadows, bring us into the light of Thy great love for us and for all mankind, Who with the Father and the Holy Ghost art God, blessed now and evermore. Amen.

Almighty God, the fountain of all wisdom, Who knowest our necessities before we ask, and our ignorance in asking: We beseech Thee to have compassion upon our infirmities; and those things which for our unworthiness we dare not, and for our blindness we cannot ask, vouchsafe to give us, for the worthiness of Thy Son, Jesus Christ, our Lord. Amen.

Then shall all say:

Our Father Who Art in Heaven . . . . Amen.

Then shall the Minister say:

The Grace of our Lord Jesus Christ, and the love of God, and the Communion of the Holy Ghost be with you all. Amen.

THE SERVICE AT THE GRAVE

When the body has been committed to the grave, the Minister shall say:

Man that is born of a woman is of few days, and full of trouble. He cometh forth like a flower, and is cut down; he fleeth also as a shadow and continueth not.

In the midst of life we are in death. Of whom may we seek for succor, but of Thee, O Lord, Who for our sins are justly displeased?

Yet, O Lord most holy, O Lord most mighty, O holy and most merciful Savior: Deliver us not into the bitter pains of eternal death.

Thou knowest, Lord, the secrets of our hearts; shut not Thy merciful ears to our prayers; but spare us, Lord most holy: O God most mighty, O holy and most merciful Saviour, Thou most worthy Judge eternal, suffer us not, at our last hour, for any pains of death, to fall from Thee.

Then shall the Minister say:

We now commit this body to the ground; earth to earth, ashes to ashes, dust to dust; until the day when the Lord Jesus Christ shall come to judge the living and the dead.

Then shall the Minister say one or more of the following Collects:

O Lord God, Heavenly Father, Who hast revealed to us through Thy Son how heaven and earth shall pass away: We beseech Thee keep us steadfast in Thy Word and in true faith; graciously guard us from all sin and preserve us amid all temptations, so that our hearts may not be overcharged with the cares of this life, but at all times in watchfulness and prayer may await the return of Thy Son and the expectation of our eternal salvation with joy; Through the same Thy Son, Jesus Christ, our Lord. Amen.

Grant, O Almighty God, that as Thy blessed Son, Jesus Christ, at His first Advent came to seek and to save that which was lost, so at His second and glorious appearing He may find in us the fruits of redemption which He wrought; through the same Jesus Christ, our Lord. Amen.

Then shall the Minister say:

The Peace of God, which passeth all understanding, keep your hearts and minds through Christ Jesus. Amen.

MISCELLANEOUS

The Committee, co-operating with the editor of *The Lutheran* arranged for an "Occasional Page" in the official organ of the Church to be devoted to the presentation of subjects in the liturgical field. Responsibility for this page was placed in the hands of Dr. Reed, with Dr. Strodach as assistant editor. A series of articles by the Chairman of the Committee has appeared during the biennium.

The Committee gave careful consideration to the action of the Savannah Convention requesting the Common Service Book "to prepare a suitable service for Rural Life Sunday" (Minutes U. L. C. A., 1934 pp. 473, 474, 475). In view of the fact that the original proposal to establish a Rural Life Sunday (Minutes 1932, pp. 446, 449) was not approved by the Church (Minutes 1934, pp. 55, 114), the Committee expressed its opinion that the preparation of such a service was inadvisable. It referred the question, however, to the Executive Board. The latter reaffirmed its previous action, and the Committee did not prepare the service. The Executive Board referred the request of the Conference of Presidents for consideration of "the desirability of a combined Confessional and Communion Service" to the Committee, with instructions to report its findings to the Columbus Convention. This request seems to have grown out of the experience of Presidents who have observed "sad departures from an orderly administration of the Sacrament" in congregations whose pastors take "endless liberties with the Liturgy when the Confessional Service is combined with it." The Committee believes that it would not be practical or advisable to print a special "Combined Service." The rubrics in the Common Service Book are simple and explicit. They should be followed accurately in rendering the service properly. It would seem to be impossible to provide a form which would absolutely protect the Church from "sad departures" and "endless liberties." Such protection can best be afforded by intelligent understanding and a loyal spirit among the clergy.

The book "Collects and Prayers for Use in Church" prepared by the Committee and authorized by the Church, appeared from the press early in 1935. It has been favorably received and should prove a serviceable work.

The Committee recommends:

1. The continuance of the devotional pamphlet "Light for Today," with commendation to pastors and congregations.

2. The approval of the Spanish Liturgy and Hymnal by the Church with the hope that the book may soon be published.

3. The adoption of The Burial Service for Those Who Die Without the Sign of Faith.

4. The approval of the purpose and general plan of the "'Daily Office Book" as outlined in this report.

Respectfully submitted,

LUTHER D. REED, *Chairman,*
HARVEY D. HOOVER, *Secretary.*

Recommendations 1, 2, 3, and 4 were adopted.

The order for adjournment at twelve o'clock was set aside so that the session could be continued to the conclusion of the order of business.

Moved and carried that the time for presentation of the remaining reports be limited to five minutes.

The Rev. G. C. Rees, Chairman, presented the report of the Committee on Church Music.

REPORT OF THE COMMITTEE ON CHURCH MUSIC

The Committee on Church Music did not meet during the biennium on account of financial conditions requiring the conservation of resources. It was upon a suggestion made to the chairman that the usual meeting of the committee was omitted. However, the committee continued to function through the individual activities of various members of the committee.

CONVOCATIONS

In accord with the announcement made at the last conveniton of the U. L. C. A. a convocation on Church Music was held at Wheeling, W. Va., in November, 1934, in which the congregations of the American Lutheran Church and of the U. L. C. A. combined their forces with very successful and satisfactory results. All of the sessions were under the general direction of the chairman of the Committee on Church Music.

At this time, it may not be amiss to remind the Church of the general plan of such convocations. Usually, three sessions are held. The morning hours are given over to the study of the musical settings of The Service, Matins and Vespers. This is followed by a practical demonstration of the best way to use such liturgical music from the standpoint of the organist, choir and congregation, in order to give the combined effect of true worship.

In the afternoon, The Music of the Hymns is considered. A study is made of the sources from which the hymn tunes have been derived, with an analysis of their character and suggestions as to their proper use. Typical tunes representing different countries, periods and composers are presented to illustrate the subject. The comprehensive character of the material is seen in merely mentioning the sources from which the tunes are derived, namely, Latin Plain Song, German Chorales, Calvinistic Psalm Tunes, English Hymn Tunes of three different periods and American Melodies.

In the evening, all the elements of public worship are combined in the Service of Choral Vespers. After the opening part of the service the order of the Church Year is followed in the reading of the Scripture passage appropriate to each season, with the singing of a hymn of the season and an anthem to re-impress the thought of each period. The anthems are chosen from widely different sources to represent the composers of church music in Russia, Austria, Germany, Italy, England and America. The organ numbers are equally characteristic of different composers and periods. With the close of such a service, comes the deep impression of the richness and beauty of the musical materials for those who desire to worship.

The Year Book List of Anthems

Following the plan adopted several years ago, the chairman of the committee requested two organist members to prepare the list of anthems for the Year Book during the biennium. Dr. Frederick L. Bach of Wittenberg College furnished the list for the year 1936 and Mr. Henry L. Seibert, organist of Holy Trinity Lutheran Church, New York City, prepared the list for the year 1937. We are deeply grateful to these men for their co-operation. With the ability of these and the other experienced organists represented in the selections of several years, our organists will be able to assemble a repertoire of the finest type of anthems for the entire Church Year.

Summer Schools

The committee appreciates the place accorded to the music of the Church at the various types of summer schools. A few of these have limited themselves entirely to the field of music while others have given music a prominent place on the program. The chairman can speak of the value of such work from his experience in again presenting the matter of church worship daily during the summer school of the Ministerium of Pennsylvania in the year 1935. In addition, he was requested to undertake a similar kind of work in several district conferences in

Eastern Pennsylvania. The experience of the chairman is like unto that of other members of the committee as well as of persons not members of the committee who would, we are sure, unite with us in urging an even greater emphasis on church music at such gatherings, also at Sunday school and Luther League conventions and similar meetings.

GENERAL CONVENTIONS

We note with pleasure the effort put forth in synodical meetings and the U. L. C. A. conventions to present the devotional sessions in a worshipfully adequate manner. Members of the committee consider it a privilege to co-operate in bringing to pass this much to be desired result. We have had the opportunity of witnessing the advancement made and are gratified at the increasing interest evidenced by all concerned.

CHOIR FESTIVALS

Our contact with the musical forces of the Church leads us to suggest that choir festivals be inaugurated wherever possible. A central place should be chosen to which the choirs and organists of a district not too large could come at least once a year for a church music festival and thereby receive great inspiration for more effective work in their respective congregations. To add zest to these festivals the competitive feature might be introduced. Such choir festivals in other countries, for example, in England and Wales, have produced quite remarkable results. In our own land there is a growing interest in festivals of this character. The Church will benefit greatly by encouraging properly directed festivals for our organists and choirs.

LITURGICAL STUDY FOR ORGANISTS

For years we have felt the desirability of liturgical study for organists. We cannot enter into the details of the subject here but we do desire to point out to organists and choir directors that they should have an adequate and a sympathetic understanding of the liturgy of the Church so that they may properly interpret it to the congregation. This will enable them to be true leaders of worship. To this end, more attention should be given at choir rehearsals to the hymns and the music of the liturgy.

UNITY OF PURPOSE AND PRACTISE

There should certainly be a unified purpose and practise in all the activities of the Church in the sphere of music. The good and tried principles of church music should not be limited to the public worship of the congregation but should find an equally important place in all the auxiliaries connected with the Church, especially in the Sunday school. To have a different spirit in any of the auxiliaries is a disturbing element in the worship of the Church. Rather, there should be a common purpose welding all elements into the one desire for the best in worship. This does not preclude any diversity necessary to meet the special requirements of different groups. However, the music of the Church is paramount and this thought should bring all musical activities of the congregation into a harmonized unity of purpose and practice.

MUSIC IN EDUCATIONAL INSTITUTIONS

We are glad to note the increasing interest in the best music in our educational institutions. The many *a capella* choirs doing uniformly excellent work in our institutions are among the gratifying evidences of this interest. The character of this music is of the best. The number of institutions thus striving for the finest has become so great as to be quite general. This is in conformity with the better trend of musical culture which is becoming quite widespread. For all this we are truly grateful, but we also see in it a challenge to the Church to use only the finest music in worship. Of course, the Church will not respond just because of this challenge, but rather for the reason that her inner spirit requires the most beautiful forms of expression.

CONCLUSION

The committee is looking forward with the hope that more favorable conditions in the near future may enable its members to carry into effect the action of the U. L. C. A. at the Philadelphia convention to provide musical material for all such parts of the Common Service Book as may yet require a musical setting. We hold ourselves in readiness to serve the Church.

Respectfully submitted,
GOMER C. REES, *Chairman.*
GEORGE R. SELTZER, *Secretary.*

Moved and carried that we recommend to every synod in this body that they appoint a committee to study, to purify and to develop Church music.

The Rev. L. D. Reed, Chairman, presented the report of the Committee on Church Architecture.

REPORT OF THE COMMITTEE ON CHURCH ARCHITECTURE

Because of the lack of projects of particular importance, and in the interest of economy, very few general meetings of the committee were held during the biennium. Dr. Luther D. Reed was elected chairman and Mr. Charles A. Scheuringer, secretary.

CORRESPONDENCE AND CONFERENCES

Between meetings the officers conferred frequently and carried on the routine work of the committee. This involved an extensive correspondence as well as conferences with pastors and building committees in various places in Pennsylvania and New Jersey. The past six months have witnessed a decided increase in these activities which indicates the likely resumption of building efforts in a large way as soon as conditions permit.

The secretary reports letters from 17 states and Canada, and the chairman letters from 22 states, Canada, Puerto Rico, Japan and China. More than three-fourths of this correspondence consisted of requests for literature, etc., or sought advice on relatively minor matters. A large number of the other letters had to do with chancel rearrangement, alterations or extensions, interior decoration, furniture, glass, etc. A number of projects involved the erection of small buildings costing from $5,000 to $15,000. In possibly a dozen instances the secretary supplied sketches for alterations, color schemes and other suggestive material. Few projects involving the expenditure of any considerable amount of money, were laid before the committee.

Some of the more important items acted upon were the following.

PLANS APPROVED

Bethany Church, Los Angeles, the Rev. H. T. Kohler. Plans submitted through Dr. Trabert, a member of the Committee, were revised and approved with the understanding that suggested changes in chancel design be adopted.

Nativity Church, Wawautosa, Wis., the Rev. A. C. Baughman, Pastor, Roy O. Papenthien, architect. Plans for a brick colonial building costing about $10,000 were approved after suggestions concerning chancel rearrangement and redesigning had been accepted by the architect.

Ascension Church, Danville, Va., the Rev. A. K. Yount. Plans for a new building prepared by a local contractor were not approved. The secretary of the committee redesigned the building and the final plans were approved by the committee and the Virginia Synod. The building was completed in June, 1935.

Holy Communion, Wautauga Mission, Boone, N. C. Revisions in plans made by Mr. E. W. Wagoner, Salisbury, N. C., covering chancel details, door openings, etc., were incorporated and final plans approved.

Messiah Church, Atlanta, Ga., the Rev. G. F. Hart, Pastor, E. B. Chaplin, architect. Plans for the first unit were approved with suggestions concerning future extensions.

Bethany, Indianapolis, Ind., the Rev. J. L. Seng. Revised plans including corrections and changes were approved.

Epiphany, Pleasantville, N. J., the Rev. R. L. McCullough. Plans for a new Sunday School wing to the existing building were approved after minor changes had been incorporated.

Holy Trinity Church, Willow Grove, Pa., the Rev. Elmer P. Truchses, Pastor, C. A. Scheuringer architect. Plans for a new church building costing approximately $7,900.00 were approved.

Messiah Church, Nashville, Tenn. R. O. Rollins, Chairman of the Building Committee. Changes suggested included the addition of a sanctuary recess, rearrangement of the chancel and redesigning of the front. Revised drawings were approved, the exterior design being commended.

Redemption, Philadelphia, Pa., the Rev. Paul Dieckman, Pastor, C. A. Scheuringer architect. Plans for new church building in colonial design were approved. The basement as a first unit was completed and dedicated in April of this year.

OTHER PROJECTS

Friedens Church, Versailles, O., the Rev. J. W. Rilling. The congregation was advised concerning the erection of an addition to the present church building for Sunday school purposes.

The Lutheran Church, Hegins, Pa., the Rev. Carl H. Moyer. Advice was given concerning the question whether to purchase the interest held by the Reformed Church in the present church building or to erect a new building for the Lutheran congregation.

St. Matthew's Church, Paducah, Ky., the Rev. M. L. Spenny. Extensive correspondence concerning adaptations of standard plan to local conditions.

St. Peter's and St. Paul's Church, Guttenberg, N. J., the Rev. George Churlick. Designs were prepared by the secretary for a proposed reredos.

Grace Church, Gouldsboro, Pa., the Rev. E. O. Steigerwalt. Advice given with sketches concerning alterations to the tower of the church building.

Redeemer Church, Atlanta, Ga., the Rev. J. L. Yost. A sketch for a small frame colonial building to serve as a temporary structure was prepared by the secretary, as well as a later comprehensive scheme for a future permanent structure.

Ascension Church, Pontiac, Mich., the Rev. Ewald G. Berger. The secretary submitted a design, with three later revisions for an addition to an existing residence building to be used as a chapel.

Friedens Church, Philadelphia, Pa., the Rev. Martin Dietrich. The secretary met with the church council and later submitted sketches for repairs and alterations to the church building.

Parma Mission, Cleveland, O., Mr. Ralph H. Orr, Columbus, O., architect. Plans received through the Rev. J. S. Herold, D.D., for a new building to cost approximately $3,500. The architect was advised to add a sanctuary recess, widen the building and redesign the exterior.

Grace Church, Oak Harbor, O., the Rev. Carl Schofer. The secretary prepared four schemes for rearrangement of the chancel and other contemplated alterations.

St. John's Church, Martin's Ferry, O., the Rev. P. W. O. Heist, pastor, J. E. Martsolf, New Brighton, architect. Plans concerning a new parish building to be erected adjacent to the present church, were considered and sketches embodying suggestions as to changes in exterior design were made.

Photographs illustrating a contemplated church and parish building for the mission at Tsing Tao, China, were received through Dr. Koller. The committee suggested the desirability of designs of simpler character and more in conformity with the architectural traditions of the country.

MISCELLANEOUS

Several church buildings have been erected by missions from one or other of the standard plans prepared by the committee, with adaptations to meet local conditions. The Prince of Peace congregation of Philadelphia, the Rev. Paul C. Empie, pastor, completed its building during the past year, using standard design "B," the only change being the erection of an additional bay. Several other missions are contemplating using one or other of these plans.

At the request of the Rev. E. A. Tappert, D.D., Divisional Secretary of the Board of American Missions, the secretary prepared a standard design for a simple chapel suitable for use by Canadian missions. The committee approved the design and prints covering the details of the same have been furnished without charge to the Mission Board.

In response to a request from the officers of the Ohio Synod, an Exhibit consisting of five panels of mounted photographs was prepared and displayed at the recent meeting of the Ohio Synod in Mansfield, O.

The chairman of the committee as president of the Associated Departments of Church Architecture, cooperated in arranging and conducting the North America Conference on Church Architecture, held at the Cathedral of St. John the Divine, New York City, May 5, 1935.

PUBLICATIONS

The committee supplies the following publications and pamphlets without cost upon request.

"Church Principles in Church Architecture"—a 20-page pamphlet prepared by the chairman.

"Practical Suggestions for Building Committees"—an 8-page pamphlet prepared by the chairman.

"Space Requirements for Church Organs"—prepared by the Rev. J. F. Ohl.

"Architectural Leaflets" Nos. 1-6, a series of four-page folders with illustrations and descriptive write-ups of successful buildings.

Leaflets 5 and 6 illustrate two designs of "Standard Plans" each with additional alternate exterior designs. These plans, designed by the Secretary for mission congregations, have been approved by the committee. Complete plans and specifications for the same can be secured by mission congregations at nominal cost.

The committee has no recommendations.

Respectfully submitted,

LUTHER D. REED, *Chairman.*

CHARLES A. SCHEURINGER, *Secretary.*

The Rev. W. H. Greever, Secretary, presented the report of the Statistical and Church Year Book Committee.

REPORT OF STATISTICAL AND CHURCH YEAR BOOK COMMITTEE

(For action on the recommendations in this report, see p. 461.)

This committee has held three meetings within the biennium, all in New York. The first meeting was on February 13, 1935, all members present. The Committee was organized by the election of Dr. George L. Kieffer, Chairman, and Dr. W. H. Greever, Secretary. Special consideration was given to the functions of the larger Committee, constituted by the advisory membership of all statistical secretaries of the Constituent Synods.

The supply of parochial blanks having been reported as barely sufficient for the 1935 distribution, special attention was given to the review and revision of the blanks, for a new edition. This work was completed at the third meeting of the Committee, April 28, 1936. Only two or three rubrics were changed, and other revisions were in clarifying notes and style of printing. The new blanks are ready for the regular distribution.

Following up the constructive work of the Conference of Synodical Statistical Secretaries held in connection with the Savannah Convention, especially in the emphasis given to the necessity for complete and accurate records and for complete, accurate and prompt reports, the Committee arranged for a similar Conference in connection with this Convention, which in reality becomes a meeting of the Advisory Committee with the regular Committee.

The following recommendations are offered for the consideration of the Convention:

RECOMMENDATIONS

1. That this Committee prepare proper blanks for reports on "State of the Church," for distribution to the Congregations, in 1937, for reports

to all Synods in 1938; that provision be made for uniform analysis and interpretation of those reports by someone appointed in each Synod for that purpose; that, such synodical summaries be forwarded to this Committee for such use as the President of the U. L. C. A. may designate; and, that, such reports be made every four years, beginning with 1938.

2. That the value of the Conference of Synodical Statistical Secretaries, authorized to be called in connection with the biennial Conventions of the U. L. C. A., be recognized as an effective means for the promotion of uniform, complete and accurate records and reports and that their attendance at these conferences is highly desirable.

3. That the wider circulation and use of the Year Book be urged upon pastors and congregations, that this official, current information concerning the state and work of the Church may serve the purpose for which it has been gathered.

4. That the Convention reemphasize certain recommendations which it has adopted at previous meetings: (1) Requesting congregations to provide records and reports through congregational statistical secretaries; (2) Requesting Synods to observe uniform size and style in printing statistical tables in their minutes, so as to make material available for proposed Statistical Hand Book; (3) Urging universal use of authorized Parish Record Book, Record Cards, Standard Blanks, etc., etc.; (4) Requesting Synods to secure statistical and graphical histories of Synods and Congregations; and, (5) Authorizing continued participation in the work of the American Lutheran Statistical Association and the National Lutheran Council in the promotion of general, uniform Lutheran statistics.

G. L. KIEFFER, *Chairman.*
W. H. GREEVER, *Secretary.*

STATISTICAL REPORT OF THE UNITED LUTHERAN CHURCH IN AMERICA FOR THE YEAR 1934

Index No.	Synod	When Organized	Pastors	Parishes	Congregations	Membership: Baptized	Confirmed	Communing	Accessions Children: Baptism	Children: Otherwise	Adult: Baptism	Adult: Confirmation	Adult: Certificate	Adult: Otherwise	Losses Children: Death	Children: Otherwise	Adult: Death	Adult: Certificate	Adult: Otherwise	Church Papers: No. Sub. to Official Papers	No. S.S. Papers Distributed	No'r Ch. P'rs to Sub. No.
1	Ministerium of Penna.	Aug. 15, 1748	485	394	600	304338	206034	146166	6255	2740	488	7054	2577	1935	352	2365	3299	1650	4423	4879	12480	5124
2	United Synod of N.Y.	Oct. 23, 1786	474	400	434	239401	162841	106148	5563	5144	446	6525	1877	4557	253	5988	2759	1061	5138	2498	9374	2353
3	United Synod of N.C.	May 2, 1803	111	92	160	38255	27006	19695	768	405	160	791	591	71	36	275	269	456	383	946	2224	4483
4	Maryland Synod	Oct. 11, 1820	141	139	139	73424	52756	14528	1289	152	140	1440	606	505	55	199	673	366	1000	1538	3453	2215
5	Synod of So. Carolina	Jan. 14, 1824	71	60	108	28815	21399	13522	415	325	53	653	507	29	21	199	222	445	348	447	1456	1478
6	Synod of West Penna.	Sept. 5, 1825	130	96	159	64031	48207	34928	1007	209	277	1321	694	401	63	170	666	455	351	901	3480	1335
7	Synod of Virginia	Aug. 10, 1829	99	78	171	27477	22129	20625	365	658	298	393	329	145	16	170	238	217	279	825	2318	2849
8	Synod of Ohio	Nov. 7, 1836	241	171	271	85690	59868	34928	1816	824	556	2027	1217	1029	83	536	940	650	809	1575	18801	1622
9	East Penna. Synod	May 9, 1842	172	127	159	78710	55830	20625	1416	124	301	1582	1079	855	62	1290	763	644	918	1207	6148	1678
10	Alleghany Synod	Sept. 9, 1842	88	69	145	44231	32614	11665	702	133	205	799	427	157	36	983	375	284	301	607	5111	757
11	Pittsburg Synod	Jan. 15, 1845	265	213	309	128725	89803	29471	2483	1284	348	1799	1135	1667	156	876	991	891	3143	1761	18218	25068
12	Indiana Synod	Oct. 28, 1848	77	72	107	24153	18374	3209	420	992	205	493	254	125	12	130	216	152	198	391	4253	455
13	Illinois Synod	Sept. 8, 1851	151	139	139	64727	44464	25293	1353	90	190	1801	764	1080	44	282	525	456	1197	785	8799	1020
14	Texas Synod	Nov. 10, 1851	24	28	29	6455	4558	416	49	30	31	213	45	282	3	16	58	52	70	167	76	28
15	Susquehanna Synod	Nov. 21, 1855	105	81	161	54473	40198	8112	898	339	153	1801	655	112	21	170	52	368	570	687	3415	431
16	Mississippi Synod	Feb. 7, 1855	7	5	11	1037	724	3055	30	181	2	15	24	107	2	63	111	12	16	39	698	309
17	Synod of Iowa	Sept. 3, 1855	33	33	33	19820	13104	15638	503	40	199	697	225	538	56	494	36	119	191	247	1684	651
18	Georgia-Ala. Synod	July 20, 1860	20	19	31	6635	4345	5481	81	378	20	136	82	181	4	142	264	44	54	221	3014	366
19	Synod of Canada	July 21, 1861	88	67	100	31382	21005	10817	796	76	36	808	137	214	23	230	141	135	543	239	3368	583
20	Synod of Kansas	Nov. 5, 1868	44	36	44	12062	8866	10748	255	253	152	335	271	339	27	184	231	86	155	327	960	133
21	Synod of Nebraska	Sept. 1, 1871	58	50	56	23410	15951	10045	681	480	185	748	571	358	20	202	163	159	163	349	859	324
22	Wartburg Synod	1875	56	47	47	23000	14814	3987	475	173	75	571	59	74	40	221	131	43	204	326	1630	397
23	Ger. Nebraska Synod	July 24, 1890	83	70	85	16432	12838	1661	462	271	75	462	67	1535	42	129	27	76	354	304	982	121
24	Synod of California	April 6, 1891	61	36	36	10585	6796	27854	315	56	29	322	422	340	6	97	84	39	393	115	112	1318
25	Rocky Mt. Synod	May 6, 1891	23	15	15	3695	2739	6226	101	1272	203	67	85	114	3	27	67	358	171	887	570	1909
26	Synod of the Northwest	Sept. 23, 1891	111	84	122	55159	36453	2139	1481	392	33	1854	91	227	8	1203	295	45	1585	112	997	156
27	Manitoba Synod	July 16, 1897	39	25	27	17113	10125	1983	795	127	29	712	78	6	6	129	84	37	131	108	156	52
28	Pacific Synod	Sept. 26, 1901	51	27	31	5848	3743	3269	118	33	10	139	140	73	8	97	67	46	96	183	195	373
29	Nova Scotia Synod	July 10, 1903	11	23	34	5859	3401	4718	156	65	20	100	100	17	3	6	53	10	16	142	1530	36
30	Synod of West Virginia	April 17, 1912	24	23	22	7442	5044	4216	137	146	16	143	143	183	8	17	68	99	35	219	21	177
31	Slovak Zion Synod	1919	26	31	33	8428	5491	4428	201	96	68	193	61	61	6	499	77	16	—	374	36	82
32	Michigan Synod	June 10, 1920	35	31	33	11260	7753	5260	309	71	22	291	140	46	8	26	19	99	1276	219	1230	177
33	Synod of Florida	Sept. 24, 1928	17	13	13	2308	1717	1308	35	95	22	81	16	26	19	19	19	16	125	95	232	82
34	Kentucky-Tenn. Synod	June 6, 1934	18	19	25	7127	5696	4696	111	71	38	152	124	130	8	70	97	36	87	144	1378	331
35	Totals for U. S. and Canada		3447	2768	3951	1529567	1066686	721749	31986	17797	5276	36932	15103	17724	1567	18133	14430	9558	24629	24843	127498	59741
36	Totals Outside U. S. and Canada				1825	181695	2249	85281	11449		3270	208	39		35	111	70	131	222		40	
37	U. L. C. A. World Total		3447	2768	5776	1711262	1068935	807030	43435	17797	8546	37140	15142	17724	1602	18244	14500	9689	24851	24843	127538	59741

STATISTICAL REPORT OF THE UNITED LUTHERAN CHURCH IN AMERICA FOR THE YEAR 1934

PAROCHIAL — FINANCIAL

Index	Sunday No.	Officers & Teachers	Sunday Scholars	Home Dep't	Cradle Roll	Weekday No.	Weekday Teachers	Weekday Scholars	Catechumens	Ministry	Deaconess	In Lutheran Inst.	In Non-Luth. Inst.	Men's No.	Men's Members	Women's No.	Women's Members	Young P. No.	Young P. Members	Church Edifices	Parsonages	School and Parish Houses
1	595	13845	132573	4581	11089	172	1470	15888	8784	99	17	262	1617	309	14191	890	36071	839	27511	22679237	2281596	2165517
2	437	8404	69627	1881	9263	99	522	5381	7676	63	8	124	1299	299	13363	801	32786	833	22384	22204093	2631538	3247794
3	157	2271	25379	490	2691	101	618	9276	2569	37	2	113	251	55	1360	177	3480	232	6609	2560000	350286	188767
4	142	3742	36250	1594	812	18	157	1515	2569	37	1	50	469	63	2405	233	9585	200	7119	6451771	714030	362600
5	107	1470	14236	1230	2994	58	484	6867	3467	23	1	106	305	26	846	159	4614	194	5099	1463893	238700	229711
6	158	4350	47345	1498	1057	20	162	2184	1386	13	1	89	393	39	2022	250	8945	172	6748	5564600	556850	292700
7	160	1889	17440	3157	3246	71	434	4583	3705	39	3	71	182	27	818	167	4276	353	4810	1898530	386560	94190
8	269	5403	51763		3302	26	143	2241	2850	31	2	245	677	142	5420	535	17630	288	8495	8103035	792821	306000
9	157	4318	41213	2184	1669	36	248	2476	1533	20	1	37	495	124	6070	351	13166	149	8221	7648422	944582	698200
10	132	2659	24339	312	5250	47	345	3705	4965	48	4	160	255	42	2483	166	5205	539	13651	3282850	427001	123000
11	303	5975	55999	314	743	59	400	4390	1996	47	1	17	737	163	5539	598	18340	121	7129	9844012	1291192	318024
12	108	1688	13392	1352	2889	13	54	767	160	6			187	36	1086	154	1131	254	4748	2251350	172150	13900
13	138	3158	27772		181	31	300	3095	1848	25	1	143	446	95	4093	296	9159	47	119	4699954	576780	275500
14	31	313	2473	42	2341	4	18	164	34	1			43	7	168	37	6916	163	2508	1368000	49950	35150
15	169	3430	33940		57	42	299	3676	1478	21	2	67	364	53	2774	226	92	7	974	4252000	481600	163250
16	11	62	453	18	733	10	34	778	249	4		18	190		626	8	2665	80	1335	34700	8675	
17	33	740	6796	126	133	7	61	558	929	3			74	17	159	73	1072	50	1715	951014	135650	3000
18	26	406	3082	61	1121	12	109	828	522	1		25	29	6	473	45	3371	95	917	649400	43420	109000
19	42	1019	7498	14	487	28	32	663	670	9		6	124	17	533	93	2684	51	1314	1120200	201350	84100
20	59	725	5893	48	1180	17	44	527	675	20	3	58	201	19	519	91	2926	80	468	1270190	166500	32900
21	41	1063	8978	45	473	13	118	1052	738	12		18	46	20	984	112	3021	61	5220	1305500	158000	18000
22	69	668	6366	135	237	28	22	293	408	8		19	68	22	59	71	1887	36	977	881577	165653	87800
23	36	488	4779	158	396	4	12	710	70	5			165	18	631	71	2328	68	691	683300	202850	13350
24	13	572	4327	10	240	11	10	113	3012			4	67	18	165	85	773	23	408	1578000	72700	18000
25	102	246	1573	66	2372	31	169	157	592	17		42	460	70	2964	32	619	212	928	458850	32200	3500
26	99	2066	16885		41	81	79	2100	169	10		13	31	3	39	193	6630	41	615	4084787	320700	153100
27	21	212	2668	71	184	8	59	2005	352	3		58	58	12	218	33	793	39	959	287475	74875	2500
28	31	255	1932		30			464	381	6		5	11	1	30	37	571	16	299	355604	39009	12750
29	21	174	1348	40	259	9	53	583	589	2		5	66	10	264	21	997	38	956	198600	31200	3000
30	30	463	3527		55	24	26	1179	66	5		4	21	3	172	43	674	20		648700	121051	2000
31	31	110	1081	61	618	8	33	333	302	1		16	90	14	299	12	1667	50		389000	84000	25000
32	20	552	4887		29	21	11	174				1	28		77	53	495	14		1052002	100000	36000
33	12	152	1130		264		7									19				367687	39500	3200
34	22	396	3554			3		73		1		5	83	15	524	58	2006	39	956	914100	111500	45500
35	3850	73284	680128	21254	57540	1092	6574	78798	57794	578	48	1805	9536	1741	71374	6190	212268	5639	155616	120107242	14004469	9167003
36	1240	203	64142			1130	13	46666	140	119			28	803	20699	703	15420	23	656	225000	56000	8270
37	5090	73487	744270	21254	57540	2222	6587	125464	57934	697	48	1805	9564	2544	92073	6893	227688	5662	156272	120332242	14060469	9175273

STATISTICAL REPORT OF THE UNITED LUTHERAN CHURCH IN AMERICA FOR THE YEAR 1934

FINANCIAL

Column groups: **Valuation of Church Property** (Endowment, Other Property, Total Valuation, Indebtedness); **Congregational Expenses** (Current, Unusual, Total); **Congregational Benevolence** — Apportioned (Paid, Excess, Deficit), Unapportioned (Education, Foreign Missions, Home Missions, Inner Missions, Other Benevolence, Total Unapportioned Benevolence); **Summary** (Total Benevolence, Total Expenditures).

Index	Endowment	Other Property	Total Valuation	Indebtedness	Current	Unusual	Total	Paid	Excess	Deficit	Education	Foreign Missions	Home Missions	Inner Missions	Other Benevolence	Total Unapport. Benev.	Total Benevolence	Total Expenditures
1	1431554	999680	29557584	3886465	1560677	575046	2135723	270204	409	245073	10389	28265	9012	43746	31427	122839	393043	2528756
2	708242	1096125	29725792	4937383	1919457	307823	2227280	157205			6518	16301	13583	5734	24766	116902	274107	2501387
3	26337	90191	3215590	266981	180446	68201	248647	32485	34	39524	1099	3537	3816	7462	7890	23804	56289	304936
4	97435	308417	7934253	1186427	505088	213138	718226	90267	798	26727	2822	15417	8945	29833	12001	69018	159285	877511
5	12600	149710	2094614	248793	118159	52372	170531	19990		24132	11200	2477	1602	6437	5663	27379	47369	217900
6	314244	133260	6861654	487833	389462	84474	473936	93389	4306	39349	1757	11309	2865	7738	11884	35553	128942	602878
7	100698	117182	2597160	169089	146897	46647	193544	26363	47	25606	383	3363	2224	9177	18976	22026	48389	241933
8	179411	282539	9663806	955014	608976	92259	701235	120374		80854	1443	9597	3858	12387	10855	46261	166635	867870
9	200985	426806	9918995	1503142	638956	141814	780770	101664	1596	43167	4395	24042	7035	32397	8009	78724	180388	961158
10	48295	145939	4027085	459980	217322	25604	242951	46936	266	24805	1225	3702	1542	3885	20714	18363	65299	308250
11	172042	808794	12434064	3008695	778768	107803	886571	104395	425	126090	6094	14189	847	33309	2182	82434	186829	1073400
12	36420	124220	2598040	124220	162388	36810	199198	27129		23140	125	1291	3225	8661	7889	13106	40235	239433
13	69019	133333	5754586		426834	52830	479664	53161	12	74786	855	7375	73	12326	1102	31670	84831	564495
14	170	9900	231970	1408550	9647	9647	19294	3460	464	8587	42	196	1135	707	4569	2120	5580	42542
15	70098	132754	5099702	37194	310470	62603	373073	54046		51279	630	6918	13	4618	204	17870	71916	444989
16		500	43875	512294	4255	952	5207	668	188	1044	3	7	443	11	2004	238	906	6113
17	5200	56703	1151567	8255	110461	10846	121307	11565		15286	390	1000	311	1154	2194	4991	16556	137863
18	20095	26061	847976	287529	45129	16047	61176	8285		6383	250	515	857	1492	2859	4532	12817	73993
19	32122	54074	1491846	131138	144362	19435	163797	22861	1231	3180	3450	1367	740	1626	1930	10159	33020	196817
20	19650	14887	150427	113779	95197	16499	111696	14928	125	11397	1181	1550	753	2391	3730	6950	21878	133574
21	5035	128762	1613297	99128	111556	14599	126155	22109	22	15378	15	1707	112	2913	355	10284	32393	158548
22	2450	12430	1149910	122827	102476	15943	118419	5679		1070	817	729	428	856	1279	2067	7746	126165
23	9800	11371	920671	50055	72014	12271	84285	5748		56362	236	939	425	1590	2734	5053	10801	95086
24	80000	40550	1789250	273864	104936	23235	128171	8229	231	8105		988	344	2691	1426	7074	15303	143474
25	58	13123	507731	222743	31726	10338	42064	4195		2658	1888	96	2103	300	9724	2384	6579	48643
26	4732	59920	4623239	1717611	349536	54548	404084	58040			256	3635	391	5322	261	22672	80712	484796
27		10935	375785	49000	44205	6643	50848	5537			430	145	36	189	1005	785	6322	57170
28	591	13726	421680	197667	30736	4160	34896	3750		2611	247	217	128	14	547	2232	5982	40878
29		7300	240100	15420	17940	1298	19238	1537		3723	177	772	43	584	1238	961	2498	21736
30	350	81940	854041	149272	54587	7728	62315	7206		5675		25	191	15	233	2899	10105	72420
31	955	3000	501955	106806	14385	910	15295	913		848	157	234	115	957	1365	316	1229	16524
32	882	20700	1209584	448452	71669	9578	81247	9883		11263	63	119	839	454	181	2904	12787	94034
33		5650	416037	153590	24980	4340	29320	2321		871	513	1162		5374	3725	932	3253	32573
34	13040	101958	1186098	179045	66845	31509	98354	6907	8	2173						11613	18520	116874
35	3662510	5622440	152563664	23797868	9488210	2137975	11626185	1401429	10256	981146	59255	163425	76257	296378	211800	807115	2208544	13834729
36		2456200	2745470		7980		7980								164926	164926	164926	172906
37	3662510	8078640	155309134	23797868	9496190	2137975	11634165	1401429	10256	981146	59255	163425	76257	296378	376726	972041	2373470	14007635

I. U. L. C. A. STATISTICAL REPORT OF OTHER COUNTRIES OUTSIDE U. S. A. AND CANADA
(Foreign Missions compiled by Board of Foreign Missions; American Missions by Board of American Missions)

Index Numbers	Country	Province	When Organized	Pastors	Congregations	MEMBERSHIP Baptized	Confirmed	Communing	Net	ACCESSIONS — CHILDREN & ADULT Baptism	Confirmation	Certificate	LOSSES — CHILDREN & ADULT Death	Certificate	Otherwise	CHURCH PAPERS No. S. S. Papers Distributed
1	India	Madras	1842	Ord. Miss. 23, Nat. Workers 2993, Unord. men & women 37	1703	168013		78176	4058	9390						
2	Africa	Liberia	1860	Ord. Miss. 5, Nat. Workers 65, Unord. men & women 10	16	480		338	149							
3	Japan	Kyushu-Hondo	1892	Ord. Miss. 11, Workers 95, Unord. men & women 9	31	4246		1535	254							
4	China	Shantung	1898	Ord. Miss. 6, Nat. Workers 128, Unord. men & women 8	36	2728		2190	476							
5	Virgin Islands*		1666	U. L. C. 4	5	1845	1209	761		52	74	10	90	50	333	15
6	British Guiana	Berbice	1889	Ord. Miss. 2, Workers 10	8	660		394	31							
7	Puerto Rico*		1898	U. L. C. 8, Workers 10	14	2038	1040	807		109	134	29	15	81		25
8	Argentina	Buenos Aires	1908	Ord. Miss. 2, Nat. Workers 31, Unord. men & women 1	12	1685		1080	200							
9	Totals Outside U. S. A. & Can.			Pastors 61, Workers 3322, Unord. 65	1825	181695	2249	85281	5168	9551	208	39	105	131	333	40

*Figures from 1935 Year Book.

STATISTICAL REPORT OF OTHER COUNTRIES OUTSIDE U. S. A. AND CANADA—Concluded
(United Lutheran Church in America)

PAROCHIAL

Index Numbers	CHURCH SCHOOLS — SUNDAY Number	Officers and Teachers	Scholars	WEEKDAY Number	Officers and Teachers	Scholars	Inquirers	Catechumens	STUDENTS Ministry	In Non-Luth. Institutions	CHURCH SOCIETIES — MEN'S Number	Members	WOMEN'S Number	Members	YOUNG P. Number	Members
1	1126		55783	1048		42230	15163		92		799	20551	691	15145		
2	10		200	13		528	199		12							
3	30		3273	10		1200	300	65	10	9						
4	30	90	1349	42		1345	580				1	80	2	40	4	148
5	6		567	4	8	105										
6	9	113	428	2		111	53		2							
7	19		2038	4	5	192		75	1	19	3	68	10	235	19	508
8	10		504	7		955	200									
9	1240	203	64142	1130	13	46666	16495	140	119	28	803	20699	703	15420	23	656

FINANCIAL

Index Numbers	VALUATION OF CHURCH PROPERTY — Church Edifices	Parsonages	School and Parish Houses	Other Property	Total Valuation	SUMMARY — Congregational Expenses	Field Contributions	Benevolence	Total Expenditures
1				1200000	1200000		144360		144360
2				80000	80000		1995		1995
3				675000	675000		9600		9600
4				185000	185000		3412		3412
5	115000	16000		30000	161000	4868		288	5156
6				61200	61200		2171		2171
7	110000	40000	8270		158270	3112		100	3212
8				225000	225000		3000		3000
9	225000	56000	8270	2456200	2745470	7980	164538	388	172906

STATISTICAL REPORT OF THE UNITED LUTHERAN CHURCH IN AMERICA FOR THE YEAR 1935

Index No.	SYNOD	When Organized	Pastors	Parishes	Congregations	Baptized	Confirmed	Communing	Ch. Baptism	Ch. Otherwise	Ad. Baptism	Con-firmation	Ad. Certificate	Ad. Otherwise	Ch. Death	Ch. Otherwise	Ad. Death	Ad. Certificate	Ad. Otherwise	No. Sub. Official Papers	No. S.S. Papers Distributed	No. Sub. Other Ch. Pr's
1	Ministerium of Penna..	Aug. 15, 1748	486	394	598	306270	208632	148215	5930	2436	502	7140	2658	2378	278	2790	3269	1653	4648	4776	11993	5360
2	United Synod of N.Y.	Oct. 23, 1786	479	394	431	245473	164641	108033	4732	4565	430	5432	1898	3021	339	4006	2186	922	5572	2592	15124	2400
3	United Synod of N.C.	May 2, 1803	117	93	160	73820	27568	31716	1413	201	56	898	566	523	29	457	299	398	208	711	2398	5156
4	Maryland Synod	Oct. 11, 1820	143	99	139	54761	41024	30165	503	427	174	1611	691	36	45	523	702	550	577	1349	8804	2157
5	Synod of So. Carolina	Jan. 14, 1824	76	108	159	29079	21896	14894	1152	163	100	625	464	458	20	36	232	321	145	561	1868	1718
6	Synod of West Penna.	Jan. 5, 1825	141	96	171	65658	49359	35414	435	534	245	1360	709	92	46	458	631	472	400	1215	2334	1183
7	Synod of Virginia	Sept. 10, 1829	96	171	272	27855	22448	50079	1725	210	376	1967	532	784	18	92	270	379	1328	703	2323	3038
8	Synod of Ohio	Aug. 1836	246	197	160	87958	61404	34816	1288	645	276	1591	1044	700	63	293	950	654	1176	1684	17272	2109
9	East Penna. Synod	Nov. 9, 1842	181	123	145	80163	56786	20741	659	150	175	743	437	223	56	784	820	665	249	1446	5580	1606
10	Alleghany Synod	May 1842	76	68	309	43107	33349	56953	414	219	343	2797	1239	404	45	700	820	279	279	664	5142	709
11	Pittsburgh Synod	Sept. 9, 1842	267	213	110	129481	90963	12132	2557	870	152	517	304	227	77	223	997	1199	185	1641	17632	25416
12	Indiana Synod	Jan. 15, 1845	86	68	139	25046	18945	31544	1321	150	356	1829	775	148	10	1120	227	185	409	469	4064	811
13	Illinois Synod	Oct. 28, 1845	158	116	29	66875	46652	25727	414	1007	29	514	217	853	37	148	425	527	186	783	8539	1065
14	Texas Synod	Sept. 8, 1851	24	29	161	6506	4638	397	131	219	216	1029	599	99	9	99	81	531	611	156	255	821
15	Susquehanna Synod	Nov. 21, 1851	107	79	11	54725	40650	25727	941	16	153	656	242	263	60	263	588	430	—	675	6113	783
16	Mississippi Synod	Feb. 25, 1855	7	5	33	1059	767	397	23	132	14	93	96	13	8	9	9	7	175	46	52	96
17	Synod of Iowa	Sept. 3, 1855	35	31	101	20434	13874	8559	476	36	23	716	255	391	5	213	119	182	134	205	2830	473
18	Georgia-Ala. Synod	Sept. 20, 1860	20	66	43	6615	4314	3010	92	393	100	244	166	151	48	13	46	55	734	266	692	312
19	Synod of Canada	July 21, 1861	90	35	57	31367	21141	15958	691	75	272	846	251	266	14	391	299	205	205	1083	1814	951
20	Synod of Kansas	Nov. 5, 1868	41	57	46	12532	9150	5590	259	307	52	645	63	384	21	151	124	100	218	179	2106	264
21	Synod of Nebraska	Sept. 1, 1875	55	43	82	24740	16963	11386	693	201	19	520	67	227	23	266	144	214	310	255	2738	568
22	Wartburg Synod	July 1871	56	69	69	22587	15138	10870	486	219	51	242	174	234	23	384	241	67	231	311	977	140
23	Ger. Nebraska Synod	July 24, 1890	85	36	15	18741	13228	10411	421	57	19	63	174	55	14	227	131	40	175	253	1037	208
24	Synod of California	April 1891	62	15	86	10665	6898	4201	307	219	217	1848	457	1496	46	234	118	73	308	280	1763	582
25	Rocky Mt. Synod	May 6, 1891	23	86	129	56992	37971	28949	76	292	10	368	89	407	46	1496	276	80	80	117	905	221
26	Synod of the Northwest	Sept. 23, 1891	103	55	54	18272	16249	6559	1388	112	25	119	101	134	11	407	39	43	325	476	3746	1067
27	Manitoba Synod	July 16, 1897	61	24	31	5686	5520	1988	663	56	2	108	70	3	16	134	61	15	362	156	153	2349
28	Pacific Synod	Sept. 26, 1901	39	26	34	6051	3475	2081	155	34	26	181	26	36	10	3	51	51	31	109	986	179
29	Nova Scotia Synod	July 1903	11	8	31	7576	5520	3484	190	8	26	94	110	155	6	70	67	13	31	172	280	17
30	Synod of West Virginia	April 17, 1912	25	34	32	8701	7820	4659	108	158	52	309	53	57	1	36	61	51	22	175	1700	412
31	Slovak Zion Synod	April 10, 1919	25	23	30	11437	6094	4401	274	80	16	86	110	155	6	155	55	67	437	221	40	65
32	Michigan Synod	June 10, 1920	34	30	13	2322	1692	1104	60	44	65	140	164	142	5	57	17	27	98	620	1544	201
33	Synod of Florida	Sept. 24, 1928	15	12	24	7354	5949	3600	104	—	—	—	—	—	—	142	87	76	78	106	278	129
34	Kentucky-Tenn. Synod	June 6, 1934	17	18	—	—	—	—	—	—	—	—	—	—	—	—	—	—	—	107	1332	152
35	Totals for U.S. and Canada	....	3487	2761	3961	1558115	1089914	736029	30625	16482	5201	35468	15706	15174	1443	16353	14073	10313	24822	24562	134414	62718
36	Totals Outside U.S. and Canada	....	—	—	1825	186916	6674	86045	8406	—	4204	43	32	—	957	30	1914	89	65	—	—	—
37	U.L.C.A. World Total	......	3487	2761	5786	1745031	1176588	822074	39031	16482	9405	35511	15738	15174	2400	16383	15987	10402	24887	24562	134414	62718

STATISTICAL REPORT OF THE UNITED LUTHERAN CHURCH IN AMERICA FOR THE YEAR 1935

Index No.	CHURCH SCHOOLS — Number	SUNDAY — Officers and Teachers	SUNDAY — Scholars	Home Dep't	Cradle Roll	WEEKDAY — Number	WEEKDAY — Teachers	WEEKDAY — Scholars	Catechu-mens	Ministry	Deaconess	Students In Lutheran Institutions	Students In Non-Luth. Institutions	MEN'S — Number	MEN'S — Members	WOMEN'S — Number	WOMEN'S — Members	YOUNG P. — Number	YOUNG P. — Members	Church Edifices	Parsonages	School and Parish Houses
1	597	13538	131488	4579	10857	161	1459	15413	9089	94	13	274	1708	337	15196	911	36042	885	27489	22697532	2194200	2263288
2	435	8367	68572	1626	9621	91	459	4742	8483	57	11	144	1360	302	13168	815	32761	870	22584	21979267	2557191	3339047
3	146	2341	25746	262	1004	59	376	5588	2674	22	4	145	286	52	1181	182	4968	231	6476	2778821	355786	192690
4	141	3776	35600	1606	3207	16	143	1384	2528	26		49	483	61	1491	243	9282	235	6932	6537052	702029	355125
5	107	1438	14386	210	778	65	505	7027	1190	15	1	134	235	36	1068	171	5438	196	5383	1474583	248700	229200
6	158	4313	47321	1174	4023	17	157	2742	3486	25		88	347	38	2280	254	9092	204	6960	1596700	561150	356700
7	158	1874	17131	603	995	78	418	4705	1181	12	3	76	196	24	767	169	4331	173	4621	1835860	339966	95490
8	273	5470	51130	1435	3122	29	195	2619	3607	42	1	267	784	141	5469	551	18338	361	8562	8247800	768445	331750
9	158	4380	40845	3008	3097	51	400	4075	2836	46		117	697	112	6013	350	13018	300	8204	7609122	925582	676400
10	136	2463	25438	721	1605	41	240	3364	1317	17	4	25	316	42	1706	168	4655	153	4134	3091250	419176	129200
11	295	5994	54859	1882	4779	65	394	4430	4492	32		207	782	156	5069	591	18102	525	12915	9712208	1280974	399886
12	110	1676	13288	276	761	18	87	886	919	4	2	19	221	38	1199	155	9667	122	2609	2304300	173700	17100
13	131	3085	26731	293	2900	30	305	2895	2207	18		132	485	95	3798	308	5240	268	7606	4698742	564537	294500
14	30	330	2501	99	134	3	18	149	187	2	1	1	57	8	196	38	1071	46	932	138100	47700	35350
15	170	3419	33734	1195	2136	39	256	3001	1685	20		68	388	42	2277	216	6671	159	4603	4278700	10300	157150
16	11	57	413		9	9	29	804	38	1		1	23	17	14	8	94		153	37300		
17	33	735	6604	82	925	11	132	1005	1081	3		21	192	8	572	74	2679	79	2490	1116811	139750	3500
18	26	375	3084		142	11	113	1125	175	4		5	80	21	170	43	1062	51	1007	622700	41100	134700
19	97	1033	7349	33	1125	30	36	661	732	6		19	40	17	552	94	3494	99	2566	1145043	204550	86600
20	42	722	5945	124	504	8	48	1197	357	4		15	109	20	561	80	2301	91	1195	1299898	180800	34500
21	59	1092	9211	103	1105	22	123	1324	951	16		67	199	23	565	114	3152	91	2183	1305950	157880	18000
22	49	655	6759		437	10	25	317	809	6		24	50	6	852	77	3070	42	1680	948475	149350	74350
23	67	505	4826	33	315	32	43	693	740	8		29	58	17	94	73	1984	68	1154	696300	218100	15250
24	35	538	4186	79	415	4	18	198	349	5	1	2	292	70	650	86	2241	24	1278	1407300	73700	33600
25	13	245	1599	113	172	4	21	331	93			36	61	6	187	31	785	195	507	459150	33100	3500
26	97	2100	16398	216	2141	29	179	2555	2969	12		9	475	17	2733	193	6402	44	5113	4089063	329500	153000
27	110	234	2934	27	49	97	95	2254	632	11		7	19	11	119	36	684	35	975	399600	76475	2100
28	22	262	1988	56	228	3	28	204	192	2		2	59	11	211	40	926	15	598	356604	39009	9750
29	33	183	1520						140	3		5	12	13	30	23	559	42	342	198600	31200	3000
30	19	473	3588	68	275	11	61	649	349	5		4	88	13	319	48	1168	16	890	848700	168851	2000
31	31	100	857		70	16	18	648	184	4		13	6	3	115	10	405	46	326	336000	44500	24025
32	13	548	4773	42	564	10	38	428	570	2		2	81	16	265	52	1586	17	783	938527	102000	85500
33	13	153	1127	26	26	2	11	158	77			13	24		61	22	513		324	370700	76000	8200
34	22	414	3688	95	255	4	14	141	144	2		11	80	16	533	60	1936	37	905	908300	105000	34500
35	3845	72888	675619	20074	57776	1076	6444	77712	56463	526	43	2020	10293	1758	69481	6286	213717	5745	154479	120465058	13805451	9598951
36	1148	2405	62990			1109	11	47448		132			15	761	20446	702	18007	48	1320	210445	50150	33650
37	4993	75293	738609	20074	57776	2185	6455	125160	56463	658	43	2020	10308	2519	89927	6988	231724	5793	155799	120675503	13855601	9632601

STATISTICAL REPORT OF THE UNITED LUTHERAN CHURCH IN AMERICA FOR THE YEAR 1935

FINANCIAL

Index Number	Valuation of Church Property — Endowment	Other Property	Total Valuation	Indebtedness	Congregational Expenses — Current	Unusual	Total	Apportioned — Paid	Excess	Deficit	Benevolence (Unapportioned) — Education	Foreign Missions	Home Missions	Inner Missions	Other Benevolence	Total Unapportioned Benevolence	Summary — Total Benevolence	Total Expenditures
1	1486549	1119956	29761525	3839435	1555796	666118	2221914	268758	287	247873	15002	26906	6853	40245	34266	123272	392030	2613944
2	904619	1237809	30017933	4828493	1950910	226597	2177507	156033		40126	6635	15625	9995	57623	21755	111633	267666	2445173
3	22050	61754	3411101	319195	188784	87373	276157	36164	1	26804	1300	3689	4531	6961	8810	25791	61955	338112
4	105561	231109	7930976	1162173	518002	177663	695665	88085	571	22726	4973	7205	7423	27936	16262	73799	161884	857549
5	435852	143834	221811	231513	116751	49588	166339	19389	88	38561	18067	2724	2193	7207	6892	37083	56472	222811
6	107398	108885	7052287	546995	413047	174214	587261	92063	3063	22557	2171	15422	2535	8697	12893	41718	133781	721042
7	194526	122960	2501674	170574	152658	49563	202221	28734	95	75027	1667	11367	4201	10200	7249	22492	51226	253447
8	216685	240852	9783373	1040585	615035	116198	731253	131293	570	43056	5362	24297	7024	11814	16942	45991	177284	908537
9	44840	383134	9810923	1450865	651401	150949	802350	103632	193	24687	4281	4360	1961	29463	11290	77436	181068	983418
10	179574	128518	3812984	280108	131070	124058	255128	44859	877	127941	733	1961	631	3541	8082	18677	63546	318674
11	32600	802082	12374724	1871680	778050	131519	909569	103179		27235	4281	11346	5821	3208	22651	76307	179486	1089055
12	75690	145777	2673477	440252	172792	49387	222179	28578		64059	137	1410	631	4287	3062	9702	38280	260459
13	170	134216	5767685	1337476	443308	64656	507964	55373	108	8676	858	6061	4270	14210	11103	36502	91875	599839
14	80379	12800	242170	28355	28355	9044	37399	3497		44883	506	240	115	734	1047	2273	5770	43169
15		90053	5083382	484015	314525	111637	426162	57908	546	767	39	6338	872	5675	5212	18603	76511	502673
16			47600	7823	3135	966	4101	532	1			7		28	142	225	757	4858
17	5800	37847	1303708	283695	108944	54581	163525	10224		16486	322	761	275	1469	2392	5219	15443	178968
18	20095	60450	879045	156692	44162	18254	62416	9008		5374	247	464	249	2227	1540	4727	13735	76151
19	70685	70085	1540345	114006	148308	24846	173154	23158	1507	2932	9606	1636	646	1900	2209	15997	39155	212309
20	22434	14804	1552436	155464	99533	10976	110509	15154	19	12332	491	1635	551	3056	2782	7939	23093	133602
21	4235	127103	1613168	124930	110162	21562	131724	20835	15	20734	640	2316	236	2930	440	11456	32291	164015
22	1000	14555	1187730		100545	33952	134497	6285	154	1052	65	556	167	1373	1516	2670	8955	143452
23	10500	15320	955470	40789	73398	10828	84226	6800		55428	268	841	430	1263	2862	4055	10855	95081
24	80000	27995	1622595	276478	99416	22337	121753	8437	6	5396	115	1090	323	1647	1370	6144	14581	136334
25	60	10377	506187	219255	31764	11290	43054	4454		2100	79	273		413		2458	6912	49966
26	6155	58285	4636003	1707541	335317	44525	379842	56916	263		945	3985	3431	4900	8605	21866	78782	458624
27		12206	490381	50070	42715	9191	51906	6699	3629	1385	118	209	113	70	572	572	7271	59177
28	615	14623	420601	189236	30743	9341	40084	3693	3	3413	269	384	194	138	969	1954	5647	45731
29	1000	5800	239600	16585	20830	3424	24254	1565		4084	231	57	100		538	926	2491	26745
30	9850	72790	1102191	201503	61517	10953	72470	7650		5211	170	517	520	584	1253	3044	10694	83164
31		4000	408525	103688	19388		19388	199		9007	73				113	186	385	19773
32	919	29891	1156837	472948	71441	13982	85423	11130	5	943	55	555	263	1488	1070	3441	14571	99994
33		5950	460850	162790	22339	16491	38830	2458		4015	95	73	131	276	408	983	3441	42271
34	18040	117415	1183255	170890	70073	38506	108579	13957	30		710	1403	6518	2480	1399	12510	26467	135046
35	4115063	5663835	153648358	22495582	9604234	2464569	12068803	1426709	12031	964870	77775	165907	75534	287043	219392	827651	2254360	14323163
36		2460256	2754501		3286		3286								241688	241688	241688	244974
37	4115063	8124091	156402859	22495582	9607520	2464569	12072089	1426709	12031	964870	77775	165907	75534	287043	461080	1069339	2496048	14558137

I. U. L. C. A. STATISTICAL REPORT OF OTHER COUNTRIES OUTSIDE U. S. A. AND CANADA—1935
(Foreign Missions compiled by Board of Foreign Missions; American Missions by Board of American Missions)

PAROCHIAL

Index	Country	Province	When Organized	Pastors	Congregations	Membership: Baptized	Confirmed	Communing	Accessions: Net	Baptism	Confirmation	Certificate	Losses: Death	Certificate	Otherwise	Church Papers: No. S.S. Papers Distributed
1	India	Madras	1842	Ord. Miss. 23, Nat. Workers 2848, Unord. men & women 37	1703	171812	80482	80482	3563	8044			2853			
2	Africa	Liberia	1860	Ord. Miss. 5, Nat. Workers 61, Unord. men & women 10.....	16	1055	401	401	79							
3	Japan	Kyushu-Hondo	1892	Ord. Miss. 11, Workers 70, Unord. men & women 9	31	4458	742	742	233							
4	China	Shantung	1898	Ord. Miss. 6, Nat. men & women 122,	36	3239	1502	1502	553							
5	Virgin Islands		1666	U. L. C. A. 4	5	1845	1209	761								
6	British Guiana	Berbice	1889	Ord. Miss. 1, Workers 12	8	661	388	388	4							
7	Puerto Rico		1898	U. L. C. A. 8	14	2144	872	691								
8	Argentina	Buenos Aires	1908	Ord. Miss. 2, Nat. Workers 27, Unord. men & women 1,	12	1702	1078	1078	17	117	43	32	18	89	95	
9	Totals Outside U. S. A. & Can.			Pastors 60, Workers 3140, Unord. 65	1825	186916	86674	86045	4449	8161	43	32	2871	89	95	

U. L. C. A. STATISTICAL REPORT OF OTHER COUNTRIES OUTSIDE U. S. A. AND CANADA—1935 Concluded

FINANCIAL

Index	Summary: Total Expenditures	Benevolence	Field Contributions	Congregational Expenses	Valuation: Total Valuation	Other Property	School and Parish Houses	Parsonages	Church Edifices
1	222370	25825	196545		1200000	1200000			
2	2227		2227		80000	80000			
3	7052		7052		690000	690000			
4	3960		3960		185000	185000			
5					156700	14200	20300	19200	103000
6	1723		1723		61000	61000			
7	3446	160		3286	151801	56	13350	30950	107445
8	4196		4196		230000	230000			
9	244974	25985	215703	3286	2754501	2460256	33650	50150	210445

PAROCHIAL

Index	Church Schools — Sunday: Number	Officers and Teachers	Scholars	Weekday: Number	Officers and Teachers	Scholars	Inquirers	Catechumens	Students: Ministry	In Non-Luth. Institutions	Church Societies — Men's: Number	Members	Women's: Number	Members	Young P.: Number	Members
1	1125	2225	55028	1044		43270	16278		105		760	20437	685	17644		
2			200	16		425	480		12							
3			3586	28		1528	479		10	1						
4			1000		11	1144										
5	5	70	636	4		107	21									
6			397	11		235			1							
7	18	110	1824	6		739	100		2	14						
8			319						2		1	9	17	363	48	1320
9	1148	2405	62990	1109	11	47448	17358		132	15	761	20446	702	18007	48	1320

Recommendations 1, 2, 3, and 4 were adopted.

The Rev. W. H. Greever, Chairman, presented the report of the Committee on Publicity.

REPORT OF COMMITTEE ON PUBLICITY

The Committee on Publicity has functioned during the biennium through informal conferences and correspondence with such meetings only as were necessary for the publicity service for this Convention. As previously, the Convention publicity is under the direction of the publicity department of the National Lutheran Council, but since the director of that agency is a member of our own Committee, the whole staff is our own.

Throughout the biennium the Committee has sought to extend the publicity-mindedness of the Church and to render specific aid wherever possible to synodical and local directors and committees. Attention has been given also to that technique in publicity so necessary in securing the service of the public press.

> W. H. GREEVER, *Chairman.*
> CHARLES K. FEGLEY, *Secretary.*

Dr. Greever introduced the Rev. C. K. Fegley who presented the following supplementary report with recommendations.

SUPPLEMENTARY REPORT OF THE PUBLICITY COMMITTEE

It is desired to make permanent record of several of the items connected with the publicity of this Convention.

The Convention is indebted to James C. Kinard, LL.D., for broadcasting a fifteen minute resume of the Convention, each morning, over Station WBNS of Columbus. He was assisted by the Rev. A. R. Naus. We recommend that both Dr. Kinard, Pastor Naus and the management of the station be thanked for their services.

We report the Committee's deep appreciation of effective service at the Press Table by a number of volunteer helpers.

A breakfast conference of publicity representatives from several synods was held during this convention and has laid foundations for fuller cooperative publicity activities in the future.

We recommend the Convention's recognition of the satisfactory news services rendered us by the wire s e r v i c e s and the newspapers of Columbus.

From clippings received, we have reason to believe that the news coverage of this convention has been more widely distributed and has been more sustained than in any past convention.

Delegates have reported that persons from their home towns have written of hearing mention of the Convention in connection with the daily radio news broadcast.

The recommendations were adopted.

There was no report of the Committee on Conference with the Y. M. C. A. It was moved and carried that the Commitee on Conference with the Y. M. C. A. be discontinued.

The Committee on Church and State reported that they had been at work and that certain documents had been filed as evidence.

The Rev. W. H. Greever, Secretary, presented the report of the Committee on Transportation.

REPORT OF COMMITTEE ON TRANSPORTATION

This is one committee in which there has been definite division of work: The Chairman, Mr. Harvey C. Miller, has always assumed responsibility for arrangement for trains and schedules for delegates to Conventions, from the larger synods in the East. Dr. Bramkamp has done all year-round work out of Chicago securing many passes, annual and trip, for Church officials, Board secretaries and officers of constituent synods, traveling on Western and Southern roads. The Secretary has performed such all-year service as was possible in the east and southeast.

The Committee sustained a sad loss by the death of Mr. Harvey C. Miller, Chairman, on July 24, 1936, and desires hereby to express the highest appreciation of his services to the Church as a member of this Committee, which membership and chairmanship he held for sixteen years.

No arrangement for special rates could be made for this convention under policies adopted by the railroads in connection with general revisions of passenger tariffs.

W. H. GREEVER, *Secretary.*

The Rev. L. D. Reed, Archivist, presented his report.

REPORT OF ARCHIVIST

The following items were received during the biennium and placed in the archives of the Church.

Official correspondence of President Knubel, 1930-32.

Official copy of the Minutes of the 1932 Convention of the U. L. C. A.

Necrology records 1932-36 from the Rev. J. F. Lambert, D.D.

Respectfully submitted,

LUTHER D. REED, *Archivist.*

Mr. S. F. Telleen, Treasurer, presented the report of the Lutheran Laymen's Radio Committee. In connection with the report for the biennium, Mr. Telleen gave a rather detailed statement concerning the current season, all of which was to the effect that the radio service had been recognized as a service of great value to the Church and therefore merits the generous support of all who are able to give.

REPORT OF LUTHERAN LAYMEN'S RADIO COMMITTEE

(For action on the recommendations in this report, see p 464)

During the years 1934 and 1935 "Sunday Vespers," the radio program of the United Lutheran Church, was on the air every Sunday during the four months from June to September, both included. In the former year the network stations cooperating reached a total of 46 and in the year 1935 a total of 53. Most of the sermons were delivered by Dr. Paul Scherer, President Knubel appearing twice in 1934 and Dr. Augustus Steimle twice in 1935. As should be known, they have served without financial compensation. The character of their service has been attested to by the thousands of letters received by them and the Committee, sent by listeners from all parts of our country and from Canada. For the current season Dr. Gould Wickey promised to serve with Dr. Scherer.

Expenditures in 1934 totalled $2,859.72 and in 1935 $2,894.34. These amounts cover payments for the quartet, a part of the administration expenses, stationery, postage, printing (which includes the cost of 1,000 copies of each week's sermon), etc. The cost to the National Broadcasting Company was many times the small amount we were called upon to pay and was in addition to the gift of the very valuable half-hour period. It is not pleasant to have to confess it, but, in spite of the widespread interest in these broadcasts, receipts each year failed to meet the amounts required and the balance needed was in each case supplied by a loan. Under the rules of the National Broadcasting Company, no solicitation of funds can be included in the program. While some listeners do send in gifts without solicitation, the Committee must rely principally on members of our Church who are interested in proclaiming the gospel message to millions of people throughout our country and outside of it, many of whom never attend church. It is therefore hoped that many individuals, brotherhoods and other church organizations which have not yet contributed will do so now and make these contributions annual ones throughout the years we are permitted to enjoy this privilege.

Another hope might be expressed here, namely, that many of the laymen of our Church will affiliate themselves with the Lutheran Laymen's Radio Committee. We should like to have the names of many in all parts of the United States and Canada who would be willing to serve their Church through this Committee. This would not involve financial participation, though it would of course be welcome.

The Committee recommends to this convention:

1. That it express our Church's appreciation to Drs. Knubel, Scherer and Steimle for services rendered and for the character and quality of the messages delivered by them;

2. That it express to the National Broadcasting Company

Its appreciation of the privilege of broadcasting "Sunday Vespers" and its thanks for the gift of the time and of the cost of the operating expenses of this radio period;

Its appreciation of, and admiration for, the high ideals which actuate the company in its relation to the great fields of religious and educational broadcasting.

Respectfully submitted,

Lutheran Laymen's Radio Committee,

HENRY BEISLER, *President.*

FRANK C. GOODMAN, *Secretary.*

S. FREDERICK TELLEEN, *Treasurer.*

Recommendations 1 and 2 were adopted.

The Rev. Harold S. Miller, a member of the Committee, presented the Report of the Committee on Army and Navy Work.

REPORT OF COMMITTEE ON ARMY AND NAVY WORK

Your committee appointed at the last Convention has not met during the past biennium, in the interests of economy. Organization was effected by correspondence. The Rev. Charles Trexler, D.D., was chosen chairman and the Rev. William Freas, D.D., as secretary. These officers together with the Rev. Harold S. Miller and Mr. Chas. H. Dahmer formed an Executive Committee which served as a committee as a whole.

Applications for appointment in the various branches of the Army and Navy come to your Committee through the General Committee on Army and Navy Chaplains. In the consideration of such applications for approval, your committee must follow the rigid requirements of both the Army and Navy—as to age, attainments, physical condition, and general standing in the community where the applicant is working. We are also very careful to recommend the best available men as the representatives of our Church. With the application made through the General Committee on Army and Navy Chaplains, Room 812, Woodward Building, Washington, D. C., we require at least five letters of recommendation. Since in many instances the applicant is not known to the Committee— these letters should contain detailed information about the applicant's character and work.

Vacancies in both the Regular Army and Navy are rare. The majority of applications to be considered are for the Army Reserve Corps. According to the latest records available, the Lutheran Church now has ten Chaplains in the Regular Army and four in the Regular Navy. At the present there is one vacancy for a Lutheran Chaplain in the Navy.

C. C. C. CAMPS

These Camps give a fine opportunity to pastors who work in the vicinity of a Camp for very effective service among the young men. We now have nine Lutheran Reserve Chaplains who are on active duty for this important work.

Your Committee, during the past biennium has considered seventeen applications, of which twelve were recommended; three for the Regular Army and nine for the Army Reserve Corps.

Respectfully submitted,

CHARLES TREXLER, *Chairman.*

The Report of the Representatives in the Advisory Council of the American Bible Society was presented.

REPORT OF REPRESENTATIVE IN THE ADVISORY COUNCIL OF THE AMERICAN BIBLE SOCIETY

(For action on the recommendations in this report, see p. 466)

Your representative in the Advisory Council of the American Bible Society herewith submits his eighth biennial report.

Two meetings of the council were held during our biennium. Your representative was present at both meetings. Of the twenty-seven ecclesiastical bodies represented in the council at the last meeting, five of them were Lutheran, namely, the Augustana Synod, Norwegian Lutheran Church, the American Lutheran Church, the United Lutheran Church and, unofficially, the Missouri Synod.

The chief function of the council is to secure a closer relation between the churches and the society. To this end the council of the American Bible Society sits with the secretaries and the treasurer in making the budget of the society and with the Board of Managers when that budget is considered. There has been a necessary curtailment of the Society's work during the past four years. But during the last biennium, with the increase of the Society's income over the preceding biennium, a corresponding increase in the budget has been possible. The normal budget of the Society is now a little less than a million dollars. The Society has realized approximately a quarter of that amount from invested funds and rentals, about $200,000 from individual gifts and annuities, and almost double that amount from sales. For the balance it must look to the churches. In 1933 the churches contributed less than $90,000; in

1934, $103,954. In 1935 the amount passed the one hundred thousand dollar mark, and in 1936 the council was able to budget $105,000. Our own contribution in 1935 totaled $2,356.65.

Three notable events marked the Society's work in 1935. First, there was the commemoration of the 400th anniversary of the printed English Bible. This event the Society celebrated in a nation-wide broadcast with addresses by Prof. Robert A. Millikan and Mr. Frank J. Loesch, while Secretary of State Cordell Hull presented a message from the President. Some six thousand theatres displayed a news reel prepared by Paramount News, while the event was celebrated by special services in other large centers. The extensive literature furnished by the Society should secure fresh attention to the Society's objective, namely, "to encourage the wider circulation of the Holy Scriptures without note or comment."

The second event of note was the reorganization of the work of the Society in the United States into eight districts and six depositories, thus greatly simplifying the Society's work.

The third outstanding event was the securing of new and more useful headquarters for the Society's offices and staff in New York City. The new Bible House, which will be occupied by the end of 1936, is located at the corner of 57th Street and Park Avenue.

The work of the Society continues to expand. In the one hundred and twenty years since its organization in 1816, the American Bible Society has put into circulation 268,588,636 volumes of Scripture in 972 languages and dialects—an increase of eighteen since the end of 1934.

Last year the Society celebrated the centennial anniversary of its work for the blind. During this period a total of 104,280 volumes have been distributed at home and 16,760 volumes abroad, making a grand total of 121,040 volumes of Scripture supplied to the blind in twenty-five languages and systems.

Your representative recommends:

1. That this body endorse the observance of Universal Bible Sunday by our churches;

2. That we endorse the work of the Society in its program of extending the circulation of the Holy Scriptures in the languages of the world;

3. And that The United Lutheran Church continue its representation in the advisory council of the American Bible Society.

Respectfully submitted,

HERBERT C. ALLEMAN.

Recommendations 1, 2 and 3 were adopted.

The Rev. J. Sittler, for the Rev. J. W. Ott, Chairman, presented the report of the Committee on Place of Next Convention.

REPORT OF COMMITTEE ON PLACE OF NEXT CONVENTION

Your Committee on place of the 1938 convention of The United Lutheran Church in America had placed in its hands the following invitations: viz., that of Omaha, Nebr.; Fort Wayne, Ind.; New York, N. Y.; and Baltimore, Md. By unanimous vote your Committee recommends that we accept the invitation from the United Lutheran Churches of Baltimore, Md., and the Synod of Maryland, granting, however, the power to the Executive Board of the Church to act, if for some unforeseen reason it should be found necessary to bring about a change in the place of meeting.

Respectfully submitted,

J. W. OTT, *Chairman.*

The recommendation was unanimously adopted.

The Rev. W. C. Davis, Chairman, presented the report of the Committee on Leave of Absence.

REPORT OF COMMITTEE ON LEAVE OF ABSENCE

Out of a possible 271 clerical delegates, 269 were present, and out of a possible 267 lay delegates, 247 were present.

The following synods have a perfect record of attendance, all delegates being registered and all present at all sessions:

East Pennsylvania	Mississippi	Pacific
Florida	Nova Scotia	Rocky Mountain
	Texas	

Again we call the attention of all delegates and chairmen of delegations to the importance of making careful reports on attendance at all sessions.

We recommend that in the future, delegation attendance report blanks be provided with a third column under each heading for special sessions in addition to the present A. M. and P. M. columns.

The report submitted by synods is as follows:

Synod	Number of Delegates Elected	Total Number of Delegates Present	Total Number of Delegates Absent All Sessions	100% Attendance All Sessions	Number of Absences from Sessions of the Convention. (Each "Absence" represents the absence of one delegate from one session) Excused	Unexcused
Alleghany	14	14			1	
California	8	8			2	
Canada	12	11	1			1
East Pennsylvania	28	28		100%		
Florida	2	2		100%		
Georgia-Alabama	4	3	1		2	
German Nebraska	12	8	4			4
Illinois	22	22			8	
Indiana	14	14			21	
Iowa	6	6			2	
Kansas	8	8			5	

Kentucky-Tennessee	4	4			3
Manitoba	2	2		4	
Maryland	20	20		7	3
Michigan	6	6		2	
Mississippi	2	2	100%		
Nebraska	10	9	1	2	
New York	74	68	6	23	
North Carolina	18	18		3	
Northwest	18	18		13	
Nova Scotia	2	2	100%		
Ohio	38	37	1	25	
Pacific	6	6	100%		
Pennsylvania Minis.	78	77	1	40	3
Pittsburgh	42	42		27	
Rocky Mountain	4	4	100%		
Slovak Zion	2	2			4
South Carolina	12	12		8	
Susquehanna	16	15	1	6	
Texas	4	4	100%		
Virginia	16	16		1	
Wartburg	10	5	5	1	
West Pennsylvania	20	20		9	
West Virginia	4	3	1		
Totals	538	516	22	7	212	18

Respectfully submitted,

WALTER C. DAVIS, *Chairman.*

The recommendation was adopted.

The Minutes of the Lutheran Historical Society were received.

THE LUTHERAN HISTORICAL SOCIETY

The Historical Society of the United Lutheran Church met in the Deshler-Wallick Hotel, Columbus, Ohio, at 5:15 P. M., Monday, October 19, 1936. President S. W. Herman called the Society to order. Rev. G. N. Lauffer offered prayer.

The Report of the Curator, Prof. A. R. Wentz, was received and adopted as follows:

The work of the Curator during the past biennium has been chiefly the routine of filing papers and periodicals, gathering the minutes of Synods, binding pamphlets and magazines, and responding to requests for information. More calls than usual have come from individuals and congregations asking for historical information. The graduate departments of universities and the Library of Congress frequently refer research students to our collection of materials.

Our extensive list of duplicates has been sent to a number of Lutheran libraries and in several cases we have been able to effect important exchange of materials.

The installation of binding machinery in the Seminary Library has enabled the Curator of the Historical Society to proceed more rapidly with the work of binding pamphlets and other materials that can better be preserved in bound volumes. Several hundred volumes have thus been bound during the past biennium.

Every effort is being made to keep our collection as complete as possible. The Curator will appreciate the help of synodical secretaries and local historians in transmitting for our files any books or papers that might possibly be used by the Lutheran historian of the future. Of special value are synod minutes, congregational histories, unpublished letters and manuscripts that bear on the life of Lutheran organizations or Lutheran personalities. Not infrequently materials that now seem utterly useless and insignificant, if preserved for future generations, become exceedingly valuable for the historian. The Library of the Historical Society offers its vault and shelves as a repository for every bit of such material.

The report of the treasurer, Mr. J. Elmer Musselman, was received and the auditor's report was adopted. The treasurer's report showed a balance of $43.18.

The following officers were elected:

President: Rev. S. W. Herman.

Vice-Presidents: Rev. W. J. Finck, Rev. John C. Horine, Rev. O. F. Blackwelder, Mr. Addison B. Freeman.

Recording Secretary: Rev. Prof. H. C. Alleman.

Treasurer: J. Elmer Musselman.

Curator: Rev. Prof. A. R. Wentz.

Additional Members of the Executive Committee: Rev. G. Morris Smith, Rev. H. F. Baughman.

After general discussion of the work of the society the meeting adjourned.

The Rev. G. H. Bechtold, Secretary, presented the report of the Lutheran Church Book and Literature Society.

THE LUTHERAN CHURCH BOOK AND LITERATURE SOCIETY

The Society continued its activities during the past biennium despite its small income.

Organized to distribute tracts and church literature to mission points, inner mission agencies, this Society has been functioning with but little support from the Church at large.

A glance at the places applying for and receiving Common Service Books, Parish School Hymnals, Light for Today, Hymns and Prayers, Catechisms, Tracts and Church School literature, reveals the wide area covered—Konnarock, Va.; Pine Lake, Minn.; Anderson, S. C.; The Pas, Manitoba; Woodbury, N. J.; Saskatoon, Manitoba (Deaf Mute S. S.); Charleston, S. C.; Nova Scotia; Panama Canal Zone (Army Post) and C. C. C. Camps in New York and Virginia.

The new tracts which should be printed and made available for free distribution cannot be published because of lack of funds.

The Society depends on the annual membership fee of $1.00 for meeting its obligations. Ours is a necessary work and we feel merits the support of the United Lutheran Church.

The officers for the biennium were as follows: Rev. F. H. Knubel, D.D., Honorary President; Rev. P. Z. Strodach, D.D., President; Rev. G. H. Bechtold, D.D., Secretary; and Mr. H. Torrey Walker, Treasurer.

The Rev. F. M. Urich, Chairman, presented the final report of the Committee of Reference and Counsel.

REPORT OF COMMITTEE OF REFERENCE AND COUNSEL

1. Availing himself of the privilege accorded delegates in connection with the closing of the discussion on the report of the Committee on Moral and Social Welfare, the Rev. B. R. Lantz, delegate from the Synod of Kansas, presented the following resolution to your Committee.

Resolved, That the Board of Publication give consideration to the matter of printing the recommendations approved in connection with the report of the Committee on Moral and Social Welfare, and that the Board be requested to send a copy to every pastor, together with information as to cost in quantities, so that pastors may be able to secure them for distribution.

We recommend that this resolution be referred to the Board of Publication.

2. We recommend the adoption of the following resolution:

Resolved, That The United Lutheran Church in America, assembled in its Tenth Convention in Columbus, Ohio, extend its most hearty thanks to the pastors and to all the members of the United Lutheran churches in this city for their warm and generous hospitality during our stay here; to the local Committee on Arrangements and to the Chamber of Commerce of Columbus for their untiring and most successful efforts in making arrangements and providing facilities for this convention; to the President and faculty of Capital University for their welcome to its halls. for the rich privilege accorded to us by them of hearing its splendid choir and orchestra in the inspiring service of sacred music especially arranged by them for our Sunday evening in Columbus, and for their courtesy in inviting our own Dr. Luther D. Reed to have part in that service; to Wittenberg College for the afternoon and evening of recreation and instruction which made our Saturday rest period so enjoyable, and to its own splendid choir for its participation in our evening services; to Sister Pearl Lyerly and to all those who assisted her in presenting the impressive pageant in celebration of the Centennial of the Protestant Diaconate; to those who entertained so delightfully the ladies in attendance on our sessions; to the Governor of Ohio for his welcome to this State; to the Mayor of Columbus for his welcome to this city and to the authorities and police of Columbus for their cooperation in insuring our comfort during our stay here; to the Associated Press and to the local press for their reports of the convention proceedings; to Mr. William H. Patrick and the Pennsylvania Railroad for the special trains made up for the eastern delegates; to the management of the Deshler-Wallick Hotel and especially to Miss Obetz for the many courtesies extended to us; and to all others who have contributed to our entertainment in Columbus.

3. The Rev. Frederick E. Reissig, delegate from the United Synod of New York, presented the following resolution to your Committee:

Resolved, That the Convention assembled urge upon the Board of Publication the consideration of a considerable reduction in the cost of "Light for Today."

We recommend the approval of this resolution.

Recommendation 1 was adopted.

Recommendation 2 was adopted unanimously by a rising vote.

Recommendation 3 was adopted.

On motion the printing of the Minutes was referred to the Executive Board.

It was moved and carried that the Minutes of the eleventh session be submitted to the Special Committee on Minutes for final approval.

At 12:50 P. M., after prayer by the Rev. G. E. Miller, the Convention was closed with the Order for the Closing of Synods.

W. H. GREEVER, *Secretary.*

Note.—On October 21, 1936, the Committee on Minutes, at a regular meeting, reviewed and approved the Minutes of the eleventh session.

C. A. PULS,
Chairman of the Committee on Minutes.

LIST OF BOARDS AND ELECTIVE COMMITTEES

1. Executive Board.
2. Commission of Adjudication.
3. Board of Foreign Missions.
4. Board of American Missions and West Indies Mission Board.
5. Board of Education.
6. Inner Mission Board.
7. Board of Publication.
8. Board of Ministerial Pensions and Relief.
9. Parish and Church School Board.
10. Board of Deaconess Work.
11. Committee on Church Papers.
12. Executive Committee of the Laymen's Movement.

LIST OF STANDING COMMITTEES, COMMISSIONS, ETC.

1. Statistical and Church Year Book Committee.
2. Committee on Common Service Book.
3. Committee on Church Music.
4. Committee on German Interests.
5. Committee on Army and Navy Work.
6. Committee on Moral and Social Welfare.
7. Committee on Evangelism.
8. Committee on Church Architecture.
9. Committee on Publicity.
10. Committee on Transportation.
11. Necrologist.
12. Archivist.
13. Such other Standing Committees as may be provided for from time to time.

SPECIAL COMMITTEES

1. Committee to Conduct the Opening and Closing Services of Each Session.
2. Committee on Leave of Absence.
3. Committee on Memorials from Constituent Synods.
4. Committee of Reference and Counsel.
5. Committee to Nominate Executive Committee of Laymen's Movement.
6. Committee to Nominate Members of Boards.
7. Committee to Nominate Members of Executive Board and all Elective Commissions or Committees.
8. Committee of Tellers.

BOARDS AND ELECTIVE COMMITTEES

EXECUTIVE BOARD

President—Rev. F. H. Knubel, D.D., LL.D., S.T.D., 39 East 35th St., New York City.

Secretary—Rev. W. H. Greever, D.D., LL.D., 39 East 35th St., New York City.

Treasurer—E. Clarence Miller, LL.D., 1508 Walnut St., Philadelphia, Pa.

Term Expires 1940

Rev. E. B. Burgess, D.D., LL.D.; Rev. H. W. A. Hanson, D.D., LL.D.; Rev. E. P. Pfatteicher, D.D., Ph.D., LL.D.; Carl M. Distler, Esq.; Robbin B. Wolf, LL.D.; Hon. John L. Zimmerman, LL.D.

Term Expires 1938

Rev. A. E. Bell, D.D.; Rev. J. L. Morgan, D.D.; Rev. R. E. Tulloss, D.D., Ph.D., LL.D.; Mr. J. K. Jensen; James C. Kinard, LL.D., Hon. Claude T. Reno.

COMMISSION OF ADJUDICATION

President—

Vice-President—Rev. W. F. Rangeler, D.D., 1643 N. Nye Ave., Fremont, Nebr.

Secretary—Rev. George J. Gongaware, D.D., LL.D., 31 Pitt St., Charleston, S. C.

Term Expires 1942

Rev. Wm. E. Frey, D.D.; Rev. L. Franklin Gruber, D.D., LL.D.; Hon. James F. Henninger.

Term Expires 1940

Rev. George J. Gongaware, D.D., LL.D.; Rev. J. A. W. Haas, D.D., LL.D.; Hon. John F. Kramer.

Term Expires 1938

Rev. John Aberly, D.D., LL.D.; Rev. W. F. Rangeler, D.D.; Hon. C. M. Efird, LL.D.

BOARD OF FOREIGN MISSIONS

President—Rev. S. W. Herman, D.D., 121 State St., Harrisburg, Penna.

Vice-President—Rev. G. A. Greiss, D.D., 38 S. Eighth St., Allentown, Pa.

Executive Secretary—Rev. Paul W. Koller, D.D., 18 E. Mt. Vernon Place, Baltimore, Md.

Recording Secretary—Rev. George Drach, D.D., 18 E. Mt. Vernon Place, Baltimore, Md.

Treasurer—Mr. George R. Weitzel, 18 E. Mt. Vernon Place, Baltimore, Md.

General Secretaries—Rev. George Drach, D.D.; Rev. M. Edwin Thomas, D.D.

Term Expires 1942

Rev. P. O. Bersell, D.D.; Rev. H. H. Beidleman, D.D.; Rev. E. E. Fischer, D.D.; Rev. P. E. Monroe, D.D.; Rev. C. M. Snyder; Mr. Frank Howard; Mr. Ralph H. Schatz.

Term Expires 1940

Rev. H. C. Brillhart, D.D.; Rev. G. A. Greiss, D.D.; Rev. L. C. Manges, D.D.; Rev. Samuel Trexler, D.D.; Mr. M. P. Moller, Jr.; Mr. W. A. Rast; Mr. S. F. Telleen.

Term Expires 1938

Rev. Robert D. Clare, D.D.; Rev. S. W. Herman, D.D.; Rev. S. T. Nicholas, D.D.; Rev. F. E. Reinartz; Mr. Chas. H. Dahmer; Mr. Claude L. Peterman; George S. Yost, Esq.

BOARD OF AMERICAN MISSIONS
and
West Indies Mission Board

President—Rev. H. J. Pflum, D.D., 81 Inwood Pl., Buffalo, N. Y.

Vice-President — Rev. J. J. Scherer, Jr., D.D., 1603 Monument Ave., Richmond, Va.

Secretary—Mr. H. F. Heuer, 52 E. Sedgwick St., Philadelphia, Pa.

Treasurer — Mr. H. Torrey Walker, 1228 Spruce St., Philadelphia, Pa.

Executive Secretary—Rev. Zenan M. Corbe, D.D., 39 East 35th St., New York City.

Asst. Ex. Secy.—Rev. Paul Andrew Kirsch, 39 East 35th St., New York City.

Asst. Gen. Supt.—Rev. J. F. Seibert, D.D., 860 N. Wabash Ave., Chicago, Ill.

Divisional Secretary of English Missions—Rev. A. M. Knudsen, 860 N. Wabash Ave., Chicago, Ill.

Divisional Secretary, Linguistic Interests—Rev. E. A. Tappert, D.D., 39 East 35th St., New York City.

Departmental Secretary of Church Extension and Finance—Mr. H. Torrey Walker, 1228 Spruce St., Philadelphia, Pa.

Term Expires 1942

Rev. A. J. Holl, D.D.; Rev. John Schmieder; Rev. Chester S. Simonton, D.D.; Rev. Emil W. Weber, D.D.; A. S. Bauer, Esq.; Mr. Louis Hanson; Heiby W. Ungerer, Esq.

Term Expires 1940

Rev. O. Garfield Beckstrand; Rev. Franklin C. Fry; Rev. J. Edward Harms, D.D.; Rev. J. J. Scherer, Jr., D.D.; Mr. Henry Beisler; Mr. A. H. Durboraw; Mr. Wm. Eck.

Term Expires 1938

Rev. F. O. Evers; Rev. L. H. Larimer, D.D.; Rev. H. J. Pflum, D.D.; Rev. L. W. Steckel, D.D.; Mr. Horace W. Bikle; Mr. H. F. Heuer; John A. Hoober, Esq.

BOARD OF EDUCATION

President—Rev. Howard R. Gold, D.D., 15 Vaughn Ave., New Rochelle, N. Y.

Vice-President—Rev. H. H. Bagger, D.D., 199 Dewey St., Edgewood, Pittsburgh, Pa.

Recording Secretary — Rev. Gould Wickey, Ph.D., 744 Jackson Place, N. W., Washington, D. C.

Treasurer—Mr. Thomas P. Hickman, 744 Jackson Place, N. W., Washington, D. C.

Executive Secretary — Rev. Gould Wickey, Ph.D., 744 Jackson Place, N. W., Washington, D. C.

Secretaries:

Rev. Carolus P. Harry, D.D., 744 Jackson Place, N. W., Washington, D. C.

Miss Mary E. Markley, Litt.D., 744 Jackson Place, N. W., Washington, D. C.

Miss Mildred E. Winston, 744 Jackson Place, N. W., Washington, D. C.

Term Expires 1942

Rev. Stanley Billheimer, D.D.; Rev. H. J. Black, D.D.; Rev. F. K. Fretz, Ph.D., D.D.; Rev. H. R. Gold, D.D.; Prof. O. F. H. Bert, Sc.D.; Mr. Frederick Henrich; Prof. R. J. Seeger, Ph.D.

Term Expires 1940

Rev. Henry H. Bagger, D.D.; Rev. E. C. Herman, D.D.; Rev. M. L. Stirewalt, D.D.; Rev. A. A. Zinck, D.D.; Mrs. Adelaide Burge; Miss Flora Prince; Hon. Charles Steele.

Term Expires 1938

Rev. G. M. Diffenderfer, D.D.; Rev. Paul H. Krauss, D.D.; Rev. W. H. Traub, D.D.; Rev. Abdel Ross Wentz, Ph.D., D.D.; Mr. H. S. Bechtolt; Mr. L. C. Hassinger; Ralph D. Owen, Ph.D.

INNER MISSION BOARD

President—Carl M. Distler, Esq., 401 American Building, Baltimore, Md.

Vice-President—Rev. G. H. Bechtold, D.D., 1228 Spruce Street, Philadelphia, Pa.

Executive Secretary—Rev. C. E. Krumbholz, D.D., 39 East 35th St., New York City.

Secretary for Immigrant Work—Rev. E. A. Sievert, 218 Seventh Ave., New York City.

Treasurer—Mr. L. Henry Lund, 39 East 35th St., New York City.

Term Expires 1942

Rev. G. H. Bechtold, D.D.; Rev. Herman Brezing, D.D.; Rev. P. D. Brown, D.D.; Carl M. Distler, Esq.; Mr. Peter P. Hagan.

Term Expires 1940

Rev. F. K. Fretz, D.D., Ph.D.; Rev. A. H. Keck, D.D.; Rev. R. E. Kern; Mr. Thos. P. Hickman; Mr. H. E. Isenhour.

Term Expires 1938

Rev. Harvey E. Crowell, D.D.; Rev. Harold S. Miller; Rev. J. L. Sieber, D.D.; Harry C. Hoffman, M.D.; Mr. L. Henry Lund.

BOARD OF PUBLICATION

President—Rev. S. W. Herman, D.D., 121 State Street, Harrisburg, Pa.

Vice-President—Mr. E. G. Hoover, 25 N. Third Street, Harrisburg, Pa.

Secretary—Rev. J. Henry Harms, D.D., 2111 Sansom St., Philadelphia, Pa.

Treasurer and Business Manager—Grant Hultberg, D.C.L., 1228 Spruce St., Philadelphia, Pa.

Term Expires 1942

Rev. Oscar F. Blackwelder, D.D.; Rev. S. W. Herman, D.D.; Rev. J. J. Scherer, Jr., D.D.; L. Russell Alden, Esq.; Mr. Henry Beisler; Mr. James L. Fisher; Mr. E. G. Hoover.

Term Expires 1940

Rev. J. Aberly, D.D., LL.D.; Rev. J. Henry Harms, D.D.; Rev. George W. Nicely, D.D.; George E. Neff, Esq.; Mr. Robert D. Raeder; Mr. W. G. Semisch; J. Myron Shimer, Esq.

Term Expires 1938

Rev. Harry F. Baughman, D.D.; Rev. John W. Horine, D.D., LL.D.; Rev. Russell D. Snyder, D.D.; Rev. H. T. Weiskotten, Ph.D.; Charles Baum, M.D.; Mr. H. F. Heuer; Mr. M. P. Moller, Jr.

BOARD OF MINISTERIAL PENSIONS AND RELIEF

President—Mr. Belding B. Slifer, 236 Summit Avenue, Jenkintown, Pa.

Vice-President — William H. Emhardt, Esq., 5521 Germantown Ave., Philadelphia, Pa.

Executive Secretary—Mr. Harry Hodges, 1228 Spruce St., Philadelphia, Pa.

Treasurer — Mr. W. G. Semisch, Integrity Trust Co., 16th and Walnut Streets, Philadelphia, Pa.

Term Expires 1942

Rev. J. H. Reble, D.D.; William H. Emhardt, Esq.; William A. Granville, Ph.D., LL.D.; Mr. H. J. Herbst; W. T. Stauffer, Esq.

Term Expires 1940

Rev. E. C. J. Kraeling, D.D.; Mr. M. P. Moller, Sr.; Mr. J. C. Rovensky; Mr. Edward Schoeppe; Mr. W. G. Semisch.

Term Expires 1938

Mr. G. Harry Ditter; Mr. Francis Seiberling; Mr. A. F. Sittloh; Mr. Belding B. Slifer; Mr. D. F. Yost.

PARISH AND CHURCH SCHOOL BOARD

President—Rev. F. R. Knubel, 330 Barrington St., Rochester, N.Y.

Vice-President—Rev. Wm. C. Schaeffer, Jr., D.D., 18 S. 14th St., Allentown, Pa.

Secretary—Rev. D. Burt Smith, D.D., 1228 Spruce St., Philadelphia, Pa.

Treasurer—Rev. M. Hadwin Fischer, Ph.D., Th.D., Gettysburg, Pa.

Executive Secretary—Rev. S. White Rhyne, 1228 Spruce Street, Philadelphia, Pa.

Field Secretary—Rev. C. H. B. Lewis, 748 E. Military Ave., Fremont, Nebr.

Editors—
Rev. Chas. P. Wiles, D.D., 1228 Spruce St., Philadelphia, Pa.
Rev. D. Burt Smith, D.D., 1228 Spruce St., Philadelphia, Pa.
Rev. Paul J. Hoh, 1228 Spruce St., Philadelphia, Pa.
*Assistant Editor—*Miss Mabel Elsie Locker, 1228 Spruce Street, Philadelphia, Pa.

Term Expires 1942
Rev. R. Homer Anderson, D.D.; Rev. Paul H. Heisey, Ph.D., D.D.; Rev. Wm. C. Schaeffer, Jr., D.D.; Mr. Clarence C. Dittmer.

Term Expires 1940
Rev. P. D. Brown, D.D.; Rev. Carl C. Rasmussen, D.D.; Rev. Amos J. Traver, D.D.; Mrs. Virgil B. Sease.

Term Expires 1938
Rev. J. D. M. Brown, Litt.D.; Rev. M. Hadwin Fischer, Ph.D., Th.D.; Rev. F. R. Knubel; Mr. George M. Jones.

BOARD OF DEACONESS WORK

*President—*Rev. William A. Wade, D.D., 505 Harwood Ave., Baltimore, Md.
*Vice-President—*Rev. H. D. Hoover, D.D., Ph.D., S.T.D., Litt.D., Gettysburg, Pa.
*Secretary—*Rev. Foster U. Gift, D.D., 2500 W. North Ave., Baltimore, Md.
*Treasurer—*Frederick J. Singley, Esq., 215 N. Charles St., Baltimore, Md.

Term Expires 1942
Rev. H. F. Baughman, D.D.; Rev. Allen L. Benner, D.D.; Rev. L. A. Thomas, D.D.; Mr. E. S. Gerberich; Frederick J. Singley, Esq.

Term Expires 1940
Rev. H. D. Hoover, D.D., Ph.D., S.T.D., Litt.D.; Rev. U. S. G. Rupp, D.D.; Rev. W. C. Schaeffer, Jr., D.D.; Mrs. Elsie Singmaster Lewars.

Term Expires 1938
Rev. George N. Lauffer, D.D.; Rev. William A. Wade, D.D.; Mr. Harry R. Hagerty; Mr. I. Searles Runyon; Edgar W. Young, Esq.

COMMITTEE ON CHURCH PAPERS

*Chairman—*Rev. Hermann F. Miller, D.D., 527 Washington St., Reading, Pa.
*Secretary—*Rev. H. F. Baughman, D.D., 3123 Queen Lane, Philadelphia, Pa.

Term Expires 1942

Rev. H. C. Alleman, D.D.; Rev. A. J. Holl, D.D.; C. G. Shatzer, Sc.D.

Term Expires 1940

Rev. Harry F. Baughman, D.D.; Rev. C. E. Gardner, D.D.; Rev. C. A. Linn, Ph.D.

Term Expires 1938

Rev. M. R. Hamsher, D.D.; Rev. Hermann F. Miller; Mr. Henry Streibert.

EXECUTIVE COMMITTEE OF THE LAYMEN'S MOVEMENT

Chairman—Mr. J. L. Clark, Ashland, Ohio.
Executive Secretary—Mr. Arthur P. Black, 700 Chandler Bldg., 1427 Eye St., N. W., Washington, D. C.
Treasurer—Mr. Harold U. Landis, Palmyra, Pa.
Chairman of the Administrative Committee — Mr. William H. Hager, Lancaster, Pa.
H. J. Albrecht; J. L. Clark; P. H. Glatfelter; W. H. Hager; J. K. Jensen; E. Clarence Miller, LL.D.; George E. Neff; W. H. Stackel; S. F. Telleen; Hon. Charles B. Zimmerman.

STANDING COMMITTEES

STATISTICAL AND CHURCH YEAR BOOK COMMITTEE

Rev. G. L. Kieffer, D.D., Litt.D. (Convener), 39 East 35th St., New York, N. Y.; Secretary of The United Lutheran Church in America, ex-officio; Rev. Ira F. Frankenfield; Rev. J. D. Krout, D.D.; Mr. Harry E. Pugh.
Corresponding Members—The official statisticians of the Constituent Synods.

COMMITTEE ON COMMON SERVICE BOOK

Rev. L. D. Reed, D.D., A.E.D. (Convener), 7204 Boyer St., Mt. Airy, Philadelphia, Pa.; Rev. Robert D. Clare, D.D.; Rev. E. E. Fischer, D.D.; Rev. H. D. Hoover, Ph.D., D.D., S.T.D., Litt.D.; Rev. E. F. Keever, D.D.; Rev. E. H. Klotsche, Ph.D., D.D.; Rev. J. C. Mattes, D.D.; Rev. J. F. Ohl, D.D., Mus.D.; Rev. H. J. Pflum, Jr., D.D.; Rev George R. Seltzer, S.T.M., Ph.D.; Rev. Carl R. Simon; Rev. A. Steimle, D.D.; Rev. M. L. Stirewalt, D.D.; Rev. P. Z. Strodach, D.D.; Rev. C. P. Swank, D.D., S.T.D.

COMMITTEE ON CHURCH MUSIC

Rev. G. C. Rees, D.D. (Convener), 211 South Main St., North Wales, Pa.; Rev. Paul M. Brosy, S.T.M.; Rev. H. Grady Davis; Rev. E. F. Krauss, D.D.; Rev. John C. Mattes, D.D.; Rev. George R. Seltzer, S.T.M., Ph.D.; Rev. E. A. Trabert, D.D.; Mr. William Benbow; Mr. Ralph P. Lewars; Harold K. Marks, Mus.D.; Mr. Rob Roy Peery; Prof. Carl P. Pfatteicher, Th.D.; Mr. Henry F. Seibert; Harry A. Sykes, Mus.D.; Prof. J. C. Williams.

COMMITTEE ON GERMAN INTERESTS

Rev. E. C. J. Kraeling, D.D. (Convener), 132 Henry St., Brooklyn, N. Y.; Rev. G. A. Benze, D.D.; Rev. F. H. Bosch, D.D.; Rev. S. G. R. von Bosse, D.D.; Rev. F. O. Evers; Rev. F. Flothmeier; Rev. L. A. Fritsch, D.D.; Rev. E. H. von Hahmann, Ph.D., D.D.; Rev. R. H. Ischinger; Rev. H. A. Kropp; Rev. Kurt E. B. Molzahn; Rev. J. L. Neve, D.D., D.Th.; Rev. T. O. Posselt, D.D.; Rev. J. Reble, D.D.; Rev. C. R. Tappert, D.D

Corresponding Members — The presidents of the German Nebraska, Manitoba, Texas and Wartburg Synods.

COMMITTEE ON ARMY AND NAVY WORK

Rev. Charles Trexler, D.D. (Convener), 28 East 73d St., New York City; Rev. J. F. Fedders, D.D.; Rev. R. H. Gearhart, Jr., D.D.; Rev. C. E. Krumbholz, D.D.; Rev. Henry Manken, Jr.; Rev. Harold S. Miller; Rev. Emil W. Weber; Mr. Chas. H. Dahmer.

COMMITTEE ON MORAL AND SOCIAL WELFARE

Rev. C. B. Foelsch, Ph.D., D.D. (Convener), 29 South Fifth St., Sunbury, Pa.; Rev. Stanley Billheimer, D.D.; Rev. Frank A. Dressel, D.D.; Rev. E. E. Flack, Th.D.; Rev. J. Henry Harms, D.D.; Rev. P. H. Heisey, Ph.D., D.D.; Rev. W. A. Sadtler, Ph.D., D.D.; Rev. G. Morris Smith, D.D.; Rev. N. Willison, Litt.D.; Rev. W. C. Zimmann; Mr. W. H. Hager.

COMMITTEE ON EVANGELISM

Rev. A. Pohlman, D.D., M.D. (Convener), 5135 Race St., Philadelphia, Pa.; Rev. R. Homer Anderson, D.D.; Rev. Russell F. Auman; Rev. J. Frederick Bermon; Rev. W. C. Davis, D.D.; Rev. Franklin C. Fry; Rev. G. Arthur Fry, D.D.; Rev. Arnold F. Keller; Rev. G. H. Kinard, D.D.; Rev. F. W. Otterbein, D.D.; Rev. C. F. Stickles.

COMMITTEE ON CHURCH ARCHITECTURE

Rev. L. D. Reed, D.D., A.E.D. (Convener), 7204 Boyer St., Mt. Airy, Philadelphia, Pa.; Rev. Wm. H. Cooper; Rev. J. L. Deaton;

Rev. H. S. Kidd; Rev. E. F. Krauss, D.D.; Rev. G. H. Schnur, D.D.; Rev. Bela Shetlock; Rev. E. A. Trabert, D.D.; Mr. Frank P. Albright; Charles Z. Klauder, M.F.A.; Prof. Warren P. Laird, Sc.D., LL.D.; Mr. Luther M. Leisenring; Mr. Charles F. Obenhack; Mr. Charles A. Scheuringer.

COMMITTEE ON PUBLICITY

Secretary of The United Lutheran Church in America, ex-officio (Convener); Rev. C. K. Fegley; Rev. A. R. Naus; Rev. L. W. Rupp.

Corresponding Members—The official publicity appointees of the Constituent Synods.

COMMITTEE ON TRANSPORTATION

Rev. W. H. Greever, D.D., LL.D. (Convener), 39 East 35th St., New York, N. Y.; Rev. J. M. Bramkamp, D.D., 1901 S. 19th Ave., Maywood, Ill.; Mr. W. H. Patrick, 7000 Lincoln Parkway, Germantown, Philadelphia, Pa.

NECROLOGIST

Rev. James F. Lambert, D.D., 415 Howertown Ave., Catasauqua, Pa.

ARCHIVIST

Rev. L. D. Reed, D.D., 7204 Boyer St., Mt. Airy, Philadelphia, Pa.

COMMISSIONERS TO THE NATIONAL LUTHERAN COUNCIL

Rev. Paul W. Koller, D.D. (Convener), 18 E. Mt. Vernon Place, Baltimore, Md.; Rev. E. B. Burgess, D.D., LL.D.; Rev. C. A. Freed, D.D.; Rev. J. A. W. Haas, D.D., LL.D.; Rev. M. R. Hamsher, D.D.; Rev. C. E. Krumbholz, D.D.; Rev. E. P. Pfatteicher, Ph.D., D.D., LL.D.; Rev. L. W. Steckel, D.D.; Hon. E. F. Eilert, C.S.D.; G. F. Greiner, Esq.

REPRESENTATIVE ON THE ADVISORY COMMITTEE OF THE AMERICAN BIBLE SOCIETY

Rev. H. C. Alleman, D.D., Gettysburg, Pa.

CONSULTATIVE REPRESENTATIVES TO COMMISSIONS OF THE FEDERAL COUNCIL OF CHURCHES

Executive Committee: Rev. A. Steimle, D.D., 174 West 93rd St., New York City; Rev. Zenan M. Corbe, D.D.

Department of Social Service—Rev. W. H. Greever, D.D., LL.D., 39 East 35th St., New York City.

Department of Radio—Rev. A. Steimle, D.D., 174 West 93rd St., New York City.

Committee on Worship — Rev. L. D. Reed, D.D., A.E.D., 7204 Boyer St., Mt. Airy, Philadelphia, Pa.

Army and Navy and the Washington Committee — Rev. C. E. Krumbholz, D.D., 39 East 35th St., New York City; Rev. Henry Manken, Jr.; Rev. Emil W. Weber, D.D.

COMMITTEE TO PREPARE A STATEMENT CONCERNING RELATIONS OF CHURCH AND STATE

Rev. C. M. Jacobs, D.D., LL.D., L.H.D., 7333 Germantown Ave., Mt. Airy, Philadelphia, Pa.; Rev. F. K. Fretz, Ph.D., D.D.; Rev. J. A. W. Haas, D.D., LL.D.; Rev. Abdel Ross Wentz, Ph.D., D.D.

COMMISSION ON WORLD CONFERENCE ON FAITH AND ORDER

Rev. John Aberly, D.D., LL.D. (Chairman), Gettysburg, Pa.; Rev. E. E. Flack, Th.D.; Rev. W. H. Greever, D.D., LL.D.; Rev. C. M. Jacobs, D.D., LL.D., L.H.D.; Rev. A. Steimle, D.D.; Rev. C. R. Tappert, D.D.; Rev. Abdel Ross Wentz, Ph.D., D.D.

COMMISSION ON INVESTMENTS

Chairman—Mr. Wm. H. Stackel, 103 East Main St., Rochester, N. Y.

Secretary—Grant Hultberg, D.C.L., 1228 Spruce Street, Philadelphia, Pa.

Members elected by the Executive Board:

Mr. Wm. H. Stackel (term expires 1941); Mr. W. G. Semisch (term expires 1940); Mr. S. F. Telleen (term expires 1939); Rev. R. E. Tulloss, Ph.D., D.D., LL.D. (term expires 1938); Robbin B. Wolf, LL.D. (term expires 1937).

Members Ex-Officio:

President of The United Lutheran Church in America — Rev. F. H. Knubel, D.D., LL.D., S.T.D.

Treasurer of The United Lutheran Church in America—E. Clarence Miller, LL.D.

Members elected by their respective Board or Agency:

Miss Flora Prince, the Women's Missionary Society.

Rev. S. W. Herman, D.D., the Board of Foreign Missions.

Mr. Heiby W. Ungerer, the Board of American Missions.

Hon. Charles Steele, the Board of Education.

Mr. Belding B. Slifer, the Board of Ministerial Pensions and Relief.

SPECIAL COMMISSION ON RELATIONS TO AMERICAN LUTHERAN CHURCH BODIES

Rev. F. H. Knubel, D.D., LL.D., S.T.D. (Chairman), 39 East 35th St., New York, N. Y.; Rev. Henry H. Bagger, D.D.; Rev. Charles M. Jacobs, D.D., LL.D., L.H.D.; Rev. Paul H. Krauss, D.D.; Rev. H. Offermann, D.D.; Hon. E. F. Eilert, C.S.D.; Mr. J. K. Jensen; E. Clarence Miller, LL.D.; Mr. Edward Rinderknecht.

COMMITTEE ON ORGANIZED WORK WITH CHILDREN
(To be appointed.)

COMMITTEE FOR NEW PENSION PLAN
(To be appointed.)

COMMISSION CONCERNING TITLE OF "BISHOP"
(To be appointed.)

COMMISSION ON WORK AMONG NEGROES IN THE SOUTH
(To be appointed.)

COMMITTEE ON CENTENNIAL IN INDIA
(To be appointed.)

APPENDIX

CONSTITUTION AND BY-LAWS

of

The United Lutheran Church in America

REVISED TO 1936.

The Constitution of the United Lutheran Church in America

PREAMBLE

In the Name of the Father, and of the Son, and of the Holy Spirit. Amen.

Having been called by the Gospel and made partakers of the grace of God, and, by faith, members of our Lord and Saviour Jesus Christ, and, through Him, of one another,

We, members of Evangelical Lutheran congregations in America, associated in Evangelical Lutheran Synods, recognizing our duty as people of God to make the inner unity which we have with one another manifest in the common confession, defense and maintenance of our faith, and in united efforts for the extension of the Kingdom of God at home and abroad; realizing the vastness of the field that God has assigned us for our labors in this Western world, and the greatness of the resources within our beloved Church which are only feebly employed for this purpose; conscious of our need of mutual assistance and encouragement; and relying upon the promise of the divine Word that He who hath begun this work will perfect it until the day of Christ Jesus.

Hereby unite, and now invite and until such end be attained continue to invite all Evangelical Lutheran congregations and synods in America, one with us in the faith, to unite with us, upon the terms of this Constitution, in one general organization, to be known as THE UNITED LUTHERAN CHURCH IN AMERICA.

CONSTITUTION

ARTICLE I

NAME

The name and title of the body organized under this Constitution shall be THE UNITED LUTHERAN CHURCH IN AMERICA.

ARTICLE II

DOCTRINAL BASIS

Section 1. The United Lutheran Church in America receives and holds the canonical Scriptures of the Old and New Testaments as the inspired Word of God, and as the only infallible rule and standard of faith and practice, according to which all doctrines and teachers are to be judged.

Section 2. The United Lutheran Church in America accepts the three ecumenical creeds: namely, the Apostles', the Nicene, and the Athanasian, as important testimonies drawn from the Holy Scriptures, and rejects all errors which they condemn.

Section 3. The United Lutheran Church in America receives and holds the Unaltered Augsburg Confession as a correct exhibition of the faith and doctrine of the Evangelical Lutheran Church, founded upon the Word of God; and acknowledges all churches that sincerely hold and faithfully confess the doctrines of the Unaltered Augsburg Confession to be entitled to the name of Evangelical Lutheran.

Section 4. The United Lutheran Church in America recognizes the Apology of the Augsburg Confession, the Smalkald Articles, the Large and Small Catechisms of Luther, and the Formula of Concord, as in the harmony of one and the same pure Scriptural faith.

ARTICLE III

PRINCIPLES OF ORGANIZATION

In accordance with the foregoing Doctrinal Basis, The United Lutheran Church in America sets forth and declares the following principles as fundamental to its organization:

Section 1. All power in the Church belongs primarily and exclusively to our Lord and Saviour Jesus Christ, the Head of the Church. This power is not delegated to any man or body of men.

Section 2. All just power exercised by the Church has been committed to her for the furtherance of the Gospel through the Word and sacraments, and is conditioned by this end and pertains to her as the servant of Jesus Christ. The Church, therefore, has no power to bind the conscience except as she teaches what her Lord teaches and faithfully commands what He has charged her to command.

Section 3. Congregations are the primary bodies through which power committed by Christ to the Church is normally exercised.

Section 4. In addition to the pastors of churches, who are *ex officio* representatives of their congregations, the people have the right to choose representatives from their own number to act for them under such constitutional limitations as the congregations may approve.

Section 5. The representatives of congregations convened in Synod and acting in accordance with their Constitution are, for the ends defined in it representatively the congregations themselves, and have the right to call and set apart ministers for the common work of all the congregations; whose representatives they thereby become, and as such also members of the Synod.

Section 6. Congregations representatively constituting the various Synods may elect delegates through those Synods to represent them in a general body, all decisions of which, when made in accordance with the Constitution, bind so far as the terms of mutual agreement make them binding, those congregations and Synods which consent to be represented in the general body.

Section 7. In the formation and administration of a general body, the Synods may know and deal with each other only as Synods. In all such cases, the official record is to be accepted as evidence of the doctrinal position of each Synod and of the principles for which alone the other Synods are responsible by connection with it.

ARTICLE IV

MEMBERSHIP

Section 1. The United Lutheran Church in America at its organization shall consist of the congregations that compose the Evangelical Lutheran Synods which have been in connection with the General Synod of the Evangelical Lutheran Church in the United States of America, the

General Council of the Lutheran Church in North America, or the United Synod of the Evangelical Lutheran Church in the South, and which accept this Constitution with its Doctrinal Basis as set forth in Article II.

Section 2.   Any Evangelical Lutheran Synod applying for admission which has accepted this Constitution with its Doctrinal Basis as set forth in Article II, and whose Constitution has been approved by the Executive Board, may be received into membership by a majority vote at any regular Convention.

ARTICLE V

DELEGATES

Section 1.   Each Synod connected with The United Lutheran Church in America shall be entitled to representation at its Conventions by one ordained minister and one layman for every ten pastoral charges or major fraction thereof, on its roll; provided, however, that each Synod shall be entitled to at least one ministerial and one lay delegate; and provided further that the delegates elected by the Synods to the last conventions of the general bodies to which they respectively belong held prior to the first convention hereunder, shall be and they are in the adoption hereof chosen by their respective Synods as their duly elected delegates to said first convention hereunder, irrespective of the basis of representation upon which they were chosen.   The ratio of representation may be changed at any regular Convention of The United Lutheran Church in America by a two-thirds vote, provided that notice of the proposed change has been given at the preceding regular Convention.

Section 2.   Each Synod shall choose its delegates in such manner as it may deem proper.   The delegates from each Synod shall elect one of their own number as chairman unless the Synod itself has designated the chairman.

ARTICLE VI

OBJECTS

The objects of The United Lutheran Church in America are:

Section 1.   To preserve and extend the pure teaching of the Gospel and the right administration of the sacraments.   (Eph. 4: 5, 6; The Augsburg Confession, Article VII.)

Section 2.   To conserve the unity of the true faith (Eph. 4: 3-16; I Cor. 1: 10), to guard against any departure therefrom (Rom. 16: 17), and to strengthen the Church in faith and confession.

Section 3.   To express outwardly the spiritual unity of Lutheran congregations and synods, to cultivate co-operation among all Lutherans in the promotion of the general interests of the Church, to seek the unification of all Lutherans in one orthodox faith, and thus to develop and unfold the specific Lutheran principle and practice and make their strength effective.

Section 4.   To awaken, co-ordinate and effectively direct the energies of the Church in such operations as the following:

(a).   The training of ministers and teachers to be witnesses of the Word.

(b).   The extension of the kingdom of God by Home, Foreign and Inner Missions.

(c).   The proper regulation of the human externals of worship, that the same, in character and administration, may be in keeping with the New Testament and the liberty of the Church, and may edify the Body of Christ.

(d). The appointment of editorial committees or editors of Church papers and Sunday school literature.

(e). The preparation and publication of such literature as shall promote the dissemination of knowledge as to the doctrines, practice, progress, and needs of the Lutheran Church.

(f). The creation, organization and development, through Boards and Committees, of agencies to carry on all departments of work.

Section 5. To lay apportionments, and to solicit and disburse the funds necessary for these and other purposes defined in this Constitution.

Section 6. To foster and develop the work of Synods, to exercise a general supervision of the Church, and on appeal of Synods to give counsel and to adjudicate questions of doctrine, worship and discipline.

Section 7. To enter into relations with other bodies in the unity of the faith and to exchange official delegates with them.

ARTICLE VII
CONVENTIONS

Section 1. A Convention of the duly elected delegates of The United Lutheran Church in America shall be held at least once in every two years, at such time and place as may be determined by the preceding Convention of the body, or by the Executive Board.

Section 2. Special Conventions shall be called by the officers at the request of two-thirds of the members of the Executive Board, or at the request of the presidents of a majority of the Synods. The delegates shall be those who represented the Synods at the previous regular Convention, provided they have not been disqualified by removal or by the election of new delegates. Vacancies in delegations shall be filled according to the rules of the respective Synods.

Section 3. A majority of the delegates representing a majority of the Synods, shall constitute a quorum.

ARTICLE VIII
POWERS

Section 1. *As to External Relations.* The United Lutheran Church in America shall have power to form and dissolve relations with other general bodies, organizations and movements. To secure uniform and consistent practice no Synod, Conference or Board, or any official representative thereof, shall have power of independent affiliation with general organizations and movements.

Section 2. *As to Internal Relations.* The United Lutheran Church in America shall have power to deal with internal matters that affect all its constituent Synods or the activities of The United Lutheran Church as a whole, except that when the operation of such power takes place within the domain of any of the Synods their consent and co-operation must first be secured.

Section 3. *As to Intersynodical Dealings.* The United Lutheran Church in America shall have power to address and counsel its constituent Synods for the promotion of intersynodical harmony. Any question of interpretation of law, rights, or principle, that comes within its jurisdiction, or any proper cases referred to it on appeal of a Synod, shall be determined by a Commission of Adjudication hereinafter provided for.

Section 4. *As to Individual Synods and Specific Cases.* If Synods have had due and legal opportunity to be represented in the Conventions of

The United Lutheran Church in America, they are bound by all resolutions that have been passed in accordance with this Constitution. But each Synod retains every power, right and jurisdiction in its own internal affairs not expressly delegated to The United Lutheran Church in America.

Section 5. *As to Doctrine and Conscience.* All matters of doctrine and conscience shall be decided according to the Word of God alone. If, on grounds of doctrine or conscience, the question be raised as to the binding character of any action, the said question shall be referred to the Commission of Adjudication. Under no circumstances shall the right of a minority be disregarded or the right to record an individual protest on the ground of conscience be refused.

Section 6. *As to the Maintenance of Principle and Practice.* The United Lutheran Church in America shall protect and enforce its Doctrinal Basis, secure pure preaching of the Word of God and the right administration of the sacraments in all its Synods and congregations. It shall also have the right, where it deems that loyalty to the Word of God requires it, to advise and admonish concerning association and affiliation with non-ecclesiastical and other organizations whose principles or practices appear to be inconsistent with full loyalty to the Christian Church, but the Synods alone shall have the power of discipline.

Section 7. *As to Books of Devotion and Instruction, etc.* The United Lutheran Church in America shall provide books of devotion and instruction, such as Liturgies, Hymn Books and Catechisms, and no Synod without its sanction shall publish or recommend books of this kind other than those provided by the general body.

Section 8. *As to Work and Administration.* The United Lutheran Church in America shall have the power to engage in the work described under "Objects" (see Article VI), to create and regulate Boards and Committees, to determine budgets, and to lay apportionments.

Section 9. The executive power of The United Lutheran Church in America shall be vested in the officers of the general body, in an Executive Board, and in various other Boards for special purposes, subject to this Constitution and the Conventions of the general body.

ARTICLE IX

Officers

Section 1. The officers of The United Lutheran Church in America shall be a President, a Secretary and a Treasurer. The President shall be an ordained minister of the Church. The officers shall be elected by ballot at each regular Convention, but shall not take office until the first day of the third month after their election.

Section 2. The President shall preside at all sessions of the Convention, shall have the appointment of committees, unless The United Lutheran Church otherwise directs; shall see that the Constitution be observed and resolutions carried out; shall sign all official papers, and shall discharge such other duties as are delegated to him by the Convention.

Section 3. The Secretary shall keep a record of the proceedings, attest all documents of the body, and publish the time and place of the next meeting at least two months in advance. In case of a special meeting he shall give a written notice thereof to the President of each of the Synods immediately upon the issue of the call, and shall publish the same at least thirty days in advance of the meeting.

Section 4. The Treasurer shall receive and disburse all moneys, and keep an account of all his transactions and submit a report of the same at each regular Convention. He shall make disbursements only upon the order of the President, attested by the Secretary. He shall be required to give corporate surety in such amount as shall be determined by the Executive Board.

Section 5. In the event of the death, resignation or incapacity of any officer in the interim between Conventions, the Executive Board shall fill the vacancy.

ARTICLE X

INCORPORATION

The United Lutheran Church in America shall be incorporated.

ARTICLE XI

THE EXECUTIVE BOARD

Section 1. The Executive Board of The United Lutheran Church in America, which shall also be its Board of Trustees, shall consist of the President, the Secretary, and the Treasurer of the general body who shall also be the officers of the Executive Board, together with six ministerial and six lay members who shall be elected by the general body for a term of four years.

Section 2. At the first election three ministerial and three lay members shall be elected to serve four years, and three ministerial and three lay members to serve two years. Thereafter three ministerial and three lay members shall be elected at each regular Convention to serve four years.

Section 3. The Executive Board shall meet at stated times. It shall be the duty of the Executive Board to represent The United Lutheran Church in America and to carry out its resolutions and attend to its business during the interim; it shall co-ordinate the work of the executive departments, receive reports as to the work and needs of the several Boards, present a budget to the Conventions with apportionments, fill vacancies not otherwise provided for, and perform such other work as may be delegated to it by the general body, to which it shall make full report of its acts.

ARTICLE XII

COMMISSION OF ADJUDICATION

Section 1. A Commission of Adjudication shall be established to which shall be referred, for interpretation and decision, all disputed questions of doctrine and practice, and this Commission shall constitute a court for the decision of all questions of principle or action arising within The United Lutheran Church in America, and which have been properly referred to it by resolution or by appeal of any of the Synods.

Section 2. This Commission of Adjudication shall consist of nine members, six ministers and three laymen, learned in the doctrine, the law and the practice of the Church. All of the members of this Commission shall be elected at the first Convention of The United Lutheran Church in America, two ministers and one layman for a period of six years, two ministers and one layman for a period of four years, and two ministers and one layman for a period of two years. As their terms expire their successors shall be elected at each Convention for a term of six years.

Section 3. The Commission shall elect its own officers, and shall meet at least semi-annually for the transaction of business. When it holds meetings, or renders decisions, due notice of the time and place of meeting shall be given by its secretary to all persons interested, and a standing notice of the time and place of its regular meetings shall be published in the Church papers.

Section 4. The consent of at least six members shall always be necessary for a decision.

Section 5. The Commission shall render a written report of all its actions and decisions to the next regular Convention, but the right of appeal from its decisions shall always be recognized.

ARTICLE XIII

BOARDS

Section 1. The United Lutheran Church in America shall determine the number of members in the several Boards which it shall create, and these Boards shall always be amenable to it.

Section 2. All members of Boards shall be elected by The United Lutheran Church in America. Vacancies occurring in any Board ad interim shall be filled by the Executive Board of the Church on nomination of the Board in which the vacancy exists. No person shall be a member of more than two boards at one and the same time.* No member of any Board, including the Executive Board, shall be a member of the Commission of Adjudication; but the President of The United Lutheran Church shall at all times have a seat and a voice in all the Boards and in the Commission of Adjudication.

Section 3. These Boards, upon the determination of the general body, shall secure articles of incorporation which must be in harmony with the purposes of The United Lutheran Church in America; but no Board shall apply for incorporation until its proposed charter shall have received the approval of the general body in Convention, or, in the interim, of the Executive Board.

Section 4. The Boards, unless otherwise provided, shall have power to elect their own officers and employees, and to carry on their work in accordance with the design of their appointment. No member of a Board shall be a salaried employee thereof.

Section 5. The Boards shall require corporate surety from their respective treasurers. At each regular Convention of The United Lutheran Church in America, they shall render full and accurate reports of their work during the preceding biennium.

Section 6. The Woman's Missionary Society, as auxiliary to Boards of The United Lutheran Church in America, shall have the right to appoint two women as advisory members of each of the missionary and benevolent Boards to the support of whose work they regularly or officially contribute.

ARTICLE XIV

SYNODS

Section 1. No Synod in connection with The United Lutheran Church in America shall alter its geographical boundaries without the permission of the general body.

---

* An amendment providing limitation of Board membership to one Board was adopted at the 1936 Convention for submission to the constituent synods.

Section 2.   Synods shall give advice to their ministers and congregations concerning doctrine, life and administration, and shall exercise such disciplinary measures as may be necessary.

Section 3.   The Presidents of Synods shall exercise an oversight of the pastors and congregations composing their respective Synods, and shall be charged with the duty of carrying out the rules and regulations adopted by the Synods.   When requested by the Executive Board they shall appear before it to represent their Synods.   They may also make suggestions to the Executive Board, or seek its advice, with respect to the conditions and work in their Synods.

Section 4.   Should any Synod in connection with The United Lutheran Church in America desire to continue its established lines of work for reasons satisfactory to the general body, such privilege may be granted.

ARTICLE XV

COMMITTEES, BY-LAWS AND AMENDMENTS

Section 1.   The United Lutheran Church in America may appoint special and standing committees.   It may adopt By-Laws for the transaction of its business, provided that they do not conflict with this Constitution. These By-Laws may be suspended or amended at any Convention by a two-thirds vote.

Section 2.   Amendments to this Constitution must be presented in writing at a regular Convention of The United Lutheran Church in America, which shall decide by a two-thirds vote whether and in what form they shall be submitted to the Synods.   An exact copy of proposed amendments shall be transmitted by the Secretary to the Presidents of the Synods for submission to their respective bodies.   If at a subsequent Convention two-thirds of the Synods shall report their approval of the amendments proposed they shall be declared adopted.

BY-LAWS

SECTION I

MEETINGS

Item 1.   Arrangements for the Conventions of The United Lutheran Church in America shall be made by the officers acting in conjunction with the pastor loci or a local committee appointed for the purpose.

Item 2.   Every Convention shall begin with The Service.   The sermon shall be preached by the President or someone appointed by him.   The first business session shall be opened by the use of the prescribed order.

Item 3.   A tentative order of business shall be prepared by the Executive Board. Boards and other representatives of causes desiring to hold meetings in the interest of their specific work shall make request to the Executive Board for a place on the program of the Convention at least two months before the regular meeting.   All appointments for religious services and public meetings in the interest of specific causes shall be left with the President.

SECTION II

DELEGATES

Item 1. A roll of the delegates of the Convention of The United Lutheran Church in America shall be prepared by the Secretary prior to each meeting. To facilitate his work each President of a Synod in connection with The United Lutheran Church in America shall forward a list of delegates elected by his Synod to the President and Secretary of the General Body at least 30 days before the meeting, signed by the President and Secretary of the Synod.

Item 2. No changes shall be made in the roll of delegates unless such change is duly authorized by the Synod concerned.

Item 3. In the absence of a quorum the delegates present may adjourn from time to time and postpone the session of the Convention until a quorum shall appear.

Item 4. Delegates, Commissions or representatives from other Lutheran Bodies not in union with The United Lutheran Church in America may be given a voice and a seat, but no vote, in the Convention by a majority vote of the delegates at any meeting.

Item 5. The mileage of all delegates shall be paid from the treasury of The United Lutheran Church, and the apportionment for the treasury shall be made sufficient to cover this expense. Other necessary expenses of delegates shall be provided for as the Synods may determine.

Item 6. Delegates shall not absent themselves from the sessions of the Convention without valid excuse, which shall be presented to the Committee on Leave of Absence. Said committee shall make a final report at the closing session of the Convention. Delegates absenting themselves without being excused shall forfeit their mileage.

SECTION III

RECEPTION OF SYNODS

Item I. The application of a Synod desiring to be received into The United Lutheran Church in America shall be presented to the Executive Board together with a copy of the Synod's Constitution. Upon recommendation of the Executive Board the Synod may be received in accordance with the Constitution, Article IV, Section 2. The delegates of such Synod upon the approval of their credentials shall at once be seated in the Convention and their names entered upon the roll.

SECTION IV

ELECTIONS

Item 1. At the beginning of every biennial Convention the President shall appoint tellers to conduct the election of officers and Boards in accordance with rules and regulations adopted by the General Body.

Item 2. Election of officers, members of the Executive Board and of the other Boards, including the Commission of Adjudication and all elective Committees, shall be by ballot. The Secretary shall prepare printed ballots for the use of voters in the Convention.

Item 3. In the election of a President, the following rules shall obtain: On the first ballot, three-fourths of all the votes cast shall be necessary to an election. On the second ballot, two-thirds of all the votes cast shall be necessary to an election. If two ballots fail to result in an election, the third ballot shall be confined to the two persons who in the second ballot receive the highest number of votes and no vote cast for any other shall be counted. In the third ballot a majority of the votes shall elect.

Item 4. In the election of the Secretary, Treasurer and members of regular Boards and elective Committees, a majority of the votes cast shall be necessary for an election.

Item 5. The result of each ballot shall be announced by the tellers to the Convention.

SECTION V

BOARDS AND COMMITTEES

A. List of Boards and Elective Committees

There shall be:
1. An Executive Board.
2. A Commission of Adjudication.
3. A Foreign Mission Board.
4. A Board of American Missions.
5. A Board of Northwestern Missions.
6. An Immigrants Mission Board.
7. A West Indies Board.
8. A Board of Education.
9. An Inner Mission Board.
10. A Board of Publication.
11. A Board of Ministerial Pensions and Relief.
12. A Parish and Church School Board.
13. A Board of Deaconess Work.
14. A Committee on Church Papers.
15. An Executive Committee of the Laymen's Movement.

B. Nominations and Appointments

Item 1. In the first Convention the Boards which shall agree to merge their interests in a common Board shall jointly nominate members for such Board. An equal number may be nominated from the floor. In either case the term of each person placed in nomination shall be indicated so that one-third of the members shall serve for two years, one-third for four years and one-third for six years.

Item 2. Thereafter beginning with the second biennial Convention of The United Lutheran Church in America, the term of each regularly elected member shall be six years. Nominations for membership shall be made as follows:

A committee appointed by the President shall nominate a number equal to the number of vacancies on each Board. The Board itself may also nominate a number equal to twice the number of vacancies. If any Board shall fail to make such nominations, the Nominating Committee shall present a sufficient number of nominations so as to present a total equalling three times as many as are to be elected. Nominations may also be made from the floor. Nominations shall not be so construed as to confine voting to the nominees.

Item 3. The membership of Boards of The United Lutheran Church in America shall consist of not less than nine, or more than twenty-one members.

Item 4. No member of any Board shall be eligible for election for more than two successive terms; and no person shall be a member of more than two Boards at one and the same time.

Item 5. Early in the session of each Convention of The United Lutheran Church the President shall appoint:

(1). A Nominating Committee of nine ministers and nine laymen to make the nominations necessary to fill all vacancies on the several benevolent Boards. Nominations made by the Boards themselves shall be referred to this Committee as soon as appointed.

(2). A Nominating Committee of nine ministers and nine laymen, to make nominations necessary to fill all vacancies on the Executive Board and on all Commissions and Committees that are to be elected by the Convention.

These Committees shall report at such time as the Convention may designate.

Item 6. A Standing Committee on Church Papers to consist of nine members shall be elected by The United Lutheran Church.

At the first Convention three shall be elected for two years, three for four years and three for six years. Beginning with the second biennium the term for the newly elected members shall be six years.

It shall be the duty of this Committee to select editors of such Church Papers as The United Lutheran Church may recognize, authorize or found. The selection of these editors shall be made, if possible, before or during the Conventions of The United Lutheran Church, and subject to its ratification. If, however, it be impossible to make the selection at the time named the Committee shall have full power to act *ad interim*. The salaries of the editors shall be determined by the Committee and the Board of Publication jointly.

This Committee shall also be charged with the general oversight of the Church Papers whose editors shall be responsible to the said Committee. The Committee shall see that the papers are conducted in accordance with the spirit and intent of the Constitution, in the interest of The United Lutheran Church and for the edification of the people.

Item 7. The President shall appoint a Standing Committee consisting of fifteen members, known as the Common Service Book Committee, to whom shall be referred all matters pertaining to the worship of the Church.

This Committee shall be responsible for the Common Service Book, with respect to text and form in all editions; it shall prepare forms and manuals of worship and devotion authorized by the Church; and shall consider such other matters as may be referred to it by the Church.

Item 8. The President shall appoint a Committee of three ministers and four laymen to nominate a Standing Committee of ten laymen which shall be known as the Executive Committee of the Laymen's Movement and shall have charge of its development and administration. It shall have power to increase its membership as deemed expedient.

Item 9. No person shall be a member of more than two appointive standing committees at one and the same time.

C. Powers and Duties

Item 1. Inasmuch as the Boards and Committees are representatives of The United Lutheran Church in America, and of its work, the general policies of all Boards and Committees shall be decided by the Church, and it shall be the duty of Boards to refer all questions affecting the principles, practice and policy of the Church as a whole, to The United Lutheran Church for decision. It shall be the duty of the Boards to carry out and administer these principles and policies thus decided; and when changes seem advisable they may suggest any changes to the Church for its approval, after which only they shall become operative.

Item 2. No official relationship with any other ecclesiastical bodies or their agencies shall be entered into by any Board or Committee of The United Lutheran Church in America without the approval of the Church. See Constitution, Art. VIII, Sec. 1.

Item 3. All Boards, Standing Committees and Commissions after each meeting shall furnish the Executive Board with a copy of their proceedings that said Executive Board may be thoroughly informed and qualified to co-ordinate the work of the entire body. Boards which seek appropriations or apportionments shall present their request for the amount desired together with a statement of financial operations to the Executive Board not less than three months before each regular Convention, to enable the Board to prepare its budget.

Item 4. No Board shall have the right to inaugurate a propaganda for the raising of funds, outside of its regular budget, without the consent of the Executive Board of The United Lutheran Church.

Item 5. The financial accounts of the several Boards and Commissions shall be submitted for audit to an accredited accountant. In connection with its report each Board shall present to the Convention the report of the Treasurer certified by said accountant. The fiscal year of all Boards shall close on the last day of the fourth month preceding the one in which the Convention of the United Lutheran Church shall meet.

Item 6. All reports of Boards and Standing Committees, with recommendations, shall be sent to the Secretary of The United Lutheran Church at least sixty days before each Convention. The Secretary shall send out a Bulletin containing reports ten days in advance of the Convention.

Item 7. All reports of Boards shall be regularly signed by their officers. All reports of Committees shall be signed by a majority of the members thereof.

Item 8. Special and institutional reports shall, as far as possible, be incorporated into the report of the Board or Committee dealing with the general subject, and where this cannot be done, shall be heard only in connection with the consideration of that report, and shall be edited before printing.

Item 9. The person first named on a temporary Committee shall act as its Chairman. Standing Committees shall be convened by the person first named, and shall elect their own officers.

Item 10. When, besides the report of the majority of a Committee, there is also a report of a minority, the former shall be read first.

Item 11. In all cases of appeal from any decision of the Commission of Adjudication rendered within the interim between Conventions of The United Lutheran Church in America, Notice of Intention to Appeal shall be given in writing to the President of the Commission at least ten days prior to the first day of the Convention following: Provided, however, that when decisons have been rendered at any Convention, or within thirty days prior thereto, appeal may be made during the Convention upon consent obtained by a two-thirds' vote of the delegates present. The Convention shall thereupon fix a time when the appeal shall be made a special order of the Convention.

Item 12. An appeal from any decision of the Commission of Adjudication can be made only at the Convention of the United Lutheran Church at which such decision has been reported, and can be entertained only when Item 11 above has been fully complied with and the appeal shall have been submitted in writing by five delegates to said Convention. After the submission and argument of the appeal it shall not be voted upon until the succeeding day, unless by reason of limited time, the Convention, by two-thirds' vote, shall decide to adjudicate the appeal on the same day. To sustain the appeal and reverse the decision from which the appeal is made, a two-thirds' vote of the members present and voting shall be necessary. In the discussion of any such appeal, the Commission of Adjudication shall be fully heard through any of its members whom it may designate, whether they be or be not delegates to the Convention.

SECTION VI
CONCERNING THE PRESIDENT

Item 1. The President shall conduct all business according to the Constitution, By-Laws, and Order of Procedure of The United Lutheran Church, and insist upon the observance of the same on the part of every member. He shall appoint all committees unless otherwise provided for.

Item 2. Robert's Rules of Order Revised shall be the governing parliamentary law except where not in harmony with the Constitution and By-Laws.

Item 3. He shall prepare a biennial report which shall briefly summarize the general conditions in the Church and his own work during the biennium and which shall be presented and assigned to Committees prior to the Convention's entering into the election of a successor.

SECTION VII
COMMITTEES
A. Special Committees

The following special Committees shall be appointed by the President at the first session of each Convention of The United Lutheran Church in America:

1. Committee to conduct the opening and closing services of each session.
2. Committee on Leave of Absence.
3. Committee on Proceedings of District Synods.
4. Committee of Reference and Council. (Its duties shall include the consideration of all general resolutions before they are submitted to the Convention, arrangements with the President for the hearing of representatives sent to the Conventions, and general assistance to the President in the daily program.)
5. Committee to Nominate Executive Committee of Laymen's Movement.
6. Committee to Nominate Members of Boards.
7. Committee to Nominate Members of Executive Board, and all elective Commissions or Committees.
8. Committee of Tellers.

B. Standing Committees

The following Standing Committees shall be appointed by the President:

1. Statistical and Church Year Book Committee.
2. Committee on Common Service Book.
3. Committee on Church Music.
4. Committee on German Interests.

(It shall arrange, in conference with the Executive Board, for any meetings of a German Conference required. It shall also be a place of counsel for any agencies of the Church when they are dealing with matters which concern especially the German-speaking portions of the Church. It shall, furthermore, have the privilege to approach any agency of the Church upon matters which are for the interest of that portion of the Church.)

5. Committee on Army and Navy Work.
6. Committee on Moral and Social Welfare.
7. Committee on Evangelism.
8. Committee on Church Architecture.
9. Committee on Publicity.
10. Committee on Transportation. (Its duties shall include all transportation interests, including the mileage and transportation arrangements for the Conventions.)
11. A Necrologist.
12. An Archivist.
13. Such other Standing Committees as may be provided for from time to time.

SECTION VIII

AMENDMENT

These By-Laws may be suspended or amended at any Convention by a two-thirds vote of the members present and voting; provided that due notice of the amendment proposed shall have been given on the preceding day.

CORPORATE TITLES

The United Lutheran Church in America, 39 East 35th Street, New York City.

The Board of Foreign Missions of the United Lutheran Church in America, 18 East Mt. Vernon Place, Baltimore, Md.

The Board of American Missions of the United Lutheran Church in America, 39 East 35th St., New York City.

The Board of Education of the United Lutheran Church in America, 744 Jackson Pl., N. W., Washington, D. C.

The Inner Mission Board of the United Lutheran Church in America, 39 East 35th Street, New York City.

The Board of Publication of the United Lutheran Church in America, 1228 Spruce Street, Philadelphia, Pa.

Board of Ministerial Pensions and Relief of the United Lutheran Church in America, 1228 Spruce St., Philadelphia, Pa.

The Parish and Church School Board of the United Lutheran Church in America, 1228 Spruce St., Philadelphia, Pa.

The Board of Deaconess Work of the United Lutheran Church in America, 2500 W. North Avenue, Baltimore, Md.

The Women's Missionary Society of the United Lutheran Church in America, 1228 Spruce St., Philadelphia, Pa.

Evangelical Lutheran Seminary of Canada, Waterloo, Ontario, Canada.

The Theological Seminary of the Evangelical Lutheran Church at Chicago, Ill., 11th Avenue & Harrison Street, Maywood, Ill.

The Theological Seminary of the General Synod of the Evangelical Lutheran Church in the United States and of the United Lutheran Church in America, Gettysburg, Pa.

The Hartwick Seminary, 259 Washington Ave., Brooklyn, N. Y.

Martin Luther Seminary of the German Evangelical Lutheran Synod of Nebraska, Lincoln, Nebr.

Northwestern Lutheran Theological Seminary, 1018 Nineteenth Ave., N. E., Minneapolis, Minn.

Pacific Theological Seminary of the Evangelical Lutheran Church, 4300 E. 45th St., Seattle, Wash.

The Lutheran Theological Seminary at Philadelphia, 7301 Germantown Ave., Mt. Airy, Philadelphia, Pa.

The Lutheran College and Seminary, Saskatoon, Sask., Canada.

Trustees of the Lutheran Theological Southern Seminary, at Columbia, S. C.

The Western Theological Seminary of the United Lutheran Church in America, Fremont, Nebr.

Carthage College, Carthage, Ill.

Gettysburg College, Gettysburg, Pa.

Lenoir-Rhyne College, Hickory, N. C.
Marion Female College (known as Marion Junior College), Marion, Va.
Midland College of the United Lutheran Church in America, Fremont, Nebr.
Muhlenberg College, Located at Allentown, Lehigh County, Pennsylvania.
Newberry College, Newberry, S. C.
The Trustees of Roanoke College, at Salem, Va.
Susquehanna University, Selinsgrove, Pa.
Trustees of Thiel College of the Evangelical Lutheran Church, Greenville, Pa.
Wagner Memorial Lutheran College, Staten Island, N. Y.
The Board of Directors of Wittenberg College, Springfield, Ohio.
Hartwick College, Oneonta, N. Y.
Hartwick Academy, Hartwick Seminary, N. Y.

Lutheran Orphans' Home in Berks County, Pennsylvania.
Tressler Orphans' Home of the Evangelical Lutheran Church of the General Synod in the United States of America, Loysville, Pa.
The Zelienople Orphans' Home Board of Directors of the Pittsburgh Synod of the Evangelical Lutheran Church, Zelienople, Pa.
The Oesterlen Orphans' Home of the United Lutheran Church of North America located at Springfield, Ohio.
The Lutheran Orphan Home of the South, located at Salem, Va.
The Nachusa Lutheran Orphanage, Nachusa, Ill.
Wartburg Orphans' Farm School of the Evangelical Lutheran Church, in the State of New York, Mount Vernon, N. Y.
Evangelical Lutheran St. John's Orphan Home at Buffalo and Sulphur Springs, N. Y., "Station D," Buffalo, N. Y.
Old People's Home of the Pittsburgh Synod of the Evangelical Lutheran Church, at Zelienople, Pa.
Evangelical Lutheran Charities Society of Charleston, S. C. (for The Jacob Washington Franke Lutheran Hospital and Home), Charleston, S. C.
The Association of the Lutheran Church Home for the Aged and Infirm of Buffalo, N. Y.
The Lutheran Church Home for the Aged and Infirm of Central New York, Inc., Clinton, N. Y. (Office at Utica, N. Y.)
The National Lutheran Home for the Aged, Washington, D. C.
The Feghtly Lutheran Home, Tippecanoe City, Ohio.
Lowman Home for the Aged and Helpless, White Rock, S. C.
Lutheran Home for the Aged, of Erie, Pennsylvania.
Lutheran Inner Mission Society of the State of Connecticut, Inc. Owner of "Lutheran Home for the Aged, Southbury, Conn."
Tabitha Home, Lincoln, Nebr.

Emaus Orphan House, Middletown, Pa.

Lutheran Home for Orphans and Aged at Germantown, 6950 Germantown Ave., Philadelphia, Pa.

The Good Shepherd Home, Allentown, Pa.

The Auxiliary Board of the Passavant Memorial Homes for the Care of Epileptics, Rochester, Pa.

Bethesda Home of the Pittsburgh Synod of the Evangelical Lutheran Church, Crawford Co., Pa.

INDEX